Modern

Guerrilla

Warfare

Modern

Guerrilla

Warfare

Fighting Communist Guerrilla Movements, 1941–1961

Edited by FRANKLIN MARK OSANKA

Introduction by SAMUEL P. HUNTINGTON

THE FREE PRESS, *New York*
Collier-Macmillan Limited, *London*

Dedicated to Those Individuals
Whose Work Appears in This Volume

CONTENTS

Part Seven

Malaya—Post-World War II

Part Eight

The Cuban Revolution and the Algerian Rebellion

Part Nine

Counterguerrilla Procedures and Policies

Research Bibliography on Guerrilla and Unconventional Warfare

PREFACE

*T*HIS BOOK is concerned with recent developments in uses of guerrilla warfare, with major emphasis on its employment by Communists* in many different situations. Some attention is given to modern non-Communist guerrilla movements and historical proponents of guerrilla activity, but the material in this volume demonstrates that today the Communists are the leading theorists and practitioners of this form of combat and that some nationalist movements have been influenced by Communist precepts and examples. Also included are accounts of successful counterguerrilla operations and proposals for remedying the long neglect of guerrilla warfare in the non-Communist world.

This volume contains more extensive coverage of recent major guerrilla movements than any other book and is the only one not restricted to a limited geographical area. It is a compilation of major research that has appeared over the past twenty years and of pronouncements from leading military and civilian authorities. Communist theorists from Lenin to

---

* At an earlier stage, this study was known as *Communist Guerrilla Movements, 1940–61*, edited by Franklin Mark (the editor's first and middle names).

"Che" Guevara are given due attention. This book also includes the most complete research bibliography yet available on the subjects of guerrilla and unconventional warfare.

This book is divided into nine sections. Beginning with a review of guerrilla warfare in the past and its modern strategic uses, there are succeeding sections on the application of guerrilla principles in various areas of the world: in Soviet Russia during World War II; in China against both the Japanese and the Nationalist regime; in the Philippines following World War II; in Greece immediately after World War II; in Indochina from the end of the Japanese occupation, after the partition, and continuing in Laos and South Vietnam to this day; in Malaya for the decade beginning in 1948; and the nationalist revolutions in Cuba and in Algeria, where fighting continues sporadically. The concluding section deals with counterguerrilla procedures and policies. Each section includes a list of Further References *in addition* to the Research Bibliography on Guerrilla and Unconventional Warfare at the end of the book; there is no duplication between the two listings.

There is a widespread popular belief that Communists invented the concept of guerrilla warfare. In fact, the Communists have merely refined, adapted, and employed with spectacular success an ancient form of warfare that has been used under a wide variety of circumstances throughout recorded history. Guerrilla activity has been an adjunct to battle operations in major wars, as well as a popular *modus operandi* of suppressed peoples in dealing with unpopular governments. It has been a favorite tactic of small and poorly armed societies against greater powers, and every country occupied by the Axis in World War II produced some type of guerrilla movement that contributed to the Allied victory.

In the atomic age, many free societies ignored or deprecated guerrilla warfare to their cost. This neglect was remedied in several instances in time to preserve the independence of entire countries menaced by the threat of total conquest, such as Greece, Malaya, and the Philippines. This volume contains a number of accounts of successful counterguerrilla operations and suggestions for more effective use of this type of combat.

Since World War II, extensive guerrilla warfare has occurred in Israel, Cyprus, Kenya, Kashmir, Indonesia, Tunisia, Algeria, Cuba, China, the Philippines, Indochina, Greece, Malaya, Laos, and South Vietnam. Some of these were wars of independence, but we are chiefly concerned with those supplied and directed by Communists.

The Communists have demonstrated great skill in utilizing social, economic, and political weaknesses as major assets to guerrilla operations. Their success has been greatest in less industrialized societies, where they have been able to identify themselves as champions of the suppressed and discontented. Some of the selections in this volume are intended to broaden our understanding of these problems. For it is not enough merely to oppose the Communists and thus appear also to be opposing social and economic progress. The development of positive programs to end the threat of Communist guerrilla movements will require greater use of our intellectual resources by social scientists as well as military strategists.

I am deeply grateful to all the authors and publishers who have granted permission to reproduce their material in this book.

I should also like to acknowledge with special thanks the following individuals for their kind interest, encouragement, and assistance: Nicholas J. Anthony, Associate Editor of *Army Magazine;* Lt. Col. T. N. Greene, Editor of *Marine Corps Gazette;* Robert C. Herber, Managing Editor of *Orbis;* Dr. Samuel P. Huntington, Associate Director of the Institute of War and Peace Studies, Columbia University; Colonel Kenneth E. Lay, Editor of *Military Review;* Eugene Methvin, Washington, D.C. office of *The Reader's Digest;* Brig. Gen. J. C. Miller, Jr., Director of the Marine Corps Educational Center at Quantico, Va.; and Dr. Stefan T. Possony, Georgetown University. In addition, my thanks go to Mrs. Chang Kim, exchange student from the Republic of Korea, and Miss Ginger Sisco and Miss Janet Sisco, students at Northern Illinois University, who helped type the original manuscript.

My special gratitude goes to F. Warren O'Reilly, Editor at The Free Press, whose interest and editorial advice are deeply appreciated.

Finally, this book could not have been produced without the patience and understanding of my wife Linda and son Jeffrey.

FRANKLIN MARK OSANKA

De Kalb, Illinois
August, 1961

Introduction

Samuel P. Huntington

GUERRILLA WARFARE

IN THEORY

AND POLICY

I. WARS AND WARFARE

GUERRILLA WARFARE has assumed a new importance in American military policy. The phrases "paramilitary operations," "unconventional war," "irregular warfare," "internal war," and "guerrilla warfare" have all blossomed forth in recent discussions of strategy. No doubt each term serves some purpose, although one cannot help but feel that semantics has perhaps outstripped theory. Whether or not the resurgence of interest in guerrilla warfare has any lasting basis depends upon the roles which it may play in world politics. These can only be understood in terms of a general theory of armed conflict. A key element in such a theory is the distinction between *types of war* and *forms of warfare*.

A war is a violent interaction between two organized political groups (governments or otherwise). Types of war are types of interaction. They may be defined in terms of the nature of the participants, the nature of their goals, the efforts they make to achieve those goals, and, broadly speaking, the resources they employ. Four types of war seem peculiarly relevant to world politics today.

1. *Total war* is a struggle between governments in which at least one aims at the destruction of the other and uses all the means at its disposal

to achieve that aim. Under present conditions total war between major powers would involve the use of thermonuclear weapons.

2. *General war* is a struggle between governments in which at least one aims at the complete destruction of the other but does *not* use all the means at its disposal. Under present conditions general war between major powers could not involve extensive use of thermonuclear weapons. World War II was a total war; if it occurred again, it would be a general war.

3. *Limited war* is a struggle between major or minor powers in which each has a restricted goal and in which each employs only a portion of its resources, usually within a defined geographical area. The Korean War was a limited war for the United States and Communist China.

4. *Revolutionary war* is the struggle between a nongovernmental group and a government in which the latter attempts to destroy the former by some or all the means at its command, and the nongovernmental group attempts by all the means at its command to replace the government in some or all of its territory. The post-World-War-II struggles in Indochina, Malaya, and Algeria were revolutionary wars.

The boundary lines between these types of war are not necessarily precise. In theory, however, the four types are mutually exclusive. Each type encompasses the sum total of the military interactions between the participants. A form of warfare, on the other hand, is one variety of military activity involving particular military forces, weapons, and tactics. It need not encompass the complete pattern of military interaction between the opposing parties. A naval blockade, a "conventional" ground forces campaign, strategic air bombardment, are forms of warfare carried out by specialized types of miiltary forces, but they are not types of war. They may appear in more than one type of war. The types of war thus set the contexts in which the forms of warfare are employed.

Guerrilla warfare is clearly a form of warfare and not a type of war. Its current significance derives from its relevance to all four types of war possible in world politics today. This relevance derives from its distinctive character. *Guerrilla warfare is a form of warfare by which the strategically weaker side assumes the tactical offensive in selected forms, times, and places.* Guerrilla warfare is the weapon of the weak. It is never chosen in preference to regular warfare; it is employed only when and where the possibilities of regular warfare have been foreclosed. Guerrilla warfare is decisive only where the anti-guerrilla side puts a low value on defeating the guerrillas and does not commit its full resources to the struggle. Except in these instances, guerrilla warfare is never self-sufficient. To achieve victory in most wars, guerrilla warfare must be accompanied by other forms of warfare. Guerrilla warfare is resorted to (1) after regular (i.e., stronger) forces have been defeated, (2) before they have been created, and (3) where they are unable to operate. All three possibilities of guerrilla warfare exist among the types of war that are likely today.

If the regular forces of one side have been defeated, or if they never existed in the first place, that side may turn to guerrilla warfare to continue the struggle as long as possible. Having lost the ability to conduct regular operations, this side resorts to guerrilla warfare in the hope that outside help may materialize or that prolonged resistance through this lesser form of warfare may induce the victorious side to accept more lenient peace terms. The term "guerrilla" itself was first applied to the bands of Spanish soldiers fighting the Napoleonic armies in Spain. This was a spontaneous development in the absence of any regular Spanish forces. Analogously, the Boers shifted to guerrilla warfare after the British had destroyed their ability to wage regular warfare. The British had to make a major new effort to break the back of the guerrilla resistance. As one Englishman observed at the time,

> If there is one certain education to be drawn from past experience it is that guerrilla tactics, when carried out by a resourceful and persistent enemy, have invariably led to a protracted struggle, during which the invading armies against which they have fought have suffered a series of minor disasters and "regrettable incidents." . . .[1]

At about the same time the United States Army was having similar difficulties in quelling the Philippine insurgents under the leadership of Aguinaldo.

Guerrilla warfare is possible in the later phases of a future total war. Such a war presumably would begin with an air-missile exchange of nuclear explosives. If one side emerged dominant from this exchange and the other side was unwilling to accept the peace terms proposed by the strategic victor, then the strategic victor might well attempt to occupy the enemy's country with its military forces. In such circumstances, the last resort of the defeated country would be guerrilla warfare. Such warfare might succeed in enhancing the defeated power's bargaining position, but it could never succeed in defeating the victorious power. Only outside intervention with new sources of power and regular military strength would reopen the prospects of victory for the defeated country. If such intervention is impossible, eventual suppression of the guerrillas is inevitable. George Kennan's proposals that the West should rely on "paramilitary" formations to defend Europe are, consequently, an argument for defeat.[2] If he assumes that such formations could by themselves dislodge the Russians from Western Europe, his assumption is false. If he assumes that they could not and that another massive invasion of Western Europe by the United States would be necessary, then his policy is pernicious.

Guerrilla warfare may also be undertaken by a side that is too weak at the opening of a war to engage in regular operations. Guerrilla warfare then

1. J. B. Firth, "The Guerrilla in History," *Fortnightly Review,* 70 (1901), 803.
2. See George F. Kennan, *Russia, the Atom, and the West* (Harper, 1957), p. 63.

becomes a way of harassing and wearing down the enemy while developing one's own strength. Unless the enemy has little interest in the struggle, the weaker side must eventually shift from guerrilla operations to regular warfare in order to achieve victory. If the weaker side is unable to develop regular forces and if the enemy is relentless in its pursuit of the conflict, the weaker side will be eventually overwhelmed. Guerrilla warfare plays a preliminary role in revolutionary war. It is not, however, identical or co-extensive with revolutionary war. Guerrilla warfare may be employed in other types of war than revolutionary war, and a successful revolutionary war requires other types of struggle than guerrilla warfare. All of this is made very plain in the writings of the principal theorist of revolutionary war, Mao Tse-tung. The key problem in revolutionary war is to calculate the timing and the means for the shift from guerrilla warfare to regular warfare. Too early a shift invites a defeat; too late a shift postpones victory.

Guerrilla warfare may also be employed as a supplement to regular operations in areas where one side is weak and the other side is strong. In these situations the importance of guerrilla warfare to a side usually varies inversely with the strength of that side. In a "regular" war both sides may organize supplementary guerrilla operations to harass the enemy's rear. Usually, the stronger a side is, the less the proportion of its total effort, however, that will be allocated to guerrilla warfare. A side that is completely confident of its ability to secure victory in regular warfare usually has little interest in or need for guerrilla warfare. A side that is dubious of its ability to secure victory through regular warfare will place a greater emphasis on guerrilla warfare. Similarly, in a regular general or limited war, guerrilla warfare will normally play a more important role in the operations of the side that suffered defeats in the early stages of the war than in the operations of the side that was initially successful. In World War II, Allied guerrillas played significant roles in Western Europe, Yugoslavia, Russia, and Burma. In the Korean War, Communist guerrillas also played an important role behind Allied lines in South Korea. In any future general or limited war, guerrilla warfare undoubtedly will be a significant supplement to regular operations.

II. GUERRILLA WARFARE AND THE *GUERRE DE COURSE*

The distinctive character of guerrilla warfare and of counterguerrilla warfare can be fully understood only if they are viewed in connection with their naval counterparts. Guerrilla warfare is to land war what the *guerre de course* is to sea war. Originally conceived by French naval officers in the eighteenth century, the idea of the *guerre de course* was further developed by the *Jeune École* of the 1880's. It was the means by which an inferior continental naval power attempted to counterbalance the naval

The Roles of Warfare in Wars

FORMS OF WARFARE	TYPES OF WAR			
	Revolutionary	Limited	General	Total
Guerrilla warfare	Dominant in early phase	Supplementary role	Supplementary role	Probable after nuclear exchange
"Conventional" land warfare	Dominant in later phase	Of major importance	Major role	Secondary role
Tactical nuclear warfare	No role	Possible but unlikely	Possible	Supporting role
Naval warfare	Peripheral	Minor to important role	Very important	Secondary, except for strategic bombardment
Strategic nuclear warfare	No role	No role	Possible on small scale	Decisive

supremacy of Great Britain. Its weapons were the frigate and privateer in the eighteenth century, the torpedo boat and cruiser in the nineteenth century, and the submarine in the twentieth century. Yet the tactics of the *guerre de course* remained essentially the same. They are also the tactics of guerrilla warfare. Each is the offensive of the weaker against the stronger. The employer of each attempts to avoid the enemy's military forces and to strike at his supply lines and communications. The motto of the *Jeune École* is also the motto of the guerrilla: "Shamelessly attack the weak, shamelessly fly from the strong."[3] Mobility, concealment, and surprise are the allies of both. Both employ the tactics of hit-and-run. The security that the guerrilla finds in rugged terrain and a friendly populace the commerce raider finds in the empty reaches and lower depths of the ocean. In both, the psychological effects of the military action often outweigh the military effects. Both attempt to spread uncertainty, panic, and disorder. The successful operation of both involves small units—guerrilla bands or individual ships—loosely coordinated and directed by a superior authority. In each case these forces must put first priority on preserving their own existence. Neither can risk a dubious battle. Each puts a premium upon daring, imaginative, resourceful leadership of these small units: Paul Jones and Gunther Prien had all the essential characteristics of a successful guerrilla. Each form of warfare eschews heavy armament. Each is relatively inexpensive to engage in and very expensive to combat. To a large extent, the success of both is measured by the resources which the enemy has to divert to defend itself against them.

The requirements of effective counterguerrilla warfare closely resemble those employed to combat the *guerre de course*. The antisubmarine warfare

---

3. Quoted in Theodore Ropp, "Continental Doctrines of Sea Power," in Edward Mead Earle (ed.), *Makers of Modern Strategy* (Princeton, 1943), p. 450.

men of the Navy and the counterguerrilla forces of the Army are confronted with similar problems. The most effective counterthrust is to destroy the base areas from which the guerrillas operate and the naval bases from which the submarines operate. A second form of counteraction is to create strong points that can defend themselves against surprise attack. In counterguerrilla warfare, this means fortifying key supply and transportation centers and the resettlement of peasants in areas where they can be protected. In antisubmarine warfare it means resort to convoys. A third tactic is to attempt to search out and destroy the elusive raiders. In counterguerrilla warfare this requires mobile columns equipped with cross-country vehicles, helicopters, and light weapons. In antisubmarine warfare, it means hunter-killer groups of fast aircraft carriers and destroyers. Finally, in each case, it is at times possible, within limits, to set a thief to catch a thief. Guerrillas can assist in the detection and elimination of guerrillas; submarines can assist in the detection and elimination of submarines. In each case, intelligence plays a critical role in the successful operations. The guerrillas and the submarines must be found before they can be destroyed. Sonar and radar are to antisubmarine warfare what spies and scouts are to counterguerrilla warfare.

The strengths and limits of the *guerre de course* are the strengths and limits of guerrilla warfare. As a supplementary weapon the *guerre de course* served its progenitors well. Some members of the *Jeune École* hoped, however, that through the *guerre de course* they could achieve a cheap victory without destroying the military strength of the enemy. They deceived themselves in thinking that they could make it more than a harassing device. Mahan easily exposed the shallowness of their arguments and the futility of their dreams. In 1916 the Germans thought that the submarine had now made possible the defeat of a superior naval power dependent upon extensive overseas commerce. But again commerce raiding failed to be decisive. In World War II a much larger German effort came closer to success, in part because the British were suffering from overconfidence derived from their World War I victory.[4] Between 1939 and 1944 the U-boats effectively tied up Allied resources in the battle of the Atlantic just as Allied guerrillas pinned down a score of Axis divisions in the Balkans. The battle was hard and close, but again commerce destruction alone was unable to tip the scales. In contrast, the American submarine campaign in the Pacific did make a significant contribution to the defeat of Japan because it was a supplement to rather than a substitute for command of the sea. The Napoleonic Wars, the War of 1812, and two World Wars reveal the potentialities and, more especially, the limitations of the *guerre de course.*

---

4. For an excellent brief summary, see Bernard Brodie, *A Guide to Naval Strategy* (Princeton, 1958; 4th ed., Naval War College Edition), pp. 136–152.

Similarly, today, it would be a mistake to overdramatize the threat or the opportunities of guerrilla warfare. At the appropriate moment in revolutionary war, limited war, general war, and total war, the guerrilla may have a major role to play; but he cannot play it for long alone and unaided. The guerrilla can destroy but he cannot conquer. God remains on the side of the bigger battalions—and guerrilla battalions are always small. Guerrilla warfare makes the most of small battalions, but guerrilla troops are no more a substitute for superior conventional forces than the torpedo boats of the *Jeune École* were a substitute for the line of battle of the Royal Navy.

III. GUERRILLA WARFARE IN AMERICAN POLICY

The most immediate problem posed by guerrilla warfare for American policy is in connection with revolutionary war. Other types of wars are possible, but they seem less likely to occur than revolutionary wars.[5] Khrushchev himself has rejected total war and limited war but has endorsed "wars of national liberation." All revolutionary wars move through a guerrilla phase. Timely and appropriate counteraction may prevent them from moving out of that phase. Communist guerrillas in Malaya, Greece, and the Philippines were effectively squelched. The strategy of both the revolutionary and the counterrevolutionary forces in a revolutionary war, however, involves far more than guerrilla warfare. A doctrine of counterguerrilla warfare is a necessary but not a sufficient doctrine in the struggle against revolutionary forces. Doctrines of guerrilla warfare and counterguerrilla warfare, moreover, may be derived from the experiences of World War II and other wars where guerrilla warfare played a supplementary role. In revolutionary war, the tactics of guerrilla warfare remain the same, but its strategic role and implications differ. Revolutionary war is a distinctive type of war, as different from the traditional interstate limited war as the Korean War was from World War II. To win a revolutionary war, it is necessary to carry on a prolonged campaign for the support of a crucial social group.[6] Guerrilla warfare and counterguerrilla warfare must be directed to this goal. Thus, the immediate problem of the United States is to develop a doctrine of counterguerrilla warfare as one element in a broader politico-military strategy of counterrevolutionary war.

What role does guerrilla warfare itself have in American strategy? At the moment undoubtedly its place is a minor one.[7] At some time in the

---

5. See my *Instability at the Non-Strategic Level of Conflict* (Institute for Defense Analyses, Study Memorandum Number 2, October 6, 1961), pp. 10–16.
6. See my "Patterns of Violence in World Politics," in *Changing Patterns of Military Politics* (Free Press, 1962), pp. 17–50.
7. See Peter Paret and John Shy, *Guerrillas in the 1960s* (Praeger, 1961), chap. V.

future, however, guerrilla warfare could become an important instrument of American policy. For this to happen will require major innovations in American strategic doctrine. Guerrilla warfare has not been an American *forte*. Guerrillas played a significant role in our eighteenth-century revolutionary war, when we were the underdog and the intervention of an outside power was necessary to secure victory. They also played a somewhat less important role on the southern side in the Civil War. In most of its wars, however, the United States has not had to rely upon guerrilla warfare. American experience with guerrilla warfare has been limited by the strength of American arms. The United States has been able to mobilize overwhelming economic and military power and to bring it to bear directly on the enemy, attacking him not where he was weakest but where he was strongest, because we were stronger still. American military doctrine has reflected this experience. It has followed the pattern of what Churchill called "the American clearcut, logical, large-scale, mass-production style of thought." British strategy, on the other hand, has traditionally followed an intermediate path. Less liberally endowed with resources and manpower, the British have relied upon what Sir Julian Corbett called a "maritime strategy" and Liddell Hart "the strategy of the indirect approach." This is one step away from the American theory of the steamroller offensive toward a strategy of the weaker.

In the future the United States may find itself forced to act in areas and in ways in which it can no longer bring to bear overwhelming military force. It may find itself forced to lead from weakness rather than from strength, its military power caught in the twin fetters of political exigency and mutual deterrence. In such situations the United States could have occasion to resort to guerrilla warfare, the classic strategy of the weaker. This is not, perhaps, a happy prospect, but it may well be one of the many adaptations that Americans will have to make in their struggle for survival in a world that they can neither escape nor dominate.

Modern Guerrilla Warfare

PART 1

REVIEW OF GUERRILLA WARFARE
AND MODERN APPLICATIONS

Guerrilla warfare is scarcely new. This section begins by recalling some instances in the long history of guerrilla warfare in Europe, North America, and the Middle East. We then turn to more modern applications, especially those of the last twenty years. Most of the major guerrilla movements since World War II are treated in more detail in the subsequent parts of this volume.

Guerrillas are known by many different labels, but, unless otherwise defined by individual authors, the term "guerrillas" may be considered to mean irregulars, partisans, bandit bands, terrorists, resistance groups, and special forces.

In the first selection, Wilkins cites some of the more historically significant guerrilla campaigns and demonstrates the influence of guerrilla history on modern Communist practices. Next, Sollom analyzes the anatomy of guerrilla forces. He points out certain governing factors necessay to successful guerrilla warfare, and notes certain limitations of the guerrilla fighter. Following that, Ney analyzes modern methods of waging guerrilla warfare and summarizes the conditions that seem necessary for effective guerrilla operations. Finally, Kutger reviews some historic examples of guerrilla warfare and contrasts them with modern applications; he concludes with an example of successful counterguerrilla operations in Malaya after World War II.

1

Lt. Col. Frederick Wilkins
U.S. Army (Retired)

GUERRILLA

WARFARE

*N*O LONGER A LIMITED MILITARY TACTIC, guerrilla warfare has political and economic consequences that can be more dangerous than the armed force employed. Guerrilla warfare is an open sore that annoys today, is a nuisance tomorrow, weakens in a month, and may cause death if not treated properly. Guerrilla warfare may be waged in the Malayan jungle, in the rear areas of Korea, or on a college campus or the councils of a labor union. The technique is the same; the end is the same.

What we now call guerrilla warfare is as old as mankind. In a thousand campaigns an invaded and overrun country has been able to keep alive the spark of national feeling by the actions of a few brave men, usually operating in mountain or forest land. These irregular bands were able to compensate for lack of numbers and military skill by superior mobility and knowledge of the countryside. By attacking small groups of the enemy under surprise conditions they achieved local success, though they seldom achieved any lasting results. Such men found a place in the legends of many lands, but they made small impression in military history.

From *U.S. Naval Institute Proceedings,* March, 1954, by permission; copyright 1954 by U.S. Naval Institute.

Some of the old campaigns did have remarkable results. During the Hundred Years' War the English lost most of their lands in France as a result of such a guerrilla campaign. Du Guesclin, Constable of France, refused to fight the English in open combat. He had studied in the English tactical system and correctly interpreted the reasons for their battlefield superiority. Since they always had inferiority of numbers, the English fought in a prepared position, using the missile action of their superb archers to shatter the French men-at-arms. Once the enemy had been disorganized by the flights of arrows, the English reserve would charge and rout the remainder. The great battles of the war all followed this pattern.

Du Guesclin simply refused to attack the English. Instead he raided them at night, ambushed their convoys, harried their fortified camps and towns. He made no effort to drive them from France; he merely made it uncomfortable for them to stay! This type of military activity greatly encouraged the French, disgusted and discouraged the English. The English gradually lost most of what they had won in battle, without ever having a chance to fight. It was an ungentlemanly, unknightly way to wage war, this system of *not* fighting, and it found little favor with the medieval warriors of either side. History, that marvelous storehouse of forgotten battles, lost opportunities, and neglected lessons, noted briefly the success of Du Guesclin. It would be many a century before his methods were again employed.

American colonial warfare developed some excellent irregular fighters, such as the celebrated Rogers Rangers. We had an outstanding guerrilla fighter in Marion "the Swamp Fox," and various of the Eastern Indian chiefs waged skillful irregular combat. There was a slightly tainted view held by the military of the day, and the irregular fighter was looked upon as neither necessary, decent, nor skilled. The best way to win a battle was to have a firm, steady line of Regulars, able to move in with a bayonet and take their losses without flinching.

It was not until the Spanish campaigns of 1808–1814 that the name and methods of the guerrilla were fully developed. When the French invaded Spain, they easily defeated the regular Spanish troops. They captured cities and towns and shattered army after army, but they never were able to dominate the countryside. Spain, was mountainous, then densely wooded; roads were few and poor. Communications between French garrisons was difficult, and the French began to suffer from the actions of irregular civilian bands. A few peasants gathered and ambushed a wagon train and fled to the hills. A courier was killed on a lonely mountain road. Cavalry patrols were lured to death in the woods. The French used cruel methods to stop these attacks, and the irregulars had even harsher answers.

It is estimated that the French lost as many as a hundred men a day to the irregulars; it was unsafe for less than twenty-five armed soldiers to venture across country; even large forces were attacked. When the irregulars became bold enough to fight pitched battles they were beaten, but they seldom offered to fight. This form of fighting the Spanish called *guerrilla*—"little war"—and so we know it today. As the guerrillas achieved local success they began working with bands in other provinces; the Spanish people took heart, and the flame of resistance, which might have died, burned brighter each year. French forces were tied up in futile marches and searches; they lost men and achieved no results, and the loss of equipment and arms was a heavy drain on French finances.

As the war dragged on the guerrilla leaders began cooperating with the English forces in Portugal and Spain. They began training for combat as regular troops, and when the final battles were being fought the Spanish guerrillas fought side by side with the English through Spain and into France. Wellington gave them great praise. It is doubtful if the English, despite their fine infantry and the not always inspired tactics of the French, could have won had not the Spanish guerrillas sapped the strength of the French over the years. Had the French been able to concentrate all their forces they would have driven the English from Portugal, however inept their tactics.

So, here was the first modern guerrilla campaign and one of the most successful. With Wellington delivering the final coup the Spanish guerrilla part in the fight was largely overlooked. The experts of the day made much the same mistakes we have made in recent years and looked on the guerrilla as a man for a local fight; he was good enough for a tactical advantage, but not to be considered in strategical planning.

Between 1814 and World War I guerrilla campaigns were waged in many parts of the world. Mexican guerrillas seriously hampered Scott's movements in the Mexico City Campaign; there were fine guerrilla leaders on both sides in our Civil War; the winning of the West was a lengthy guerrilla fight; the British fought such bands in several out-of-the-way corners of the Empire; and the Russians engaged the Turkoman tribes in various guerrilla battles. Not one of these guerrilla campaigns had any hope of eventual success, and they all gave way after local tactical victories. At the time no one saw that these failures were due to faulty, or lacking, over-all plans. Guerrilla combat was a measure of desperation, not a planned strategical scheme. For that reason all guerrilla campaigns were eventual failures, even though the guerrillas often won many local battles.

What guerrillas can accomplish with a proper *strategical* plan was shown by T. E. Lawrence in the 1916–1918 campaigns in Arabia and Palestine. This is not the place for a discussion of Lawrence; that has been done before and will be done in the future. One Englishman dismissed him as a "comical little bastard," and others have been lost in beauties of his prose and word portraits of Arab life. Whatever the truth about Lawrence may finally be, he was the first man to reduce guerrilla warfare to a set of rules. Where others had fought because it was all they could do under the circumstances, he adopted guerrilla warfare after careful thought. He was the first leader to see that the true objective of guerrilla warfare is not necessarily fighting.

While not a trained military man, Lawrence had read all the military classics and was convinced of the soundness of the Clausewitz doctrine that the enemy field army must be destroyed. Sent to Arabia to organize the Arab tribes and lead a revolt against Turkey, Lawrence and his Arabians had a measure of success at first. Mecca was captured, but efforts to take Medina failed. The Arabs were beaten in open battle, and the rebellion seemed in danger of collapse.

When he was recovering from an illness, Lawrence began trying to find the cause for their failure. Clausewitz might be a good guide for European war, but they were not in Europe. It began to dawn on Lawrence that they were trying to fight a European war in a non-European theater. He was trying to fight regulars with irregular troops. No matter how much the British instructors tried to build an Arab army, they would never be able to stand against the Turkish forces in open battle. When Lawrence decided that this was not necessary, he went on to evolve a plan for guerrilla warfare that has been the model ever since.

In *Seven Pillars of Wisdom* Lawrence explained the plan that eventually defeated the Turks in Arabia. "In the Turkish Army materials were scarce and precious, men more plentiful than equipment . . . the aim should be to destroy not the army but the materials." Eventually 35,000 Turkish casualties resulted from the new change in methods, but they were incidental to the attack on enemy material. The plan was to convince the Turks *they couldn't stay,* rather than to drive them out.

Using English demolition specialists Lawrence had the Arabs blow up railway bridges and tunnels, cut rails, harass fortified railway stations. Medina was no longer the primary objective; the railway to the city was the target. Isolated posts and garrisons were threatened, so that the Turks reinforced them. No further attacks were made, as the heavily reinforced garrison sat about and ate up their rations. In a short time the Turkish troops had additional supply problems. No open battles were allowed by Lawrence. Whenever the enemy concentrated to crush the rebellion, he had his tribesmen scatter and avoid raids. Lulled into a false feeling of security the Turkish forces would resume their garrison positions—whereupon the raids would start again.

The Turkish position gradually became impossible in Arabia. Garrisons withered and the effectiveness of the Turkish field force was largely on paper. Lawrence even wanted to keep it in being in Arabia, as the necessity for feeding the scattered units placed a heavy drain on the already burdened enemy supply system. As they had local success the Arab tribes were gradually joined into one unit, or such was the plan. That it did not ever come to final accomplishment was no fault of Lawrence. In the final victorious sweep of the Allied forces through Palestine and Syria the necessary ground work done by the Arab guerrillas was lost in the clash of combat. Allenby and Syria was much like Wellington and Spain. Despite this parallel, Lawrence had made too much of a name to be forgotten. He wrote an article for one of the leading reference works and reduced his views on guerrilla warfare to final form. He almost converted the tactics of the guerrilla to a science and claimed that no enemy could occupy a country employing guerrilla warfare unless every acre of land could be occupied with troops.

His work, however, was appreciated more in Russia and China than among his own people. The spread of Communism saw his methods copied in two major theaters of conflict and in many lesser fights. To his basically military system the Chinese and Russians grafted economic and political concepts that have radically expanded and altered guerrilla warfare.

Shortly after Lawrence, Lenin was writing on the best methods for revolutionary movements to use. Like Lawrence he advocated avoiding the enemy strength and adapted guerrilla warfare to the business of world revolution and destruction. Intelligence of enemy movements, while keeping your own plans hidden, is a basic guerrilla—and Communist—tactic, perhaps the one prime tactical secret. By employing small, rigidly controlled units the Communist—or guerrilla leaders—can out-maneuver larger, less mobile forces. By concentrating on vital objectives the guerrilla —or revolutionist—weakens the enemy, while encouraging his own people. During the time actual physical attacks are being made, the enemy is being slowly weakened by creating disunion, distrust, and loss of morale among his forces, whether military or civilian. The non-military emphasis is on talk and discussion, rather than action. The entire Communist movement was reduced to a giant guerrilla campaign. One new feature was added to earlier ideas—the use of fear. The deliberate use of terror as a means of breaking down resistance, while keeping your own people under control.

Lenin was not the only Red leader to write on guerrilla warfare. A soon-to-be famous Chinese wrote a short discussion of guerrilla warfare in 1937 that is one of the classics in this field. At the time he wrote, Mao Tse-tung was somewhat less to be feared than today, which qualifies him as the prime example of the local guerrilla making good. Mao's work is a blend of Communist party line, his own field experience, and the writings of Sun Tzu, a Chinese writer of about 500 B.C. Mao made one major contribution to guerrilla strategy, only partially developed by Lawrence. This was the view that a guerrilla force would eventually grow to a regular army. This was largely due to the long period Mao and the Chinese Communists had been fighting and the Asiatic contempt for time.

A few leftists appeared when the Manchu Empire was breaking up at the turn of the century; by the twenties and the struggle between the war lords in China, a definite Communist Party was active. At first they actually cooperated with Chiang, but when it was clear that he was destined to win control, they broke and became his bitterest foe. Open war started in 1927, and between 1931 and 1934 Chiang fought four major campaigns against the Reds and finally drove them on the famous long march to Chansi Province. Chiang was never able to completely destroy the Communist Army in China, as internal troubles and the Japanese kept him from making an all-out effort. So, on the edge of the nation, the Chinese Communists managed to establish a firm base. The people who knew the real nature of this settlement naturally didn't talk, and the world came to look on Mao and his people as "agrarian reformers."

The Japanese invasion gave the Reds a chance to play the part of patriots. In 1937 Mao issued his pamphlet on guerrilla warfare, which was widely read throughout China. This study is a fine blend of military advice, Red preaching, political guidance, and economic control. It is a lot plainer now than in 1937 just how connected the fields are and were in the Chinese guerrilla forces. Mao carefully explained the nature of his guerrilla forces, answering the charges of the Nationalists that his men were no more than bandits. However his politics may be taken, Mao had correctly estimated the Chinese situation and the Japanese weakness. Certain selected portions of his work will show his main points.

> In a war of revolutionary character guerrilla operations are a necessary part . . . these guerrilla operations must not be considered as an independent form of warfare. They are but one step in the total war; one aspect of the revolutionary struggle. . . .

> During the progress of hostilities guerrillas gradually develop into orthodox forces that operate in conjunction with units of the regular army. . . .

> What is the relationship of guerrilla warfare to the people? Without a political goal guerrilla warfare must fail, as it must if its political objectives do not coincide with the aspirations of the people and their sympathy, cooperation and assistance cannot be obtained. . . .

> Because guerrilla warfare basically derives from the masses and is supported by them it can neither exist nor flourish if it separates itself from their sympathies and cooperation.

> All guerrilla units must have political and military leadership. These . . . must be well educated in revolutionary technique, self-confident, able to establish severe discipline, and able to cope with counter-propaganda. . . . What is basic guerrilla strategy? Guerrilla strategy must primarily be based on alertness, mobility and attack. . . .

> An opinion that admits the existence of guerrilla war but isolates it is one that does not properly estimate the potentialities of such war.

Isolated quotes, however honestly selected, are not a substitute for the whole, but these contain the main points of Mao's work on guerrilla warfare. In his tactical discussions, which are brief and subordinate to political guidance, Mao leans heavily on Sun's ancient book, even to exact phrasing. All guerrillas have used the ancient teachings of Sun, for this is the only way a guerrilla band can fight—with deception, speed, surprise.

Mao did devise a strategical plan to fit the Chinese topography and military capabilities, as well as the Japanese weakness. He estimated that the Japanese could only spare a certain force for China and must win a victory as quickly as possible. As long as the invaders could concentrate their forces and had good communications they could probably defeat any force the Chinese could put in the field. Therefore, the guerrilla strategy would be to fight them on a broad front, forcing them to disperse, while attacking their communication and supply systems.

In order to pose as patriots the Communist forces had to fight the Japanese—this also afforded a practice ground for their future conflicts with Chiang when the Japanese had been defeated and gave them secure control over provinces they liberated from the Japanese. The Chinese Red Eighth Army and the New Fourth Army fought largely as regular troops, though they did assume the role and tactics of guerrilla bands when necessary. These regular troops established guerrilla districts and areas and set up control headquarters. They screened the local population for friendly and unfriendly civilians and organized regular guerrilla bands. Ranking below the organized guerrillas were "armed peasants," who fought as guerrillas, though without a definite organization. No accurate reports were kept, but it is estimated that the Eighth Army had nearly a half-million guerrillas and armed peasants in its area. The New Fourth Army controlled something over a hundred thousand.

These groups were given training in the use of weapons, sabotage, demolitions—and political science, Russian style. As weapons were brought in or captured military operations were stepped up. Careful propaganda made it appear that only the Red guerrillas were fighting the Japanese; they did play a large part, though not as much as the world was led to believe. On a few raids they struck massive blows. During August, 1940, a concerted series of raids blasted two hundred miles of vital railway track and five hundred miles of highway; bridges and telegraph systems were blown up. Japanese communication throughout North China was largely shattered for a considerable period.

Like the Arabs, the Chinese guerrillas made no effort to fight a pitched battle. The Japanese were weakest in their equipment and communication fields, and the guerrillas struck at the material side of the Japanese invaders. They were a steady drain on the Japanese homeland, while preventing the invaders from consolidating their mainland conquests. The invasion of China was to have had a profitable return for the Japanese; the guerrillas not only kept them from showing a profit, they made the whole affair a financial loss. And while all this was going on, Mao and his guerrillas were training and getting ready for the day when the Japanese would leave and the final showdown with Chiang would come about.

It came with the end of the war. The Russians took over the Japanese forces in Manchuria and turned their arms and equipment over to the guerrillas. When the Nationalists adopted a policy of static defense, much as had the Japanese, the guerrillas cooped them in the towns, cut communications, and began their change from guerrillas to field armies. Province after province, city after city, China fell to the Reds. The old-time guerrillas had developed into the rulers of the new China.

Russian leaders had influenced the course of the Chinese guerrilla movement. In World War II they organized a campaign second only in size to that of the Chinese. *The Russian Partisan Directive of 1933* laid down the general plan of guerrilla warfare in the event Russia was invaded. Despite this planning, there was very little guerrilla action during the initial stages of the German invasion. The massive blows of the *Panzer* formations smashed the Russian border units and drove deeper into Russia. German combat units, initially, acted as occupation troops in the overrun areas. While they were strict enough, they were fair and generally treated the Russians as human beings; on the whole there was not too much resentment among the civilian population. In the Ukraine the Germans were accepted as friends.

When the German combat units moved deeper into Russia, the occupation mission was turned over to political troops. To these troops the Russians were nothing more than slave labor; they seemed to do everything possible to create resentment. After the initial shock of invasion, thousands of by-passed Russian troops began raiding as guerrillas, operating in the extensive forest and swamp areas. The Russian high command was not slow to take advantage of this new feeling. The local civilians were aroused against the invaders. Actual terror acts were blamed on the Germans; if there were no incidents, they were staged. The Russian civilians shifted from their previous hands-off stand to one of aid and comfort to the growing guerrilla bands. By late 1941 sniping and sabotage were common in the German rear areas.

Russian propaganda seized on the Partisans as heroes, which many of them were. The leaders were written up in the press as unselfish men and women, leading their children against the foe. Actually, the typical guerrilla leader was a pretty hard character. If a civilian, as most were at first, he rose to command through strength of character, guts, and luck. Within a short time commanders with tested military background began taking over many bands. Political advisers began joining; it became just as important for the guerrillas to be politically correct as to be militarily successful. In doubtful areas, such as the Ukraine, it was more important.

Party doctrine and discipline was ruthlessly enforced by the guerrilla leaders. Once a person was in a partisan group, he was in for life. Suspected traitors were slain without mercy. The local civilians were used as spies and for food supplies; any village that did not cooperate was destroyed. Civilians were used as decoys and as shields when attacking German bases. In time the guerrilla fight became a simple matter of survival, with the poor villager caught between the Russian and the German, each determined that he would not help the other.

Russian tactics were much the same as all guerrilla tactics. They operated in small groups, at least initially, using bases in the swamps and forests. The Russian road net was poor, and German supply was by means of the railways. These became the chief Partisan objective, with communications and German command posts secondary targets. The Russian guerrillas planned to slow the German supply system and disrupt troop movements by cutting the railroads. Attacks on the communication centers would bring about confusion and lack of cooperation among German troop units, while the attacks on command posts would further disrupt control. As these attacks increased, it would be necessary for the Germans to pull back front-line troops to protect their rear areas.

These plans were quite successful. By 1942 Russian guerrillas were fairly well organized and under some top-level control, though many smaller bands operated independently. Air drops became common, and the capture of German supplies enabled more men to take the field. During 1943 the Russian guerrillas became a serious threat and the Germans began giving thought to the best way to stop this menace. Special hunter groups were formed and extensive "round ups" of suspected areas were made. The movement was too extensive by now, and during 1944 the German rear area troops spent more time fighting guerrillas than they did in their normal missions. All forms of transport and communication were seriously hampered. Some of their actions were carefully coordinated. The night of June 19–20, 1944, Russian guerrillas placed 15,000 demolition charges in the sector of German Army Group Center and managed to explode over 10,000. Besides the actual damage, the confusion resulting from such a mass attack can well be imagined.

Not all of the guerrillas' missions were successful, however. Like most individuals the groups could not stand success and were destroyed attempting missions too ambitious for their capabilities. Some bands grew to such size they could not hide or move fast and were hunted down. Some large bands tried to fight it out with the Germans in the open and were destroyed. Often the guerrillas tipped the Germans to planned attacks by their actions in a quiet sector. Though they had severe losses at times and listed failures with their victories, the Russian guerrillas made a substantial contribution to the final victory. In the last stages of the Russian counter offensive they cut off stragglers, ruined roads, made lateral communication difficult, and caused units desperately needed at the front to be diverted for protection of command posts and railways.

The end of World War II did not mean the end of guerrilla action. With a battle-tested technique the Reds started guerrilla campaigns in many places, following Mao's teaching of a widespread war. Greece, Malaya, the Philippine Islands, Indo-china and various lesser guerrilla actions show how well the Reds have used the guerrilla method to undermine their enemies.

There is a sameness about these campaigns, however much they may be separated geographically. The very fact of separation is also part of the plan—if the West tries to help all at the same time a serious economic burden is placed on a system that the Reds believe is already tottering. If we do not help, then they can win the countries. All of these guerrilla campaigns have taken place or are taking place in rough country, whether the Greek mountains or the jungles of the Far East. A great claim to be representing the people has been made, whether the native against the European, as in Malaya and Indo-china, or the patriot against the oppressive tools of the foreign Capitalists, as in the Philippines and in Greece. In all cases the war has been waged with a callous disregard for life and property, and guerrilla actions have been little more than a campaign waged by bandits. In only one place, Indochina, have the guerrillas made a serious effort to drive the outsiders from the country.

It would be the most dangerous kind of thinking to minimize these movements for this reason, or to fail to recognize them for the vital danger they are, simply because they seem to partake more of the nature of robbery and arson than regular warfare. What the Communist leaders have done is make a simple military estimate of the situation and launch an attack on the part of the West that offers the best chance of success, with the least cost and effort. Some of these guerrilla actions have been going on for seven years; only the Greek guerrillas have been crushed.

Had Greece fallen to the Reds the Balkans would have been solidly Communist, and Turkey would have been in a dangerous pincers. Despite American and British aid, the Greek Communist guerrillas waged successful war against their fellow countrymen for several years. They were well supplied by Red agents north of the border and could move into Bulgaria and other Balkan countries whenever they needed to rest and refit. The guerrillas were well armed and had high morale, the result of combat success and constant Red training and teaching. At the height of the guerrilla movement there were some 73,000 guerrillas in action. They completely wrecked the national life of a nation of seven million and forced over seven hundred thousand people to flee from their homes; entire regions of Greece were devastated and the economic life of the country was ruined.

Red tactics were based on a destructive process—as they are in Asia. The two main strongholds were in the northern mountains, but the guerrillas had scattered bands operating throughout Greece. These pockets kept the nation disturbed, ruined crops, forced people to leave their homes, raided small villages and towns, and kidnapped people to be held as hostages. The failure of the National Government to stop these attacks cast discredit on Athens and bolstered guerrilla prestige. While the people as a whole opposed them, the guerrilla managed to get cooperation in many areas by fear of reprisal.

After extensive British and American aid and advisers had been brought in, a major effort was made to defeat the guerrillas. Local defense forces were organized to protect the villages and curb the fear of reprisal. A minimum field force was established to contain the guerrilla forces in the northern mountains, while a major cross-country sweep was made to eliminate the bands in southern Greece. Suspected and known Reds were rounded up, so that the guerrillas would not have intelligence of the coming attacks. Then the guerrilla pockets were attacked night and day, with field forces moving on a broad front and giving no opportunity for the beaten guerrillas to rally, or slip northward. The Vitsi sector was reduced and then the Grammos Mountain area, the attacking forces giving the beaten Reds no chance to rest or reorganize. This all took longer than the telling, but a winning *military* formula had been evolved.

Unfortunately, this formula cannot be so readily applied in Asia. The guerrilla war in Indochina has grown into full-scale combat, with the guerrillas making the change from raider bands to regularly organized divisions. Extremely difficult terrain in Malaya and the Philippine Islands hampers antiguerrilla work in these lands. Political and economic factors in Europe have prevented the all-out war that was possible in Greece. The Greek guerrillas were well established and occupied definite areas. The Malayan guerrilla may be a farmer today, a merchant tomorrow, a guerrilla at night.

At no time have more than 5,000 guerrillas been active in Malaya; the British and native police forces have probably killed this many, but the Reds are able to recruit new fighters, or slip them in from China. This small force ties up many times its own numbers in troops and costs over a million dollars each week to fight. They stir up resentment between the British and the local rulers and try to split the Malay and Chinese into rival camps. And they make raids on the tin and rubber mines and plantations, killing, burning, driving away native workers, killing white leaders. This is more than banditry. It is a well planned campaign to destroy British economic wealth. Rubber and tin are major British offerings in the world of trade; without Malayan tin and rubber the British position world-wide is seriously weakened.

As long as the Chinese in Malaya believe they are being treated as an inferior race, they will support and aid the guerrillas. If the Malays believe they have nothing to fight for, they will not take a major part in defending their country. The answer is not a military one alone. Killing bandits is not enough—seven years of bandit killing have not solved anything. The British now realize this, just as the Philippine government is now fighting guerrillas on a different plan. The guerrilla has a weakness, just as those he fights.

When there are no economic and political foundations for the guerrilla movement, there will be no guerrilla movement. The bulk of any guerrilla force joins out of belief in what it is doing; the hard core of leaders keeps going because of political beliefs. If the bulk of the band find they can live as decent human beings, do not have to rob to live, and can have land and homes, they will be poor guerrillas from then on. If the great mass of the population knows it will be protected by a strong, just government, it has no reason to cooperate with the guerrillas, and the system of intelligence and supply that sustains all guerrilla movements breaks down. Without popular support the mopping up of the hard-core die-hards is fairly easy.

The West will have guerrilla campaigns to combat as long as East and West sit on opposite sides of the fence. We have a serious situation in Korea today. North Africa and the Middle East offer possibilities for a half-dozen vicious guerrilla movements. These areas are vital to the West, both economically and geographically. We must be prepared to fight the guerrilla in two ways—militarily and politically. We can contain guerrillas temporarily by force, but the only lasting way to destroy a guerrilla movement is by removing the foundation upon which it stands. The belief that only out-of-the-way corners of the world offer shelter for guerrillas must be changed to a more realistic view. A guerrilla band can fight just as well in a large city as in the Malayan jungle. It would be well if we did not forget this.

Guerrilla warfare is a two-edged sword. While we are perfecting tactical techniques for military destruction of the guerrilla, we must make plans for actually taking the guerrilla campaign to the enemy. Guerrilla warfare is no longer a poor relation in the military family.

2

Lt. Col. A. H. Sollom
U.S. Marine Corps

NOWHERE

YET

EVERYWHERE

STUDENTS OF MILITARY HISTORY are sometimes bemused upon discovering what appears to be, at least on the surface, a strange paradox. That of a strong, well-equipped, well-trained army being unable to cope with an irregular force which may sometimes be composed almost entirely of poorly equipped civilians with little if any regular military training. This happened to Napoleon in Spain and later in Russia. The Japanese in WWII were never able to fully control the Philippines even though all regular U.S. units had been defeated. The Germans in the Second World War had more than their share of this irregular warfare; in Russia, France, Italy, Norway and in the Balkans armed civilians rose to thwart their operations.

The partisan has made his appearance innumerable times through the past ages, and we are indeed in error if we assume that he will not be on the fringes of the battlefield in future conflicts. Whether our aim is to utilize friendly partisans in conjunction with our own operations or to protect ourselves from the actions of enemy partisans, it is necessary to

From the *Marine Corps Gazette,* June, 1958. Copyright 1958 by the Marine Corps Association and reproduced by permission.

understand just what this pseudomilitary man is, why it is possible for him to successfully combat regular forces, and what types of operations he is capable of accomplishing.

The partisan movement is like a hothouse plant which blossoms only under the most exact conditions. Civilians do not ordinarily desire to disrupt the pattern of their day-to-day living with the violence of military conflict. Let us say then that there must be a motivating force which will cause a widespread spirit of resistance to the extent that the majority of the population will support the partisan group if not joining its active membership. The force which most often comes to mind in this respect is an invasion of an area by a foreign power such as occurred when Napoleon invaded Spain and when, in more recent times, Hitler overran Norway. However, an equally effective motivator can be political or revolutionary, such as is occurring at the present time in the far east.

The Chinese Communist leader, Mao Tse-tung, no amateur in this field, once wrote a pamphlet, *Problems in Guerrilla Warfare,* in which he asserted:

If guerrilla warfare is without a political objective, it must fail; but if it maintains a political objective which is incompatible with the political objectives of the people, failing to receive their support then this too must fail. This is the basic reason why guerrilla warfare can only be a form of a revolutionary war and why it cannot be utilized by any kind of counter-revolutionary war. This is because guerrilla warfare is basically organized and maintained by the masses, and once it is deprived of these masses, or fails to enlist their participation and co-operation, its survival and development is not possible.

If a country is ripe for the formation of partisan bands, in that the bulk of the people will support them, who then are to become the active members—the doers so to speak? If a person has much to lose from taking certain actions he will logically refrain from doing them; therefore, we find that the more wealthy members of the community are more content to support the partisan movement in a covert role, if at all. It is those who have nothing to lose who ordinarily become the active members. The peasant farmer, the poorer rural dweller are in this category. These are general statements; it would be inaccurate not to say that there are idealists and patriots among the wealthier classes who are willing to risk all for their country or for an ideology. Former soldiers may also take an active part in the movement. No matter from what source he springs, the active partisan must have the willingness and courage to face death and extreme hardship.

From these active groups of doers it is natural that a few individuals will appear as leaders to control the actions of the majority. They may not be the best qualified, the most moral or the most intelligent, but in the rough and tumble world of the partisan band it is safe to say that they will be the strongest and most determined.

Consider the partisan leader Páez, who can be ranked second only to Bolivar himself, in South America's struggle for independence. Here was a man who could neither read nor write but in spite of this, as well as a complete lack of military training, by the age of 20 he had gathered around him a formidable force of irregular cavalry, recruited from the wild Llaneros, whose home was the vast Venezuelan grasslands. His men revered him and performed impossible tasks for him because he was as wild and untamed as they. Páez would compete with them in their violent sports and emerge the winner. On the battlefield he was the most fierce of all—charging madly into the fray, he would hack away at the enemy until he fell, covered with the blood of his foes, in the throes of a sort of epileptic seizure. This same man later rose to the presidency of the Venezuelan Republic, but at the time he was engaged in guerrilla warfare he rode at the head of his band because he was the strongest among men who regarded physical strength as a virtue and also because he possessed the cunning of a predatory animal ranging through its native habitat.

The leader of the partisan band maintains control through inflexible discipline and often by the ruthless elimination of the opposition. The biblical axiom "Those who are not with me are against me" could very well be applied to the attitude of the partisan leader. Until the leader appears to direct the will and determination of the group into positive action there is no real, effective partisan movement.

The national spirit of resistance, the formation of active bands and the emergence of leaders, all of which we have discussed briefly, might be termed "human factors" in the growth of the partisan movement. Another factor which influences the formation of these irregular forces is that of terrain. Because of partisan limitations, which we will discuss later, favorable terrain must be available in which the partisan force can carry out its particular type of warfare. If such terrain is not available, the partisan may be ferreted out and destroyed. In rural areas will be found terrain suitable for partisan groups organized to conduct "open" military activities.

During WWII the Russian partisans would operate from bases located in swamps such as those near the Narva River. The only access to these strongholds was by following paths constructed below the water level or by the use of swamp skis which closely resemble snowshoes in giving the wearer the ability to traverse spongy surfaces common to swamps.

The communist-sponsored partisan forces which were such a menace in Greece following WWII had their strongholds in the Vitsi and Grammos mountains and it was not until these bases were destroyed in the summer of 1949 that the partisan movement in Greece collapsed.

Large cities provide suitable areas for the activities of partisans engaged in actions which are not usually considered military in nature. Perhaps the activity of the French underground in Paris in WWII is the best example of the utilization of this type of "terrain."

A third factor in the growth of partisan forces is that of supply. There must be food, shelter and tools of war available to the partisan. His food is usually obtained from the civil population which supports his actions and is in sympathy with his intentions. If this food is not delivered voluntarily, the civilian may be forced to provide for the partisan's needs. However, such action by the partisan may alienate the civil support the partisan needs if he is to flourish.

In favorable climates his needs for shelter may be few, a cave or a lean-to may suffice, but under less temperate conditions he must again turn to the civilian supporter for assistance.

The arms, ammunition and other tools of war required by the partisan may come from raids on enemy installations, battlefield salvage and from external sources. The partisan may operate small factories for the manufacture and repair of weapons and equipment.

The final factor is that of outside support. The full potential of a partisan movement is seldom realized until it receives assistance, particularly along logistical lines, from external sources. England in supporting the Arab partisans in WWI is said to have spent about 10 million pounds to keep the movement alive and effective. This outside support may also include providing personnel to assist in the training of partisans in a variety of military subjects. Advisor teams may be provided to assist the partisan commander in military and technical matters and also to coordinate the partisan operations with those of an outside, regular force. Perhaps the most publicized and best known of these advisors was the controversial figure of Col. T. E. Lawrence who guided and advised the Arabian tribes in their activities against the Turks in WWI.

Now that we have an idea of the source of the partisan forces and under what conditions they form let us examine what their characteristics are, or perhaps we might say, what their strengths and weaknesses are. First we will look at those characteristics which contribute to their capability of carrying on their operations.

Partisan forces usually operate in rear areas where regular forces are least prepared, equipped or trained to combat them. German officers in WWII who were unfortunate enough to become involved with the Russian partisan found that their troops had difficulty defending themselves against this type of warfare. The effectiveness of these irregular operations had been underestimated and even front line troops who were well trained for orthodox warfare were lacking in the experience and training necessary in antipartisan warfare. This lack of training was an even more serious weakness when present in those troops who occupied rear area installations and who operated along the lines of communications, as these are the usual targets for partisan attack. Partisans are usually formed into numerous small units dispersed over a wide area. In other words in depth.

Another characteristic contributing to partisan success is that the partisan is most often native to the area in which he operates. This gives him two distinct advantages. First, when he is not fighting, he may blend in with the surrounding population which is also composed of natives. This gives him a perfect disguise. US Marines who participated in the Pohang Guerrilla Hunt in Korea in the early part of 1951, are aware of the difficulty encountered in the differentiation of the North Korean partisan from the South Korean civilian. The second advantage gained in being native to the area of operation is that the partisan will have an intimate knowledge of the terrain in which he operates. He will be able to move swiftly through apparently impassable terrain because he will know the hidden trails. He will be able to exist in arid areas, for he will know the hidden water holes. The hiding places, the shelters, springs, rivers and trails are all known by him and secret from the outsider.

As we said earlier, one of the factors contributing to the development of a partisan movement was the presence of suitable terrain in which to operate. We include in such terrain: swamps, mountains and forests where mobility is limited to movements on foot and in light vehicles. The fact that the partisan operates in such terrain will be to his advantage for in an environment of this nature the regular forces lose the use of their vehicles and artillery as well as the ability to mass superior members. In essence, the terrain reduces the better equipped, better trained, and better armed regular force to a level where the partisan is its equal. It has been estimated that approximately 5,000 communist partisans in Malaya were being hunted by 230,000 regular soldiers and police, a seemingly overwhelming majority, but the jungle is the equalizer. In this jungle it took 1,000 man-hours of patrolling to make one contact with the partisans and 1,500 man-hours for each partisan killed. In open terrain the future of these partisans would be something less than secure.

Another characteristic which lends to partisan success is that the partisan has the support of the civilian population in the area of operations. As Mao, the leader of the Chinese Communist government, has stated, the people are the water in which the partisan fish swims. If the water becomes unhealthy the fish will die. The partisan, although he may at times assist in some of the work carried on in the community, cannot be considered as one of its self-sufficient or even contributing members. He is, therefore, dependent on his civilian supporter for his food and shelter. Because the civilian populace is willing to provide the partisan with the necessities of life, he is able to travel about without being too much concerned with a great many of the logistical problems which are always with the regular armies. Also, the partisan in his isolated stronghold has, in the civilian population, a ready-made outpost and intelligence system. For whom does the civilian of an invaded country normally have a feeling of sympathy and loyalty? The invader, or his own relatives, friends, and countrymen who compose the partisan force? The answer is obviously the latter. Because this is true, almost every civilian is a potential intelligence agent combined with an early warning system. It would be almost impossible for an enemy force to pass through such a community without the partisan learning every move perhaps even as it was taking place.

Russian partisans operating behind German lines were capable of moving as far as 45 miles in a day's time. Such a capability was not unique to the Russian partisan, it has been a characteristic of most partisan bands regardless of nationality. Irregular partisan cavalry, active against the Spanish in the South American revolutions, had the amazing ability of covering over 100 kilometers in 24 hours, which compares favorably with the mobility of modern mechanized units. How is such desirable mobility attained? Partisan forces are lightly armed. It is seldom that they will have artillery, tanks or other cumbersome weapons which would decrease mobility. The partisan force is organized into small units which travel rapidly and independently through the country with the ability of converging on a target, striking a strong blow ("un golpe terrifico" the Mexican partisan Poncho Villa termed it), and once again dispersing, a capability of more than passing interest in this age of nuclear tactics.

The partisan's characteristic which is the most important contributing factor in the success of his operations is the ability to conduct operations which achieve surprise. The partisan failing in this ability to achieve surprise would cease to be a problem, for then the regular force would be prepared to meet and defeat him. The partisan, however, does have this capability. If you know the enemy's movements, if you know the features of the terrain and if you can move your forces rapidly to a point of concentration and just as rapidly withdraw and disperse, you should be able to achieve surprise. As we have previously discussed, the partisans have all three of these abilities: intelligence sources, knowledge of the terrain, and great mobility, all of which contribute to the major capability—that of achieving surprise.

These have been characteristics which contribute to the capabilities of the partisan forces. While most publicity and discussion is about the successes which partisans have achieved, these irregular forces have some definite limitations in their operations. Let us now look at some of the characteristics which limit the scope of the partisan in his operations.

The partisan force, springing as it does from the civil population, may be composed of individuals who have never had any formal military training. It is also possible that a partisan leader, who maintains his position through the strength of his personality backed up by the strength of his arm, will be the most ignorant of all. A lack of instructors and training literature may prevent the remedying of this situation. Also there may be a lack of training facilities as well as the inability to muster the number of partisans necessary to conduct anything but small unit training. For such a group of military "amateurs" to challenge a regular force in anything but a hit-and-run engagement would be to invite disaster.

Modern warfare requires the employment of many tools which are not available to the partisan for his use. He may not be able to get them, and, indeed, his type of warfare may preclude his using them. Then, too, there is the problem of procurement of the trained personnel required to operate these technical tools of war. Tanks, artillery, aircraft, vehicles and heavy equipment are some of these implements of modern warfare not available to the partisan.

Another characteristic which limits the partisan in the scope of his operations is his inability to concentrate a large force for extended periods of time. The partisan in massing his troops becomes himself a lucrative target for attack. The regular force, instead of being faced with small units in great depth, now has something tangible to attack with its superior numbers, armament, and equipment. Because the partisan force lives off the civilian population and has little capability of transporting supplies, it may be difficult for the partisan supporters in a local area to provide the necessary shelter and quantity of food for a large group for an extended period.

The members of partisan bands have signed no contracts or enlistment papers, they are truly volunteers who have joined because they want to fight; however, if they do not feel like fighting tomorrow, they may not be available. The members may decide to go home and help with the harvest or to visit the old folks, so the partisan commander, unless he has unusually strong control, may find his muster rolls vacillating with the season and with the whims of his command. The fact that the majority of the members of a particular band may be from the same community can result in a particular sensitivity to casualties and defeats. T. E. Lawrence, in his book, *The Seven Pillars of Wisdom,* makes a statement which not only demonstrates this point but also describes the delicate relationship which exists between the native partisan and the alien advisor. He states,

> To me an unnecessary action or shot was not a waste but sin. I was unable to take the professional view that all successful actions were gains. Our rebels were volunteers, individuals, local men, relatives, so that a death was a personal sorrow to many in the Army.

Gen MacArthur, in order to sustain the courage of the partisan forces resisting the Japanese in the Philippines, reiterated at every opportunity that he would return to those islands and that the efforts of the partisans were not in vain. "I shall return" became a famous slogan which was not only broadcast by radio but which also appeared stenciled on the boxes of supplies which were surreptitiously delivered to the partisans by aircraft, submarine and small boat.

Perhaps the greatest limitation of all in the success of partisan operations is in the very nature of "guerrilla"-type tactics. Partisans cannot, by themselves, employing these tactics alone, defeat a determined regular army. They may help regular forces win wars, but unless they drop their guerrilla tactics and fight as a regular army, they cannot force a decision. When the partisan does quit his guerrilla tactics, and stands and fights, he no longer presents a special problem as he can then be defeated by regular forces much better equipped, trained and commanded to conduct normal military operations. Mao Tse-tung has expressed this opinion regarding the relationship of regular tactics and guerrilla tactics:

> Although guerrilla warfare may occasionally become the chief form of operation in the entire anti-Japanese war, it is the general chief form in the rear of the enemy. But taking the war as a whole, regular warfare is undoubtedly the main and basic form and its strategical role is decisive, whereas guerrilla warfare is its auxiliary.

Considering the characteristics, or strength and weaknesses, we have just examined, what then is the partisan capable of accomplishing? The operations conducted by the irregular groups can be placed into two major classifications: covert (clandestine) and overt (open).

Covert operations are usually associated with partisan groups operating in cities or built-up areas and are not considered to be really military in nature. These operations include the organization and instigation of civil disturbances such as labor strikes, work slowdowns, protest meetings and riots. Then, under the confusion of these disturbances, the partisan can employ the most effective weapon of the covert variety, sabotage. While these clandestine operations are of more than mere academic interest to the military man, the operations which are apt to affect him more directly are those of the overt or open classification.

Overt operations are generally associated with partisan forces organized along military lines and operating from suitable terrain in rural areas. The enemy, in using partisan forces in direct, quasi-military action, seeks to cause enough harassment and to interfere with operations in the rear areas to such an extent that substantial forces, which could better be utilized in the main battles, will have to be diverted to combating partisans and protecting rear installations and lines of communications. As the partisan force becomes better organized and better trained and its actions become more closely coordinated with the action taking place on the front lines, these operations assume greater significance. Important developments at the front will often result in extremely lively partisan activity, with the disruption and destruction of lines of communication the goal. The Germans in Russia, during one of their major attacks, had the unpleasant experience of having the main line of a railroad cut at 2,000 points in a single night. So effectively was the operation of the railroad disrupted that all traffic was stalled for several days. Such large-scale operations obviously had the effect of seriously hampering the supply of front-line troops and by doing so affected the outcome of the battle. The dollars-and-cents value of the material destroyed was little, and the number of personnel lost as a direct result of this action were few, but when interrupting the lines of communication at a time when the Germans were engaged in important operations at the front and thus preventing them from getting needed men and materials to critical points, the partisans could no longer be regarded as a mere annoyance and some positive action had to be taken by the Germans to protect themselves from this menace.

In a final analysis, the enemy seeks to divide our forces, to cause us to fight in two places, the normal front against his regular forces, where the decisive actions are taking place, and in the rear areas against his partisan forces.

The ambush, the sudden surprise attack from hiding upon a moving enemy, can be considered the forte of the partisan force. With the extensive intelligence screen, provided by civilians to learn of enemy movements, coupled with the intimate knowledge of the terrain and inherent mobility, the partisan is able to effectively establish ambushes directed against rail, vehicular, and foot movements. In his book, *American Guerrilla in the Philippines,* Ira Wolfert, describing the experiences of Lt Richardson, USN, has this to say about ambushes:

> The Japs sent heavy-weapons squads with their patrols. The guerrillas let them go by. Then, in the evening when the Japs came dragging back all loose and tired from maybe a 15-mile march on which they had found nothing, the guerrillas hit them. For the ideal ambush, you need a long, deep ravine on the tops of which your troops can stand and fire down from both sides. You need it long so that you can let the whole Jap column get into it before firing. That prevents them from deploying and coming in on your splitup forces. You need it deep so that your own people won't hit into each other when they fire.

Another common partisan operation is the surprise raid with the object of destroying or capturing arms, equipment, supplies, and personnel. Raids are also conducted against bridges, power plants, communication centers, and other installations which may be of importance to the enemy.

Only partisans who have attained a state of organization and training equal to that of regular forces, and who are well armed and supplied, are capable of successfully executing an attack in force against strong enemy garrisons and combat units. Operations conducted on this scale so closely parallel regular offensive combat that it is doubtful that they should be included as a partisan capability.

It is considered most unusual for the partisan force to engage in defensive combat. By going into a defensive position the partisan loses the characteristics which have made it possible for him to engage a regular force. He normally does not possess the necessary artillery, tanks, and other means to engage in this type of operation. The partisan can be expected to engage in temporary defensive combat to prevent enemy penetration of important partisan-controlled areas; however, he usually utilizes these operations to gain time to move to a new base of operations rather than engage in a prolonged position type defense.

The partisan is a civilian who has taken up arms.

He springs from the people and must have their support.

He can operate against regular forces because he capitalizes on his strong points and avoids those types of combat which expose his weaknesses.

To be most effective, the partisan carries on operations, both overt and covert, which complement the efforts of a regular force which is also engaging the common enemy.

The partisan who knows and stays within his own capabilities can be a useful ally or an adversary deserving the respect of the regular. . . .

3

Colonel Virgil Ney
U.S. Army (Retired)

GUERRILLA WARFARE

AND MODERN

STRATEGY

G UERRILLA WARFARE is as ageless as war itself. From the times of Alexander, Hannibal, and Caesar, the resistance of small bands to regular soldiery has constituted an important form of military conflict. The term "guerrilla warfare," however, passed into the military vocabulary only after the French invasion of the Iberian Peninsula in 1807, when Spanish irregular forces played a large role in the defeat of Napoleon.[1] By definition, the word "guerrilla" means a "little war." By usage, it gradually came to denote the irregular, nonprofessional civilian-soldier who accepts the challenge of the invading or occupying force either by supporting his country's professional army or by substituting for it.

From *Orbis*, Spring, 1958. Copyright 1958 by the Foreign Policy Research Institute, University of Pennsylvania, and reproduced by permission. Also see Virgil Ney's *Notes on Guerrilla War* (Washington, D.C., 1961).

The author is indebted to the Foreign Policy Research Institute, which permitted him to draw on extensive documentary material and a series of case studies on guerrilla warfare. The author gratefully acknowledges the assistance of FPRI Fellows Alvin J. Cottrell and James E. Dougherty.

1. The effectiveness of the Spanish guerrilla forces against the French in 1807 is vividly described in two novels by C. S. Forester, *The Gun* and *Death to the French*. See, also, "Yank" Levy, *Guerrilla Warfare* (New York, 1942), p. 56.

Guerrilla warfare, with its hit-and-run tactics, raids, terrorism, and sabotage, mocks the formality which is the hallmark of the traditional military profession. That a peasant or worker, armed with nothing but musket or rifle, could pose a serious challenge to well-equipped and highly trained professional troops was, for a long time, scarcely deemed credible by orthodox military tacticians.[2] Yet guerrilla bands have shown their military worth in the history of modern warfare. The Spaniards in 1807 and the Russians in 1812 and 1941 furnished classic examples of the effectiveness of guerrilla activity in support of professional armies.[3] Since the beginning of the second World War, this form of guerrilla action—i.e., a substitute for conventional warfare—has become much more prominent. Among the many instances in which guerrilla forces have been used successfully in lieu of regular armies, we may cite the war between Mao's Communists and Chiang's Nationalists, Tito's Partisans and the Nazis, and the current struggle in Algeria between the insurgents and the French army.

The main strength of guerrilla warfare is found in its very lack of military formality. Peasants or workers by day, guerrilla fighters by night: this formula tells not the whole story, but a good part of it. It is a conflict which is characterized by armed bands sallying forth to harass the enemy within his own lines and then fading back behind the curtain of the local population. Guerrilla warfare is conducted by civilians who usually have little formal military experience and little patience with the science of tactics by which modern mass armies operate. The abiding impetus which spurs

---

2. Even in Russia, which has experienced considerable success with guerrilla fighting, a controversy arose over the role of partisans in the defeat of Napoleon. For some time following the War of 1812, the exploits of the partisan leaders were praised, but a reaction later set in and "the generals and officers of the regular army, the heroes of Borodino and Maloyaroslavets, were reluctant to accept as their equals these daring raiders who submitted to no one, who came from nowhere and spent half their time in hiding, who captured baggage trains and shared the spoils, but were incapable of standing up in a pitched battle with regular French units." Eugene Tarlé, *Napoleon's Invasion of Russia* (Toronto, 1942), p. 349.

3. The idea to use guerrilla warfare to combat Napoleon in 1812 was prompted by its success in Spain. "Colonel Chuykevich, who wrote his *Reflections on the War of 1812* during the war itself (though the book was published only in 1813), recalls the Spaniards and cites them as a model: 'The rapid success of the French arms in Spain are explained by the fact that the inhabitants of that country, burning with desire to take revenge on the French, relied too much on their personal bravery and the justice of their cause. Hurriedly mobilized recruits were opposed to the French armies and were beaten by an enemy superior in numbers and experience. These disastrous lessons induced the brave Spaniards to change their methods of fighting. They magnanimously chose a protracted struggle that would be to their advantage. Avoiding general battles with the French forces, they divided their men into small units . . . frequently interrupted communications with France, destroyed the enemy's supplies, and exhausted him with ceaseless marches . . . !' " *Ibid.*, p. 345. For a discussion of the role of guerrilla forces following the Nazi invasion in 1941, see Edward Meade Earle, "Lenin, Trotsky and Stalin," in *Makers of Modern Strategy*, Edward Meade Earle, ed. (Princeton, 1944), pp. 361–363.

the guerrilla is the intense desire to expel the invader, the occupier, or the colonizer. The most powerful assets at his command are native shrewdness, familiarity with local environmental factors, keen understanding of his own people, and—especially in the present era of protracted conflict—the political know-how which enables him to exploit latent conflicts inherent in the international situation. To the highly disciplined mind of the military professional, schooled in classical strategy, who must cope with the guerrilla, the latter's method of fighting often appears promiscuous, unpredictable and illogical. One of the most distinctive features of the guerrilla strategy is its lack of a "logical" procedure which can be anticipated and thwarted by the enemy.

In this age of missiles and nuclear weapons, there is a growing and pernicious assumption that all of the older modes of warfare have been rendered obsolete. One of the most pressing problems confronting the military establishments of the Western allies springs from the West's relative lack of experience in coping with guerrilla strategy. The great strides made in military technology since 1945 may help to prevent the massing of conventional military forces in future wars.[4] Guerrilla warfare, with its informality, loose formations, and unique capabilities for independent action may offer the most workable solution to the dilemma facing the planning staffs of modern armies. The guerrilla of tomorrow will operate independently or in support of widely dispersed, highly mobile, logistically self-sufficient, small-sized military units which can fight the enemy either in coordinated or independent combat actions.

The day may come when nations, with their cities leveled and communications systems destroyed, will be forced to rely upon extremely decentralized organization and highly flexible strategy in order to survive. But even if the need for a desperate post-atomic strategy were never to arise, the problem of guerrilla warfare will continue to harass the West for a long time to come. While the use of organized military force is inhibited by the "equilibrium of terror," guerrillas remain relatively free to operate; in fact, the guerrilla alternative seems more attractive than ever. Since the end of the second World War there has been a rise in the incidence of guerrilla activity throughout the world: in Greece, China, Indochina, Malaya, the Philippines, Egypt, Oman, Ifni, Aden, the French Cameroons, Kenya, Algeria, Cyprus, Hungary, and Cuba. Probably the most significant success of guerrilla strategy has been in its use as a politico-military method of winning national independence by posing the kind of challenge which the technically superior Western military powers have been least prepared to meet effectively. In view of the increased significance of guerrilla warfare, the factors which determine its conduct invite the closest attention of statesmen and strategists.

---

4. Edward Teller, "Alternatives for Security," *Foreign Affairs,* XXXVI (January, 1958), pp. 206–207.

THE CRITERIA OF GUERRILLA WARFARE

The principles of guerrilla war, like those of regular war, are immutable. They can be applied in a variety of combinations. The guerrilla cannot ignore the general principles of military strategy which govern the choice of the objective, offensive operations, the massing of force, the economy of force, mobility, the use of surprise, the maintenance of security, and the coordination of operations. But in addition to these, the guerrilla is governed by several criteria which are peculiar to him: (1) the environment, (2) the unity of his movement, (3) community support and security, (4) division of functions, and (5) proximity.

Environment

The environment, which exerts a considerable influence, for better or for worse, on guerrilla operations, should not be conceived of merely in geographical terms, however significant these may be. Environment also embraces climate, terrain, the road and communications network, local economic conditions, the location of villages and towns, and the attitudes of the indigenous population. Ethnic factors, too, are extremely important; language barriers, for example, can have a decided bearing upon the effectiveness of guerrilla operations. Finally, the system of religious belief—indeed, the entire pattern of a people's culture—may determine how a people will behave under the conditions of guerrilla warfare.

Guerrilla operations are most successful wherever regular armies are hampered in their movements by topographical obstacles such as jungles, mountains, deserts, and delta country. This, unfortunately, is the type of terrain which predominates in the greater part of the so-called "gray areas." The character of the jungle war in Indochina, for example, goes far in explaining the reluctance of American military leaders to commit U.S. forces, air or ground, in that area.[5] In Malaya, the Communist Malayan Races Liberation Army was able to establish a network of jungle camps, ingeniously camouflaged against air attacks and carefully defended against ground approach.[6] Moreover, the fact that, during the early phase of the

---

5. *Soldier: The Memoirs of Matthew B. Ridgway* (New York, 1956), pp. 275–277.

6. The sentry post is sited some distance from the camp on the only line of approach—for it is rarely possible to approach a camp except by way of the main track, and on hearing a shot from the sentry a rear guard holds the track for a few minutes while the rest of the bandits get away and march off without difficulty to another camp which is waiting for them. They may leave tracks, but the pursuers are tired before they have to return for supplies. . . . The fact remains that not even the most experienced troops of any race, accompanied by trained trackers and all the advantages in arms and tactics that have yet been devised, have yet been able to effect a complete surprise on a bandit camp in the jungle." "The Campaign in Malaya: Tactics of Jungle Fighting," *World Today,* V (November, 1949), 480.

Malayan "emergency," 500,000 Chinese squatters lived in villages along the edge of the jungle made it relatively easy for the guerrillas to maintain a steady flow of supplies into the jungle. Obviously, an isolated village located on flat or desert land does not constitute a suitable base for guerrilla operations, since it can be easily surrounded and captured by regular army units.

> The most effective method of support for army operations by partisan movements lies in the creation of what are known as "redoubts." These are rising in mountainous regions, particularly those which adjoin lines of strategic importance to the enemy. These mountain fastnesses can in time become real fortresses of the guerrilla movement. The French had quite a number of redoubts, especially in the south and southeast of France. They became rallying points for guerrillas and the campaign centers which went by the name of "Maquis." Begun in 1942, they displayed an activity very disagreeable to the Germans well before the American invasion. Similar nests were built in the marshy and wooded regions of Poland and Russia as well as the mountains of Yugoslavia.[7]

The guerrilla commander must be keenly sensitive to environmental factors. When the environment thwarts his movements, he should move on to more hospitable ground. The astute guerrilla leader will determine the suitability of an operations base only after personal reconnaissance and study. He cannot make his decisions on the run; they must be weighed carefully and with a cool appreciation of their widest strategic implications.

Strategic-geographical factors which influence the selection of a site for a guerrilla campaign comprise a significant part of the environment in question. The external environment may often prove even more important than the internal one. Territorial contiguity with independent states friendly to the insurgents simplifies the problem of supplying the guerrillas with war materiel and furnishes to the guerrillas a convenient avenue of temporary retreat to a safe haven, or "sanctuary." Thus guerrillas were able to operate effectively along the northern border of Greece after World War II because it was easy for them to vanish behind the Yugoslav frontier. More recently, Algerian rebels, based in the Aures Mountains, have often evaded their French pursuers by fading across the border into independent Tunisia. (The FLN launched its first attack in November, 1954, when it was obvious that a new international status for Tunisia was only a matter of months away. The French, unwilling to offend the Tunisians while negotiations were in progress and reluctant to violate their territorial integrity after granting them independence, refrained from carrying the war across the border until February, 1958.)[8]

In seeking supplies, access to the sea may be just as advantageous as

---

7. F. O. Miksche, *Secret Forces* (London, 1950), pp. 151–153.
8. Cf. Alvin J. Cottrell and James E. Dougherty, "Algeria: Case Study in the Evolution of a Colonial Problem," *U.S. Naval Institute Proceedings*, LXXXIII (July, 1957), 179–180.

physical contiguity with a friendly country. This is especially true if the guerrilla war is waged in an independent island country which possesses no navy of its own, as, for example, in Cuba, where the rebel leader, Fidel Castro, has been able to make arms deals in the United States.[9] Access to the sea, however, may have only marginal or diminishing value for guerrilla forces fighting against an opponent who controls the high seas. In the early stages of the Malayan war, the communist guerrillas received sea-borne supplies from friendly Chinese sources in Southeast Asia until British naval patrols closed the sea approaches. France's greatest problem in quelling the Algerian rebellion has been to cut off the flow of arms supplies overland from the adjacent Arab states of Libya, Tunisia and Morocco. Two major efforts by the rebels to obtain shipments of arms via the Mediterranean from Egypt and Yugoslavia were blocked by the French with relative ease.[10]

Unity of the Movement

The problem of unity is a particularly acute one for guerrilla forces. Technological powers, in possession of regular armed forces which boast long traditions of discipline and loyalty, rarely, if ever, experience open conflict within their military establishments; unity of command in wartime is no problem for them. But guerrilla movements, especially those in technically less advanced societies, invariably are rent by factionalism. A guerrilla organization develops slowly and unevenly; a considerable amount of time is needed for the establishment of institutional procedures which can cope with the problems of loyalty and unity. Given the limitations on communication in underdeveloped areas, topographical barriers often isolate guerrilla forces from one another; the stage is thus set for an internecine struggle for power among independent guerrilla bands and leaders. Such a struggle can become extremely bitter wherever, because of the smallness of the theater of operations, guerrilla leadership cannot be shared. Many factors other than geographic, of course, are involved in the struggle for leadership. Personal rivalry, for example, is invariably present. Whatever the causes, however, there are many instances where guerrillas turn their guns from the enemy and point them at their own compatriots.

9. Cf. *New York Times*, February 14, 1958.
10. In October, 1956, a Greek ship carrying arms from Egypt, the *Athos*, was captured in Algerian waters. Her cago included mortars, machine guns, rifles, and pistols—enough to equip 3,000 rebels. According to Reto Caratsch, in *The Swiss Review of World Affairs*, April, 1957, the arms were intended for an attempted conquest of Tlemcen, a town near the Moroccan border which the rebels hoped to make their provisional capital. In January, 1958, the Yugoslav cargo ship *Slovenija* was captured by French warships in international waters some fifty miles from Oran. She was carrying 6,000 weapons and 95 tons of ammunition for delivery to agents of the Algerian rebel movement in Casablanca.

Mutual liquidation of guerrilla bands is, therefore, a contingency which antiguerrilla strategy must take into account. There were several instances in the second World War when fratricidal guerrilla conflict was successfully exploited by the power most anxious to weaken the guerrilla movement. In Yugoslavia, for example, the Germans liberally supplied "Chetnik" General Draja Mihailovitch, who initially fought the Germans but later directed some of his operations against the Communist partisan bands of Marshal Tito. In recent years, the Algerian rebellion has been marked by a bitter struggle between the dominant resistance group, the National Liberation Front (FLN), and its principal rival, the Algerian National Movement (MNA). The Melouza incident in May, 1957, when the entire adult male population of a village, numbering some 300, was massacred, was generally interpreted as an act of reprisal by the FLN against the village for cooperating with the more moderate MNA.[11] So intense has been the internecine battle between the two Algerian nationalist groups that it has been carried across the Mediterranean to the alleys of the Algerian "Casbah" in Paris. During the summer of 1957, more people were killed or wounded along the "second front" in the French capital than in Algiers itself. Apparently, the issue at stake was the control of the rebels' most lucrative source of funds; the half-million Arabs residing in France, including many merchants from whom monthly contributions were extorted.[12]

Community Support and Community Security

A guerrilla force can neither survive nor function without community support. At first glance, the problem of how, when and where a clandestine guerrilla force, operating within an enemy-held zone, can obtain the necessary food, shelter, clothing, arms, ammunition, medicines, motor fuels and funds may appear insurmountable.

Basically, the guerrilla may have access to three sources of supply: the local native community, friendly parties outside the theater of operations, and the enemy himself. A guerrilla movement, when directed against a formidable colonial power in complete occupation of the territory, cannot, after initiating the rebellion, depend on local stockpiles of arms. There have been instances where guerrillas could supply themselves liberally from arms caches abandoned during World War II.[13] Generally, however,

11. C. L. Sulzberger, "The Nationalist Strategy of Terror in Algeria," *New York Times,* June 5, 1957.

12. United Press report, July 23, 1957.

13. British Force 136 of the Southeast Asia Command delivered arms by parachute drop to the communist guerrillas in Malaya's jungles during the spring of 1945, preparatory to a planned joint offensive against the Japanese. The offensive proved to be unnecessary and the communists stored many of the weapons in jungle hideouts. These were used subsequently against the British-Malayan forces afer 1948. Lucien W. Pye, *Guerrilla Communism in Malaya* (Princeton, 1957), p. 70.

the guerrilla must rely on a generous and continuous flow of arms from abroad. The occupying power, if it hopes to quell a guerrilla rising, must stop the flow of arms to the insurgents. The inability to intercept arms shipments to the Algerian rebels from adjacent Tunisia and Morocco has been, according to the French, the main reason for their failure to end the war after more than three years of bitter fighting. The French estimate that the rebels receive 2,000 weapons per month from Tunisia alone, only 400 of which are captured by the French.[14]

The guerrilla, once he possesses the arms for the initial offensive, can augment his arsenal with arms garnered in ambushes of enemy soldiers and in commando-type raids against isolated enemy supply depots and convoys. By the time the occupying power can assess the threat to its forces and supply lines, the guerrilla may possess enough striking power to attract attention to his cause from abroad. Once he gains military "respectability," the guerrilla is in a more favorable position to arrange for the importation of arms from foreign sources.

While the modern guerrilla depends increasingly upon the international community for military aid and diplomatic support, he must rely almost exclusively on the local community for all the immediate necessities of war—food, clothing, shelter, funds, cover and intelligence. Lawrence of Arabia pointed out decades ago that community support need not be an "actively friendly" one:

> It [the rebel movement] must have a friendly population, not actively friendly but sympathetic to the point of not betraying rebel movements to the enemy. Rebellions can be made by 2 per cent active in a striking force, and 98 per cent passively sympathetic.[15]

Where voluntary community support is not spontaneously forthcoming at the outbreak of the struggle or cannot be sustained at the desired level, the guerrilla movement almost inevitably will resort to terrorism to compel such support. In the twentieth century, terrorism has become an orthodox part of guerrilla strategy. The use of terror, to be effective, must be absolute. Terror, the guerrilla leader's most potent weapon, is used by him not only to demoralize the enemy and extort the support of his own people, but also to exact unswerving loyalty from the individual guerrilla, who is made to understand that defection or betrayal is punishable by death. In extreme cases, the guerrilla may be so disciplined that he will not spare even members of his immediate family if they threaten the security of the movement. The grisly oath administered to recruits of the Mau Mau in Kenya, for example, included the command: "If your Father, Mother, Brother or Sister refuses the Mau Mau in any way, you will kill them."[16]

---

14. *New York Times,* February 19, 1958.

15. T. E. Lawrence, "Guerrilla Warfare," *Encyclopedia Britannica* (London, 950), X, 953.

16. Sir Philip Mitchell, "Mau Mau," in *Africa Today,* C. Grove Haines, ed. (Baltimore, 1955), p. 491.

Among primitive tribal societies, guerrilla leaders may rely upon the pagan superstitions of their followers to prevent defections. In more advanced societies, the threat of physical reprisal is invoked to intimidate wavering guerrillas or unenthusiastic civilians. Terror may be used to force untrained members of the populace to carry out sporadic guerrilla assignments against their will. An observer of the conflict in Cyprus described the plight of "a secondary schoolboy who had signed the EOKA oath and who one day found himself in a small room with three masked men who ordered him to place a time-bomb or commit a murder—*or else pay the price.*"[17]

The Algerian rebels, when they launched their concerted attack against the French on November 1, 1954, numbered between a few hundred and three thousand. At the time of this writing, the total rebel strength is estimated at 20,000 full-time guerrilla troops and an even larger number of part-time combatants. This growth in rebel strength can be attributed primarily to the wide-spread use by the rebel leadership of terrorist methods against the Moslem population. From the outset of the fighting, the nationalist forces in Algeria have attacked Moslems who have either openly collaborated with the French or refused to cooperate with the rebel movement—a fact which is brought out clearly by the official casualty lists of the Algerian War: of a total of 8,650 civilians killed, 7,450 have been Moslems. These terrorist methods not only have compelled the tactical support of the Algerian Moslem population but have also given many nationalist guerrillas a personal source of revenue and thus a vested interest in the prolongation of the conflict.[18]

Terrorism is thus the most powerful weapon at the disposal of the guerrilla leader. When wielded against his own people, it establishes the needed community support. Its use against the enemy confronts the latter with a formidable dilemma. The enemy, in order to forestall casualties and prevent the demoralization of his forces, must be prepared to meet terror with terror. And yet such draconian measures are alien to a civilized power. Even Field Marshal Albert von Kesselring, a product of the austere school of German militarism, faced this dilemma in the partisan warfare in Italy during World War II. He wrote in his memoirs:

> In view of the brutal, indeed very often inhuman, behaviour of the (partisan) bands, for one critical period I had to order drastic use of weapons to curtail the extraordinary casualties we were incurring from a certain nonchalance and out-of-place mildness on the part of our soldiers. Unless one wanted to commit suicide, the Partisan war involved a reversal of natural feelings, which in itself concealed grave dangers.
>
> As a matter of principle, I abstained from the use of bombers, which would naturally have been the most effective means, because in inhabited places I could not take the responsibility for injury to the civilian popu-

17. Lawrence Durrell, *Bitter Lemons* (London, 1957), p. 203.
18. Anthony Nutting, "Report on Algeria," *New York Herald Tribune*, May 14, 1957.

lation. Events have taught me that this consideration is rewarded with very little thanks. In the future, such scruples will have to go by the board—unless guerrilla warfare is universally banned.[19]

The pattern of guerrilla warfare during the last decade shows that neither communists nor extremist nationalist movements are inhibited in the promiscuous use of terror. Their tactics are prompted in part by the recognition that the more stable and mature powers of the West, with their deep-rooted humanitarian concepts, react to bloody and protracted conflict with a troubled conscience and will not meet terror with terror. The French, for example, cannot employ the same sort of brutal methods to end the Algerian rebellion which the Soviet Union used in Hungary. The French are judged by themselves and by others according to humanitarian standards; the Soviets, with no liberal tradition behind them, can commit totalitarian barbarities with relative impunity.

Even when a Western nation momentarily sheds its moral scruples, as the French did when they bombed a Tunisian village in February, 1958, the guerrilla retains the psychological advantage. The effort by the French to destroy the rebel sanctuary in Tunisia weakened the international position of the French and commensurately strengthened the bargaining position of the Algerian nationalist movement, which has always sought to have the Algerian problem "internationalized." Drastic measures by the occupying power to cope with guerrilla terror invariable increase the hostility of the local populace and thus strengthen community support in favor of the guerrilla.

Community support enhances community security—the safety of the guerrilla unit or fighter from betrayal by his people. The community must be induced to make common cause against the enemy; under no circumstance should it be alienated. The guerrilla must not become, in the eyes of his people, a mere parasite who devours the community's substance without giving anything in return. Even when he cannot reimburse the community with money, the guerrilla must persuade the community that he has dedicated his life to its liberation. His cause must be made dramatic enough to induce others to take the risk of screening his presence and activities. Hence, guerrilla operations should be planned and executed in such a way as to minimize the disruption of the natives' normal community life. The successful guerrilla leader is the one who can lift the community's esprit and enhance the local population's sense of pride, daring, and adventure. Community support and security are thus safeguarded best when the native population identifies itself spontaneously with the fortunes of the guerrilla movement. In a protracted conflict, however, absolute and spontaneous support is a rare commodity. Sooner or later the guerrilla will find it necessary to take up the instruments of terror.

---

19. Albert von Kesselring, *A Soldier's Record* (New York), 1954), p. 276.

Division of Functions

Successful guerrilla operations demand a complex organization, which can be constructed only with patient, painstaking effort. Normally, guerrilla warfare is carried on by both full-time and part-time personnel. The full-time fighter often makes a complete break with community life and withdraws to the jungle or the mountains for training, indoctrination, and military operations. The guerrilla movement, once it gains prestige and resources, may very well establish a formal organizational structure, replete with uniformed units and ranks, which will help to give the movement the appearance of a "going concern." The part-time guerrilla, however, cannot afford the luxury of recognition as a soldier. He does not withdraw from community life: in fact, his very effectiveness depends upon his ability to lead "two lives." In the Indochina campaign, for example, French troops moving through the countryside rarely came upon an enemy soldier: they would see only harmless peasants working in the fields. Suddenly, without warning, the "peaceful" nha que would turn into an armed Viet Minh guerrilla. Entire regions of the Vietnam delta which were, during the day, nominally under French control would revert under cover of darkness to the Viet Minh.[20]

By living in the community and remaining in daily contact with the enemy, part-time guerrillas are well adapted to carry out indispensable missions of intelligence and covert sabotage. The experience of the second World War demonstrated the value of intelligence and sabotage activities carried out in support of conventional military operations.[21] They are, if anything, even more valuable to guerrilla movements. Guerrillas, to operate with maximum effectiveness against enemy conventional forces, need a highly sensitive intelligence system which enables them to know when and where they can strike profitably and at minimum risk or when they must move quickly to avoid being trapped by a superior enemy force. Covert sabotage serves the guerrilla not only as a means of harassing enemy forces, but also as a weapon against local collaborators and business interests who, voluntarily or not, supply or support the occupier.[22]

20. Ellen J. Hammer, The Struggle for Indochina (Stanford, 1954), pp. 126, 292 et passim.

21. Prior to the landings of the American forces in the Philippines in 1944, Filipino guerrillas had fed a continuous stream of information via radio and submarine contacts to General MacArthur's headquarters in Australia. This intelligence was essential to the planning and execution of the Allies' island-hopping liberation campaign against the Japanese in the Pacific. R. L. Eichelberger, Jungle Road to Tokyo (New York, 1950), pp. 217–218. For a general discussion of the importance of sabotage in guerrilla operations, cf. F. O. Miksche, op. cit., pp. 124–130.

22. Luis Perez Rios, a leader of Fidel Castro's anti-Batista guerrilla movement in Cuba, announced on February 2, 1958, that the movement would concentrate on industrial sabotage. "We have been doing sporadic bombings in the cities as well as burning sugar-cane fields and tobacco drying sheds in the countryside," he explained. "This will continue. But now we will cripple sugar mills, tobacco factories, public utilities, railroads and refineries." New York Times, February 3, 1958.

Part-time guerrillas may never carry a weapon or wear a uniform; they support their full-time comrades by ripping up railroad tracks, cutting telephone lines, destroying farm property and burning down industrial plants.

Complete deception is indispensable to the success of these covert operations. Security measures must be absolute. The fewer the persons who know the identity of a part-time guerrilla—even within his own family —the more easily can he execute his missions and then retreat behind the screen of normal civilian life. The clandestine existence of these part-time guerrillas makes it almost impossible for the enemy to assess accurately the movement's over-all strength. In Algeria, for example, the number of full-time fighters has, according to French estimates, never exceeded 30,000. But the fact that these regular fighters have been reinforced by part-time rebels, numbering anywhere from 20,000 to 100,000, has made it necessary for the French to withhold about a half-million French regular troops from European defense in order to deal with the Algerian rebellion.[23] At the height of the Malayan "Emergency," the communist guerrilla army, the MRLA, which consisted of 5,000 to 6,000 fighters, was supported by the *Min Yuen*, a group of about 10,000 communist sympathizers who were willing to act as intelligence agents, couriers, food gatherers, and carriers of propaganda.[24]

A number of factors enter into a local guerrilla commander's decision of whether to emphasize operations by full-time or part-time fighters. Among these considerations are: proximity of the enemy; the mission of the enemy's military units; the location of his installations; the degree of mobility enjoyed by the enemy; the friendliness of the environment; the attitude of the local population; and the general military situation, especially the proximity of friendly armed forces with whose campaign the operations of the guerrilla units can be coordinated.

Proximity

Proximity in guerrilla warfare denotes the degree of physical, geographical and psychological closeness among the guerrilla forces, the enemy army and the indigenous population. It determines the nature, the direction and the method of the struggle. In the earliest instances of partisan warfare in modern European military history—i.e., in Spain and Russia during the Napoleonic period—guerrillas were used primarily for direct harassing attacks against the enemy's military forces. In the twentieth century, there have been several instances—and their number appears to

---

23. Cf. Hanson W. Baldwin, "Tempo of Algerian War," *New York Times,* August 28, 1957.
24. To combat the guerrillas, the British eventually had to commit 40,000 troops in Malaya. These were supported by a quarter million native police and home guards. Cf. *Annual Reports of the Federation of Malaya* (Kuala Lumpur, 1949–1955).

be on the increase—in which the guerrilla force deliberately avoids a direct engagement with the enemy. This is particularly true where the guerrilla force opposes not an invading army but an established colonial power and where the movement does not enjoy ready-made community support. In a society which can bring to bear a strong sense of national unity and independence against an invader, on the other hand, guerrilla forces need not grapple unduly with the problem of evoking community support and can turn their exclusive attention to fighting the invading army.

There is no doubt that, from a purely military point of view, guerrilla operations are more effective when employed in support of regular armies. In the absence of a friendly army, a guerrilla commander is compelled to proceed with the greatest circumspection while building up his own strength. This caution is required especially in the early phases of a guerrilla war, when relatively inexperienced and ill-equipped rebel forces confront a disciplined enemy in full command of an area. During World War II, the Japanese in the Philippines generally followed the policy of garrisoning towns. This concentration of enemy forces in urban centers forced patriotic village and town residents to become part-time rather than full-time guerrillas. Their compatriots in the thinly occupied rural areas, however, were able to organize more direct, full-time opposition.[25]

Guerrillas, whenever they cannot count upon friendly conventional armies to engage the enemy and force him to concentrate his troops, may find it increasingly difficult to maintain coordinated, full-time forces. Their only chance for survival against mounting enemy military pressure may then be to shift to dispersed, part-time terroristic operations, which are intended to have more of a political and psychological, rather than military, effect. Thus Fidel Castro, faced in January, 1958, with growing pressure from government troops in his Oriente Province stronghold, launched a campaign of widely dispersed attacks against small military outposts in the mountains of Las Villas Province to force the Government to lessen its pressure in the Oriente district.[26] At the same time, the Cuban rebels announced their intention to step up their sabotage tactics and to disrupt the national economy in an effort to prevent the impending presidential election.[27]

CONCLUSIONS

Heretofore, Western military writers have considered guerrilla warfare almost exclusively in purely military terms. They have been concerned

25. General Headquarters, USAFPAC, 1948, *The Guerrilla Resistance Movement in the Philippines*, I, 83.
26. *New York Times*, July 11, 1957, and January 28, 1958.
27. *Ibid.*, February 3 and 10, 1958.

primarily with the effectiveness of guerrilla tactics when employed against conventional armies. There is no question that valuable lessons can be gleaned from such a military study, for the modes of guerrilla organization and operation may come to have increasing significance in an age when technological developments make decentralization, flexibility, and mobility of regular ground forces more necessary than ever. The future importance of guerrilla warfare is assured, for it is now clearly recognized as the safest method of waging open conflict within the restraints of the "balance of terror."

But guerrilla warfare, during the last quarter of a century, has undergone an important transformation from a type of warfare the objectives of which were chiefly military to a mode of conflict the objectives of which are conceived in a larger political dimension. The Western nations are confronted today with the new challenge of guerrilla warfare posed by the strategists of international communism and national liberation movements in the "gray areas." It matters little whether this or that liberation movement is linked with communism: inasmuch as it places a heavy drain on the West's conventional military strength and seeks to dislodge a Western power from an established position of strength on the periphery of Eurasia, its immediate strategic objectives will parallel those of the Sino-Soviet bloc.

Modern guerrilla movements are armed with elaborate psycho-political weapons. Guerrilla wars waged against colonial rule have wrought havoc upon Western coalition diplomacy. Guerrilla leaders today operate in a world linked by mass communications: every action in a remote area of the globe is instantaneously transmitted to the nerve centers of world opinion. The daily and detailed coverage which the Western press gave to the small-scale irregular uprising of mid-1957 in Oman, for example, was in sharp contrast to the world's almost total lack of awareness of previous outbreaks in this remote region before the advent of the airplane, the wire services and the mass-circulation dailies.

It is the communications network, more than anything else, which enables the contemporary guerrilla to amplify the political effects of his terroristic methods. The deep-rooted cultural tradition of the West renders it an easy prey to blackmail by protracted guerrilla terror. Unlike the average citizen of a democratic country, the guerrilla does not feel ill at ease in the presence of conflict. Since he regards conflict as the best—indeed, the sole—means of achieving his objectives, he is able to come to terms with terror, violence, and abiding insecurity. By fomenting conflict and instability, the guerrilla levies blackmail upon the humanitarian West's longing for peace and thereby enhances his political bargaining power: the *quid pro quo* is the granting of territorial independence in return for the termination of the exhausting conflict.

4

Lt. Col. Joseph P. Kutger
U.S. Air Force

IRREGULAR

WARFARE

IN TRANSITION

Background

D

ESPITE WEAPONS SYSTEMS of unforeseen destructive magnitude, an observation on irregular warfare made by Karl von Clausewitz nearly a century and a half ago has lost none of its original validity:

> . . . when, as in Spain . . . the war is for the most part carried on by means of a people's war . . . a truly new power is formed and . . . people's warfare introduces a means of defense peculiar to itself.[1]

Irregular warfare comprises all those types of warfare alien to the conventional warfare of the period involved. It is usually employed against an adversary as a *means* of minimizing his relative advantages, either in numerical strength or in the technology of his weaponry. It has been em-

---

From *Military Affairs,* Fall, 1960. Copyright 1690 by the American Military Institute and reproduced by permission.

1. Karl von Clausewitz, *On War* (Berlin: The Ministry of National Defense, 1957). P. 416. The German text reads: ". . . wo es, wie in Spanien, durch einen Volkskrieg diesen Kampf der Hauptsache nach selbst führt, so begrieft man, dass hier nicht bloss eine Steigerung des Volksbeistandes, sondern eine wahrhaft neu Potenz Entsteht, und dass wir also die Volksbewaffnung oder den Landsturm als ein eigentümliches Mitel der Verteidigung anführen können." [Clausewitz, *Vom Kriege* (Berlin 1957), Sechstes Buch, Sechstes Kapital, die Seite, 416.]

ployed in many ways throughout the ages, namely, as an internal rebellion against an established government; as an overt or covert aid to friendly forces engaged in a struggle with a potential enemy; as a subversive alien element in attempting to develop open rebellion in another nation; as an adjunct to the native conventional forces engaged in conflict with the enemy; and as the only means of fighting the superior forces of an enemy, after defeat of the regular armed forces. In the performance of such sundry roles it has paraded under the banner of a variety of names, such as unconventional, unorthodox, underground, guerrilla, and partisan warfare. Today we find that almost all types of irregular actions are commonly referred to as *guerrilla actions.*

The long and colorful history of guerrilla warfare far antedates the very birth of the language from whence this present sobriquet came. It is generally conceded that the term *guerrilla warfare* derives from the period 150 years ago when, after Napoleon's victorious 1808 sweep through Spain, the Spanish army in defeat was dissolved and reorganized into small independent units capable only of fighting limited actions. As a consequence, the Spanish diminutive suffix was added to their word for war—*guerra*—the resultant, *guerrilla.*

The first warlike acts of primitive society, wherein one village would fall upon another by surprise and completely destroy it, should by its very nature be termed irregular warfare. The Old Testament relates how Gideon smote the enemy hip and thigh and how the Maccabees fought a partisan campaign against the Syrian armies. For over 2,000 years astute delaying and harassing actions have been termed "Fabian" tactics, in tribute to the brilliant, unorthodox tactics of Fabius Maximus, who, in refusing to face Hannibal and certain defeat in conventional battle, succeeded in diverting him from his objective—Rome.

Modern Concepts, Strategy, and Tactics

The history of the Latin American revolutions for liberation against external control and the recent and continuing revolutions for independence in Africa as well as in the Middle and Far East have helped to establish the picture of *guerrillas* as illegally established amateurs challenging the authority of the presently constituted government. Contrary to such impressions (as mentioned earlier), the forms of irregular or guerrilla warfare are numerous, and many of the guerrillas are either members of the formal forces of their nation or, at least, are carried on the rolls. Seaborne assault troops are in essence *amphibious guerrillas.* Various forms of combat teams, infiltration units, and deep penetration units designed to be self-sufficient are also types of guerrilla forces.

In those cases where guerrilla forces have taken up arms of their own volition, we find that as their relative weaknesses and shortages are over-come (through raiding of enemy supplies and bases and gaining manpower through local popular support), there is a trend towards abandonment of guerrilla tactics—because guerrilla actions are not able to achieve the complete defeat of the enemy. Such ultimate transition of guerrilla cam-paigns was seen in Tito's triumph in Yugoslavia, Mao Tse-tung's in Red China, Ho Chi-minh's in northern Viet Nam, and Fidel Castro's in Cuba.

During World War II most of the irregular or guerrilla activity took the form of partisan actions such as the *Maquis* in France, the Italian partisans, the Belgian underground, the Russian guerrillas, the Philippine guerrillas, and the aborted German *Werewolf*. Extensive covert activity normally preceded and often later accompanied any overt actions. Covert activity refers to that clandestine type which usually develops in urban areas best suited to their tactics of sabotage, espionage, subversion, opera-tion of secret presses and radios, and the less dramatic but equally com-pelling force of passive resistance. This latter technique includes such functions as the wastage of industrial materials, shoddy workmanship, slow-downs, and acts designed to irritate and aggravate the enemy—taunts of children, acts of noncooperation, obvious avoidance of contact with occupying forces, and the like. Any attempt to convert *covert* to *overt* action usually depends upon preplanned coordination with military opera-tions to insure the rapid relief of the partisan forces. This conversion was successfully performed by the French uprising in Paris in 1945, which synchronized with the arrival of the Allied Forces. In contrast, one recalls the horror of the tragic ordeal suffered by the hopeful but fully uncoordi-nated plans of General Bor's (Komotowski) Polish uprising in Warsaw during the fall of 1944. In this case the Russians, having reached the eastern bank of the Vistula, across from Warsaw, treacherously incited action on the part of the most patriotic of the Poles and then stood off deliberately while the Germans completely annihilated General Bor's forces. In this fashion they cunningly used their enemy to eliminate Bor's friendly partisan troops, who represented the flower of Polish nationalism and could therefore prove most troublesome to the postwar Soviet plans for Poland.

Several years ago the news media carried stories about the U.S. Army Special Forces, hitherto held in secrecy. These men were trained for all phases of guerrilla- and antiguerrilla-type activity. Their commander, Colonel Edson Raff, led hit-and-run raids which harassed the German *Afrika Corps* in World War II. One rarely finds a reference in historical documents about the African campaigns to such men as Colonel Raff. This is not unusual, since in almost all accounts of the major wars there is a paucity of documentation for guerrilla actions. Perhaps this is due to the fact that professional soldiers have been prone to ascribe little recogni-tion to the irregular soldier. This attitude is understandable, albeit it seems both remarkable and paradoxical that, among professional military writers, a dearth of interest in the subject of unconventional tactics and warfare still exists today. Yet it is becoming increasingly evident that future land forces must be small, highly mobile, and self-contained. The essentially mysterious character of guerrilla warfare has made it difficult for military historians to analyze its motives, but this can no longer excuse the tendency to neglect it. Can a student of military history deny the logic or the plausibility of conceiving guerrilla activities as the only ones possible after an all-out nuclear holocaust? Perhaps French Colonel Nemo (a nom de plume in the *Revue Militaire Générale of France*) has the answer to the lack of appreciation of the role played by irregular warfare exhibited by military historians. He claims that:

> Regular armies have almost never succeeded in gaining the ascendancy over guerrilla operations of any importance. Perhaps it is because of a subconscious desire to hide this impotence that the great commanders have minimized the role of guerrilla operations.[2]

The revolution in weapons and delivery systems brought about by the tremendous technological strides of the last decade has set many a military man to seriously contemplating just how valid the principles of warfare will be in a thermonuclear war.

Since the appearance of von Clausewitz's great classic, *Vom Kriege,* there has been a tendency to study war and to be concerned with strategic doctrine. Usually this has been centered on the conventional aspects of warfare. But carried to the ultimate by the doctrine of *massive retaliation,* many theorists have argued that large-scale war has at last become virtually impossible. In 1954, Britain's Sir John Slessor, then Marshal of the Royal Air Force, wrote: "The first and most far reaching consequence of this revolution (in weapons and delivery systems) is that total war as we have known it in the past forty years is a thing of the past."[3] During the "no war, no peace" situation of the present, conspiratorial and unconventional techniques have played the major rather than the minor role. The sporadic flare-ups of various types of irregular warfare and the almost continuous condition of guerrilla warfare in parts of Africa, the Near East, and the Far East would appear to emphasize a need for us to re-examine our war plans and strategic doctrine.

Thus, today, the Soviet Union no longer considers the various defensive positions and reserve forces backing up ground forces engaged in battle as representing a *defense in depth.* As will be discussed later, this is the greatest fault the Russians see in our concepts of warfare. The new param-

2. "The Place of Guerrilla Action in War," translated and digested from a copyrighted article by Colonel Nemo in *Revue Militaire Générale* (France) (January, 1957), *Military Review,* C&GS (U.S.), Vol. XXXVII (November, 1957), p. 99. Hereafter *Mil. Rev. U.S.*

3. Dr. James D. Atkinson, "American Military Policy and Communist Unorthodox Warfare," *Marine Corps Gazette,* Vol. XLIII, No. 1 (January, 1958), p. 22.

eters involve, according to their thinking, the concept of *territorial war,* which involves a defense in depth equal to the entire area of the nation behind the line of action. If, through partisan and guerrilla warfare, the Communists expand the tactical principle of defense in depth to its fullest employment, the doctrines of warfare as now developed by the western nations, can be classified as designed primarily for *frontal* offense and defense.

In May, 1959, one writer on the future potential of guerrilla warfare pleaded for our strategic doctrine to incorporate provisions for its exploitation in these words:

> The United States must develop a guerrilla potential as quickly as possible, based on the best available information and experience. . . . Naturally the first step should be an exhaustive study of guerrilla warfare. . . . We must create a sound theory for a resistance movement . . . we must glean every lesson from existing guerrilla literature. More than this we must search out guerrilla leaders who have not published their experiences. Full development of any theory waits upon this accumulation of information.[4]

To employ operations of a guerrilla nature, a relatively simple strategy masks the difficult and demanding techniques that are required to successfully engage in this type of warfare. It entails development of a doctrine based on what might be termed the *negative offensive.* Thus it refuses the challenge to positional combat, it does not seek to engage in decisive battles, and it calls for avoidance of contact with major elements of enemy forces.

Surprise is the main element of guerrilla tactics. Mobility, deceit, and ambush are among its strongest weapons. These tactics require great skill, courage, cunning, and imagination. Accurate intelligence as to enemy strengths and positions is a *sine qua non* if the guerrilla leader is to know where to strike with a relative superiority. He must also be adept at hit-and-run tactics, because prolonged contact with the enemy hazards the risk of the enemy massing sufficiently to wheel and destroy him. Generally his tactics include, but are not limited to, the following:

1. Initiation of attack after careful planning.

2. Avoidance if possible or withdrawal before superior enemy forces. Harass the enemy at any time he relieves pressure. If enemy can be exhausted, to undertake limited offensive action, and take full advantage of pursuit should the enemy flee.

3. Concentration on isolated and/or weaker elements of the enemy's forces; not overlooking the opportunities to strike stronger forces, while in movement, with swift determined surprise attacks on their flanks, or at some vital spot along their line.

---

4. Edward F. Downey, Jr., "Theory of Guerrilla Warfare," *Mil. Rev. U.S.,* Vol. XXXIX, No. 2 (May, 1959), p. 54.

4. Preparation for immediate dispersal to preselected positions when unfavorable conditions develop.

5. Solicitation of assistance of local citizenry.

6. Destruction or pirating of enemy communications.

7. Diversion and exploitation of the enemy, to force him to dissipate sizable forces for his own internal protection.

8. Collection of valid intelligence behind enemy lines.

9. Demolition and harassment activities far behind the enemy's front lines.

10. Developing guides for potential friendly invasion forces.

11. When applicable, performing special services such as beach and coastal reconnaissances.

Irregular Actions during the American Civil War

A century ahead of their time, the Virginia Confederates of the American Civil War stumbled upon one of the secrets of ultramodern war. Their techniques of resistance within occupied territory presaged that of the Russians during World War II. One better appreciates the difficulties faced by Grant during the Wilderness–Cold Harbor campaign, when it is realized that the Army of the Potomac moved southward almost like a ship at sea—the waters closing in behind it—for any line of supply that extended more than a few miles was certain to be ravelled and tattered by the attacks of the irregulars.

That Grant was fully aware of the drain on his capabilities caused by the guerrillas is evident in a message he sent to Sheridan on August 17, 1864. In violation of the then code of international warfare, Grant instructed:

> The families of most of Mosby's men are known, and can be collected. I think they should be taken and kept at Fort McHenry or some secure place, as hostages for the good conduct of Mosby and his men. Where any of Mosby's men are caught hang them without trial.[5]

John Singleton Mosby had long been a southern guerrilla leader. Formerly an officer in Jeb Stuart's cavalry, he requested and received a transfer to the guerrillas in 1862, shortly after almost all the partisans had been persuaded to join the rolls of the regular Confederate forces, in order to extend to them the protective rights established for prisoners of war under international law. His men had been operating in the Shenandoah Valley and were causing Sheridan substantial trouble.

Previous orders issued to Union troops, while Halleck was general-in-chief of the U.S. Army, were based on the recommendations of Dr.

---

5. *The War of the Rebellion: A Compilation of the Official Records of the Union and Confederate Armies* (Washington, GPO, 1880–1901), Vol. XLIII, Pt. 1, p. 811.

Francis Lieber, recognized internationally for his study of the usages and customs of war. Dr. Lieber, in a lengthy response to a letter from Halleck, stated that guerrillas were legitimate soldiers as long as they were properly enrolled with the regular establishment.[6]

Union General Benjamin F. Kelley, who commanded along the Baltimore and Ohio R.R., was constantly involved in battles with Confederate guerrillas until, near war's end he was actually kidnapped from his bed by Jesse McNeill's rangers. The daring and boldness that led to the capture of "Old Ben" Kelley compares equally with any of Skorzeny's escapades during World War II, including his fabulous rescue of Mussolini from the mountain stronghold where the Italians held him prisoner.[7]

In February, 1865, McNeill's band and the partisans fighting under Blake Woodson had developed a great deal of friction due to overlapping efforts. To remedy the situation, a Major Gilmor was sent to take command of all rangers in the South Branch Valley. He was not only given a decidedly cool welcome by both McNeill's and Woodson's men, but his capture shortly afterward by Union forces was not seriously contested by the Rebel horsemen, althoug they had ample opportunity to do so. While news of this event was being received by Early, McNeill and his rangers put into action a well-planned scheme to kidnap General Kelley from the hotel room he lived in at Cumberland, and, learning that General George Crook, the head of the Department of West Virginia was quartered in a nearby hotel, they captured him also. The recounting of the escapade reads like a melodrama, executed with a brilliance that underscored McNeill's thorough preparations.

Jubal Early, thoroughly incensed by the treatment given to Major Gilmor, requested that both McNeill's and Woodson's rangers be disbanded as independent outfits, stating:

> The fact is that all those independent organizations, not excepting Mosby's, are injurious to us, and the occasional dashes they make do not compensate for the disorganization and dissatisfaction produced among other troops.[8]

Early's request was quickly indorsed by General Lee, but it was returned from the Army's Adjutant General marked "No Action," as McNeill's rangers had in the meantime brought sudden and unparalleled acclaim upon themselves by capturing the two Yankee generals in a single raid.[9]

Undoubtedly the claims and counterclaims of the successes of the partisan bands were exaggerated, but their effect and influence was substantial and merit far more attention than is usually given in any history

---

6. Virgil C. Jones, *Ranger Mosby* (Chapel Hill, N.C., 1944), pp. 89–95.
7. For an excellent narrative of this episode, see *ibid.*, pp. 356–361.
8. As quoted in *ibid.*, p. 356.
9. *Ibid.*

of the Civil War. The South was not alone in employing guerrilla tactics; Grant used Grierson to sally forth through Louisiana and Mississippi, and Grierson's raid caused such confusion and consternation that it compounded Johnston's difficulty in deciding whether to go to Vicksburg and combine his forces with Pemberton's or to pursue the raiders. This gave Grant sufficient time to get his army between the two main Confederate forces and, after forcing Johnston to retreat to the northeast from Jackson, Grant was able to turn his forces westward and drive Pemberton back into Vicksburg, where, in six weeks, he compelled Pemberton's surrender. There were other instances of Yankee ranger actions such as Colonel James H. Wilson's cavalry sweep through Tennessee.

Guerrilla Actions during World War II

During World War II, the allies received untold aid from the partisan and guerrilla forces which sprang up in practically every country that the Nazis or the Japanese occupied. General Eisenhower thought the assistance rendered by the French *Maquis* during the allied landings in France equal to at least 12 divisions.[10] Tito's partisans tied down an average of 30 German divisions in Yugoslavia.

Russian partisan raids on German rear installations assumed such serious proportions that the occupation troops were forced to employ expensive and complicated protective measures. The vast Russian forest area as well as the swamp regions like the Pripet (or Pinsk) Marshes served as natural sanctuaries for the development of partisan cells. Elements of the Red Army that escaped destruction or capture as the Nazi juggernaut rolled onward were able to hide in almost inaccessible places and provide the nuclei around which the partisans rallied. The hardy partisan bands were well acquainted with the normally inaccessible terrain, and the Germans were faced with a ruthless guerrilla war in the woods and swamps well within and behind the combat zone.[11] Toward the end of the war the situation become so critical that a special warning radio channel was included by the Germans in their signal operation instructions for the exclusive transmission of urgent calls for assistance.[12]

There is little doubt that the Soviet partisan movement, which arose in the wake of the German invasion, was the greatest irregular resistance movement in the history of warfare. During the two years the Soviets conducted this partisan type of activity, they claim to have killed more than 300,000 Germans, including 30 generals, 6,336 officers, and 520

10. Colonel R. W. van de Velde, U.S.A., Ret., "The Neglected Deterrent," *Mil. Rev. U.S.*, Vol. XXXVIII, August, 1958, p. 7. See also Colonel Virgil Ney, "Guerrilla Warfare in the Philippines, 1942–45," unpublished MS., Georgetown University.

11. "Combat in Russian Forests and Swamps," *Dept. of the Army Pamphlet No. 20–231* (Washington, GPO, 1951), p. 33.

12. *Ibid.*, p. 34.

airmen; they also claim the derailment of 3,000 trains, the destruction of 3,262 railway and highway bridges, 1,191 tanks and armored cars, 4,027 trucks, and 895 dumps and warehouses.[13]

During his court-martial, Field Marshal Fritz Erich Von Manstein was asked how many partisan attacks took place every day. He replied:

> I cannot give you an exact figure from my experience in the Crimea, but as an example I would say I remember in 1944, in the Army Group Center, in the course of seven hours nearly a thousand raids took place on roads and railways in the rear, and in the Crimea these raids happened every single day.[14]

The experiences of the Germans pertaining to the maintenance of their *rear area security* during their invasion of Russia is worthy of thoughtful study. Therefore, it should be discernible to the student of military history that *rear areas* can no longer be treated in the traditional sense as being merely zones of communications. Partisan operations as conducted by the Russians well support the contention that the *front-behind-the-front* is a theater of operations in its own right.[15]

The allies during World War II were by no means the sole beneficiaries of this irregular type of warfare. Perhaps the most legendary figure to come out of the war was the German soldier-adventurer, Otto Skorzeny, whose exploits ranged from the recapture of Mussolini, the abduction of Admiral Horthy, the destruction of the Nymwegen bridge, to the command of special squads of soldiers dressed in American uniforms and fluent in English, whom Hitler planned to use to create confusion behind the enemy's front when he threw into execution his ill-fated Ardennes offensive of December, 1944, which, after a brilliant beginning, petered out, bleeding the last ounce of strength from the German western front before the general Anglo-American assault began. A study of *SS Sturmbannführer* Skorzeny's exploits should demonstrate to the serious student of military history that the basic principles of *Objective, Surprise* and *Simplicity,* coupled with a daring use of the *Offensive,* make properly organized assault actions well-nigh invincible.

The Indo-Chinese Case

After the Korean conflict subsided, the attention of the Western powers shifted to the Indo-Chinese scene. Fears were expressed that the Red Chinese would now be freed to send so-called volunteers to the aid of the Vietminh.

---

13. Brigadier C. Aubrey Dixon, O.B.E., and Otto Heilbrunn, *Communist Guerrilla Warfare* (New York, Frederick A. Praeger, 1955), p. 56.

14. *U.S. War Crimes Trials against Field Marshal Von Manstein, et al.* (Nuremberg, 1946), pp. 1923 *ff.* of the transcript.

15. "Rear Area Security in Russia, the Soviet Second Front behind the German Lines," Dept. of the Army Pamphlet No. 20–240 (Washington, GPO, 1951), p. 35.

Some six months before the Korean armistice, President Eisenhower took the stand that any Korean settlement must include guarantees that Red Chinese forces would not violate the territory of Indo-China, and this became the official U.S. position. The French government received assurances of assistance by U.S. Forces if Red China's volunteers came to Ho Chi-minh's aid. But Ho's forces needed antiaircraft artillery and sundry military supplies rather than manpower.

During the final phases of the Indo-Chinese campaign, the French were sorely embarrassed by the guerrilla infiltration of their air bases and the destruction of their critically needed aircraft. American press insults, alleging the disgraceful lack of security measures and the apparent futility of American efforts to support the French war effort, added to their chagrin. The French had taken every possible precaution, but were no more able to stop the destruction than Rommel had been against the British Special Air Service Unit of commando-type personnel in North Africa.

Rommel was plagued during the entire campaign from El Alamein to Tunisia by these British infiltrators who often hit hundreds of miles behind his lines. Attempts were made to thwart them by wiring the air-base boundaries, locating machine guns on the roofs of airport buildings, equipping the gunners with infrared glasses, and the like. Still the destruction of Rommel's aircraft continued, even when guards were heavily increased and a sentry placed aboard each airplane.

This British Special Air Service Unit actually accounted for the destruction of more Nazi and Fascist aircraft on the ground than the RAF destroyed in the air. More than 100 German airplanes were destroyed in one night of such an infiltration raid.

The difficulties suffered by Rommel in North Africa and the French in Indo-China, in attempting to combat this type of guerrilla antiaircraft action, bear serious consideration.

Both the French in Indo-China, and recently the Cubans under Batista's dictatorship, insured their ultimate defeat by disregarding the one theme of Clausewitz's which unlike many of his other themes has never been disputed by any other military theorist. In general it can be said to emphasize that no war, and particularly one against an adversary utilizing irregular tactics, can be won by remaining on the defensive.

Moscow-trained Ho Chi-minh fathered most of the psychological and political phases of the war. Both he and his counterpart, General Ngo Nguyen-giap, who commanded the Communist military forces, were true disciples of Mao Tse-tung's brand of guerrilla warfare. Mao's three basic principles were adhered to even in defeat:

1. Yield any town you cannot hold safely.
2. Limit yourself to guerrilla warfare as long as the enemy has numerical superiority and better weapons.

3. Organize regular units and pass over to the general counteroffensive only when you are sure of the family victory.

The Malayan Case

Perhaps the Malayan case deserves far more attention than most military historians accord it, since it represents the only one in the Far East where a successful strategy was developed against a formidable communist guerrilla force. The struggle between the Malayan Race's Liberation Army (MRLA) and the British can be instructive in understanding some of the factors involved when (as seems to be the unavoidable sequence of events in the *gray areas*), guerrillas fighting for national independence pit themselves against the regular military establishment of an alleged oppressor. This is not meant to imply that the combination of countertechniques used by the British—political, social, economic, psychological and military—would be applicable *per se* in other areas where the political problems and environmental factors involved are dissimilar.

Initially the British attempted to penetrate the jungle in battalion strength, but even if the attempt was performed in squad file formation they were constantly frustrated, as the word of their approach traveled faster than they did. Any inclination to leave the main trails found them so impeded that their movement was often reduced to only 100 feet per hour. British army officers on rotation leave to Singapore, in discussing the status of the war with the author, during one of his visits to that city in 1953, stated that before 1950, when such tactics were regularly used, if they were fortunate enough to actually reach a guerrilla campsite, they would find the guerrillas had faded off with the elusiveness of the will-o'-the-wisp. A single warning shot by one of the guerrilla sentries alerted the others, and, individually, they would move through the jungles to a prearranged new location. British pursuit would have been useless, but as an added precaution the guerrillas usually left a small rear guard to act as a reception committee, and insure the effective delay of any pursuit by the British.

General Sir Gerard Templar served as High Commissioner in Malaya for some three years prior to his retirement in May, 1954. During these years the threat of the Communist guerrillas was effectively reduced, and he is credited with developing the successful plans, although another British general, Sir Harold Briggs, actually instituted the political-military measures which accomplished the most successful anti-Communist offensive during the current decade (1950–1960).[16]

In the realization that one of the most pressing problems confronting every guerrilla organization was the maintenance of an adequate flow of food and other supplies, General Briggs devised a plan to cut off the

16. James E. Dougherty, "The Guerrilla War in Malaya," *U.S. Naval Institute Proceedings*, Vol. LXXXIV, No. 9 (September, 1958), p. 45.

guerrillas from their necessities and, at the same time, cut the ground from under the Communist social propaganda. Over half a million people were living near the fringe of the jungles. He recognized them as the contact linking the guerrillas with supply sources. He therefore set up an enormous resettlement program to move the jungle fringe squatters into hundreds of villages that were built away from their habitat.

The severe embarrassment suffered by the British regulars during 1948 and 1949 had been due to the guerrillas' complete tactical mastery of surprise. Even when attempting an offensive penetration of the jungle, the British were in reality held to a defensive attitude, seldom able to seize the initiative. Sole possessors of air support, the British found even this element incapable of effective operation. The first two years of the war saw the guerrillas inflicting telling damage in almost every mission they undertook, and seldom failing to achieve most of their limited objectives.

General Briggs' astute observations did not end with his massive resettlement program. He recognized the need for aggressive action and concluded that the British must gain a better understanding of the enemy's *modus operandi* in order to step up pressure against the guerrillas in the jungle. To gain an understanding of how Communist activities were adapted to the thought patterns of the indigenous population, he established a ferret force comprised of hand-picked British, Malayan, Gurka, and Chinese personnel. This force was assigned to live in the recesses of the jungle for several months performing patrolling missions and obtaining good intelligence concerning the Communist organization in action. After their return from this arduous mission the personnel of the unit were assigned as information and intelligence cadres among the various British military units in order to get the maximum benefit from their experience. As may be suspected, the former tactics of jungle penetration with battalion-sized units was quickly abandoned. Squads and platoons were filtered into the jungles using the same furtive techniques as the guerrillas to avoid detection by enemy scouts. These units severed their supply lines and, for periods ranging as high as a month, operated like the guerrillas. Frequent changes of location were made and a high degree of maneuverability was developed together with skill in ambush techniques.

The guerrillas started to feel the pressure of the squeeze. The difficulty of maintaining local supply lines after the relocation of the jungle fringe squatters reduced them to depending on crops raised in jungle clearings. This at last presented the British air arm with suitable targets. The RAF would observe the area and at the propitious moment dampen the spirits of the beleaguered guerrillas by spraying the food plots with poison or setting afire a field about to be harvested.

The British Navy also exerted additional pressure on the MRLA by making it impossible for them to import any arms aid or foodstuffs. Inexorably the pressures on the Communist guerrillas began an attrition that could not fail to exact its toll on their morale. Next the British worked out a rather novel propaganda campaign with the utilization of helicopters equipped with loudspeakers usually employed at night over the Communist camps.

The declining guerrilla forces were bombarded with announcements con-cerning the hopelessness of their situation, and they were given the choice of defecting from the Communists and accepting a rehabilitated life in urban Malaya or resigning themselves to (as the author recalls it) a rotten jungle existence probably culminating in death. The scope of the effort was impressive. By mid-1954, security forces were dropping 2,000 leaflets every week in pursuance of this propaganda campaign, and planes were broadcasting to about 15 jungle targets each week.[17]

An amusing sidelight of this rather successful psychological warfare offensive was that many of the guerrillas who surrendered fairly early in the campaign indicated their major difficulty in taking advantage of the amnesty offer lay in attempting to make their way out of the dense jungle at night. These guerrillas dared not make their move during daylight, as they were somewhat vulnerable to their unit's displeasure, normally evidenced by a hail of gunfire, being the *bon voyage* extended to those attempting to flee to the British. The British (renowned for their gracious hospitality) thoughtfully provided colored searchlights and sound trucks to serve as guides to the nearest army or police post.

The Malayan campaign, in the author's opinion, is the guerrilla warfare case deserving the closest scrutiny, because from it can be gleaned positive potentials in the successful combating of guerrilla actions. Unfortunately, far greater emphasis is usually placed on the campaigns that have culminated in defeats for western democracy. These can do little but fill us with a sense of frustration, not only by awakening us to the intrinsic danger of Communism slowly approaching its present obvious object of communizing all of Asia and Africa, but also because they fail to provide a basis for objective operational planning and development of successful antiguerrilla tactics.

History is replete with the accounts of guerrilla activities that gradually gained more and more popular support while using their harassing and plundering forays (as well as in some cases sympathetic external sources) to gradually build up their strength to the point where they are no longer confined to their unorthodox techniques of warfare. Then, to the consternation of the ruling authorities (foreign or native), they awaken to the further painful shock that even a segment of their own armed forces is not to be depended on. The consistent failure of most ruling authorities, faced with incipient guerrilla activities, to insure that an offen-

---

17. "Summary of Sir Gerard Templar's Farewell Press Conference," *Chronology of International Events,* Vol. X, No. 11 (London, British Royal Institute of International Affairs, 1954), p. 354.

sive attitude is instilled in their armed forces is noteworthy. Whether this apparent attitude of indifference or complacency is based on an over-confidence in the ability of their troops to remain superior in a final showdown, or because of the difficulties and hardships entailed in the assumption of an offensive conducted on the terms laid down by such guerrillas, is of little consequence. What is important is that invariably in comparison with the guerrilla forces, the government troops involved are somewhat softer due to their less rigorous existence. In addition, the failure to properly energize their fighting spirit gravely lowers their effectiveness when faced with the fiery enthusiasm diligently whipped up by the guerrilla leaders.

The students of military history must find it simple indeed to prophesy the eventual outcome of any struggle oriented along such lines. The failure of any government to willingly endure the costly and perhaps somewhat distasteful task of excising terrorist forces before their maturation can only result in its being visited with a stern judgment of Mars, for having defaulted to the enemy the mastery of almost all the principles of war—Objective, Offensive, Simplicity, Maneuver, Surprise, Security, and even Mass.

During the current decade (1950–1960) both the French Indo-Chinese War and Castro's revolt in Cuba were case examples involving the failure of a ruling authority fully to appreciate the basic requirement of assuming the offensive and maintaining it until fulfillment of the objective. Since the assumption of any antiguerrilla offensive must recognize the necessity of conducting it on the terms laid down by the guerrillas themselves, it is a *sina qua non* that it involves the use of equally unorthodox tactics as the guerrilla foes involved. From time to time the world was treated to expensive claims and exhortations on the part of both French premiers and Cuba's former dictator, Batista. In retrospect one can only conclude that pious exhortation is particularly pointless and that exchanging messages and purposeless displays of force, or diplomatic utterances unbacked by either the ability or will to enforce them, are completely sterile in effect.

The long list of unsuccessful operations conducted against guerrilla activities is a product of the inflexibility of many literary leaders as well as their intransigent attitude concerning the abandonment of conventional tactics. This military arteriosclerosis has existed down through the ages and is most evident toward the end of each epic period in the style of warfare, symbolized by a major transition of the conventional warfare of the day. The words of the late George Santayana echo the grim prospects awaiting future commanders who evidence symptoms of this cancerous military affliction: ". . . those who will not learn from history are condemned to repeat it."

Further References

BOOKS

Blacker, I. R., ed. *Irregulars, Partisans, Guerrillas: Great Stories from Rogers' Rangers to the Haganah.* New York: Simon & Schuster, 1954.

Crozier, B. *The Rebels: A Study of Post-War Insurrections.* Boston: Beacon, 1960.

Sanderson, J. D. *Behind Enemy Lines.* New York: Pyramid Books, 1961.

Standing, P. C. *Guerrilla Leaders of the World: From Charelte to De Wet.* Boston: Houghton, 1913 (London: S. Paul, 1913).

ARTICLES

Dening, B. C. "Modern Problems of Guerrilla Warfare," *Army Quarterly,* January, 1927.

East, C. H. A. "Guerrilla Warfare," *Australian Army Journal,* October, 1956 (condensed, *Military Review,* September, 1957).

Esson, D. M. R. "The Secret Weapon—Terrorism," *Army Quarterly,* July, 1959.

Griffith, S. B. "Guerrillas," *Marine Corps Gazette,* July and August, 1950.

Raymond, E. A. "Peoples' War," *Combat Forces Journal,* December, 1952.

Saundby, R. "Irregular Warfare," *Air Power,* Winter, 1956–57 (condensed, *Military Review,* December, 1957).

Sloman, J. H. "Guerrilla Warfare," *Australian Army Journal,* September, 1954 (condensed, *Military Review,* July, 1956).

PART 2 SOVIET RUSSIA

The history of Russia is dotted with instances of guerrilla activities. In the War of 1812, Russian peasant guerrillas harassed and disorganized Napoleon's retreating forces. In World War I small Russian raiderlike groups were active behind the German lines. Partisan guerrilla groups of many political shades were involved in the civil war of 1918–1921. Finally, partisans played an active role in the defeat of German forces in Russia during World War II.

Most western students of the Soviet partisan movement in World War II contend that the Soviets had anticipated the German invasion and had prepared cadre and stored arms in various sections of Russia. Understandably, Soviet historians make the counterclaim that the movement was a spontaneous result of the invasion of the Fatherland.[1]

In this section we are primarily concerned with modern guerrilla activity in Russia, especially during World War II, and with some of the countermeasures employed by the Nazis in their attempt to squelch the Soviet partisan movement. (Some discussions of current Soviet unconventional warfare strategy will be found in Part Nine.) In the lead article Jacobs analyzes some inconsistencies in Soviet claims for guerrilla warfare, including the Soviet partisan movement in World War II. This is followed by the translation and analysis of Lenin's theories of partisan warfare. McClure's account of Soviet guerrilla tactics is based on captured documents and training manuals. Dohnányi provides one of the better accounts of the Soviet partisan groups and German countermeasures; he also suggests organization policies for counterguerrilla forces of the future.

---

1. Walter D. Jacobs (see Further References at the end of this section) has translated a recent Russian article by V. I. Kulikov that severely criticizes western students of the Soviet partisan movement who "have been striving in every possible way to belittle and degrade the role of Soviet partisans, using the methods of falsification in this effort." Kulikov emphatically denies and proves to his own satisfaction at least that the Soviet government had not prepared for partisan warfare before the Nazis invaded Russia. Despite the article's origin and tediousness of "bourgeois falsification," its 45 pages merit consideration by objective western students.

Finally, Codó discusses the guerrilla activities of the Ukrainian partisans, who not only fought the Germans but the Soviets as well; he suggests that the Ukraine is ready to resume its anti-Communist guerrilla activities in the event of another war.

5

Walter D. Jacobs

IRREGULAR

WARFARE

AND THE SOVIETS

L ENIN'S EARLY VIEWS on the utilization of the form of partisan warfare contain the core of much of his thinking on armed insurrection. In an essay published in 1906 he stated that the character of partisan military activities should "produce knowledge of offensive and surprise military actions."[1]

The idea of the educational value of engaging in partisan warfare, in Lenin's opinion, is supplemented by its value as an example, within reality, of the flexibility required of a revolutionary, conspiratorial organization.

Reprinted from *Military Review*, May, 1958, by permission. The following applies to all *Military Review* articles reprinted in this volume: "The Military Review, a publication of the *United States Army*, provides a forum for the expression of military thought and a medium for the dissemination of Army doctrine of the division and higher levels. The *views* expressed in this magazine *are the authors'* and not necessarily those of the Army or the United States Army Command and General Staff College."

1. *V. I. Lenin o Voine, Armii i Voennoi Nauke* (V. I. Lenin on War, the Army and Military Science), Moscow, Voennoe Izdatel'stvo, 1957. Two Volumes (hereafter cited as *Lenin o Voine*), Volume I, p. 220.

"In the period of the civil war," Lenin continued in his essay (and by civil war he meant the struggle of class against class within prerevolutionary Russia), "the ideal party of the proletariat is a fighting party." Therefore, he considered it necessary to engage in activities which might be militarily inexpedient. The disorganizing tendencies of partisan warfare should indeed be recognized and studied, but "every military action in any war to a certain extent disorganizes the ranks of the fighters." One cannot, for that reason, abandon the fight—"One must learn to fight. That is all."

Partisan Warfare

The lesson of flexibility and what it means to an insurrectionist group can be learned from the choice of partisan warfare as a form. Lenin pointed out that:

> At different periods Social-Democrats [Communists] apply different methods, always qualifying the choice of them by strictly defined ideological and organizational conditions.

In the course of a few years Lenin and the Communists passed from armed insurrections directed against the Imperial government to holders of power in the Soviet Republic. One of their first tasks was the fighting of a civil war.

That a peculiarly Communist concept of irregular warfare did not develop out of the events of the 1917 November Revolution nor out of the subsequent civil war is due to the following factors.

Limited Military Action

The Bolsheviks seized political power in the original instance without the necessity of extensive military action, regular or irregular. In the major cities of Russia, power was seized virtually without military action. Those military clashes which did occur were of short duration and involved limited numbers of troops. The Soviet forces committed were unconventional, but their unconventionality varied from place to place. There was no regularity in their irregularity.

The irregular actions of the civil war were on a larger scale and of a less varied nature. The types of irregular action can be divided, for purposes of convenience, into two—those occurring in the mountains and those occurring in the plains.

Irregular actions which took place in the plains were restricted largely to the Ukraine. The plains irregulars of the Ukraine were a source of despair to the centralizing tendencies of Lenin and Trotsky.

Trotsky

Lenin and Trotsky were attempting to build a military force of the traditional type from the material provided by the Red Guards. The tradition in the Ukraine, however, was with the local atamans and decentralization. These local traditions were castigated by Lenin in his speech of 4 July, 1919, "On the Present Situation and the Immediate Tasks of Soviet Power," when he said:

> The peasants simply took up arms, chose an ataman and instituted a power of their own there and then. They paid no heed to any central power and each Ukrainian ataman thought he could solve all his country's problems without bothering about events in the capital.

Lenin's attitude was reflected by Trotsky, who had said:

> It is necessary ruthlessly to cleanse the commanders of the Third Army . . . (I)n some units of the Third Army there are still surviving the habits of the guerrillas or atamans to discuss combat orders and to fail, under all kinds of pretexts, in carrying them out.[2]

Voroshilov, Budenny, and other early Red Army leaders who came from the ranks of the guerrillas later attempted to evolve a concept of military doctrine based on the proletarian character of the force. This doctrine was best put into written form by M. V. Frunze.[3] Frunze's doctrine emphasized speed and the offensive. It cannot, however, be viewed as a concept of irregular warfare in spite of the origin of its composers.

Creation of Regular Army

In any event, with the establishment of Soviet power the central government began to turn its back on the irregulars. According to Raymond L. Garthoff in his *Soviet Military Doctrine,* the Soviets called for the creation of a "regular" army on 10 June 1918. There was no provision for incorporation into that army of the traditions of the irregulars.

Neither the official acceptance of the regular army concept nor the later attempt of the Frunze group to put forward a "unified" military doctrine rules out the possibility of the development of a Communist doctrine of irregular warfare. The irregular forces of the mountain areas, especially those of the taiga and the Soviet Far East, did not come under the same general condemnation from Moscow as did the plains guerrillas. But a doctrine of irregular warfare did not come out of the east either.

---

2. Quoted in Dimitri Daniel Fedotoff White, *The Growth of the Red Army,* Princeton University Press, Princeton, N.J., 1944, p. 64.

3. Mikhail V. Frunze, "Edinaia voennaia doktrina i Krasnaia Armiia" ("A Unified Military Doctrine and the Red Army") in *Izbrannye Proizvedeniia* (Selected Works), Voennoe Izdatel'stvo Moscow, 1950, pp. 137–159.

It produced epic heroes of Soviet literature rather than giants of military doctrine.

While no doctrine was produced in the pre-World War II Soviet Union which could be said to be the "official" view on irregular warfare, a sort of operational code did develop. It can be summarized as follows: irregulars who fight for the central government and accept its authority will receive a temporary blessing; no endorsement of partisan warfare as a form is intended by this temporary blessing.

World War II

When the Wehrmacht drove into Soviet Russia in the late summer of 1941, there existed no generally available Soviet doctrine of irregular warfare.

Stalin's famous Order of the Day of 3 July 1941 was not the signal for the unleashing of hordes of previously prepared partisans. Hitler's troops did not originally encounter a hostile Soviet populace steeped in tales of fabled Communist irregulars such as Chapaev, Frunze, Budenny, Chu Teh, and Mao Tse-tung.

Although there was little or nothing on 22 June 1941, by the end of the war—and even earlier when victory seemed certainly to be on the side of the Soviets—a partisan movement of notable scale occurred in the occupied areas of the Soviet Union.

It appears that by the time of the German invasion the Soviet Government had prepared certain official groups, for instance, the Red Army, the NKVD (Soviet Secret Police), and Party leaders, to operate as leaders and organizers of irregular resistance against enemy troops. The examples of early resistance attest to such preparations. The limits of the preparation are reflected in the very friendly receptions given to the invading German columns by the natives. Whatever the preparation or lack of it, the implementation of the partisan movement on the scale on which it took place is a marvel of organization and supervision.

Partisan Movement

From the first days of the war the Soviet authorities realized the value of irregular opposition to the Germans. From the beginning they attempted to establish some type of central authority over the partisans.

The methods employed included the official organization of the partisan movement under General Mechlis of the Main Administration of the Political Propaganda of the Red Army.[4] General Mechlis issued orders

4. Major Edgar M. Howell, *The Soviet Partisan Movement, 1941–1944,* Department of the Army, Washington, 1946, p. 47.

for the composition and employment of irregular units. Command channels of small or isolated units frequently flowed through available Red Army officers, NKVD members, and Party functionaries in the area. Moscow attempted to maintain control by means of improved communications and by making the irregulars party dependent on the center for supplies. The use of the airplane in partisan warfare is a Soviet "first." In early 1942 the central government of the Soviet Union began the publication and distribution of the guide and reference book, *Sputnik Partizana* (Partisan's Handbook).

In spite of all these activities the partisan movement did not become widespread or achieve popular progovernmental support until the activities of the German occupiers came to the aid of the beleagured Communists in Moscow.

Nazi Policy

Soviet civilians were treated as *Untermensch* ("subhuman") and the soldiers of the Red Army were told:

> The regulations of the Hague Rules of Land Warfare . . . are not valid inasmuch as the USSR is dissolved. (T)he Geneva Convention for the Treatment of Prisoners of War is not binding in the relationship between Germany and the USSR.[5]

The beginnings of the Soviet partisan movement can be traced to the continued fighting of Soviet troops cut off by the first German thrusts. As Major Howell has indicated, these groups were led by Red Army officers and Party members.

Initially, the partisan movement did not have the support of the citizens in the area. In *Panzer Leader,* General Heinz Guderian tells of a deeply moving welcome of Germans into Roslavl in August 1941. He adds:

> Unfortunately, this friendly attitude toward the Germans lasted only so long as the more benevolent military administration was in control. The so-called "Reich commissars" soon managed to alienate all sympathy from the Germans and thus to prepare the ground for all the horrors of partisan warfare.

As stated by Alexander Dallin in *German Rule in Russia, 1941–1945,* the spread of partisan activity in the Soviet Union can be attributed more to hatred of Erich Koch ("Reich commissar" for the Ukraine) than to love of Josef Stalin. Stalin's call for extensive partisan activity did not enjoy popular support until the nature of Nazi policy became known to the citizens of the Soviet Union and to the members of the Red Army.

One result of Nazi policy in the U.S.S.R. was to force civilians into partisan activities in preference to enduring the rigors of the Koch occupa-

5. *Ibid.,* pp. 109–110.

tion and to force bypassed and abandoned Red Army soldiers into irregular formations in preference to a questionable prisoner-or-war status.

Young Communists specifically trained for their tasks represented a third element in the partisan movement. This element was small and relatively unimportant in the over-all irregular movement.[6]

Tactics

The Soviet authorities attempted to take full advantage of the fact that large numbers of individuals were drawn or forced into the partisan movement. The tactical concept which issued from Moscow was in the traditional mold. After-action studies almost uniformly indicate that Soviet irregulars placed an emphasis on surprise, speed, mobility, flexibility of plans and of maneuver, night actions, bases in inaccessible areas, and the need for the support and assistance of the local populace. The most frequently employed offensive tactical means, according to Colonel General V. S. Popov in *Surprise and the Unexpected in the History of Wars,* were "traps, ambushes on forest roads, ambushes in mountain passes, ambushes at river crossings, and at exits from populated points."

Popov goes to the essence of the partisan tactical concept when he states:

> Mobility, flexibility of maneuver based on knowledge of the area, good continuous information of the adversary through their own intelligence and from local inhabitants—all this permitted partisan detachments to know beforehand, without fail, the intentions of the enemy and in turn to attack enemy troops with surprise and unexpectedly on the move and in populated points.

The Soviet concept of the strategy of irregular operations during the Second World War varies in some aspects from previous irregular doctrine although the general comparative view is similar.

Political Character

The political character of the movement was its overriding characteristic. It is always difficult to draw a line separating political and military aims and operations. It is even more difficult in operations of an irregular nature. It is practically impossible in irregular operations directed by the Communist Party. Stalin characterized Bolsheviks as a sort of modern-day Antaeus drawing their strength from contact with the masses.[7] Contact

---

6. Lieutenant General Wladyslaw Ander, *Hitler's Defeat in Russia,* Henry Regnery Co., Chicago, 1953, pp. 168–172. 211.

7. *History of the Communist Party of the Soviet Union (Bolsheviks): Short Course,* Foreign Languages Publishing House, Moscow, 1950, p. 447.

with the masses was, not surprisingly, the most frequently emphasized strategic element of the partisan movement in Soviet writings.

"(U)nlike the guerrilla movements in previous struggles," reported a wartime account, ". . . the guerrilla units have safe bases to operate from."[8]

When the partisan hero, General Kovpak, visited Stalin in the Kremlin, the Communist chief kept repeating, "The most important thing is to keep stronger links with the people."[9]

Another trait of identification of the Soviet concept of irregular warfare at the strategic level was the plan to integrate "little wars" of the partisans with "big wars" of the regulars. Captain N. Galay suggests one reason for this integration. He maintains that the anticentralistic inclination among subject peoples of the Soviet Union is great and has been and will be expressed at every opportunity. In order to suppress such inclinations, therefore, the Soviets in the center are forced to coordinate all actions, regular or irregular.[10]

No Authoritative Doctrine

The concept of irregular warfare which is held by Soviet Communists is revealed through observation of partisan actions in World War II. There is no single source outlining the official Soviet views on irregular warfare in the sense that Mao Tse-tung's writings have given the Chinese Communist line. The works of Kovpak, Fiodorov, Popov, and others are instructive. They can hardly be viewed as authoritative in the same sense that Mao's works are authoritative. The explanation for the Soviet lacuna perhaps is more political than military.

The *yu chi chan* concept in China was consolidative (from the Communist point of view), while the partisan movement in the Soviet Union tended to be centrifugal. The irregulars in China were the force around which Mao Tse-tung and Chu Teh were building the nucleus of their apparatus for the seizure of power. To Moscow the partisan movement was as much an attempt to hold down desertions of citizens and soldiers as it was to organize a supplementary military force. The force of anticentrical irregulars had been turned against a Communist government in Moscow during the years of the civil war. When Mao was expounding his concept of *yu chi chan,* the Chinese Communists had never held central power and, of course, had no prejudicial opposition to irregulars. For all the romanticiz-

---

8. *Guerrilla Warfare in the Occupied Parts of the Soviet Union,* Foreign Languages Publishing House, Moscow, 1943, p. 8.

9. Major General S. A. Kovpak, *Our Partisan Course,* London, Hutchinson, n.d., p. 79.

10. Captain N. Galay, "The Partisan Forces," in H. Liddell Hart, ed., *The Red Army,* Harcourt, Brace & Co., New York, 1956, pp. 163–171.

ing of him in times of war and stress, the irregular is out of place in a society peopled by Soviet men.

Conclusion

The Soviet concept of irregular war appears to be one of congruism. The guerrilla is effective to the extent that he is resourceful, creative, bold, and independent. These are traits which are not conducive to the building of good Communists on levels below the summit. The Soviets, however, are willing to award grace to the irregular. They are not willing to see in him the ideal type.

However, he may be useful against the enemy in a future war. Lieutenant General S. Krasil'nikov had this to say in a 1956 essay:

> In wars of imperialism against the camp of socialism, the creation in the rear of the imperialistic front, where it will be possible, of a "partisan front" will be characteristic. The partisan front is usually formed in the course of war on the basis of popular resistance in territories occupied by the aggressor, but also in colonies and in countries dependent on imperialism which do not want to bear the shameful yoke of slavery and national oppression. However, the conditions of partisan war and its conduct will be different than they were in the last war.

6

V. I. Lenin

PARTISAN

WARFARE

L ENIN'S ARTICLE ON PARTISAN WARFARE—that is, on the use of terrorism, robbery, and ambush in the revolutionary struggle—is one of the most important "operational" writings from the pen of the founder of bolshevism. It is his most outspoken unclassified contribution to communist conflict doctrine. Under the title of *Partisanskaya Voina,* this article has been reprinted in all five Russian editions of Lenin's *Sochineniya (Collected Works). . . .*

For reasons which are too obvious to require comment, the communists —to the best of our knowledge—so far have neglected to publish an English translation of Lenin's revealing piece. Since the article has remained virtually unknown even among American experts on communism, the editors of *Orbis* believe that the time has come to close this dangerous gap in "English literature."

Students of protracted warfare will discover in this article the original writ of the communist operational doctrine. Here is the model of the many terroristic wars which the communists, since 1945 or so, have been fanning

From *Orbis,* Summer, 1958. Copyright 1958 by Foreign Policy Research Institute, University of Pennsylvania and reproduced by permission.

in the so-called "underdeveloped" areas. It appears that the concept of protracted conflict did not originate with Mao Tse-tung—who, however, remains its most incisive and comprehensive protagonist—but with Lenin, who conceived it, on the basis of contemporary experience, no less than fifty-two years ago.

Lenin's text, originally published on October 13, 1906, in No. 5 of his newspaper *Proletari,* is somewhat heavy-handed and occasionally confusing. Fortunately, its main message is clear and penetrating. Hence, the editors of *Orbis* deemed it preferable to print an accurate translation rather than "edit" Lenin's article. For a better understanding of the author's many references to events of the Russian revolution of 1905–1906, the editors have appended footnotes prepared by Stefan T. Possony. In some instances, words were added to make the original text more comprehensible; these words have been placed between brackets. The italics are Lenin's own.

The translation was prepared by Regina Eldor from Volume X of the Third Edition of *Sochineniya* and from Volume X of the German *Saemtliche Werke,* an authoritative translation prepared by the Lenin Institute in Moscow.—EDITORS, *Orbis*

I

The question of partisan actions has aroused great interest within the party and among the workers.[1] We have mentioned this topic repeatedly

1. The term "partisan war" or "partisan actions" is a euphemism. It does not mean "guerrilla war" in the modern sense but stands for terrorism, holdups and robberies. So-called "expropriations" of money were directed against banks, taxation agencies, post offices, customs houses, railroad stations and similar establishments where large sums of cash were likely to be stored. However, small firms, such as bakeries and village shops, as well as affluent individuals, also were victimized. In many instances, the "expropriations" were planned by professional "fingermen" and executed by expert robbers. Terror was practiced on policemen, soldiers and officials, both in cities and in the rural areas. Operations in the cities were conducted by small "combat groups"; forays in the countryside were sometimes executed by large armed bands which, under the convenient guise of "partisan warfare," made looting and pillaging a profitable profession. Originally, the social democrats had rejected terrorism, which was a major *modus operandi* of the social revolutionaries. During 1905 and 1906, however, the incidence of terror increased greatly and the bolshevik faction of the Social Democratic Party supported it wholeheartedly. In fact, a large percentage of the bombs used in "partisan warfare" was fabricated in a secret bolshevik laboratory run by Leonid B. Krassin. Most mensheviks were opposed both to terror and "expropriations," but it is interesting that G. V. Plekhanov, the founder of Russian Marxism, favored them, at least for a time. The Russian socialists who opposed terrorism argued that "European means of struggle" be used. They feared that terrorism was harming the reputation of the social democrats and worried about the fact that many, if not most, of the "expropriations" were perpetrated by criminal elements, for purposes of their own personal enrichment.

In reading Lenin's discourse, it should be remembered that, in practical terms, before. Our present intention is to redeem our promise and summarize our position on this subject.

Let us start from the beginning. What are the basic questions every Marxist must ask when he analyzes the problem of the types of struggle?[2] First of all, unlike primitive forms of socialism, Marxism does not tie the movement to any particular combat method. It recognizes the possibility that struggle may assume the most variegated forms. For that matter, Marxism does not "invent" those forms of struggle. It merely organizes the tactics of strife and renders them suitable for general use. It also renders the revolutionary classes conscious of the forms of the clashes which emerge spontaneously from the activities of the movement. Marxism rejects all abstract thinking and doctrinaire prescriptions about types of struggle. It calls for a careful study of the *mass struggle* which actually is taking place. As the movement develops, as the consciousness of the masses grows, and as the economic and political crises are becoming more intense, ever new and different methods of defense and attack will be used in the conflict. Hence, Marxism never will reject any particular combat method, let alone reject it forever. Marxism does not limit itself to those types of struggle which, at a given moment, are both practical and traditional. It holds that, owing to changes in social conditions, new forms of battle will arise *inevitably,* although no one can foresee what the character of these future encounters will be. In this field, if we may say so, Marxism is *learning* from the practice of the masses. It is far from claiming that it should *teach*

---

he was advocating an alliance between revolution and crime: Lenin did, in fact, enter into agreements with criminal elements during the partisan warfare period. Later, during World War I, he even recommended a notorious highwayman to the Germans for sabotage operations. (The man received pay but did not commit any acts of sabotage.)

While Lenin was penning his treatise on "partisan war," the terrorist phase of the first Russian revolution was reaching its peak. In October, 1906, alone, 121 terror acts, 47 clashes between revolutionaries and the police, and 362 expropriations were reported. [See Boris Souvarine, *Staline, Aperçu Historique du Bolchevisme* (Paris: Plon, 1935), p. 92.] While it is impossible to draw up exact statistics of the total terror campaign, there is no question that it cost the lives of more than 5,000 policemen and officials. Several millions of rubles were "expropriated" by criminal and revolutional elements.

2. The terms, "types" or "forms of struggle," and their variations, such as "combat tactics" and "methods of battle," all of which sound awkward in English, denote a key concept in communist conflict doctrine. The term "struggle" is a short notation for "class struggle." Lenin contends that the tactics and techniques of the class struggle must be altered as situations and conditions change. Socialists should have no dogmatic attachment to one particular type of tactic or a particular weapon but should employ those procedures and means which, singly or in combination, are expedient and effective. The point is important, since American policy-makers often assume that the communists are wedded to one particular "type of struggle" and that the communists, once they begin to apply one specific method, will continue to do so. Such an interpretation of bolshevik theory can be reconciled neither with the writings nor the actions of international communism.

the masses tactics elaborated in the abstract by strategists of the pen. We know, as Kautsky stated when he was analyzing the different forms of social revolution, that the coming crisis will present us with new and unpredictable forms of action.

Second, Marxism asks that the various types of struggle be analyzed within their *historical* framework. To discuss conflict outside of its historical and concrete setting is to misunderstand elementary dialectic materialism. At various junctures of the economic evolution, and depending upon changing political, national, cultural, social and other conditions, differing types of struggle may become important and even predominant. As a result of those [sociological] transformations, secondary and subordinate forms of action may change their significance. To try and answer positively or negatively the question of whether a certain tactic is usable, without at the same time studying the concrete conditions confronting a given movement at a precise point of its development, would mean a complete negation of Marxism.

Those are the two basic concepts which must serve as our guide. The soundness of this approach has been confirmed by numerous examples from the history of Western European Marxism. At present, European socialists regard parliamentarism and trade unionism as their main method of struggle. Previously, they favored the armed uprising.[3] Contrary to the opinion of liberal-bourgeois politicians like the Russian Cadets and the Bessaglavtsi,[4] the European socialists are perfectly willing to favor the uprising again should the situation change in the future.

During the 1870's, social democrats rejected the idea that the general strike could be used as a panacea tactic and as a nonpolitical method suitable for the immediate overthrow of the bourgeoisie. But after the experience of 1905,[5] the social democrats fully recognized the political

---

3. Lenin alludes here to one of Friedrich Engels' last publications in which, to the chagrin of the radicals, he discussed the difficulties of an armed uprising against a government armed with modern weapons. Engels went so far as to question the usefulness of that revolutionary symbol, the barricade. Lenin also alludes to the gradual shift at that time taking place in practically all European socialist parties toward forsaking revolution in favor of evolutionary methods.

4. This refers to a weekly magazine entitled *Bes Zaglavia* (*Without Title*), of which sixteen issues were published between February and May, 1906, by S. N. Prokopovich, E. D. Kuskova, and others. The editors of this magazine were moderate socialists who believed in democracy. They were friendly to the objectives of the left wing of the Constitutional Democrats (Cadets).

5. Lenin refers to the mass strike movement which began in August, 1905, and in October culminated in one of the most complete general strikes of history. It was this strike movement, and particularly the railroad strike, which forced the Russian government to proclaim the so-called "October Manifesto" by which a semiconstitutional regime (Max Weber described it as "sham constitutionalism") was promulgated. Incidentally, these strikes neither were called nor run by the socialist leaders but by the liberal-bourgeois parties, especially the Cadets. Lenin's wording suggests that he was completely aware of this historical fact, which, however, he was loath to admit in writing. Lenin and other revolutionaries did not return

mass strike as *a* means which, under *certain* conditions, could become necessary. Similarly, during the 1840's the social democrats recognized the utility of barricades. By the end of the nineteenth century, conditions had changed and the socialists rejected the barricades as unsuitable. However, after the experience of the Moscow rising, which, in Kautsky's words, demonstrated new tactics of barricade fighting, they were willing to revise their position and again acknowledged the usefulness of barricades.[6]

II

After this exposition of general Marxist doctrine, we want to discuss the Russian revolution. Let us consider the historical development of the various action types to which the revolution gave rise. First, there occurred economic strikes by the workers (1896–1900), then political demonstrations by workers and students (1901–1902), peasant unrest (1902), subsequently the beginnings of political mass strikes variously connected with demonstrations (Rostov, 1902, strikes during summer of 1903, the affair of January 22, 1905[7]), political general strike with local barricade fighting (October, 1905), mass barricade battles waged by large numbers [of revolutionaries], as well as armed uprising (December, 1905), peaceful parliamentary struggle (April–July, 1906) local military uprisings (June, 1905–June, 1906), and local peasant uprisings (fall, 1905–fall, 1906).

Such was the development of the struggle before the autumn of 1906.

---

to Russia until an amnesty, late in October, 1905, made it safe for them to do so. Only after the middle-of-the-road parties, whose outstanding demands were met by the "October Manifesto," withdrew from the revolution, did the socialists assume leadership of the revolutionary movement.

6. Alexander Helphand, better known as "Parvus," discussed this vexing problem of barricades as early as 1897—that is, two years after Engels had expressed his doubts. "Parvus" pointed out that barricades, while perhaps no longer militarily useful, could serve as rallying points for the aroused and fighting masses. He considered barricades as a predominantly psychological device suitable for bringing the masses into the streets. Obviously, Lenin, who feared "Parvus" as an intellectually superior competitor, did not want to give him credit for this correct prediction, nor did he want to acknowledge that he now adopted "Parvus'" interpretation of barricade tactics.

7. The "affair of January 22, 1905" is better known as "Bloody Sunday." Lenin's undramatic description of this event, which was the tragic overture to the revolution of 1905, probably is due to the fact that neither the social democrats nor the bolshevik faction played any significant role in it. The revolution had started without their assistance. The leading revolutionary figure of Bloody Sunday was Father George Gapon, who originally had been involved in "police socialism" and was cooperating with the social revolutionaries in initiating the revolution.

Absolutism opposed these types of struggle with Black Hundreds pogroms.[8] These pogroms were initiated in spring, 1903, at Kishinev and ended with the Siedliec pogrom in 1906. During this period, the organizing of Black Hundreds pogroms and the tormenting of Jews, students, revolutionaries, and class-conscious workers continued unabated and steadily increased in ferocity. Mob violence was paired with military violence perpetrated by reactionary troops. Artillery was used on villages and cities. Punitive expeditions were dispatched, and all over the railroads there were moving trains crowded with political prisoners.

This, then, has been the general background of the situation. From this background there has emerged the phenomenon of *armed struggle*.[9] Our paper is devoted to the study and evaluation of this new occurrence. Although merely a secondary and incidental part of the whole, armed struggle has been pushed into the foreground. What is armed struggle? What are its forms and its causes? When did it originate? What has been the frequency of its occurrence? What is its significance for the general course of the revolution? What is its connection with the proletarian class struggle organized and waged by social democracy? After having described the general background of the problem, we shall now address ourselves to these questions.

Armed struggle is waged by small groups and individuals, some of whom are members of revolutionary parties. In certain regions of Russia, however, the *majority* [of the partisans] are not affiliated with any revo-

---

8. The "Black Hundreds" were combat groups set up by parties of the extreme right in order to fight the revolutionaries. They might be considered the ancestors of the Nazi SA and SS, though their organization was not as strong and their membership fluctuated greatly. The Black Hundreds were openly tolerated by the Tsarist police; there is, in fact, the strong possibility that the police itself secretly created these forces. The Black Hundreds rarely, if ever, succeeded in fighting the revolutionaries directly. They were used for anti-Semitic pogroms, mostly in poor Jewish districts. The pogroms were launched in the hope that counterterror ultimately would intimidate the revolutionaries. (It may be added that, according to the official version, the pogroms were "spontaneous.") This hope was based on the mistaken notion, prevalent within the Russian government and the police, that the revolutionary movement was largely the creation of Jewish international circles on whose financial and political support it depended. The assumption was that, if the Jews in Russia were made to pay for the crimes of the revolutionaries, the Jewish world leaders, in order to save their coreligionists, would call off the revolution. The frequency and violence of the pogroms have been overrated, and the utility of this antirevolutionary tactic was very much debated within the Russian government. When it became apparent that pogroms were totally ineffective in halting the revolution, the Black Hundreds gradually fell into disuse. Their very existence, however, provided the revolutionaries with excellent arguments for their own terror operations.

From 1906 onward, under the premiership of P. A. Stolypin, the revolutionary movement was incapacitated by systematic arrests of revolutionaries, summary executions, exiling to Siberia, and punitive expeditions against partisan bands.

9. The term "armed struggle" is another expression for "partisan action." Lenin had in mind violent actions executed by small groups for secondary objectives such as terrorism and robbery. The term does not denote armed uprising.

lutionary organization. Armed struggle aims at two *different* objectives which must be distinguished *sharply* from one another. The first objective is to kill individuals such as high officials and lower-ranking members of the police and army.[10] The second objective is to confiscate money from the government as well as from private persons. Portions of the captured money are used for party purposes, other portions for arms and the preparation of the rising, and the rest for the sustenance of persons engaging in the struggle described by us.[11] The money seized in the great expropriations (more than 200,000 rubles in the Caucasus and 875,000 rubles in Moscow) was allocated to the revolutionary parties primarily.[12] Smaller expropriations were used mainly, and sometimes exclusively, for the livelihood of the "expropriators." This type of struggle came into widespread use during 1906, after the December uprising [at Moscow]. The aggravation of the political crisis to the point of armed insurrection, and especially the ever growing pauperization, famine and unemployment in villages and cities, were among the most potent causes leading to the emergence of armed combat. The *déclassé* elements of the population, the *Lumpenproletariat* and anarchist groups, chose this struggle as the main and even *only* form of the social war. Autocracy answered with the tactics of martial law, conscription of younger military classes, Black Hundreds pogroms (Siedliec), and court-martials.

---

10. According to the official legend, the bolsheviks are opposed to terrorism. Lenin's article should dispel any false notions about the bolshevik attitude to political assassinations. Lenin makes it perfectly clear that a true bolshevik never can be against terrorism as a matter of principle: he should oppose terror only if and when murder is inexpedient and ineffective. The bolshevik, by the same token, should favor political assassinations whenever they promise to advance the communist cause.

11. Thus, Lenin admitted that many of the so-called "expropriations" were simply robberies. While Lenin did not openly advocate robberies as a convenient source of income for professional revolutionaries, the "expediency" which he championed was broad enough to include such use of "expropriations."

12. According to the Lenin Institute, Lenin was describing an expropriation which took place on March 26, 1906 at Dushet, near Tiflis, and which was carried out by six men disguised as soldiers of the 263rd Infantry Regiment. The Lenin Institute stated that 315,000 rubles were expropriated. If Lenin's party treasury received only the 200,000 rubles to which he was referring, then 115,000 rubles must have remained in the hands of the "expropriators." Souvarine commented that the robbers were socialist-federalists (that is, they belonged to one of the many splinter groups of the Social Revolutionary Party) and that the bolsheviks got hold of this money "by ruse" (*op. cit.,* p. 91). In other words, true to their Marxian philosophy, they expropriated the expropriators. Note that the action of Dushet was *not* the expropriation in which Stalin participated. Stalin earned his laurels as a bank robber on June 26, 1907, in Tiflis. In the course of that raid, no less than ten bombs were thrown and 431,000 rubles (or $170,000) seized. The Moscow expropriation was carried out on March 20, 1906, by twenty armed men who attacked a bank, disarmed four guards, and took 875,000 rubles, just as Lenin indicated in the text. For a useful discussion of some of these events, the reader is referred to Alexandre Spiridovich, *Histoire de Terrorisme Russe* (Paris: Payot, 1930).

III

Armed struggle often is considered to be anarchism, Blanquism, old-style terrorism and, at any rate, an activity perpetrated by isolated individuals out of touch with the masses. The acts of armed struggle are judged to demoralize the workers. Allegedly they divorce broad strata of the population from the toilers, disorganize the revolutionary movement and hurt the revolutionary cause. Examples supporting this type of evaluation are drawn easily from the daily press.

But how good are these examples? Let us look at one case. Partisan struggle reached its *greatest* popularity in the Lettish districts. On August 21 and September 25 [1906], the newspaper *Novoye Vremya*[13] complained bitterly about the activities of the Lettish socialists. The Lettish Social Democratic Party, a branch of the Social Democratic Workers Party of Russia, disclosed a list of police agents. This disclosure was inserted in the party newspaper (circulation: 30,000) and was accompanied by the comment that it was the duty of every honest person to help bring about the liquidation of those spies. The police collaborators were "enemies of the revolution," their property was declared liable to seizure, and they themselves were designated for execution. The social democrats have instructed the population to contribute money to the party, but against stamped receipts only. In the latest budget, there was listed among the party's annual receipts totaling 48,000 rubles an item of 5,600 rubles expropriated by the Libau organization for the purchase of weapons. Of course, *Novoye Vremya* is outraged by such "revolutionary legislation" and by this "terror regime."

No one would dare call those actions by the Lettish social democrats anarchism, Blanquism or terrorism. Why? Simply because the armed struggle *clearly* is interrelated with the uprising which took place in December. Such uprisings are bound to reoccur. If Russia is considered as a whole, then this relationship [between armed struggle and armed uprising] is not so clearly noticeable, but it does exist. After all, there is no question but that "partisan" struggle reached its greatest popularity after the December rising. Those actions are related not only to the economic crisis but also to the political crisis. Traditional Russian terrorism was the work of plotting intellectuals. Now, workers or unemployed persons who

13. *Novoye Vremya* was a leading conservative paper. During 1906, the Lettish revolutionary movement was very well organized and registered some of the more notable successes of the first Russian revolution. The Baltic provinces were the scene of a great deal of partisan action in the modern sense, which it took Russian military forces considerable time to suppress. Socialist ideology contributed only mildly to the Lettish movement's strength: nationalist feelings were a more significant factor. This is one of the first instances of the socialist-nationalist "amalgam" in guerrilla war.

are members of combat groups usually are leading this struggle.[14] People who like to generalize according to abstract patterns easily may think of anarchism or Blanquism. In the face of an insurrectionist situation as it clearly existed in the Lettish area, such phrases learned by rote obviously are meaningless.

The Lettish example demonstrates that the usual method of analyzing partisan action without regard to the status of the uprising is completely wrong, unscientific, and unhistorical. The [concrete] situation must be taken into consideration. The characteristics of the transition periods between large uprisings must be taken into account. The types of struggle which, in a given period, are becoming inevitable should not be criticized with a few clichés such as anarchism, plunder, and *Lumpenproletariat,* as is customary among Cadets[15] and the *Novoye Vremya* crowd.

It is said that partisan actions disorganize our work. Let us see to what extent this evaluation is justified, especially with respect to the period after December, 1905, and to the areas under martial law and [suffering from] Black Hundreds pogroms. What is it that disorganizes the movement in such an area more: the lack of resistance or the lack of [a well] organized partisan struggle? Compare the situation in Central Russia with that of the Western border regions, such as Poland and Livonia. There is no doubt that in the Western provinces partisan struggles occur far more frequently and have reached a higher stage of development. Contrariwise, there is no doubt that in Central Russia the revolutionary movement in general, and the social democratic movement in particular, is far *more disorganized* [than in the West]. Certainly we would not think of concluding that because of the partisan struggle the Polish and Lettish social democratic movement has suffered from disorganization less [than the movement in Central Russia]. No. The point is merely that the partisan struggle is not responsible for the disorganization of the Russian social democratic workers movement [which occurred] during 1906.

In this connection, frequent reference has been made to the peculiarities of national conditions. Such arguments disclose the weakness of the customary objections to partisan struggle. If it is a matter of national conditions, then obviously it is not a matter of anarchism, Blanquism, or terrorism, but something else is involved: general Russian or even specifically Russian sins. Analyze this "something else" more *concretely,* gentlemen! You will find that national oppression or national antagonisms explain nothing. These conditions always were present in the Western border regions, yet partisan actions have occurred only in a special his-

---

14. Lenin wanted to imply that the partisan actions usually were carried out by authentic "proletarians." There is no evidence to support this statement. The "plotting intellectuals" continued to play a dominant role, and peasants were at least as important in this struggle as workers.

15. This is a reference to the Cadet Party led by P. N. Milyukov.

torical period. There are many regions where national oppression and antagonisms have been rampant, and yet no partisan struggles are taking place. The fact is that sometimes partisan struggles develop in the absence of any national oppression[16] A concrete analysis of this question would show that it is not national oppression but the development of the uprising which is decisive. Partisan struggle is an unavoidable form of action at a time when the mass movement has matured to the point of insurrection and when the intervals between the "big battles" of the civil war are becoming shorter.

The movement has not been disorganized by partisan struggles but by the weakness of the party, which does not know how to *take those actions into its own hands.* Consequently, the indictments against partisan warfare, so customary among us Russians, go together with secret, accidental, and unorganized partisan actions which, indeed, do disorganize the party. If we do not understand the historical conditions of partisan warfare, then we shall be unable to eliminate its darker sides. In spite of everything, partisan operations occur [because they] are created by powerful economic and political causes. Since we are unable to get rid of those causes, we are unable to prevent this type of struggle. Our complaints about partisan warfare are nothing but complaints about the weakness of our party [which is incapable of] organizing the uprising.

What we said about disorganization also applies to demoralization. Partisan struggle as such does not produce demoralization, which results rather from *disorganization,* undisciplined armed actions, and lack of party leadership. Demoralization, which *unquestionably* has set in, cannot be overcome by disapproving and rejecting the [concept of] partisan struggle. Such censures are by no means sufficient to prevent events which result from profound economic and political causes. It could be objected that, while we may not have the capability of suppressing abnormal and demoralizing happenings, no purpose would be served if the party were to use anomalous and demoralizing tactics. Such a non-Marxist objection would be of a purely liberal-bourgeois character. No Marxist should consider partisan warfare, which is just one of the forms of civil war, as abnormal and demoralizing. Marxists favor class struggle and not social peace. In periods of grave economic and political crisis, the class struggle develops into civil war—that is, into an armed struggle between two parts of the people. In such periods, every Marxist is *obliged* to endorse the cause of civil war. From the Marxist point of view, moral condemnations of civil war are entirely unacceptable.

In situations of civil war, a *combat party* is the ideal type of a proletarian party. This is indisputable. We admit that one may try to prove,

---

16. While Lenin's analysis is accurate, he did underrate the importance of the national question during the first Russian revolution. Subsequently he assigned a far higher value to nationalism as a revolutionary factor.

and perhaps may be able to prove, the inadvisibility of this or that type of struggle at this or that juncture of the civil war. From the point of view of *military expediency,* criticism of the various forms of civil war certainly is justified. We agree that the decisive voice in such questions belongs to those experienced socialist leaders who are familiar with the practical conditions in each locality. But, in the name of Marxist principles, we must insist that civil war be analyzed seriously and that shopworn phrases such as anarchism, Blanquism and terrorism not be thrown into the debate. Senseless partisan actions, such as were indulged in by this or that organization of the PPS[17] in this or that situation, should not be abused for a scare argument against socialist participation in partisan warfare.

One must accept assertions that partisan warfare disorganizes the [socialist] movement with skepticism. *Every* new form of struggle which involves new dangers and new sacrifices inevitably will "disorganize" organizations unprepared for the new tactics. Our old study groups become disorganized when agitational methods were adopted. Later on, our party committees were disorganized when the party took to demonstrations. In every war, new tactics carry a degree of disorganization into the battle ranks. Yet this is no argument against fighting a war. It merely follows that one must *learn* how to wage war. That is all there is to it.

When I meet social democrats who proudly and self-righteously declare, "We are no anarchists, no thieves, no robbers, we are above [such violent forms of struggle], we reject partisan warfare," then I ask myself: "Do these people understand what they are talking about?" Violent incidents and armed clashes between the Black Hundreds government and the people are happening all over the country. This is inevitable at the present stage of revolution. The population reacts to the attacks by Black Hundreds troopers with armed *coups de main* and ambushes. Because they are spontaneous and unorganized, these counterattacks may assume inexpedient and *evil* forms. I understand quite well that, owing to weakness and lack of preparation by our organization, the party may refrain from assuming, at given places and times, the leadership of such spontaneous actions. I understand that this question must be decided by local practitioners and that the strengthening of weak and unprepared party organizations is not an easy task. But if a social democratic theoretician or writer fails to be saddened by such lack of preparedness and, on the contrary, displays proud self-satisfaction, and conceitedly and enthusiastically repeats slogans on anarchism, Blanquism, and terrorism which he memorized in his early youth, then I consider this to be a degradation of the world's most revolutionary doctrine.

---

17. Lenin was referring to the Polish Socialist Party, of which Joseph Pilsudski was the most prominent leader. It is significant that Pilsudski personally led one of the most daring expropriation attacks on a Polish post office himself. Lenin never participated in any of the partisan actions he was advocating so fervently.

It is asserted that partisan actions lower the class-conscious proletariat to the level of drunkards and bums. This is correct. But from this follows only that the party of the proletariat never should consider partisan warfare to be its only or even its chief means of struggle. This particular technique must be integrated with other tactics and be in harmony with the most important methods of combat. Partisan warfare should be enobled by the enlightening and organizing influence of socialism. Without this *last* condition, *all*—clearly all—means of struggle will move the proletariat [which lives] within a bourgeois society close to various nonproletarian strata, whether they stand higher or lower [in social rank].[18] If they are allowed to develop spontaneously, such techniques will lose their effectiveness and their original form and will become prostituted.[19] Strikes which are left to take a spontaneous course degenerate into "alliances," i.e., agreements between business and labor *against* the consumer. Parliament becomes a brothel where gangs of bourgeois politicians are bargaining, wholesale and retail, about "people's freedom," "liberalism," "democracy," republicanism, anti-clericalism, socialism, and other brands of popular commodities. Newspapers turn into cheap procurers and into tools corrupting the masses and flattering the lowest mob instincts, etc. The socialists know of no universally applicable combat method which would separate the proletariat, as though by a Chinese wall, from those classes of the people which [socially] are situated slightly higher or slightly lower. Socialists use different means at different periods. Those means are chosen in *strict* accordance with ideological and organizational conditions the nature of which must be determined *accurately* [by the Marxian dialectic method].

The bolsheviks[20] have been accused frequently of an unthinking party-oriented [and positive] attitude toward partisan actions. It seems necessary, therefore, to reiterate that the *particular* bolshevik faction[21] which approved partisan warfare defined in its draft [of a social democratic party resolution] the conditions under which armed struggle would be permissible: "Expropriations" of private property are entirely forbidden. "Expropriations" of government property are not recommended, but are *permitted* provided they are accomplished *under party control* and pro-

---

18. This obtuse sentence is of significance only to firm believers in the Marxian doctrine. Lenin wanted to say that some types of struggle would bring the proletariat closer to the middle classes, while others would lead it into closer relationships with the *Lumpenproletariat* and, possibly, with the very poor peasants. His point was that the socialist ideology would preserve the pure class character of the proletarian movement, regardless of the means of struggle employed by it.

19. Lenin presumably meant that if the party loses control over operations, other social forces may be able to exploit the proletarian movement for their purposes.

20. The following paragraph was written by Lenin as a footnote to his article. We have inserted it into the main text to enhance clarity.

21. Not all the bolsheviks were in favor of partisan action.

vided the captured money is used for the *purposes of the uprising*. Terrorist partisan acts against representatives of the violent regime and of active Black Hundreds groups *are recommended*[22] but are subject to the following restrictions: (1) the popular mood must be taken into account; (2) local conditions under which the workers movement is operating must be considered; (3) care must be taken that no proletarian forces are wasted unnecessarily. The *only* practical difference between the resolution accepted by the unification congress of the [Social Democratic] Party[23] and our draft resolution is that [in the former] "expropriations" of government property were entirely forbidden.

IV

The Russian revolution differs from bourgeois revolutions in Europe in that it displays an immense variety in the methods of struggle. Kautsky predicted this in 1902, at least to a point, when he said that the coming revolution (and he added: *perhaps* with the exception of Russia) will not be so much a struggle of the people against the government as a struggle of one part of the people against the other. In Russia we witnessed a broader development of the *second* kind of struggle than during the burgeois revolutions in the West. The enemies of our revolution have but few followers among the people, but as the fight develops, the opponents are getting better and better organized and are gaining support from reactionary groups of the bourgeoisie. Thus, it is natural and unavoidable

---

22. This amounts to Lenin *recommending* terrorism.
23. Lenin was referring to the resolution adopted by the Fourth Congress of the Russian Social Democratic Workers Party at Stockholm during April and May, 1906. The difference between Lenin's views and that of the majority of the "unification congress" was considerably greater than indicated here, but Lenin at that time found it necessary to keep his peace with the party, especially since he was not certain of the wholehearted support of his bolsheviks. The Stockholm resolution opposed theft, the expropriation of private funds and of bank accounts, forced contributions, the destruction of public buildings, and railroad sabotage. Lenin succeeded in convincing the congress that it should allow the confiscation of government funds, provided expropriation could be carried out by a revolutionary organization and on its orders. The congress also approved terrorist actions in cases of self-defense.

In September, 1906, the Moscow Bolshevik Party Committee issued a resolution that came out far more radically in favor of partisan war. It proclaimed "offensive tactics" to be the only useful tactics. The party was called upon to organize partisan war in cities and villages against the government. The party was to liquidate the most active representatives of the government and to seize money and arms. The resolution suggested that the population at large be invited to support the partisan war. Lenin was in favor of this more radical policy. This article in its entirety is essentially a polemic against the softer resolution of the Stockholm congress.

that in *such* periods, in a period of political general strikes, *the uprising* cannot assume the traditional form of a single blow, limited to a very short time and a very small area.[24] [Under such circumstances], it is natural and unavoidable that the uprising assumes the higher and more complicated form of a protracted civil war enmeshing the entire country—that is, the form of armed struggle by one part of the people against the other. Such a war must be conceived as a series of a few big battles, separated by comparatively long intervals, and a large number of small engagements, which take place during these interim periods. If this is so—and it undoubtedly is so—then the task of social democracy is to create organizations most suitable to leading the masses both in the big battles and, so far as practical, in the smaller actions. At a time when the class struggle is developing into civil war, social democrats must consider it their task not only *to participate* in this civil war, but must play the leading role in this conflict. The Social Democratic Party must educate and prepare its organizations in such a way that they will become true *belligerents* who will not fail to exploit opportunities through which the strengths of the opponent can be sapped.

Unquestionably, this is a difficult task. It cannot be accomplished at once. Similarly, as an entire people is transforming itself in the course of civil war and is learning from the struggle, so our organizations, if they are to fulfill their mission, must be educated and reorganized on the basis of experience.

We do not presume at all to impose on comrades who are carrying on with their practical work any theoretical ideas about tactics, let alone to decide from the vantage point of a desk what role this or that form of partisan struggle should assume during the civil war in Russia. We shall not confuse particular *political orientations* within the social democratic movement with specific partisan actions.[25] But we consider it our task to provide a correct *theoretical* evaluation of the new forms of struggle which life has created.[26] Our business is to fight pitilessly against the

---

24. This important sentence refers to uprisings in capital cities. Many revolutionaries believed that the seizure of power could be accomplished by a sudden one-thrust insurrection against the seat of government. Lenin's remark foreshadows the development of Mao Tse-tung's operational doctrine and basically enlarges the concept of uprising into that of civil or guerrilla war.

25. This unclear sentence presumably means that it is wrong to confuse tactics with ideology. Factions of the socialist movement, distinguished from other factions largely by ideological differences, usually had a preference for specific forms of struggle. Conversely, a group specializing in one particular type of combat might be inclined to a correlated ideological orientation. Lenin suggested that the tactics of the revolutionary movement be discussed on their own merit and that ideological questions be discussed in ideological terms.

26. Commenting on Lenin's assertion that the party, instead of teaching the masses, is being schooled by them and that partisan war emerged spontaneously as a riposte to actions by the Black Hundreds, the army, and the police, Souvarine said that Lenin's point could be summarized in this fashion: "All that is spon-

clichés and prejudices which are hindering the class-conscious workers from posing a new and difficult question in the right manner and hence from solving it correctly.

---

taneous is necessary." This is a paraphrase of a statement by Hegel, all too frequently quoted by Marxists: "All that is real is reasonable." Note the value which Lenin ascribed to spontaneity—a value quite at variance with the subsequent development of the "Leninist-Stalinist doctrine," which claimed to be opposed to spontaneity and placed instead the highest value on organization.

7

Brooks McClure   RUSSIA'S HIDDEN ARMY

*T*HIS ARTICLE HAS ITS BASIS IN a large mass of material made
available to *Infantry Journal* by a German citizen, known to the Journal in
pre-World War II days. We are withholding his name at his request. It has
been rewritten by Brooks McClure, a veteran of World War II, and now a
Washington newspaperman.

The material itself gives evidence of its sources: Russian documents
captured by the Germans and reports of all echelons of German commanders on the Eastern front.—EDITOR, *Infantry Journal*

The blitzkrieg victory so confidently predicted by Hitler seemed assured almost from the moment German troops invaded Russia in June,
1941. The *Wehrmacht* swept relentlessly through Russian-occupied Poland, into the Ukraine and Crimea and to within fifteen miles of Moscow
before the year was out. . . .

The first appearance of partisans in the Battle for Russia was shortly
after the *Wehrmacht's* deep penetration of the country, but they were then

From *Infantry Journal,* July and August, 1949. Copyright 1949 by Association
of the U.S. Army and reproduced by permission.

ineffective and betrayed little of the extensive training and organization which later became apparent. It was not until the Germans had extended their lines hundreds of miles in depth and across a 2,000-mile front that the Russian guerrillas began full-scale operations. Within a year, fighting bands behind the German lines were stalling transport, interrupting communications, destroying reserve supplies, and taking a heavy toll of German lives. So effective were these "irregulars" that a German army of more than 100,000 troops was unable to keep clear the arterial supply routes to the front.

Partisan forces, working as spies and saboteurs as well as soldiers, also struck at war production as far back as Germany itself, cutting the output of some factories ninety per cent. In desperation, the Germans moved plants back to home soil while the partisans virtually dominated the hundreds of miles between German sources of supply and front-line troops.

Partisan coordination with operations of the Red Army was excellent. Hours before a Russian attack, partisans cut German communications, destroyed their supplies, diverted their strength, and undermined their morale to the point where successful operations were impossible. Extensive reconnoitering and spying supplied partisans with details of German positions, and in some cases these operations included theft of *Wehrmacht* battle plans, raids on German staffs, and tapping German telephone lines.

The vast quantity of intelligence data collected in this way was added to other information obtained through interrogation and even torture of captured soldiers and from Russian civilians and forwarded to the Russian Army. Then, when the attack began, partisan forces simultaneously struck the Germans from the rear in forces as large as regiments. Advancing Red Army troops could expect to find repaired and new roads—built in advance by partisans behind the German lines.

Thus, it might be said that partisan warfare by the Russians was the margin of victory. As the war progressed into its second and third year, the ruthless guerrilla forces made it more difficult for the Germans to fight the Red Army on anything like equal terms. Coupled with the severe winters and strategic blunders by Hitler and the party bosses of the army, the guerrillas first eliminated the initial advantage held by the Germans and then turned from "defensive" tactics to join in the final drive to oust the invaders from Russian soil.

Fighting for Time

Germany went into the Russian campaign with 3,000,000 of the best-trained, best-equipped troops of that time. Against this force Russia could array only 2,000,000 of her total armed strength of about 3,000,000 men, many of whom were inadequately equipped. The Russians, therefore, were fighting above all for time—time to train and outfit their unlimited reserves; time to get material aid from abroad; time to let the elements wear down the invader as they had Napoleon's army in 1812.

Russia's hope of victory lay with a long war of attrition, costly in men and resources on both sides. Hitler knew this and his strategy called for a short campaign of great intensity. This is probably why he would permit nothing to distract his attention from delivering the knockout blow against the Red Army and why he refused to heed pleas for a change of plans to cope with partisan warfare.

Although the partisans had already made themselves felt through sabotage and harassment, their real importance as a fighting force developed as the siege of Moscow reached its decisive stage in the winter of 1941–42. It was then that the irregular forces behind the German lines coordinated their operations with those of the Red Army to prevent the quick victory sought by Hitler.

Der Führer, trying to meet his deadline for victory before the end of 1941, had ordered Field Marshal Feodor von Bock to attack on October 2, over the protests of the High Command, which warned that mud and snow soon would hamper *Panzer* operations. Within a few days, Russian Marshal Semyon Timoshenko's army group had lost approximately 640,-000 men as prisoners and was beaten back by ferocious German assaults. Spearheads of the German *Panzer* divisions on the left wing, commanded by Colonel General Erich Höppner, penetrated as far as Kalinin almost without resistance, and the right wing of the attack, led by Colonel General Heinz Guderian, struck through Orel to Tula. Colonel General Günther von Kluge, attacking in the center, drove forward until, on October 18, his forces were practically at the gates of Moscow.

General Weather Takes Command

Then, with victory almost in sight, the weather changed suddenly as Hitler had been warned, and within a few hours snow and rain converted the firm ground into a sea of mud—impassable for armored units. All major forward movement stopped. Once again, in the middle of November, the first frosts made the ground hard, and Hitler ordered a new attack. This time, however, the issue could not be forced. The elite . . . German shock troops had suffered heavy casualties, and the weeks of bad weather had reduced the efficiency of both equipment and men. The disorganized supply system could barely provide for three per cent of the front-line forces. The last desperate drives for Moscow failed for lack of ammunition and reinforcements.

Winter now was arriving, with the Germans in a weakened condition and exposed to the elements. The situation was ideal for infiltration, and the partisans boldly set up positions behind the enemy lines. A month later, in January, 1942, guerrilla forces dominated almost the entire rear area, and it took every effort of the Germans to keep their one remaining supply route open. . . .

Exploiting this situation, the Red Army sent cavalry through the thin German lines to join the partisans, which continually attacked convoys on the last main supply line, the Smolensk-Moscow road. The attacks now were intensified, virtually imprisoning the German army before the Soviet capital.

Without adequate ammunition and provisions, buried under heavy snow and paralyzed by the coldest winter recorded in the area in decades, the Germans were held fast within grasp of Moscow, the city they were never to capture. At last . . . Hitler yielded to the pressure of his generals and ordered the troops back into winter quarters, which had to be hastily improvised. The battle of Moscow was decided, and the partisans played an important part in the outcome. For the first time they gave vital tacti-cal assistance to the Red Army.

Direct Cooperation with Army

Often in later operations, partisan units cooperated directly with Red Army troops which penetrated the German lines. In the summer of 1942, for instance, a large Soviet Army detachment, reinforced with engineers and artillery, reached the Dnieper River with the tactical aid of partisans all along the route of advance. The detachment was able to complete its mission of destroying a pontoon bridge and, covered by partisan fire, fight its way back to its own lines with only light casualties.

Although partisans often operated in this manner—to assist a specific army mission or lend their weight in a decisive battle—coordination of guerrilla and regular troops operations in general combat was not customary. The highly organized and disciplined partisan movement had no relationship on paper to the Red Army and took no orders from it. Rather, the guerrilla forces had a chain of command all of their own which reached to Stalin himself. Merging of partisan units with the advancing Soviet Army was prohibited; in fact, the partisans were directed to avoid all contact with regular troops for reasons of policy and discipline. When the battle line moved beyond them, the guerrillas were ordered to reinfiltrate through the German lines immediately and operate as before.

Probably the outstanding example of partisan tactical coordination with the Red Army was in the crucial battle of the war, when the Russians broke the German lines in the Brobruisk-Vitebsk area at the end of June, 1944. Even before the Red Army attacked, the Germans' central positions were seriously weakened by partisan assaults in the rear. . . . Huge areas behind the German lines were dominated by partisans and practically removed from German control. Between and sometimes through these areas ran the *Wehrmacht* communications lines. . . . Fortified points, camps, and airfields in the rear were constantly raided and could be protected only by considerable forces.

Partisan Activity

In the weeks before the Soviet general attack, the partisans became more and more active. German strongpoints were attacked, wires cut, trains derailed, roads mined, and supply convoys destroyed. Russian planes carrying supplies to the partisans at night increased steadily, the guerrilla radios became more active with messages from the central staff in Moscow, and German reconnaissance planes reported that the partisans were preparing to rebuild destroyed bridges, remove roadblocks, and repair highways—particularly those running East and West.

About June 20, 1944, a wireless message from Moscow was intercepted. It ordered all partisan units to intensify their activities without regard even for the civilian populace.

The night before the Red Army attacked, the partisans made more than 10,000 raids cutting off all German supplies and wire communications and paralyzing the command. Then Red armored units, breaking through the weakened front, cut swiftly North and South of the Minsk-Mogilev highway and advanced from one partisan area to the next until they enveloped Minsk and the German staff headquarters. Retreating German troops suffered heavy losses as they ran into successive pockets of partisans. With savage fury, the guerrillas hunted down small groups of German infantry and slaughtered them in the woods where they sought to escape Soviet tanks. The Soviet regulars pushed their attack without concern about mopping up.

History of a Band

The psychological, physical, and moral makeup of the partisan fighter is best described in the history of a guerrilla band. One of the more dramatic such units was formed in the village of Fomino, in German-occupied White Russia, early in December, 1941. A number of men and women secretly met, founded a partisan *otrjad* and selected as their leader young Sergei Vladimirovich Grischin. Although only 24 years old, Grischin had earned a reputation for being intelligent as well as rowdy, and his election was approved by the leader of the partisan movement in the Smolensk area, who had been invited to the meeting.

The elite of Grischin's band were a few hardy young people and several escaped Russian prisoners of war. As word of the new organization spread, volunteers from nearby villages swelled the band until it couldn't take any more. Several times Grischin had to send groups of 300 to 400 candidates through the lines to the Russian Army because he couldn't arm them. . . .

Grischin always insisted on careful reconnoitering before an attack and his operations never failed. His band destroyed plants, sawmills, and dairy farms in the occupied area and killed German-sponsored village officials and policemen together with their families as "enemies of the people." Grischin took no prisoners. Only when captives were sought by the NKVD *politruk,* the commissar provided by higher headquarters to maintain discipline in the band and evaluate intelligence, were Germans brought in. After interrogation, they were shot.

The Grischin *otrjad* in time became a *polk,* a force roughly comparable to a regiment in size, and expanded its activities. Its fierce spirit is reflected by these random messages:

In the fight, nine Russian policemen were slain, nine were taken prisoner and eight of these slain; one deserter remained alive.

Patrol leader Tschubukov seized a naked German in the woods, but he was taken from him by a captain of the 14th Partisan Brigade, from whom the German had escaped before being killed.

On the battlefield, a German feigned death. Partisan Skvorzev brought him back to life by a stab with a poniard; then, by another, caused him never to rise again.

It is perhaps characteristic of partisan forces that, ruthless as they were in dealing with the enemy and Russian collaborators, they were at least as severe in maintaining discipline among themselves. The slightest infraction of *polk* regulations often brought immediate execution, as shown in the following orders issued by Grischin:

October 13, 1943: For arbitrarily leaving position, the squad leader Bacharev is to be shot.

January 19, 1943: The [partisan] spy Andrejenkova is to be shot because repeatedly she has not performed orders to reconnoiter.

May 11, 1943: Repeated licentiousness in dealing with women has caused pregnancy in seven cases. These women are a bother for the *polk.* Shoot them.

September 22, 1943: Platoon Leader Lukjanov extorted brandy and caroused with his platoon. Shoot him.

In spite of Grischin's severe discipline, new applicants continued to flock to his famous *polk.* Typical of this expansion was the report received by the *polk* from a subordinate *otrjad* leader in September, 1943:

In the last two days we were joined by 41 deserted policemen, 17 railway workers, six sanitaries from Tscherikov, and 19 escaped prisoners; 83 men altogether. People of all classes are arriving—without arms generally, sorry to say.

On September 10, 1943, the *polk* was divided into six battalions, two *otrjadi*, a staff company, a reconnaissance detachment of special services —2,224 men all told.

Grischin, always a stickler for thorough reconnaissance, got special assistance from innumerable civilian agents, who vied with each other to collect important information for the band. Women and children often provided the most valuable data, picked up from Germans who had become careless or confiding. All this material was organized and studied by an NKVD officer attached to the *polk* and then sent to the Red Army through the front, where it sometimes proved to be of vital strategic importance.

Meanwhile, the *polk* itself based its operations on this information. Several times Grischin's forces, using the cover of woods, blew up trains and sections of railroad track between Vitebsk and Smolensk and between Orsha and Smolensk. . . .

Luck was running out for Polk Grischin. During 1943 the powerful, battle-hardened band became progressively bolder, making daring raids from the wooded and marshy terrain between the Dnieper and Sozh Rivers, where they had shifted their operations. The Germans, however, were at last making headway with their antipartisan action, and the *polk* found itself trapped by the enemy on November 11, 1943. . . .

In the fight that followed, the partisans of the renowned Polk Grischin fought bravely till exterminated. Only Grischin and a few followers could escape at night across the Dnieper.

War on Economy

If the combat record of the partisans was the most dramatic feature of their operations, it was probably no more important than the sabotage of German war industry in the East. Because of heavy air bombardment from bases in England, the Germans had to move much of their war plants out of the Reich to comparative safety in the East. Furthermore, raw materials vital to armament production were located in the Slavic countries, so the region had double economic importance.

Thus the . . . war economy of Germany relied on production in the East, and the partisans made elaborate plans to attack this vulnerable spot. Through sabotage, propaganda aimed at factory workers, and terror raids, the partisans methodically and tirelessly hacked away at Hitler's sources of supply. The results, according to a German report made in August, 1944, were devastating.

Even at that time, with the end of the war still nine months away, the partisans were interfering with production in Prussia—part of Germany itself. East Prussia was reported full of small groups of partisan paratroopers, who, however, had so far confined their activities to scouting and made few terror raids. Still, by frightening the inhabitants, they made harvesting difficult, and in a region 210 miles northeast of Berlin they seriously hampered the yield of wood. . . .

Long Tradition

Guerrilla fighting has a long tradition in Russia, and many of the old folk songs tell of partisan heroism in other generations and centuries. Thus the first psychological basis for a national partisan organization was established. In addition, the Russians have two prerequisites for a successful guerrilla force: hardy, tenacious people capable of being rigidly disciplined; and swampy, wooded and hilly terrain with few roads, affording ideal cover for partisan activities.

Capitalizing on these natural qualities of people and country, the Soviet leaders provided for an endless training program under officers chosen for ability and initiative. During the war, recruits from among peasants and townsfolk constantly swelled the partisan ranks and got their training together with combat experience. There was, however, a nucleus of expert partisan fighters indoctrinated before the war which provided leadership and instruction. This cadre had been trained, registered, and provided with special manuals long before Russia was invaded.

It therefore was no improvisation—contrary to Hitler's interpretation —when Stalin, in a speech to the country on July 3, 1941, proclaimed the partisan war in these words:

In the area occupied by the enemy, partisan units on foot and horseback must be established. Moreover, bands of saboteurs must be organized to fight hostile detachments . . . blow up bridges and roads, interrupt phone and telegraph communications and set camps and depots afire. In the occupied areas, insufferable conditions must be created for the enemy; you must follow him everywhere and annihilate his forces.

Hitler saw despair in these "burnt soil" tactics, but it soon became evident to the *Wehrmacht* if not to *Der Führer* himself that they were a carefully conceived method of warfare. The order issued by Stalin laid down a broad program for partisans in areas from which the Russian Army retreated. It included the destruction of all property useful to the enemy, creation of a spy and propaganda network, organization of new partisan bands, establishment of concealed bases for sustained guerrilla operations, and designation of assembly points for straggling soldiers and escaped prisoners of war.

Partisan Successes

Although a surprising pro-German sentiment by much of the Russian population in occupied areas hampered the work of the partisans, the chief of the Soviet propaganda office, Losovski, was able to report with some justification on July 21, 1941: "Hundreds of partisans keep attacking the German communications. Everywhere there are tens of thousands of men sufficiently armed for fighting the invaders."

The next year showed marked improvement in both the strength and tactics of the partisans, and in August, 1942, the Politburo of the Central Committee of the Communist Party decided on an elaborate expansion of guerrilla warfare. Top partisan officers were summoned to Moscow and put through intensive courses in organization and fighting techniques. They were then returned to their units either by air or reinfiltration of the front lines in the winter of 1942, and by May of 1943 *Pravda* could report that partisan activity had developed into a mass movement capable of prolonged independent military action. Increasingly frantic calls for help from German units and the Nazi civil administration confirmed this announcement.

Central Organization

Behind the sensational partisan successes was an organization which had solved the problem of central control for units of irregular size operating with a great deal of tactical freedom over vast areas. The Central Staff of the Partisan Movement was the high command, directed by Lieutenant General Ponomarenko, Secretary of the Central Committee of the White Russian Socialist Soviet Republic. Although it was a creation of the Party, the Central Staff enjoyed the same status as the Central Committee of the Communist Party and the Supreme Command of the Red Army.

Under the Central Staff were regional staffs which operated at major Red Army headquarters at the front. These commands directed the strategic operations of the partisan forces beyond the front and were responsible for the coordination of guerrilla activities with the army's operations. The next lower partisan echelon, the Operation Group, was situated on the other side of the battle line and dictated general tactics in each region. Communications to the higher command were handled by radio, plane courier, and runners who made their way through the enemy lines. . . .

Organization of Lower Echelons

In the lower, operational echelons, the basic unit was the brigade, which in turn was divided into sections, or *otrjadi*. Sometimes the designation of regiment and division occurred, but these had no relation to the conventional military strengths and, in fact, varied greatly in size.

Leaders of partisan bands were in most cases officers specially trained for guerrilla fighting and then assigned commands in occupied areas. Occasionally, however, adept civilians who assumed authority when bands formed were recognized as leaders, and in some instances even criminals became commanders.

Political and military discipline was maintained in every unit through the use of the *politruk,* or NKVD commissar. The partisan *politruk* examined newcomers carefully and kept an eye on the activities of all the guerrillas. He would notify the NKVD to exile relatives of deserters and cowards and reward those of heroes. An NKVD section for larger units provided severe punishment for violations of regulations, to help commanders maintain iron discipline.

Family punishment was the strongest weapon of the NKVD, but the secret police also knew the advantage of reward, as indicated in a directive captured by the Germans which read:

> The connection of the partisans with their families is of greatest importance. Make the postal system known to all partisans. We shall send planes for the mail. Gather requests for searching for missing families with all clues to identity. We shall take all possible measures.

The personnel of almost every unit varied widely in origin. Some were assigned to an area and flown in at night over the battle front. Others included escaped Russian prisoners of war, deserted Russian legionnaires from the German Army, and natives of the region who either volunteered or were terrorized into joining. Many women were among them.

While maintaining their trade, many peasants and townsfolk temporarily fought with the partisans or helped them as scouts, couriers, or agents. This was particularly true in open terrain, where larger bands could not find sufficient cover to operate and smaller units needed help. . . .

Partisan Equipment

The equipment of the partisans was never standard. At the beginning of the Russian campaign, the clothing and arms of guerrillas were improvised. Later the partisans were able to get the latest and best equipment, some of it captured German materiel and the rest sent by the Americans and British. Mass fire effect was stressed as was individual marksmanship and proficiency with all arms. Usual equipment included submachine guns, light machine guns, mines, mortars, and small-caliber, armor-piercing cannon. Explosives were abundantly supplied and used throughout the operations.

The guerrillas had no special uniform, although they did not hesitate to wear Red Army clothes if they could get them. They also dressed in odds and ends of civilian clothes and parts of German uniforms. Sometimes they disguised themselves as German soldiers.

Transportation was makeshift, with pack animals, wagons, and occasional automobiles being used. Sometimes the inhabitants of whole villages were impressed as bearers. Prisoners also were used and often killed when their job was done.

Supply System

Partisans usually lived off the country and at first resorted to wide-scale robbery to get provisions. When the staff commands decided to try winning over the unfriendly populace, however, the guerrillas were ordered to pay when possible for food. Violators of this regulation were severely punished. As the movement expanded, planes operating at night brought in food supplied by the Americans. The Soviet civil air service was used on these missions, dropping provisions at prearranged points.

Larger partisan camps, sheltered by dense woods, had facilities for butchering, baking, and repairing arms. Hospitals were set up and reserve stores of food and ammunition were buried and camouflaged in the surrounding area.

In some cases, when partisans were able to stay in one locality for a long time, they set up an administration of their own, enlisted recruits, formed new units, and conducted regular military training.

Training and Tactics

The plans and training function of the partisan movement was an extensive one, with a steady stream of publications and radio talks refreshing the guerrilla fighter on his earlier training and offering new ideas developed in the field. During the war a series of special partisan manuals were printed, including "Notebook for Partisans," "Handbook for Partisans," "Instructions of the Central Staff of the Partisan Movement," the "Comrade of the Partisan," and even "Technical Instructions of the People's Commissariat of Defense."

These publications were supplemented with radio talks and personal appearances by Red Army officers and noncoms who lectured on their specialties.

Although many of the bands were formed on a "choose-up" basis, the Central Staff tried to bring all units up to a minimum fighting standard with the infusion of men trained at partisan schools far behind the Russian lines. Some of these men reached their assigned units by sneaking through the German lines where marshes, dense forests, or rough ground offered good concealment. The others were dropped behind the lines by parachutes at night. . . .

Scant attention was paid to technique in making the jumps, and injuries were common. The jumps were usually made from altitudes of 1,000 to 1,300 feet and the margin of safety was narrow. . . .

A whistle or animal call by the leader summoned the landed partisans, who, whenever possible, carried their parachutes for later use as tents and shelters. After assembling, the guerrillas moved off some distance—usually not more than a mile or two because of the injured who had to be carried—and established a defensive position. Extra weapons, ammunition, and food were immediately dug in and camouflaged.

Permanent camp sites for larger units were carefully chosen for concealment, inaccessibility to the enemy, defensibility, and quick route of escape. These installations studded the partisan areas behind the German lines in marshes, impassable woods, gorges, and hidden caverns. They were usually protected by mine fields, strategically placed observation posts, and weapons emplacements.

Smaller units, on the other hand, made practically no defensive preparations for their camps, relying instead on concealment, an alert guard, and mobility for escape if attacked.

It was SOP in all cases to establish one or two alternate camps some distance from the existing position and stock them with arms and provisions. Outposts were arranged in depth and were mutually supporting. When a region had a heavy concentration of partisan units, an effort was made to arrange smaller camps as outposts in turn for bigger installations, and defensive reconnaissance extended to nearby towns, where friendly civilians helped provide an effective warning service.

Deployment

Partisan forces were deployed so as to provide maximum security and offensive strength while offering as small and elusive target as possible on the defense. Like bits of mercury, the guerrilla bands could combine quickly into a large force for a single mission and then, just as swiftly, split into a score of parts and melt away when the Germans took counteraction. The basic theory of defense was to avoid grappling with the enemy in a conventional test of strength; mobility and flexibility were the strongest tactical qualities of the partisans. On the offensive, the rule was to attack repeatedly and relentlessly.

The Russian guerrilla forces marched usually at night under the strictest discipline. Strong security was maintained, and the route of march was carefully plotted through difficult country, using little-known roads and crossing rivers at remote fords. Constant use of the same route, however, trapped partisan bands on many occasions. The Germans learned that guerrillas followed what they called a *Bandenwechsel—Wechsel* being the usual path taken by big game—and they ambushed partisan forces on the march.

In unfamiliar terrain, the partisans marked their route for bands following behind by simple and unobtrusive signs, such as cracked twigs or blades of grass, artificial animal scents, or small stones arranged to show directions. Whenever possible, however, they used visual contact between bands on the march.

Reconnaissance

Reconnaissance and spying were the essentials of successful partisan operations—indeed, these were an end product as well, for the guerrillas provided much valuable intelligence data to the Red Army. Some of the information was provided by scouting by the bands themselves, but the greatest bulk was supplied by a well-organized espionage network among nonpartisan Russians.

A constant stream of news flowed from innumerable peasants and workmen, and from spies among the *Hilfswillige*—members of Russian volunteer units under German command. Information, including the most trivial occurrences, was analyzed by trained NKVD intelligence officers with the partisans.

Often the most valuable data came from pretty girls, old women and children who won the confidence of Germans and made exhaustive reports of conversations. For purely tactical information, partisan scouts disguised as townspeople, peasants going to market, and even German soldiers were generally used. Tapping of telephone lines was common, and partisan spies even answered unheeded calls to try to get information.

Russian-language newspapers run by the Germans frequently conveyed hidden messages, and small children were used as unsuspected couriers from town to town, and eventually to partisan camps, after the Germans had attempted to regulate all adult travel.

The NKVD *politruks* were constantly on guard against spies in the partisan ranks and others who provided misleading or erroneous information. In order to combat false reports and trap German agents, the Central Staff of the Partisan Movement prepared a form divided into 21 sections and containing 172 questions to be answered by partisans collecting intelligence. The questions were so worded as to draw out all possible information, test the powers of observation and reliability of the reporter, and trap spies in inconsistencies.

Intelligence

Lower partisan staffs added many of their own questions to cover local conditions, and the total mass of paper work tended to mire down the most cunning liar. The questionnaires and supplemental interrogation were handled by the NKVD *politruk,* especially trained for the task. Upon him rested the final responsibility of sifting out only the reliable information for use by the partisans and the Red Army.

Once equipped with all the data that could be collected through the spy system and military reconnaissance, the partisans acted with exceptional daring—"courage touching insolence" as the "Comrade of the Partisan" once characterized it. Surprise assaults were made on kitchens, quarters, small troop units, individual soldiers, transport trains, supply columns, and straggling vehicles. The watchword was set forth in the manual: "Attack by surprise, using unexpected, bold strokes."

Demolition also was an important job for the guerrillas. Roads, bridges, and railroad tracks were blown up, together with any kind of depot or installation useful to the enemy. Vehicle and antipersonnel mines were laid in quantities along German supply routes to hamper enemy operations further.

Communications were a constant target. All the common tricks for cutting lines were described in the "Comrade of the Partisan" and other handbooks: cutting sections out of phone lines, felling trees across overhead construction, shorting out power lines, driving pins through insulation to make trouble-shooting difficult, and ambushing signalmen sent out to repair cut lines. . . .

Attack! Attack! Attack!

In attempting to summarize guerrilla activity into a creed, the "Comrade of the Partisan" had this to say:

Enumerating all sorts of partisan combat is impossible. But think of one thing: The fundamental law of the partisans is attack, attack and attack again! If you act half-heartedly and stick to your place, you will waste your strength to no purpose and deliver yourself to the enemy. Resolve an offensive activity—these are the pledges of success in in the partisan war!

The offensive spirit was not lacking, and the NKVD *politruk* was there to be sure it was not. The partisans attacked with a ferocious zeal and, while they usually avoided a fight with a superior enemy, they battled stubbornly against all odds when cornered.

The manual was explicit on the way to conduct a partisan attack. The first rule was to take advantage of any opportunity for surprise or ambush and design the whole operation accordingly. When the target—a town, enemy garrison, radio station, airfield, motor pool, or any other kind of installation—was chosen, the initial requirement was careful reconnaissance. The objective was located on maps, and all possible information on troop strength, location of heavy weapons, guards, and vulnerable points was collected for briefing the raiders.

The leader of the band then drew up a detailed scheme of attack, assigning men to specific tasks and drilling them until they were prepared for every foreseeable development. Each man was given all the information needed for his mission, and the group was assigned one or more covered routes of advance to exploit the surprise element to the utmost.

Since most attacks were made at night and the covered route of approach frequently was through woods, dense brush, and swamps, it was necessary to acquaint every man with the terrain in detail. This was done both by map study and inspection of the ground itself where feasible. Again, friendly compatriots at the objective often provided valuable information on surrounding terrain as well as a plan of the installation itself.

Method of Attack

Considering the difficulty of the approach march, special care was needed to plan a simultaneous attack from all sides of the objective. Standard tactics called for a surprise assault at a given signal, with officers' quarters and weapons emplacements as the initial objective. Heavy firing from all sides helped create the impression that a much larger force was actually involved and that the installation was hopelessly surrounded. Arrangements were made just before the attack to cut all the installation's communications with the outside, and this had both a tactical and a psychological effect.

Partisans used plenty of ammunition and hand grenades in the attack, which almost always was timed just before dawn. The enemy was confused and disorganized after the first encounter, and then, as day began breaking, the partisans could see enough to complete wrecking the installation, mop up any remaining force capable of pursuit, and escape by prearranged routes. Slightly wounded partisans were carried away, while those badly hurt were shot. Prisoners were taken only for interrogation and then shot.

On the subject of preparing an ambush, the partisan manual is especially dramatic.

"Small groups of partisans, about six to eight men to each, are lying in wait for the enemy in a thicket, in a wood joining the roads, in roadside ditches covered with brambles," the "Comrade of the Partisan" envisions. "Hide yourself well so the enemy can't find you. Choose for an ambush a spot offering a good fire zone toward the road.

"Look! The enemy appears! Let him come within 20, even 10 meters, and then suddenly fire with rifles, machine guns and hand grenades. The enemy must not have time to use his firearms. After that, if necessary, start fighting hand-to-hand! Push with your side arm! Beat with your spade! Strike with your rifle butt! Stab with your knife! Don't let the enemy take the initiative for even a moment."

The manual urges the use of grenades against vehicles but notes that road ambushes are generally successful only during the day because "at nightfall the Germans stop the traffic on roads. The cowardly fascists are afraid of partisans!"

"If you make such raids without useless noise—without unnecessary shooting, explosions, shrieking—they will be even more efficient than the kind just described," the instructions continue. "In this case you can use a small-bore weapon which makes little noise. You can wound a driver and his companion, then kill them noiselessly with the cold arm."

In such a way, the manual points out, nearby German forces are less likely to be attracted and go to the aid of the attacked column. The partisans, then, have time to unload the trucks and carry the supplies away.

When the initiative was with the enemy, the partisans behaved according to their strength and mission of the moment. Larger bands usually fought back when surprised if they thought they were a match for the German force. Smaller groups retired quickly, especially if they feared being surrounded. When trapped, their standing order was to attack repeatedly in hope of finding a weak point in the enemy line through which to force an escape. Often the terrain was such that individuals and small groups of partisans could filter out of the trap and hide in swamps, caves, or dense brush until the enemy withdrew.

Terroristic Methods

German intelligence reports show the partisan to be as cruel as he was resourceful and intrepid. Part of the guerrilla reign of terror, used as a weapon in psychological warfare, called for torture of prisoners. Wounded and captured Germans and collaborators were disemboweled, blinded, castrated, and otherwise mutilated. This phase of the partisan program was carried out under the direction and supervision of the NKVD *politruk,* according to the *Wehrmacht.*

The purpose of this brutality was to paralyze the enemy with fright and horror, and it amply succeeded. Not only were collaborators terrorized into turning against the Germans, but Nazi troops themselves developed a mortal fear of the partisans. Word of this torture, as well as of the cruel winters and savage fighting quality of the Russian Army, reached deep into the western front, and some soldiers killed themselves on being notified of a transfer to the East. The stories about the partisans could hardly have been exaggerated, for the Germans found evidence of cannibalism in guerrilla camps—the alternative of starvation.

The *Wehrmacht* classed all partisan activity as "illegal," although no part of it—including the torture—actually was outlawed. The Soviet Union had refused to be obligated under The Hague Convention of 1907, setting up rules of warfare, and today subscribes to no treaty restricting them in their weapons or combat methods. The natural law of retaliation, then, is the only possible limiting factor. . . .

However crafty and capable the partisans were, though, they had some qualities which gave the NKVD headaches. Despite the practice of punishing relatives of partisans who misbehaved, many serious infractions of discipline were reported in partisan dispatches intercepted by the Germans. Drinking often led to sexual outrages and violence against Russian civilians, which, particularly early in the war, increased the popularity of the Germans in the occupied areas. A strange inconsistency of mind sometimes caused guerrillas to panic and even revolt on the slightest inadequacy of a leader, although with proper direction the same men fought bravely and showed indifference to their fate when captured. When the Germans finally used specially conditioned troops to root out the partisans toward the end of the war, they found the Russians often unable to cope with their discipline and tactics if the strengths were anything like equal.

German Measures against Partisans

. . . Heinrich Himmler, head of the Gestapo and creator of the *Waffen-SS,* was put in charge of all antipartisan operations except those in the zone extending from the front to the occupation command, where the army provided its own protection. Hitler apparently was confident that Himmler's ruthless efficiency would wipe out the partisan menace, but his choice was prompted by other considerations as well.

The Germans, with cocky self-assurance, had set up a civil administration in occupied Russia shortly after the invasion—much too soon. Reestablishing army control in the rear areas, at that late date, even for so vital a job as combating the partisan menace, would have been an admission of failure. It was a matter of prestige to fight the guerrilla menace with "police" instead of troops.

Making antipartisan operations a responsibility of the Nazi Party instead of the army proved to be a grave mistake even before the guerrillas succeeded in disrupting the entire German communications system. The brutal measures used by Himmler did no harm to the partisans and made enemies of the friendly Russians who became victims of mass reprisals.

German Failure

Furthermore, the organization had practically no competent leaders aside from the *Gestapo* chief himself. If Himmler had selected a capable SS general and a force of elite Nazi troops for the job, it is possible the guerrilla warfare could at least have been checked in 1943. But he chose instead a team of political favorites who were unable to organize and direct effective operations. Except for a few isolated cases, such as the police commander at Minsk, the regional chiefs failed completely.

Himmler set up under his immediate command a staff organization known as "Chief of the Units Fighting Partisans" and put at its head a Nazi bureaucrat with the rank of police general. This agency became little more than a clearinghouse for squabbles and jealousies among the *SS*, the party hierarchy and the *Wehrmacht* command.

The intelligence and operations work of the staff was of little value, in contrast to the performance of army units assigned to combat guerrillas in forward areas. The army general staff painstakingly collected accurate data on partisan activities and took prompt countermeasures. Daily reports were issued, positions were constantly plotted on situation maps and background information was provided regularly to troops.

Strategic plans of the partisans were anticipated through the study of monthly surveys of their operations, captured documents and interrogation of prisoners. One monthly army paper, *Nachrichten über den Bandenkrieg,* carried translations of partisan documents as well as summarizing intelligence data and providing hints on tactics.

The *Wehrmacht* gave consideration to how captured partisans should be treated. Russian guerrilla fighting was branded as illegal by the Germans, who pointed to the terms of The Hague Convention. The partisans among other things wore no "distinct" badges which can be seen from a distance and therefore, in the opinion of the Germans, did not qualify for treatment as prisoners of war. . . .

Unit commanders continually pressed headquarters for an SOP on handling partisan prisoners, and finally the army and Himmler agreed to a policy in August of 1943. It provided that partisans generally would be treated as prisoners of war, except when they were caught wearing German uniforms. Such "spies" would be shot, but only under order of an officer with rank of division commander or above. Deserters, regardless of their dress, were to be spared.

The army made appreciable progress in its antipartisan campaign. After a while it was able to keep a zone 40 kilometers back from the front clear of large guerrilla units. But in the rear areas the situation grew steadily worse. Himmler's police made no headway against the partisans, and Nazi corruption and ineptitude created a hostile force in every town. All physical security for the Russians disappeared, and a growing black market made living still harder.

Partisan Propaganda

At the same time, the partisans were exploiting these difficulties in their propaganda appeals. They taunted the police by ridiculing their failure, bringing more bitter reprisals against helpless civilians, and they also capitalized on the split between the army and Himmler's organization to show the enemy's weakness.

The Gestapo force managed to form a few *Jagdkommandos,* or hunting groups, but these proved too weak to make any impression on the partisans. As failures mounted and the guerrillas grew stronger and bolder, a more ambitious undertaking or *Grossunternehmen* was attempted. Strong forces, well armed and equipped, were put into the field, but those were no match for the Russians. Even when they trapped a band, they seldom crushed it, and losses were heavy.

Valuable lessons were learned by both the rear-zone police and the army's antipartisan forces, and a huge mass of reports from both quarters accumulated over the years. But these were filed without attracting attention until the fall of 1944, when at last the *Oberkommando der Wehrmacht,* or army high command, and Himmler's organization began cooperating in a final attempt to stop the partisans. A valuable manual for fighting guerrillas resulted called *Bandenbekampfung,* Attack on Bands.

Too late, a clear policy extending from staff organization to squad tactics was laid down. *Bandenbekampfung* cited the need for a single commander for all antiguerrilla operations, and urged imitation of the partisans' methods in fighting them. It called for small, powerful units trained and outfitted at *Jagdkommandos* to live and fight like guerrillas. It stressed attack by surprise, ambush and relentless pursuit as the only means of combating the enemy.

"The fighting of bands is no second-rate fight," the book cautioned. "It requires soldiers who are particularly agile, cunning, fighting like hunters, hardened and frugal. Only continuous vigilance protects troops from serious casualties.

"A hunting section should not be smaller than a platoon nor stronger than a company. Fights with superior forces should be avoided."

Emphasizing that antipartisan operations are a great hunt for a strong, crafty and deadly enemy, the manual said: "Hunting is an intensified, indefatigable kind of pursuit; its aim is outrunning, bringing to a stand and crushing or capturing the prey."

The key tactic in all antipartisan operations is known in German by a vivid hunting term, *Kesseltreiben. Kessel* means either kettle or circle, and the first object of the hunt is to encircle the prey. *Treiben* means to beat, signifying both the scaring of game into a trap and the mortal battle which follows.

The Germans issued a supplemental booklet, *Merkblatt für Bandenbekampfung* or "Booklet on How to Fight Bands," which dealt with air support for the *Jagdkommandos*. It covered bombing, reconnaissance, tactical assistance, parachute supply, evacuation of wounded and distribution of propaganda.

The German forces, both military and police, had only a short time to use the practical information which was brought together finally in manual form. As a last resort, even in the face of greater pressure than ever from the Red Army, the *Wehrmacht* had to divert substantial strength to fight the enemy in the rear. The partisans had succeeded in one more principal objective by this relieving the pressure at the front, and even then escaped serious harm. They were too strong, the Germans were too exhausted and demoralized, and the war was nearly over.

Probably Hitler's greatest tribute to the partisans was paid when the war had been lost. Casting about for some way to delay Germany's certain defeat, he called on the civilians who remained at home to take up arms as guerrillas. The pathetic *Wehrwolf* campaign never materialized, but the disorganized mass of old men, women and children who were to hold the final line of defense had a special guidebook, "Guerrillas—Hints for Hunting Units."

Here was an outline of the partisan tactics used so effectively against the Germans in Russia, but combined with a curious defeatism and undertone of despair:

"Without any clear political aim the guerrilla, even if skillfully led in action, can have only temporary success. Lasting results can be expected only if military and political forces are strong enough to make the most of guerrilla accomplishments."

8

Ernst von Dohnányi   **COMBATTING SOVIET**

GUERRILLAS

GUERRILLA WARFARE has become an essential part of modern strategy, a factor which should not be overlooked by the military leaders. This was sufficiently proved by the guerrilla and resistance movements in almost every occupied European country during World War II, in Indonesia, Indochina and Korea.

It seems, however, that the possibility of guerrilla warfare has been completely overlooked by the military planning staffs of the Western World. Consequently, the modern soldier is being trained to use every conceivable weapon to defend himself against the most terrible tools of destruction on land and in the air, but he still remains unprepared to cope with the equally dangerous and exacting work of combatting guerrillas. This negligence on the part of general staffs may prove to be as disastrous in the future as it was for the German armed forces during World War II.

The dogmatic attitude of the German General Staff during the Soviet campaign was, undoubtedly, one of the main reasons for its failure, originally to prevent and later to suppress the Soviet guerrilla movement which

___

From the *Marine Corps Gazette,* February, 1955. Copyright 1955 by the Marine Corps Association and reproduced by permission.

inflicted so many losses upon the German fighting forces. Depending on the success of the blitzkrieg and the political weakness of the Communist regime in the Soviet Union, the Germans failed to make preparations for the severe Russian winter and apparently completely excluded the idea of a possible guerrilla threat from their minds. The arrogant and foolish policy of the German civil government in regards to the Soviet people cannot be accepted as an excuse for the narrow-minded planning of the military authorities. Practically the identical shortsighted attitude as that of the German General Staff during World War II was displayed by the U.S. military command during the Seminole Indian War in Florida under Jefferson's and Van Buren's administrations. The government troops dispatched to pacify the Indians were certainly sufficiently trained for orthodox battle but, not being familiar with Indian fighting in the woods, they paid a terrible toll in blood for their eventual success.

In order to comprehend the amazingly swift development of guerrilla bands it is necessary to review the events of 1941. Seeking to attain their main objective—the annihilation of major Soviet forces—German spearheads rushed eastward, broke through Soviet defenses, surrounded entire armies and spread confusion in the Soviet rear; but unfortunately, they paid little attention to dispersed units and scattered personnel who remained in the occupied areas. Naturally, Soviet officers and enlisted men who did not care to surrender disappeared into the countryside. Some exchanged their uniforms for civilian clothing and sought refuge in villages; others hid in swamps and forests; the more active of them organized guerrilla bands.

The early winter, the unexpected setback at Moscow, the inadequate supply of winter clothing and the breakdown of supply lines, forced the German troops onto the defensive. Deep snow and severe cold compelled the poorly clothed and equipped troops to stay in settlements, which in turn permitted the still small guerrilla bands to remain undisturbed in the woods. By the spring of 1942 it was too late—numerous guerrilla groups had gained complete control over the territory not directly occupied by German forces. Innumerable assaults on communication and supply lines (and even on small German garrisons) forced the German units to concentrate solely on defending these vital arteries.

The organization of Soviet guerrilla bands was comparatively simple. Recruited from military personnel and fanatical communists, the bands established their headquarters and camps deep in inaccessible woodlands and swamps. If no direct threat of a German attack was expected, they billeted themselves in villages and small towns from which, in case of emergency, they could fall back to their hiding places in the forests. The population, being given no protection by German forces, willingly accepted and supported them. The bands varied in number from approximately 15 to 200 depending on the terrain, the availability of volunteers and the attitude of the populace towards the German invaders. Smaller bands were led by a detachment commander and a political commissar. Leaders of task groups or sabotage squads—dispatched to intercept a German supply truck, to destroy a railroad bridge, or to procure food—were appointed from among the most efficient members of the group.

Later, large guerrilla bands were subdivided into platoons and squads. Two or three bands were loosely organized into brigades. In time, communications were established between bands and brigades to the Soviet Supreme Command across the front lines. Procurement of arms and ammunition was easily accomplished from equipment thrown away by the soldiers of the routed Soviet armies. Food supply was available in villages and collective farms which, in most cases, had not been dissolved by the Germans and were frequently still managed by the same Soviet functionaries—an error which proved to be of great assistance to the guerrillas. On the other hand, the lack of clothing and medical supplies appeared to be a considerable handicap to the guerrilla bands.

Their operations were chiefly limited to sabotage, cutting of German supply lines, mining of railroad tracks and roads and occasional assaults upon small German units. These missions were usually executed by small groups at night. In comparatively few cases did the guerrillas attack larger German units, and then only under the most advantageous circumstances. Thus, in the winter of 1941–42 a German engineer battalion was annihilated, while embarked on a train moving west of Bryansk. Having stopped the train by removing the rails in a cleared area, the guerrillas opened fire with four or five heavy machine guns and succeeded in killing most of the Germans before they managed to evacuate the train and reach a snow covered embankment. However, it offered no better protection than had the train against the murderous fire. The above incident was an isolated case; generally the guerrillas disappeared into the woods as soon as the approach of a German unit was reported by their sentries.

Greatly alarmed by the new threat, the German command initiated intensive study for appropriate methods of suppressing the guerrilla activities. To accomplish this, each commanding officer was authorized to do what he deemed best. Certain of them tried to hunt down the guerrilla bands by dispatching combat units into the woods. This method proved to be unsuccessful. If not confronted by superior guerrilla forces, or decimated in a trap, the companies or battalions returned after an abortive search with empty hands. The great advantage of guerrilla bands in woodlands lay in their mobility and ability to disperse and disappear among the population, their excellent communication with the local inhabitants and, in the clumsiness of regular army units inexperienced in backwoods fighting.

Efforts to eliminate the guerrilla movement through retaliatory measures against the population were even more disastrous. The endangered population fled into the same inaccessible areas and joined the guerrillas.

It was often like an endless chain: small German units or supply trains were attacked in a village and routed. German reinforcements arriving later found no trace of guerrillas. The population was reluctant to give any information regarding the attackers, as they knew that after the departure of the Germans, they would have to account for their "treason" to the guerrillas who were the actual masters of the unprotected farmer. Their reluctance to speak seemed to the Germans to be a manifestation of loyalty to the banditti. Enraged by the sight of their dead comrades, the German soldiers frequently took revenge by shooting some innocent peasants or by burning down a part, or all, of a village. These unjust acts merely increased the hatred of the native for the Germans and either led him to join the guerrilla bands, or made him a willing spy for them.

Large scale operations conducted by several regular divisions did little harm to the guerrilla movement. These thoroughly planned and expertly executed offensives might have guaranteed victory over a regular army unit operating in an orthodox manner, but they were not effective against a foe who had no permanent bases, who acted as an organized armed force one day and became a group of peaceful farmers the next. Having surrounded a large guerrilla-controlled area the battalions would spread out in a line, create a tight circle around the objective and advance slowly through the brush and swamp in a combing operation. Whenever such a unit met opposition, reserves reinforced by tanks and artillery would be dispatched to break the opposition and to annihilate the band. In spite of clever planning the majority of the guerrilla bands usually managed to escape from the endangered area before the operation started, simply because they had been forewarned by the increase of troops in the region, or by local informants.

In addition to the active measures described above, the German command was forced to employ many divisions for the static defense of roads, railroads and other means of communication. These vital lines had been fortified—thousands of bunkers, palisades and entrenched posts had been built along the railroads and roads; patrols walked from post to post in order to prevent sabotage on the tracks and to detect hidden mines. This task was performed chiefly by German guard regiments, Hungarian and Rumanian units and indigenous volunteer units. None of them were very reliable: the German units because of age and quality of personnel (either too old or physically disqualified for service in combat units), the allies because of their unwillingness to fight for the German cause, the indigenous volunteers because they had no real reason to fight.

It was a dangerous situation for the Germans. All of these efforts had failed to eliminate the danger of guerrilla raids which, in fact, were growing in frequency and ferocity.

In spite of this apparently hopeless situation some German generals and commanders did find appropriate means to meet this threat. Their flexible plans enabled them to adopt unorthodox tactics and, in doing so, finally to succeed in either forcing the guerrilla bands to withdraw or to reduce their activities.

The most outstanding example was conceived by the commanding general of the German Second Panzer Army, Generaloberst (ColGen) Schmidt. In early December, 1941, this army had been stopped south of Moscow and had fallen back to the stabilized line Zhizdra-Orel-Kursk. It was discovered that almost the entire rear, with the exception of larger towns like Bryansk, Bezhitsa, Karachev, Dmitrovsk, Dmitriyev, and Sevsk was under control by the guerrillas. The supply lines for the whole army consisted of a single railroad Orel-Karachev-Bryansk-Unetcha-Orsha-Minsk and the highway Orel-Bryansk-Roslavl'-Smolensk. The areas south of Bryansk including Lokot' and Trubchevsk, and north of this city including Dyad'kovo and Lyudinovo, were controlled by strong guerrilla bands which were a constant threat to these supply lines. In the spring of 1942 the towns of Dyad'kovo and Lyudinovo had been cleared of guerrillas by German troops. However, their garrisons were connected with one another only by means of one road and a branch railroad line which were also subjected to frequent guerrilla attacks.

The area south of Bryansk is divided by the Bryansk-l'gov railroad into a wooded section west of the railroad and plains east of it. The eastern section was soon brought under control by the Germans. Garrisons were stationed in Karachev, Brassovo, Navlya, and Lokot'. The district enclosed by these towns, with the exception of its northern part, offered no protection to guerrilla bands and was quickly abandoned by them. On the contrary, the area between the railroad and the Desna River was covered with woods and swamps, which formed perfect terrain for guerrilla hiding places and camps. An estimated 6,000 guerrillas and an equal number of farmers and their families populated this area. The available German reserves—some Hungarian regiments—were ordered to guard the Bryansk-l'gov railroad line. The commanding general of the Second Panzer Army assigned only a small number of other troops to check the guerrilla assaults.

The tactics formulated by Generaloberst Schmidt to suppress guerrilla operations south of Bryansk deserve a special study which, unfortunately, cannot be made at this time. However, a brief description of the events may suffice to demonstrate the ingenuity of his plan.

In March, 1942, a horse drawn sled arrived from Karachev in Navlya and Lokot', bringing a small group of Russian civilians. The chief, one Kaminski, a slender, energetic middle-aged man, presented to the German garrison commanders "to-whom-it-may-concern" orders signed by Generaloberst Schmidt, which requested German units to render every possible assistance to the bearer of the order. Furthermore, the order appointed Kaminski as governor of the area including the towns of Navlya, Lokot',

Dmitrovsk, Dmitriyev, and Sevsk. He was authorized to act independently, to appoint local officials, to organize the economy of the area and, what is more important, he was responsible only to Generaloberst Schmidt. No German officer in this area was to interfere with Kaminski's activities.

The new governor immediately appointed *Buergermeister* (mayors), proclaimed the abolishment of the collective farm system, supervised the distribution of the remaining implements and stock among farmers, and started the organization of local militia for the protection of this area against guerrilla raids. This reorganization changed the situation entirely. From then on, every cow, horse, pig and loaf of bread were the private property of the farmer Ivanov or Petrov. The population went to work with great eagerness. At last, it seemed, the Germans were acting as they had been expected to: at last they began to abolish the hated collective farms; to give the population self-government and to limit their own influence merely to military needs. At the same time the newly created property owners turned their wrath against guerrillas who still visited their villages at night seeking food. Prior to Kaminski's time, the farmer had watched apathetically while the foraging bands confiscated collective farm stock; however, now "he" was directly affected, "he" was going to lose his own property, his cow, or pig. Many young men enlisted in the local militia and were treated by the population with the greatest respect. By the summer of 1942 the marauding guerrilla bands were met with fierce resistance. Every step outside of the protecting woods became dangerous; for every bit of food seized in a village during a night raid they had to pay with blood. Both parties were at home in this territory; both fought for their livelihood; both fought without mercy. Gradually the antagonism between guerrillas and farmers began to overshadow the events of the war, politics and even their dislike of the Germans. The militia, unassisted by the Germans, equipped itself with what could be found in the woods—left there by the retreating Soviet army. Efforts were made to repair and employ some of the ex-Soviet heavy equipment— tanks, anti-tank guns, howitzers, mortars, machine guns, etc. Finally, Kaminski's force became a formidable brigade, consisting of 5 or 6 battalions of 500 to 600 men each, a tank unit with 10 to 12 light tanks and an artillery battalion with some 20 guns. This number was not only sufficient to stop the guerrilla raids on the villages and towns of the area, but also to launch counterraids and, with the assistance of some German units, even a counteroffensive in the spring of 1943. During this offensive, Kaminski's militia drove the guerrillas from practically the entire area between Dmitrovsk, Dmitriyev, Sevsk and Lokot' and pushed the borders of the "liberated area" 10 to 15 kilometers northwest of Lokot' and about 7 kilometers west of the Bryansk-l'gov railroad line. Considering the fact that he received neither arms nor supply from the Germans, Kaminski's success exceeded all expectations. No doubt, had not the German retreat interrupted this development Kaminski would have succeeded in his task of pacifying the entire area entrusted to him. Events, however, forced the indigenous militia to join the German forces in their retreat west. A few weeks later Kaminski's militia, having lost their primary reason for fighting, deprived of their property and knowing that there would be no pardon by Soviet authorities, became a mere gang of bandits who plundered the population, indulged in drinking, quarrelled with the Germans and among themselves, refused to fight, and at last were disbanded by the German command.

Sound ideas were sometimes also born among field personnel of the German army. Some battalion, company and platoon leaders formulated methods for effective small-scale antiguerrilla warfare. If properly developed, these ideas could serve as a basis for the organization of special antiguerrilla units in the armed forces of the Western World.

After the retreat from Moscow in the winter of 1941–42, a German communications battalion was ordered to occupy Bezhitsa. As has been mentioned, this surrounded town and its outskirts were repeatedly raided by guerrilla bands, which were hiding in the woodlands north and northwest of the town. In order to keep these unpleasant neighbors away from Bezhitsa, the battalion commander established several outposts on the periphery of the city. The most advanced post was stationed in the village of Chaikovichi, about 3 kilometers north of Bezhitsa. . . . Fortunately, the commander of this post was a German who had spent many years in the Soviet Union and was familiar with Russian customs, the Russian mind and the Russian language. Having no definite orders, this officer was at liberty to wage war in his own way. The post garrison consisted of 15 German soldiers and about as many native volunteers (sons of kulaks, persons persecuted by the Soviets for political or criminal reasons and some adventurers). It required no special intelligence to discover that guerrilla scouts were watching this post from a very short distance, that some of the villagers were guerrilla spies, and that every German move was immediately reported to the headquarters of the guerrilla band. With insulting impudence the guerrillas constantly mined the road from Bezhitsa to Dyad'kovo just outside of Chaikovichi. Almost every day, trucks proceeding in convoy to Dyad'kovo were destroyed on this unpaved road. The commanding officer of the Chaikovichi post decided that some action must be taken. Having picked out a group of 12 reliable Germans and natives, he undertook to reconnoiter the surrounding area. For several days this squad criss-crossed the entire region, avoiding deliberately the woods and ravines until everyone became familiar with the terrain. Then, paying attention to utmost secrecy, the patrols were shifted to night-time. At irregular times, without confiding his plans even to the German personnel, the post commander summoned his squad and left the village using a covered route in order to avoid observation. Having reached the extensive woods north or west of the village, the squad waited until dawn. This precaution was necessary in order to deceive the guerrilla sentries watching the German post from various points during the day, and perhaps from the village itself at night. An encounter with guerrillas in the forest was not to be feared. The squad was equipped with automatic weapons and hand grenades and was thoroughly indoctrinated for such a fight. If worst came to worst, a retreat would present no difficulties: the tree trunks offered sufficient protection against rifle fire; an envelopment by the enemy would be extremely difficult to perform; the fire-power of automatic rifles and submachine guns was sufficient to create a gap in a comparatively thin guerrilla line. Moreover, it was unlikely that a guerrilla band would stand and fight a German unit whose strength was unknown to them.

After a period of approximately four weeks, during which time scouting was carried on almost daily, the squad had sufficiently explored the area to determine the approximate location of the guerrilla camp. Scouts discovered fresh paths and guerrilla messages or warnings written on the bark of trees. Most of the paths led from the margin of the woods to a swampy district some 4 kilometers inside the forest. The first important work had been accomplished. The commander realized that his unit was too small for an attack on the hideout. Consequently, reinforcements were requested. The request was approved and the reinforcements promised for a date in the near future. Meanwhile the reconnaissance squad in Chaikovichi shifted from scouting to ambush tactics. Leaving the village with the same caution, the squad marched after sunset across the country to places from which they could watch the Bezhitsa-Dyad'kovo road, which frequently was mined by guerrilla saboteurs. The patience of the squad was put to a considerable strain; having spent a night at one place, the ambush party learned that mines had been laid at another site. However, one night, while lying in the grass on a flat knoll dominating the road, the scouts saw three or four figures moving on the road. At a signal from the leader the squad opened fire. The surprised guerrillas ran into the dark without firing a single shot, but left one of their party, a boy of about 17 who had been killed by a burst of machine gun fire. This rather small victory would not be worth-while mentioning, had it not caused the discontinuance of mine laying on this road. The guerrillas seemed to be greatly surprised and apparently frightened since they did not know how many such ambushes were laid, from whence the enemy came, and how strong he was.

Some days later, returning from a reconnaissance trip into the woods, the squad surprised a man lying under a tree about 100 meters in front of the woods. In a semi-circle, concealed by the high grass, the scouts approached the man. Startled by a crack of a dry branch or some other sound, the stranger jumped to his feet, and seeing several Germans, took to flight. A few bursts brought him down. A second man, unnoticed so far, jumped down from the tree with raised hands. It appeared that this was a sentry post watching the traffic on the road to Dyad'kovo. In addition, this post was to notify the guerrilla camp back in the woods of approaching danger.

At last the promised reinforcements arrived in Bezhitsa. It was important not to arouse the suspicions of the guerrillas in Chaikovichi. Therefore, both the infantry company and the reconnaissance squad were embarked on tarpaulin-covered trucks in Bezhitsa and, together with the usual convoy, departed as if for Dyad'kovo. The assault force dismounted from trucks deep in the woods above Chaikovichi and northeast of the suspected guerrilla camp. The captured guerrilla sentry was to be the guide. Having his hands tied and led on a rope, the prisoner was made to understand that disobedience or treachery would mean certain death to him. After about a 2-hour march the unit arrived without incident at the swamp. Disclosures of the guerrilla indicated that the camp was pitched about 500 meters farther sowthwest on a hill in the middle of this area. The swamp appeared to be only waist deep. The company spread out and the soldiers advanced at an interval of 5 or 6 paces in order not to lose sight of one another. In spite of this the left wing of the company advanced too quickly and three or four men popped up in the guerrilla camp long before the rest of the company had arrived. The surprise was complete. The band had just started their breakfast which was served in primitive pots on rough hewn tables. Terrified by the sudden appearance of the Germans, the guerrillas, amongst whom there were several women, fled in panic in all directions, leaving everything behind. Those who ran towards the approaching German line were either killed or captured; others managed to escape into the protection of the brush and high grass. In all probability the major part of the routed band found other guerrilla groups and continued their activities in another district. At any rate, the area between Bezhitsa and Dyad'kovo seemed to be taboo for guerrillas from this time on. Not a single assault, not a single mine were reported or discovered until the retreat of the German troops in August, 1943.

Neither of the two examples—Kaminski and the Chaikovichi squad were decisive victories over the guerrilla movement. But, and this cannot be sufficiently stressed, they demonstrated one very essential thing: namely, that guerrillas cannot survive in an area where they are deprived of a food supply and freedom of movement. To achieve this objective, methods other than those prescribed for normal combat must be adopted.

II

The effectiveness of a regular military unit depends chiefly upon its combined firepower and coordinated action. If control is lost so that each small unit must operate without this overall coordination, it loses a great deal of its strength. Consequently, when a unit is forced to fight in a strange country over unfamiliar terrain, this unit will prefer to fight in the open, where control is easier and firepower can be fully utilized.

On the other hand, the very nature of guerrilla bands accounts for their preference for close country and woodlands; areas where they can easily retreat and hide themselves. Since there is no central authority such as the State to enforce discipline, it is almost impossible to forge a guerrilla band into a unit which would be the equal of a regular command and which could offer battle in the open.

But in their native mountains, forests or swamps, guerrillas are far superior to regular forces since they can attack their enemy whenever they hold the advantages of time and terrain and are assured of a safe retreat. From their hidden camps they can easily watch the enemy, maintain communications with their agents in occupied settlements and between their own bands. It requires no special intelligence work for them to find out the location of enemy troops as well as their vulnerable supply and communication lines. Knowing these things, a guerrilla can live and move about in his area without great danger. He can even enter the villages and towns which are under the control of the invading forces.

Apart from the purely political and psychological means of preventing or suppressing a guerrilla movement, it remains to be considered what can or cannot be done from a strictly military point of view. The answer does not seem to be very complicated: *guerrillas must be fought with guerrilla methods* by specially trained units which can be trained and equipped without great cost and without detriment to the major force. However, it is necessary that serious consideration be given to this problem by the responsible command.

As soon as an army penetrates into foreign territory it must assign a certain number of units to guard its supply and communication lines as well as for garrison duty. The employment of some of these units for active suppression of guerrilla bands would tend to decrease their number rather than require additional personnel. But these antiguerrilla units must be previously organized and trained in order to achieve success.

German experiences during World War II proved that:

a. Units assigned to guerrilla warfare must operate directly under a corps or army staff.

b. They must be completely mobile in summer and winter.

c. They must consist of appropriately equipped, independently operating companies or battalions.

d. The personnel must be carefully chosen and thoroughly trained for this special task.

A suggested organization for such an antiguerrilla battalion is as follows:

(1) *Personnel:* If possible, volunteers; to be chosen from such professions as: rangers, woodsmen, professional and amateur hunters, as well as from the rural population of wooded and mountainous areas. People who are acquainted with the terrain and language of the presumed enemy country are to be preferred. Volunteers from urban areas may also become proficient. Age: between 18 and 40. Special requirements: well developed ability to find one's bearings, be a good marksman with several weapons, maturity and good physical condition.

(2) *Training:* Basic military training. Have a thorough knowledge and be expert in use of all organic weapons and, if possible, those of the enemy. Operational training in woods, swamps and mountains: operating alone (the fear of fighting when alone against guerrillas must be taken from the fighter), or within a squad or in platoon formation; training in the systematic search of towns and villages; accurate snap-shooting; the use of mine-detectors; laying and removal of mines; skiing; conduct of operations in the winter; use of snow as shelter and woodsmanship. In addition, lectures should be delivered regarding the way of life and the customs of the presumed enemy people; the best ways to treat them in order to win their friendship and support; rules of land warfare and how they are to be applied in case of guerrilla warfare (justly but severely) and economic conditions of the occupied country.

(3) *Organization and Equipment:* The organization of a Marine Corps battalion with its squads sub-divided into fire teams and its great firepower would roughly meet with the requirements of an antiguerrilla battalion. Its equipment may generally be the same. However, keeping in mind the fact that companies, platoons and even squads may be forced to operate independently, some additional equipment must be supplied to these units. Squads dispatched into woods or mountains must be provided with means of communications, that is to say light, portable radios with sufficient range (at least 3 miles); platoons need more powerful sets in order to maintain communications with the company headquarters which may be located at a greater distance. The battalion must be equipped with a sufficient number of trucks to guarantee the mobility of the unit and its sub-divisions. The availability of one or two armored cars would greatly facilitate the mobility of battalion and company commanders, as well as being a valuable asset where greater fire support is needed. Since in some places guerrillas use fortifications (dugouts and bunkers), the assignment of two or three recoilless guns and perhaps a flame-thrower team, would prevent unnecesary casualties. Mine detectors should be available to every platoon.

(4) *Operations:* The antiguerrilla battalion, being directly attached to the army or corps headquarters, may be used for guard duty, search of towns, etc., until the receipt of information on the presence of guerrilla bands in a certain area. Then, depending on the supposed number of

guerrillas, a platoon or company is dispatched to the endangered sector. Company headquarters may be set up in the town which is the nearest to the area of operations. A platoon of this company may be sent into a village in the immediate neighborhood of the supposed guerrilla hiding place. This comparatively small unit will not unduly alarm the guerrillas and will leave them unprepared for a possible round-up. Squads will reconnoiter the nearby woods and swamps, to intercept guerrilla runners and sentries and lay ambushes for guerrilla mining teams, until positive information on the location and strength of the guerrilla band is obtained. Then the company, and if necessary the battalion, may be called in and can be skillfully directed to assault and to annihilate or, at least, disperse the band. During these preparations the members of antiguerrilla units must establish contact with the population and support their fight by psychological treatment of the natives. They must be always ready to help the farmer, to protect him and, if possible, to win him as an associate and co-fighter. Members of these units must always be on their guard against treachery. *Patience* and *caution* are the first and most important rules for a successful operation and for the prevention of unnecessary casualties.

If the military antiguerrilla activities are assisted by a resourceful and flexible policy, perhaps as displayed by Generaloberst Schmidt during WWII in the Bryansk-Lokot' area, the task of suppressing a guerrilla movement, or at least of reducing it to insignificance will be greatly facilitated.

It must be emphasized that in order to wage an effective antiguerrilla campaign the responsible leaders must be well acquainted with not only the physical aspects of the enemy force, but also they must fully understand the psychology of the indigenous population. This knowledge will enable them to establish a policy which the population will recognize not only for its effectiveness but, what is more important, for its humane and just consideration of the welfare of the local inhabitants. Guerrillas starve without the support of the people.

9

Enrique Martínez Codó   **GUERRILLA**

WARFARE

IN THE UKRAINE

HE PERVERSION OF HISTORICAL FACT to accomplish Soviet propaganda ends is no more evident than in studies concerning guerrilla operations behind the German lines in 1941–44. The Soviets would have us believe that all guerrillas, and particularly those operating in the Ukraine, were Communist and that they fought under Soviet control against the Germans. Many Western writers, relying on the accuracy of abundant Soviet information sources, innocently have cultivated the literary fields in which the Soviet propagandists have planted the seeds of distortion, misplaced emphasis, and half-truth. Of such ingredients the military reputation of "General" Khrushchev is made.

It is true that Red guerrillas were active in the Ukraine. But they were mostly remnants of the regular forces which the Germans scattered during the first few months of the war or they were special troops parachuted behind the German lines. Their actions were of little consequence in the years 1941–44.

The Ukrainian people never backed the Soviet guerrillas. They were

Reprinted from *Military Review,* November, 1960, by permission.

not only anti-Communist but also anti-Russian by tradition. The Ukrainians fought both the German Army of occupation and the Soviet guerrillas who attempted to operate in their country.

This was a natural consequence of the country's history. The Ukraine had declared its independence from Russia in 1917 and in 1920 was subjugated by the Red Army. Since then, various secret Ukrainian anti-Communist movements have operated with the objective of liberating their country from Soviet rule.

Thus, because of a well-defined patriotic and political feeling, it was not astonishing that the Ukrainian people welcomed the German troops as liberators when they invaded Russia on 22 June 1941. Nor was it a strange circumstance that the deepest German penetration and the largest encirclements took place in Ukrainian territory.

Soldiers of Ukrainian nationality in the Soviet units defending the Ukrainian front deserted in large numbers at the sight of the approaching German Armies. They had no desire to fight in defense of the regime imposed on them. Entire units, headed by their commanding officers, surrendered without firing a single shot. In the great Battle of Kiev alone, fought in September, 1941, more than 675,000 men, a large proportion of which were Ukrainians, surrendered to the Germans.

After the Battle of Kiev, the Germans found Marshal Kryvonos, Commander of the Military Region of Kiev, and 17 officers of his general staff dead. Ukrainian sources believe they were shot by the NKVD (Soviet Secret Police) on the suspicion that they were Ukrainian Nationalists ready to surrender the entire army group to the Germans.

Nightingale Battalion

The German High Command (OKH), aware of the nationalistic feelings among the Ukrainian people, created a special unit called the Nightingale Battalion manned by Ukrainian Nationalists. The German political administration, however, always in disagreement with the German Army authorities, bungled this mutual understanding which would have gained for Hitler the collaboration of a country of 40 million inhabitants and, more important, the security of his rear area.

General Heinz Guderian confirms in his *Memoirs* the favorable reception tendered the Germans by the Ukrainians and the subsequent deterioration of the good relations between the two, when he says:

> It is a pity that the friendly attitude of the Ukrainian people toward the Germans lasted only under the benevolent military administration. The so-called "Reich Commissars" did a good job in destroying in a short time the friendly attitude of the Ukrainians toward the Germans, and prepared the ground for the rebel or partisan struggle.

On 30 June 1941, scarcely one week after the invasion started, the Ukrainian people liberated the city of Lvov and announced over the radio the restoration of their national independence. This surprised the German politicians who ordered that the members of the recently formed Ukrainian national government be arrested and confined in various concentration camps.

This action served as a warning that the German "liberators" were not going to recognize their independence—they were merely new oppressors.

Thus, in 1941 the first anti-German guerrilla bands were formed and the Organization of Ukrainian Nationalists came into being. Finally, on 14 October 1942 the small detachments of guerrilla fighters were organized under one single command, taking the name of *Ukrainska Povstancha Armia* (UPA), Ukrainian Guerrilla Army.

The Ukrainian resistance movement had the following missions:

1. To organize politically and militarily the mass of the Ukrainian population, and reorient them to oppose the new invader.

2. To organize a network of revolutionary forces in the Ukraine and instruct them in anti-German sabotage (disobedience to German orders and instruction in self-defense against the Gestapo).

3. To organize campaigns against the forced employment of laborers in German agriculture and industry.

4. To organize activities to prevent grain exports to Germany and to instruct the people in how to hide provisions, clothing, and other goods from the German requisitioning patrols.

5. To organize an information and propaganda campaign to expose the true purposes of the Nazis and Bolsheviki in the Ukraine.

6. To organize schools to teach clandestine resistance procedures to political and military leaders.

7. To collect arms, ammunition, and other military equipment to be used by the future Ukrainian armed forces.

8. To clear the Ukrainian territory of Bolshevik secret agents, who under various guises were able to join the German agencies, including the Gestapo, to help the Germans destroy the Ukrainian resistance.

Reinforced by the transfer of members from the police forces of the principal Ukrainian cities and other sources, the UPA promptly acquired an unexpected capability for combat action. Numerous contingents of Ukrainian troops which had deserted the Red Army joined the UPA, as well as contingents from other traditionally anti-Communist nationalities, such as Georgians, Tartars, Azerbaijani, and Turki.

The German reaction was not slow in appearing. In the spring of 1943 bloody battles were fought in the vicinities of Sarny, Stolyn, and Volodymirz, in all of which the UPA succeeded in disrupting the German support organizations. Violent guerrilla attacks followed against the concentration camps of Kremenets, Dubno, Kovel, Lutsk, and Kyvertsi, which resulted in the liberation of political prisoners who promptly joined and strengthened the guerrilla ranks.

By the summer of 1943 the anti-German campaign was in full swing. The Germans controlled only the large cities and large military installations. Even strongly guarded German movements were restricted to daytime and were always vulnerable to sabotage and direct attack from guerrillas.

The Ukrainian people accepted the UPA government and supported it actively and voluntarily with money and goods.

Notable Accomplishments

In May, 1943, the Ukrainian guerrillas ambushed and killed the German SA Commander Victor Lutze and his escort, an incident which the German Press played down referring to it as a "traffic accident." During 1943 the Ukrainian guerrillas fought successfully in a series of pitched battles. At Volyn in July, 1943, an attack of a mixed German-Hungarian division was repelled successfully by guerrillas. In May, 1944, a German division was forced to retreat after a battle in the Chorny Lis (Black Forest) region of the Stanislav province. In July, 1944, the guerrillas repelled the attack of two German divisions against UPA positions at Lopata Hill. A 10-day fight, from 6 to 16 July, between Skole and Bolejiv, climaxed this series of battles and resulted in heavy losses to the attacking German-Hungarian division.

From this moment on, in view of the crumbling German front in Russia, the Germans changed their political tactics and sought to coordinate anti-Soviet actions with the UPA. However, the UPA rejected such negotiations. The German plan failed, and the anti-German period of the Ukrainian guerrilla war ended. It should be noted that during this period (1941–44) there was little activity of Red guerrillas in the Ukraine, because the German forces, as well as the UPA, had chased them out of the region.

The most serious Red guerrilla attempt to penetrate the Ukrainian region was made under the leadership of the Soviet General Kovpak. The force came from White Russia after crossing the Pripet River and headed toward Galitzia with the intention of reaching the Carpathian Mountains. But the village militia and the regular units of the UPA pursued and harassed them to the point of almost complete annihilation. Only 700 men succeeded in escaping from the UPA attacks. They returned to the Soviet lines exhausted and unable to gain sympathizers among the Ukrainian people.

UPA Organization in 1944

By the end of the German occupation it is estimated that the UPA had about 200,000 armed guerrillas organized in units assigned to four territorial operational regions and to a series of independent operational groups.

These regions were:

The Northern Region, comprising the province of Polesie and the northern part of the Volyn province.

The Southern Region, formed by the northern part of Bukovina and the provinces of Kamenets Podolski and Vinnitsa.

The Eastern Region, formed by the northern forest sectors of Kiev and Zhitomir.

The Western Region, the best organized of all, comprising the provinces of Galitzia and the Carpathian Ukraine (sectors of Lvov, Ternopol, Stanislav, Chernovtsy, Drogobych, Przemysl, Lemkishchyna, and Jolm).

The independent operational groups carried on their activities with success in the Donets River Basin, in Dnepropetrovsk, Kharkov, Krivoi Rog, Odessa, Kremenchug, the city of Kiev, Uman, and other Ukrainian cities and in the Crimean Peninsula.

Each region was subdivided into military districts, each consisting of a determined number of guerrillas formed in companies, battalions, and regiments.

The tactical operational unit was the company. Only in special situations would three or four companies unite to form a battalion, or two or three battalions to form a regiment. Battalions and regiments were formed only on personal orders from the commander of the military district who would generally assume command of the larger unit thus formed. The most able and competent company commanders were assigned as battalion commanders.

Only in exceptional defensive situations were the battalions allowed to join on their own accord if it was not possible to obtain orders or the consent of the district commander. This was rare because the command posts of the military districts were mobile and were continuously supervising the situation where danger was the greatest.

The company organization . . . was not rigid, but generally followed one of these two types:

1. The *light type* company consisting of 168 men armed with rifles, light machineguns, submachineguns, hand grenades, and demolition materials. Its principal mission was to effect hit-and-run raids. When an engagement against tanks was anticipated, the companies were reinforced

with antitank rifle (*panzerbusche 43,* 88-mm bazooka) teams and anti-tank bazooka teams.

The company was organized in the triangular system (three platoons of three squads each) but the strength of the squads was flexible. The rifle platoons were equipped with 50-mm light mortars.

2. The *heavy type* company consisted of about 186 men, its organization also following the triangular concept. The armament was similar to the light company, but it was reinforced by a three-piece heavy machinegun platoon, and a three-piece 82-mm mortar platoon. The missions of these companies were the attack of important areas, the defense of certain objectives, and open battle against enemy forces.

Mounted guerrillas fought in the Northern Region. They formed special heavy squadrons sometimes equipped with light artillery.

Artillery was used only on rare occasions and then almost never organically, for the cannon constituted a great hazard for the guerrilla fighter. It is a heavy crew-served weapon whose characteristics of employment, even for the light mountain type, are not readily adaptable to guerrilla warfare. The gun fixes the guerrilla fighter activities, minimizes their mobility and speed, and, unless it is of the mountain type, ties the fighters to the roads, giving the enemy a chance for pursuit.

The guerrilla fighter, tied to this crew-served weapon, cannot keep close tab on the situation and is not aware of danger until it is too late to avoid defeat. This happened to the Communist guerrillas under General Kovpak in their fight against the UPA forces. Guerrillas preferred mortars and made good use of so-called "potential artillery." Groups of infantry-artillery would seize the enemy guns and use them against their former owners in the same engagement. The captured guns that were retained were used only in the defense of strong points and to train the potential artillerymen in the use of the weapon.

It is evident that had recoilless rifles been available at that time they would have been the "artillery of the guerrillas."

The UPA forces considered light automatic weapons best suited to guerrilla tactics. The most popular among these was the submachinegun due to its easy handling and firepower which made it the most powerful shock element in ambush and close combat. The standard hand grenade of the German and Soviet Armies, as well as those manufactured by the guerrillas themselves, were also favorite weapons. The efficient German *panzerfaust* and the *panzerbusche 43* were used, as well as a variety of antitank mines.

The source of armament for these forces was the German and Soviet arsenals seized in raids and major engagements. The seizure of weapons and ammunition was a permanent objective of the Ukrainian guerrillas, inasmuch as they had no outside help whatsoever and depended entirely on their own resources. Thus, during the German occupation period

(1941–44) the German weapons and those of their allies were widely used by the UPA. During the Soviet occupation period, starting in mid-1944, they used Russian weapons almost exclusively.

In addition to the units already described, which might be called "regular" within the irregularity of guerrilla organizations, self-defense detachments or village militia existed for the protection of small towns and villages. They were particularly effective at night against German and Soviet foraging parties and raids. This technique, which arose spontaneously in the Ukraine, also had been practiced in China during the Japanese occupation, and later appeared in Indochina between the French and the Vietnamese. Thus, the "regular" UPA troops were something like the Indochinese *Chulic,* while the Ukrainian village militia was similar to the *Dan-Quan* of Vietnam.

The Commander in Chief of the UPA was assisted by a general staff with an operations section, intelligence section, organization and personnel section, logistics section, miltiary instruction section, and political instruction section. . . .

The *operations section* planned tactical operations, coordinating them by means of general instructions or concrete orders; planned and directed the politically and strategically important raids; evaluated the general situation; and prepared military maps and sketches. Officers of this section were attached to each regional command so they could develop the plans of action on the ground, and, at the same time, direct local large-scale operations. When the mission required the commitment of personnel of other regional commands, the organization and direction of the forces was a responsibility of the general staff.

The *intelligence section* had over-all direction of the intelligence and counterintelligence effort. The collection of information was of primary importance for the movement of the guerrillas. The guerrillas had the backing of the civilian population in these operations. The intelligence system was so effective that as soon as the German troops and Soviet guerrillas started any operation, the UPA General Staff knew of their course of action and their strength. The cooperation of the civilian population is *conditio sine qua non* for guerrilla operations.

The *organization and personnel section* was in charge of preparing the tables of organization, of personnel replacement, of operating a roster of guerrilla fighters, and of the mobilization of military regions.

The *logistics section* had the difficult and important task of supplying food, ammunition, and clothing. Its mission included also the repair and maintenance of all material. In these tasks the cooperation of the people was essential. This section also was in charge of the establishment of large subterranean supply storage bunkers, four to 10 meters underground, facilitating the problem of supply during the winter.

In combat the UPA guerrillas wore military uniforms and their leaders wore distinctive insignia, such as the Ukrainian triden* In other words, they conformed to the laws and rules of land warfare and normally would have been considered regular troops—a fact ignored most of the time by both the Soviets and Germans.

The *military instruction section* was in charge of writing directives and manuals for the cadre schools and for the military instruction therein. The problem of organizing competent cadre (officers and noncommissioned officers) was critical due to the growth of the UPA and the consequent growing need for better and larger cadres. The section was in charge of two officers' schools which operated in the Northern and Western Regions. There were noncommissioned officer schools in every military district. The military instructors for these schools were Ukrainian military men who had pursued their military careers in the armies of Poland, Czechoslovakia, Romania, and Russia; from the cadres organized in Germany before the war (cadres from the Nightingale Battalion); and the old leaders of the Ukrainian National Army of 1917–22.

In addition to the actual military instruction, the section was in charge of editing the directives, manuals, and tactical regulations of the UPA. Among these works there is one deserving special mention: *The Practical Manual of Guerrilla Warfare,* a 364-page volume of tactical concepts for these forces.

The *political instruction section* (psychological action) had one of the most important missions. Because the UPA depended strictly on voluntary enlistments, it had to win the good will of its people as well as that of the people of foreign countries. Thus, it was necessary to have a psychological warfare apparatus to raise the morale and political standards of its men and make the UPA a strong political force. To accomplish this, two official tracts were published and circulated among guerrillas and civilians alike: *The Povstanets* (The Guerrilla Fighter) and the excellent review *Do Zbroi* (To Arms). These supplemented the clandestine press of the Ukrainian movement for national liberation which published more than 20 titles. They also operated several clandestine radio stations which broadcast Ukrainian propaganda and anti-German and anti-Soviet counterpropaganda to the Ukrainian people and the peoples of subjugated neighboring countries. This section also was in charge of liaison with other Ukrainian political organizations, particularly with the Organization of Ukrainian Nationalists.

An underground *communication and liaison service*—which used the most varied communication means imaginable, ranging from technical equipment to foot messengers—was operated by the general staff in addition to the aforementioned activities.

During the German occupation the organization of a central technical liaison team was started but was not completed until the beginning of the Soviet occupation in 1944. Time needed to train specialists and to assemble equipment, which was obtained mainly from the enemy or built locally, prolonged the organization.

In those areas not occupied by the enemy (during the German occupation), Ukrainian forces communicated over existing conventional telephone and telegraph lines by codes or prearranged messages. They sent messages in the clear only to give orders calling for immediate action. The messenger service, whether on foot, mounted, or motorized, was organized in such a way as to ensure delivery of messages to the UPA Headquarters within 24 and to the regional commands within 12 hours. A permanent system of relay couriers was operated regularly for this purpose.

The combat units (companies, battalions) in the field used the conventional communications means employed by regular armies—low-power radios (walkie-talkies), and visual signals (semaphores, flags, and panels).

The UPA Headquarters had under its direct command a headquarters security force (generally a reinforced company), a medical service, and a counterespionage service.

The *medical service* (Ukrainian Red Cross) labored under critical conditions due to its precarious means of evacuation and the lack of security in the rear area which forced the field hospitals as well as the recuperation centers to operate entirely clandestinely. Furthermore, medical supply was sporadic and dependent upon captured enemy material or contributions by generous civilians at great personal sacrifice. For this reason the German and Soviet ambulances and hospitals were favorite targets for the UPA groups as sources of supplies. However, they were careful not to disturb the welfare of wounded personnel.

Another problem the medical service faced was the recruiting and training of specialists. Generally speaking, the UPA volunteers were reluctant at first to serve in these noncombat units. The positions were filled by women and elderly men. In due time the importance of this service became evident and the number of volunteers increased. The enemy never recognized the Ukrainian Red Cross, and its posts were attacked and looted as any ordinary military objective. Thus, the UPA aid men became active combat soldiers.

Nursing schools were established for men and women, and special textbooks were prepared for them. Due to the shortage of drugs and patent medicines, medicinal herbs were widely used. These were gathered by civilians, particularly school children, for the UPA groups. The medical service published a small manual called *Medical Plants and Their Use* which was used by all echelons of the medical service in the fighting forces and also by the civilian population.

The lowest medical service echelon was the aid man in each guerrilla squad. Next in line was the company surgeon whose mission was to supervise first aid treatment, to administer emergency treatment, and to dispense morphine injections, when necessary. Serious cases were taken to camouflaged special centers and clandestine laboratories where they received final treatment to include surgical operations. The battalion surgeon was responsible for these clandestine centers and administered the treatment and performed the operations.

The Ukrainian Red Cross also had to help the population of the free zones over which the occupying force had no control. This was an additional strain on the overtaxed medical service. Thus, the service was split into two divisions: a civilian division whch operated among the civilian population, and eventually supported the combat units when these were engaged in combat in its zone of responsibility, and a military division which operated exclusively with the UPA troops.

The *security or counterespionage of the UPA* was another important service whose mission was to uncover the Communist and Nazi agents infiltrated through the Ukrainian lines. The Communists, in particular, sent secret agents to obtain exact information concerning Ukrainian strength and armament and logistic bases, as well as information about their contacts with the Ukrainian civilians. It was a difficult task to fight these infiltrators, because Soviet agents were excellently trained and it was fairly easy to disguise themselves as Ukrainians or refugees of various nationalities who had escaped from prison camps. However, the counterespionage service of the UPA was successful by virtue of effective counter-measures and in spite of the refined and cunning methods employed by the enemy espionage agents.

Also operating directly under higher headquarters were the inspecting officers, a group of active officers whose mission was to control the UPA activities in the entire territory where the guerrillas operated.

The regional staffs followed the organizational pattern of the general staff, and had similar sections and services, but operated with fewer personnel. The military district staffs did not have inspecting officers and the various sections operated with even fewer people.

With this general organization the UPA faced the new occupation of their territory by Soviet troops and administration. It is noteworthy to mention that the Germans—who up to this moment had called the Ukrainian guerrillas by such epithets as "Bolshevik spies," "bandits," and "criminals" —now reversed their propaganda line and started calling the Ukrainian guerrillas "heroes of the anti-Bolshevik struggle" and "Ukrainian freedom fighters." The Soviet propaganda began to refer to them as "traitors," "Fascist Nationalists," and "Bandera's murderers" (named after the Ukrainian leader, Esteban Bandera, who was murdered in Munich on 15 October 1959 presumably by Kremlin agents).

Anti-Soviet Activities

As soon as the German troops were forced by the Soviet offensives to withdraw from the Ukrainian territory, the UPA took advantage of the situation and collected all the material and equipment abandoned in their withdrawal. Thus, when the Communist Armies entered the Ukraine, they met a strongly oganized and well-supplied resistance.

It did not take long for the Soviet administration to start its usual purges of the "people's enemy" and to make mass deportations of Ukrainians to far-off Siberia. The UPA reacted with a series of raids against Soviet installations. The first battle of importance against the Red forces occurred in the winter of 1944 with the ambush against Marshal Vatutin and his powerful escort which included armored vehicles. It was in this battle that Marshal Vatutin was fatally wounded. Unfortunately, the Northern Region Commander of the UPA and his Chief of Staff also lost their lives in the battle. Soviet newspapers suppressed the facts, and Marshal Vatutin's death appears officially in many professional and civilian publications, Soviet and even some Western, to have been due to "wounds received at the battlefront."

After replacing the regular Soviet troops—who appeared to be lukewarm to, or even sympathizers of, the Ukrainian guerrillas—with NKVD selected personnel, the Soviets launched a series of offensives. The first of these was commanded by the "Ukrainian" Minister of Interior, Lieutenant General Ryassny, under the direct supervision of the Ukrainian "Premier," "General" Nikita Khrushchev. The Soviet propaganda ministry announced the end of this "greatly successful" offensive in October, 1945, and declared that it had demolished the "resistance of the Ukrainian Fascists." On 31 October, five battalions of the UPA attacked and captured the city of Stanislav, capital of the province of the same name, clearly demonstrating that their resistance was alive and acting with relative impunity.

When a second Soviet offensive was launched, preparatory measures designed to ensure the success of the campaign included such activities as setting forest fires, forced conscription by territorial quotas, contamination of water, sale in the "black market" of medicines contaminated with typhus, and forced evacuation of populated zones. During this offensive, a UPA detachment set an ambush near the railroad station at Tiaziv in Stanislav province, where the commander, General Moskalenko, and his staff were due to arrive on 3 May 1946. The general's armored car was hit by an antitank shell killing all its occupants.

Efforts to Crush UPA

In spite of the official declaration of "victory" by the Soviets, the Ukrainian guerrillas continued their activities. On 29 March 1947, in another spectacular ambush, the UPA killed Poland's Vice Minister of War, General Swierczewski, who had achieved fame as "General Walter" during the Spanish Civil War at the head of the international brigades.

Impressed by this act, the Soviet Union, Poland, and Czechoslovakia (whose Minister of Interior was Communist) signed a tripartite pact on 12

May 1947 calling for the joint action of the armies of the three countries to complete destruction of the UPA. Shortly thereafter, joint operations were launched with units in division strength comprising Polish infantry, Czechoslovakian mountain troops, Red partisans, Soviet armored troops, infantry of the NKVD, paratrooper units, and Soviet Air Forces, plus Hungarian and Romanian units made up of gendarmes and frontier guards.

This concerted attack, conducted at full speed and on a wide front, could not wipe out the UPA resistance. Their forces dispersed into small detachments and avoided the open combat the Communists sought. The guerrilla forces took refuge in the mountain and forest bunkers, and sometimes waited there for months until the enemy pressure subsided. Afterward, the UPA Command sent groups of men on propaganda missions to Eastern European countries—even to Russia—to prove the existence of the Ukrainian resistance. Some of these groups were able to cross the "Iron Curtain" to freedom in Western Europe.

However, in Western Ukraine (Galitzia) the struggle between the UPA and the tripartite pact forces continued. On 5 March 1950, near the town of Bilohorsha, the commander of the UPA, General Roman Shujévych, better known by his cover name of "Tarás Chuprynka," was killed in action. He had served as Commander in Chief of the UPA for nine years.

From then on, in view of the attrition of the fighting units, it was decided to shift the emphasis from active combat to psychological warfare, and the UPA went underground. The fundamental objectives of the struggle remained the same, only the means and methods were altered. The UPA groups were scattered and absorbed by clandestine armed organizations which had the following missions:

1. To maintain and develop the subversive, clandestine organization in all Ukrainian territory occupied by the Soviet Union.

2. To maintain and strengthen the Ukrainian people's ideological and moral status, disseminating the ideals of liberty and independence, and fostering sabotage and even raids against determined Soviet objectives.

3. To publicize the Ukrainian revolutionary spirit and spread the idea of anti-Communist revolution to all the countries subjugated by the USSR.

4. To make known to the Free World the fight that the Ukrainian people—particularly their armed organization, the UPA—had sustained against the Red occupation and the Communist oppression, and the possibilities offered to the Western strategists in another World War.

Conclusions

This is the present situation of the Ukrainian resistance movement. It has not ceased to carry on active propaganda campaigns and unexpected sabotage acts against the Soviet administration. This is the reason for the brief "police" reports which appear periodically in the Communist Ukrainian press mentioning the capture of "reactionary elements" and such news as trials and death sentences, such as the ones which occurred in 1959 in the cities of Kiev and Rovno. This is also the reason the combined troops of Soviet Russia, Poland, and Czechoslovakia "maneuver" in the Carpathian Mountains, in the western areas of Eslovakia, and other regions. Their true objective is to flush out and wipe out the UPA guerrilla fighters who still perform sabotage and engage in propaganda activities as attested by the patriotic demonstrations which took place in March, 1959, in the cities of Mukachevo, Uzhgorod, and Just.

The resistance movement also carries on passive resistance activity among the people with the purpose of sabotaging and retarding the Communist production program. They have perfected alibis to justify the feigned sickness of laborers, waste of time at plants and collective farms, low production, and demands for more personnel.

The UPA represents a potential force to resume guerrilla warfare in the event of another war.

Further References *

BOOKS

Agapov, B. *After the Battle* and *Notes of a Guerrilla Fighter*. London: Hutchinson, 1943.

Anders, W. *Hitler's Defeat in Russia*. Chicago: Regnery, 1953.

Armstrong, J. A. *Ukrainian Nationalism, 1939–1945*. New York: Columbia University, 1958.

Bamm, P. *The Invisible Flag*. New York: John Day, 1956 (London: Faber, 1956).

Burks, R. V. *The Dynamics of Communism in Eastern Europe*. Princeton, N.J.: Princeton University, 1961.

Chamberlin, W. H. *The Ukraine: A Submerged Nation*. New York: Macmillan, 1944.

Dallin, A. *German Rule in Russia, 1941–45: A Study of Occupation Policies*. New York: St. Martin's, 1957 (London: Macmillan, 1957).

Dixon, A., and O. Heilbrunn. *Communist Guerrilla Warfare*. New York: Praeger, 1954 (London: Allen & Unwin, 1954).

Federov, A. F. *The Underground Carries On*. Moscow: Foreign Language Publishing House, 1949.

Garthoff, R. L. *Soviet Military Doctrine*. New York: The Free Press, 1953.

Guerrilla Warfare in Occupied Parts of the Soviet Union. Moscow: Foreign Language Publishing House, 1943.

Hart, L. ed., *The Red Army*. New York: Harcourt, Brace, 1956 (London: *The Soviet Army*. Weidenfeld & Nicolson, 1956).

Heilbrunn, O. *The Soviet Secret Service*. New York: Praeger, 1956.

Heinman, L. *I Was a Soviet Guerrilla*. London: Brown, Watson, 1959.

Ignatov, P. K. *Partisans of the Kuban*. Tr. by J. Fineberg. London: Hutchinson, 1945.

Kovpak, S. A. *Our Partisan Course*. Tr. by E. and M. Lesser. London: Hutchinson, 1947.

Kuzin, I. *Notes on a Guerrilla Fighter*. Moscow: Foreign Language Publishing House, 1942.

Lawrynenko, J. *Ukrainian Communism and the Soviet Russian Policy toward the Ukraine: An Annotated Bibliography, 1917–1953*. New York: Research Program on the USSR, 1953.

Manning, C. A. *Twentieth Century Ukrainian*. New York: Bookman Association, 1951.

---

* Consult Raymond L. Garthoff, *Soviet Military Doctrine* (New York: The Free Press of Glencoe, 1953) for references in the Russian language.

Martovych, O. *Ukraine Liberation Movements in Modern Times.* Edinburgh: Scottish League for European Freedom, 1951.

Poliakow, A. *Russians Don't Surrender.* New York: Dutton, 1942.

Ponomarenko, Lt. Gen. *Behind the Front Lines.* Tr. by A. Gritsuk. London: Hutchinson, 1945.

Reitlinger, G. *The House Built on Sand: The Conflict of German Policy in Russia, 1939–1945.* London: Weidenfeld & Nicolson, 1960.

Ukrainian Congress. *Ukraine Resistance.* New York: Ukrainian Congress Committee of America, 1949.

Ukrainian Insurgent Army in Fight for Freedom. New York: United Committee of the Ukrainian-American Organization, 1954.

Vershigora, P. *Men with a Clear Conscience.* Tr. by M. Parker. Moscow: Foreign Language Publishing House, 1949.

We Are Guerrillas. London: Hutchinson, 1942.

ARTICLES

Anderson, N. J. "Guerrilla Warfare," *Military Review,* April, 1942.

Atkinson, J. D. "The Communist Revolution in Warfare," *U.S. Naval Institute Proceedings,* March, 1953.

Bjelajac, S. N. "Soviet Unconventional Warfare Capabilities," *Military Review,* November, 1959.

Burke, W. A. "Guerrillas without Morale: The White Russian Partisans," *Military Review,* September, 1961.

"Comments on the Present War—Guerrilla Warfare," *Military Review,* April, 1942.

Dallin, A., and R. S. Mavrogordato. "Rodionov: A Case Study in War-Time Redefection," *American Slavic and East European Review,* February, 1959.

Engels, F. "Frederick Engels on Guerrilla Warfare," *Labour Monthly,* August, 1943.

Feehan, S. "Russian Guerrillas," *Military Review,* September, 1944.

"German Tactics of Combatting Guerrillas," *Military Review,* June, 1944.

"Guerrilla Attacks on Populated Places," *Military Review,* August, 1944.

Kovpak, S. "Russian Partisans," *Army Quarterly,* January, 1945.

Kreidel, H. "Agents and Propaganda in Partisan Warfare," tr. by and condensed in *Military Review,* November, 1959.

Kulikov, V. I. "Against the Bourgeois Falsification of the Soviet Partisan Movement," tr. by W. D. Jacobs (4948 33d Rd., North, Arlington 7, Va.), 1960, n.p.

Marr, L. M. "Rear Area Security," *Military Review,* May, 1951.

Munzel, J. J. "Hit Hard and Vanish," *Military Police Journal,* November, 1959.

"Partisan Warfare," tr. by W. D. Jacobs, *Military Review,* January, 1959.

Schafer, Major. "The War against Guerrilla Fighters," tr. and condensed in *Military Review,* September, 1943.

"Soviet Guerrilla Warfare," *Cavalry Journal,* September–October, 1941.

"Soviet Partisan Warfare," *Army Information Digest,* February, 1951.

Szoda, W. E. "Red Soldier—Mentality and Tactics," *Armor,* July–August, 1961.

Wolff, L. L. "The Soviet Partisan Movements," *Military Review,* May, 1955.

Woodmer, J. A. "A Limited Study of Communist Guerrilla Warfare," *Canadian Army Journal,* July, 1956.

Wyndham, E. H. "Russian Partisans," *Army Quarterly,* January, 1945.

DOCUMENTS

Air Force. Human Resources Research Institute. Intelligence Division:
Partisan Warfare in the Dnepr Bend Area of the Ukraine, no. 24, vol. 1, 24p., 1954.
Soviet Partisan Movements in North Caucasus, 1942–1943. Maxwell AFB, Ala. no. 24, vol. 5, 139p., 1954.
The Role of the Partisan in Soviet Intelligence, Maxwell, AFB, Ala., no. 6, vol. 1, 52p., 1954.

Department of the Army. Government Printing Office, Washington, D.C.:
Combat in Russian Forest and Swamps, no. 20–231, 39p., July, 1951.
Small Unit Action during the German Campaign in Russia, no. 20–269, 283p., July, 1953.
Howell, E. M. *The Soviet Partisan Movement,* no. 20–244, 1956.
Military Improvisation during the Russian Campaign, no. 20–201, 110p., August, 1951.
Rear Area Security in Russia, the Soviet Second Front behind the German Lines, no. 20–240, 39p., 1951.

Office of Strategic Services. Research and Analysis. Washington, D.C.:
Soviet Guerrilla Warfare, no. 1356, 1943.

PART 3 COMMUNIST CHINA

In the 1920's the Communist Party of China broke away from Chiang
Kai-shek's Kuomintang and fled to the rural and desolate regions of China.
Civil war broke out and lasted until the Japanese invaded China, at which
time a United Chinese Front was formed to repel the invaders. The Chinese
guerrillas yielded towns and industrial areas to the enemy, but they never
lost control of the interior provinces and rural areas. Here they played
havoc with the enemy's overextended communications network, ambushed
his patrols, and cut off and annihilated his small outposts. It was at this
time that the once obscure Peiping librarian Mao Tse-tung developed his
strategy of war—strategy that he would later use to win China and that
still later was to be applied in other areas of the world.

After the Japanese war the Soviets provided the Chinese Red army
with a huge amount of supplies surrendered by the Japanese in Manchuria.
Battle-tested and well-equipped, Mao Tse-tung resumed the civil war that
culminated in 1949 with the retreat of Chiang Kai-shek's forces to Formosa.
The Chinese Reds won by using a combination of guerrilla and conventional
tactics. Some months later, battle-tested Chinese guerrilla "volunteers" began to appear in various trouble spots in Southeast Asia.

In the first article Katzenbach and Hanrahan analyze Mao Tse-tung's
revolutionary strategy, balancing its success with its limitations. Dinegar's
detailed descriptive analysis of the Chinese Reds' "long march" demonstrates that the experience of that unique trek brought about a refining of
Mao Tse-tung's own earlier theory of guerrilla warfare. Hanrahan describes
the Chinese Red Army's guerrilla warfare practices: how they were applied
against the Japanese in particular and what countermeasures were developed by the invaders. Finally, Jacobs cautions that Mao Tse-tung may
have received too much credit as an innovator of guerrilla strategy. Jacobs
contends that Mao's theories of guerrilla combat are but one facet of an
over-all concept of revolutionary warfare and that tactics and principles
developed in China are seldom useful elsewhere.

PART 3 COMMUNIST CHINA

10

Edward L. Katzenbach, Jr.,   **THE REVOLUTIONARY**
and Gene Z. Hanrahan

STRATEGY OF

MAO TSE-TUNG

. . . the main form of struggle is war, the main form of organization is the army . . . without armed struggle there would be no place for the proletariate, there will be no place for the people, there will be no place for the Communist Party, and there will be no victory in revolution.

—MAO TSE-TUNG[1]

THE WHITE MAN'S BURDEN, so it is generally agreed, was considerably lightened by the marvelous works performed by the Maxim machine gun. It was Western military technology that established white supremacy in Africa and the Far East. It was the iron warship, first used against the Chinese, that fabulous whistle on "Chinese" Gordon's river boat, the dumdum bullet, the mountain-type "75," and eventually the light reconnaissance plane that so lowered the cost of colonial warfare as to make it, and keep it, attractive to the peoples who paid the bills. But recent developments in colonial warfare would seem to indicate that absolute technical superiority cannot of itself win cheap wars.

In other words, the success of Western military technology in the past can only be explained with an addendum to the effect that the tactics of the indigenous armies made its use possible. Whether it was the Fuzzy-Wuzzies, the Boxers, or the troops of Haile Selassie, indigenous peoples

From *Political Science Quarterly*, September, 1955. Copyright 1955 by The Academy of Political Science, Columbia University, and reproduced by permission.
1. Cited by Chu Te, "25 Years of the Chinese People's Liberation Army," *NCNA*, Peking, August 1, 1952.

fought Western troops on terms favorable to the latter, namely their own. It is this error of strategy, with the ensuing tactical errors concomitant thereto, that explains their defeat. At least this would be the explanation of the theorist of anti-colonial warfare, the Dictator of Communist China, Mao Tse-tung.

I

Mao Tse-tung has done for war what Lenin did for imperialism and Marx for capitalism: he has given war "scientific" schemata. And as such his writings have been given a Communist-world-wide circulation.[2] His work has been studied in Russia where it was used as the theoretical base of Russian guerrilla tactics,[3] although, according to the Chinese, the Russians did not really understand the subject.[4] In simplified form his writings are the military Bible of the Viet Minh in Indo-China, of the Huks in the Phillipines, and of the insurgents in Malaya.[5]

Mao's military philosophy did not flow from his agile mind a finished product. His first important military piece, *The Struggle in the Chingkang Mountains* (1928), is dated. His most important work, *On the Protracted War* (1938), purports to be, and probably is, a classic and timeless. The first deals with a set of problems, the last with a set of premises. Mao, in other words, finally universalized his own experience. And that is why his work has become a primer for action for all those whose situation was and is in any way comparable.

In Mao's Communist cultural heritage there has been great interest in military affairs as well as some remarkable thinking. Marx, Engels, Lenin, Trotsky and Stalin agreed on the historical necessity of war as a con-

2. Until his works were brought out by Lawrence and Wishart in England and by International Publishers in the United States in 1954, Mao's writings, which had been translated and were available, were virtually unobtainable in the United States. Including the Library of Congress, they were simply unavailable, except for a stray pamphlet here or there. They were not even in the Service libraries where one would certainly expect to find them.

3. Brigadier C. Aubrey Dixon and Otto Heilbrunn, *Communist Guerrilla Warfare* (New York, 1954), p. 29.

4. Charles P. Fitzgerald, *Revolution in China* (New York, 1952), pp. 96, 97.

5. An analysis of Maoist doctrine as it is being applied today in Malaya appears in Gene Z. Hanrahan, *The Communist Struggle in Malaya* (New York, 1954), in particular pp. 109–129. Communist revolutionary strategy in Indo-China has been outlined in *Yueh-nan jen-min fan-ti tou-cheng shik.* (*A History of the Vietnamese People's Anti-Imperialist Struggle*) (in Chinese) by Lu Ku (Shanghai, 1951), chapter 6, and also by General V. N. Giap in Bernard B. Fall, *The Viet-Mink Regime* (New York, 1954), pp. 79–83. Huk strategic doctrine has been outlined in a memorandum issued by the Central Executive Committee to the Central Committee, Philippine Communist Party, dated November, 1952.

comitant of revolution. Hence all at one time or another expressed an interest in the special problems of a people's war.[6] Their studies, however, were not systematized within an ideological framework, as are those of Mao. Mao claims to have applied to warfare the "immutable laws" that fellow-Communists have detected in socio-economic behavior. Essentially he discovered these for himself.

From his ideological forebears, most frequently from Lenin, Mao borrowed quotations—apparently more to give tone to his argument, like Biblical quotations to political orations, than for any other reason. And, of course, he borrowed an angle of sight, the notion that war is the mid-wife of revolution, and that war like revolution follows a course which is "scientifically ascertainable." Chang Kuo-tao, a former Chinese Communist leader and for many years an intimate of Mao, has characterized Mao as "a calculating and practical Chinese schemer gold-plated with Com-munism."[7] For a one-like sketch of Mao's military-political thinking this approximates the truth.

Nor does Mao's thinking seem to have been extensively influenced by Western military thinkers. Mao read, as had Lenin and Trotsky and Stalin before him, some Clausewitz in Chinese translation as early as 1928. What he learned about Western military thought from Chu Te (now Commander-in-Chief of the Chinese People's Liberation Army and second only to Mao in the party hierarchy) who had Western military training is unknown. And some of Mao's later concepts are much like those expressed by Jomini in his study of *The Art of War*.[8]

There can be no doubt of Mao's intimate acquaintance with the great military classics of Sun Tzu and lesser Chinese military thinkers. Yet, al-though much of his thinking is like theirs, direct influence is difficult to trace. He uses his military classics, however, as he uses his Marxist classics, simply as a mine of good examples and corroborative quotations for what appears to be his own independent thinking. True, there is much in guerrilla warfare that can be traced back even to the American Indians, but never before has it been given so clear and concise a synthesis. Mao, like Clausewitz, in regular military theory, did not invent something new. His ability lies, rather, in pulling together a group of previously unrelated and

---

6. Dixon and Heilbrunn, *op. cit.*, chap. 1; F. O. Mitsche, *Secret Forces: The Technique of Underground Movements* (London, 1950), chap. 1. In general see Edward Mead Earle, ed., *Makers of Modern Strategy* (Princeton, 1952), chap. 7, "Marx and Engels," and chap. 14, "Lenin and Stalin." See also Isaac Deutscher, *The Prophet Armed* (New York and London, 1954), pp. 477–485, and Raymond L. Garthoff, *Soviet Military Doctrine* (New York, 1953), Part I.

7. Chang Kuo-tao, "Mao—A New Portrait by an Old Colleague," *New York Times Magazine*, August 2, 1953, p. 5. See also Ch'en Yi, "Learn from the Marxist-Leninist Creative Style of Work of Chairman Mao," *NCNA*, Peking, July 31, 1951.

8. Antoine H. Jomini, *The Art of War* (Harrisburg, 1947), p. 70. Mao's analysis of the nature of the defensive offensive is remarkably parallel to that outlined by Jomini here.

unstudied techniques—shaping these into a single operational pattern. He is the man who has written it down for others; the man who has presented the Communist revolutionary with the workable blueprint. As such it is a remarkable theoretical extrapolation from his own experience with fixed politico-military conditions in China—hung loosely on a Marxist framework.

II

The war which Mao Tse-tung fought from his early days as a peasant organizer and agitator in South China in 1927 was one in which the first rule was simple survival.[9] So as the cornerstone of military planning Mao Tse-tung has placed a politico-revolutionary sense of time. Whereas Western military men have spent most of their lives considering the problems of the concentration of force *in time,* Mao has spent his life and thought on how to gain *time to.*

In the Western view, war is usually seen as a struggle which, like a football game, has a series of critical points at no one of which is a certain outcome foreseeable. Crises are usually attributed, as are defeats, to failures to have a flotilla or division at the right place at the right time. If Grouchy had arived in time at Waterloo . . . if Hitler had moved more troops from the Southern to the Northern Russian front in time . . . and so on.

In Western thought time is considered in terms of hours and days, months and years. In these terms time not specifically saved is considered time wasted. Particularly in United States military thought economy of time is considered far more important than the principle laid down in the texts—economy of force. That is to say, in American planning the least militarily necessary in terms of increments of force has been thought to be the most obtainable. This has been our operative principle from the Civil War to date. The war of attrition—i.e., one in which the principle of economy of force not time comes first—has been considered simply an auxiliary form of war.

"The ten years' revolutionary war we have fought may be surprising to other countries, but for us it is only like the presentation, amplification and preliminary exposition of the theme in an . . . essay with many exciting paragraphs yet to follow," wrote Mao in 1936.[10] Time, Mao believes, can

---

9. For details on his life see Mao Tse-tung, *Autobiography* (Canton, 1944); Lionel M. Chassin, *L'ascension de Mao Tse-tung, 1921–1945* (Paris, 1953); Pierre Fromentin, *Mao Tse-tung, le dragon rouge* (Paris, 1949); P. S. R. Payne, *Mao Tse-tung: Ruler of Red China* (New York, 1950).

10. *Selected Works of Mao Tse-tung* (New York, 1954), "Strategic Problems of China's Revolutionary War," vol. 1, p. 248.

be made to defeat technology. And unlimited time depends primarily on unlimited space. Unlike Western writers Mao does not concentrate on the problem of ending a war quickly. His problem is to keep it going. Again and again he returns to this theme: "Our War of Resistance cannot be quickly won and can only be a protracted war."[11] Again, "as 'a distant journey tests the strength of a horse and a long task proves the character of a man,' [so] guerrilla warfare will demonstrate its enormous power in the course of a long and ruthless war. . . ."[12]

Western military thought in the 1930's, when most of Mao's important military work was written, was concerned with industrial problems: industrial mobilization and its converse, industrial destruction. All Western thinkers shared an interest in the impact of industrialization on strategy. Some were interested, as were Douhet and Mitchell, in industrial destruction by bombing the industrial heart. Others, the tank men—de Gaulle, Fuller, Guderian—thought to achieve the same end by cutting off the roads and railways, the arteries of the industrial state. Navies saw the problem of war as one of cutting off the industrial intake of raw materials by blocking the sea lanes. But all were thinking, even the navies, in terms of limited space—which Mao was not.

Space in military terms may be described as square mileage plus obstacles minus a workable communications network. Thus ten square miles of mountainous jungle might be equal to a hundred square miles of rolling plain, and this in turn might be equal to a thousand square miles cut by roads and railroads. That space in China could be made to yield time, and time, revolutionary organization, and political cohesion, victory —this is the basis of Mao's optimism.

From the military point of view how then does Mao think that space can be made to yield time?

III

The Chinese Revolutionary Army was born in sublime poverty: no clothing, no guns, no cash, no food. Recognizing this as hard fact, Mao had to rerank the elements necessary to win a war. He pointed out that "in studying the guiding laws of war of different historical stages, of different characters, of different places and of different nations, we must keep our eyes on their respective characteristics and their development,

---

11. *Selected Works of Mao Tse-tung* (London, 1954), "On the Protracted War," vol. 2, p. 183. Compare with Stalin's comment: "We shall act as we did in the Red Army: they may beat us a hundred times, but the hundred and first time we shall beat them all."

12. *Ibid.,* p. 225.

and must oppose a mechanical approach to the problem of war."[13] He told his readers that "[we had to] familiarise ourselves with all aspects of the enemy's situation as well as our own, to discover the laws of the actions of both sides, and to take these laws into account in our own actions."[14]

Mao did not merely rethink but initially formulated a philosophy of war based on a reëstimate of strength ratios. Guns were few in the early days of the struggle and Mao, from necessity, found that arms were not the only effective tools in a revolution. "Weapons are an important factor in war but not the decisive one; it is man and not material that counts," he wrote.[15] With neither military nor economic means he was forced to emphasize that "the ratio of strength is not only a comparison between military and economic strength, but also between manpower and the minds of men."[16] Mao would scoff at the tale, which has at least the status of the apocryphal in the Western world, of the loss of the nail from the shoe of the horse, which lost the battle and then the empire. His theory is, in essence, a theory of substitution: substitution of propaganda for guns, subversion for air power, men for machines, space for mechanization, political for industrial mobilization. The theory was formed intuitively in day-to-day practice. Reflection then turned practice into a theory of war.

In his early pronouncements Mao stressed two points: the first, the necessity of political education; the second, the need for a "democratic" army. But those features of his democratic army which so impressed foreign military observers at first,[17] such as complete equality between officers and men, tended to be less emphasized as the Red Army grew. And Mao's commentaries ceased to mention them. The emphasis on political education has, of course, remained, and with it that essential concomitant; the inculcation of "iron" discipline. It was political education which time was to yield. And it was political discipline which was to yield more time.

Political mobilization, Mao believes, "is the most fundamental condition for winning the war."[18] And elsewhere he gives the reason in a simile,

13. *Ibid.,* "Strategic Problems of China's Revolutionary War," vol. 1, p. 178.
14. *Ibid.,* p. 183.
15. *Ibid.,* "On the Protracted War," Vol. 2, p. 192.
16. Cited in Kuo Kau-jo, "On the Occasion of the 15th Anniversary of the Publication of 'On the Protracted War,' " *Jen-min Jih-pao,* June 3, 1953, p. 4.
17. See Evans F. Carlson, *The Chinese Army: Its Organization . . .* (New York, 1940).
18. *Selected Works,* "On the Protracted War," vol. 2, p. 241. See also Mao's "Interview with the British Correspondent James Bertram," *ibid.,* pp. 92 *et seq.* In this, Mao is consistent with sound Marxist-Leninist doctrine. One of Communist China's foremost theoreticians, Kuo Hua-jo, attributes this to Mao's study of the works of both Marx and Lenin. See Kuo Hua-jo, *Chun-shih pan-she (Military Dialectics)* (Peking, 1951), in particular chaps. 2 and 3. This doctrine, of course, was applied in the Russia Red Army as well. See Erich Wollenberg, *The Red Army* (London, 1938), p. 184.

a form he dearly loves: "The people are like water and the army is like fish."[19] "With the common people of the whole country mobilised, we shall create a vast sea of humanity and drown the enemy in it. . . ."[20] Mao holds out military salvation, in a truly ideological sense, as a concomitant of political conversion.

Year after year Mao returned to the problems involved in creating a political revolution through a protracted armed struggle. In 1929 he complained in a resolution presented to the Ninth Conference of the party organization of the Fourth Army that any separation of the political task from the military task of the Army would make both impossible. He warned:

> When the Red Army fights, it fights not merely for the sake of fighting, but to agitate the masses, to organise them, to arm them, and to help them establish revolutionary political power; apart from such objectives, fighting loses its meaning and the Red Army the reason for its existence.[21]

And as the Red Army is the torch of revolution, so is war the flame that purifies the revolution. ". . . [War] is an antitoxin . . ." he wrote, "not only capable of expelling the evil influences of the enemy, but also of purging ourselves of all impurities."[22] A curious and ancient thought!

Political mobilization, however, depends not only on routing out the dissidents and equipping military units with mimeograph machines, and "chalk cans and big brushes" for cartoon warfare. Political mobilization depends directly on military tactics. Mao recognizes that there are two politico-military dangers. The first is too great a penchant for heroism—desperadoism, he calls it. The other is, as one might expect, a willingness to give up too soon.[23]

Discouragement requires that war must be at once constantly successful and most cautiously fought. Losses must be kept at a minimum, and local successes must be continuous. The very price of survival is caution. Hence Mao's repetitive insistence on the necessity of local superiority: five and even ten against one is his formula. The political control necessary to maintain the formula undiluted in a situation in which revolutionary ardor is present is, of course, extraordinarily difficult. It accounts for Mao's insistence on absolute discipline.

----

19. Mao Tse-tung, *Aspects of China's Anti-Japanese Struggle* (edition of Bombay, 1948), p. 48. This work is included in *Selected Works*, vol. 2, pp. 119–156, under the title of "Strategic Problems in the Anti-Japanese Guerrilla War." This London publication is perhaps more grammatically correct than the Bombay edition, but the picturesqueness of the Bombay edition deserves quotation at times.

20. *Selected Works*, "On the Protracted War," vol. 2, p. 204.

21. *Ibid.*, "On the Rectification of Incorrect Ideas in the Party," vol. 1, p. 106.

22. Cited in Hsiao Hua, "The Communist Party of China and the Chinese People's Liberation Army," *NCNA*, Peking, July 25, 1951.

23. *Selected Works*, "On the Protracted War," vol. 2, pp. 223, 224.

IV

Guerrilla warfare is the great timeserver of military strategy. Guerrilla operations are the muck, the quicksand in which military machinery bogs down in futility. And it is the cheapest kind of war to wage. It can also be the most futile, if left undirected. Like mud it can stave off defeat, but it cannot bring victory. Because he could not himself direct all operations, Mao outlined his doctrinal position on this type of war in a series of pamphlets: *Strategic Problems of China's Revolutionary War* (1936), *Strategic Problems in the Anti-Japanese Guerrilla War* (1938) and finally in *On the Protracted War* (1938).

Mao deals in one way or another with one central problem in all these works of his. The problem is one of combining dispersion with concentration. Local insurrection corps "armed with spears and fowling pieces,"[24] the "special feature,"[25] of revolution in agricultural China, had to be combined with the use of the regular Chinese Red Army. The local corps, by being dispersed, were to disperse the enemy. The army was to defeat said enemy in detail. There is nothing new certainly in this concept. What Mao did, however, was to set the concept in the context of time. In doing so, he plotted the course of war, as Marx had plotted the pattern of history, as thesis, antithesis, and victorious synthesis.

Mao, according to his own lights, has taken the "if" out of warfare. War, always given adequate space, has not only a predictable outcome, but clearly defined phases. In this sense, Mao has used Marxism-Leninism as a "telescope or microscope in matters political and military."[26] The "laws of China's revolutionary war—this is a problem which anyone directing China's revolutionary war must study and solve," he writes.[27]

To Mao, that is to say, the pattern of the future has the same relentless inevitability as the pattern of the past. A protracted war—the point is made dogmatically—*must* pass through three stages to victory. The first of the three stages is one in which the enemy is on the strategic offensive, and Mao is on what he calls the "strategic defensive." The second is a stalemate stage in which the Communists prepare to seize the initiative. In the third stage there is a shift to the strategic offensive on the Communists' part, forcing the enemy onto the strategic defensive, and eventually out of the war altogether.[28]

There are certain assumptions that Mao makes regarding the first stage. The first is that the loss of the means of production to the enemy does

24. *Ibid.*, "The Struggle in the Chingkang Mountains," vol. 1, p. 84.

25. *Ibid.*, p. 100.

26. *Ibid.*, "Strategic Problems of China's Revolutionary War," vol. 1, p. 222. See also Garthoff, *op. cit.*, pp. 253 *et seq.*

27. *Selected Works*, "Strategic Problems of China's Revolutionary War," vol. 1, p. 175.

28. *Ibid.*, "On the Protracted War," vol. 2, pp. 184 *et. seq.*

not mean the loss of the war. The second is that the enemy is committed to a quick war, and will strike with the totality of power possible. During this period Mao expects fighting, but primarily he also expects to retreat. "Is it not self-contradictory to fight heroically first and abandon territory afterwards?" he asks rhetorically. Rhetorically he answers with another question: "One eats first and then relieves oneself; does one eat in vain?"[29]

The first stage is said to slip into the second for two interdependent reasons. In that the war is seen not to be over, a sense of futility creeps up both among the opponents' troops and on their home front where there is a "change for the worse" because of casualties, expense, and so forth.[30] Communist morale by this very token begins to rise. When the see-saw of war reaches a state of equilibrium, the strategic stalemate, or stage two, has been reached.

An increase in guerrilla warfare, supplemented by mobile warfare fought by increasing numbers of regular Communist troops will then— despite defeatism, economic difficulties and "collaborators' subversive activities"—turn stage two into stage three. Finally, as this stage moves toward its culmination, guerrilla warfare becomes supplementary, and the more regular forms of warfare become once more the order of the day.

Mao pursued the three stages of warfare outlined in his *On the Protracted War* throughout the Sino-Japanese conflict. The first stage, the strategic defensive, was marked by a broad Japanese offensive in North and Central China in which, as Mao himself pointed out, the Chinese "retreated in space but advanced in time." This phase was concluded with the fall of the Wuhan cities (China's "Chicago") on October 25, 1938. In October, 1939, the Chinese Communists announced officially that the second phase of the war, the stalemate phase, had finally arrived. The Red high command was not unduly optimistic, for shortly thereafter the Japanese offensive reached its climax in the foothills of Western China. The Japanese advance averaged only five miles a day in 1938. By the following year it had fallen to two miles a day, and finally it shrank to but a single mile in 1940.[31]

Reflecting on Chinese Communist strategy during this period, General Nieh Jung-chen recently stated:

> What deserves particular attention is that such an extensive as well as protracted guerrilla warfare is something of a novelty in man's entire military history and this state of affairs is inseparable from the fact that

29. *Ibid.*, p. 235.
30. *Ibid.*, p. 189.
31. *K'ang-chen chung-ti chung-kuo chun-skih (Chinese Military Operations During the War of Resistance)* (K'ang-chan shu-tien, n.p., n.d.), p. 66. One notable exception to this pattern was the large-scale Japanese assault against Chinese-U.S. air bases in 1943–44.

times have progressed from the 'thirties to the 'forties in the twentieth century.[32]

The Japanese sued for peace before the Chinese Communists could embark upon the strategic offensive, the third and final stage in Mao's strategy. The question as to whether the Chinese Communists could ever have defeated the Japanese by using Mao's blueprint is largely an academic one, for it appears that Pearl Harbor required that both the Communists and Nationalists alike revise their war plans. There is indeed sound evidence to support the contention that, following the entry of the United States into the war, both these political groups decided, independently of course, that the United States would insure the eventual defeat of Japan and that military operations against the Japanese—aside from purely defensive measures—were now of secondary importance. A new but unannounced strategy was in the offing, i.e., jockeying for position in North and Central China with both sides attempting to reach a status of strength and influence in order to insure their own control over the China mainland once the war was brought to a close.

Because their commitments to the Allies were less demanding, and because of the expertness of their guerrilla operations, the Chinese Communists found this new strategy easy indeed to implement. In fact, after 1941, Red commanders concentrated more on political indoctrination, building up their forces, and expanding their mass base than on conducting aggressive military operations against the enemy.

This strategy paid off; for, following the Japanese surrender, the Nationalists found themselves in much the same position that the Japanese had been. Their forces reoccupied areas that remained hostile despite the new-found peace. In fact, much of North and Central China remained essentially enemy territory—land dominated by Communist-led guerrilla and mass organizations—land where the people regarded the Nationalists with something less than trust, friendship and loyalty.

The outbreak of the civil war between the Communists and Nationalists in 1946 was a logical development of Mao's strategic plan. In fact, there was no essential shift or change in Communist strategy. This was a point which the Nationalists regrettably failed to grasp. Because the nature of the enemy had changed, the Communists reverted to Mao's first phase, i.e., to the strategic defensive. Nationalist advances were, territory-wise, nothing short of spectacular during the first year of the war. But, whether they knew it or not, they were fighting a war dictated by Communist military doctrine.

Mao was trading space for time and cities for men. In his "rear base," Manchuria, he was organizing, training and arming a strong force that

---

32. Nieh Jung-chen, "How the Chinese People Defeated the Japanese Fascist Aggressors," *People's China,* July 1, 1951, p. 29.

was to remain uncommitted until the second phase, the stalemate, could be realized. Meanwhile, Chinese Communist military commanders in North China continued their policies of attrition of the enemy, capitalizing upon Chiang Kai-shek's habit of giving his commanders certain definite time limits for achieving their objectives. The "European-style" war fought by the Nationalists played into the hands of the Red strategists.

The all-out assault on the Communist capital at Yenan in 1947 is a case in point. The Nationalists lost many men, used up valuable time, drew off divisions that could well have been used more advantageously elsewhere, and overextended their lines of communications and supply in order to take the Red capital. Ch'en Yi, the Communist military commander in the area, summed up the campaign at the time when he told reporters:

> According to orthodox military policies the Communists should deploy their best troops in defense of their capital city. We should be considering how best to defend Yenan and how long we can hold it. Actually, we are not taking any of these measures. Instead, we are only concerned with how many of Chiang's troops we can annihilate. [33]

Maoist strategy paid off in late 1947 and early 1948 with the arrival of the military stalemate. The second phase was a brief one, largely because the Communists had laid their plans well. The war after 1948 was almost preordained. The Communists took full advantage of the overextended Nationalist armies, now wallowing deep in the Red-controlled areas. The Nationalists found themselves unable to take advantage of either time or space—both were now on the side of Mao.

The third and final stage was at hand when General Lin Piao led his Manchurian forces in the initial counter-offensive against the enemy. Pivoting from the Manchurian provinces, the Communist armies swept through the key Shanhai pass and into the vast North China plain. Joining up with other Red forces the Communist armies found little difficulty in breaking the back of the main Nationalist armies and eventually in completing the conquest of the China mainland. The civil war was a classic in Maoist strategy—a strategy clearly outlined over ten years previously, in 1938. The fact that neither the Nationalists nor the West took heed of the pronouncements of this prophetic strategist is attested to by the failure of the Nationalists and of the West to counter the advances made by Communist China since 1946.[34]

The Korean conflict was a different type of war—with different objec-

---

33. Cited in Gene Z. Hanrahan, "Red China's Top Field Commanders," *Marine Corps Gazette*, February, 1952, p. 61.

34. This is not to imply that it was Communist strategy along which won the civil war. Certainly such factors as Nationalist morale and leadership, American indecision, Russian protection in Manchuria, etc., played their part. However, it is believed that Communist strategy—so important to the outcome of this struggle —has been little appreciated by students of Chinese affairs as of this writing.

tives and conditions. And yet, we can see that much of Mao's doctrine obtained even there. Red military operations were largely those laid down by Mao in his study of the *Strategic Problems of China's Revolutionary War*—this despite the fact that China was engaged in its first "modern war" against the West.[35] Mao's concept of time was aptly demonstrated in the protracted stalemate period when the Communists, seemingly indifferent to losses, conducted what appeared to United Nations observers as wasted military operations. But the Red high command had two very important reasons in mind. First, it was argued that the side which continued to be aggressive and held the initiative—despite the fact that peace was imminent and the truce lines were drawn—could be considered, at lease propaganda-wise, the victor. In this way the Communists showed no aversion toward utilizing their men to gain a political or psychological victory through military action; even though in so doing they might take heavy losses. Such a means could never even be considered by United Nations forces. Secondly, the Communists hoped to learn more about positional (or trench) warfare at this time. Captured enemy documents reveal that the Red military leaders were willing to expend their manpower in learning this "Western-style" warfare. The Communists were preparing for the next war in the closing phases of the Korean conflict.

But the Communist high command knew that the campaign would be written as a whole, and not in terms of any one of its parts. Time and, indeed, setbacks were not only secondary, but could in fact be turned to the ultimate advantage of the Communists. In Maoist strategy, military victory in the field is valuable only in so far as it pertains to ultimate political success. And this latter is the only true criterion of victory in the Communist sense.

It need hardly be underlined that the war in North Vietnam likewise followed Mao's formula: stage one—1945–1948; stage two—1948–1950; stage three—1950–1954. Conditions were, of course, virtually perfect from the Communist point of view.[36] Because of a combination of jungle, mountain and swamp, the degree of mobility enjoyed by the armed forces depended directly on the degree to which they were *not* mechanized and motorized. Furthermore, radio communication in areas in which other means of communication were lacking gave partisans an opportunity to coordinate their activities so that concentration of local forces could be used to create diversion. It was almost as if the peninsula were being torn by groups of men dropped from an unseen plane to carry out a given

---

35. A competent analysis of this is given in Lt. Col. F. B. Nihart, "Mao's Strategic Defensive," *Marine Corps Gazette,* November, 1952, pp. 51–59. See also Gene Z. Hanrahan, "The Chinese Red Army and Guerrilla Warfare" [Chapter 12 of this volume].

36. For details see Edward L. Katzenbach, Jr., "Indo-China: A Military-Political Appreciation," *World Politics,* vol. IV, No. 2 (January, 1952), pp. 186–222.

mission of destruction, and then disappear. And politically, of course, the situation was as favorable to the Communists as it was geographically, for each defeat of the Franco-Vietnamese forces further disrupted their common front. Indeed, in retrospect, one of the more macabre aspects of that macabre war was the fact that each military defeat was in a sense a political victory for a fraction of the defeated. For, when Franco-Vietnamese forces were defeated, it gave the Vietnamese politicians an opportunity to press the more firmly for those political rights which the French granted only on the morrow of defeat.

It would seem undeniable that Mao's strategy, wherever applied, has been remarkably and tragically successful.

V

Indo-China was a graveyard for the reputations of fine and valiant French generals—for Valluy, Leclerc, Carpentier, Salan, Navarre. Each arrived on the field with a prophecy of victory, and left with words of despair. In Malaya such highly respected leaders as Sir Edward Gent, Major General Charles Boucher and Let. Gen. Sir Harold Briggs have been something less than brilliantly successful. The United States Secretary of Defense, Charles E. Wilson, admitted with his usual candor that the war in Indo-China was a failure not of arms but of strategy. The outcome of the war in Indo-China would not have been any different had the United States Army been "twice as big as it is, if the Navy [had] twice as many ships afloat, and the Air Force had [had] 200 wings," he said.[37] The fact of past failure is amply documented.

Mao has always maintained that his is the last just war, the war to end wars, after which will emerge a historically unprecedented new era for mankind in which there will "no longer be any wars."[38] There is, however, no indication that this war for a "new world of permanent peace and permanent light"[39] will end before the world is made safe for communism. He believes that the willingness to compromise has a class basis, and that therefore compromise by its very origin cannot be successful.[40] Nor can there be any question as to his views on means. Referring to the courtesy of an ancient nobleman who turned over, in courtly fashion, the initiative to the enemy, he remarked: "We are not Duke Hsiang of Sung and have no use for his stupid scruples about benevolence, righteousness

---

37. *New York Times,* July 20, 1954.
38. *Selected Works,* "Strategic Problems of China's Revolutionary War," vol. 1, p. 179.
39. *Ibid.,* "On the Protracted War," vol. 2, p. 199.
40. *Ibid.,* p. 175.

and morality in war."[41] This would appear to be the way of the future.

But Mao's theory of war is based, as is any theory, on a set of postulates. And his structure is no stronger than its foundations. The first and most important of Mao's premises is that he and those who think like him have a monopoly on patience. This monopoly is comfortably cushioned, moreover, by the flexibility built into Mao's doctrine of the inevitability of ultimate victory. For the shift from one stage of war to the next is not always progressive. There may be setbacks depending on what in another society would be called "acts of God." (In his view, for example, there is presently a shift back to the strategic defensive in the Philippines.) Euphonically this is called the "Revolutionary Flow." As Mao puts it: ". . . although our chart may not coincide with, but will be amended by, future developments, it is still necessary in formulating the strategic plan for carrying on a protracted war firmly and purposefully."[42]

Indeed, it is the faith of the Communists in Southeast Asia in their monopoly on patience that has made Mao's the ubiquitous gospel it is. In Malaya the Communists argue that the "anti-British national revolutionary war will be protracted, uphill and violent," and that Mao Tsetung's "concepts . . . are imperatives in the course of the struggle."[43] In the Philippines, the Huk leaders recently reported that "the war continues in revolutionary stages and cannot be counted by the day or month."[44] For the partially defeated, there could scarcely be a more comforting analysis.

The second premise, perhaps a corollary of the first, is that the anti-Communist front is committed to quick victory, and therefore cannot, and will not, underwrite a long-drawn-out war. The effects of the stalemate in Korea on public opinion in the United States and of the long-drawn-out war in Indo-China on the French serve as illustrations of what Mao had in mind when writing, back in the 1930's, with particular reference to Japan.

It is in this connection that he believes that initial tactical self-sacrifice in the first stage of war is the necessary price of eventual victory. But the yeast of this process is, in the Communist view, the maintenance of the initiative after and even during the expected initial setbacks. In operational terms this means that local victories must be cheap and continuous. Moreover, the lesson of the war in China and Indo-China is that in such a war military initiative has very little to do with technological superiority.

This leads to the third postulate: that the Communists can maintain

---

41. *Ibid.*, p. 217.

42. *Ibid.*, p. 184. The same insistence on planning runs throughout all his writing. See *Selected Works*, "Strategic Problems in the Anti-Japanese Guerrilla War," vol. 2, p. 131.

43. Translated Malayan Communist party documents which appear in Hanrahan, *The Communist Struggle in Malaya*, pp. 103 and 117.

44. Memorandum of the Secretariat of the Philippine Communist Party, *supra*, note 5.

the initiative from both a military and a political standpoint—if one can make the distinction. They reason that they can, largely because they know that a "people's war," operating under strict party discipline, has an enormously flexible arsenal. Communists understand, what is frequently forgotten, that it is not simply the weapons one has in one's arsenal that give one flexibility, but the willingness and ability to use them. Assassination, sabotage, ambush, "spontaneous uprisings," or mass attacks in fanatical waves, the more typical form of revolutionary warfare, are all a part of this arsenal.

VI

Perhaps one should—indeed, one must—conclude with a word of caution. None of Mao's recent remarks seem to contradict the impression given by his older works—that in the atomic age his views may be quite unrealistic. Mao's mind may still envision catastrophe, like victory, as a cumulative effect. He may, therefore, fail to appreciate the dangers of atomic war, the war of massive and instantaneous destruction. It is a dismal fact that Mao has a psychological immunity to what he considers to be temporary suffering. His values are in a different balance from those of the Western world. The threat of atomic warfare may be no deterrent to his plans.

Similarly, the very concept that assisted so much in winning the Chinese revolution may, today, be more of a drawback than an asset to the Chinese Communists. Guerrilla warfare has its place, but it cannot be effective at all times and under all conditions. It was this idea of "guerrillaism" that worried the Soviet high command following the civil war in Russia. In the 'twenties, everything possible was done by the Russians to stamp out the remaining vestiges of this in their own armed forces.

In China, almost every leader—be he essentially in the military or political sphere—has had decades of guerrilla experience behind him. The question whether these men—and this includes Mao Tse-tung himself—can now divorce themselves from their deeply ingrained backgrounds is an important one and worthy of serious consideration by us. We do know that Mao, even today, does not rate our technical advancements as highly as the Russians do, and that he still thinks at least partly in terms of the revolution and the wars he knew in the 'thirties. We can only conjecture as to how much this clouds his and his associates' thinking on more contemporary matters.

In the Korean conflict, for example, the Chinese insisted on making strong efforts to raise guerrilla forces, operating out of rear bases, in South Korea. P'eng Te-huai, the Communist commander there (and currently head of the Department of Defense in the Chinese Communist government), is known to have argued strongly for a combined guerrilla-regular force strategy in the Korean conflict. This did not work and the Communists lost much, in terms of both troop strength and material, in this program. Whether the Communists themselves have realized their own faults on this matter we do not know. But it is difficult indeed to rid oneself of thirty years of training and experience—especially if it is that experience which gained so much for one in the past. The problem of "guerrillaism"—whether it be in leaders or basic concepts—may remain one of the great intangibles to plague the Communist Chinese for some time to come.

There is also room for another word of optimism here. From the war in Malaya, from the war in the Philippines, and from the failure in Indo-China, there is now available tactical doctrine for a war against the Maoists. Like any tactical doctrine, it is rooted in a general strategic concept. And like any strategy it makes demands. Over the years, with tough professional troops, whose job everyone, including themselves, knows to be fighting, and with the promise of free political participation, the desirable may come within the range of possibility without total commitment. Putting first things first, the logical first step remains what it has always been: the breaking of Mao's monopoly on patience. This would seem primarily a problem in self-education.

11

Captain Wilbur W. Dinegar
U.S. Marine Corps

THE "LONG MARCH"

AS EXTENDED

GUERRILLA WARFARE

FOR A RATHER SPECTACULAR example of the development of Communist guerrilla tactics, one need only study the Chinese Red Army's famous "Long March." Here is a story which has never been more pregnant with significance than it is today.

By 1927 the differences of opinion between the left wing of the Kuomintang and Chiang Kai-shek had widened to a definite breach. The breach was caused by a complex of ideas based on political, economic, and personal feelings. It had developed to such an extent that by April 11, 1927, Chiang had decided it was time to be done with the Communists—and violently!

Though bloody even by Oriental standards, Chiang's purge did not obliterate the Reds. Mao Tse-tung, a young Red agitator, attempted to organize a revolt in the fall of '27—known as the "Autumn Harvest uprising"—but failed badly. His forces fled principally into the interior of Kiangsi province. By 1934 Mao had administrative control of much of Kiangsi, and soviets had been established in the provinces of Fukien, Hunan, Honan, Hopeh, Anhui, Szechuan, and Shensi.

From U.S. Naval Institute *Proceedings,* by permission. Copyright 1952 by U.S. Naval Institute.

Throughout these seven years of Red growth, Chiang and his Nationalists had not been inactive. From December, 1933, to October, 1934, five major "annihilation" drives were sent against the Communists, requiring over a million and a quarter Nationalist troops.

Four of these the Reds drove off with varying losses to the Nationalists. The cost began to show on the Reds, however, since their territories were completely surrounded by the Kuomintang.

The fifth "surrounding" began in October, 1933, with the mobilization of some 900,000 troops by Chiang, for a drive against the Reds in the Fukien-Kiangsi area. About 400,000 of these saw action against Communist forces totaling 180,000 "regulars" and guerrillas, and 200,000 lesser partisans. The Reds could muster only about 100,000 rifles for these men, no heavy artillery, and were short in all categories of equipment and ammunition. The Nanking troops, on the other hand, were well equipped throughout, with much mechanized and air support, of which the Reds had none.

Chiang had learned many lessons in the four costly campaigns preceding, and they were put to good use in the fifth. Rather than attempt, for the fifth time, to trap a highly mobile foe in the field, Chiang turned to the tactic of compressing the enemy into nothing. A veritable ring of iron and a "fiery wall," advancing from all sides simultaneously, robbed the Reds of the advantage they had possessed by extreme mobility, and emphasized the disadvantages of smaller resources and numbers.

Also, this tactic denied Mao the cooperation of the local peasantry. The area was literally scorched, and, where necessary, depopulated. The Kuomintang admits over 1,000,000 peasants were massacred, in this campaign alone, to effect the economic and psychological blockade of Mao's forces. The new policy was very effective, too; in addition to restricting Mao's mobility, it terrified the peasants to the extent that, despite their sympathies, they would not supply, or cooperate with, the Reds. That of itself was bad enough, but it also forced the Reds to exploit the peasants, as had the Kuomintang—thus destroying much of their faith in the Reds' good intentions.

This latter aspect is very interesting in view of the differing regards held for the mass of peasants by Mao and Chiang. Mao had always considered the peasants the backbone of power, and later wrote of them in such a way in *Yu Chi Chan*. Chiang perhaps began to look on Mao with suspicion because of this feeling.

Chiang had always felt peasant movements dangerous to organized authority. Militarily he held the opinion, "The task of the peasant is to provide us with information concerning the enemy, food and comforts for our encampment, and soldiers for our armies." But a peasant-run army—never!

Throughout the fifth campaign, Chiang's troops never repeated the mistake of exposing themselves as they had before. This time they went forward cautiously, never venturing in advance of the ring of forts they projected before themselves, and never without armor, artillery, and air support.[1]

Denied the aid of peasants, outnumbered, outmaneuvered, and outgunned, Mao and Chu Teh now found themselves being forced into positional warfare against vastly superior forces.[2] The Red commander could no longer lure Nationalist troops deep into their interior, and then attack with concentrated force against their weakest point. By August, 1934, the Reds had lost 80,000 or more men. Chou En-lai (then a leader of the First Red Army Corps) admitted the Communist armies had lost 60,000 in a single protracted siege.

The positional warfare into which the Reds had been forced was entirely against Mao's military principles. He was feeling the effects of an up-to-date, motorized army pushing into his positions. That army was no longer overextending itself, leaving flanks and columns exposed to attack, but was moving as a solid mass. True, the Nationalist losses were severe, but with five times as many troops, they were in a much better position to sustain heavy losses than was Mao. Already a third of his army was gone.

In late August, Mao and Chu Teh met at Juichin and went over the situation. It was clearly evident that unless something was done, this was the end. Mao was later to write:

> . . . guerrillas must not permit themselves to be maneuvered into a position where they are robbed of initiative and where the decision to attack is forced upon them. . . . Even in defence all our efforts must be directed towards a resumption of the attack. A defence or withdrawal is entirely useless as far as extinguishing our enemies is concerned, and only of temporary value as far as the conservation of our forces is concerned.

Yet, this was just the problem that faced Mao and Chu Teh. They had been robbed of the initiative and in defense had to direct all their efforts to a resumption of the attack. The only course was withdrawal. But not "withdrawal" alone, because they were surrounded—first they had to break out.[3]

---

1. This departure, in the fifth "surrounding," from previous tactics was not original with Chiang, but was the work of his foreign (German) military advisors. In *Red Star over China,* Snow says the fifth campaign was the work of General von Seeckt, one time Nazi chief-of-staff.

2. The chief Red military adviser, Li Teh, was blamed for this. Like the Nationalist advisers, he too was a German.

3. In order to impress the Chinese people and the world at large, the Reds had declared war on Japan when that nation first invaded Manchuria. This was purely propaganda, as there were no soviets bordering on Japanese held territory at the time. Later, when established in north Shensi, the Reds made great claim that the march was organized so that they could move to an area from which they could attack the Japanese. I doubt very much the war with Japan greatly concerned Mao in Kiangsi in '34!

Mao and Chu Teh ordered the abandonment of Juichin. The Red arsenal was taken apart and buried. Everything that was not of use was destroyed. What was of use was either buried, for possible future recovery, or loaded on to pack animals. Later, these vast amounts of baggage were to prove a great bother, and before the march was finished all was buried, abandoned, or lost en route. It was surprising that Mao tried to take as much as he did, being so conscious of vital mobility as he was. As if in justification (and perhaps he was justified) he wrote: ". . . Equipment cannot be furnished immediately, but must be acquired gradually." But, in being reluctant to abandon former gradual accumulations, he lost sight of what possibly lay ahead.

Mao recognized defeat when he saw it staring him in the face; and he was able to remember it later (unlike many lesser military figures). He had no hesitation in later reflecting:

> . . . We did not plan organically; we had not thought out the campaign. . . . The enemy's supreme command was far sighted in its strategy: we only thought of what was under our noses. There are three essentials: an assurance of victory, an understanding of the campaign as a whole, and a knowledge of the next strategic move. We panicked and we fought stupidly.

Surely the circumstances demanding the abandonment of Juichin and the embarkation on the Long March were well in mind when Mao wrote later:

> . . . When an army loses the initiative it loses its liberty: its role becomes passive; it faces the danger of defeat and destruction. It is more difficult to obtain the initiative when defending on interior lines than it is while attacking on exterior lines. . . .
> When the enemy attacks guerrillas with more than one column, it is difficult for the latter to retain the initiative. Any error, no matter how slight, in the estimation of the situation is likely to result in forcing the guerrillas into a passive role. They will then find themselves unable to beat off the attacks of the enemy. It is apparent that we only can gain and retain the initiative by a correct estimation of the situation and a proper arrangement of all military and political factors. . . .
> When a guerrilla unit, due either to poor estimate on the part of its leader, or pressure from the enemy, is forced into a passive position, its first duty is to extricate itself. . . .
> Dispersion, concentration, constant change of position—it is in these ways that guerrillas employ their strength. In general, guerrilla units disperse to operate.

The Communist main forces were ordered to assemble in southern Kiangsi—at Yutu—for at that place was a weak point in the Kuomintang circle. Chiefly by forced night marches, with rainy skies and no moon preventing Nationalist air patrol, Mao's group reached Yutu in two days (October 14–16, 1934) and combined with other groups, totaling about 90,000–100,000—having been forced to leave behind some 20,000 wounded from the battle at Kwanchang, who could not be carried. Skirmishes occurred all along the route from Juichin to Yutu, and had it not been for the weather and night marches, things might have gone much worse, since no aid was forthcoming from the local peasantry, terrified by Chiang's methods.

Although the Kuomintang troops were sporadically in contact with the Reds on the way to Yutu, they had no idea what was going on. Local partisan units and peasant guards occupied towns and field positions as the troops of the main body groups moved out. Just to make sure this ruse worked, two diversionary columns were formed. One, under Fang Chih-min, was to establish pressure in northeastern Kiangsi, while the second, under Han Ying, was to establish itself in the mountains to the south on the border of Fukein and Chekiang. The first was wiped out, but not before it had done its job. The second was able to hold out, and eventually made its way independently to Shensi, arriving four years later. As late as 1938, the Kuomintang announced a "final" drive to mop up the south Kiangsi area.

In this instance Mao and Chu Teh used smaller guerrilla units to cover the repositioning and subsequent operations of a larger guerrilla body. This is more properly a function of guerrilla forces in relation to larger regular forces, but we must realize that we are not here dealing with a guerrilla band, but with a large guerrilla army. Only in this way was the main Red column allowed the requisite freedom to "disperse" in accordance with the five criteria Mao set forth as to the time for dispersal:

1. When the enemy is in over-extended defense and sufficient force cannot be concentrated against him, guerrillas must disperse, harass, and demoralize him.
2. When encircled by the enemy, guerrillas disperse to withdraw.
3. Disperse when the nature of the ground limits action.
4. Disperse when the availability of supplies limits actions.
5. Disperse in order to promote movements over a wide area.

On October 16, 1934, the Long March began. Smedley says that only the top leaders knew what lay ahead, but Mao himself frankly stated that at the time no definite plan had been prepared. The immediate task was to break through the encirclement and attempt to join up with Hsiao-Keh, who had broken out in August with 10,000 men.

In the six weeks immediately following, four lines of Kuomintang defenses were penetrated, each supported by concrete machine-gun nests and blockhouses. Five days after the jump off from Yutu the first line was broken in Kiangsi. The second, in Hunan, was pierced on November 3, and the third, also in Hunan, a week later. On November 29th Nationalist troops of Kiangsi and Hunan gave up the fourth. In all, nine battles were fought during those first 38 days, costing the Reds some 25,000 men.

The deplorable state of Communist thinking at the time is exemplified by the fact that once through the last Kuomintang line the Reds turned northward and made straight for Szechuan, where Hsu Hsiang-chien was established with 100,000 men. This move was all too obvious to Chiang, and he was able to handle the Reds severely all the way as long as they kept it up. While the Reds maintained their undeviating north-westward advance, the Nationalists were able to mobilize some 110 regiments in their path and even construct elaborate road blocks.

Up to this time the Communist armies had used a straight-point disposition for advance. The grievous losses the Reds were forced to absorb, they could ill afford. If the rate at this time were to continue, they would be wiped out in six weeks. Just why Mao and Chu Teh abandoned the tactics of deviation and diversion that had seen them safely through four campaigns, I have not been able to ascertain, nor have I found any opinions or discussions along that line. I can only believe the situation to have been brought about by a complete demoralization of the top command, due to the stunning blows and the debilitating effects of the compressive "fiery wall."

But now, in the comparative open and beyond the Nanking encirclements, the Communist heads began to clear. Distraction, once more, became the theme of their tactics. As many as four columns at a time operated on the flanks of the main body, while the van developed a double pronged, or pincer, disposition.

Already Mao was beginning to see, perhaps, the folly of attaching so much importance to the spoils of Yutu. The "impedimenta" had occupied as many as 5,000 men at a time, to date, and had definitely slowed the entire advance. The equipment of the soldiers was now cut to a minimum, and much of the baggage was buried by the way. Still, night marches only were instituted at this point to save the baggage train from destruction by bombing.

Mao was headed to cross the Yangtze Ho into Szechuan (the Golden Sand River in Yunan), and Chiang knew it! The Generalissimo shifted heavy forces to the west from Anhui, Hupeh, and Kiangsi; ferries were drawn to the north bank, the crossings heavily fortified, roads blocked, and large areas stripped of grain.

It took 15 weeks for the Reds to cross the Yangtze. Two long counter marches were executed, but finally with excellent strategy and the aid of weather—low clouds cover much of Kweichow province this time of the year for five straight months—it was accomplished. During the period the Reds stayed clear of cities and large towns. Mao was essentially working from the standpoint of "agrarian reform," and rightly saw the larger portion of power in China residing in the overwhelming mass of peasants. He was never too enthusiastic for industrial labor organization and saw little long-run political and military value in cities.⁴ Thus it was that Mao fought desperately to stamp out the still existent influence of Li Li-san, and strictly forbade any operations towards the capture of the capital of Kweichow (Kweiyang), though the army as a whole was eager to try. On the subject in general he advised:

> There is no way to accomplish this with the resources we command. The desire to fight positional wars and to capture cities springs from the same adventurism. Our duty is to fight a protracted war, avoiding the enemy if possible, never engaging him unless it can be made certain in advance that it is to our advantage.

The operations in Kweichow are excellent depictions of the principles of guerrilla tactics and strategy. Here, in truth, Mao selected "the tactic of seeming to come from the east and attacking from the west." By speedy concentrations Chiang had blocked all direct routes to the Yangtze, and hoped either to trap the Reds in the southwest or drive them into the wastelands of Tibet. Suddenly, in early May, Red columns drove south, as if in attempt to capture Yunanfu, causing the precipitous flight of Chiang and his wife from that place. The Nationalists hurried after them, only to find, too late, the main body driving westward with the obvious design of a crossing at Lenghai. With all boats burned (he thought) and crossings fortified, Chiang closed for the kill. The main communist body advanced on Lenghai, with the van already there constructing a bamboo bridge.

Chiang saw no great rush, since weeks would be required to erect a bridge. But, one night, a single battalion broke off from the main body and arrived the next day at Chon Ping Fort, eighty-five miles away, dressed in Kuomintang uniforms. The Nationalists on the north bank obligingly sent over a boat for their "comrades." (They had seen no necessity to carry out Chiang's orders and burn the boats here, with the nearest Reds known to be almost 300 li away.)⁵ Once over, the Reds disarmed the unwary garrison busily engaged in mah jong.

Meanwhile, the main body and van had also reversed themselves and arrived by noon the next day. In nine days the six available boats had ferried the Red Army into Szechuan. They then burned the boats, necessitating a 200 mile detour by the Nationalists, who arrived on the south bank two days later. Chiang's only hope now was to prevent a further crossing at the Tatu.

It was apparent that the Reds were now back in form. They had re-

---

4. Chiang, on the other hand, was quite fond of cities. After the defeat of Japan and the resumption of civil war between the Reds and the Kuomintang, it was a favorite expression of Mao's to say that he had sold Chiang a city for men—meaning, the loss of 100,000 men to Chiang was well worth a city to Mao, and that he'd trade like that any time Chiang wanted. It would appear that Mao drove the harder bargain.

5. One mile = 2.78 li. The Reds refer to the Long March as the "25,000 Li March."

cruited over 20,000 men, destroyed five Kuomintang divisions, and were in Szechuan at last. Never more justly was Mao to boast: "Thus, to take a long and circuitous route after enticing the enemy out of the way, and though starting after him, reach the goal before him, shows knowledge of the artifice of deviation."

Ahead lay the rugged forested land of the Lolo tribesmen, who for centuries had been oppressed by the Chinese around them. They recognized no difference between Red and White Chinese, hating Chinese in general with a fierce feeling. Many Chinese armies in the past had perished in attempting to pass through these lands. Those that had succeeded in passing through were hardly recognizable as an army when they emerged.

Chiang was counting on the Lolos to cause the Reds a long delay. The dense forests had hidden the Red advances from the Kuomintang air patrols, a fact that was to prove unfortunate for Chiang.

Gen. Liu Po-ch'eng had had experience with Lolo tribesmen serving in previous commands of his. Several chieftans imprisoned by the Nationalists were liberated by the Reds, and to these Gen. Liu was able to explain what the Reds were trying to do, and that they were common enemies of the Nationalist Chinese. Mao took a chance that Sun Tzu (the Chinese Clausewitz) never countenanced and gave arms to the Lolos when they requested them for defense against the Whites. This won over the Lolos, and the Reds were able to pass through with a minimum of trouble.

Thus the Reds fell on An Jen Chang, capturing the local Kuomintang commander, dining with his in-laws, on the south bank; while Nanking reenforcements proceeded leisurely—the Reds not expected to emerge for several weeks yet.

This was May, and the great Tatu Ho was in spring flood. It required two hours for the commander's boat, filled with Reds, to cross. The guarding regiment was routed, and for three days three ferries were worked constantly, until nearly a division was across. By the third day, progress had slowed dangerously. Nanking planes were raiding daily, and large concentrations were closing in from the north and southeast. The entire march was bottlenecked here and in danger of being trapped against an impassable river.

About 200 li westward was an ancient chain bridge, and in hasty conference with Lin Piao, Chou Teh, Chou En-lai, and Peng Teh-huai it was decided to attempt its capture. The only alternative was to retraverse Lololand, reenter Yunnan, and march 1,000 miles to cross at Likiang in Tibet.

What followed is as breathless a tale as I have ever heard. To recount the drama of it would be quite out of place here. Marching night and day with only a few ten minute rests, the Red van on the south bank won the 60 mile race against the Nationalist troops on the north who had dispersed the Red "division" already across. The taking of the bridge—after sixty miles forced marching over rocky cliffs and through rocky defiles where a determined Nationalist company could hold off the whole 10,000 of the Red van—was no less dramatic than the race, and abounded with acts of brilliant individual gallantry. The division downstream had re-formed and arrived in time to scatter the guarding regiment—but not before the bridge had been won by the "Heroes of Tatu . . . to whom soldiering was not merely a rice bowl, but youths ready to commit suicide to win." By nightfall on May 30, 1935, the Reds were at Szechuan. The only comment Mao could offer was: "We were always at our best when faced with impossible odds; we knew that there was every reason to believe that we would fail; that is why we did not fail."

Now, in June, they press onward through the militarily "open" country of Szechuan province, where the blockhouse chains had not been extended. Many were to perish in the Ma An Shan pass at 10,000 feet. Great Snow Mountain—rising to 16,300 feet—was of necessity transversed in a single daylight march. As night falls on that peak, violent winds can blow a man off his feet, eccentric pressure drops can asphyxiate a marching man, and he can be "brained" by enormous hailstones. Half the remaining pack animals failed to survive the crossing.

By the 20th of June they had reached northwest Szechuan and effected a rendezvous with the Fourth Front Army of 50,000 under Hsu Hsiang-chien and Chang Kuo-tao, now at Ta-wei. Here Mao and his troops rested for nearly a month. The First, Third, Fifth, Eighth, and Ninth Corps could by this time muster less than half the hundred thousand they began with. By far the greater portion of the difference had been lost as casualties, but still, many had been left along the way in small cadres, to organize local guerrilla groups to harass and divert the Kuomintang flanks. Ho Lung, joined by Hsiao Keh, was particularly active in southern Hunnan, with his Second Army, and was not to be dislodged for a year—and then only after he had received orders to move into Szechuan.

Throughout the March to date, wherever possible, the Reds had armed and fed the peasants, expropriated local landlords, torn up deeds, and redistributed the land. For the Army itself, only the finance section was authorized to apportion spoils. It was, by regulation, informed by radio of all seizures, and thus could assign quantities, on the spot, to various units stretching over a fifty mile line of march.

Since he wanted to establish for the winter in northern Shensi, by the first of August, Mao was feeling the need to move on. He had decided definitely by this time that the northwest was the only place to go with or without the added strength of the Fourth Army. In that area the Communists would be relatively beyond the reach of Chiang, in a position to implement their declaration of war against Japan, and nearer a possible source of material supply from Russia.

Chang, chairman of the Honan-Hupeh-Anhui soviets, was eager to establish Communist power south of Yangtze Ho. Much time and energy might have been spent in argument, had not a rising river between the two forces made it impossible for them to join together had they wanted to. Besides, the ubiquitous Chiang was closing in for a new threatened encirclement.

With the First Corps in the van of an Army of now about 30,000, Mao moved on northward with Chou En-lai, the greater part of the Central Committee of the Communist Party, and the Kiangsi Central Government. Chu Teh was left behind to await the arrival of Ho Lung and the Second Front Army, expected in a year or less.

Chiang was now pressing in, and the western route to Shensi was the only one left open. Along that path lay unmapped country inhabited by savage tribesmen—the Grasslands of the Mantzu.

The Mantzu tribes took to the hills at the advance of the Reds, who for the first time faced a population united in hostility against them. Some few local tribesmen acted as guides, but it usually turned out that these were guiding them into ambush. It was unsafe to venture beyond a hundred yards on either side of the column; many were lost to snipers hiding in the chest-high grass that gives the area its name.

Here, perhaps more than anywhere else on the March, their sufferings were the greatest. The rains converted the ground into a swamp, into which disappeared whole columns at a time. The mud caused painful and poisonous swelling of the flesh, for which the only aid was cold water—the last of the pack animals had sunk into the swamps with the medical supplies. No fire wood was to be found to heat cleansing water or to cook what wheat and vegetables they were lucky enough to find.

Disinhabitation of the land by the Mantzus made foraging almost useless, and dangerous too because of snipers in the grass. Those that fell, ill from the mud or mosquitoes, or wounded, were abandoned; it was simply impossible to carry them on litters where everyone had to fight for survival. Battles were fought for a few head of cattle, and the saying was that one sheep cost the life of one man. As Edgar Snow wrote in *Red Star over China,*

> . . . Their sufferings on this part of the trip exceeded anything of the past. They had money, but could buy no food. They had guns, but their enemies were invisible. As they marched into the thick forests and jungles, and across the head waters of a dozen great rivers, the tribesmen withdrew from the vicinity of the March. They stripped their houses bare, carried off all edibles, drove their cattle and fowl to the plateaus, and simply disinhabited the area. . . .

Mao learned a good deal from the passage through the Grasslands. In a way, one might say that the master guerrilla himself was out-guerrillaed by these primitive people. He was to speak later with admiration of the various forms of camouflage they used. But most importantly, he had learned what it meant to lose 10,000 men to hostile irregulars. As he later wrote:

> Many people think it impossible for guerrillas to exist for long in the enemy's rear. Such a belief reveals a lack of comprehension of the relationship that should exist between the people and the troops. The former may be likened to water and the latter to fish who inhabit it. How may it be said that these two cannot exist together? It is only undisciplined troops who make the people their enemies and who, like the fish out of its native element, cannot live.

Only a few sharp and short engagements remained to be fought with Nanking, Tungpei, and Moslem troops across their projected advance. Theoretically, any one of these groups should have been able to finish them off, but the Reds were too near their goal and had too much invested in the past year to be stopped now. They pushed through with relative ease, and even made up for the lost pack animals by capturing many horses from the Mohammedan cavalry.

On October 20, 1935, the Red Army crossed the border into northern Shensi province, connecting with the Twenty-Fifth, Twenty-Sixth, and Twenty-Seventh Armies, which had maintained a small base there since 1933. Of the Army of one hundred thousand that left Kiangsi just a year before, only 20,000 now remained, and the vast majority of that number were recruits picked up along the way.

To Mao, this largest adaptation of "the wide curve" he had employed in the annihilation drives proved not only the tactical, but the strategic mobility of guerrillas, in escaping beyond the effective reach of the Kuomintang bases in the south:

> A revolution does not march in a straight line. It wanders where it can, retreats before superior forces, advances wherever it has room to advance, and is possessed of enormous patience.
>
> Sometimes it will not be profitable for a unit to become engaged in a certain area, and in that case it must move immediately. When the situation is serious guerrillas must move with the fluidity of water and the ease of the blowing wind. Their tactics must deceive, tempt, and confuse the enemy. They must lead the enemy to believe they will attack from the east and north and they must then strike him from the west and the south. They must strike and then rapidly disperse. They must move at night.

Surely the story I have retold is in some measure responsible for the development of the basic military principles of Red China today. I have tried, in some degree, to show by example how various ancient principles were developed and followed in the early days of the Chinese Communists, and how further the lessons of those days lead to newer development of military thought.

Later practice of these principles in the continuing civil war in China have not as yet been fully analyzed.[6] Little material on the subject has left China and it is classified. But certainly the story in which the leaders of China today played stellar roles is the point of departure for the study and subsequent understanding of the military thought we face in Korea and may yet have to face in all of Asia. "Hence the saying: If you know the enemy and know yourself, you need not fear the result of a hundred battles. If you know yourself and not the enemy, for every victory gained you will also suffer a defeat. If you know neither the enemy nor yourself, you will succumb in every battle," so wrote Sun Tzu 1,500 years ago in his *The Art of War*.

6. But some studies, notably "The Chinese Red Army and Guerrilla Warfare" by Gene Z. Hanrahan [Chapter 3 of this volume] and *Red China's Fighting Hordes* by Lt. Col. R. Rigg, have laid an excellent foundation for further research.

12

Gene Z. Hanrahan

THE CHINESE RED ARMY

AND GUERRILLA

WARFARE

ALTHOUGH THE CHINESE Communist Government is comparatively new, its army has operated as a military fighting entity for the past twenty-three years. Of this period, over nineteen have consisted of a series of individual battles for bare existence, defensive non-positional fighting against, in most cases, superior numbers, equipment and fire power. It is only natural that the Red military minds of China should develop a mobile "unorthodox" theory of fighting, resulting in a complex form of guerrilla warfare well worth serious study by the student of military tactics.

Guerrilla warfare requires three things: a vastness of land and fighting area; a backward nation, made up of essentially rural underdeveloped country; and finally, inadequate communications and transportation facilities.

China fits this formula more exactly than any other you might name; not even excepting the Union of Soviet Socialist Republics. China is a land with more than ninety per cent of its area and population classified as rural.

From *Combat Forces Journal,* February, 1951. Copyright 1951 by Association of the U.S. Army and reproduced by permission.

It has tremendous space and woefully inadequate communications system. Given these conditions guerrilla warfare would be inevitable in China.

The present leader of the Chinese Communist Government, Mao Tsetung, is also the founder of the Chinese Red Army. The Red Army commander, Chu Teh, joined Mao a short time later and has since been in joint control of the Chinese Red forces. Although Mao's military theory developed indigenously, with little foreign influence, Chu Teh is a product of the German military schools. He later, however, turned to the Soviets, whose interests he believed more closely coincided with the existing problems of China.

During the long, protracted period of defensive fighting, both Mao and Chu were drawn more closely to the theory and practice of guerrilla warfare. With the advent of the Sino-Japanese War, the Chinese Red armies developed their guerrilla troops until they reached a high state of military perfection.

In this article I will describe the ideas of the Chinese Red military tactician, and his doctrine of active guerrilla warfare—along with some of the counter measures instituted by the opposing forces who came into contact with this mode of fighting.

To the Chinese Red general, guerrilla warfare consists of three phases. This factor remains constant regardless of the size and scope of the operation. The first phase consists of intelligence, followed by movement, and finally by action.

Intelligence for these guerrilla units consists in a knowledge of the enemy, his movements, supplies and potentialities. Where the organized army makes use of various professional intelligence services, the guerrilla units utilize the peasants and farmers within their particular area of operations. These civilians are organized into a highly developed spy network. Their knowledge of troop concentrations and movements are, with amazing speed, forwarded by mouth to the guerrilla unit commander. This phase also consists of definite overt action by small, individual guerrilla elements which are constantly at work—feigning, harassing outlying elements and cutting means of communication and transportation.

In the second phase the guerrilla unit commander must show unusual ability and daring. His element must execute a series of movements in respect to obtaining a temporary position for an all-out attack or ambush of the enemy forces. The advantage here is maintained by superior knowledge of both the enemy and the terrain, supplemented by the mobility of the unit. Each individual soldier carries only what is absolutely necessary for the individual operation and is hence able to move with surprising speed over the most rugged of terrain. The Chinese Red Army tacticians feel that in their movement phase, the tactical maneuvering that is executed parallels in importance the actual fighting. In his book, *Strategic Problems,* published in 1941, Mao Tse-tung has said, "Our strategy is one against ten, while our tactics can be formulated as consisting of ten against one."

In the final phase the battle is the payoff. However, annihilation and defeat of the enemy is secondary in the individual campaign to the capture of spoils. The unit commander must remember that he is not fighting a war of attrition.

In defensive fighting, one can draw no clean line of demarcation between the guerrilla forces and the larger armies. Both are equally dependent on each other and closely associated with each other. The Chinese Communists make a clear distinction between their terminology of a "guerrilla force" and a group of "individual, armed and organized peasants." An army breakdown of troops would be as follows: (1) regular troops and fighting units; (2) guerrilla forces; (3) armed and organized peasants.

Under satisfactory conditions, the guerrilla forces are integrated as a member of the larger army element. The size of each particular unit is determined by the area covered and the strength of the enemy forces in that specific area. The guerrilla units are commanded by regular army officers who are specifically trained in guerrilla techniques. They organize and run all units on the same basis as that of the regular army. All military operations, whenever possible, are operated under command of higher echelons.[1]

During the Sino-Japanese War, the two large fighting forces of the Chinese Red Army consisted of the Eighth Route Army and the New Fourth Army. The Eighth Route covered an area of approximately four provinces in North China with an estimated population of some thirty million Chinese. The actual organization of the army could be compared to that of an iceberg. The regular personnel of the army directly opposing the Japanese on an established front amounted to approximately a hundred and thirty thousand men. The guerrilla elements of this army, operating behind the Japanese lines, supplemented by armed peasants, consisted of five hundred thousand men.

The New Fourth Army area was spread over three provinces in Central China. In 1941 the estimated strength of this unit, in regular troops, was a hundred and fifty thousand, which in turn was supplemented by a corresponding number of guerrilla units and armed peasants.

Of primary importance is the location of their bases, movements and fighting, all of which were conducted within the Japanese invasion and occupation areas. The statement of Chen-yi, the commander of the New

---

1. We should note that this situation existed only under ideal conditions. Because of the great distance and lack of communications during the Sino-Japanese War, many of these individual units, which had been cut off from the main army for a length of time, degenerated into bandits. The Red Army leaders instituted measures to counteract this by placing political officers with the elements of more dubious loyalty in an attempt to weed out the potential undesirable bandits.

Fourth Army, in regard to his army's operations, conducted wholly behind the Japanese lines, illustrates this point: "Our policy of transferring the invader's rear into fronts and thus reducing the scope of the Japanese occupation to mere points and lines in this region, has achieved great success."

A large army such as the Eighth Route could be termed as mainly a central dispersing and strategy center, facilitating and training smaller units, and maintaining guerrilla zones. The central army headquarters exerted control over all lesser units. The effectiveness of this control varied with the distance, size and loyalty in the respective groups.

The controlling echelons of the army attempted to develop land areas into self-sustaining and fighting entities, which later could assume semi-independent control over the particular fighting units within their command.

All guerrilla operation zones were broken down into guerrilla *bases* and guerrilla *areas*—the essential difference being in the amount of control exerted by the guerrilla forces within their given zone. Those zones which were only under temporary control by the guerrilla units were termed *areas;* those which were maintained in a permanent status, were called guerrilla *bases*. In most cases, guerrilla bases were maintained in mountainous zones. Guerrilla areas included plains and embraced rivers, lakes and harbors. The first mission of the commander of an individual guerrilla base was the extension of his control to plains and the development of the areas into guerrilla bases. Mao Tse-tung realized the difficult task of turning a guerrilla area into a base, and saw that two important tasks had to be completed before this could be accomplished. These tasks were the annihilation of the enemy and the awakening of the masses both in morale and physical support of the guerrilla elements.

The guerrilla base is the most highly developed and complex form of organization for guerrilla warfare. In the overall plan, the base forms the actual rear for the guerrilla forces, and is indispensable for the existence and development of this form of warfare. The Eighth Route Army broke its major control area down into eleven large semi-self-sustaining bases known as "Anti-Japanese Bases." From these bases military, political and civil officers engaged in one or another phase of guerrilla activity. The military spread out and took charge of independent guerrilla units in the area. They trained new troops and attempted to keep contact, as close as possible, with the higher army echelons. The political officers operated in much the same way as in the Soviet Army. They also worked in conjunction with the civil officers supervising and teaching the peasants and farmers sabotage techniques, along with Marxist dogma.

Most of the fighting from these bases and areas consisted of individual small-scale operations. However, these guerrilla engagements developed into intensive battles, and caused the Japanese high command a great deal of trouble. In August, 1940, one of these engagements, known as the

"Hundred Regiments Battle," consisted of a correlated force of 500,000 men, along with the assistance of a 150,000 armed peasants. They smashed the communications and transportation lines throughout North China. This combined operation, estimated by some to be one of the widest guerrilla actions in history, succeeded in disrupting Japanese civilian and military personnel, blowing up seventy-six bridges, destroying two hundred miles of railroad track, 500 miles of highway, nineteen railway stations, eight tunnels, and sixty-seven concrete forts, along with the capture and destruction of large amounts of Japanese weapons and equipment.

It is obvious that the Japanese command realized the disastrous consequences of these extensive guerrilla operations. The Japanese strategy in guerrilla-dominated areas consisted in advancing along railroad lines and capturing strategic points. Their positions were consolidated by pushing forward a network of forts and blockade lines, each a self-sustaining unit, protecting a vital communications or supply area. This however, did not restrict the guerrillas, and they were forced to facilitate this method by adopting semi-guerrilla tactics themselves. They learned to dispatch small, highly mobile elements to offset the guerrilla forces, and at the same time balance their positional elements. They were still under the handicap of lacking adequate knowledge of the movements and headquarters of the enemy and of the terrain.

The Japanese realized the value of the villagers and farmers to the guerrilla units. They knew that the peasants and villagers besides forming a perfect intelligence network, performed other helpful duties for the guerrillas. They cared for the wounded, supplied food and clothing to the soldiers, and served as a means of warning and communication for the individual units. The young men of the villages and farms, when properly indoctrinated into the Communist camp by the civil and political officers, served willingly as soldiers either in the regular Eighth Route Army or in a guerrilla base unit. The Japanese technique of dealing with the villagers and peasants wavered from attempts at wooing them into the Japanese camp by propaganda, to slaughtering wholesale villages of men, women and children as an example to the anti-Japanese elements. Neither produced any effective results.[2]

The extent of the guerrilla activities in North and Central China became so grave that in 1940, of the thirty-six Japanese divisions in China, eighteen were placed in the north to curtail the activities of the Eighth Route Army, and in Central China, the area of the New Fourth Army, the Japanese high command placed four divisions, four independent brigades, and two hundred thousand puppet troops. These puppet troops, most of whom were

---

2. For a time, the Japanese made small, intermediate villages directly responsible for railroad tracks and roads in their area, which were not personally guarded by Japanese troops or forts.

forced or coerced into fighting for the Japanese, were of little value in actual combat.

Following the surrender of Japan, the Chinese Nationalists under Chiang Kai-shek, followed essentially the same strategy as that of the Japanese. The Kuomintang forces, of which there were some twenty divisions wholly or partially equipped by the United States, held the centers and rail points. Here, as in the same case during the Sino-Japanese War, the Red forces held the countryside. Again the theory of extension into guerrilla-dominated areas by operating on lines and points. Had not the Nationalist forces been so corrupted both in morale and fighting efficiency, their development of tactics against the Red guerrilla activity would have been interesting to follow.[3]

Some observers have reported a high correlation between the tactics of the Soviet partisans and those of the Chinese Red guerrillas. Although the Soviets studied the Chinese guerrilla tactics, one can observe some essential differences. The Soviet armies as a whole made little use of their regular troops for actual guerrilla operations. The partisan troops of the USSR would more closely parallel the "armed and organized peasants" of the Chinese Red forces.

The Soviets also made use of extensive forests and swamps to hide and retreat in. In Central and North China there are no swamps and few trees. The guerrillas in this area must rely more on distance, rapid movement and rugged terrain.

The German troops developed a different mode of operations against the Soviet partisan forces. They attempted to surround the enemy partisan units, with an ever diminishing circle consisting of several echelons of troops. The Japanese attempted this early in the war, but failed to realize any satisfactory results.

It is axiomatic that guerrilla warfare is a defensive arm of war and has little use in any offensive operation. It can, however, be used as a means of paving the way for a force that is in the process of changing over from the defensive to the offensive. The Chinese Red Army when attacking, as in the last years of the civil war, had little use for guerrilla operations on a large scale.

In his text, On a Prolonged War, Mao Tse-tung stresses that the Chinese Reds must keep in mind the necessity of casting aside guerrilla defensive war for offensive large-scale mobile war whenever possible. In the area,

---

3. This writer does not wish to take any political sides or assume any definite arguments that led to the defeat of the armies of Chiang Kai-shek. However, it appears evident that the morale of the Nationalist forces fell to such an extent that a majority of their unit casualties in the latter period of the civil war consisted of desertions. Direct sales of weapons and equipment by the Nationalist military forces to the Red Army are reported, even while they were in preparation for battle with these enemy elements.

taken as a whole, the large-scale mobile war is of primary importance. It is only in breaking down the whole into individual component parts, that guerrilla warfare can be utilized effectively.

There appears to have been some obvious fear on the part of Mao that his Red forces, so long on the defensive, would be reluctant to leave their guerrilla warfare technique when engaged in the offensive. The fact that he somewhat overestimated this, however, can be seen in the rapid advance made by the main Chinese Red armies through Central China in pursuit of the retreating Nationalist forces.

At the present time, the need for active guerrilla warfare on the part of the Chinese Reds is almost nonexistent. However, we can logically assume that in the advent of any enemy invasion in force, or a serious defeat of their armies in the field, would be followed by a reversion to their old-time proven guerrilla tactics.

An invasion or occupying force must be prepared to cope with guerrilla activities that would equal or better those in existence during the Sino-Japanese War. The Chinese peasant and farmer, even though he is not a Communist, would side with his own people and government, whatever its kind, against the non-Chinese invader armies. The term *wai kuo jen* (foreigner) still carries as much distrust and suspicion as of old, for the average Chinese.

It would be tantamount to defeat if the occupying and attacking forces in China did not take direct action to counteract guerrilla activities in their areas. The necessary steps to be taken in meeting this situation are too broad and detailed to be handled in this study; however, they deserve consideration both on the strategic as well as the tactical level.

I have only scratched the surface of the problem of guerrilla warfare in underdeveloped areas as pursued by a determined organized military power. I hope others will continue the investigation of this problem in the light of more recent military techniques.

13

Walter D. Jacobs

MAO TSE-TUNG

AS A GUERRILLA

—A SECOND LOOK

*T*HERE IS NO SHORTAGE of commentary on the value of Mao Tse-tung's theory of guerrilla warfare. By some sort of tacit agreement, westerners now accept Mao as the father or at least as the perfector of guerrilla warfare in its modern application.

This agreement deserves a second examination.

First, it should be noted that what Mao was writing about in most cases was not guerrilla warfare but *yu chi chan*. This expression is derived from the root words for (1) travel, roam; (2) strike, attack, rout; and (3) war, battle. The translation "guerrilla warfare" may be a convenient one but it can hardly be viewed as completely accurate.

Association with Chu Teh

Second, it should be noted that Mao's reputation rests on the later success of the Chinese Communists and on Mao's association with Chu Teh.

From *Military Review*, February, 1958, and reproduced by permission.

The success of the Chinese Communists is due to a number of factors, not excluding, but not exclusively, guerrilla warfare.

Mao's collaboration with Chu Teh is the basis for a great number of western commentaries on Chinese concepts of guerrilla warfare.

Chu Teh's early history includes training at the Yunnan Military Academy, a sojourn in Germany (from where he was expelled by the government), a period as an opium addict, and a habit of selling his sword to the highest bidder.[1]

In May, 1928, he combined forces with Mao Tse-tung. The Chu-Mao combination did much to put the Communists in power in China. It provided history with an elaborate example of the supposed unity of theory and practice in that Chu and Mao not only articulated a theory of irregular warfare but executed that theory.

It is suggested that the picture of Mao (and of Chu) as father of a new or universal theory of irregular warfare is as erroneous as the earlier acceptance of Mao and his band as agrarian reformers.

Historical Influences

Western writers have indicated that a number of historical influences had a bearing on the framing of the Chu-Mao concept of irregular warfare.

In her book, *The Great Road: The Life and Times of Chu Teh,* Agnes Smedley cites the influence of Sun Tzu, of the Chinese and Mongol armies of ancient times, and of the Taipings. She recalls that Chu Teh quoted with approval the advice of an old Chinese bandit, who was known as Old Deaf Chu, to the effect that "You don't have to know how to fight; all you have to know is how to encircle the enemy." Miss Smedley maintains that there was little or no Russian influence on Chinese Communist strategy and tactics.

According to Robert Elegant, "the first textbook on large-scale partisan warfare" which was used by Chu was "a short work on the tactics employed by General George Washington."[2] Mr. Elegant continues that Washington's example was particularly apt, because Chu Teh, too, was fighting with inferior forces for the establishment of a new form of government against an unenthusiastic enemy. Since Washington and his Continentals had modeled their tactics or those of the American Indians, presumably of Asian origin, the lesson had come full circle.

According to Haldore Hanson, the fabulous T. E. Lawrence exerted

---

1. These summary remarks on Chu Teh are based on *The Great Road: The Life and Times of Chu Teh,* Agnes Smedley, Monthly Review Press, New York, 1956, *passim.*

2. Robert S. Elegant, *China's Red Masters: Political Biographies of the Chinese Communist Leaders,* Twayne Publishers, New York, 1951, p. 82.

his influence. Mr. Hanson visited the headquarters of General Lu Cheng-ts'ao, the commander of the Central Hopeh guerrillas. In *Humane Endeavor, the Story of the China War,* Mr. Hanson reports that General Lu had a Chinese translation of *Seven Pillars of Wisdom* in his tent and that General Lu and other commanders in China considered Lawrence's work "one of the standard reference books on strategy."

Robert Payne says that Mao Tse-tung and Lawrence of Arabia are the only scholar-soldiers who have fought and won extensive guerrilla campaigns in recent history. In his book, *Mao Tse-tung: Ruler of Red China,* Payne adds, however, that:

> When the Chinese Communists were told of his [Lawrence's] exploits, they were tempted to disbelieve their informant, as though guerrilla warfare was their own invention, the legacy of the 222 wars fought in the "Spring and Autumn Period" and the countless Chinese wars which followed.

Washington, Lawrence, and Old Deaf Chu all may have influenced the Chu-Mao concept of irregular warfare although there is no readily discoverable evidence to indicate that any of them had an overriding influence. A study of the writings of Mao and of the imitative writings of other Chinese Communists prominent in military affairs—such as Chu Teh, Nieh Jung-chen, P'êng Têh-huai, Kuo Hua-jo, and others—indicates that the important influences on the Communist concept of irregular warfare were the situation and the terrain. These influences are clearly evident in the writings of Mao.

Guerrilla Warfare and Environment

Mao emphasized the peculiar Chinese character of his concept in an essay, "Strategic Problems of China's Revolutionary War," in Volume I of his *Selected Works.* He criticized three groups which did not understand that China's revolutionary war "is waged in the special environment of China."

The first group "declare(s) that it is enough to study merely the laws of war in general. . . ." Mao maintained that the laws of war in general should indeed be studied, but "although we must cherish the experiences acquired by people in the past at the cost of their blood, we must also cherish experiences at the cost of our own blood."

The second group suggested that "it is enough to study Russia's experiences of revolutionary war. . . ." "They do not see," said Mao, "that these laws of war and military directives in the Soviet Union embody the special characteristics of the civil war and the Red Army of the Soviet Union." He added that "there are a great number of conditions special to the Chinese revolution and the Chinese Red Army."

The third erroneous group wanted to base its theory on the Northern Expedition of 1926–27. Mao rejected this theory as he contended "we should work out our own measures according to our present circumstances."

Mao summed up the peculiarities of his concept and its design for the situation and terrain in China as follows:

> Thus the difference in the circumstances of wars determines the difference in the guiding laws of wars: the differences of time, place, and character.

> In studying the guiding laws of war of different historical stages, of different characters, of different places, and of different nations, we must keep our eyes on their respective characteristics and their development, and must oppose a mechanical approach to the problem of war.

Basic Principles

Mao stresses that the basic principles of guerrilla warfare can be summarized in the famous slogans of the Chinese Communist Forces:

1. Enemy advances, we retreat.
2. Enemy halts, we harass.
3. Enemy tires, we attack.
4. Enemy retreats, we pursue.

These slogans consist of four Chinese characters each. In an attempt to capture a similar pattern in the English translation, this somewhat awkward form has been produced.

These statements—as well as the influence of time, place, and character —have been elaborated by Mao in "Strategic Problems in the Anti-Japanese Guerrilla War," Volume II, *Selected Works*. This essay is presented as an effort concerning the anti-Japanese war and is not intended as positing general rules for guerrilla warfare. There are, in fact, six specific problems of the anti-Japanese war which are discussed as problems peculiar to the time and place considered by the essay. In addition, Mao, from time to time in the course of the essay, permits himself to speak of warfare in general terms. Since Mao is at such pains to distinguish between the specific and the general, it is only fair that the two not be confounded and a sincere and continuing attempt has been made in that direction in this study.

Specific Problems

As pointed out by Mao in Volume II, the specific strategic problems of the anti-Japanese guerrilla war are:

> 1. On our own initiative, with flexibility and according to plan, carry out offensives in a defensive war, battles of quick decision in a protracted war, and exterior-line operations within interior-line operations.

2. Coordinate with regular warfare.
3. Establish base areas.
4. Undertake strategic defensive and strategic offensive.
5. Develop into mobile warfare.
6. Establish correct relationship of commands.

While describing and developing these six specific problems in the essay, Mao elucidates the following general principles:

1. Conservatism in guerrilla warfare must be opposed.
2. The principle of preserving oneself and annihilating the enemy is the basis of all military principles.
3. Guerrilla warfare is different from regular warfare only in degree and in form of manifestation.
4. The basic principle of guerrilla warfare must be one of offensive, and its offensive character is even more pronounced than that of regular warfare.
5. The offensive is the only means of annihilating the enemy as well as the principal means of preserving oneself, while pure defense and withdrawal can play only a temporary and partial role in preserving oneself and are utterly useless in annihilating the enemy.

Undoubtedly, P'êng Têh-huai thought he was reproducing Mao's thoughts when he told Edgar Snow, "Partisans must not fight any losing battles."[3]

Analysis of Specific Problems

Mao's statements and their mirrorings by such as P'êng are more than blandness. For example, the first specific strategic problem places the task of carrying out offensives in a defensive war and of conducting exterior-line operations within interior-line operations. In an exterior-lines situation principal communications and land are held and the troops are somewhat dispersed. In an interior-lines situation less space is held, the forces are usually encircled, they are more centralized, and hence more easily concentrated.

The anti-Japanese war was purely a defensive one from the Chinese Communist viewpoint and the Communists clearly were weaker than the Japanese. Had the Communists adopted a defensive approach under such conditions, one of two situations would have resulted—the adoption of positional defenses, or the abandonment of opposition to the Japanese. Either situation would have been fatal to the political and military plans of the Communists.

The problem of coodinating guerrilla warfare with regular warfare is viewed by Mao as a problem peculiar to the time and area of the anti-Japanese war. In earlier situations there had been no regular warfare with which to coodinate. In later situations, when guerrilla warfare had transformed itself into mobile warfare and into regular warfare, there would be

---

3. Edgar Snow, *Red Star over China*, Random House, New York, 1938, p. 276.

no guerrilla warfare to be coordinated. The concurrent existence of regular warfare and guerrilla warfare made such coordination possible and, being possible, necessary at this specific time.

The establishment of base areas seems, at first glance, to be incompatible with the concept of guerrilla warfare (or to be more nearly exact, *yu chi chan*). Mao maintains that guerrillas without base areas are roving insurgents and can have no connection with the political aspirations of the indigenous population. The thoroughly political character of Mao's theory makes such a concept anathema. While serving a political purpose, the base area also serves a definite military purpose. They usually were located in the mountains, for obvious military reasons, although Mao did not rule out plains areas. Chu Teh has given a description of the military role of the base areas in his remarks concerning the Wutai mountains area. He said:

> Our regulars can return to such bases for rest, replenishment, and retraining, guerrilla forces and the masses can be trained in them, and small arsenals, schools, hospitals, cooperative and regional administrative organs centered there. From these strongholds we can emerge to attack Japanese garrisons, forts, strategic points, ammunition dumps, communications lines, railways. After destroying such objectives, our troops can disappear and strike elsewhere.[4]

In counseling the guerrillas to undertake strategic defensive and strategic offensive, Mao merely is saying that there will be an alternation of periods during which the guerrillas will be now on the defensive, now on the offensive.

The injunction to develop into mobile warfare goes to the heart of the Mao concept. He views guerrilla warfare as a prelude to regular warfare. The guerrillas will be transformed into regulars. In the best Marxian sense, Mao holds that by increasing their numbers and improving their quality guerrillas will transform themselves into "a regular army which can wage a mobile war."

Discipline Required

The establishment of the correct relationship of commands is synonymous to the establishment of discipline. Guerrilla units traditionally have been notable for their lack of discipline to the disdain and discomfort of commanders at successively higher levels. Mao has maintained elsewhere[5] that "it [discipline] should increase with the size of the unit." Mao is calling for better command control while, at the same time, trying to avoid the restriction of the very essence of the guerrillas—their mobility.

The elimination of the six specific problems of the anti-Japanese guer-

---

4. Smedley, *op. cit.,* p. 360.
5. Quoted in Lieutenant Colonel Robert B. Rigg's *Red China's Fighting Hordes,* The Military Service Publishing Co., Harrisburg, Pa., 1951, p. 226.

rilla war leaves little of a universal nature in the famous Mao essay. The general principles listed here are of such a nature as to make further discussion redundant. Most analyses of Mao's writings on guerrilla warfare give a prominent place to "Strategic Problems in the Anti-Japanese Guerrilla War." This is as it should be for this is Mao's most important work on *yu chi chan.* However, they almost uniformly ignore Mao's own caution that the principles discussed apply to a distinct historical moment and to a definite geographical location. If the strategy and tactics which Mao adopted in the anti-Japanese war are applicable elsewhere, that applicability would seem to contradict Mao's reiterated warning that every historical stage and every geographic site must be considered separately. It is not Mao Tse-tung who urges that Chinese Communist concepts of guerrilla warfare be imitated elsewhere.

Basis of Theory

Mao's contribution was not so much in providing war with "scientific" schemata as it was in recognizing the peculiarities of the time and place in which he operated and in adapting his theory of irregular war to the existing situation.

His theory of war, as outlined in Volume II, was based on the statement that "Every Communist must grasp the truth: 'Political power grows out of the barrel of a gun.'" He maintained that "In China, without armed struggle the proletariat and the Communist Party could not win any place for themselves or accomplish any revolutionary task." His concept of irregular warfare evolved from these assumptions.

Guerrilla warfare was never suggested by Mao as a desirable or eternal form of war. He freely and frequently deprecated it. In 1936 he said:

> This guerrilla character is precisely our distinguishing feature, our strong point, our means for defeating the enemy. We should prepare to discard this character, but we cannot yet discard it today. Someday this character will definitely become a thing to be ashamed of and therefore to be discarded, but today it is invaluable and must be firmly retained.

Conclusion

Mao made a virtue of necessity. His theory of warfare, in general, and his theory of irregular warfare, in particular, were adapted to the circumstances of his time and place. The success which crowned the efforts of Mao and the Chinese Communists should not induce observers to discover elements which are, in fact, not there. Mao's theory has universal applicability only in its repeated warnings that every situation must be considered in the frame of its historic development and geographic setting.

Further References

BOOKS

Band, C. and William. *Two Years with the Chinese Communists*. New Haven: Yale University, 1948 (London: *Dragon Fangs*. Allen & Unwin, 1947).

Bertran, J. M. *Unconquered: Journal of a Year's Adventure among the Fighting Peasants of North China*. New York: John Day, 1939 (London: *North China Front*, Macmillan, 1939).

Carlson, E. F. *Twin Stars over China*. New York: Dodd, 1940.

———. *The Chinese Army: Its Organization*. New York: Institute of Pacific Relations, 1940.

Epstein, I. *The People's War*. London: Gollancz, 1939.

Fitzgerald, C. P. *Revolution in China*. London: Cresset, 1952.

Gelder, S. *The Chinese Communist*. London: Gollancz, 1946.

Homer, J. *Dawn Watch in China*. Boston: Houghton, 1941.

Lao Pin Pei. *It's Dark Underground*. New York: Putnam, 1946.

Lindsay, M. *The North China Front*. London: China Campaign Committee, 1947.

Liu, F. F. *A Military History of Modern China: 1924–1949*. Princeton, N.J.: Princeton University, 1956.

Mao Tse-tung. *On the Protracted War*. Peking: Foreign Language, 1954.

———. *Strategic Problems in the Anti-Japanese Guerrilla War*. Peking: Foreign Language, 1960.

Mao Tse-tung on Guerrilla Warfare. Tr. by S. B. Griffith. New York: Praeger, 1961.

Mowrer, E. A. *The Dragon Wakes: A Report from China*. New York: Morrow, 1939.

Rigg, R. B. *Red China's Fighting Hordes*. Harrisburg, Pa.: Military Service Publishing Co., 1951.

Simpson, B. L. *The Fight for the Republic of China*. New York: Dodd, 1937.

Smedley, A. *Battle Hymn of China*. New York: Knopf, 1938.

Snow, E. *The Battle for Asia*. New York: Random House, 1941.

———. *Red Star over China*. New York: Random House, 1944.

Sues, J. R. *Shark's Fins and Millet*. New York: Doubleday, 1944.

Suigo, C. *In the Land of Mao Tse-tung*. London: Allen & Unwin, 1953.

Sun Tzu Wu. *The Art of War*. Tr. by Lionel Giles. Harrisburg, Pa.: Military Service Publishing Co., 1953.

Stratton, R. O. *Saco—The Rice Paddy Navy*. Pleasantville, N.Y.: Palmer, 1950.

Tipton, L. *Chinese Escapades*. London: Macmillan, 1949.

Warner, Denis. *Hurricane from China*. New York: Macmillan, 1961.

———. *Out of the Gun*. London: Hutchinson, 1956.

White, T. H., and A. Jacoby. *Thunder out of China.* New York: Sloane, 1946.
Wint, G. *Dragon and Sickle: How Communist Revolution Happened in China.* London: Pall Mall, 1959.

ARTICLES

Arlington, H. "North China Patrol," *Marine Corp Gazette,* June, 1949.
Carlson, E. F. "The Unorthodox War Continues," *Amerasia,* March, 1939.
————. "Whither China?," *Amerasia,* December, 1939.
Chang, Y. "China Not All Red Yet," *Saturday Evening Post,* June 30, 1951.
Fuller, F. F. "Mao Tse-tung: Military Thinker," *Military Affairs,* Fall (November), 1958.
Griffith, S. B. "Organization for Guerrilla Hostilities in China," *Marine Corps Gazette,* September, 1941.
Guelzo, C. M. "The Communist Long War," *Military Review,* December, 1960.
Kalischer, P. "I Raided Red China with the Guerrillas," *Collier's,* March 28, 1953.
Mansfield, W. R. "Ambush in China," *Marine Corps Gazette,* March, 1946.
Mao Tse-tung. "Mao's Primer on Guerrilla War," tr. by S. B. Griffith and condensed by the *New York Times Magazine,* June, 1961.
"Mao's Strategy and Tactics," *Atlas,* June, 1961.
Miles, Milton E. "U.S. Naval Group China," *U.S. Naval Institute Proceedings,* July, 1946.
Nihart, F. B. "Mao's Strategic Defensive," *Marine Corps Gazette,* November, 1952.
Rigg, R. B. "Campaign for the Northeast China Railway System," *Military Review,* December, 1947.
————. "How the Chinese Communists Wage War," *Infantry Journal,* February, 1949.
Rudolph, J. W. "Partisan Warfare," *Infantry Journal,* January–February, 1940.
Smith, C. R. "Military Lessons from the Chinese-Japanese War," *Military Engineer,* January–February, 1940.
Taylor, G. E. "The Hegemony of the Chinese Communist, 1945–1950," *Annals of the American Academy of Political and Social Sciences,* September, 1951.
Yen Hsi Shan. "The Fundamental Principle of China's Guerrilla Warfare," *Modern China Monthly,* December, 1950.

DOCUMENTS

Air Force. Directorate of Intelligence. Stewart AFB, N.Y.:
   Guerrilla Organization on the Chinese Mainland, no. 62, 9p., 1951.
Department of the Army. Collection and Dissemination Branch. Washington, D.C.:
   Chinese Communist Guerrilla Tactics, ed. and tr. by G. Z. Hanrahan. 134p., 1952.
Department of State. Office of Intelligence Research, Washington, D.C.:
   Chinese Irregular Forces in Burma, ORO Report no. 6507, 23p., 1954.

PART 4 THE PHILIPPINES —POST-WORLD WAR II

While the majority of the Filipino people were enjoying a hard-won, well-earned peace after World War II, Communist elements were waging a covert war. They began by exploiting the widespread social disorganization that can follow any major war. The Philippine government was pictured by Communist propagandists as an incompetent body that cared little for the problems of the average man. The Communists made special appeals to the farmers, the majority of whom were suffering from the shortage of farm implements.

By 1951 the Communists built up a guerrilla force numbering close to 10,000. Using the terrorist tactics advocated by Lenin, they began widespread attacks on villages, kidnapped dignitaries, and placed political informers and commissars in virtually all of the towns. Communist guerrillas ambushed government troops and designated certain areas as guerrilla owned.

The first government reaction was an all-out military offensive. Later, as it became obvious that military measures in and of themselves would not solve the problem, the government put into effect a larger program, a program that took into consideration the social, political, economic, and psychological conditions then existing. Only by carrying out a broad program of social and economic progress in connection with renewed military offensive was the Communist guerrilla movement in the Philippines actually destroyed.

One important factor in successful counter-guerrilla operations that is not spelled out in the subsequent articles is explained by a Philippine Army officer who fought the communist guerrillas:[1]

Foreign troops are certain to be less welcome among the people than are the regular armed forces of their own government. The local populations will shelter their own people against operations of foreign troops, even though those they shelter may be outlaws. For this reason, native troops

---

1. L. A. Villa-Real, "Huk Hunting," *Combat Forces Journal*, November, 1954, is an excellent account of counterguerrilla operations in the Philippines.

would be more effective than foreign forces in operations against native Communist conspirators. It would be rare, indeed, if use of foreign troops would not in itself doom to failure an antiguerrilla campaign.

Hammer's article provides a concise review of some of the historical events necessary to a thorough understanding of the postwar crises in the Philippines. Bashore recounts the salient features of the Communist offensive and explains the Philippine government's countermeasures. He also presents a valuable portrait of Ramon Magsaysay, the late president of the Republic of the Philippines, whose courage and love of freedom played such a large role in the eventual defeat of the Communists. Finally, Tirona, former chief of the Philippine air staff, analyzes Communist tactics applied in his country. He describes in detail, from his own experience, how and why the Philippine government's counterguerrilla program operated so successfully.

14

Major Kenneth M. Hammer   **HUKS IN THE**
U.S. Air Force

PHILIPPINES

W HEN THE JAPANESE invaded the Philippines in World War II, the people took the occupation in their stride. Although the people realized that their arms were defeated, they faced the situation with the typical self-confidence that is characteristic of an agricultural community reliant on the family and village system. They maintained an admirable solidarity.

In central Luzon the peasant fought. During the day he took up his plow. During the night he struck. Central Luzon became a no man's land for the aggressor. Out of this first struggle was born the Hukbalahap (Huks), the peasant militant movement of resistance. This organization became the chief concern of the Japanese police and the puppet government.

The leader of the Huks was Luis Taruc, a Filipino born of peasant stock. He participated in forming the Huk movement which was conceived in December, 1941, and formally organized on 29 March 1942 at Cabiao on the Pampanga border. "Hukbalahap" is a word coined from the syllables

Reprinted from *Military Review*, April, 1956, by permission.

of the Tagalog title *Hukbo Na Bayan Laban Sa Hapon,* or People's Army (to Fight) against Japan. The original group of Huks were Communists, intellectuals, politicians, and army personnel. A report to Colonel Gyles Merrill, a guerrilla leader, in March, 1944, stated that the Huk "numbers among its members an estimated 30 percent of properly inducted United States Army Forces Far East men."

The Huks attempted cooperation with other guerrilla forces in central Luzon. On 21 May 1942 Luis Taruc effected liaison with Lieutenant Colonel Claude Thorp who was then in command of other guerrilla activities in central Luzon. With Taruc, Thorp drew up a plan of resistance to harass the enemy rear and "make this island uninhabitable for the enemy."

Coordination

Efforts to coordinate the guerrilla forces were pressed and on 7 July 1942 Colonel Thorp's staff entered into agreement with the Huk military committee to form a joint guerrilla command in central Luzon. Main points of the accord were mutual collaboration with the establishment of a central headquarters of the Central Luzon Command, independent action of the Huk on organizational or political matters, and mutual assistance between the guerrilla units on military supplies and equipment.

When Colonel Thorp was captured by the Japanese and executed at Tarlac, the pact did not materialize. Thorp's successor, Colonel Merrill, kept in touch with Taruc because he recognized the fighting ability of the Huks and was anxious to coordinate guerrilla activities.

The political activities of the Huks brought about many clashes with other guerrilla groups. Conflicts with other guerrilla units were frequent and by mid-1944 the Huks were actively fighting their guerrilla neighbors. When they realized that the other guerrilla forces were receiving arms and equipment from the Americans, the rivalry flared into open warfare. For example, there was a clash between the Huk squadron under Colonel Cantindig and the San Isidro unit of Anderson's guerrillas under Irineo Alberto which broke out in March, 1945, at San Isidro, Nueva Ecija. The fighting lasted three days and was ended by the arrival of the American forces.

The relations between the United States Forces in the Philippines (USFIP) under Merrill and the Huks deteriorated, however, despite the efforts of Merrill and Huk leaders to come to a common understanding. This was partly due to the tactlessness of officers under Merrill's command whose air of superiority was resented by Huk leaders. The basic issue was, of course, political. Terming the puppet officials, rich landowners, and pro-American Filipinos as "tools of imperialism" and "instruments of capitalism," the Huks directed much of their efforts toward elimination of these elements which they believed would be an obstacle to the attainment of their political and economic motives.

Lieutenant Colonel Roy Tuggle, United States Army, who was assistant to the executive officer of the USFIP, wrote the Huks a few days before the Leyte landing. He said:

> Any organization which fails to cooperate will be regarded by incoming troops as unlawful armed bands . . . United States Army does not recognize any political aims or ambitions and it is the position that in time of war, the only political activity which is legal is political activity aimed at maintenance of the loyalty of the masses of the established, the legal government.

The efforts of reconciling the USFIP and the Huks continued until the American landing on Luzon in January but deep-rooted suspicions already separated the groups. Tuggle wrote Taruc on 16 January 1944:

> I am instructed to also issue warning to all guerrilla units that the killing of any person or the taking of any Filipino, except in case that person may be proved beyond all question of doubt to have attacked with armed force or to have actually betrayed the guerrilla cause to the enemy, will be considered murder or kidnapping with threat to murder.

Attacks on Japanese

During 1942 and 1943 the Huks had made attacks on Japanese shipments, garrisons, and convoys and some disruption of the enemy supply line to Manila from the north was achieved. They were most active in the year 1943 when other guerrilla units were inactive in accordance with orders from General Headquarters, Southwest Pacific Area.

The Huks had a fighting strength of at least 5,000 men, 10,000 lightly armed reserves, and about 35,000 unarmed reserves. Most of their original arms were obtained from Bataan or captured from the Japanese. By February, 1945, when Manila was liberated, the Huks had killed about 25,000 Japanese spies and collaborators. It had fought over 1,200 engagements with the enemy and puppet constabulary. During the liberation campaign in Luzon the Huks helped the American operations and contributed in no small degree to the final defeat of the Japanese. At the end of the war little interest was shown by the United States Army in recognizing Huk units and the peasants themselves lost interest when they saw the opportunistic groups and even collaborationist elements being recognized and rewarded with back pay by the United States Army. The nonrecognition of the Huk fighting forces and the later hostility of Army authorities toward the Huk organization, because of the Marxist tendencies of its leaders, caused bitter resentment among the Huks.

The United States Army Counter Intelligence Corps arrested Taruc and Casto Alejandrino on charges of murder and sedition and kept them in jail for over seven months at the end of World War II. Casto Alejandrino is a fanatical, able, energetic, and brutal Communist and the son of one of the largest and most oppressive landowners on Luzon. Alejandrino was released first and turned over to the Philippine Commonwealth authorities for prosecution. No case was found against him and his release was ordered. With Alejandrino released the Army authorities then released Taruc. Both men capitalized on their arrest and the failure of their men to receive back pay; they immediately resumed command of the Huks and continued to carry on their political and economic movements which now were directed toward the landlords, the constabulary, and the Philippine Army. What then did the Huk want? Their goals included the elimination of collaborators from positions of power and the broadening of democracy in the Philippines by the increased participation of the workers in the government. They wanted to be independent and not enslaved peons. They wanted to own the land that they tilled and the crops they harvested. The root of unrest in the Philippines was and is the fact that the autocracy of the Philippines imposed its own solution to the problems of another class, the peasants. To understand this it is necessary to examine the status of the peasant. The late Manuel Quezon said in 1938 of the Filipino worker:

> As he works from sunrise to sundown, his employer get richer while he remains poor. He has to drink the same polluted water his ancestors drank for ages. Malaria, dysentery, and tuberculosis still threaten him and his family at every turn. His children cannot go to school, or if they do, they cannot finish the whole primary instruction.

As late as 1940 the majority of Filipinos lived under an agricultural system based on feudal practices. Millions of peasants were still bound to the soil in a state no better than peonage with the average daily wage of the agricultural worker being 22 cents. The census showed that 1.3 percent of the population owned the large farms with an area of 20 hectares (about 50 acres) or more. The landlords collect from 20 to 22 percent a year on their investment. In the Philippines even today 1.5 million farm families are below the subsistence level—small wonder that there is serious agrarian discontent in the provinces.

Little Accomplished

President Quezon, a landlord in his own right, sought remedial legislation but little was accomplished because he failed to recognize that the farmer could not make a decent living under a 50-50 crop division. President Osmena tried to meet this problem after the liberation. In September, 1945, he named a cabinet committee which brought together the landlords and tenants and a 60-40 crop division was adopted. This was a good beginning for a program of progressively increasing the tenant's share to enable him to live decently.

The Quezon administration did find one practical solution to the tenancy problem which was the purchase by the Government of the large estates and their resale to the tenants on the installment plan. They also undertook the program of land resettlement projects in Mindanao, the most successful of which was the Koronadal Valley Project. The Government "transplanted" about 2,000 peasants and their families to Koronadal in 1951 and the settlers transformed the valley into a self-sufficient agricultural colony. The Economic Development Corps opened 2,960 hectares (about 75,000 acres) in Kapatagan, Lanao, in February, 1951, and of 89 families that have resettled there, 55 are Huk families. The land projects opened by the Armed Forces of the Philippines at Kapatagan, Lanao, have succeeded in bringing about some of the needed reform. But Kapatagan will become an idle dream unless the Government follows through with proper legislative action to expand land ownership.

In 1949 the Huk name was changed to *Hukbo Ng Mapagpalaya Sa Bayan*, the HMB or People's Liberation Army. The HMB campaign scored successes following the 1949 balloting. Taking advantage of the low morale of the people, it launched a series of determined attacks against the Government, raiding weakly defended towns, kidnapping authorities, and placing organizers in captured territory for espionage, kidnapping, and recruiting activities. The HMB bands swept through central Luzon villages seizing arms and supplies.

The situation grew worse to the point where conditions in the Philippines were considered gravely critical. Although the HMB was apparently not strong enough in force to undertake the overthrow of the Government directly, it possessed the capabilities to command any given situation by its hit-and-run tactics.

By 1950 the HMB numbered at least 20,000 and roamed at will over much of Luzon. They were well armed and under the control command of an astute Politburo operating from Manila. By April, 1950, the Huks had spread from central Luzon to other provinces providing a serious threat to the very existence of the state. In some places they levied taxes, ran their schools and newspapers, and maintained a group of production centers.

Ramon Magsaysay

But the press was still free and critical, the inaudible masses were eager for better conditions, and there were still a few incorruptible politicians. Among them was Ramon Magsaysay.

He had studied engineering at the University of the Philippines. Later he took a job as a mechanic with a bus company and advanced to become its general manager. At the time the war broke out he went to work for the United States Army and ended the war as commander of a guerrilla army of 10,000. In 1950, as Chairman of the House National Defense Committee, he attacked his own party, the Liberals, demanding a real fight against the HMB.

His actions caught the eyes of Manila's newspapers who supported him. President Quirino was diplomatically persuaded that a cleanup of the army and constabulary was overdue, and that Congressman Magsaysay was just the man for it.

Magsaysay got the job. A reorganization of the entire Armed Forces was begun in September, 1950, to create a more effective combat force to meet the critical situation. He took to his role as a man of action. He combed the army for corrupt officers, promoted good officers, and put a revitalized force into the field, with one mission, "kill Huks." The Philippine Constabulary (which was held in distrust by the people because of the abuses it had committed) was reduced in strength and its troops were absorbed in the new Armed Forces. The army expanded from 10 battalion combat teams to 21 with a total strength of 22,500 officers and men.

To the demoralized population in HMB country, Magsaysay sent civil officers to explain the new army and to solicit their support. He posted rewards for Huks, dead or alive, and saw to it that they were paid. He went after the Huks with their own tricks. They picked at army communications with phony messages and fake letters; Magsaysay disrupted their communications even more with the same tactics and with sharp, well-planned forays.

But most important of all he struck at the source of the HMB strength, the social conditions that make them what they are. He sent out word that all who surrendered would be spared, and offered each Huk 10 hectares (about 25 acres) and a Government-built house in a liberal resettlement program in the fertile underpopulated island of Mindanao. "They are fighting the Government because they want a house and land of their own," said Magsaysay. "All right, they can stop fighting, because I will give it to them." The Huks began to come in, at first a trickle, then by the hundreds.

The HMB is still a force to be reckoned with, although large areas of the country have been pacified. They are no longer a threat to Manila, or along the main highways through central Luzon. A number of the powerful leaders have been rounded up or killed. Magsaysay paid over 8,000 pesos to an informer who notified him of the Manila hideout of the Communist Politburo for the islands. The mass arrest of 105 members of the Politburo (including five members of the Secretariat) was made and the HMB underground in Manila was virtually wiped out. At least two HMB regional commands have been disbanded. A total of 70,000 pesos was paid for the roundup of 18 HMB commanders on the island of Panay. With their capture the HMB movement on Panay collapsed. When Magsaysay took over the Huks numbered an estimated 16,000. Now there are less than 8,000. Luis Taruc, the dyed-in-the-red general of the rebellion with a 100,000 pesos price on his head, became so distrustful of his own comrades that he would let only his family approach him. Taruc surrendered in May, 1954, and was tried and sentenced to 12 years' imprisonment. A price of 130,000 pesos was offered for the capture of Jesus Lava, the Communist leader.

The remaining tasks for the Philippines still loom formidable and difficult. In the military sphere the army must destroy the hard core of the HMB movement—Lava and Alejandrino—to render the dissidents impotent. In the socioeconomic field additional reforms are needed to further eliminate the inequalities, poverty, misery, and injustices from which the dissident movement sprang to life and on which it continues to grow.

15

Major Boyd T. Bashore   **DUAL STRATEGY**
U.S. Army

FOR LIMITED WAR

*T*HE PLANE ROARED FORWARD IN THE MOONLIGHT and lifted from the palm and bamboo fringed airstrip. Painted in white script on the polished aluminum nose of the C-47 was the name Mount Pinatubo—the dominant peak in the Province of Zambales north of Bataan. Here, Ramon Magsaysay, as a young guerrilla leader, fought the World War II Japanese occupation troops.

Minutes later in a violent blinding crash 3,000 feet high on the jungle-covered slopes of another Philippine mountain, Ramon Magsaysay—President of the Republic of the Philippines for almost three and a half years —died. Perhaps more than any other single event in recent years this tragic accident marked the end of one of the most ignored wars in military history; marked the end of an era of approximately 11 years which was a milestone not only for the Philippines, but for the entire Free World.

Unfortunately, perhaps, it also marked the beginning of an era during which, more and more, variations of the type of war that Ramon Magsaysay fought may become the only mode of conflict possible for ground

Reprinted from *Military Review*, May, 1960, by permission.

armies operating within the twin shadows of the aggressive ambitions of world communism and the forced atmosphere of tranquilization generated by the presence of tactical and strategic nuclear weapons—the age of limited wars.

Lieutenant General James M. Gavin, Retired, in his book, *War and Peace in the Space Age,* predicts:

> In fact this is the most probable nature of future war, a slow, almost imperceptible transition of a bad economic and political situation into internal disorder. Arms will be provided by the Communists to the side they choose, and sometimes which side they choose is not very important. They will throw out the original leaders and substitute their own, including their own revolution of the "proletariat" at a time of their choosing. Thereafter, sufficient force will be used, until combatting it no longer seems worth the effort to the West, or until the West is decisively defeated.

This is, in effect, one important phase of the classic Communist concept of "protracted war" as formulated by Mao Tse-tung. This is *almost* what happened in the Philippines.

Study Desirable

Americans should study the Communist campaign which was waged in the Philippines because it may be a harbinger of a type of warfare to come, a classic example of one type of limited war. In addition, it should be studied because Magsaysay won his war and thus became the only democratic leader in Asia, and one of the few in the world, who for all intents and purposes completely defeated an *overt* communistic armed rebellion in his country.

Today, 600 miles west of the Philippines, the mainland of China lays totally under Red domination, a festering cancer which is spewing out the germs of world communism and encouraging neutralism throughout all of Asia. To the north, Korea remains divided—north and south—both sides glaring covetously toward the 38th Parallel, the split breeding all the hatred and frustration that an unfinished war can produce. To the west, Indochina also lies divided with North and South Vietnam, like Korea, the frustrated victims of an unfinished war and a distasteful compromise truce of the type that may become progressively more frequent in the peripheral or brush fire type war.

Of all the countries of Asia which have been subjected not only to the theoretical siren's song, but also the flaying fists of international communism, only the democratic Philippines has emerged *completely* victorious. This is a free undivided nation which certainly is no question mark on the ledger; a nation that has not had to weaken its government by compromise and accept a split country or dual leadership with the Reds.

The Republic of the Philippines is, in fact, one of the few countries in Southeast Asia which have dared to outlaw the Communist Party within the shadow of the slumbering Chinese dragon.

By 1953 the backbone of the Hukbalahap, the Tagalog name for the military arm of the Philippine Communist Party—the Huks for short—had been broken effectively as a serious threat to the freedom of the Philippines. But as a result of a series of Huk atrocities as late as the spring of 1956, Magsaysay suspended all training and schooling in the Philippine Army. He deployed the 26 battalion combat teams of the army into the field throughout Central Luzon. This campaign was meant once and for all to bring the Communists to heel.

On the day Magsaysay died, 17 March 1957, the Philippine armed forces still were engaged in this anti-Huk peace-and-order campaign, although admittedly the effectiveness of their purely military combat operations was coming to the end. That this final campaign was essentially successful can be seen in the fact that in the spring of 1958, one year after Magsaysay's death, the reorganized Philippine Army conducted its first joint division-size maneuver since before World War II. For the first time since the founding of the new Republic, the Philippine Army is out of the business of fighting Huks, stripped of its internal security mission, and is beginning to take its place as an available force in the Southeast Asia Treaty Organization (SEATO).

Significance

It may be significant that the government which won this particular war was neither a true nor a constitutional monarchy; neither a "democratic" dictatorship nor a colonial government controlled from a distant parent nation. This war was won by the only nation in Asia, and perhaps the world, which has a republican government that is somewhat like our own, modified only by the realities of the country itself, its geography, and the heritage and temperament of its people.

Political, economic, technological, psychological, and sociological factors, of course, are all extremely important, and must be considered in any realistic appraisal of the history of this Huk compaign. These are the *strategic* factors of the cold war. Unless each individual government, no matter what its form, can offer the majority of its people something better than communism, then the bitter seeds of communism will continue to nourish and grow. Under our concept of government and world aid these internal factors, no matter how important they may be in the outcome of the struggle, cannot be controlled by the American statesmen and military men whom we entrust with the responsibility of winning this cold war. Essentially, we are pledged to support the *status quo*. As differentiated from the Communists in their protracted war, we are *not* committed to the principle of making over other nations and governments in our own image.

Robert Strausz-Hupé has stated:

> The West has neither a doctrine of protracted conflict nor an international conspiratorial apparatus for executing it. What is more, we do not want such a doctrine or such a political apparatus, for it would be a tragic piece of irony if the men of the Free World, in trying to combat the communist, should become like them.

Thus these most important factors remain only the internal responsibilities of the people of a nation themselves, their political, economic, and religious leaders. As Americans we must concern ourselves not so much with these strategic factors, as with the *tactical* aspects of winning this type war. Unfortunately, we will see that in Magsaysay's kind of war the strategy and tactics sometimes become so intermingled that they cannot be considered separately.

Bitter War

The Huk campaign was a war as bitter, unglamorous, and thankless as any ever fought. It was guerrilla warfare at its worst. Countryman was pitted against countryman. It was a war in which the rules of land warfare and the Geneva Convention were unknown. Often it showed itself only in criminal acts such as extortion, kidnapping, and murder. It was fought by an enemy who varied from a single sniper in the cogon grass to battalion-size organizations—an enemy who seldom wore uniforms or markings, only the local civilian dress, and who one minute could appear to be a peaceful farmer or worker, and then the next minute could become a dangerous killer. No neat order of battle showed on the map with the traditional armies, corps, and divisions squared-off symmetrically against each other. It was certainly a hot war, but one in which at times all the expensive machinery of modern warfare—the airplanes, the tanks, and the heavy artillery and trucks—stood by idle. They were not worth the services of a single planted informer who would empty his carbine into the sleeping bodies of the Huks who mistakenly might have accepted him as one of them.

Militarily this was initially a war of company and battalion-size units. Patrols and check points were spread out at great distances from one another, searching for and sometimes finding and fighting an illusive enemy who usually had all the advantages of fighting or not depending on his whim—an enemy who further chose his own time and place for the scrap with infinite care. In its later phases, in between small unit clashes which became less and less frequent, it degenerated primarily into a war of intelligence and psychology.

A student of today's changing military doctrine immediately will see certain sketchy similarities between the spreadout fluid war that the Filipinos fought initially and some of the tactics that are beginning to emerge as the accepted techniques of the United States Army in nuclear warfare. Certainly, there were no new "principles of war" developed in this Huk conflict, but the emphasis that was laid on the various time-worn principles is interesting and unique in many cases, as were the methods of application.

Review of History

Before studying the tactical and strategic lessons learned during this Huk campaign, it would be well to review the history of the Philippines briefly. In order to understand this civil war, one also must be aware of the fairly well-known goals of international communism, something of the Filipino people, and what came before the years 1946–57.

The Filipinos, individually and in small bands, have desired and fought continually and bravely for freedom since before Chief Lapu Lapu killed Magellan within a few miles of where Magsaysay's plane crashed. And yet, due to the caprice of nature which divided their country into 7,000 islands, and all that such a configuration has meant since the dawn of history to communications, ethnics, and national unity, they have been for years essentially a divided people and, consequently, more easily subjugated to imperialism and colonialism of various types. China, Spain, America, and Japan at one time or another have controlled all or major portions of the islands, and each country in its own way has fanned the same sparks of nationalism among Filipinos that are burning fiercely elsewhere throughout the Far East from India to Korea.

A detailed study of why the seeds of communism grew in the Philippines will not be attempted here. Some knowledge of this local brand of Philippine communism, however, is necessary to understand the initial mistakes that were made in combating it and the tactical principles that finally were successful.

Philippine communism was married officially to international communism some time between 1928 and 1930 with the foundation of the Communist Party of the Philippines (CPP). The CPP was admitted to the Comintern in 1932. The seeds of this movement probably were sown in 1920 during the Congress of the People's of the East at Baku, when the Communists met with the ultranationalists from all over Asia and attempted to breed communism with nationalism and anticolonialism. The seeds were nourished locally in the Philippines by the same discontent

which had bred communism in other countries throughout the world—
poverty, lack of work, exploitation of people in certain classes, and perhaps
an intellectual class with no place to go.

Major Differences

There were, however, major differences between the Communist movement that occurred in the Philippines and the "pure" Marxist revolution
that the intellectuals felt should occur. The economy of the Philippines is
primarily agricultural even today. Because the industrial revolution has
not yet profoundly affected the island's economy, there is only an extremely small class of industrial "workers." As envisioned by Karl Marx,
of course, the Communist revolution will evolve in various countries
throughout the world as a result of the subjugation of the new working
class, the industrial proletariat.

Lacking this force base of discontented workers, the Filipinos, as in
other agrarian countries, seriously had to modify the theory of pure Marxian communism and attempt to evolve their own brand.

This requirement was not new. At the time of her revolution, Russia
was largely agricultural; China is today. The successful revolutions in these
agrarian countries have exposed the fallacy of pure Marxist communism.
The fact that the successful "revolutions" have occurred in the nonindus-
trial countries, while the peoples of the truly industrial nations have held
aloof, has led to the acceptance of the modified Leninist concept of communism which basically substitutes the struggles between states and peoples
for the struggle between classes. This Leninist concept, after a considerable
incubation period, is the modern-day popular brand of international communism practiced by Russia.

In evolving a popular nationalistic brand of communism, the Filipinos
have not been so successful as their international compatriots. During the
early years the leaders of the local party continued the classic strength-
sapping internal debate between Marxist purists and "heretics" about
whom should form their "mass" base—the farmers or the workers?

For years the democratic Filipino was fortunate to have this senseless
internal debate raging within the Communist Party, a factor which retarded
the spread of communistic theory to the masses during the early years.
Essentially, communism first was limited to leaders of the peasants and
factory workers who debated furiously among themselves. This debate
lasted almost up to the beginning of World War II.

The impoverished Filipino tenant farmers who live in the rice and
coconut growing provinces north and south of Manila, however, long
have been ripe for some type of "revolution," whether economic, socio-

logical, or industrial. For years they were subjected to many forms of abuse by various factions. The people still are poor, they are discontented, and naturally they want to better themselves and their lot. This is human nature. This also is a cause and the effect of modern Philippine communism. The field long has been ripe for something—anything.

Fighting Qualities

The volatile Filipinos have never loathed a fight. As a rule they are fearless individual fighters, proud and sensitive, cunning, generally in good physical condition, and unrelenting and aggressive in the clinch. The Filipinos fought the Chinese pirates, they fought the Spaniards, they fought the Americans, and they fought the Japanese. Approximately 500 minor and 25 major disjointed uprisings occurred prior to the time the Filipinos finally were given their sovereignty. The fighting spirit certainly was not lacking. What was lacking, in the early days, perhaps, was a strong leader with ability to unify and the facilities to communicate. And the greatest "failure" of all in the sphere of international relations at any time was the simple crime of being too weak industrially to demand and get their way. In spite of Communist claims to the contrary, these first Filipino rebellions—whatever they lacked in coordination and unification with one another—certainly were not communistic in nature. Few of the fighters had any goals other than freedom or personal power. The rebellions were the effects of a growing nationalism, not communism.

When the United States quite unexpectedly and unintentionally found herself guardian of the Philippines at the end of the Spanish-American War, we fell heir to these problems. Unwittingly we perpetuated many of the social and economic abuses under the Treaty of Paris in which we guaranteed that the economic *status quo* in the islands would remain essentially unchanged. This can neither be held for nor against us. In those days of colonialism, "total war" was unknown and we could hardly have been termed a nation bent on revolutionizing the existing economic situation in any country.

With the fall of the Spanish, because of what we considered to be a lack of any capable national Philippine government, we gradually developed the sound national policy of educating and training the Filipinos toward eventual self-government and independence. This sociological goal we lived up to faithfully.

During this period of American control, the small elite nucleus of the CPP continued to grow and operate under various guises, even though driven underground in October, 1932, when the Supreme Court of the Philippines declared the CPP illegal.

When the Japanese occupied the Philippines in World War II, there was little question but that the Filipinos would continue to fight wherever possible. This they did. They fought under their own local democratic leaders—Lim, Magsaysay, and Garcia. They fought under Americans like Anderson, Volckman, Lapham, and Parsons. And they fought under such Communists as Taruc, Jesus Lava, Mateo del Castillo, and Alejandrino.

Huks Organized

On 29 March 1942 the CPP formally established a guerrilla force called Hukbalahap—*Hukbo ng Bayan Laban sa Hapon:* "People's Army against the Japanese." Initially, the Huks were led by a coalition government. The two main factions were Socialists, who actually were the remnants of the driven underground Communists of 1932, and the pure militant Communists. These groups began to vie for power. When they did, the Huk movement lost direction.

Chinese Communists were ordered to the Philippines to help reorganize the Huks when these local leaders began to fight for power among themselves. Ong Kiet was the Chinese "field general" who crushed the pseudocoalition of Socialists and Communists. By 1943 the Hukbalahap was completely in militant international Communist control.

The commanders of Huk units were most powerful in the critical rice and coconut growing areas in Central Luzon north and south of Manila where the Communist and Socialist causes always had found the greatest support. They divided their area into military sectors, districts, and regional commands. These areas, to all intents and purposes, they controlled effectively. During the Japanese occupation their strength continued to grow. To form their logistical base, the Huks activated the Barrio United Defense Corps (BUDC). In 1946, during the Huk-Constabulary conflict, the BUDC was reactivated as the National Peasant Union (PKM). Both the BUDC and PKM collected supplies and arms for the Hukbalahap, and were used also as vehicles for spreading communism to the peasants. Eventually, the Huk strength rivaled that of the guerrilla units that were organized and supported by the United States Armed Forces Far East (USAFFE). (MacArthur, in a far-seeing decision, refused to give arms to the Huks. The Huks, in turn, refused to join or accept orders from the USAFFE.)

The growth of the Huks at this time can be attributed as much to a popular patriotic desire to fight the Japanese, as to any true understanding or acceptance of the principles of communism by a *majority* of the guerrillas. No matter under what guise, the Huk leaders, in the eyes of many Filipinos, now had skillfully welded their cause with both nationalism *and* the patriotic battle against the Japanese. The Huks' long-range mission was clear, however, from their combat objectives. They often fought as aggressively against the non-Communist USAFFE guerrilla units as they did the Japanese.

The pattern of Huk strategy before and after the war ended was familiar. Basically, the same over-all plan was followed with minor local variations in almost every country devastated by World War II. Into a vacuum of government and economy left by the fighting, the Communists turned on their weakened countrymen and attempted to gain control of the government by force.

Series of Reverses

However, at this critical time the Huks lost face in a number of fields. Two of their duly elected politicians, Luis Taruc and Jesus Lava, were unseated in free elections. Government troops committed alleged "abuses" against many of the Huks and their sympathizers. A number of Huk leaders were killed or imprisoned. In addition, the Americans continued to refuse to recognize or pay any except one Huk ex-guerrilla unit as "legitimate." Unfortunately, at this time there was no practical alternative to not recognizing the Huk units, although certainly this helped drive the Communists into the hills. The power, prestige, and funds that would have accompanied official American recognition of the already powerful Huk leaders would have galvanized the Communist cause at the very birth of the infant Philippine Republic. Even more power would have flowed into their legal "Parliamentary Struggle." Frustrated and infuriated by this series of reverses in which they lost face, the Huks initiated an orgy of grudge and revenge killings.

At first the new Philippine democratic government considered the Huk military actions to be primarily a "police matter." During this same period many non-Communists, who were more outlaws and bandits than ex-guerrillas, fell into the embrace of the Huks because they lacked anywhere else to turn. Because of this association with criminals, the Huk depredations in so many instances looked like an upsurge of the lawlessness that sometimes flourishes after any war. There have always been bandits and outlaw bands in the Philippines.

A trial and error police-style campaign of combating the dissidents was initiated. The former Secretary of National Defense, Jesus Vargas, summed up those early attempts by saying:

> A remedy would be applied, and when it did not seem to work out, it was revised or discarded for another. In this we were fortunate that the situation allowed for a certain degree of experimentation.

"Mailed Fist"

When Manuel Roxas became the president of the newly created Republic in 1946, he tried to persuade the Huks to disband their military units, surrender their arms, and return to peaceful living. The Huks defied Roxas and continued their reign of terror. To counteract this display of force, Roxas implemented his "mailed fist" policy in September, 1946.

Troops from the National Police Force, the Philippine Constabulary, were deployed in the areas of maximum disturbance. But what was already a festering situation was made worse by committing untrained military police units to an extremely delicate mission. This first use of troops afforded little security to the people. Depredations continued. Farms, and in some cases entire barrios (villages), were abandoned. This further weakened an already strained national economy. Travel on highways became dangerous.

As noted, a serious weakness appeared in the ranks of the democratic Philippine Constabulary. The choice of many of the Constabulary officers and men had been haphazard. After four years of occupation, their training at best had been cursory or spotty. They were sent into a battlefield that was both military and sociological. With little firm guidance other than "use force," some returned abuse for abuse, frequently treating their own countrymen as people of an occupied territory. The "mailed fist" often was indiscriminately applied to civilian friend as well as military foe. Soon many Filipino farmers and civilians feared the Constabulary troops as much or more than the Huks. This destroyed the respect and confidence in many of the people, not only in their armed forces, but in the central government. In many areas of Luzon the people now openly supported the Communist troops.

At this point a reaction against brute force occurred and the government, now under President Quirino, decided to attempt a new policy of amnesty. After months of fruitless naive negotiations, rampant with Red duplicity, this amnesty policy collapsed and in 1948 the government again resumed the "police action." The respite had given the Huks an opportunity to reorganize, rehabilitate, replenish, and stockpile critical items such as ammunition and medicine.

Name Changed

By 1949 the success of Mao Tse-tung in China and the Ho Chi Minh struggle for Indochina further invigorated the Communists in the Philippines. Should the plans of international communism be fulfilled, all of Asia, except possibly Japan, soon would be Communist dominated. The CPP now changed the name of the World War II Hukbalahap. The new army took the more appropriate revolutionary title of "People's Liberation Army," *Hukbong Mapagpalaya ng Bayan* (HMB). No longer was there any question about the basic intent of the renewed Huk conflict— this was revolution!

The year 1950 was the most critical for the young Republic. The HMB's were at the peak of their power. They stepped up their rampage of terrorism with kidnappings, murder, arson, and looting. Although the HMB guerrillas were only moderately well-equipped with light weapons, and certainly were not well-trained in anything above individual and small unit tactics, they had on their side the greatest advantage in combat— they were on the offensive.

The HMB's, of course, were only the armed forces of the CPP, with "Major General" Luis M. Taruc as the chief of staff. As in any Communist state, the HMB was an instrument of the party. Pyramided above this military was a complete revolutionary civilian government. The secretary general of the party, Dr. Jesus Lava, a disillusioned intellectual, probably could be considered the leader of the Communist Republic of the Philippines. Filipino estimates vary, but most agree that the Communist strength consisted of around 19,000 active Huks, supported by 54,000 sympathizers. By 1952 the Reds felt they would have an armed strength of 173,000 Huks, supported by a mass base of 2.5 million active sympathizers to carry their revolution.

Further fanning the fury of the HMB attacks, the North Korean Army struck south in an attempt to unify Korea into a single communistic state. The Huks now successfully staged large-scale raids near Manila, and plundered several important towns in central and southern Luzon. Fertile fields and towns were deserted. HMB's controlled other major portions of the countryside, governing towns and barrios, collecting taxes, tributes, and ransoms, occupying the farms, and running military and civilian schools. They rode high on the hostility that was inherent in the tenant-landlord relationship in central Luzon, and the fear that had been instilled in many places for the Philippine Constabulary forces. One-half of their Politbureau flourished in Manila; the other half worked in the "field" with the troops.

In all the confusion, however, one thing was certain. The newly born democratic Philippine Republic was approaching economic chaos. Graft and corruption plagued the government. In the face of a vacillating governmental policy toward the Huks, compounded by the army's own weakness within its ranks, the armed forces were ineffective.

Indeed, the Filipinos were in grave danger of losing their limited war. These were dark days for "The Showcase of Democracy" in Asia.

Secretary Vargas said:

> About the only redeeming aspect of the situation was the realization by the officials of the government and later by the nation that the solution of the

problem was well beyond the reach of normal police action and that a more integrated national effort had to be exerted. . . . The Armed Forces were called upon to spearhead the antidissident campaign, which originally was entrusted to the Philippine Constabulary alone.

Ramon Magsaysay

At this point Ramon Magsaysay began to play his ever-increasing role in the Huk campaign. During World War II, Magsaysay had been active in the resistance movement against the Japanese in his home province of Zambales. As a young USAFFE guerrilla leader, he participated with the American forces in the liberation of Zambales. After the war he had been elected to Congress where, as a member of the House of Representatives, he eventually was appointed chairman of the powerful Committee on National Defense. Thus although Magsaysay certainly was not a professional soldier, he was a proved civilian leader who had a splendid background in the Philippine military field. Therefore, on 1 September 1950, President Quirino appointed Ramon Magsaysay Secretary of National Defense.

As the newly appointed Secretary of Defense, it was Magsaysay's job to cut out the Huk cancer and prescribe the cure. His first step was to reassess the Communist problem and determine why and where the government had failed in the past. Although technically his field of responsibility was restricted to the military, Magsaysay quickly saw that the military tactics of the antidissident campaign were unavoidably chained to the entire spectrum of the strategy of national internal policy.

In his research, the strategic crux of the entire fight against communism was discovered—or rather again realized—by Magsaysay. Simply stated it is:

Any "democratic" government is neither of necessity nor automatically better in the eyes of the common man than a communistic government. *In order to stamp out communism, the local government must clean its own house. A* status quo *that has bred virulent communism cannot remain unchanged. Communism seldom flourishes where the people are content and prosperous basically.*

Magsaysay decided that popular support for Philippine communism existed for the following reasons.

1. In high circles the new democratic Philippine Government had drifted slowly toward what some people term the "traditional" Asian acceptance of inefficiency, graft, and corruption as the prerogatives of those in power.

2. The people had received abusive treatment from some of the military.

3. A lack of any national socioeconomic reforms, compounded by the people's almost universal poverty, caused great masses to feel that the national government was not interested in them, while the Communists were.

National Policy

Communism showed itself most dramatically in the Huk military campaign. Magsaysay realized, however, that in order to combat it there had to be, in addition to military action, a many-faceted political, psychological, technological, and socioeconomic operation in the Philippines. Magsaysay implemented a sweeping national policy. His tools were the "left hand" and "right hand" efforts: The government extended its left hand in friendship, while the right hand was used to deal ruthless military blows. All-out force and all-out friendship were combined. Simply stated, the government promised mercy and help to those misguided elements who voluntarily sought peace and renounced communism; it promised all-out force against those who continued to defy the government. Each of these policies was to be emphasized on a priority basis. First, of course, a military victory was needed through the application of all-out force.

The Filipinos now realized that if their armed forces were going to counter this small unit hit-and-run type of Huk guerrilla warfare, they needed to be reorganized and revitalized completely. The company-size military police units that had been bearing the brunt of the Huk fighting had proved weak and ineffective. However, the Philippine armed forces themselves consisted mainly of administrative, service, and training elements that had assisted in the World War II USAFFE liberation campaign. Fighting organizations were lacking. There were only two infantry battalions available. However, conventional divisions or regiments were not necessarily appropriate for this impending fight.

The solution was the activation of 26 self-sufficient battalion combat teams (BCT's). The combat elements of the BCT's consisted of three infantry rifle companies, a heavy weapons company, a field artillery battery (whose members doubled in brass as infantrymen), and a reconnaissance company. The administrative and service portion consisted of a service company, a headquarters and headquarters company, an intelligence section, a psychological warfare section, and a medical and dental detachment. The table of organization and equipment strength stood at a high of 1,047 officers and men, although actual strength varied from full to reduced strength depending on the tactical missions of the unit.

The BCT's were under a unified sector command which had a small tactical headquarters. Two or more BCT's were attached to sector as needed based on the situation. The sector commander was capable of massing units for larger scale operations similar to a combat command or armor. When the Philippine Constabulary was integrated into the re-organized command forces, the total strength of the military establishment was about 30,000 officers and men.

Strategic Reserve

Small mobile Scout Ranger teams were the army's "strategic reserve." Flown or driven into a critical area, the rangers backed up the BCT's when and where needed. In splendid physical condition, these squad-size units were capable of sustained scouting and patrolling for as long as seven days without resupply. They carried the battle to the Huk in the jungle wilderness of the Sierra Madre Mountains and Candaba Swamp, the heart of their final bastions.

Detachments also were stationed throughout the country to secure key terrain features that did not justify the use of a BCT, such as water holes, road junctions, and small barrios. Liberal experiments were conducted with every type military unit that might help in the fight, from scout-dog platoons, horse cavalry, and close air support to airborne troops. Their further use depended on proved results. Most of the sophisticated methods of modern combat, it was found, could not do the job of the "traditional infantryman" and they were dropped.

"Civilian commandos," able-bodied armed civilians representing a menaced community, were led by regular servicemen and equipped to fight back against the Huks. Their mission was mainly defensive, to secure a community, thus freeing the regular troops for offensive combat opera-tions. To settle the inevitable misunderstandings, Civilian Advisory Com-mittees were established.

As in any warfare, the mission of this right hand effect was to destroy the HMB army. To facilitate this, tactical training was improved. Constant conventional patrolling and small unit combat were initiated. An effective all-out drive to eliminate the HMB sources of food and supply was started. Every conceivable type of unorthodox operation was combined with the "conventional" guerrilla warfare: sniping; ambuscades; surprise raids on HMB schools, camps, and supply points; individuals and entire combat patrols disguised as Huks infiltrated the HMB areas; periodic surprise patrols by civilian commandos; and total screening of entire barrios when the HMB's mingled with the civilian populace.

Favorable Results

These plans gave quick and noticeable results. Fatalities in fire fights began to average eight to one in favor of the BCT's and Scout Rangers. Within months it became difficult to find dissident concentrations in sizable numbers. Where before battalion and company-size bivouacs of 100 or more Huks could be found, they now split into itinerant groups of from 20 to 30 and avoided conflict. Later the groups shrunk even further. By 1957 bands of three to five men became common, vainly trying to exist, finally acquiring the instinct of the hunted animals they had become. This is the situation today with less than a few hundred armed diehard HMB's still roaming the jungles and swamps.

As the following figures indicate, the Huks had sustained heavy casualties by 1954:

9,695 killed in combat
1,635 wounded
4,269 captured
15,866 surrendered

By various means, 43,000 assorted firearms and 15 million rounds of ammunition had been rounded up; in contrast, only 1,578 Philippine armed forces personnel had been killed and 1,416 wounded.

An important lesson appeared during this period of gradually dwindling enemy strength. As it becomes more and more difficult to make combat contact with the enemy guerrilla units, a needle-in-the-haystack stage is reached where the effectiveness of "conventional" military antiguerrilla operations becomes unproductive budgetwise in simple terms of dollars spent to support the combat forces in the field, graphed against the number of enemy killed or captured. By conventional military intelligence means, such as scouting and patrolling, it is no longer possible to find a worthwhile concentration of enemy against which to commit combat units. At the same time, a deceptive feeling of security pervades the government and people.

Unfortunately, at this point, the guerrilla is *not* beaten. The classic military mission of destroying the enemy's forces and their will to fight has not been completely accomplished. In fact, the guerrillas who remain now probably have the most dangerous *potential* of any in the entire span of the fight. These are the diehards, the Moscow-trained leaders, the dedicated Communists around whom a new uprising can spring if they are permitted a respite.

To a degree the Filipinos were fortunate in their campaign to eliminate the hard-core leaders. In one bold government raid in the heart of Manila in 1950, they captured one-half of the entire Communist Politbureau. Later, such leaders as Taruc, Capadocia, and the American William Pomeroy also fell, although greater success certainly would have been welcomed. Jesus Lava, one of the ranking leaders of the Communist Republic of the Philippines, for example, today still roams the hills and jungles of Luzon, a sick, hunted man, but as the top Filipino Communist, one who has never surrendered.

When the needle-in-the-haystack stage is reached, combat troops gradually should be drawn out of their unproductive combat mission, and set about other tasks or demobilized, retaining only a mobile reserve, such as the Scout Ranger Regiment for emergency missions. In the Philippines, BCT's were initially kept in position for security reasons and assigned semimilitary public works tasks, as described later. By 1957 they were reorganized into conventional SEATO ground force divisions and regiments and taken completely out of the fight. However, the money thus conserved by decreasing the military operations should not be considered "saved" and the military budget reduced by that amount.

Scale of Rewards

The psychological and covert war is most important throughout the antiguerrilla campaign. But it becomes predominant in the latter "final crushing" stages. A graduated scale of rewards for the capture or for information leading to the capture, dead or alive, of ranking leaders of the movement is continued and emphasized. This makes the hard core and their units even more wary of exposure at the very time they should be able to relax because of the slackening of conventional military activity. The payment of informers and rewards must be decentralized to the lowest field commanders. In order to motivate the flow of current useful information, immediate full payment, or at least a partial payment, must be made wherever possible. The rewards also must be worthwhile, and should approximate cash sums for which the average citizen would work months—and in important cases years—to acquire and save in ordinary labor. In the Philippines, rewards ranged from a high of $65,000 down. Even rewards of this magnitude were not entirely successful due to red tape, slowness of payment, and conflicting claims.

This phase of the operation obviously begins to depend less on pure military strength and more and more on the mass support of the people, on the civilian citizens of the country itself. It is virtually impossible to destroy the complete combat potential of the guerrillas by military force alone. If, as in the Philippines, the guerrillas are supported extensively by the civilian population, a winning over of the people must occur. This is the goal of the "left hand effort."

One of the keys to winning the support of the people, and to the success of both the "right hand and left hand" policies in the Philippines, was a thorough housecleaning not only in the armed forces but in the entire government. Magsaysay attempted to eliminate corruption and abuse wherever he found it. This he considered as important as the hot war against the HMB. Initially, in the military, broad powers were given to field commanders to discharge or otherwise discipline men under them.

Spot decorations, rewards, and promotions were made. Commanders also were summarily relieved and demotions made. Personal leadership and frequent field inspections of troops and units were stressed by all military authorities. A positive attitude was instilled in the armed forces, replacing the defeatism that had been present.

Outside Assistance

Early in such a fight a decision must be made as to who will do the fighting. Is outside help needed? This is an extremely important decision and, of course, depends entirely on the situation within the country itself. It has much to do with the winning over of the people. The Filipino leaders had to decide whether the situation was serious enough to ask the United States to send in troops. They decided against this action.

Whatever the initial requirements for outside help, every effort should be made to require the nation itself to take over the fight *completely* at the earliest possible moment. Lieutenant Colonel Villa-Rial in his article *Huk Hunter* says:

> Foreign troops are certain to be less welcome among the people than are the regular armed forces of their own government. Local populations will shelter their own people against operations of foreign troops, even though those they shelter may be outlaws. For this reason, native troops would be more effective than foreign forces in operations against native communist conspirators. It would be rare, indeed, if the use of foreign troops would not in itself doom to failure an anti-guerrilla campaign.

Also to be considered is the need for lesser degrees of aid than foreign physical intervention in a threatened country. These opportunities appear primarily in the fields of advice, and in economic and material aid. The United States gave generously to the Philippines in all of these fields, and the place of this aid in winning the Huk campaign cannot be gauged accurately in black and white percentage figures. Needless to say, without the means to wage war, no battle can be won.

Certainly, the Joint U.S. Military Advisory Group in the military field and the International Cooperation Administration in the economic sphere did splendid jobs and contributed immeasurably to the defeat of communism in the Philippines. The Free World was indeed fortunate that the geographical location of the Philippine Islands made it unrealistic for Red China or Russia to give similar economic and military aid to the Communist government on the Philippines. If the Reds had helped the CPP as they did in other Asian countries, the story in the Philippines may not have had the same ending.

When the combat situation became relatively quiet, reduced strength BCT's still were stationed throughout the critical areas. Major General

Joseph H. Harper, the last U.S. Military Advisor to President Magsaysay, compared their mission to that of the U.S. Army units stationed at the cavalry and infantry posts throughout Indian country during the opening of our Western frontier. The Filipino troops could not be sent home or demobilized immediately due to the possibility of a resurgence of communism. The detachments spread a feeling of security to the people.

To counteract the ill feelings of the "mailed fist" that had turned the people against the military in the early stages of the campaign, these units were given semimilitary public works projects. Assured that the soldiers would stay in their localities as long as the threat to their lives and property was present and that the HMB could not retaliate, the people began to have trust and confidence in and cooperate with the troops. The stock in Magsaysay's armed forces began to rise.

Magsaysay Elected President

Magsaysay so captured the confidence of the people that in 1953 he was elected President of the Republic of the Philippines. In this capacity he was able to extend the anti-Communist principles in which he believed to the entire internal Philippine government. It is easiest to review the "left hand" effort from Magsaysay's tenure as President, rather than as Secretary of National Defense, because in this capacity he was able to bring the theory into full play.

It must be remembered, however, that the "left hand" effort was initiated and for the first few years carried out almost entirely by the Philippine Defense Department. Certainly, the Department of Defense of the Philippines, because of this, was unique among defense establishments throughout the world. It made itself felt in every corner of the "civilian" government. It controlled or participated heavily in such seemingly nonmilitary fields as: agrarian reform; economic aid; public works (in the rural development program); medical aid; justice (it provided "Courts on wheels" to arbitrate agrarian problems and institute harmonious landlord-tenant relationships); ferry and transportation service; and the conduct of many mercy missions.

As President, Magsaysay was further able to extend these principles to the entire sphere of the public administration. Perhaps to the extreme of undermining the morale of some of his cabinet members and lesser governmental officials, he relieved officials ruthlessly, no matter what their social position or rank. He prosecuted corruption whever he found it. In some cases he incurred the criticism that he had been overhasty and arbitrary in his action, but the people recognized what he was doing and applauded the motive.

On the governmental level he further stole the thunder from the Communists' slogans, like "land for the landless" and "equality for all." Countering each of the CPP rallying cries, he continued the far-reaching economic and sociological programs of the Defense Department. Where the fulfillment of the Communist promises were *years* away, Magsaysay offered the people something *tangible* and *immediate*.

He offered land to the reformed Huks and landless peasants. He backed this up with government loans to aid them over the rough initial period of becoming independent farmers. A commission was appointed to arbitrate the tenant-landlord problems. New farm settlements were established in the jungles, supported by government funds, made up of ex-Communists and peasants from the congested areas. He required the armed forces, when they were not fighting, to build such public works as bridges, barrio roads, wells, and school houses. Aids to small businesses and farmers were established, such as the Land Tenancy Commission, Agricultural Credit and Cooperative Financing Association, and the Farmer's Cooperative Marketing Association. He outlawed the Communist Party. And to counter Communist charges, he did his best to insure that all elections were free and honest. "Positive Nationalism" was his answer to the distorted brand of Red nationalism.

Conclusion

So much had the climate of communism changed in the Philippines when Magsaysay met his tragic end, that his death certainly marked the end of an era. It is not meant to imply that Magsaysay fought this battle singlehandedly. It was a national *democratic* revolution, the likes of which have seldom been seen before, in which the entire Filipino population took part. Never before in the history of Asia has militant communism been beaten so decisively.

16

Lt. Col. Tomás C. Tirona
Philippine Air Force

THE PHILIPPINE

ANTI-COMMUNIST

CAMPAIGN

W ITHOUT FANFARE, the eight-year-old Republic of the Philippines is concluding major operations in a successful limited war against Communism. This article will briefly recount the typical pattern of Communist conquest, and the tactics of the eight-year, bitter campaign the young Republic conducted against it.

The Communist Party of the Philippines was overtly organized on 7 November 1930. As a political party it was insignificant and never did assume any major legitimate political stature. But within the first two years of its existence it made manifest its aims of subversion through violent strikes and seditious political campaigns. On 26 October 1932, the Supreme Court of the Philippines declared the party to be illegal under the Philippine Constitution. Subsequently its leaders were tried and found guilty of illegal association.

The Socialist Party of the Philippines was organized just as formally and overtly as the Communist Party. Founded a year after the Communist Party went underground, the Socialist Party's aims were highly

From *Air University Quarterly Review*, Summer, 1954, and reproduced by permission.

indicative of heavy Communistic leanings. The Constitution of the Socialist Party of the Philippines described Philippine Socialism as differing from that of the United States and Europe and "condemned the counterrevolutionary role of Trotskyites and accepted the principles of scientific socialism enunciated by Marx, Engels, Lenin, and Stalin." In 1938 both parties were merged under the banner of the Communist Party of the Philippines. Its flag proudly announced the affiliation of the Party with the Communist International.

From 1938 to 1941 the Communist Party succeeded in organizing various social, political, cultural, and economic groups of the Philippines under a variety of fronts. In December, 1941, at the outbreak of World War II in the Pacific, the Party and its various fronts went underground. During the war thousands of Filipinos, impelled by a common desire to resist the Japanese, joined the armed faction of the Communist Party with no knowledge of the aims of the organization. This strong guerrilla organization became widely known as the *Hukbo Nang Bayan Laban Sa Hapon* (People's Anti-Japanese Army) or Hukbalahap. Its war-time record was one of numerous engagements against both the Japanese and other Filipino guerrilla units.

In 1945 the United States armed forces furnished arms to various guerrilla organizations in order to expedite the campaign in the Philippines and to hasten the attack against the Japanese mainland. Since the Huks were fighting the Japanese as vigorously as the others were, they were also furnished arms. However, most of these arms were deposited in secret caches. All Huk units, with the exception of one regiment attached to the U.S. Eighth Army, showed no more than sporadic and token resistance to the Japanese after the receipt of these arms. When these facts became evident, the United States armed forces came to distrust the Huks and confined their top leaders in a Philippine penal colony. The rank and file continued to terrorize the Philippine countryside. In 1946 the new Philippine Republic initiated a drive to return normalcy to the nation. The top Huk leaders were released from confinement to help in this campaign by contacting their dissident followers and encouraging them to surrender themselves and their firearms. While these leaders were ostensibly engaged in the pacification campaign, the *Hukbalahap* was redesignated *Hukbong Magpalaya Nang Bayan* or HMB (People's Liberation Army). All the various armed units were reorganized under a GHQ and prepared intensively for all forms of prescribed Communist struggle. The Republic subsequently declared the HMB and its affiliate organizations illegal.

Communist Strategy for Conquest

The strategy for conquest adopted by the Communist Party of the Philippines and its armed force, the HMB, was laid out in a memorandum to the Central Committee by the Communist Party of the Philippines (CPP) Secretariat. This memorandum reads in part:

Aim: To establish the New Democracy (People's Democratic Republic) by overthrowing American imperialism.

Direction of the Main Blow: Isolation of the national bourgeoisie and other elements who compromise with imperialism and the winning over of the masses.

Main Forces: The proletarians and landless peasants.

Reserves: The middle class and rice peasants, the Soviet Union, and the New Democracies (other Communist States).

Disposition of the Main Forces and Reserves: Alliance of the working class and peasantry.

Revolution:

1. Period of preparation—Battle for reserves or strategic defense.
2. Seizure of National Power—Military offensive or strategic offense.

The absence of a valid objective to present to the masses may be noted in the announced aim of the CPP. The prescribed Communist Party line for Asia stressed the liberation of the masses from colonialism, but how could one liberate from colonialism and independent Republic of the Philippines? So the Communist Party of the Philippines substituted "American imperialism" in place of "colonialism."

From 1946 until 1951 the Communists prepared themselves for the drive to power. The years 1951 and 1952 were to be the period for the military offensive. This plan was carried out by the HMBs in the central and southern provinces of Luzon. The HMB Finance Department levied stiff cash and crop contributions on farmers to support the military drive. Crops of large estates owned by absentee landlords were harvested by HMB units. The loot from highway robberies was divided equally between the Communist Party Headquarters and the unit involved. Their widespread depredations in the rich rice, sugar, and coconut lands of central and southern Luzon dropped agricultural production to a new low. This worsened the serious economic problems of the young Republic which was only beginning to recover from the effects of two major campaigns of World War II and of Japanese occupation and exploitation.

Early Government Counter-HMB Operations

From 1946 to 1948 the HMBs were forced to lay more stress on their military activities as a result of punitive drives conducted by the national police force, the Philippine Constabulary. In spite of this diversion, the Organization and the Education Departments of the CPP actively carried out the political conversion of the masses. The government had considered the campaign and extension of its anti-banditry drive and employed quasi-military police methods to stamp out the menace. But the undermanned and lightly armed Constabulary soon found itself unable to check the worsening situation.

An evaluation of the government campaign from 1946 to 1950 shows that the Republic overemphasized military operations and paid too little attention to the socio-economic, political, and psychological aspects of the problem. The socio-economic problems of the Philippines have been endemic to the country for centuries. The CPP and its armed HMB capitalized on the failure of the government to make the needed improvements. The Communists more than held their own militarily, and progressed in their political drive by stepping up their propaganda and other proselytizing activities. Their propaganda made much of the failure of the government to intensify the amelioration program for the masses. In 1950, emboldened by the successes of the ragged HMBs, the HMB command attacked towns adjacent to the city of Manila. They threatened Manila with a force of 10,000 armed HMBs, supplemented by fifth-column forces in each city district. The plan of attack called for the burning of the city by fifth-column arsonists, with the armed HMBs slipping into the city during the confusion. The plan failed when the government called the Armed Forces of the Philippines to defend the city.

In 1950, at the height of their successes, the HMB force stood at 15,000 armed and 80,000 active HMBs, with a mass-support base of 500,000. In the large areas where the people did not sympathize with the Communist movement, the CPP used intimidation and reprisals to keep them from cooperating with the government. They sought to alienate, divide, and conquer. The nation was in danger of falling into a tragic state of apathy and discord.

The New Counter-HMB Plan

Alarmed by the deteriorating state of peace and order, the government marshalled its forces and adopted a new campaign plan. The plan welded the socio-economic, political, and military aspects, supplemented by a vigorous psychological warfare program. To counter the CPP propaganda offer of "land for the landless," the government stepped up the drive to resettle farmers from the congested and marginal-producing farm areas of Luzon to the virgin public lands of Mindanao. A long-range industrial and economic program was financed by new issues of government bonds. Health and social welfare activities aided indigent families and victims of nature's holocausts. Tenants were assured 70 per cent of the harvest. Small-crop loans and a vigorous anti-usury drive helped the tenants finance their farming. A new minimum wage law prescribing minimum wages for the various categories of skilled, semi-skilled, and unskilled labor nullified the effects of CPP propaganda on the labor front. As a guarantee of order and honesty in elections, the armed forces were employed at the polls to safeguard the ballot. Two clean and orderly national elections and the rigorous drive against graft and corruption, spurred by a militant press and aroused civic organizations, gradually restored the people's confidence in the ability of the government to counteract the physical menace posed by Communist insurrection and to offer a positive, legitimate social and economic program to offset Communism's grandiose promises.

The Revised Military Plan

At the height of the Communist successes in April, 1950, the Republic called the armed forces to join the Philippine Constabulary in the military campaign. When the armed forces considered the over-all government plan, they realized that socio-economic and political annexes to the main military plan would be required. Since the public normally looks askance at local military operations by the armed forces, a psychological warfare plan with wider coverage was also approved. Prior to the implementation of these plans, substantial improvements were made in the armed forces. Military areas were organized. A framework for the combined operations of the four major commands (Philippine Army, Philippine Air Force, Philippine Navy, and Philippine Constabulary) was laid out, subject to polishing as the campaign progressed.

The Philippine Army reorganized its units into battalion combat teams, hard-hitting and well-trained units capable of sustained operations. An airborne battalion, a cavalry squadron, a dog team (K-9), and scout rangers were activated and fielded to supplement ground operations. The old plan of placing small garrisons in threatened areas was abandoned. Military areas were subdivided into sectors with two to three battalion combat teams (BCTs) each. These BCTs, together with Air Force and Navy units, formed task forces to conduct combined operations. Ground forces covered the sectors with fast mobile forces supported by strong reserves. While Air Force armed reconnaissance aircraft scoured the rugged mountains and the plains, the Philippine Navy patrolled the long Philippine shoreline. Dog teams and scout rangers worked together in ferretting out HMB hiding places and in reinforcing scout ranger units. These tactics brought the fighting to the enemy deep in the jungles. The cavalry squadron and airborne troops provided more mobile troops to seal off enemy escape routes or to purse retreating enemy units. These were special operations supplementing the combined operations which were conducted whenever the enemy was located in sizable force. Military intelligence teams operated in the cities and towns, breaking up Communist cells and destroying the enemy's communications system. Six months after the armed forces took over the operations, the military intelligence service captured the entire CPP Politburo in Manila.

To complement the purely military aspect of the campaign, the armed forces initiated a policy of "attraction and fellowship." This policy embraced several levels of action against individual Huks, depending on the degree of the individual's complicity. Against those who knew nothing but the language of naked force, a system of rewards was instituted for information leading to their apprehension or death. The rewards ranged from $50 to $75,000. In 1951 the top CPP leader, at the time actively organizing cells in the central Philippine Islands known as the Visayas, was killed by a civilian commando unit. The reward of $50,000 was distributed among the 21 members of this unit. As the system of rewards attracted more cooperation from civilians, including HMBs themselves, suspicion and dissension cropped up among the HMB rank and file. Top HMB leaders, on whose heads high rewards were placed, hardly dared move outside their mountain hide-outs. They surrounded themselves with none but the most loyal bodyguards.

For the HMBs and Communists who understood and accepted the terms of the attraction drive, the armed forces provided for their return to peaceful society. Several Economic Development Corps (EDCOR) settlements were cleared in virgin public lands by the armed forces engineers. The ex-HMB was given 6 to 8 hectares of land (roughly 15 to 20 acres) initially cleared by the armed forces, a modest hut which he helped build, subsistence allowances and crop loans to tide him through the first harvest, a work animal, and farm implements. The engineers built community centers and cooperative marketing buildings. The community centers featured the traditional Philippine plaza flanked by a chapel. Armed forces medical personnel provided medical care. The plan today envisions the transfer of these settlements to civil agencies for administration when normalcy returns. Recently the armed forces, now able to relax the past intensive campaigns, have turned several hundred officers and men to the task of clearing several thousand acres of swamp land around San Luis, Pampanga, hotbed of Communism and home of Luis Taruc, the HMB leader. The proposed resettlement project in this area is expected to take the steam out of local Communist opposition.

The armed forces psychological warfare plan embraces the dissidents, the general public, and the armed forces itself. The plan provided programs for each of the following:

Primary target—the dissident group.

1. The hard core—die-hards thoroughly indoctrinated in Communist ideology and irrevocably against democracy as a political society. These understood only the language of force.

2. The soft core—misguided peasants, workers, opportunists, fugitives

from justice, and adventurers. These were won over by the policy of "attraction and fellowship." Persons who surrendered were given good treatment and opportunities for a new and better life. They were encouraged to surrender by shows of force and vigorous military action that demonstrated to them the futility of resistance and pitted their professed belief in Communism against the age-old instinct of self-preservation.

Secondary target—the mass base, consisting mostly of peasants, laborers, landlords, business men, students, professionals, and government officials. These elements were continually informed on government activities in the fight against Communism. A systematic propagation of information on established democratic ways and the Communist conspiracy was pushed in all types of media. Support of the mass base was enlisted.

Tertiary target—the armed forces of the Philippines. The program generally presented to the men the reasons for fighting Communism, relations with the public, and an overview of the world situation. The intensive information and education program rapidly contributed to the rise in prestige of the armed forces.

As a result of the intensive implementation of the revised military plan, the HMB force was reduced to 1500 armed HMBs, about 2500 active followers, and a mass base of about 33,000. HMB Supreme Luis Taruc, relentlessly pursued by the armed forces and quarrelling with CPP brass, surrendered in May, 1954. This surrender of the top leader of the HMB does not conclude the campaign against Communism in the Philippines. Various methods of struggle are still available to those who elect to defy the government. But the surrender of Luis Taruc will have far-reaching effects on Communist morale and possibly future tactics.

Lessons from the Philippine Campaign

The lessons presented here are derived from the personal observations and opinion of the writer and do not necessarily reflect the official views of the armed forces of the Philippines or any other instrumentality of the Philippine Government. In many respects the problems of Communism elsewhere in Asia today bear the same aspects as those of the Philippines. These lessons are therefore presented here with the hope that these may prove worthy of consideration by others interested in similar operations.

In any country with a terrain similar to that of the Philippines, characterized by heavily-forested and rugged mountains, swamps, and jungles, the topography defines sharply the roles of each of the arms and services. A specific example is the role of the tactical air arm in this type of operations. Counter-air operations may not be necessary, but tactical air will be important from the military and psychological warfare aspects. Over areas declared free of friendly forces, armed reconnaissance limits enemy movement, prevents construction of large cantonments, and inflicts casualties on the careless. Interdiction of production bases, bivouacs, and trails important to enemy logistics forces the enemy to scatter his forces and to move frequently. Denied security, rest, food sources, and adequate shelter, the enemy becomes demoralized, succumbs to diseases, and defects or surrenders. In the various phases of the attack and pursuit, aircraft prove valuable in disorganizing the enemy and delaying his retreat so that friendly ground forces can pin them down. In mountainous areas troops air-landed by properly designed helicopters can cut off the enemy retreat. Helicopters are especially effective for air-landing special troops operating deep into enemy territory and for resupplying these troops in pre-designated areas.

Countries unable to support a large and highly technical air force can support an economical and highly effective aerial campaign by employing lighter conventional fighter-bombers of good dive and climb performance. Where the enemy does not possess considerable antiaircraft firepower, some of the modern high-performance, conventional trainer aircraft designed to be armed with guns, bombs, rockets, and napalm may be more feasible and more suitable firepower platforms. Fire bombs are not very effective against targets in heavily-forested tropical areas because containers break at tree-top levels. The wide dispersion of the jelly and the rank, humid vegetation prevent effective fires. Butterfly bombs sown in a wide pattern are more effective against personnel in these areas. Five-hundred-pound general-purpose bombs uncover natural and artificial camouflage and are lethal within a radius of 200 yards against personnel entrenched in deep ravines and river beds. The blast effect, confined by the sheer walls of these ravines, causes more casualties than the fragments themselves. In rugged terrain, strafing is more effective as a psychological weapon than as a weapon of destruction. Fire bombs and rockets continue to be the most effective weapons against enemy positions in caves.

In combined operations in this type of terrain, the employment of forces must be well coordinated. Indoctrination in the capabilities and limitations of the various forces employed will instill confidence, especially among the supported forces. The enemy is skillful in the use of terrain and knows the area better than the attacking forces, so that operations require careful planning and coordination to maximize surprise, deception, and the principle of the offensive. Bomb lines have to be set as close to the advancing surface forces as possible to enable them to move in on the enemy immediately after air attack has ceased. This poses a difficult problem of identification, in which proper communications are essential. Surface forces maneuvering over difficult and heavily-forested terrain require lightweight, portable, waterproof transceiver sets capable of contacting both support aircraft and adjacent ground sets. Communications are probably the most important single factor bearing on close support problems in this type of operations.

Enemy tactics are elastic. Unless the friendly forces are trained in tactics similar to accepted Communist guerrilla tactics and are provided superior materiel with which to wage operations, the forces employed against Communists will very likely be bewildered and outmaneuvered by the hodgepodge of tactics and techniques employed against them. The enemy excels at deception. Forces employed against these guerrillas must adapt their tactics to those of the enemy. The employment of garrisons in fixed bases in outlying areas merely fritters away any superiority enjoyed by friendly forces. In accordance with the "elastic disengagement" tactics, Communist guerrillas attack only when they enjoy local superiority, even if it be temporary in nature. Isolated, fixed garrisons will always be subject to attacks by a numerically superior enemy. A more effective employment divides these outlying areas into sectors and subsectors patrolled by hard-hitting mobile forces backed by alert reserves and welded into cohesive action by an effective communications net.

More troops are generally needed to combat guerrillas than are normally required for other operations of comparable scope. If friendly areas and areas liberated from Communist control can be organized for their own defense, the battlefield will be localized to a more manageable size. A suitable plan for the organization of these areas must embrace the socioeconomic, political, and military aspects of the problem. The psychological warfare program must be immediately applied to these areas. Success of such a unified plan depends on the sincerity of purpose, concreteness of ideas, and the acuity of the appraisal of the situation. It cannot operate in a vacuum, but must be based on actual, demonstrable facts. As trust and confidence are restored, the populace can be organized into paramilitary forces for the defense of their communities. A good intelligence screening and the effective application of psychological warfare programs can obviate the danger of these forces falling into Communist control. These forces may be under either civil or military control. They are intended as defensive or delaying-action forces and should not be used in strictly military operations. The well-organized community gains the courage to resist and is therefore less apt to cooperate with the enemy. This is the fatal blow to a guerrilla force, which by definition lives on and derives its support from the local populace. Without this support the enemy must withdraw from these areas because his security is compromised and his sources of information and supplies are no longer available.

In the conduct of an all-out campaign against internal defection, military intelligence teams play as important a role as combat forces. While combat forces scour the countryside for the armed enemy, military intelligence teams root out the covert enemy forces in towns and cities. Special troops like rangers and commandos can go on intelligence forays deep into enemy territory. Both special and military intelligence teams need civilian guides and informers. The British in Malaya and the armed forces of the Philippines have had considerable success in using these civilians. Rewards and security attract a number of erstwhile non-cooperative civilians and lukewarm Communists to provide these services.

Conclusion

The problems of Southeast Asia are basically socio-economic. World War II brought these problems into sharp focus and the leaders of Asia's voiceless millions believe that the existing political order must be changed if the solution of these problems is to be expedited. Communism, ever-ready to take advantage of nationalistic and political movements, does not offer a solution, but all too often leaders awake too late and find themselves irretrievably enmeshed in the Communist expansion program.

Communists have long recognized the need for the support of the mass of the population. Unfortunately the democracies have stressed the military aspects of the peace-and-order problem. They have tended to ignore the other facets of the dilemma, and by default have allowed the Communists to assimilate the masses into their ranks. The campaign against Communism requires the application of sound socio-economic, political, military, and psychological warfare plans. It requires the wisdom, sincerity, and determination of a well-informed nation. Unaided, no single nation in Asia today can withstand the burrowing campaign of Communism. If the free world abandons the complicated and sometimes strange play of power politics and resists cohesively, Communism can be defeated.

Further References

BOOKS

Appel, B. *Fortress in Rice.* New York: Pocket Books, 1960.

Baclagon, V. S. *Philippine Campaigns.* Manila: Graphic House, 1952.

———. *The Huk Campaign in the Philippines.* Manila: Colcol, 1960.

Romulo, C. P. *Crusade in Asia.* New York: John Day, 1955.

Scaff, A. H. *The Philippine Answer to Communism.* Stanford, Calif.: Stanford University, 1955.

Starner, F. L. *Magsaysay and the Philippine Peasantry: The Agrarian Impact on Philippine Politics, 1953–1956.* Berkeley: University of California, 1961.

Taruc, L. *Born of the People.* New York: International Publishers, 1953.

ARTICLES

"American Responsibility—The Philippines," *Amerasia,* November, 1949.

Bowers, F. "The Land-locked Pirate of the Pacific," *Harper's,* June, 1955.

Gunabe, L. I. "The Cover-up in the Peninsula," *Philippine Armed Forces Journal,* January, 1957.

Mata, B. "Ten Years of the Pacific Campaign," *Military Historical Review,* December, 1955.

Villa-Real, L. A. "Huk Hunting," *Combat Forces Journal,* November, 1954.

PART 5 *GREECE—POST-WORLD WAR II*

In 1946 Greece found itself in danger of Soviet control through the efforts of a guerrilla force directed and led by Communists. The guerrilla movement, covertly active prior to World War II, became overtly aggressive in 1946. By 1949 the Greek government, with both material aid and advisers from the United States and Britain, had successfully thwarted Communist designs on Greece as a Soviet satellite.

The guerrillas began by murdering local officials, spreading terror, and attacking and occupying small villages in an effort to show that the current Greek government was unable to maintain order and protect its citizens. The aim of these tactics was to force the government to surrender control to the Communists.

In October of 1948, the Greek government requested General Alexander Papagos to take supreme command of the Greek land forces. Papagos accepted only on condition that he would be given complete control of all military operations. These conditions were agreed upon and Papagos began his campaign that would end the war seven months later. According to Murray, in his excellent study "The Anti-Bandit War,"[1]

> No development could have been more fortuitous than the appointment of Papagos. . . . He restored discipline in the army by the ruthless removal of unsuitable officers. He stressed aggressive action and ordered the Greek armed forces into a series of offensive operations that deprived the guerrilla of the initiative and afforded him no respite. He gave the guerrillas no opportunity to recruit replacements for increasing battle casualties, but harried them until they were driven from Greece.

In the first article Wainhouse presents an overview of the politico-military situation in Greece from 1946 to 1949. This is followed by a summary of the Greek effort to isolate and then eliminate the guerrillas by Field Marshal Papagos.

---

1. Marine Corps Colonel J. C. Murray's study (see Further References at the end of this section) is most comprehensive and deserves the attention of all students of Communist guerrilla movements.

17

Lt. Col. Edward R. Wainhouse, **GUERRILLA WAR**
U.S. Army

IN GREECE, 1946–49:

A CASE STUDY

*T*EN YEARS AGO THE SOVIET UNION, through the Communist Party of Greece (KKE), turned to military pressure in an attempt to extend its influence and control to the Mediterranean. Had the effort been successful, a satellite Greece would have appeared in the Soviet orbit and a centuries old dream of Russian rulers—outflanking the Turkish Straits— would have been realized. In addition, Crete, the largest of the Greek Islands, occupying a strategic position in the eastern Mediterranean 200 miles off the North Africa Coast, would have provided an excellent base for continued unconventional warfare operations against the Middle East complex.

Other than its geographical position, Greece possesses none of the elements which a foreign power could consider as valuable war potential. Natural resources are largely undeveloped and limited in variety, while Greek industrial capacity is small and, by western standards, technologically backward. The land area, about 50,000 square miles, is only one-fourth arable and is insufficient to support the population of under eight million.

From *Military Review,* June, 1957, and reproduced by permission.

The Rugged Arena

Terrain, which is an influencing factor in any type of military operation, is of critical importance in the conduct of guerrilla warfare. Craggy, mountainous terrain with crude roads and poor communications is ideally suited for guerrilla operations. Forests, swamps, jungles, marshes, and similar geographical features which reduce the mobility of and hamper control by conventional forces provide the required protection and strongholds for guerrilla units. In areas of this type heavy weapons, artillery, and air support are considerably reduced in effectiveness.

The mountains of Greece cover more than two-thirds of the mainland and in normal times are the homes of about 40 per cent of the population. The remainder of the population is concentrated in cities with about one-seventh of the entire population living in the Athens-Piraeus area. There are no large towns in the mountain areas, but the land supports small groups in widely separated villages. Few areas are uninhabitable for there is usually grazing for sheep and goats, and from these animals and the poor soil the mountain dwellers eke out a bare existence.

Of the major mountain masses in Greece, the Pindus range, extending from the Albanian frontier southeastward to the Gulf of Corinth, forms the central core and largest area of sparse population.

The second important massif, the Kaimakchalan-Vermion-Olympos, runs in a semicircular arc along the western coast of the Gulf of Thermai (Salonika). The third is the southern end of the Rhodope range, which lies between the Strimon and Nestos Rivers in Macedonia, and drops sharply to the plains bordering the Aegean Sea south of Bulgaria.

The interior road net in Greece is a primitive one. Consequently, the towns guarding the mountain passes are of special importance in the planning and execution of operations. Examples are Métsovon, which guards the pass on the road from Ioánnina to Kalabaka, and Karpenísion, astride the road from Lamía to Agrínion.

Topographically then, the country provides almost optimum conditions for waging guerrilla warfare.

Strategic Requirements

Three basic strategic requirements must be met in the conduct of successful guerrilla warfare. The first basic requirement is to insure the support—material, moral, ideological, and psychological—of a large part of the population of the area in which operations are to be carried out. Lacking this support by the population, guerrilla troops are faced with almost insurmountable difficulties in recruiting, intelligence and information collection, and supply. Without a doubt there is a decided advantage to the guerrilla force if this support by the population is voluntary and enthusiastic.

However, this support can, if necessary, be induced by widespread measures of terror and repression.

Although the extent to which the Greek population supported the Communist guerrilla movement during 1946–49 cannot be validated, there was, at least initially, a great degree of sympathy for the Communist Party of Greece. This sympathy had been generated by the activities of the KKE's World War II military arm, ELAS (National People's Liberation Army), during the German occupation.

By the end of 1943 the ELAS forces had about 20,000 guerrillas and a highly organized underground which had been trained and in operation even during its period of suppression prior to World War II. The prewar organizations of the KKE were abundant and included not only hard-core Communists but sympathizers representing almost the entire spectrum of national life and culture. The Communist Party thus afforded the Greek people a multiplicity of organizations in which membership was possible for people in almost all age, sex, occupational, and social categories. The list of Party-controlled organizations shows the Communist facility for achieving unity among population elements of diverse personal interests.

Party-Controlled Organizations

AKE—Communist Agricultural Party

DAS—Democratic People's Army (post-World War II guerrilla organization)

EAM—National Liberation Front (during German occupation)

ELAS—National People's Liberation Army (military arm of EAM)

EPON—Communist Youth Organization

ERGAS—Communist Labor Organization

ETA—Supply Organization of the DAS

KEN—Seamen's Partisan Committee

KKE—Communist Party of Greece

KOEN—Communist Organization of Aegean Macedonia

KOSSA—Communist Organization of the Army and Security Corps (secret cells inside the Greek National Army)

NOF—Slav-Macedonian Organization (promoting Macedonian independence)

OENO—Maritime Organization

OPLA—Protective Organization of the People's Fight

PDEG—Democratic Women's Organization of Greece

Must Have Logistic Support

The second basic requirement for the successful employment of guerrilla force is continuous logistical support from outside the area of operations. Since guerrilla forces do not maintain or operate the extensive industrial facilities required for the manufacture of arms, ammunition, technical equipment, and critical expendables such as demolitions and explosives, their ability to conduct offensive operations is dependent upon an uninterrupted supply of war material from allied sources.

This second strategic requirement initially was solved by the Greek guerrilla forces through the logistical support given them by the Communists and allowed to flow into Greece from her Communist neighbors—Albania, Yugoslavia, and Bulgaria. This logistical support included not only clothing, rations, arms, and ammunition, but training camps, transit areas, replacement centers, field hospitals, and supply depots, all easily accessible in safe areas across the northern borders.

The third basic requirement necessary in order to realize the objective of guerrilla warfare (to assist in the attainment of ultimate victory) is the close coordination of operations between guerrilla forces and conventional forces. The closer and more efficient this operational coordination, the greater will be the military advantages accruing to both forces. The Greek guerrilla forces fought as an independent military organization which could not consolidate its military gains because of the nature of the type of warfare in which it was engaged. Having failed to meet the third basic requirement, the guerrilla forces were forced to rely on attaining ultimate victory through political strategy. The objective was to demonstrate the Greek Government's inability to maintain law and order and to emphasize the deteriorating economic conditions stemming from the conflict, thereby forcing the government to sue for a cessation of hostilities on terms dictated by the guerrilla high command.

Prelude to Violence

Following the surrender of Italy in September, 1943, many Italian occupation units in Greece, at the urging of British agents in contact with them, moved into the mountain areas supposedly to cooperate as Allies of the Greek resistance forces. Instead, they were disarmed by ELAS forces. In this way the Communist guerrillas were able to build up sizable stocks of arms, ammunition, and equipment.

In October, 1944, German forces withdrew from Greece and the Greek Government-in-Exile, composed of representatives from the major political parties, including KKE, returned from Cairo to Athens. General Sir Ronald MacKenzie Scobie, Commander of Allied Forces in Greece, which consisted mainly of British and a few Greek units, ordered the disbandment of all resistance groups. The ELAS forces refused to comply with this order and their political representatives resigned from the government on 2 December. The surface political unity was broken and on the following day an armed revolt by ELAS forces broke out in Athens. For two months civil war raged but the KKE was defeated in its attempt to seize control of the government. On 12 February 1945 the Communist and the newly formed government reached an agreement which ended the short but bloody uprising.

KKE leaders and commanders of the ELAS forces left Greece and took refuge in Albania, Yugoslavia, and Bulgaria. Other groups of ELASites took to the mountains and formed small bands which conducted sporadic harassing activities in the countryside. The reestablishment of the monarchy in 1946 was followed by an acceleration in Communist guerrilla activity aimed at disrupting the internal security and economic rehabilitation of Greece.

Followed Familiar Pattern

As in other European countries where the aftermath of World War II found the population destitute and ideologically confused, conditions in Greece offered a fertile area for the spread of communism. The three and one-half years of the German occupation of Greece were a record of despair —collaboration, inflation, hunger, oppression—and the political, economic, and social disintegration of a population subjected to the total impact of the "Übermensch" philosophy.

From its inception in 1942 the Communist guerrilla movement, organized and directed by hard-core Party members, attracted a motley collection of blind idealists, political opportunists, regenerate criminals, and misled individuals who honestly thought the KKE could alleviate the occupation and, later, the postwar misery of Greece.

During 1947 the guerrilla forces conducted small-scale operations, concentrating their efforts on an intensive recruiting campaign in the rural areas. The campaign was aimed at acquiring volunteers but also carried out a considerable number of forced abductions. By the end of the year Communist led guerrilla forces in Greece totaled approximately 23,000 armed troops, of whom 20 per cent were women, with about 8,000 armed replacements in training centers in the neighboring Soviet satellites. "General" Markos Vafiades, who had been political commissar of the ELAS forces, was made commander in chief of the postwar guerrilla forces.

Government Measures Weak

During the early stages of the guerrilla rebellion, the countermeasures undertaken by the Greek Government and Greek National Army (GNA) failed to have any significant effect on reducing the offensive activities of the guerrilla forces. Basically, the reason for this failure was attributable to political interference in the deployment of the GNA. Influential politicians in Athens insisted on "adequate protection" for the areas which they represented. Under this pressure the GNA had dissipated its tactical capabilities by piecemeal deployment of most of its available units to the static defenses of towns and villages throughout the country. In addition, when military commanders found it necessary to redeploy any of their units they had to seek authority through channels with final approval retained by the Greek General Staff.

In a politico-military situation of this type it was practically impossible for field commanders to adhere to the basic principles of war. The principles specifically violated were those of unity of command, mass, economy of force, maneuver, and, above all, the offensive. It was under these conditions which destroyed the GNA's initiative that the guerrilla forces, capably and fanatically led, were able to carry out their program of systematic devastation.

By the end of 1947 the guerrilla reign of terror had forced approximately 700,000 people of the farm population to flee to the larger cities for protection, further seriously complicating an already deteriorating political and military situation. The problem of providing shelter and food for these refugees was a tremendous economic burden on a nation which was already extremely short of dwellings and food supplies.

The Armed Conflict

During 1946 and 1947 the guerrilla bands scattered throughout Greece, each numbering 50–100 in strength, periodically descended from their mountain hideouts and carried out harassing raids against unprotected villages in order to collect food and clothing, recruit personnel, extort funds, sabotage lines of communications, and produce a general disruption of movement throughout the country. At this stage of the guerrilla campaign the Communist units were lightly equipped and seldom concentrated in large formations. They adhered largely to the three principles of successful guerrilla operations—surprise, shock action, and mobility.

Although the GNA had carried out a number of small-scale clearing operations during 1947, these only succeeded in pushing the guerrillas from one area into another, and in the north the guerrillas would simply escape into Communist satellite territory, subsequently reappearing in another part of Greece.

As is the case with any type of combat force, the guerrillas were faced with the problem of replacing losses in personnel, equipment, and supplies. Personnel losses were replaced through three principal sources:

1. The KKE supplied volunteers from among its members and sympathizers throughout Greece, especially from the larger cities where the underground's ability to operate is greatly enhanced.

2. Slav-Macedonian elements along the northern border areas, motivated by the hope of an autonomous Macedonia, supplied the recruits and formed a few small combat units of ethnic homogeneity.

3. Forced recruiting and abduction of villagers. Guerrilla raiders obtained the "cooperation" of the abductee by threat of death for him and his family should he attempt to escape or show lack of enthusiasm in combat.

Originally, the guerrillas obtained arms and ammunition from two sources: first, from Allied air drops made to the ELAS forces operating in the mountains of Greece during the German occupation, and second, from the disarmed Italian units following Italian surrender during World War II, and from German army supplies which the guerrillas were given in exchange for permitting an unhampered withdrawal of German forces from Greece in October 1944. The replacement of arms and ammunition during the postwar period of guerrilla operations was accomplished through logistical support by way of Albania, Yugoslavia, and Bulgaria.

Sound Intelligence Net

In the field of intelligence the guerrilla combat forces were aided by "self-defense" or informer personnel in most of the populated centers of Greece. These "self-defense" personnel operated clandestinely through local "YIAFKA's"[1] or cells, into an excellent intelligence net which kept the guerrilla forces informed of all GNA movements. In addition to their information function, YIAFKA members collected funds, carried out supply and recruiting activities, and were used to effect reprisals against individuals suspected of aiding the Greek Government forces in any way. At the end of 1947 "self-defense" personnel throughout Greece were estimated at about 50,000 with some 750,000 more sympathizers, some in high political positions, aiding the Communist cause in varying degrees.

Supply operations for support of guerrilla forces in the interior of Greece were difficult and hazardous because of terrain, distance, and possible interception by the GNA. The guerrillas solved the problem adequately by using pack animal trains moving mainly at night. Interior supply operations also were organized around guerrilla area units with an average strength of 56 to 60 men. The area units had the missions of collecting and forwarding information, concentrating and guarding food and ammunition

---

1. From the Russian term ЯВКА, meaning place of meeting, usually of a conspiratorial nature.

caches, providing clothing, and arranging for the care of sick or wounded guerrillas. These area units were prohibited from leaving their area of responsibility and, consequently, during clearing operations by the GNA the units would spit up into small groups and remain hidden in their areas until the situation permitted the resumption of activities.

At the beginning of 1948 there were 182,000 government troops in the field, supported by two Spitfire squadrons of the Greek Air Force, against 23,000 guerrillas without air support. Terrain obstacles and the impossibility of sealing the northern borders of Greece were the principal reasons an armed force of this size had to be organized to conduct an antiguerrilla campaign.

To provide coordinated operational and logistical advice to the Greek Armed Forces, a Joint United States Military Advisory and Planning Group (JUSMAPG) under the United States Army Group was established in December, 1947.

Guerrilla Tactics Sound

As a result of the combined efforts of the Greek General Staff and JUSMAPG, by the spring of 1948 the GNA was able to begin a series of planned major operations against guerrilla strongholds. In spite of well-conducted offensives which had cleaned out a number of guerrilla infested areas and reportedly cost the guerrillas 32,000 casualties in killed, captured, and surrendered, the total number of guerrillas in Greece at the end of the year remained about 23,000. Intensive forced recruiting inside Greece netted approximately 24,000 civilians. By virtue of this and the influx of reserves and recovered wounded from the border countries, the guerrilla high command managed to replace its losses during 1948.

The guerrillas had fought tenaciously and efficiently. Their tactics, ideally suited to the terrain, generally were of two types—the defense, for a limited time only, of an important area; and the hit-and-run raids of roving units.

In the limited time defense of an area, an outer ring (or outpost line of resistance) and an inner ring (or main line of resistance) were organized. These lines consisted of machinegun pillboxes dug into the ground and covered with 3 to 10 layers of logs with dirt filler in between. These pillboxes were mutually supporting, particularly at places where there were few, narrow avenues of approach to the defended position. In coordination with this area of defense, guerrilla saboteur squads operated in the rear of GNA lines mining roads and rail nets, destroying bridges and telephone communications, and ambushing supply columns. Guerrilla leaders placed great stress on the use of saboteurs and snipers for operations in areas under GNA control.

Raids Carefully Planned

In the hit-and-run raid the roving guerrilla forces of the interior assembled two or more units at some distance from the objective. The number of units depended on the scope of the operation to be carried out. By a forced march of up to 10 hours, and carefully avoiding observation, these units reached their objective and attacked, usually at night. Good intelligence had supplied the attackers with a plan of the town defenses, locations of the homes of Nationalist sympathizers, important government and public service installations, military headquarters, factories, well-stocked shops, and a list of recruitable persons. The bulk of the guerrilla force would attack and enter the town while supporting detachments isolated the town by mining the approach roads and trails, blowing up bridges and rail lines in the vicinity, and occupying commanding heights outside the town in order to prevent the arrival of any GNA reinforcements. When the attacking force withdrew it left behind burned and gutted houses, government installations, utilities, factories, and shops. Lying murdered where the guerrillas found them were the Nationalist sympathizers and their families.

Despite the fact that the guerrillas at the end of 1948 still were 23,000 strong, the initiative had passed to the GNA and a confident, more experienced, and better trained national army was ready to launch its offensive in the spring of 1949.

Guerrilla Strategy Changed

Toward the end of 1948 the KKE realized that its initial objective of destroying the Greek economy was doomed to failure so long as U.S. aid to Greece continued. Therefore, to attain its final goal of seizing power, its immediate objective became the delivery of a decisive blow against the major obstacle—the Greek National Army. Consequently, in November, 1948, the guerrilla high command reorganized its units along conventional lines with unit designations to include brigades, divisions, and corps. The brigade totaled 600 to 800 men, with a division consisting of two or three brigades, and a corps of two or three divisions.

Shortly after this reorganization General Markos was relieved as supreme commander of the guerrilla forces. Based on what is known of the internal political struggle in the KKE at the time, it is probable that Markos' relief from command was due to his differences with Nikos Zachariades, secretary general of the KKE, who succeeded him as supreme commander. These differences concerned the strategy of resistance, with Markos favoring the retention of small unit operations, while Zachariades insisted on meeting the GNA forces in large-scale attacks.

The key to the success of the guerrillas until 1949 was due largely to the excellent operation of their intelligence net which provided them the information necessary to determine when and where to engage GNA forces. However, in each of the series of successful operations executed by the GNA in 1949, army and police security forces took steps to destroy or render inoperable the guerrilla intelligence net in an area prior to the start of any operation. This involved the arrest and temporary internment of known Communist sympathizers or suspected informers. As a result the armed guerrillas, operating without their "eyes and ears," could no longer avoid surprise attacks by GNA units. Guerrilla leaders and their forces were killed or captured in a number of quickly executed GNA operations beginning in the Peloponnesus and working north toward the satellite borders.

Two noteworthy operations, carried out in August, 1949, involved the destruction of the major guerrilla strongholds in the Vitsi area and Grammos mountain area of northwestern Greece. The guerrilla high command had made the strategic error of deciding to hold and defend these areas along conventional lines. The result was destruction of the bulk of guerrilla forces in Vitsi and Grammos. Those guerrilla remnants which escaped into Albania could no longer be reconstituted as an effective fighting force. By the end of 1949 a few small, starving, and desperate guerrilla bands were left in the mountains, their entire effort directed toward survival. They were militarily incapable of any significant activity. The KKE had failed in its objective of bringing a satellite Greece into the Soviet orbit. As an anticlimax the "Free Greek Government" announced that it had ceased to continue further operations in order to save Greece from destruction. This hypocritical explanation was motivated entirely by the desire to sugar-coat the very bitter pill of defeat.

Conclusion

International communism, operating in the Greek arena, used all of the typical stratagems of unconventional warfare in its drive for power—misleading Party names and alliances, "united front" association with worthy causes, organization of clandestine cells of hard-core members, infiltration and attempted subversion of the armed forces and government ministries, industrial violence and sabotage, espionage for foreign powers, and the stratagem of desperation: armed insurrection.

The failure of the KKE in its postwar bid for control of Greece was the cumulative effect of a number of factors, not the least of which were the Communists' fallacious evaluation of the psychological factors inherent in this type of warfare and their organizational and operational blunders such as reorganization into conventional, identifiable units which reduced mobility and tended to dictate conventional warfare. Other important factors, generally beyond the control of the KKE, were: Yugoslav denial (beginning in the spring of 1949) of supply routes into northern Greece; improved capabilities of the Greek Army as a result of U.S. training and logistic support; and the gradual replacement of old and incompetent Greek division commanders by more capable officers.

The war in Greece was a civil war, for the most part conducted on the KKE side through guerrilla operations designed to harass, delay, and disrupt the military operations of the Greek Army. If such a people's war is to be successful, it must appeal to the fundamental political, moral, and ethical values of the people among whom it is waged. An intensive psychological warfare campaign must precede, and be conducted concurrently with, guerrilla warfare operations if the necessary support of a significant segment of the population is to be obtained. To maintain this support the tendency toward blind excesses of terror and destruction must be avoided at all costs, as this will finally lead to complete alienation of the populace.

Who can say what the course and duration of the war would have been had the Communists earned the voluntary support of a significant segment of the Greek people in the areas of their guerrilla operations? Instead, the KKE and its guerrilla forces resorted to indiscriminate rapine, extortions, assassinations, reprisals, abductions, arson, and terrorism which contributed a great deal toward sealing the military doom of the Communist guerrilla campaign in Greece.

18

Field Marshal
Alexander Papagos
Greek Army

GUERRILLA

WARFARE

W HEN WE SOLDIERS SPEAK OF WAR, or warfare, the term implies combat conducted by a regular army, with all its rules and ramifications, its orthodox precepts for the handling of larger and lesser units of strength, its intricate over-all pattern of communications and supply. It is this kind of warfare which has been the object of analysis and study by generations of military experts and writers and which is taught in our military schools and academies; it is to the requirements and objectives of this kind of warfare that our entire unit organization and training are geared. And the outstanding characteristic of this kind of warfare may well be said to be that its theater of operations is clearly and discernibly divided into two distinct and separate zones—enemy and friendly—by the line of the front.

In the course of past centuries, however, there have been cases—one is tempted to qualify them as heretical—wherein irregular armed forces have

From *Foreign Affairs*, January, 1952. Copyright 1952 by Council on Foreign Relations and reproduced by permission.

conducted military operations on their own or have participated in the campaigns of regular armies. Although such activity has almost always had unfavorable effects on the opponent—and sometimes done him critical injury—it has never, so far as I am aware, been treated by high commands and general staffs as a serious subject of study. Though it is mentioned in some classical military textbooks, military investigators have given it scanty attention. It seldom has been considered worthy of advance planning or of premeditated use.

During the past decade, Greece has been a theater of war in which irregular forces formed one of the opposing sides. I will endeavor to sketch here briefly the circumstances in which their activity arose and how they conducted it, and to reach certain conclusions as to the practical extent to which one may generalize the Greek experience and apply its lessons to other countries. It seems necessary to describe the setting of the operations in question because without this the reader cannot evaluate them. Since it is somewhat audacious, of course, to draw broad conclusions from local experience alone, I shall proceed warily in this respect. It will remain for the qualified military student, on the basis of his coordinated knowledge of many such case histories, to reach final generalizations.

II. THE OCCUPATION OF GREECE—THE LIBERATION

In May, 1941, after a sustained and victorious war against the Italians, and while the major part of the forces were still engaged against them, Greece was attacked by the Germans in strength, and succumbed. The Greek people quickly rallied, however, and despite the severity of their struggle for mere subsistence did not lose their morale. Their inherent—and inherited—love of freedom did not for a moment allow them to doubt their continued responsibility to fight for that freedom. Hardly had enemy rule been established in the country when they set themselves to devise practical ways of continuing the struggle, not only by passive resistance, but aggressively. At first these efforts were sporadic and individual, but gradually became better focused and more and more coordinated.

At that time, the Greek Communist Party was extremely restricted and had few adherents and little influence among the people. But it was quick to take advantage of the psychological climate prevailing. Under the banner of resistance against the invader the Communists endeavored to assemble the people into what appeared originally to be a democratic movement of no specific political hue, inspiringly if misleadingly designated the National Liberation Front (known generally by the Greek abbreviation, EAM). The armed forces of EAM were known as ELAS—the People's Army of Liberation Thousands of patriotic citizens, young men in particular, eager to fight the Germans, flocked unsuspectingly into the EAM ranks. With their lifelong experience as conspirators and their rigid adherence to Party precepts and directives, the Communists were able gradually to consolidate their hold over the two organizations. All the key posts passed into the hands of trusted Communists.

As soon began to be apparent (and as confirmed by subsequent events), the object of the leaders of the Greek Communist Party was not the restoration of national independence. They were not concerned with fighting the Germans, who, they foresaw, were doomed in any case. Their chief concern was to retain ELAS intact and to increase its strength sufficiently to give its Communist leadership complete control of the country. Consequently, under a limited show of armed resistance against the Germans—the bare minimum necessary to camouflage their true purposes—the ELAS confined their military operations in occupied Greece almost exclusively to annihilating non-Communist movements.

From the organizational point of view, the ELAS was primarily in irregular force. Initially it consisted of small individual bands of armed guerrillas, and though it attempted, as it grew, to assume the form of a regular army, with units designated as divisions and so on, this was superficial, done for its effect on the Allies in the Middle East, and in pursuit of political rather than military purposes.

Moreover, since the arms and equipment available did not allow the maintenance of a large force on continuous active service, the system of the ELAS reserve was invented. All the able-bodied inhabitants of regions under ELAS control were compulsorily registered in this so-called reserve. As a result, the ELAS always could speak in large terms, even though its actual fighting strength was considerably smaller.

Through the use of this irregular armed force, the Communists aimed at gaining control over extensive mountain areas; and in this they gradually succeeded. The foreign occupation forces, concerned primarily with maintaining their lines of communication, left the mountain strongholds of the ELAS unmolested. There was no necessity for them to deal with the Communists, who caused them no trouble; and they lacked sufficient forces with which to insure an efficient occupation of the areas in question even if once they conquered them.

Until the beginning of December, 1944, that is, until about two months after the liberation of Greece, the Communist organization remained concealed—for appearances' sake—under the designation EAM. Then, however, it shed its mask and undertook to win control of the entire country by armed action. Its main target was the British liberation force which had meanwhile landed in Greece. As a result, all-out military operations developed in the Athens area between British and Greek national forces on the one hand and the Greek Communists on the other. There were considerable losses on both sides, and, in addition, there were barbarous Communist atrocities against the general population. After a bitter struggle lasting two months, the Communist leaders abandoned their efforts and came to terms; but under the Varkiza Agreement, signed in February, 1945, these turned out to be notably favorable to them.

From the history here very briefly told of the development of an armed Communist force, and from an understanding of its purposes, we Greeks have gleaned the following lessons:

(a) The first essential element in the organization and operation of a movement of this sort is the existence of a suitable general undercurrent. In the case described, there existed a highly malleable mass resentment against the German and Italian conquerors. The Communists exploited it with subtlety and craft. The secret machinery of the Communist Party ensured that in the end the popular movement would come under its control.

(b) The masses, far from being Communist, did not even have Communist sympathies. In order to decoy the people, the movement had to make its appearance under the banner of armed resistance against the invaders and conquerors.

(c) To swell their ranks, the Communists used both persuasion and force. Persuasion took the form of lectures to the peasants, playing on their patriotic instincts and their desire for liberation. Force was used both directly, by the compulsory enlistment of the population, and also indirectly. Under the latter method, individuals refusing to join the Communist ranks were dubbed collaborators of the enemy, a charge which involved the death penalty or at least the burning down of the delinquent's home. Peasants who saw this happen and feared similar treatment joined the Communist ranks.

(d) In order to convert their recruits into an armed force the Communists needed arms and a cadre of leaders. The arms were procured from three main sources: first, the arms hidden in the villages by Greek soldiers after the German occupation and the disintegration of the Greek Army; second, considerable quantities parachuted into the mountains by the Allies; and third, after the armistice with Italy, the arms of the former Italian occupation forces. A cadre was formed of reservist noncommissioned officers and junior officers of the former Greek Army, lured in the manner described above. Since these ex-Army men were not always trusted by the Communists, the dual system of command was instituted, whereby each military commander was accompanied by a Communist political commissar who really controlled the unit.

Under such a system these armed units could not have really effective combat qualities. Most of the regular army officers joined nationalist resistance movements. The few that joined the ELAS were eyed askance. Rather than risk losing control, the Communists were willing to have their fighting potential against the Germans reduced.

(e) These armed bands were called regular army units. However, when they took part in battles against regular army forces (British and Greek) after the liberation in Greece—battles with definite locations, not involving guerrilla tactics—they were unable to gain the ascendancy. The fact that the fighting continued for two months was due not to any particular fighting capacity of the Communist bands, but to the anomalous conditions under which it was conducted. For example, a chief concern of the British and Greek forces was to confine to a minimum the damage inflicted on the city of Athens.

(f) The skill with which the Communists conducted their propaganda was noteworthy. It not only won over numbers of individuals who had originally been bitterly opposed to Communism, but also succeeded in creating the impression abroad that the movement was a pure resistance movement in accord with the sovereign right of the people to choose their own form of government.

That, in brief, is the outline of how in a specific case a force of armed irregulars was formed and developed. From it certain general conclusions might be deduced:

1. In numbers, Communism is a restricted force. In order to become an active operational force it requires allies, "fellow-travelers." To acquire them is the first concern of the Communist leaders. They have a variety of methods at their disposal. A classic one is that of the "united front" or "popular front." They do not hesitate to appear under the banners of causes entirely contrary to that of true Communism. And we may be certain that they have not exhausted their repertoire, and that they still will spring new surprises.

2. The only weapon against such tactics is an intensive, unremitting and aggressive campaign of public instruction and enlightenment—not so much vague anti-Communist propaganda as concrete arguments to meet specific cases. And here I would put a question that often recurs in my mind: Why, in these days when so many efforts are being made to rally the free democratic countries to common defensive action against an eventual attack from behind the Iron Curtain, is there no coordinated effort in the field of public enlightenment? Why has there not been set up a joint Western headquarters for such an educational movement?

3. Communism operates on a long-term basis. It does not concern itself exclusively with immediate results, but looks also to far objectives. We saw this in Greece, where the ELAS army was developed not to help the Allies win the war but to help Moscow win the peace.

4. The military objective of the Communists is subordinate to their political requirements. Thus there were no noteworthy operations against the conqueror, since that was not the political purpose for which the guer-

rilla army was created. But as soon as the Communist political chiefs decided that to use the guerrilla army against the British and Greek liberation troops would advance their political aims they did not hesitate to do so.

III. GUERRILLA WARFARE: 1946–1947

By signing the Varzika Agreement in February, 1945, the Communist leaders did not relinquish their ultimate purposes but merely deferred them temporarily. It was an example of the Communist tactic of a provisional withdrawal in order to renew the attack later under more propitious circumstances. Proof that they had not renounced their plans is apparent in the fact that after the signing of the Agreement the ELAS did indeed hand over their old and useless arms, but hid and retained all the serviceable arms and ammunition possible.

The year 1945 went by peacefully. During the last quarter of that year and the early months of 1946, the Communist Party tried to reestablish its organization and to expand it in the form of nuclear groups. It maintained contact with foreign Communist leadership throughout the Balkans, and under the directives of the latter the first Communist bandit groups were formed and reappeared on the scene in northern Greece. In the beginning these bands were small and few in number; but in the spring of 1946 they were sufficient to resume guerrilla warfare. Their activity was confined for the most part to the regions immediately adjacent to the frontier, where they attacked small isolated army outposts. Occasionally they succeeded in wiping out all of these, after which they would attack and loot the nearby village and then vanish into neighboring foreign territory. Gradually, as the strength and number of these bands increased, they extended their operations southward, as far as Thessaly. Their weapons were chiefly those hidden after the December, 1944–February, 1945, revolution, along with some supplied by neighboring states to the north.

In this period the military activity of these bands consisted, briefly, of attacks against main lines of communication, not as yet by means of mines, but by strikes at vehicles, civilian or military, traveling alone or in small convoys; attacks against small isolated army detachments or gendarmerie posts; harassing actions against larger army units, by long-range firing; and attacks against defenseless villages.

Their tactics were based on the following principles:

1. When deciding to attack a post or village, the Communist bands first made sure that its armed strength was considerably less than theirs,

so that they might achieve their objective quickly, certainly and with few casualties.

2. In cases when the target was larger they mustered enough additional bandits to cut all the routes by which reinforcements might arrive. But wherever possible they chose isolated posts. If the operation was not successfully completed within a predetermined time it was abandoned.

3. The objective was not to capture, occupy and consolidate certain areas but only to make swift strikes, achieve local results and then withdraw rapidly to distant strongholds—preferably, if proximity to a frontier permitted, to foreign soil.

Parallel to this activity, and helped by it, the Communist leaders engaged in intensive underground activity. The purpose here was to organize a network of spies, informers, suppliers and recruiting agents to support the guerrilla activity. This organization, called by the misleading name "self-defense," succeeded in establishing invisible control over large regions, mostly mountainous, which the bandit groups could not occupy openly. Through terrorism and propaganda the invisible administrative hierarchy exacted subservience, concurrence or, at least, non-resistance from the inhabitants of a considerable number of villages in those areas. Villagers who opposed it were either killed or forced to abandon their homes and seek refuge in the cities.

The national military forces and the gendarmerie were unprepared for this kind of warfare. After each operation the armed bands disappeared, so that when the military arrived they found no sign of the enemy except perhaps a few parting shots from afar. The attacks against the lines of communication made it necessary for all vehicles to move under armed escort. The raids against the defenseless villages, which brought desperate appeals for protection, necessitated a piecemeal allotment of a large part of the existing armed forces to guard key points. Not merely were these detachments static, but being isolated were extremely vulnerable to bandit attack. In addition, Communists had managed to insinuate themselves not only into the state machinery but even into the ranks of the Army. Towards the end of 1946, then, the situation was critical. The national struggle against Communism had begun to disintegrate.

Although known and unknown Communists in the various Army units were forming Communist cells, disseminating propaganda, and obtaining and passing on information, no mass mutinies occurred, and desertions to the Communist bands were few and far between. The Communists who had infiltrated were instructed to stay in the Army units and gradually erode them. The Greek Army commanders were well aware of the situation, but the government hesitated to adopt special measures against the Communists without indisputable proof of guilt, and only rarely were the Communists careless or artless enough to provide it. However, there were two or three cases where, during attacks by bandits against small Army units, Communist soldiers turned against their comrades, killed their officers and helped the bandits to win.

It is perhaps difficult for outsiders to realize the psychological stress of this period. The situation in itself was extremely unpleasant, and in addition it contained the distinct threat of dangerous developments in the near future. Helped by their conscious or naïvely unconscious allies, the Communists had succeeded in erasing the memory of the atrocities they had committed little over a year ago. They succeeded in creating a general belief that appeasement measures could end the bandit activity, which, they alleged, resulted exclusively from excesses by the "Right." Nor was this belief confined to Greek public opinion alone; it received widespread credence abroad.

During the winter of 1946–47, in those regions where the guerrilla bands were most active, the Army, for the reasons outlined above, was concentrated around the main cities and towns and their lines of communications. The small detachments hitherto scattered over the countryside were withdrawn and grouped together. Simultaneously, under the pressure of events and in view of the seriousness of the situation, the first measures were taken to rid the units of Communist soldiers and confine them in a separate camp. Virtually no active cleaning-up operations against the guerrilla bands were undertaken during this period. Taking advantage of the situation, and favored by the fact that heavy snowfall had rendered many routes impassable, the Communists were able to gain complete control over large mountain areas, whence they would frequently emerge to the nearby plains to raid villages or harass troops. A study of the positions thus occupied reveals that they extended progressively southward, reaching out towards the ultimate objective—Athens, the capital. Moreover, an unbroken network of mountain corridors linked the strongholds to one another and to the northern frontier; not all the corridors were under Communist control, but the guerrilla bands had comparative ease of movement and supply from the north.

On the whole, the operations of the bandits during the year 1946 were designed first of all to achieve psychological results which, in turn, would yield material results. We cannot actually be certain whether this was the original Communist plan, or whether it developed with the trend of events. Even the professional soldier, whose teaching and experience has been connected with regular army warfare, finds it hard to appraise with certainty the material gains of the Communist bandits. It is a fact that the national forces were numerically superior to the guerrilla bands. Also, they were better armed, their leaders were tried veterans of the 1940–41 war (some even were veterans of previous wars as well) and their casualties negligible. No large-scale battles were fought, no mass enemy movements occurred. And in these negative factors lay the strength and effectiveness of the guerrillas' interconnected cold and hot war. The hot element remained smaller than the cold, so that the national forces were in danger of losing the war without fighting it.

IV. THE YEARS 1947 AND 1948

During the late winter of 1946–1947 the command of the country's armed forces examined the situation and reached certain general decisions.

Extensive cleaning-up operations would be initiated in the spring. As the available forces were not deemed sufficient for simultaneous operations of this kind in all the districts infested by Communist bandits, plans were laid to progress gradually from the south to the north. It was estimated that by the end of the year the Communist bands would have been liquidated. While the principal operations were in progress in a certain district, such forces as were available in other infested areas would also attack the bands there in order at least to hinder their further development.

These cleaning-up operations would consist at first of a pincer movement around a chosen area, with the points of the pincer gradually converging toward the center. It was hoped thus to capture a large number of bandits or, at least, force them into battle and exterminate them. The second period, estimated to be very short, would be given to mopping up the remnants. Following this, the bulk of the armed forces would be available to assume similar operations in the next area. However, a few forces would be left to deal with the last remnants of bandits and the local Communist "self-defense" organization. By now all understood that this was quite as dangerous as the bands themselves, who could not thrive without it.

It was also decided that the units of the Army would be systematically purged of Communist soldiers. These would be sent to a special camp to undergo a moral rehabilitation. Those who sincerely abjured Communism, into which they had been inveigled, would be returned to their units.

However, these operations did not go according to plan for several reasons. The Communist bandits were informed of impending attacks in given districts in time to withdraw, for the most part, to some neighboring district which had not yet been cleaned up. Even when they did not withdraw ahead of time most of them usually succeeded in leaking through gaps in the pincers. When the cleansing of a district from the "self-defense" organization and the liquidation of its remnants proceeded satisfactorily, much more time and much larger forces than had been estimated were required. In order to encourage the inhabitants to support the Army in its job, they had to be convinced that the Army would not withdraw and leave them unprotected. And when the cleansing had been successfully effected in some of the early operations, the Communist rebels elsewhere withdrew not only their bands but also the greater part of the local "self-defense" machine.

Moreover, to clear a district of rebel bands and keep it clear demanded the stationing on the spot of larger forces than had at first been estimated. In an effort to overcome this disadvantage armed peasants under military leadership were at first employed on a small scale; but they tended to be ineffective. The result was that as the main operations were carried northward the number of available government troops was continually reduced and finally was insufficient to cope with the situation. By avoiding battle, the Communists endeavored, at times successfully, to reenter the districts from which they had been expelled, either by infiltrating through gaps in the cordon or by circuitous movements.

Finally, despite their losses and numerous defections, the Communist bands succeeded in refilling their ranks through compulsory recruiting of peasants. They also retained their fighting spirit. In June they actually attacked a significant urban center with large forces. That attack failed, but it was another proof that the numerous military operations undertaken against them had neither destroyed their fighting ability nor curbed the warlike disposition of their leaders. During the summer of that year the Communist bands for the first time received designations as regular army units (battalions), and their leaders endeavored to organize them in accordance with regular army standards—adjusted, of course, to the means at their disposal and to the lessons they had learned in guerrilla warfare. They were reinforced, moreover, by cadres freshly trained in military schools functioning in the neighboring satellite countries. And simultaneously, the supply of arms and ammunition reaching them from the neighboring countries was intensified.

The result of the 1947 operations was disheartening. Though the progress of the bandits had been checked the Communist threat was by no means ended. In the winter of 1947–1948 the bandits reorganized their forces and set to work to increase them. They returned to the districts from which they had been driven and prepared to meet the Army's new attacks in the coming spring. Moreover, the efforts to intercept the supplies dispatched from neighboring countries were not successful and the rebels now came into possession of artillery.

Along with these developments, the Communist leadership endeavored to assume a more official appearance. The leaders announced the formation of a government and endeavored to occupy some urban center adjacent to the border with the intention of using it as a "capital." They failed in this, however. According to the Greek Government's information, had they succeeded in this they would have received official recognition from the Communist countries, followed probably by open military aid.

The leaders of the Communist bandits also strove to create a "free area" which would be securely in their hands. This was a political necessity for them after forming a "government," and it was a military move as well, since if they were to extend their operations they needed a stable base on Greek territory. They selected as a base the mountainous region of Grammos-Vitsi, near the Greek-Albanian-Jugoslav border, and fortified it during the winter with military works, barbed wire and some minefields. The bulk of the Communist bands were assembled there. Several attacks were also made upon points guarded by the Greek Army, but they were of little avail.

The Greek command changed its tactics in 1948. It was decided that after a rapid cleaning-up operation from the south to the north, the Army's main effort would be concentrated against the Communist fortified area, in the hope that the enemy would give battle, and, forced to withdraw to the neighboring countries, would sustain serious losses. The seizure of this territory would seriously hamper, if not cut entirely, the supply lines by which the Communists maintained their troops in the interior.

The past year's experience had shown that the government forces were insufficient for their task, and thanks to American aid the size of the Army was notably enlarged. More of the quasi-military units called M.E.A., composed of armed peasants under military command, were organized. Operations began in the spring, when the Army's forces were concentrated opposite Mt. Grammos. The fighting continued for more than two months, with considerable losses on both sides, and in the end the area was taken. The remaining Communist forces escaped through Albanian territory, however, and reentered Greece in the Vitsi area, farther to the north.

In the beginning of autumn the Army attacked this mountain mass, but failed in the operation and incurred serious losses. The losses of the Communist rebels were heavy also, but they were not dislodged. Clashes occurred continuously through the country, and the Communist bands extended their activity to the southernmost tip of continental Greece and to some of the islands. Supplies reached them at these distant points by sea from Albania. They mined the roads and railways, and the destruction of communications forced the Army to disperse its efforts. Thus by the end of 1948 and the beginning of 1949 the whole situation was deteriorating. Communist bandits reestablished themselves on Grammos during the winter. Two years of hard and bloody effort seemed to have ended in failure. The end of the ghastly affair was not in sight.

By spring the Communists had made good their losses, mainly by the compulsory recruiting of peasants, and supplies from the neighboring Communist countries were reaching them in ever-increasing quantities, including heavy armament, especially artillery. As a result they were enabled to attack even important towns successfully. The Communist excesses, as well as the executions by the reactionaries, had caused numbers of peasants to abandon their homes and seek safety in guarded towns. This created an enormous refugee problem. The year's fighting had shown that the concentration of Army efforts on uprooting the Communist base (Grammos-Vitsi) close to the border had simply enabled the bandits to extend their activity in the interior. Moreover, the Communist forces had now taken the shape of a regular army, thanks to the abundant supplies pouring in from abroad and the training of officers in the military schools of the satellite countries. The situation was critical. Communism seemed an unconquerable hydra.

V. THE YEAR 1949

Three years of indecisive guerrilla warfare were indeed a terrible price for a weary and impoverished nation to pay for learning the correct method of finally defeating the Communists who had taken up arms against the legal government. The fellow-travelers were still advising appeasement. Nobody else doubted that this would mean in fact handing the country over to Communism and that this would be followed by its subjugation by the Slav satellites of Moscow. Even so, some people doubted whether a victory by the national forces was possible. The writer was not one of these. He believed that, on the contrary, Communism could be defeated, that the measures applied for this purpose in the past had failed because they were either inadequate or uncoordinated, that a radical change would lead to victory, but that there was no time to waste.

The change in the command of the Greek armed forces took place in January, 1949. The wide powers with which the new command was invested were, one may say, the fundamental reason for the subsequent improvement in the situation. The immediate and most important result was the recovery in morale of both the people and the Army. The new general plan of action, drawn up in agreement with the American and British military missions, was plain and simple. It was based on an analysis of existing Communist activities. In the first place, the Communists had firmly occupied a certain number of areas close to the border, with their rear resting on friendly foreign territory; these areas, mainly Grammos and Vitsi, were well fortified with barbed wire and minefields and were defended by important forces well supplied with artillery and ammunition. Second, they had operated throughout the rest of the country by normal guerrilla activity—that is, by bands which evaded pitched battles but tried to control a whole area by visiting the different districts in it from time to time and dealing out severe punishment to unfriendly peasants.

The one possible way to deal with the firmly-held areas close to the border was to undertake an offensive action based on the usual rules employed by regular forces to annihilate an opponent. To deal with the Communist bands scattered through the country different tactics were necessary. In the first place, they must be pursued ruthlessly and relentlessly by day and night, by sufficient forces, proceeding from different directions, so that they would be obliged either to give battle or to disperse. Secondly, stern measures must be taken to liquidate the "self-defense" setup which provided them with essential intelligence, recruits and supplies.

As the available Army forces were not sufficient for the simultaneous execution of both tasks, plans were laid for a gradual advance from south to north. The cleaning-up of the Peloponnese had begun at the end of 1948, but fresh measures were needed to make sure that areas once cleared of guerrillas would not be reinfected. Militarized units of armed peasants under the command of Army officers were assigned this task. Meanwhile, sufficient forces for the occupation of Grammos and Vitsi had to be concentrated. To guard against Communist inroads among them, all personnel under suspicion were removed and sent to a special camp for national rehabilitation.[1]

The general plan, matured with American aid, was applied with strict attention to the minutest details. The new combined force, aided by the local military units, successively cleared one district after another from south to north. They accomplished their tasks virtually within the designated time limits. Fresh units replaced worn ones as the main force moved to new areas, and light battalions were left behind to hold the ground gained. Their job was not too difficult, for the campaign had been so thorough that all but a small number of the roving bandits had been exterminated and the local "self-defense" organizations which maintained them had been wiped out. Finally, most of the Army's divisions were drawn up in imposing array before the Vitsi-Grammos fortified area. It fell after a swift drive. Victory had been achieved in nine months.

The Communists had reacted to these operations both tactically and strategically. By attacking with one echelon in the Vitsi-Grammos area in coordination with an offensive by roving bands in the interior they attempted to distract the Army's main forces from the cleaning-up operations further south. At another time they tried to occupy an important town near the Vitsi area; and later they resorted to a strong raiding action in depth. But they failed both tactically and strategically. They could not compel a change in the general plan or force the Army to withdraw from the main effort in order to protect the threatened areas.

VI. GENERAL CONCLUSIONS

Let me now summarize my conclusions from our experience in Greece.

Communist guerrilla warfare has two methods of operation: attack by arms and propaganda. Propaganda precedes the armed action and con-

---

1. The rehabilitated men later were formed into separate units, some of which distinguished themselves in the field.

tinues during and after it. The cold and hot war are closely coordinated, and one helps the other; but the emphasis is on the cold war. Communism cannot sustain its efforts alone; it requires allies, that is, the help of fellow-travelers. Without an auxiliary organization for obtaining information and giving general support guerrillas are condemned to early extinction. Parallel with their military operations, the Communist guerrillas seek to disintegrate their opponent—the army, the people, the state—by subversive propaganda and by reducing as many of the population as possible to destitution. To create a huge wave of hungry and ragged refugees they resort to any sort of ferocious and criminal action.

The first and principal antidote to these activities is timely diagnosis and ruthless suppression. Any leniency shown will inevitably be paid for later with blood and treasure. In saying this I wish not to be misunderstood: I do not imply that social problems are to be solved by the use of violence. On the contrary, it is the primary duty of a truly democratic government to seek and find just and generous solutions to such problems. But by now it has become quite clear that Communism is concerned only to exploit social problems; it seeks to aggravate rather than solve them because it thrives on unrest. The forcible measures which I advocate are to be used only against the professional dealers in subversion, the Communists and Communist agents who speculate in human lives. For them, no quarter. Our experience in Greece showed, however, that a considerable number of those who have accepted Communist leadership can with proper treatment and guidance be reclaimed and made into good members of the community. This should be one of the nation's chief aims. But the fanatic and hardened incorrigibles must be prevented from spreading their poison.

Public education and psychological warfare must be used intensively in order to counteract the Communist propaganda. Every democratic citizen should understand the Communist challenge.

When a nation reaches a point where it is forced to engage in military operations against guerrillas, the Communists have already won the first round. Thereafter the process will be painful. To suppress them will take much larger armed forces than those in the guerrilla bands. Moreover, activity must be directed simultaneously against the guerrillas and against the unseen organization which supports them. The members of this must be sought out everywhere, even in districts where guerrilla activity has not yet come into the open. The particular form of the military operations used against the elusive guerrillas themselves will be determined by local conditions, but in general the best procedure is continuous, relentless, unremitting pursuit, especially by night, so as to exhaust them and to force them either to fight or disintegrate.

Further References

BOOKS

Chandler, G. *The Divided Land: An Anglo-Greek Tragedy.* London: Macmillan, 1959.

Kousoulas, D. G. *The Price of Freedom: Greece in World Affairs, 1939–1953.* Syracuse: Syracuse University, 1954.

Leeper, R. *When Greek Meets Greek.* London: Chatto & Windus, 1950.

Sarafis, S. *Greek Resistance Army: The Story of Elas.* Tr. by Marion Pascoe. London: Garleigh, 1951.

Voigt, F. A. *The Greek Sedition.* London: Hollis & Carter, 1949.

Woodhouse, C. M. *Apple of Discord.* London: Hutchinson, 1947.

ARTICLES

Anthem, T. "The Challenge in Greece," *Contemporary Review,* March, 1948.

Balcos, A. A. "Guerrilla Warfare," *Military Review,* March 1958.

Black, C. E. "Greece and the United Nations," *Political Science Quarterly,* December, 1948.

Curtin, E. P. "American Advisory Group Aids Greece in War on Guerrillas," *Armored Cavalry Journal,* January–February, 1949.

Falls, C. "Communist Campaign against Greece," *Military Review,* May, 1949.

———. "Greek Army and the Guerrillas," *Military Review,* March, 1948.

Loomis, F. H. "Report from Greece," *Military Review,* April, 1950.

Murray, J. C. "The Anti-Bandit War," *Marine Corps Gazette,* January, February, March, April, and May, 1954.

Papthanasiades, T. "The Bandit's Last Stand in Greece," *Military Review,* February, 1951.

Siapkaras, A. "The Importance of Greece to NATO," *Military Review,* August, 1961.

Zacharakis, E. E. "Lessons Learned from the Anti-Guerrilla War in Greece, 1946–1949," *Revue Militare Generale,* July, 1960 (Extract of the same, *Marine Corps Gazette,* December, 1960).

DOCUMENTS

Greece. Modern Army. Intelligence Directorate, Salonika, Greece:
Guerrilla Warfare—The Organization and Employment of Irregulars, 56p., n.d.

Office of the Chief of Military History. Washington, D.C.:
Suppression of Irregular (Bandits) Operations, tr. by the writing of Deputy Chief of Staff, Greek Army, n.d.

PART 6 INDO-CHINA, LAOS, AND VIETNAM —POST-WORLD WAR II

The complex history of the Communist guerrilla movements in Indochina and Laos repays study from many aspects. To recount the full story is beyond the scope of this book. The contributions in this section offer some explanations for the Communist success against the French and an examination of current guerrilla activities.

Between 1945 and 1954 the French and Ho Chi-minh's Communist guerrillas fought a protracted and exceedingly bloody war. The Communists emerged the victors, which split Vietnam into Free South Vietnam and Communist North Vietnam. In 1960 civil war broke out in Laos, where the Communist insurgents were supplied from bases in North Vietnam. While peace terms are now (1961) being negotiated in Laos, sporadic fighting still continues. Daily fighting also occurs in South Vietnam, which is plagued with Viet Cong guerrillas supported and directed by Ho Chi-minh's Communist North Vietnam. At present writing guerrilla activities are limited to murdering South Vietnam officials at a high rate and terrorizing into submission the population of the rural areas. Though the objective of the original Communist guerrilla organizations was ostensibly the ousting of the French from the region, independence from France has not brought peace anywhere in this region.

Linebarger's article provides illuminating and sometimes startling analysis on events in Indochina up to 1951. Next, Fall discusses military operations up to 1953. Geneste describes some of his impressions as a French soldier fighting Communist guerrillas. This is followed by Rigg's comparison of Ho Chi-minh's tactics to the principles which Mao Tse-tung used with success in China. Warner explains how the guerrilla campaign continues in South Vietnam today. And, Jonas and Tanham analyze recent guerrilla activity in Laos and the role these activities play in the strategy of Communist revolution.

19

Paul M. A. Linebarger INDOCHINA:

THE BLEEDING WAR

RECENTLY I HEARD A MAN ASK, "What's this country Indo-china that the Reds are invading? Or have they invaded it?"

They are hard questions to answer.

Indochina is not a country. The Communists can't invade it because they are already there. The war in Indochina is as hot as the war in Korea, but—like the British conflict with the Malayan Chinese communists—it is an unacknowledged and undeclared war.

Indochina is not one country. It is either five countries or three, depending on how you count them. Before World War II, Indochina was a weird colonial composite within the French empire. The direct French colony of Cochin China, inhabited by Annamese, Chinese, French, Cambodians, Siamese, Hindus, and a few Laotians, was owned directly by France just like the island of St. Pierre of French Somaliland. The empire of Annam lay just north of Indochina. It had moved from being a loose Chinese dependency to becoming a very tight dependency instead

From U.S. Combat Forces Journal, March, 1951. Copyright 1951 by Association of the U.S. Army and reproduced by permission.

under French colonial overlordship. Between Annam and the frontier of China proper there lay the rich Annamese province of Tonkin. West of Cochin China and Annam lay the decadent but beautiful kingdom of Cambodia, still inhabited by the Khmers, whose ancestors—in their one and only fit of political, esthetic, and artistic zeal—built the dream city of Angkor Wat between about 750 and 1250 A.D., only to let Angkor sink like a treasure ship beneath a sea of jungle. Finally, north of Cambodia, west of Annam and Tonkin, running along the border of Siam, there was the high, wild, poor country of Laos.

Cochin China, Annam, Tonkin, Cambodia, and Laos—these were the five constituent countries of Indochina before the war.

Today there are three countries in Indochina:

Viet Nam, under French protection, is composed of the French-controlled parts of Cochin China, Annam, and Tonkin.

Cambodia, little changed except for a lone and uninterested sort of rebellion on the part of a few Cambodians who have set themselves up as Free Cambodians (*Khmer Issarac*), simply because everybody else in Asia has guerrilla movements and the Cambodians, languid though they may be, must have guerrilla movements too.

Laos, relatively quiet so far as the natives are concerned, but criss-crossed by exceedingly violent and dangerous Annamese.

These are the three governments of Indochina recognized by our State Department, recognized as existing by most of the UN facilities, and defended by a French army which includes a high proportion of *Wehrmacht* veterans who have enlisted in the French Foreign Legion.

But there is a fourth power, the one that is causing all the trouble—trouble characterized chiefly by superb infantry performance against the French and their lackadaisical local allies.

This fourth power is also called Viet Nam. It also covers prewar Tonkin, Annam, and Cochin China. A communist movement with na-tionalist support, or a nationalist movement under communist control—and nobody, not even the experts, can be sure which phrase is more descriptive—anti-French Viet Nam is usually referred to, not by the name of its government, but by the name of the political movement, which tries to destroy the Viet Nam set up by French power, recently reinforced by American aid, and tries to replace it with a pro-Stalin, pro-Mao, Viet Nam.

That power is the Viet Minh. . . .

Much of the confusion over Indochina arises from the kind of mixup that might occur in the mind of an intelligent *lama* from Shangri-la who was told, by the first British visitor he had ever met, about England, Britain, Great Britain, the United Kingdom, the UK and the British Isles. He might think that they were six different countries somewhere near each other, or he might think they were all different names for England, which would not be true either. You can keep the picture straight if you remember that Viet

Nam is the ancient patriotic name which Annamese (who inhabit both Annam and Tonkin, as well as most of Cochin China) have for their own realm. Therefore, the French use of the term "Viet Nam" represents a concession by the Paris authorities as to the label of the country; the French are trying to give *their* Viet Nam enough self-respect to make it an ally of France instead of a victim of Gallic imperialism. Cambodia and Laos remain relatively unaffected by what is in old-fashioned language a new Franco-Annamese war.

The other Viet Nam, which is being fought *for* by the Communist-dominated Viet Minh, represents a wartime leftover, in which emergent Asian nationalism has turned out to be a movement of men fighting, not for their right to be like Americans, but for their right to be like Russians.

No one now living can foretell how long the struggle in Indochina will go on. It has a patriotic base. The French did not complete the conquest of Annam until 1885 when the old empire of Annam-Tonkin passed from a light nominal and benign Chinese overlordship to a tight, real one, exploiting French control. In the fifty-five years of undisputed French control, the Annamese saw the French build more prisons than schools, more colonial palaces for French officials than universities for the natives.

Fifty-five years is not forever. The Annamese were restless under French rule, but the French gave them a sop to their pride by perpetuating the formal institutions of the ancient Annamese empire: Even after the Chinese empire fell in 1911–12, the ancient empire of Annam maintained the quaint imperial ceremonies which Annam had copied so faithfully from China a thousand and more years before. French rule was not atrocious, but neither was it a model of colonial practice.

When France itself fell in 1940, the local French authorities in Indochina stayed loyal to Vichy and did not join the Free France of General de Gaulle. These French colonial rulers were well rewarded—with a bitter and paradoxical kind of reward. They were allowed to be the stooges of the Imperial Japanese Army in the area, so that between 1940 and 1945 the peoples of East Asia saw a fantastic sight indeed. Proud French colonial officials served as the front men for a Japanese military regime, while having as their front men the political relics of the ancient Annam empire. The common Annamese peasant thus saw himself governed by a nominal imperial Annamese mandarin, supervised by a French colonial officer, who was supervised in turn by an Imperial Japanese officer. Through the war years the common people of Annam and Tonkin had three empires on top of them—Annamese, French, and Japanese.

I myself was in Stilwell's G-2 office, which later became Wedemeyer's, between 1943 and 1945. Part of the story of Indochina is absurd, contradictory, and fantastic beyond all the dreams of a Milton Caniff or a George Wunder. Neither Terry and his pirates nor Steve Canyon ever faced adventures in the comic strips to compare with some of the escapades of our

American and British contacts with the anti-Japanese forces in Indochina. We will have to wait a long time before enough American materials are declassified for the American public to know just how we supported the French against the Japanese, while supporting the Annamese against the French, while supporting the communists against the nationalists, while supporting the nationalists against the communists. If there was anybody in the entire area other than senior Japanese military personnel who did not get some kind of Allied aid to fight somebody else in the area of Indochina, I do not know who it could have been!

At the end of the war the Japanese were ready to leave, but the French weren't there. With V-J-day the last remnants of Vichy had disappeared and the Japanese in the Far East, with a superbly bold political warfare gesture, tossed out their French stooges and offered the Annamese any kind of independence which the Annamese might wish to set up for themselves.

(How many persons, even today, realize that Japan, just as the atomic bombs were falling at Hiroshima and Nagasaki, won some of the greatest *political* and *psychological* victories of modern times by giving Indonesia, Annam, and Korea their independence? Some Japanese staff officers did the modern world's finest single stroke of political warfare on that occasion, but I have never seen an article or document which said just who it was in the Japanese government or the Japanese military staff who recouped great Asian political victories out of the bitter darkness of Japan's surrender.)

Japanese-granted independence under the nominal emperor, Bao Dai, did not last long. By inter-Allied military agreement the Chinese and the British took over Indochina from the Japanese. (Could a situation be more complex than that? For a few weeks the Annamese peasant was under an Annamese official, technically under a French official, recently under a Japanese official, and currently under the British or Chinese army.) The British marched in, helped the French ashore, and marched back to their ships. The Chinese came in, stole everything that was portable, gave everything else to the bystanders, whether nationalists or communists, thumbed their noses at the French while letting the French in, and went back to China.

But what did the French find when they came in?

They discovered that the politics of 1940–1945 had unrolled with the breathless kaleidoscopic nonsense of an early Buster Keaton or Harold Lloyd comedy. Complexity had been compounded until it became chaos.

Out of chaos there stepped Ho Chi-minh. Ho Chi-minh was a tough, wiry, devoted little man. He is a hero and a great national leader, full of statesmanlike sagacity, if you like him. He is a tired, stupid, wornout, nationalistic Communist, if you don't like him. On estimates of his character you can pay your money and take your choice.

There is no doubt as to his performance. Out of the last year of Japanese control, out of the confusion attendant upon Japanese dismissal of their docile Vichy stooges in 1945, out of help from world Communism and help from our own OSS, help from Chiang and Mao, both of them, an army had arisen. And a government had been proclaimed.

This was the Republic of Viet Nam.

The French tried to deal with these inexperienced and crude Asiatic bandits who were presuming to set up a nation of their own. French officers and officials had high confidence in their own capacity to outsmart the rude leaders of a peasant rabble. French political strategy was simple. France and Viet Nam agreed by the Hanoi Agreement of March, 1946, to accept the Republic of Viet Nam as part of an Indochinese federation under the French empire (which took on the more grandiloquent and democratic-sounding name of "The French Union"). Subsequent conferences between Viet Namese and French were held at Dalat and Fontainebleau in 1946. But even while the two nationalities, Annamese and French, conferred with one another, they were fighting.

What were the realities?

On the Asian side there was a national movement of liberation in which the tough Annamese yearned for freedom so as to be able to resume their pre-French aggressions against Laos and Cambodia. Liberation did not mean lying down like lambs amid the lions in a political paradise. It meant the right to be themselves. And to be Viet Namese or Annamese means being tough, turbulent, bright, and aggressive. The Annamese share with the Siamese the reputation of being the two fiercest nationalities of southeast Asia. Overlorded and goaded by French, Japanese, Chinese, British, and their own imperialism, they added communism to their struggle for liberation. The communism was not an insidious addition from Moscow. In the pre-1940 years most anti-French Annamese had turned to Moscow because the United States was not in the liberating business at that time and because Chiang's Kuomintang, though technically a revolutionary party, was willing to support little more than a sister-Kuomintang of Annam on paper. Only the communists were tough enough to double-cross everybody and start with grass-roots armies recruited from peasantry. Only the communists had the faith and the courage to face French bestiality or Japanese torture in rebelling during the war years.

On the European side a beaten and dishonored France had communists in its cabinet at home while it behaved like an old-fashioned empire overseas.

The reconciliations were a double double-cross. The French condescendingly negotiated with Ho; Ho contemptuously negotiated with the French. Each spied on the other. Each got ready for a fight.

The fight came. Since 1946 the Communist-led Viet Minh version of "Viet Nam" has been gained. The victories of Mao Tse-tung in neighboring China seemed world-shaking in adjacent Tonkin and Annam. The communist regime changed from being a hit-and-run movement of pure guerrillas to a Yenan-styled Communist insurrectionary republic, moveable but not concealable, which governed all of the country part of the time and part of the country all of the time. When the Chinese Red Army reached the Indochinese frontier, endless reserves of ammunition, equipment, and training facilities were opened up. The Annamese or Viet Namese are roughly, sixteen million out of the twenty-three million people in Indo-china, and most of them clung to the communist-led patriotic movement.

Indochina and Korea are the only two areas which can be reached effectively by Chinese Communist infantry power across the Yalu and Red Rivers, respectively.

What did Ho accomplish between 1946 and 1950?

He promoted his military movement two steps up in the communist scheme of things. Guerrilla bands had become a well equipped national army, all infantry. His technicians had begun to manufacture good local bazookas. His "Viet Nam" had been recognized by the USSR and had even been offered recognition by that heterodox communist prankster, Marshal Tito of Yugoslavia. The hinterland of Ho Chi-minh, once Mao came to power in China, reached back six thousand miles and more to the in-dustrial complexes of Russia, while the French hinterland reached only to the coast and then had to be picked up by a long and expensive shipping route back to Europe.

On the French side there was the moth-eaten grandeur of Bao Dai, who (having been brought up a stooge) found it easy to keep on in the stooging business. But the French had thrown away with bad political warfare and bad psychological warfare everything that they gained with tough and efficacious infantry tactics. Paris stabbed Paris in the back—not by treason or conspiracy but by crudeness and unperceptiveness.

The French in Indochina did not trust Bao Dai enough to let him be a real national leader even if he could. The French military conquered villages and then alienated them. Throughout the French-held territory the communists operated a terroristic underground which tossed hand grenades, collected taxes, murdered "traitors," and mocked French power. If the French had succeeded, by the kind of genius which led the British to give up India in a tactful and profitable way, or by the kind of toughness which the Japanese had used in massacring any bystander who so much as looked like "opposition," *either* in creating a despotic but safe colonial regime *or* in setting up genuinely pro-French Viet Namese nationalists, they might have gotten one hundred per cent return from their military campaign against the rebels.

But from 1946 to the present the French threw away in the cities what they gained in the country. They did not trust any Annamese enough to let Annamese nationalism grow on the French side. Ho changed from being the leader of fugitive bands to becoming the leader of a chain of Communist peasant republics. In 1950 he began consolidating these very swiftly into a small, tough, Asiatic communist power. Behind him lay Communist China, and behind Communist China lay Communist Russia.

Therefore the war in Indochina is a bleeding war. A majority of the French regular troops, badly needed for the defense of Western Europe, are tied up in a fight against manpower—right at that one place on earth where manpower is cheapest of all. The Americans have done what they could to circumvent French crudeness and tactlessness by getting the French to allow direct U.S. diplomatic representation at the capitals of Viet Nam, Cambodia, and Laos. Last summer the Far Eastern Military Aid Program Commission led by Major General Graves Erskine of the Marine Corps and Ambassador John Melby of the Department of State, surveyed the situation, and recommended aid. In 1950–51 American equipment began to pour in, but no American combat personnel.

Indochina and Korea are not comparable. Korea had a quiet military frontier between 1945 and 1950 when the Communist North Koreans broke loose. Indochina has not known peace yet. The Communists can't open aggression because they have been at it for years. Nothing they now did could be drastic enough to mark a "beginning."

Indochina has suffered strangely. The French are usually noted for their political suavity and tact, but here the French have lost with bad politics and worse propaganda what they have gained with good fighting. DeGaullist veterans and *Wehrmacht* veterans, fighting side by side against Annamese guerrillas across the paddy fields, the jungles, or the forested hills of Indochina, have died in vain because nobody on the democratic side of the world knew how to take a patriotic movement away from its communist leadership.

Combat forces can do the job—when it's a combat job.

Combat forces can win tactical victories.

But tactics become strategy when victory makes sense. And the French have not been able to present, by politics or by propaganda, a victory that made sense to the common people of Viet Nam. American aid may help. Communism is bleeding France in Indochina and Communism will bleed us, too, if we go in with nothing more than weapons to offer.

War is a totality. If the Communists can bleed the French and us, we can bleed Mao and Stalin. But we cannot fight them with repeated tactical victories which are lost as soon as they are won. A democratic victory in Indochina can be a testing ground in which we learn the new kind of skills thrust upon us by the communist version of warfare.

Is it possible that World War III will never come? Is it possible that in its stead we have entered a historic period which no one of us has yet named—a period in which the old wars *between* nations are gone and the new wars *within* nations have come to stay? Are we not, perhaps, already in the middle of the First World Civil War? And if this is the First World Civil War, isn't Indochina a good place to take off the blinders of conventional thinking? Can we win if we keep on distinguishing between "political" and "military," keep on drawing lines between "American" and "French" and "Viet Namese"?

We Americans are good at inventing things. If we turn our imaginations from the mechanical and the technical to the strategic, we can still give the communists the shock of their lives. But it will have to be by the sheer and awful *newness* of our strategy. I don't know the whys or hows. Nor perhaps do you. But I think that we as Americans are smart enough to think up *new* things. If we are half as good at that as we were on the military hardware job, we can give the communists in Indochina and elsewhere a real shock.

Perhaps the last shock of their political lives. . . .

20

Bernard B. Fall

INDOCHINA:

THE SEVEN-YEAR

DILEMMA

ON 19 DECEMBER 1953, the war between the French Union Forces and Ho Chi Minh's Communist-led Vietminh will be 7 years old and there are but few indications at hand to point toward its possible end either through military victory or negotiation.

However, the situation has matured sufficiently to enable the military student to take stock of the various factors which might make the war in Indochina a useful example for future operations in other areas with similar climatic and terrain features.

Prior to World War II, the Indochinese Federation, as it then was called, was composed of three protected kingdoms, Laos, Cambodia, and Annam; one protected territory, Tonkin; and one French colony, Cochin China. France had consolidated her control over Indochina during the last 30 years of the nineteenth century and uprisings against French rule had been both few and completely unsuccessful. The only revolt of any consequence occurred at Yen Bay, Tonkin, in 1930. This was ruthlessly put down, and practically eliminated all major anti-French leaders—who were

---

Reprinted from *Military Review*, October, 1953, by permission.

exiled to the penal colony of Poulo Condore Island off southern Indochina.

With the outbreak of World War II, France was compelled to withdraw her best troops from Indochina in order to use them in the European theater. The result was that Indochina—particularly after France's defeat in June, 1940—was left wide open to ever increasing Japanese pressures. The Japanese, in particular, sought to obtain control of the Haiphong-Yunnan railroad in order to attack Generalissimo Chiang Kai-shek's main supply bases around Kunming.

Indeed the armistice with Germany had hardly been signed before a Japanese military mission under General Nishihara appeared in Hanoi. On 30 August 1940, Japan began to occupy a transit base at Haiphong and all major airfields of Tonkin. On 29 July 1941, Japan further occupied naval and air bases at Saigon and Tourane, and shortly after Pearl Harbor, Indochina was in fact as much a Japanese-occupied territory as any of the other southeast Asian countries which were overrun by the Japanese forces. The only difference being that the French still maintained their internal administration and lightly-armed military forces. It is estimated that the total French military forces available in Indochina did not exceed 15,000 men. However, with the war situation turning to the advantage of the Allies, the Japanese decided to eliminate the slight threat to their communications lines which the small colonial army represented, and on 9 March 1945, Japanese troops and secret police wiped out all French resistance. Only a few units succeeded in escaping the Japanese *coup* and succeeded in fighting their way through the jungle into Free China. Among these units was a task force of a few thousand men under the command of Generals Sabatier and Alessandri.

At the same time, all French administrators and civil servants, as well as most of the white or Eurasian civilian population, were imprisoned in various internment camps. Some of these internment camps achieved a notoriety in the Far East comparable to that of Dachau and Buchenwald in Europe.

The Vietminh

While the Japanese eliminated the French, the various nationalist and Communist groups began to reorganize themselves in order to take over as rapidly as possible whatever regions the Japanese did not occupy. Soon, such groups controlled seven provinces in Upper Tonkin as well as large tracts of land in Annam. The elimination of the French brought about a complete breakdown of Allied intelligence which, hitherto, had mainly relied upon its French contacts and this factor favored the activities of these groups. The new situation resulted in numerous contacts between the guerrillas and OSS as well as Chinese Nationalist intelligence groups. Many new weapons (bazookas, submachine guns) as well as radio sets and instructors were parachuted to them so that certain of the guerrilla units soon gained an appreciable amount of combat strength and efficiency. No distinction was made as to whether the groups in question were subordinated to a recognized liberation movement or whether they pursued aims of their own or of a particular political party. As it happens, it was the Communist groups under their Moscow-trained leader Ho Chi Minh which possessed not only the necessary strength but also the adequate purposeful leadership necessary to exploit the existing situation to the fullest.

On 6 August, the first atom bomb gave the signal of the beginning of the end of Japan's military might. On the following day, Ho Chi Minh's guerrillas became the "Vietnam Liberation Army." A shadow government, called the "Vietnam People's Liberation Committee" was set up during the following days. In the meantime, the Japanese handed over control powers to a newly-created "government" of their own choosing just as they had done in the Philippines and in Indonesia. However, the latter had but little chance of survival against the organized onslaught of the Communist forces, and on 20 August 1945, the Vietminh solidly held the whole north of Vietnam (as the three coastal territories of Indochina collectively were now called) while the Japanese quietly abandoned their puppets to shift for themselves. In fact, on 25 August, the Emperor of Annam abdicated and handed over his powers to Ho Chi Minh. On the same day, a "Provisional Executive Committee for South Vietnam," including seven Communists among its nine members, took control of Saigon. Within a fortnight after Hiroshima, the red flag of the Vietminh flew over all of Vietnam.

Return of the French

After VE-day, the French began to plan for an eventual re-occupation of Indochina within the framework of the operations planned by Admiral Mountbatten's South East Asia Command (SEAC). The initial force set aside for that operation was composed of two infantry brigades, equipped with British materiel, from Madagascar and the Cameroons; one United States-equipped armored brigade from the 2d French Armored Division; and one composite parachute commando unit, for special missions behind the lines.

Shipping difficulties were encountered because of the impending assault on Japan which prevented an early departure of the assigned units. As a result of the Potsdam Conference it was decided that French troops were not to enter Indochina for the time being and that it was to be split into two zones along the sixteenth parallel; the northern part to be occupied by Chiang's Kuomintang troops, the southern part to be administered by the British.

This was a serious blow to the French—the more so in view of the fact that they had not been invited to the Potsdam Conference. General de Gaulle, then the premier of the French Government, decided to send all available forces to Indochina on whatever shipping could be found. Thanks to the help of SEAC, one armored brigade of the 2d French Armored Division and elements of the 9th Colonial Infantry Division were finally on their way to Indochina by the beginning of autumn 1945. In the meantime, teams of French paratroopers and newly-appointed colonial administrators were parachuted into Indochina, in order to re-establish "law and order." These people were massacred with but a very few exceptions.

A small British force of 2,500 men under General Gracey was landed in Saigon on 25 September to occupy a territory that was slightly larger than Korea. It was clear that they could do little more than hold their own in Saigon, where the Japanese garrison alone numbered more than 5,000 troops.

On 2 October 1945, the first French elements arrived in Saigon. One company of paratroopers of the 5th Colonial Infantry Regiment was airlifted to Cambodia and another to Laos, while the remainder established a hedgehog position around the Saigon key area. General Leclerc, Commander in Chief of the French Expeditionary Forces, knew that one element alone played in his favor—speed. He knew that he had to make the utmost of the mobility of his airborne units and of his armored brigade (which had landed toward the end of October, 1945) so as to occupy the strategic points of the country *before* the Vietminh had had time to concentrate an appreciable number of troops around the southern key areas. Within less than 5 weeks and with less than a full division (the French troops who had been detained in Japanese prisoner of war camps being too exhausted for anything but limited garrison duty), Leclerc cleared an area of about 70,000 square miles. The Vietminh dissolved its "divisions" and "regiments" in the south and returned to guerrilla warfare. The French had won the first round.

It would be useless to go into the details of the political squabbles that finally brought about the complete breakdown of negotiations between the French and Ho Chi Minh's revolutionary government, still solidly entrenched in the north under the protective wing of the Kuomintang generals. It is quite obvious that they were conducted in a spirit of mutual bad faith and incomprehension, not to speak of the various factors of the cold war that began to play their part in the matter.

Nonetheless, the Vietminh agreed to let French troops land peacefully in Hanoi and to place small garrisons of between 500 to 850 men in several important border posts. However, multiple incidents between French and Vietnamese as well as Kuomintang troops created an extremely tense atmosphere which eventually became so explosive that one spark was all that was needed to bring about a general conflagration. The case in point was a matter involving a Chinese junk which the French customs guards had impounded because it assertedly had carried illegal arms for the Vietminh. Road blocks were erected by the Vietminh in Haiphong and when a French bulldozer crew, detailed to remove the block, was attacked, the French, in turn, shelled the city. A few days later, on 19 December 1946, the Vietminh attacked French installations throughout Indochina in a supreme effort to sweep the French into the sea. The "seven-year war" between France and the Vietminh had begun.

The War Situation

At the outset, the position of the French seemed desperate. Hampered by thousands of European and Eurasian civilians and 14,000 miles from its supply bases, the bulk of General Leclerc's mobile troops was bottled up in many small garrisons thinly spread over an area of jungle forests and steep mountains which was four times the size of Korea. General Leclerc's principal assets were massed firepower and air transport. It was the judicious use of both that saved Leclerc's troops from annihilation. The armored brigades swiftly swept a path from Hanoi to Haiphong; paratroopers and light bombers relieved the pressure from the small garrisons—some of which, such as Nam Dinh, were besieged for 4 months. Soon, most of the Red River Delta and Upper Tonkin, including the key cities of Lao Kay, Cao Bang, and Lang Son, were under French control.

The French troops, however, were already too weakened by the recent attacks and their overextended communications lines to be able to dislodge Ho Chi Minh from his mountain strongholds. The situation slowly degenerated into a stalemate.

For the Vietminh, the stalemate proved to be a welcome respite. The guerrillas were reorganized on a battalion basis, officer training schools were established, and the eventual victory of Mao Tse-tung over Chiang Kai-shek on the Chinese mainland brought about a welcome flow of ammunition, equipment, and instructors. Soon, General Valluy, the new French commander after Leclerc's departure and death, was now faced with 30 regular Vietminh battalions under the command of Vo Nguyen Giap, while in the south, guerrilla units under Nguyen Binh cut off Saigon from the hinterland and occupied the Transbassac—Indochina's rice bowl.

Despite the dangerous overextension of their lines in view of the number of troops available, the French persisted in maintaining their line of outposts along the Chinese border, in spite of the advice of General Revers, then Inspector-General of the French Armed Forces, to concentrate French forces around the vital urban and rice areas. General Revers had advocated this line of action as early as the middle of 1949, when it became apparent that the Chinese Communists would soon reach the confines of Indochina.

Giap's troops attacked in the fall of 1950, when atmospheric conditions all but nullified French air power. The French, at this time, under General Carpentier, desperately attempted to disengage their outlying garrisons by sacrificing some of their smaller posts. Nevertheless, the destruction of the forts of Lao Kay and Cao Bang—with nearly all their troops—were real disasters and French morale reached its lowest ebb.

In France, in view of the lengthening casualty lists, the public clamored for a recall of the French Expeditionary Forces and all available ships were directed to Indochina to evacuate the 20,000 to 30,000 French civilians who remained there. On the other side, Ho Chi Minh's radio announced that he would enter Hanoi, his former "capital," on the fourth anniversary of the beginning of the war, 19 December 1950. It was then that France decided to send General Jean de Lattre de Tassigny, her best combat commander, to Indochina.

It is a controversial matter whether the sudden change for the better was the result of the new commander's presence or was the result of a crucial error in the tactics of the Vietminh—to operate in the plains where the French flat-trajectory weapons and armor could be brought into full play. Still, the fact remains that De Lattre smashed the Vietminh attempt to break through to Hanoi via Vinh Yen on 18 January 1951, and the follow-up attempts to capture the vital port of Haiphong, North Vietnam's "iron lung"; while a third successful battle, on the Day River, assured the French of the control of the northern rice bowl.

In the meantime smaller but strong commando groups and French marine units had broken open the main communication bottlenecks in the south around Saigon and French naval and air units in turn blockaded the Transbassac so that the Vietminh could not harvest its rice to trade on the black markets of Singapore. Cambodia and Laos, with the exception of a few guerrilla areas, were entirely in French hands. A more resolute French policy at home and stepped-up American aid increased the strength of the French Expeditionary Force to about 250,000 men. Under the guidance of De Lattre, Vietnam began to recruit and train its own armed forces, which soon reached a total strength of about 130,000 men. Another of De Lattre's achievements was the construction of a fortified line of bunkers and concrete emplacements, supplemented by centrally located heavy and medium artillery positions, covering the entire vital northern Delta. Using this fortified Delta as a base for future offensive operations, De Lattre executed several deep stabs into Vietminh positions, using paratroopers and armored units.

On the other side, Ho Chi Minh's Vietminh underwent one of its most severe command crises. Giap's position, for a time, seemed severely shaken, and there were even rumors that Ho Chi Minh had been relegated to the background. The truth of the matter seems to be that he was following the three basic principles for Communist warfare in Asia as laid down by Mao Tse-tung, which were:

1. Yield any town or terrain you cannot hold safely.
2. Limit yourself to guerrilla warfare as long as the enemy has numerical superiority and better weapons.
3. Organize regular units and pass over to the general counteroffensive only when you are sure of the final victory.

The Vietminh high command had mistakenly underestimated French capabilities and passed from step 2 to step 3, with disastrous results. Since a scapegoat had to be found, it was found in the person of Nguyen Binh, the Vietminh commander in the south, who had been an ardent advocate of the general counteroffensive Nguyen Binh was ordered north to Giap's headquarters—a 1,200-mile march through the jungle—and was killed by a French Union patrol in Cambodia.

French Tactics—1952

On the French side, the army experienced a very serious loss when Marshal de Lattre died last year shortly after his only son had been killed in action in Indochina. General Salan, who took command as acting Commander in Chief, French Expeditionary Forces, Extreme Orient, apparently let the initiative slip back into the hands of the Vietminh—a most dangerous situation, the more so in view of the existence of a fortified line behind which French Union Forces could be lulled into a state of complacency. It cannot be denied that a certain "Maginot Line" or "wall psychology" spirit had developed in the French High Command. More than 10,000 forts, bunkers, and concrete emplacements, totaling more than five million tons of concrete, were built in and around the delta. The whole tactical concept was built around the theme of *hold that line*. Costly battles were fought for the possession of these forts, while their occupation—at one squad per fort, and many have company strength—immobilized at from 120,000 to 140,000 troops. And by no means do those forts prevent the infiltration of Vietminh elements! Battles involving nearly a whole Vietminh division were fought last year well within the fortified line and conservative intelligence estimates place the number of Vietminh troops operating within the delta at around 30,000 men.

One other result of the "wall" tactics was the holding of nearly half a dozen isolated fortresses far behind Vietminh lines, some as far as 300 miles inside Communist territory. Most of those fortresses appeared in the fall of 1952, when Vietminh elements—realizing that the Delta was too well defended to be attacked through a general counteroffensive—turned towards the elimination of the remaining French posts in northwestern Vietnam. Offensives were launched in the plateau area between the Red and Black Rivers, with the resulting destruction of the French garrisons at Son La and Nghia Lo. Na San, a third post, however, was fortified swiftly and provided with an airfield capable of supporting C-47s. As a result, about 12,000 troops with their vehicles, pack animals, and 105-mm howitzers had been airlifted into the stronghold within a short time. The ensuing Vietminh attacks were met by the withering fire of the defenders, and Na San still holds out. The same applies to Lai Chau, near the Chinese border, to Phong Saly in northern Laos and to several smaller points. In short, the French Far Eastern Air Force constantly maintains at least three to four airlifts over distances from 120 to 400 miles inside enemy territory, not to speak of tactical airlifts to front-line troops operating in Laos. During the Na San offensive, for example, the freight turnover between Hanoi's Gia Lam airport and Na San was higher than that on Europe's biggest airport, Orly Field. It is clear that such operations are prohibitive both from the point of view of equipment as well as from that of financial expenditure. The tactical value of having about 20,000 to 30,000 excellent troops bottled up hundreds of miles behind enemy lines in the jungle cannot be justified readily. Dispersed as they are, these troops cannot operate deep break-throughs or sorties into enemy supply lines—which, by the way, have long since been using bypass routes far around the French hedgehogs. Yet these troops are a serious liability to the French supply services particularly during the rainy seasons, and would be a most welcome tactical reserve against Communist infiltrations on the main fronts. Their value in the case of a highly problematic Franco-Vietnamese general counteroffensive could hardly justify their maintenance indefinitely.

On the other hand, by mounting an attack against Laos, the Vietminh command gave proof of a versatility and imagination which the opposing command has yet to show. Having realized that the major objective in the north, the Red River Delta, was too tough a nut to crack with the presently-available forces, the Vietminh command veered off at a 90 degree angle to the west and invaded thinly-populated Laos—one and a half million population spread over a territory twice the size of Pennsylvania—which was held by a force of about 15,000 Laotians and a few battalions of French troops. Within a few weeks, most of northern Laos was overrun and the French Union forces around Luang-Prabang and Vientiane were fighting for their lives. Again, the French Air Force came to the rescue and a hedgehog was set up in the Plaine des Jarres—and was promptly bypassed by the Vietminh forces which soon made their appearance within a few miles of the Thailand border. As suddenly as it had begun, the Vietminh tide then began to recede. There was no panic or air of defeat over the withdrawal. It was an orderly retreat toward their nearly impregnable jungle positions to the north.

Reports that the Vietminh attack had been a failure since it fell short of capturing the main urban centers will need additional substantiation. The fact remains that the French High Command was forced—and still is—to withdraw badly-needed troops hurriedly from other points in Indochina in order to protect Laos, and that, from now on, it will have to leave important garrisons in various Laotian key areas in order to forestall a repetition of such an invasion. In other words, by establishing a *second front* in Laos, the Vietminh command considerably softened certain other of his [?] main objectives, and the increased rate of attacks against the Red River Delta—which began a few days after the Vietminh withdrawal from Laos seems to bear out the contention.

Of course, it is true that the Vietminh, while on the attack, is faced with a tremendous supply problem. A former Vietminh quartermaster officer told this writer that, for the Nghia Lo operation alone, a large number of coolies—men, women, and children—were used to carry the supplies for the attack force. One can imagine the hordes of supply carriers who were needed to launch the Laos offensive which, after all, was mounted at least three Vietminh divisions of about 10,000 men each. Because of the mountainous terrain, no coolie can carry more than about 60 pounds for over 15 miles per day. On the other hand, he also has to carry his own sustenance (about 2 pounds of rice per day). Therefore, any large-scale operation far from the original Vietminh bases—such as the Laos offensive—implies the establishment of several intermediary supply depots and a huge expenditure of scarce rice for the transport of a ridiculously small "payload." Trucks are available in limited numbers but can only circulate during the night in view of French air superiority. It is obvious, therefore, that, in view of the lesson learned during the general counteroffensive of 1951, the Vietminh High Command will probably avoid a final showdown with the French Union Forces until such times as its Chinese Communist ally will be able to divert enough heavy equipment to fulfill Mao Tse-tung's theory of pass to the general counteroffensive only when you are sure of the final victory.

The Outlook

As the situation stands at present—barring the occurrence of such events as the appearance of MiG-15s in the Indochinese sky—the military aspect there points to a stalemate similar to the one in Korea. Although slightly superior in numbers and far superior in heavy equipment, the French Union Forces seem compelled to divert the bulk of their manpower to the defense of highly vulnerable communications lines, where the Vietminh is at liberty to attack any of the three main and several secondary fronts that exist throughout Indochina. Hopes are high that the arrival of General Henri Navarre the new Commander in Chief, French Expeditionary Forces, Extreme Orient, and of General Cogny, the new Commanding General, North Vietnam—who commanded one of the hardest-hitting combat teams during the last offensives under De Lattre— will bring a "new spirit" to French tactics and get the bulk of the forces out of the bunkers. It appears that the new Commander in Chief might advocate the methods used by General Merrill and General Wingate during the Burma Campaign—units *without* surface communications lines operating deep behind enemy lines, resupplied by air. This would exploit to the utmost the basic French superiority in mobility in supply and firepower and would also transfer the initiative to the French.

The establishment of 54 commando-type Vietnamese battalions who are familiar with both the language and the terrain also should contribute greatly to the eventual success of such a method of fighting.

There are those who—mindful of General MacArthur's ill-fated Yalu River campaign—fear that too much pressure against the Vietminh might bring about the appearance of several hundred thousand Chinese troops on the Indochinese battlefields. This is within the realm of possibility, however, a glance at the map of South China will indicate that such a mad appearance is unlikely—Yunnan and Kwang-Si, with their rugged terrain and wretched communications, are not like the highly-industrialized Manchurian Plain. The Soviet Union's and Red China's industrial centers are nearly 3,000 miles away so that, for once it would be the Communists who would have to struggle with the most severe problem of logistics. On the other hand, it is obvious that a Communist jet air force with a Red Chinese sanctuary would provide a nearly insuperable problem to the French. The air "infrastructure" of Indochina, already severely taxed by the various airlifts, is far from satisfactory, and the number of airfields capable of accommodating jets now is desperately small.

In the meantime, the 7 years of war in Indochina presents an ever increasing burden to French finances. Human losses have been heavy— 43,000 dead, 40 per cent of these casualties were regular French officers and noncommissioned officers who are sorely needed for the infrastructure of the new French North Atlantic Treaty divisions.

There are high hopes for the new Vietnamese Army, under General Nguyen Van Hinh. Vietnamese units have in the past given a good account of themselves and now number seven divisions. About 30 of the 54 planned commando-battalions are expected to be ready by the fall of 1953. Nevertheless, there is little hope that an appreciable number of French troops could be withdrawn from the murderous climate of the jungle battle lines in the near future. Nor is there hope that these units, now badly needed in North Africa or France, can be withdrawn. Like Korea, there seems to be no *substitute for victory* in Indochina. Or, as a French civilian official here put it: "How do you think it feels to fight alone for 7 years a war that is militarily hopeless, politically a deadend street, and economically ruinous?"

Conclusions

1. Contrary to general expectations, there are only a few general lessons that can be drawn from the Indochina conflict. It cannot be considered a modern war since one of the opponents is entirely devoid of armor and air power. Both parties, however, do make considerable use of modern light armament, so that one could call the Indochinese war an *old-type war with modern weapons.*

2. A great deal of rigidity in tactical thinking has been displayed by the French High Command. Add to this the fact that the French forces have used heavy tanks and artillery, which were designed for use on the firm soils and open plains of Western Europe, in rice paddies and jungle terrain.

3. More than heavy weapons and new concrete pillboxes, the situation in Indochina requires the kind of "offensive spirit" so remarkably displayed by Leclerc and De Lattre with much smaller and poorer-equipped forces than those now at the disposal of the French High Command. No war, and particularly no guerrilla war, can be won by remaining on the defensive. The French will have to adopt Mao Tse-tung's advice and fight the war, with hit-and-run stabs.

At the present time, the entire French order of battle appears to be based on the hopeful assumption that the opposing side will *never* receive an air force or armor for it is quite obvious that under the present conditions no airlift of any consequence could be maintained in the face of enemy fighter opposition. Already the hitherto invulnerable concrete bunkers are victims of the enemy's new recoilless guns and shaped charges and increasing enemy efficiency has to be expected and reckoned with.

The future alone will show whether the recent reorganization of the French High Command in Indochina has brought about this change of spirit.

21

Lt. Col. Marc E. Geneste
French Army

GUERRILLA

WARFARE

WITHIN SIX MONTHS after the end of World War II, pictures of Communist leaders and anti-French slogans began to appear in this small village in Indochina to which my unit was sent at the end of the war. Now, all the jungle has been undermined. Somebody from abroad has given these people an ideal—something to fight for—and promised them a better life. They have read so in the leaflets and listened to their chiefs. Those who doubted the word had their throats cut. If they escaped, their families were slaughtered. Now terror reigns in the jungle. People are silent.

Always and everywhere the same pictures and the same slogans appear. This is a strange fight, indeed. There are no apparent objectives; however, we French soldiers know that the enemy is here. In the mornings we find our friends killed, their houses burned. Ambushes destroy convoys, soldiers are shot in the back, mines are placed on the roads and bombs blow up here and there killing women and children. Every time

---

Reprinted from *Infantry Magazine,* January–February, 1961, by permission of *Proceedings of the U.S. Naval Institute;* Copyright © 1960 by U.S. Naval Institute.

we arrive the enemy has vanished in the jungle or is mixed-in with the population. People do not talk. There is no intelligence.

Our planes (they have none) have the absolute mastery of the skies; our navy (they have none) controls the sea; our tanks, our armament and technical skill are unchallenged. All this material—all this military strength—appears to be useless. Is this a new type of war? Not at all. Partisans have always existed. What is baffling is the way we civilized people are forced to fight. We are hamstrung by the rules of war.

Probably the first rule of war was to make fighters wear uniforms (indeed, this must have been one of the first steps of civilization) in order to save the civilian population from indiscriminate massacre. In the past when those uniform-wearing fighters were defeated, the war was over. But here in Indochina, the Communists have changed the rules of the game. Everybody is a fighter without uniform. Some carry weapons. Others help by gathering information. Still more assist by simply being silent (under penalty of death). When we appear, weapons are concealed and we get smiles. Each village is friendly or inimical, depending on our strength.

In the old times, this too-simple trick would not work with us because the village as a whole or some hostages were held collectively responsible for any hostile act. But the Communists have noticed that our determination has vanished. Our idealism prevents us from using these radical remedies, which are the one and only way out unless we use a fantastic number of soldiers. The Communists in France, however, will prevent our government, through public opinion, from sending adequate reinforcements.

All our friends at home and abroad believe that we are fighting here an old colonial-style war. Nobody cares to think about the fact that we have forever given up our old colonial policy simply because, time and again, eastern propaganda sticks on our back the label of "colonialists." The Communist organization plays with the idealists' minds like a cat with a mouse. Americans in Hong Kong print papers favoring Ho Chi Minh and we know that they approve his action, which is the worst blow to our enterprise—the worst blow to our morale. Contributions are made, even in France, for the heroic "resistance" of the Vietnamese people. No one knows the facts except a handful of soldiers lost in this jungle. Our government is unable to give way to the truth because democracy means the contrary of propaganda; it ignores psychological weapons and has already forgotten the success of Doctor Goebbels. We soldiers, our government and our friends are trapped in the net of the Organization. A world-wide machine carefully and shrewdly built, backed by world power of a great people which has succeeded in defeating Hitler's armies—all this machinery is on the move and could crush us. These thoughts make heavier the hot and heavy air we breathe in this deep equatorial forest. Our lonely fight—is it hopeless? We'll fight it anyway. How? Our units were organized to fight against Germany in World War II battles.

Here, the enemy has been organized according to our tactics. Within a few weeks, we have occupied practically the whole of the Indochinese Peninsula. We hold the towns, the roadnets, the harbors and the airfields. In the offices of our G3, no classical military problem appears. In G2, intelligence people are perplexed. We hold everything, but the enemy is everywhere. We have seen leaflets which say, "If you want to join Viet-Minh (the Communist organization in Indochina), leave the highways." But our World War II organization ties us to these roads to get fuel, ammunition, food and supplies. If we leave the road to fight, our vehicles bog down in the swamps and rice fields. If we go on foot, we are lost in a terrible terrain of jungles, mountains, and forests where malaria and dysentery are the worst of our foes. In any event, we have not enough strength—barely 30,000—to mop up everything. Mop up what? Civilians?

In daylight, however, we succeed in keeping order because our planes and our vehicles can quickly bring Infantrymen to search the jungle. Only Infantry is usable—other weapons have no targets.

By night, Indochina belongs to the VietMinh. Our night patrols are spotted when they leave the posts. Dogs bark and disclose our ambushes. "Tam Tam" calls in the jungle mark the progress of our men. The rebels know all the trees in the forest; they fight on the spot where they used to play when they were children.

The Organization has made each village a military entity—a little theater of operations self-sufficient with its cells, its political commissar, its tax collector and its supply system. We have discovered the "medical" organization of one village: only women. They confirm that, willingly or not, everyone has a role. Even children bring messages or weapons. No modern army could cope with such a problem without using the old radical methods of reprisal. We need at least 500,000 Infantrymen trained for this special warfare. We don't even have 50,000 and we do not play the same war game as the enemy. We seldom meet. There is no hope to get reinforcements. Public opinion in France, undermined by Communists and idealists of all kinds, will never agree to send draftees. Modern weapons can help to conquer land; but Communists conquer people. To control land and lines of communication among hostile people who become, when necessary, hostile fighters, a considerable number of soldiers is required.

As weapons systems become more and more complicated, the more we will depend on sophisticated and vulnerable logistics and lines of communications. In theaters where the Organization has thrown its underground nets, quality cannot replace quantity. To the contrary, quality—which is almost useless here—requires quantity. This is the new military challenge of Communism whose Infantry of millions is already spread throughout the world. We need soldiers and more soldiers; nothing can replace the old Infantry, the only all-weather and all-terrain weapon.

Are not our military chiefs a little lured by the promises of scientists and led into dangerous concepts of warfare, relying too much on machines and forgetting men?

Obviously here the machines fail. In this environment they work only in daylight and if it does not rain too much, only on limited portions of the ground. They are useful one-half of the time and over only one-tenth of the terrain. The rest belongs to the foot-soldiers—to the numbers.

The machines, of course, will remain necessary, but in themselves, they will never be sufficient. Some illusions of World War II vanish in the swamps, the forests, the monsoon and the nights of Indochina.

. . . At last we have met them, entrenched to guard a mountain pass. They have built pillboxes. My tanks have objectives.

When the easy fight is over we find only corpses—no prisoners, no wounded, no weapons. The survivors have fled into the forest with their wounded and all their weapons. They do not have one rifle per soldier— only one for two or three riflemen. A cord is tied to the weapon and if the first man is killed, the second pulls on the cord and gets back the gun in his foxhole.

In a pillbox hit by my tank, I find only one forearm cut at the elbow by a shell. The man has fled. But he has left his weapon with his right hand—a crossbow.

This rugged Communist Infantry is courageous, too. We have underrated them. Communism, as Nazism and Fascism, provides an ideal— right or wrong—and this makes men fight.

They have numbers. If they get more weapons. . . .

22

Colonel Robert B. Rigg
U.S. Army

RED PARALLEL:

THE TACTICS OF

HO AND MAO

THE PARALLEL BETWEEN TACTICAL PATTERNS and growth of the Viet Minh and of the Red Chinese in the Chinese civil war is so precise that even the circumstance of today's truce predicts tomorrow's trouble.

Mao Tse-tung's ten military principles have been consistently applied by Red warlord Ho Chi-minh. The Viet Minh began war on a guerrilla basis and has emerged to its brigade- and division-level period. Before long it will enter its army-level era of organization and operation.

Viet Minh foot mobility has been of the highest order, and on a parallel with that of the Chinese Reds. It is the Asiatic rebuttal to machine-age war. Ho Chi-minh's guerrillas have followed Mao Tse-tung's axiom: "We march more than we fight, but every march is for the sake of a fight." This tactic multiplied Viet Minh members and confused opposing intelligence officers and commanders. A formal army, like that of the French and the Chinese Nationalists, arrives at a point of justified desperation when it cannot find, much less oppose, the enemy opposite it. The mobility and the elusiveness of the Viet Minh greatly prolonged the Indo-

From *U.S. Army Combat Forces Journal,* January, 1955. Copyright 1955 by Association of the U.S. Army and reproduced by permission.

china war. It was so designed by the Communists for two purposes: to allow the Viet Minh forces time to grow to full military stature, and to bring war weariness to the people of Indochina. They followed the Mao Tse-tung philosophy of "not fearing long wars" but wanting decisive campaigns within long wars.

It was the ninth of Mao Tse-tung's Ten Military Principles that accelerated his rise to power from 1946 to 1949. This principle said, in simple terms, "capture from the enemy so as to arm yourself." As the Chinese Reds gained new weapons and material in the Chinese civil war, the number of offensive moves increased and they became more aggressive. While the source of supply was different for the Viet Minh, its aggressiveness and concerted military action was in direct ratio to the armament it gained, and it gained the majority of its arms from the Chinese Reds. Organizationally the Viet Minh grew larger and more formal as Red China supplied advisers, technicians, and weapons.

Red China's Ten Principles are simple rules designed for beginners in warfare. They are tailored for the patient, and they fit the ultra-patient Asiatic. Palace revolutionists or daring revolutionists would be contemptuous of their cautious and conservative advice. But they are sure and certain rules for men who have the patience and endurance to apply them. Ho Chi-minh is such a man.

First among the ten principles of the Chinese Reds is: ". . . strike at scattered and isolated enemies, and later strike at the . . . powerful enemies." Foremost in consistency and chronology was the Viet Minh's application of this axiom, which might be called the tactics of digestion without indigestion, a principle which was proportionate to the means at hand. The Viet Minh attacked the outposts (strategic and tactical) of the French Army in this succession, and scored some very important gains in 1950–51, especially in Tonkin. Over the years the Viet Minh adhered well to the first principle but did err now and then in gauging the next degree of target to attack. For example, the Red attack on Na-Sam (November–December, 1952) was apparently preceded by faulty intelligence, or overconfidence, or a combination of both. This bloody Viet Minh attack had much of the character of the 1947 attack the Chinese Communists made on the Shantung city (a formidably walled one) of Tsining which, like Na-Sam, was an attack eventually abandoned after heavy Red casualties. Neither place had any real (local) strategic importance, yet in both instances there is now reason to believe that the Reds attacked in the hope of establishing military prestige.

Viet Minh adherence to the second principle ("first take the small towns; later the large") was leading to the application of the third: "We take the annihilation of the enemy's fighting strength, and not the holding of cities . . . as the major objective. . . ."

Ho's regular forces always tried to apply the fourth principle: "In every battle, concentrate absolutely superior forces. . . ." This they did at Dien Bien Phu.

Consistently choosing its own conditions of battle, the Viet Minh adhered to the fifth principle: "Fight no unprepared engagements. Fight no engagements in which there is no assurance of victory. . . ."

Throughout all of their campaigns with regular and irregular forces, Ho's warriors were subjected to the sixth principle, which is "fear no sacrifice, fatigue," and train to fight successive engagements within a short time.

Ambushing French columns with regularity, Viet Minh forces regularly applied the seventh principle successfully: "Strive to destroy the enemy while he is in movement. . . ."

Hanoi and Haiphong stood in 1954 as Mukden and the port city of Yingkow did in 1947. The Chinese Reds eventually took Yingkow, and Mukden became an air-supported island that was later submerged into the Communist sea. Like the Chinese Reds, the Viet Minh was patient and abided by the eighth principle: "With regard to the question of assaults on cities [take] . . . those which are weakly defended. At favorable opportunities wrest all of those which are defended to medium degree. Wait until conditions mature to wrest [those] . . . strongly defended." As the 1954 negotiations in Geneva reached their crisis the Viet Minh began militarily to choke Hanoi and Haiphong. Conditions had matured with the fall of Dien Bien Phu. Obviously, Ho Chi-minh had wanted these cities for a long time, but he abided by the eighth axiom that Mao had demonstrated to be so successful. There is no doubt that Ho's forces would have attacked and tried to divide, so as later to devour, the delta region had the truce not been established at Geneva. Another Viet Minh aping of the Chinese Reds—and an old Communist military-political combination—was their backing with military victories of their representatives at the diplomatic table. Asiatic Reds regard it as axiomatic and necessary to arrive at the conference table with victories current enough to force favorable diplomatic arguments. The Chinese Reds set their pattern when General George C. Marshall tried to settle the civil war, and they applied it in Korea. It must always be expected that when a Red regime is ready to negotiate it is also ready with some soon-to-be-applied war plans.

Examine the tenth principle (which the Viet Minh used) and you find yourself reading between the lines or paraphrasing its real lines:

"Be skilled at using the intervals between two campaigns for the resting, regrouping and training of troops. (Do not rest too long.) . . . Do not let the enemy have breathing space." This principle concedes that the Communists at this particular military stage of development do not always have the logistical capability of "carrying through" and that their drives will often spend themselves, yet they must always seek to resume their pressure on the enemy. Logistically the Viet Minh was not up to prolonged attacks as was demonstrated in several instances when they hit the hard core of French defenses.

The French military problem over the years was much like that of the Chinese Nationalists. Unfortunately, the French technique was parallel. Pillboxes, islands of resistance, and bristling defenses were created to ward off the Red mosquito attacks, but as Communist aggressiveness increased, the French came to rely more on these fixed defenses. In the fury of the tasks and troubles at hand the French were often blind to the potential and power of mobility. In the jungles aerial reconnaissance and intelligence were useless. What was most needed was more effective ground intelligence or information from natives made ultra-friendly by political means. British General Sir Gerald Templar proved this point in Malaya. The French wanted to engage the foe in open battle; the Viet Minh forces avoided brutal contests until they were ready, and the French lacked timely enough information upon which to launch forces to catch the Communists. Thus the French were unable to concentrate on worthwhile Red concentrations.

In the sober application of these ten principles it must be conceded that Red Chinese advisers to the Viet Minh had their influence, and Ho Chi-minh and his officers can be credited with endurance and patience, but not with originality. The Chinese Reds spent many war years perfecting these principles, which will in the future provide the basic guide to all other Red revolutionary moves in Asia.

Dien Bien Phu, the target of much opportunity, was enveloped vertically, just as Chanchun was in 1946 when the Chinese Nationalists airlifted twelve thousand troops into the Manchurian capital, air supplied them, and lost them to Red concentric envelopments on the ground. Like the heoric defenders of Dien Bien Phu, the soldiers of Chiang Kai-shek fought at Changchun until their perimeter was only a few hundred yards in diameter—and even then resisted until they were physically overrun and captured at point-blank range.

After seeing this battle in Manchuria I could only conclude that to survive at all, such an airhead must move and keep moving on the ground, so as to force the enemy to realign his forces and prevent him from concentrating them. To stand still (and Nationalist heroism was equal to that demonstrated at Dien Bien Phu, although the skill was somewhat less) is to invite disaster.

Dien Bien Phu was a blocking effort and an attempt to engage Viet Minh forces in open battle so as to destroy their numbers. But the key to Viet Minh acceptance of battle here lay in the Red consideration of the odds and the "favorable conditions" which Red China's great tactician and strategist, General Lin Piao, summarizes several times in his written texts and in one place says: "Calculated risk engagements . . . should not be undertaken at random . . . and only if there is a 70 per cent prospect of victory."

The Battle of Dien Bien Phu goes deeper than the French decision to establish a blocking airhead there. Whose initiative really caused the conflict? Ho Chi-minh moved certain of his troops into Laos in a maneuver that was used by Chinese generals. The "One-Eyed Dragon," Chinese General Liu Po-cheng, executed such a move in 1947 when he moved his army group from a long-established battleground in Shantung and "fled" hundreds of miles southwest to the Taipeh Mountains, where he could fight in a new area and force the Nationalists to realign their strategy. In short, Liu diverted the enemy and forced him to fight in an area favorable to his own forces.

At the time of the Laos invasion the French were reported to have explained the disappearance of the Viet Minh 316th Division by saying that it had been "wiped off the battlefield." The Chinese civil war proved to U.S. Army observers that one must beware of the Red division that "disappears," because it always turns up again at a very embarrassing place. The 316th Division did just that.

The Viet Minh organization of divisions on a regional rather than operational basis is taken from Mao Tse-tung's concepts of consolidation in guerrilla war, which he wrote many years ago. As Colonel Samuel B. Griffith, USMC, translated it: "Without consolidation, one will have no strength for further expansion. In guerrilla warfare, if only one thinks about expansion but forgets consolidation, he will not be able to stand up against the enemy. . . . The correct policy is to expand on *bases* of consolidation." Logistically the regional organization provided the Viet Minh with bases of food, manpower and intelligence because the Reds forced the allegiance of the people within the particular countryside. Politically it allowed them to dominate the people and indoctrinate them.

In viewing Red regional organization on a local or tactical basis, it is important to look at the Viet Minh regional, or base, organization on a strategic level. Here we find the real logistical base of the Viet Minh in South China just as the Red Chinese base for their operations in Korea was in Manchuria—or, more realistically, in the Soviet Union. Yet in both cases the bases were outside the war zone and relatively safe because to bomb or invade them was to invite a bigger third power into the war.

The Viet Minh was a "twilight army" whose strength at night could exceed the numbers usually manifest in daylight. This army, like that of the Chinese Reds up until 1949, had two parts—the guerrilla and the formal—which acted in combination and coordination with each other. In most cases either portion could avoid battle by hiding its arms and merging into the countryside as peasants. This feature of momentary obscurity in one's own land was in direct contrast to the necessary formality of the French forces which had the mission of preserving the government and vital territories. However, the Viet Minh force possessed, and still possesses, the capability of operating portions of its body on this basis.

Like the Chinese Reds until 1949, the Viet Minh force has lacked an air force. Ho Chi-minh's forces have also, like their Chinese predecessors, operated with a fair minimum of motor transport, and have utilized motor vehicles for supply rather than for tactical mobility.

Oriental tactics of encirclement are not those of the half-moon diagrams we are prone to draw on maps. Instead, they are more subtle, and often part of the circle is a permanent guerrilla base which only needs the regular or more formal army to close with it. The Viet Minh's approach was often based upon this concept, long ago projected by Mao Tse-tung: ". . . if we analyze our various [regular army] bases and their interrelation, plus the relation of multiple guerrilla bases to the regular army's front lines, then we are encircling portions of the enemy. This is [a] second form of encirclement."

Ho Chi-minh's forces must now be measured in light of the progress of the Red Army of China since 1949. The "twilight army" of today will not resemble that army of the future. The Viet Minh forces are going to take on modern and formal aspect with Chinese assistance, especially now that it is not fighting.

In June, 1946, a truce was superimposed on the Chinese civil war fighting in Manchuria. At that time General Lin Piao, the Communist commander in Manchuria, had an irregular to half regular collection of well-disciplined, hardened troops. He had failed, however, in the Battle of Ssupingkai (1946) to stand up successfully against the more formal and formidable fire power of the Nationalist armies. The truce, for all of its well intended purpose, gave Lin Piao a period of many months. He utilized this interval to recruit, retrain, re-cadre, and reorganize his motley army. Logistically, he strengthened his army and made many technical improvements. It was this army, rebuilt during a truce period, that eventually attacked the Nationalists and swung the balance in favor of the Communists. Lin Piao's army was the avalanche that started the Red sweep of China.

The truce in Indochina now offers Ho Chi-minh the same opportunity and period of grace. He can now rebuild his army along more formal lines, cadre new units from among his veterans, train without having to fight at the same time, and strengthen his forces logistically and technically. The Viet Minh will not neglect to capitalize on the truce period.

Should the war be renewed, it could well be with an entirely new type of Viet Minh army.

23

Denis Warner

THE INVISIBLE

FRONT LINES

OF SOUTH VIETNAM

*T*HIS CAPITAL CITY OF SOUTH VIETNAM and the first twenty miles or so of road leading south through the rice fields of the Mekong Delta reflect an improving economic situation brought about by the American aid program. Results have not been dramatic, but they have been impressive in a quiet way.

The general air of well-being does not extend very far from Saigon, however. For most of the ten million Vietnamese who live south of Saigon, the improvement in living standards has been almost imperceptible.

Security and well-being are in direct proportion. Immediately beyond the city limits of Saigon, military jeeps travel only with armed escort. South of the Mekong and west along the Cambodian border, one moves through dreary and obviously poor hamlets and only partly tilled lands, escorted by armored cars front and rear and infantry in armored troop carriers. Buses and other civilian traffic are subject to unscheduled halts by rebel Viet Cong forces. Passengers on the "wanted" list are liable to find themselves abducted and shot; others may have to pay a tax levy.

From *The Reporter,* August 17, 1961, by permission.

Some of Vietnam's current difficulties may certainly be attributed to the shortcomings of the administration of President Ngo Dinh Diem. But isolated from Communist influence, South Vietnam under Diem and with American aid would certainly have prospered: it was beginning to prosper when terror hit the countryside and halted rice deliveries to Saigon. Even if Diem had been more liberal and democratic and his associates had all been beyond reproach, it is doubtful whether the Communists would have been prevented from gaining ground in the rural areas.

It is not true, either, that some of Diem's most bitterly criticized rural policies have been brutally and unnecessarily repressive. The resettlement of isolated peasants in twenty-one new towns, or agrovilles, was ineptly handled, causing resentments that the Viet Cong exploited, but only a small fraction of the rural population was involved. Nor does an examination of the even more bitterly criticized Law 10/1959, establishing special military tribunals to deal summarily with Communist acts of insurgency and treason, reveal the excesses of which it has been so often accused.

Diem was not alone in interpreting the Communist threat in conventional military terms. This was SEATO's interpretation and Washington's also. But in a generally gloomy situation there is now some reason for optimism. Many American Military Assistance Advisory Group officers in the field with the Vietnamese Army are familiar with the Viet Cong's tactics. "Most of us are sure that this problem is only fifteen per cent military and eighty-five per cent social and economic," Lieutenant Colonel Arthur P. Gregory, a MAAG officer assigned to the southern delta, told me. "It's not just a matter of killing Viet Cong but of coupling security with welfare."

The army has abandoned the task of guarding the frontiers against improbable conventional invasion and has turned seriously, and often effectively, to the task of fighting the insurgents. The appointment of a senior general, hitherto occupied with strategic planning, as field commander, and the division of the country into three territorial regions are moves designed both to improve efficiency and to prevent President Diem from continuing to intervene directly in the conduct of military operations. Sixty companies of rangers, trained by MAAG officers in guerrilla tactics, have added flexibility to the army. The badly paid and wretchedly equipped fifty-eight-thousand-man Civil Guard, which bore the brunt of the fighting last year and early this year, is also being expanded, retrained, and reequipped with assistance from the United States.

Finally, a major effort is being made to improve security communications. Most isolated hamlets and villages have had to rely on runners to send word of a Viet Cong attack to the nearest Civil Guard or army post. In future, village defense units will be able to radio for help.

"A Warless Area?"

In principle, therefore, the right military steps have been taken. When the monsoon rains end in October and the new campaigning season begins, the Viet Cong will find itself opposed by a much more impressive-looking deterrent force.

Yet there are many causes for disquiet. Saigon rumbles with discontent. An abortive paratroop coup last November lowered the flash point, and Diem's failure to respond to advice since the coup has brought about some profound changes in what passes in Saigon for public opinion. The government has not become more broadly based, is not more liberal, and remains, in effect, in the hands of an extremely limited group centering on Diem, his brother, Ngo Dinh Nhu, and the secretary of the presidency, Nguyen Dinh Thuan. Diem still commands personal respect and even admiration, but many Vietnamese have lost confidence in his leadership.

The army is still dissatisfied with slow promotions (some lieutenants and captains have had no promotion since 1954), and having saved Diem once, the senior officers now realize that they are the base on which his authority rests. Since comparatively few of the top twenty can be regarded as staunch Diem supporters, the possibility of another attempted *coup d'état* cannot be dismissed.

Another possibility now being openly advocated in Saigon by independent politicians, intellectuals, and students, seems even more likely to play into the hands of the Communists. The Movement for National Unification has no links with North Vietnam, but its manifesto, which was distributed in Vietnamese, French, and English at a recent crowded public meeting in a Saigon hall, could scarcely fail to meet with full Communist approval. It was Utopian and dangerous to rely on one group of imperialists to oust another, the manifesto said. In a world of cold war, the choice of a friend implied that of a foe. The proper solution, therefore, was to throw out all foreign advisers and to unite with neighbors to form a "warless" area in Southeast Asia.

Against this background of uncertainty, and a hope that neutrality may produce something better than alignment with the West has, the Viet Cong has made rapid progress.

From a network of village and hamlet cells, the Viet Cong has created a series of political bases extending even into the tribal regions of the central plateau, which Saigon once regarded as secure. The army controls a region while it is there in force; when it moves, the Viet Cong takes over again. Scores and even hundreds of village headmen and others suspected of cooperating with the government have been disemboweled and decapitated, and their families with them.

Every village has its undercover Viet Cong agents who act as the eyes and ears of the regular full-time forces and the regional part-time guerrillas. The Viet Cong rarely attempts to "hold" a village in force for more than a few hours, however, and then for specific purposes, such as tax collections, summary executions, and propaganda. The propaganda cadres, which are always unarmed, are careful to avoid suggesting that a take-over by North Vietnam is implicit in their plans.

Orders from Hanoi

The chain of Viet Cong command originates in Hanoi, and the Viet-minh directs, coordinates, and supplies the Viet Cong's operation. Hanoi itself makes no secret of the fact, and Peking is a firm and consistent ally. The Laodong Party congress in Hanoi last September called for an up-surge of revolution in the South. "Our compatriots of the South have no alternative but to stand up and fight with whatever weapons they can lay their hands on," the congress agreed. "The overthrowing of the U.S.–Diem clique and the liberation of the South constitute a task consistent with history's law of development and with the Geneva Agreement." Again on April 12 of this year, in the National Assembly in Hanoi, Nguyen Van Vinh, director of the Central Reunification Committee, said: "This multiform struggle [in South Vietnam] is entirely consistent with the line laid down by the national congress of the Laodong Party and with the manifesto of the Moscow Conference of eighty-one parties." Consistent also, he might have added, with the policy enunciated by Chou En-lai, who as recently as June 12 reaffirmed full Chinese support for "the Viet-namese people's struggle against U.S. imperialist aggression" and Diem's "terrorist" rule.

Hanoi announced the formation of a National Liberation Front in January. This was followed by the creation of a Liberation Press Agency and also an Association of Students for the Liberation of South Vietnam. A month or so later, the National Liberation Front and the National Liberation Army set up headquarters in eastern Cambodia close to the South Vietnam border and soon achieved effective administrative and military coordination in the rebel areas of South Vietnam. What these headquarters in Cambodia amount to in terms of men and materials is anybody's guess. The Cambodians indignantly deny their existence, but both the Vietnamese Army and western military attachés in Saigon are certain of their general whereabouts and certain too that they maintain constant radio communication with Hanoi, whose orders are in turn trans-mitted to the three regional Viet Cong commanders inside South Vietnam.

Only about half of a force of perhaps 15,000 guerrillas have firearms. Some of the rifles and almost all the mines and booby traps are home-made and, though lethal enough, are extremely primitive. They were also extremely primitive, it is useful to recall, during the Indo-China war. In

1954 one Vietminh regiment, which tied down three French mobile brigades on the Hanoi-Haiphong road in the Tongking Delta, operated entirely on captured French supplies. It did not receive a round of ammunition, a single weapon, or a pound of explosives from the Vietminh main supply. The Viet Cong, it is clear, is being raised on the same hard rations.

An Unfortunate Playback

It is also being opposed by tactics that are often tragically reminiscent of the tactics used by the French. The Civil Guard, in its concrete block-houses and compounds protected by barbed wire and minefields, lives in isolation from the people it is supposed to protect, just as the French Expeditionary Force in the identical blockhouses used to live, and sometimes to die, in isolation years ago.

Recently I went south from Saigon to Vinh Binh Province to watch six army and Civil Guard battalions with artillery and naval support launch a major drive along the peninsula stretching toward the South China Sea. This first major action by the Vietnamese Army since just before the April elections would have been much more impressive if I had not seen a precisely similar operation with identical intentions conducted by the French Expeditionary Force in Thai Binh Province in the Tonkin Delta eleven years earlier. Whether at divisional headquarters over a six-course, two-hour French lunch, agreeably served on a white damask tablecloth with adequate quantities of Algerian wine, or forward at the much simpler and more warlike regimental headquarters, I had the curious impression that I was watching an old and familiar movie.

Five armored cars and an armored troop carrier were detailed to act as escort for me and two Vietnamese correspondents on the fifty-mile drive from the Mekong River crossing to divisional headquarters at Tra Vinh. When we moved out as far as the regiments, we went in convoys containing tens of vehicles and almost a company of men. Once again it was an army that thought in terms of towns and roads—and an enemy that thought in terms of people and countryside.

The Pattern of Laos

Certainly military action is necessary against the Viet Cong. It is also inevitable that of the approximately four hundred "Viet Cong" killed each month, many should be innocent bystanders. So many camp followers and women guerrillas are mixed up with the Viet Cong that any estimate of the numbers killed in error is at best only a fairly wild guess. Some western military attachés put it at twenty-five per cent—a clue to the impact these "errors" may have on the peasants.

The psychological-warfare and political-warfare teams that follow the army with movies and lectures in the hope of winning converts face an uphill task. Too often the peasants are interrupted in their own tasks of personal rehabilitation and asked to repair roads and installations for the military, and no money is available to replace pigs and poultry or reconstruct lost homes. Though the problem is largely social and economic, it is still treated as if it were purely military and political.

As many Americans now in the field understand very well, economic aid at the center and military efficiency in the field are not in themselves enough to cope with a revolution of this type. First, there is a need for a national spirit, or at least a will to fight. "The Americans can train soldiers in three months but they won't be able to teach them to love their country in three years," one Vietnamese said. If Diem had fulfilled early hopes, the inspiration might have come from the top.

This is not to suggest that Diem no longer has a part to play. His downfall could well prove an unqualified disaster. If it is too late to hope that Diem may change, it is not too late to find the resources for rural welfare, in particular for welfare of a type that will persuade the peasants that their role is something more than victims in this war. In addition to the army and its psychological-warfare teams, there is a crying need for rural-aid teams with the means to inspire at least the hope for a better future and perhaps, in the process, to create some sort of national consciousness.

There is not much time left. The Viet Cong, in the best Maoist tradition, clearly regards the peasants as the "sea" in which they will "swim" to victory. They have begun an intensive recruiting campaign in the rural areas to fill the ranks depleted by casualties that have averaged more than a thousand a month for the past eighteen months. They hope to proclaim a "liberated" area, probably not in the Mekong Delta, where the terrain is unfavorable, but in the central plateau.

In Paris and Geneva, representatives of a hundred or more Vietnamese expatriates, including prominent political figures of the Bao Dai era, have been scurrying around the Vietminh camp in the hope of establishing a relationship between the anti-Diem neutrals and the Viet Cong. This fits precisely with Communist plans for repeating the pattern that worked so well for them in Laos. If the situation deteriorates after the monsoons, and Hanoi leaves no doubt that this is its intention, the establishment of a "liberated" area and the creation of a rival "neutralist" government in South Vietnam, appealing alike to the peasants and the frustrated intellectuals, middle class, and students of Saigon, is the obvious next step.

24

Anne M. Jonas and
George K. Tanham

LAOS: A PHASE IN
CYCLIC REGIONAL
REVOLUTION

THE COMMUNISTS WAGE REVOLUTIONARY WARFARE continuously, but often their activities remain hidden and the gradual deterioration of the situation goes virtually unnoticed. Suddenly, well-organized forces appear and precipitate civil war and international crisis.

Current communist moves in Laos conform to this pattern. After the cease-fire in Indochina in 1954, overt communist military activity in Southeast Asia virtually ground to a halt. Nevertheless, terrorism, political subversion and guerrilla actions served to set the stage for a new revolution. The results of this seven-year effort are visible in Laos today.

Laos, however, is but a small part of the broader battlefield of the globe. If the communists are to exploit successfully any one of the spate of "national liberation" conflicts which continue to flare in Asia, Africa and Latin America, they must carefully mesh local actions with global strategy. Above all, they must avoid local moves which might trigger unfavorable or dangerous developments at the international level, including a world war.

From *Orbis,* Spring, 1961. Copyright 1961 by the Foreign Policy Research Institute, University of Pennsylvania, and reproduced by permission.

Khrushchev has indicated that the level of devastation the USSR would be required to absorb in a central nuclear war is considered by him unacceptably high, at least for the moment. Hence, his present strategy is to seek a *modus vivendi* with the major Western powers. It is essential to the success of this strategy that he avoid too overtly aggressive a policy anywhere on the globe. Cyclic regional revolution waged by proxy and masked as an "internal conflict" may very well be the way out of this dilemma, and Southeast Asia appears to be the ideal proving ground for this tactic.

I

What are the key characteristics of cyclic regional revolution? From the pattern of events, as they have evolved in Southeast Asia between the end of World War II and early 1961, six successive steps may be discerned.

First, the area earmarked for conquest is to be prepared for revolution, primarily through political subversion. Second, a revolutionary guerrilla war is to be waged along the lines postulated years ago by Mao Tse-tung. Third, if it is expedient, a partial victory may be accepted and a cease-fire concluded when both local military considerations and developments on the international political scene are estimated to be the most favorable. Fourth, the revolutionary base thereby acquired is to be strengthened, and to be used simultaneously to initiate immediately a new revolutionary war. Fifth, this new phase of the regional revolution is to be pushed to its own decisive stage, as events permit. Sixth, local insurgents are to continue to operate in this fashion, until the whole region has been conquered.

If this hypothesis is correct, the first war in the Southeast Asian cycle lasted from the end of World War II to the middle of 1954, when North Vietnam became the permanent revolutionary base for the area. The decisive stage of the second war seems now to have begun in Laos. Should the Pathet Laotian guerrillas, in turn, succeed in gaining permanent control over at least a part of Laos, a new conflict can be initiated elsewhere. Its exact form cannot, of course, be predicted. But there is no question that the communists' successes have considerably widened their range of future alternatives.

II

An essential element in the communist formula for waging cyclic regional revolution in Southeast Asia has been the active application of Mao

Tse-tung's earlier theories of revolutionary war, adapted to meet local requirements.

Mao envisaged a war in which initially inferior communist forces ultimately could defeat the enemy in an attritional, protracted conflict. According to Mao's concept, the struggle would proceed through three distinct stages, each unpredictable in length. During stage one, the inferior revolutionary forces would be indoctrinated and organized in small groups, and would carry out limited sabotage and terror operations. As the capabilities and strength of the guerrillas increased, during stage two the operations would take on a more formal cast, and some regularized forces would begin to fight in small-scale engagements. When the communists felt their forces were superior to those of the enemy, the decisive phase would begin with the launching of the counteroffensive.

Even before Mao had succeeded in seizing power on the Chinese mainland, Ho Chi Minh and his Viet Minh guerrillas in 1945 and 1946 initiated their struggle with the French to gain control of what then comprised Indochina. After a few false starts, the Viet Minh conducted their operations during the first two phases of the war along the lines Mao had prescribed: while the guerrillas engaged in terrorist operations, political indoctrination of the population, and subversive maneuvers designed to weaken the enemy, a regular revolutionary force was recruited, trained and equipped. These measures were designed to prepare for the decisive third phase of the war—the launching of the communist counteroffensive.

By 1950, the military Commander-in-Chief of the Viet Minh, General Ngo Nguyen Giap, had codified a specifically Viet Minh military doctrine which refined Mao's earlier concept of when and how to conduct the counteroffensive. While Mao had never denied that guerrilla operations would retain their important role even after the counteroffensive had been launched, he had envisaged, during this decisive phase of the war, battles conducted along conventional lines between the enemy's troops and the regular forces the communists meanwhile had built up. By contrast, General Giap viewed the decisive counteroffensive phase of the war as being composed of several sub-phases: only in the last of these would there be formal battles, in the traditional sense.

In Giap's view, even during the final drive to victory, mobility was to be the key to all operations, offensive as well as defensive. Like the guerrillas, the regular forces were to slip away when threatened by attack from superior enemy troops and to refuse to accept battle in unfavorable situations. The guerrillas were to strike to harass, confuse and demoralize, while during the "showdown" phase of the counteroffensive the regular forces, although employing the very same tactics, would strike to annihilate.

With only a few exceptions, Giap's principles subsequently governed the conduct of the actual Viet Minh military counteroffensive. The decisive victory came, however, when he deviated from his tactical doctrine during the battle at Dien Bien Phu and accepted a static battle situation.

III

True to his own—and Mao's—doctrine, General Giap, when he mounted his attack on Dien Bien Phu in late 1953 and carried it through to successful negotiation of a cease-fire in July 1954, was closely in touch with communist assessments of related developments on the international political scene. His military counteroffensive was timed to take account of the interplay of events in the international arena as well as the opportunities afforded by the local military situation. It was this careful timing which permitted the Viet Minh to conclude an armistice on favorable terms.

The first post-Stalin conference of the Big Four Foreign Ministers opened in Berlin on January 24, 1954, and Indochina was one of the many outstanding problems crying for attention. France was convinced of her inability to resist the rising popular pressures at home to end the war in Indochina and alarmed by the increasing effectiveness of the Viet Minh on the battlefield. She was, therefore, keenly susceptible to Molotov's proposal that the Big Four Foreign Ministers meet once more, this time with Communist China and "other interested states," to try to work out a peaceful settlement of the protracted Indochinese war. Ultimately, it was agreed to meet at Geneva late in April. During the intervening months, the coordination of Viet Minh military operations to coincide with—and attempt to influence—developments on the international scene reached a high point. Mass Viet Minh attacks on Dien Bien Phu during March and early April exacted a heavy toll from the French defenders. A series of hurried high-level conferences among France, Great Britain and the United States failed to produce any immediate agreement on how to cope with the worsening military situation.

While pressing their attack on Dien Bien Phu, the Viet Minh were conducting simultaneous forays into Laos and Cambodia.

The Big Four powers, Communist China, the Royal Governments of Vietnam, Cambodia and Laos, and the Viet Minh met at Geneva on April 26, but procedural questions for a while delayed meaningful discussions on Indochina. Just as these problems had been solved, Dien Bien Phu fell on May 7. There followed an intensive exchange of proposals and counterproposals for a cease-fire. Meanwhile, the Viet Minh troops were moving in for an assault on the delta region around Hanoi and Haiphong, while continuing smaller operations in Cambodia and Laos.

By June 17, the French government had fallen, and high-ranking participants in the Geneva discussions had returned home for a recess. The new French premier, Mendès-France, immediately went on record that he would resign unless he could work out a way to end the Indochinese war by July 20. Formal negotiations at Geneva were not resumed until July 17, and prompt conclusion of a cease-fire therefore became a matter of extreme urgency. By July 21, the West, under pressure, had agreed to the partitioning of Vietnam. By giving the communists all rights in the northern half of that country and by creating tripartite commissions to safeguard communist adherence to the armistice terms, the West hoped to devise some means of containing the Viet Minh threat and assisting South Vietnam, Laos and Cambodia to attain political stability.

Under the armistice terms, France agreed to withdraw her few troops from Cambodia, but retained the right to leave officers and men to train the Royal Laotian Army. By contrast, the Viet Minh were to withdraw all their forces to North Vietnam. Neither the United States nor the Royal Vietnamese government signed the armistice agreements. Instead, each issued a separate unilateral statement, thus reserving some future freedom of action.

The French proceeded in good faith to withdraw their forces in accordance with the armistice terms. For the most part, the Royal Armies of Vietnam, Laos and Cambodia already were confined to the areas stipulated by the armistice agreements. But the Viet Minh, thanks to their ethnic ties in the neighboring states and their guerrilla organization, were able to leave a fairly large clandestine cadre in South Vietnam, a "hard core" in Laos, and lesser numbers of guerrillas in Cambodia. Even while the majority of the Viet Minh forces were being evacuated northward, some guerrilla forays continued in Vietnam near the supposedly demilitarized zone around the area of the demarcation line. The second war in the cyclic regional revolution had begun.

IV

In the years between the cease-fire in 1954 and the launching of a counteroffensive in Laos by the Pathet Lao guerrillas late in 1960, the Viet Minh concentrated on two objectives: (1) strengthening the regional revolutionary base—North Vietnam—economically and militarily; and (2) infiltrating neighboring countries to wage revolutionary war clandestinely, thereby keeping unrest and political instability alive while preparing the indigenous rebels for their own "internal revolutions." Some Viet Minh guerrillas moved back and forth across the borders to assist local insurgents in their terror operations, to engage in training, to help indoctrinate the population with the ideology of communism and to transport and secrete caches of arms and ammunition. Others, in North Vietnam, helped train new recruits for the modernized regular army the Viet Minh were building up, and, along with the regular forces, participated in the over-all effort to repair the war damage, indoctrinate the population, and improve the status of that country's civilian economy.

Viet Minh opportunities to conduct the first two phases of the second war in Southeast Asia during a period of ostensible peace were enhanced by the fact that the international supervisory control commissions (composed of Poland, India, and Canada) were powerless to compel the communist belligerents to observe the armistice terms. Poland, of course, showed favoritism to the Viet Minh, and India was inclined to permit the countries of Southeast Asia to settle their internal problems without outside interference. Canada was in the minority. Furthermore, Viet Minh violations, being clandestine, were extremely difficult to prove. Assisted by the Pathet Lao, and, to a lesser extent, by the Khmer in Cambodia, the Viet Minh were essentially unchallenged in carrying forward the regional revolution.

Up to early 1961, Viet Minh infiltration of surrounding nations was heaviest in Laos, South Vietnam and Cambodia. But extensive operations also had been carried out in Thailand. While groups of non-Communist nationals were attempting to establish stable governments in these nations, the indigenous communist guerrillas, with Viet Minh assistance, were sabotaging these efforts by indoctrinating the population, expanding, training and improving their own revolutionary forces and engaging in sabotage and terror operations.

V

Laos proved fertile ground for Viet Minh infiltration. It is not surprising, therefore, that this tiny, unhappy country should have become the site of the current effort to establish another communist regime in Southeast Asia.

After the 1954 cease-fire, the Pathet Lao had opted against integration with the Royal Laotian forces and, until 1957, succeeded in retaining armed control over their traditional home stronghold, the two provinces of Phong Saly and Sam Neua, along the border between North Vietnam and Laos. Consequently, the Viet Minh had little difficulty in moving back and forth across the border to help fan Laotian unrest and strengthen local revolutionary cadres. Even the Vientiane agreements of 1957, by which the Pathet Lao supposedly had merged their military forces with those of the Royal Army in return for the legalization of the Communist Party, did not, in essence, alter the situation. Only a few of the Pathet Laotian troops who were integrated with the Royal Army left their traditional stronghold.

The vast majority remained stationed in the two northeastern provinces, kept their own officers, and continued to operate in semi-autonomy. Moreover, Kayson Phomivhane, the guerrilla military commander, went completely underground with some of the hard core. Internal unrest continued, therefore, marked by a succession of coalition governments, some strongly anti-communist, and by skirmishes between Kayson's guerrillas and the Royal Laotian Army. By early September, 1959, the situation had deteriorated to a point where Laos had appealed to the United Nations to send an emergency force to stop what it termed "flagrant aggression" on the part of North Vietnam. The UN responded by sending a fact-finding commission. Its report, submitted to the Security Council on November 6, 1959, did indicate that North Vietnam had furnished equipment, arms, ammunition, supplies and political advice to the Pathet Lao. But all identifiable Viet Minh personnel meanwhile had been withdrawn temporarily across the poorly demarcated border, and justification for UN intervention was deemed insufficient.

The year 1960 brought a new upsurge of military skirmishes incited by the Pathet Lao, and the Royal Government proved totally unable to form a stable regime. By this time, the non-communists were split into several factions. At one end of this non-communist spectrum were the extreme rightists; at the other, the supporters of Souvanna Phouma, who claimed to want a completely middle-of-the-road and neutralist policy for Laos. Between them, several factions were battling for recognition. While these various non-communist groups struggled for power, the Pathet Lao were successfully preparing for the final stage of the war, the counteroffensive.

By the end of the year, Souvanna Phouma had once more lost control of the government and had fled to Cambodia. The Pathet Laotian troops had emerged from hiding to launch massed attacks in a war of movement designed to capture the important area of the Plaine de Jarres. On the international political level, the pattern was remarkably similar to the moment, in late 1953, when the Viet Minh had launched their counteroffensive on the battlefield. This time, however, the major communist powers, and even the Pathet Lao, are utilizing a non-communist figure head as "temporary ally." Souvanna Phouma, whom they acclaim as "the rightful ruler of Laos," provides them with a convenient shield behind which to carry on their aggressive activities. Should their bid for complete power fail, the communists can justify their recent military operations with pious protests that their objective was merely to reinstate a neutral leader.

The communists in Laos are conducting the second war of the cyclic regional revolution in Southeast Asia under far easier conditions than those the Viet Minh faced earlier. First, they have been assisted by the Viet Minh in training their guerrillas. Second, they have General Giap's war doctrine and military experience to guide them. Third, they are fighting local nationals split among themselves and highly susceptible to political indoctrination. Fourth, they have entered the final military phase of the counteroffensive relatively equal in battle readiness to the opponent (Western materiel furnished the Royal forces has been offset by similar assistance rendered to the insurgents by the communist bloc). Finally, they have a sanctuary in North Vietnam to which they can retreat, if necessary.

With North Vietnam as an established revolutionary base, the communists have gained considerable flexibility in deciding the timing and nature of future operations in Laos and other parts of Southeast Asia. Such flexibility is essential because local operations are responsive to Western countermeasures, both local and international, as well as to the effectiveness and speed of the communist counteroffensive. True, the growing Soviet weapons arsenal may have reduced the likelihood that the West will intervene directly—under the aegis of the UN or by unilateral actions. Moreover, the situation has been deliberately beclouded to the extent where the West would be hard-put to justify plausibly any formal intervention. Yet this does not rule out the possibilities of Western pressures on Moscow that, in turn, would have their effect in Southeast Asia.

Should the Pathet Lao succeed in seizing power in Laos, they, in conjunction with the Viet Minh, may decide to expand the miiltary conflict to other countries of the area. Alternately, they may choose to step up guerrilla terror operations to exploit existing instability in neighboring nations, which a communist seizure of power in Laos would serve to intensify. Still another possibility would be to follow the earlier Viet Minh example of agreeing to a cease-fire and formal partition which would furnish a second base from which to launch the third war in the regional revolutionary cycle. The USSR must tailor its support to the limits imposed by its own policy objectives vis-à-vis the United States and other major Western powers. It is worth noting that, thus far, the Soviet Union continues to uphold Souvanna Phouma, while restricting its overt military assistance of the local guerrillas to logistical support.

VI

What advantages can the communists hope to gain by the cyclical-revolutionary technique?

First, in Southeast Asia the leaders of international communism have gained experience which can be applied to waging revolutionary warfare by proxy in any area where national boundaries do not conform to tribal and ethnic lines of demarcation. Already, communist actions in Africa and Latin America signal the new strategy, boldly proclaimed by Khrushchev, of supporting local rebels who show promise of being able to establish revolutionary bases in areas previously closed to the communist offensive.

Second, many of the conflict principles involved in the conduct of cyclic regional revolution are equally applicable to the exploitation of "revolutionary opportunities" arising in any single country.

Third, the Viet Minh, as the near fulfillment of their revolutionary mission in Southeast Asia, will become increasingly free to assume a larger role in providing "proxy" aid to indigenous rebels elsewhere. They already have consolidated their power, modernized their army, and built up the economy of their own country to a point where, if necessary, they could eventually assume the prime responsibility for clandestine or even overt training of local guerrilla leaders from other underdeveloped areas. In that case, Moscow and Peking could more easily confine their own direct support of such guerrilla operations to the limits imposed by the necessity to avoid retaliatory moves by the major Western nations.

Fourth, this potential strategy would have the added virtue that, should matters get out of hand, Moscow and Peking could extricate themselves from involvement in an allegedly "internal affair," even if it meant officially rebuking the Viet Minh for "aggression."

Cyclic regional revolution, then, is a conflict technique which admirably serves one of the two main objectives of current international communist policy: the exploitation of "national liberation movements." And this technique, better than any other, minimizes the jeopardy to the Soviet Union's simultaneous efforts to promote "coexistence" and negotiate with the United States at the highest level.

Further References

BOOKS

Champassak, S. *Storm over Laos: A Contemporary History*. New York: Praeger, 1961.

Cole, A. B., ed. *Conflict in Indochina and International Repercussions*. Ithaca, N.Y.: Cornell University, 1956.

Fall, B. B. *The Viet-Minh Regime: Government and Administration in the Democratic Republic of Vietnam*. Ithaca, N.Y.: Cornell University, 1954.

———. *Street without Joy: Indochina at War, 1946–1954*. Harrisburg, Pa.: Stackpole, 1961.

Fishel, W. D., ed. *Problems of Freedom: Vietnam Since Independence*. New York: The Free Press, 1962.

Friang, B. *Parachutes and Petticoats*. Tr. by James Cadell. London: Jarrolds, 1958.

Hammer, E. J. *The Struggle for Indochina*. Stanford, Calif.: Stanford University, 1954.

Human Relations Area Files, Inc. *Laos, Its People, Its Society, Its Culture*. New Haven, Conn.: HRAF, 1960.

Lancaster, D. *The Emancipation of French Indochina*. New York: Oxford University, 1961.

Riesen, R. *Jungle Mission*. Tr. by James Oliver. New York: Crowell, 1957.

Tanham, G. K. *Communist Revolutionary Warfare: The Viet-Minh in Indochina*. New York: Praeger, 1961.

ARTICLES

Bashore, B. T. "Soldier of the Future," *Army Magazine*, September, 1961.

Chassis, G. J. "Lessons of the War in Indochina," *Interavia*, 1952.

Crocker, H. E. "The General Situation in Indochina up to September, 1953," *Army Quarterly*, January, 1954.

Fall, B. B. "Indochina: The Last Year of the War," *Military Review*, October and December, 1956.

———. "South Viet-Nam's Internal Problems," *Pacific Affairs*, September, 1958.

———. "Street without Joy" (Chapter 7 from his book, *Street without Joy*, listed above), *Marine Corps Gazette* (Special Guerrilla Warfare Issue), January, 1961.

Geneste, M. E. "Danger from Below," *U.S. Naval Institute Proceedings*, November, 1960.

Hotchkiss, V. C. "Laos—Country of Conflict," *Military Review*, June, 1961.

Karnow, S. "Diem Defeats His Own Best Troops," *The Reporter*, Jan. 17, 1961.

Katzenbach, E. L. "Indochina: A Military-Political Appreciation," *World Politics,* January, 1952.

Koch, H. G. "Terrain Tailors Tactics in Indochina," *Army Combat Forces Journal,* April, 1954.

"The Last Months in Indochina," *Marine Corps Gazette,* January, 1955.

McQuillen, J. F. "Indochina," *Marine Corps Gazette,* December, 1954.

Malgankar, M. D. "The Situation in Indochina," *Military Digest,* October, 1951.

Merglen, A. "Two Airborne Raids in North Vietnam," *Military Review,* April, 1958.

Norman, M. E. "Dien Bien Phu and the Future of Airborne Operations," *Military Review,* June, 1956.

Nomdeplume, Col. "A Military Briefing on Laos," *Marine Corps Gazette,* April, 1961.

O'Ballance, E. "The Campaign in Indochina: Fighting in Laos, 1953–54," *Army Quarterly,* April, 1955.

Prosser, L. M. "The Bloody Lessons of Indochina," *Combat Forces Journal,* June, 1955.

Rose, J. A. "The Fight for Rice in Divided Vietnam," *The Reporter,* October 12, 1961.

Soixante. "Defeat in the East," *Royal United Service Institute Journal,* August, 1961.

Soustelle, J. "Indochina and Korea: One Front," *Foreign Affairs,* October, 1955.

Souyris, A. "An Effective Counter-Guerrilla Procedure," tr. and condensed in *Military Review,* March, 1957.

Topping, S. "Indochina on the Razor's Edge," *Foreign Affairs,* April, 1951.

Warner, D. "The Loss of Laos," *The Reporter,* July 6, 1961.

DOCUMENT

Department of State. Office of Intelligence Research. Washington, D.C.: *Prospects for the Resolution of the Conflict in Indochina,* Report no. 44, 11p., n.d.

PART 7

MALAYA—POST-WORLD WAR II

In 1948 the Communist party of Malaya began overt terrorist operations. Its timing was nearly perfect. The Malayan police force was untrained and ill-equipped. The token force of British troops was not prepared or equipped to fight an antiguerrilla war. Using arms supplied by the British in World War II and supplies acquired from the defeated Japanese, the Communists put into effect phase one of a three-phase operational plan.

The first phase consisted of guerrilla actions designed to terrorize the population and weaken the people's confidence in the government's ability to protect them. The second phase was to consist of continuous attacks on communication networks and the taking over of small selected areas. These occupied areas were to have served as temporary bases that would facilitate the next phase. That third phase would involve taking over local administrative control in these temporary base areas, conversion of the guerrilla elements into conventional formations, and turning the occupied areas into permanent bases of operation.

Fortunately, the British and Malayan government forces were able to prevent phases two and three from occurring and eventually brought peace to Malaya once more. It took over ten years. The success was not due solely to military operations; a combination of political, social, economic, psychological, and military actions eventually defeated the Communists in Malaya.

The jungles of Malaya still hold a small scattered force of die-hard Communists who find comfort in the thought that it took Mao Tse-tung's forces thirty years to win China. They are confident, too, that the West, with its "forgive and forget" values, will eventually let up pressure. Then, with the West's attentions on another part of the world, and with supplies from Comrade Mao Tse-tung, they may once more attempt what they see as their rendezvous with destiny.

In the first selection Linebarger presents an overview of the international complexities of the situation in Malaya as they appeared during the fighting. This is followed by Dougherty's comprehensive yet concise summary of the guerrilla problem—how it was met and the final outcome. Finally, there is Crockett's eye-witness account of a counterguerrilla patrol in action.

25

Paul M. A. Linebarger   **THEY CALL 'EM**

BANDITS

IN MALAYA

MALAYA IS A MILITARY PARADOX. Strategically it is a well secured portion of the British Empire—that inner empire still governed as a chain of colonies from London. At the same time it is one of the most successful areas of Communist guerrilla activity. Both the British and the Communists are doing well. Each has dented the other very perceptibly. But in three years of open warfare neither one has put the other out of business.

One of the basic factors behind the paradox lies in the fact that neither side is fighting a war. The Communists are waging a "liberation" and the British are using combat forces for an "emergency." It's something like a field with a basket at one end and goal posts at the other, with two husky teams, one playing basketball and the other football, and each determined not only to win, but to win in its own peculiar way.

To start with, British Malaya isn't British Malaya; there is no such thing. There is the Crown Colony of Singapore, a large island with a big

From *U.S. Army Combat Forces Journal*, January, 1951. Copyright 1951 by Association of the U.S. Army and reproduced by permission.

Chinese city on it. Singapore has some Malays, somewhat more than there are American Indians in New York City. Singapore is governed by a British governor. It has all the machinery of a democracy. As one of the local bigwigs told me, the Hindus run the political parties, the Chinese do the voting, and the Scots get elected.

The rest of British Malaya is the Federation of Malaya. Part of this is British and part of it merely a British protectorate. Both parts are in the Federation, so that George VI, in the role of local sultan for the old cities of Penang and Malacca, sits vicariously as a co-equal with the other sultans (of Johore, Negri Sembilan, Perak, and so on) under a high commissioner who represents the British King in London. Just to keep the situation from being too simple, the British have installed a policy-making official called the Commissioner General for Southeast Asia who coordinates not only Malaya with Singapore, but both of them with British Hong Kong and British Borneo.

The British military command is divided up between the three services and the two governments in British Malaya. Coordination is effected by Lieutenant General Sir Harold Briggs, a brilliant improviser who, since he is a key military personage in British Malaya, obviously serves in a civilian capacity. Otherwise his role would be unparadoxical and probably that might be un-British. It is up to General Briggs to coordinate everything he can find—governments, police, land forces, naval forces, air forces, and so on—in a unified campaign to suppress persons whom the British authorities do not describe as "Communists," but as bandits whose "rebellion" is labelled an "emergency." And warfare against them is not "war" but "operations."

Do you begin to see the picture?

The British are conducting operations against bandits, not a war against Communists. If they did, you see, the insurance rates would go up. Besides, if they used ordinary Anglo-Saxon words for what they are doing, even the British home public might wake up to the fact that the British are fighting the Reds in Malaya, trading with them in Hong Kong, buttering them up in Peking, and shooting them dead in Korea—and that would be a little too paradoxical even for the British home public. Hence, the British in Malaya find it much safer to use the magic words, "bandits" and "operations."

But all of this gets back to infantry.

The jungle is so thick in most of Malaya that a man disappears completely six feet from a trail. Hot pursuit is out of the question. Even atomic weapons could not clear the thousands of square miles of fantastically rich jungle growth. The few thousand Chinese Communist guerrillas who leap out from the jungle to harass the British with murder, sniping, sabotage, and arson cannot be found by any forthright clearing of forces out of the country. This is especially the case since the Communists are not fighting a war either. They are conducting a liberation.

On their side the Communists of Malaya are mostly Chinese by race, language, and national origin. There are some Malays and a few Indians, but these do not amount to much. The Communists are organized into the Malayan Races Liberation Army, called MRLA for short. The bases of this army consist of camps accommodating from half a dozen to several hundred men. These camps are logistically supplied from within British territory. The actual Chinese who do the fighting make a point of trying to act like an army with real uniforms, genuine flags, and guns that really shoot.

Though the Malayan Communists are Chinese, they are not Chinese Communists. Chinese Communists are people with whom the British Empire is at peace. It is perfectly legal to be a member of the Chinese Communist Party in Singapore, though it is not legal to be a Chinese *and* a member of the *Malayan* Communist Party. Therefore, the Chinese Communists who are not Chinese Communists, and who aren't very Malayan either, are fighting a Britain which is at peace with Communist China.

Their chief tactics are what ignorant Americans would call murder and arson.

Rubber, unfortunately for the British, burns very readily and a great deal of the effort of the MRLA has been centered on the burning of stocks of sheet rubber. When I was in Singapore last summer they burned up several million dollars' worth in a fire which built up a cloud with a distressing resemblance to an atomic bomb explosion. When the Communists are not burning rubber they are shooting people. They prefer to shoot soldiers, but they will also shoot children, women, or anyone else handy. They particularly enjoy torturing informers to death inexpertly but slowly.

Let us look at this war again. Five thousand Chinese plus or minus are committing as many murders as they can and setting as many fires as they can in order to destroy British rule in a territory which is solidly under British military, naval, and air control. They have frightened a large part of the local Chinese population into an attitude of neutrality or silence. Opposing them are many times their number of British regulars, local militia, police, plantation guards, and other armed men. The anti-Communists try to find the Communists and then arrest them according to the best British standards of good police procedure. When they have to they even shoot them, but they do not do what the Chinese Communists do in China—take hostages. Nor do they do what both the Japanese and Chiang Kai-chek did against Communists at other times in China—take mass reprisals.

The guerrilla forces in Malaya are Chinese and they are Communist. They do not appear to be the Mao Tse-tung variety. Their tactics and weapons derive much more from British training given them during the war as part of the underground anti-Japanese campaign than from anything Communist armed forces have learned in the struggles within China itself. The local Communists are fighting a war along the standard Moscow pattern for guerrillas, but they are doing so under immense logistical and communications handicaps.

Singapore looks close to China on a map of the world, but it would not be much easier for Mao Tse-tung's land forces to walk from China to Singapore than it would for Peron's land forces to march overland from Argentina to Nicaragua.

From the United States the Far East seems to be all one piece. It is only locally that one realizes the immensity of the natural barriers. Only in Singapore is one forced to remember that the Japanese troops which conquered Singapore from the landward side were not brought to Malaya overland, but by ships, and dumped ashore along the peninsula not too far from their final points of attack. The prospects of overland Chinese Communist reinforcements from Mao's Red China are virtually nil.

General Briggs is a real individualist, a man of bold and unorthodox military thinking, who reminded me in some ways of Stilwell or Lawrence of Arabia. Faced with a war that is not a war, against enemies who commit murder, opposed by an army without a government and supported, not by one government, but by more different British governments than he could count, General Briggs is meeting the Communist attack with a counterattack as weird as it is effective. He is waging what might be called sociological warfare. . . .

General Briggs is applying the tactics of big-game hunting to the Communist guerrillas and he is cleaning them out by procedures more nearly resembling pest control than Clausewitzian concepts of strategy. In order to destroy the enemy he is breaking up the nesting places of the pests.

Hundreds of thousands of Chinese squatters have moved to inaccessible villages in remote parts of the jungle. These squatter villages have neither British law, nor British police, nor British health services, nor British postal connections, nor British schools. (Of course, all these British services would be supplied by Malay sultans, but we can leave that complication aside and refer the interests of the reader to that fascinating document, *Annual Report on the Federation of Malaya, 1949.*[1]

These outlying villages form the prime base of the anti-British guerrillas. The Chinese squatters can be intimidated precisely because British authority cannot protect them. Therefore General Briggs is proposing to absquat, unsquat, or desquat the squatter villages, whichever it is he has to do to a squatter village to make it an ex-squatter village. One of his chief weapons is cadastral—that's a term I never saw in a military dictionary before. It consists of giving land titles to the Chinese squatters, settling

1. Printed at the Government Press by H. T. Ross, Government Printer, Kuala Lumpur, 1950, price $5.00 or 7s.

them legally and officially on new pieces of land which can be policed by the British. The resettlement project is proceeding along the lines of a coordinated police, civilian government, army and RAF campaign. Unless world Communism moves in with measures of support, the British expect to clean up Malaya within two or three years at the latest.

Meanwhile, strategic responsibility for this part of the world is carried on the British side by one of the Empire's most seasoned political leaders, Mr. Malcolm MacDonald, and by one of the ablest of all British theater commanders, General Sir John Harding. It is up to them to see that the Alice-in-Wonderland politics of the British Empire, plus Communism, plus the Far East, do not interfere too much with the consolidations effected under General Briggs' "operations." The British are learning some mighty valuable lessons on that strange and necessary art, "How to Stay Alive Despite Guerrillas in Your Neighborhood." The British civilians and the pro-British Chinese and Malay foremen on the plantations are showing inventiveness and heroism in avoiding the Chinese youths who like to shoot people in the back at dusk. It is nothing, for example, to see a British woman driving a Ford V-8 which has been armored at home until it looks like a cockroach-sized tank. The British planters have to conduct virtually a reconnaissance patrol to collect their precious rubber sap from the trees, but they are collecting it. From the prices currently quoted on the New York market for rubber, it is well worth anyone's while to go out on patrol to get this precious juice.

Everyone is making money. I was even told in Singapore that some of the most enthusiastic friends of the Communists cannot resist sympathizing with Mao on the one hand while they build up large balances of Malayan dollars with the other. Peace and war, murder and infantry, prosperity and terror—all these seem to go hand in hand in Malaya.

The British are learning how to patrol communications lines in settled areas with small bodies of police and troops. They are learning how to stage response raids. They are learning to hunt enemies who are so scarce and previous that they must be hunted one by one. Someone once said that the only beast more dangerous than the tiger was man: the British are having to learn the lessons of tactical insecurity within the framework of profound strategic security. Communism has bred a generation of human tigers in Malaya. I am afraid this is not the last place nor the last time that democratic soldiers will try to fight a war against people who don't believe in waging war, but who would much rather commit ordinary murder and arson instead. The fight in Malaya is a long fight and it is a fight for keeps. The British will win, and the *how* of their winning may become one of our most valuable codes of military training and doctrine.

26

James E. Dougherty

THE GUERRILLA WAR

IN MALAYA

URING THE YEARS since World War II, guerrilla warfare in many areas of the world has challenged the power of the Western nations. The Malayan "emergency," which began ten years ago last June, provides a valuable case study in this type of conflict. Its primary significance consists in the fact that the British in Malaya finally devised a successful strategy against a formidable Communist guerrilla force. By employing a combination of counter-techniques—political, social, economic, psychological, and military—the British prevented the Malayan Races' Liberation Army (MRLA) from achieving its major objectives. Today, when the NATO powers face the threat of spreading guerrilla wars, a reexamination of the Malayan experience may prove instructive. This is not to imply that the strategy applied to the British in Malaya should or could be applied in other areas, where the political problems and environmental factors involved are dissimilar. But a review of the Malayan war can cast light on the nature of the struggle which arises in the "Gray Areas" when guerrillas, fighting for "national independence," pit themselves against the regular military arm of a Western industrial state.

Reprinted from *U.S. Naval Institute Proceedings,* by permission; copyright 1958 by U.S. Naval Institute. Appeared in the September, 1958, issue.

To understand the Malayan guerrilla war in its full context, one must know something about the background of Communism in that peninsular country and about the country itself. When Communist organizers from Indonesia, following Lenin's mandate to penetrate the West's colonial territories, moved into British Malaya in the 1920's, they got a cool reception from the Malays. The rural Malayans, most of them devout Moslems, were satisfied with their simple pattern of village life. Those who migrated into the urban areas for an education usually entered the army, the service industries, the police force, or the government and enjoyed friendly relations with the British. The Indian Tamils, who comprised somewhat less than ten per cent of the population, were also hard to stir with Marxist doctrine, since they already benefited from welfare programs arranged jointly by the Indian and Malayan governments. But there was one large and influential ethnic minority in Malaya which felt sufficiently "rootless" to be attracted by Communist preachments. This was the "overseas Chinese" community, which constituted two-fifths of the total population in 1931, the year in which the Malayan Communist Party (MCP) was founded. Most of these Chinese, although they enjoyed a strong position in the commercial life of Malaya, looked to China as their homeland. Hence it is hardly surprising that Communism, when it finally came to Malaya, was imported not from Russia but from China.

Until 1939, the British Protectorate of Malaya had seemed so securely guarded by the naval bases at Singapore and Hong Kong that no sizable native army had been trained to defend it. The Japanese seized Singapore and overran Malaya within three months after Pearl Harbor. At that point the MCP seized its golden opportunity to become the chief vehicle of national resistance sentiment. The party withdrew to the jungle and organized a guerrilla opposition. The British, while fighting a delaying action against the invader felt constrained to adopt in Malaya (as they have so often elsewhere) a wartime policy which contained the seeds of serious postwar problems. The British authorities recognized frankly that the Communists were the only ones in the country who could be counted upon to remain enemies of the Japanese. The Communists had no other choice, since the Japanese had put a price on their heads. The British, therefore, hurriedly set up a special training school and taught the Communists guerrilla tactics and sabotage methods.

Beginning with about 200 hand-picked and well disciplined Chinese Communists, the guerrilla force undertook harassing activities behind the Japanese lines. Initially, it armed itself by searching the battlefield for abandoned weapons. By the time Force 136, headed by British officers from the Southeast Asia Command, landed from a submarine in May, 1943, to contact the so-called Malayan People's Anti-Japanese Army (MPAJA), the latter boasted some 3,000 men. Early in 1945, Lord Mountbatten's Command reached an agreement with the guerrillas under which the British supplied them with food, clothing, and weapons and parachuted training officers into them preparatory to a planned joint invasion against the Japanese. In view of Japan's sudden collapse late that summer, the projected invasion proved unnecessary. That was a turn of good fortune for the British. Their postwar troubles in Malaya would no doubt have been greatly compounded if the Communists had played an actual role in the liberation of the country.

Even as matters stood, the MPAJA emerged from the war with a grossly inflated sense of its own contribution to the defeat of the Japanese. As a matter of fact, the guerrillas had engaged much more in propaganda, training, indoctrination, and morale-building than in fighting the enemy. When the war ended, about 7,000 guerrillas came out from their jungle campsites and took over control of the countryside, establishing their own government in many towns. They were extremely reluctant in September, 1945, to relinquish their power to the incoming British Military Administration. To facilitate the disbanding of the potentially revolutionary MPAJA, the British offered $350 to every man who would turn in his arms. More than 6,000 responded to the offer, but the Communists made certain that several caches of arms and ammunition, both British and Japanese, remained hidden in the jungle.

After the war, the British were anxious to reestablish their position in Malaya, for that colony was potentially, by virtue of its rubber and tin resources, the biggest earner of American dollars in the sterling area. But all through South and Southeast Asia, the historical tide seemed to be going against the prewar colonial empires as new nationalist forces arose to demand independence. The French were having trouble in Indochina, as were the Dutch in Indonesia. India and Ceylon were about to achieve status as Commonwealth members, and Burma was ready to separate completely from Great Britain. If Malaya had been ethnically homogeneous, the British would probably have encountered a great deal more difficulty than they did in that area. But the Malays, now outnumbered by the Chinese in the Malayan Federation and Singapore, were for the most part content to see the British come back.

The years 1945–1948 witnessed unsteady attempts by the British to institute some sort of federal self-rule system in the face of considerable dissatisfaction from the Chinese, the Indians, and a small minority of Malays who desired union with Indonesia. The MCP resorted to strikes as a means of prolonging the country's economic disorganization and thereby embarrassing the British, both politically and financially. Besides infiltrating the labor unions, the Communists founded Youth Corps, Women's Associations, and numerous other front organizations and schools. After the announcement of the Marshall Plan, the party newspapers urged sabotage of the national productive effort to hinder the "imperialist" Marshall Plan. Nevertheless, the Malays, the Indians, and even a majority of the Chinese refused to shift their allegiance.

Throughout Europe and Asia, as it became apparent that the Communists were not yet able to ride into power by peaceful political means, the party line hardened. Just as Czechoslovakia was falling victim to a *coup* in February, 1948, a revised strategy for the Communists in Asia, especially Southeast Asia, was laid down in a series of meetings in Calcutta. These meetings were followed by a noticeable increase in agitational activities in India, Burma, Indonesia, and Malaya. Following a period of labor unrest, demonstrations, and sporadic sabotage, the MCP retreated into the jungles once again and began to engage in full-scale violence. Not all the party members were eager to return to the rigors of guerrilla life, but they were warned that if they stayed behind they would be identified as party members and punished as traitors.

Approximately half of the "old timers" answered the party summons and joined the guerrilla force, which finally became known as the Malayan Races' Liberation Army (MRLA). New recruits, including thugs and criminals, brought the army up to a strength of 5,000 or 6,000. Against them, the British and Malayan authorities were ultimately compelled to mobilize a total of 40,000 regular troops, 60,000 police, and about a quarter of a million home guards.

The Communists embarked upon a variety of offensive activities after June 20, 1948. Armed gangs carried out payroll robberies to obtain operating funds for the movement. Other gangs, to intimidate the population with a show of strength, slashed or burned thousands of rubber trees and bombed installations at the tin mines. Railroad tracks were ripped up and telephone lines cut. Well-to-do Europeans, Chinese, and Malays were kidnaped for ransom or murdered for reasons of sheer terrorism.

The MRLA, upon taking up its abode in the jungle, reactivated and extended its wartime network of campsites, which were ingeniously camouflaged against air attacks and carefully defended against ground approach. Generally speaking, the military position of the MRLA in the early phases of the conflict was quite good. The wartime weapons caches provided sufficient strength for the initial terroristic operations, and the guerrilla leaders undoubtedly hoped that in due time additional arms could be obtained from external sources. There was some doubt at the time as to whether the MCP was under the immediate direction of Moscow or whether it was taking orders from the Chinese Communists. The British were mainly concerned over the possibility of Chinese Communist attempts to support the MCP. But as the Malayan rebellion broke out, the Chinese Communists, then mounting their final offensive against the Nationalists, were scarcely in a position to divert sizable quantities of equipment to the MCP—assuming that they could have overcome the formidable transport difficulties of sending aid to the east coast of the peninsula or down through Thailand.

One of the most pressing problems confronting every guerrilla organization is that of maintaining a steady flow of food and other necessary supplies. The Malayan Communists found a solution ready at hand in the presence of some 500,000 Chinese squatters who lived along the edge of the jungle. These people, mostly illiterate, had little political consciousness, and whatever vague convictions they did hold were usually anti-government. Back in the days of the resistance against the Japanese, they had played a major role in provisioning the guerrillas. Now they were hardly surprised to be visited regularly once again and assessed by the *Min Yuen,* the MRLA's supporting arm. The *Min Yuen,* numbering perhaps 10,000, served as a link between the guerrillas and the native community. It performed courier, food-gathering, propaganda, intelligence, and recruiting service in the external zone of operations. Most of its members, as might be expected, were Chinese. Not a few of them led a double life, carrying out missions for the guerrillas by night and blending into the civil occupational pattern by day. The operations of this community support organization, half above- and half under-ground, often made it difficult for the British to distinguish between friendly and enemy territory.

During the first two years of the war, the British relied almost exclusively on conventional military measures to put down the rebellion. But they gradually realized that the orthodox modes of warfare taught at Sandhurst were not applicable against an elusive jungle foe who was bent on protracting the conflict as long as possible. The British offensive strategy was simply not geared to the Malayan jungle. In Malaya, the jungle covers four-fifths of the country, furnishes a covered approach to worthwhile targets in many areas, and contains so many unfamiliar, mysterious obstacles as to prove virtually impervious to Western combat forces trained for a very different type of ground action.

There was, first of all, the problem of reconnoitering the enemy. Foot reconnaissance was out of the question for regular troops that had not been trained to distinguish native from guerrilla trails. Jungle aborigines helped the British in some instances, but they had different names for every place plotted on the military maps and this gave rise to considerable confusion. Sometimes the jungle-dwelling aborigines would start out on a guidance mission for government units, only to end by leading the troops on a wild goose chase rather than run the risk of enemy reprisals. The British next tried reconnaissance by helicopter, but whenever the guerrillas suspected that their camouflage had been penetrated and a revealing photograph produced, they abandoned the campsite for a few weeks. Army groups found that as they moved into the jungle in squad files, the word that they were coming moved faster than they did. If they avoided the main trails, they ran into brush so thick that they could advance no faster than 100 feet per hour. As they approached a guerrilla campsite, a sentry fired a warning shot and a small rear guard held the track for a few minutes while most of the fighters made their getaway to another campsite, perhaps one which they had abandoned weeks or months previously. The pursuers rarely caught up with the guerrillas before having to return to their base for supplies. Small wonder, under such conditions, that it took some crack British battalions from three to six months of combing operations before they were able to report any guerrilla casualties or prisoners.

The British became painfully aware that they were unable to turn against the guerrilla his own prime tactic—surprise. Through 1948 and 1949 the MRLA remained the master of surprise, retaining its freedom to strike at any selected point near the jungle which happened to be poorly protected. The British, on the other hand, even when apparently undertaking an offensive penetration into the jungle, invariably labored under a defensive mentality and were seldom able to seize the initiative. They possessed one instrument of surprise—the RAF—but its sudden attacks proved less efficient than those of the guerrillas, who were able to inflict telling damage in almost every mission they undertook.

By early 1950, the British had recognized the fact that they were making little or no headway against the MRLA. They began to devise new approaches, which required a fuller strategic perspective of the situation. In April of that year, General Sir Harold Briggs was appointed Director of Operations for the Emergency. The British were beginning to see that the key to success consisted in isolating the guerrilla force from the civilian community while at the same time developing more adequate techniques to deal with the guerrillas inside the jungle. There was a grave danger that, as time went on, the Chinese component of the Malayan population would become increasingly sympathetic with the political objectives of the Communists, particularly in view of the Communist triumph on the Chinese mainland. The British, consequently, were faced with a subtle dilemma. The fact that the guerrilla army was almost entirely Chinese made it relatively easy to enlist the support of the Malays for counteroperations. But the British were reluctant to emphasize the ethnic character of the conflict, for this might have driven many Chinese from involuntary to voluntary cooperation with the MRLA. If the British were to minimize the chances of full scale civil war, it was necessary for them to drive a wedge between the Communists and the great majority of the Chinese.

General Briggs realized that military measures alone were not sufficient to solve the problem. He worked out a plan to sever the logistical link between the terrorists and the Chinese farmers who lived along the edge of the jungle in villages that were highly vulnerable to guerrilla pressure and almost impossible to protect. Between June, 1950, and the end of 1953, more than a half million Chinese were resettled in new villages removed from the jungle and easier to guard. Altogether, more than 600 new communities were constructed at a considerable cost to the government. Those which were located in rural areas closest to the jungle were enclosed by barbed wire and their perimeters were lighted at night. All of them were kept under constant police surveillance. This resettlement program, which moved the poorest tenth of Malaya's population into more viable areas with good roads, sewage, water, and electricity, helped to solve one of the country's most serious social problems. It gave large numbers of Chinese peasants security in land title for the first time and brought them into a friendlier relationship with the government. Politically, the transfer program contributed toward a reorientation of thinking among the people who had hitherto comprised the most unstable and least reliable element of the civilian population.

The resettlement program undoubtedly hurt the Communist guerrillas, for it disrupted their chief source of supply and forced them to rely more heavily on the jungle aborigines. The degree of physical, psychological, and political proximity which the guerrillas had enjoyed *vis-à-vis* the local Chinese community declined perceptibly. Lines of communication between the guerrillas and the party cells in the villages were strained almost to the breaking point, at least for a time. The extension of their supply lines rendered the members of the MRLA and the *Min Yuen* more vulnerable than ever to ambush as they moved in and out of the jungle. The number of terrorist attacks fell off by more than half. Meanwhile, Federation authorities were able to mount their own ideological offensive to offset the effect of the "liberation" propaganda which had gone practically uncontested for several years.

The hard-core Communists did not allow adversity to dampen their ardor. The guerrillas attempted to maintain flagging morale by boldly risking dangerous expeditions into the new government-built villages. Occasional murders and other acts of terror continued to occur, giving rise among the Chinese to some resentment against the government for its inability to guarantee absolute security. In that type of war, of course, it is practically impossible to secure the native population completely against terroristic attacks, so long as large numbers of guerrillas can live undetected within the civilian community.[1]

Gradually, civilian morale improved. Normal railway and road communications were restored and private property, especially the rubber plantations and tin mines, became less susceptible to destructive raids. The popularity of the Communists declined steadily as greater blame was laid to the party for prolonging the troublesome situation. Consequently, the MCP felt constrained to switch its strategy. A party directive dated October 1, 1951, ordered all members to desist from the following practices: seizing identity and ration cards, burning new villages, attacking post offices, reservoirs, and other public facilities, derailing civilian trains, burning religious buildings and Red Cross vehicles, and committing sabotage

---

1. From the start of the Emergency until the end of 1952, some 30,000 persons were arrested for known or suspected acts of terrorism, and during the same period nearly 15,000 Chinese were deported.

against the major industries, thereby causing workers to lose their jobs. Communists were urged to emphasize the indoctrination of the masses, propaganda against conscription, the obstruction of government policies by non-violent means, and penetration of the trade unions. Violence, however, was not ruled out completely. It was still quite proper to kill British and Gurkha troops, senior civil servants and police officers, members of the Kuomintang and the Malayan Chinese Association, "stubborn reactionaries," and British industrial managers, but not British health officers or engineers. Perhaps the party directive was a face-saving device, designed to convey the impression that the change in the Communists' policy was freely chosen rather than forced upon them. The resettlement program had significantly altered the relationship between the guerrillas and the local Chinese community upon which they had depended for support. Such a change invariably compels a guerrilla army to modify its tactics drastically.

Meanwhile, the British stepped up their pressure against the guerrillas in the jungle. To do this, they had to obtain a better grasp of the enemy's *modus operandi*. Although the British possessed a superior "map knowledge" of the Malayan terrain, they initially lacked an understanding of the manner in which Communist activities were adapted to the language, customs, and though patterns of the indigenous population. A "ferret force" was formed, comprising hand-picked British, Malayan, Gurkha, and Chinese personnel. This ferret force went to live in the recesses of the jungle for six months, carrying out patrolling activities and observing the Communist organization in action. The personnel of this force were then distributed among other military units to spread the benefits of their experience. Efforts were made to win over the aborigines who furnished the Communist fighters with rice, acted as scouts for them, and warned them of the approach of hostile troops. But this turned out to be an extremely difficult task, since the aborigines had known some of the veteran guerrillas for upwards of a dozen years, whereas they had previously come into only superficial contact with the British and Malayan officials.

After carefully assessing the military problem, the British adopted new methods of carrying the offensive to the guerrillas. Head-on penetration and attack by battalion-sized units based outside the jungle was abandoned. Smaller units, such as squads or platoons, were sent into the jungle under a screen of deception to thwart the Communist scouts. These units lived like guerrillas for a month or more at a time, shifting their location frequently and solving their own supply problems. The Gurkhas showed themselves especially adept in this phase of the campaign. Whereas under the earlier operational plans, marching units became tired out in fruitless tracking only to find themselves in the end an easy target for ambush, the new counterguerrilla groups developed their own initiative and skill in ambush techniques. Improved ground-air radio communications enabled the RAF to increase the demoralizing effect of its sudden strafing and bombing missions. The guerrillas were further beleaguered when their food plots in jungle clearings were sprayed with poison.

The more intensive techniques raised the average number of guerrilla fatal casualties from about 600 per year in the 1949–1950 period to more than 1,000 per year from 1951 onward. Despite the fact that new recruits kept the Communist strength from falling much below its normal level of 5,000 to 6,000, British intelligence indicated that enemy morale was crumbling. The Malayan Communist Party had not succeeded in gaining either international political support or external arms aid to sustain its struggle. To exploit the psychological factors implicit in the decline of dynamism within a guerrilla army, the British worked out an ingenious propaganda campaign which relied heavily on the use of "voice aircraft"— helicopters equipped with loudspeakers to broadcast at night over Communist locations. The general theme stressed was that the guerrillas, caught in a hopeless military situation, were free to choose: a rotten jungle existence probably culminating in death, or a rehabilitated life in urban Malaya following their surrender. Messages from MRLA men who gave themselves up one night were tape-recorded for "pinpoint delivery" over the campsites of their erstwhile cohorts the very next night. Thousands of leaflets urging defection were dropped over the jungle each week. Since one of the main hindrances to the would-be deserter was finding his way out of the thick brush at night, the British furnished colored searchlights and soundtrucks as guides to the nearest army or police post. During 1953, more than 350 individual surrenders were reported.

The Communists' military victory in Indochina and their diplomatic successes at Geneva sent the MRLA's stock climbing for a while in 1954. By and large, however, it was obvious that the war was going against the Communists in Malaya. The guerrillas were gradually being forced deeper into the jungle to more decentralized positions, from which their operations became necessarily less efficient. Their morale and logistics problems were compounded in proportion to their increasing isolation from the civilian community. Outside the jungle, the "white areas," where security was sufficiently established to permit the lifting of curfew and other restrictions, were being steadily extended.

The MCP finally convinced the international leadership of the party that, if additional military support was not forthcoming, a shift would have to be made to political maneuvers to reduce the Federation's pressure and to halt the defections. In September, 1954, Communist delegates to the British Trades Unions Congress sounded the call for a cease-fire in Malaya. No doubt they hoped that truce proposals in Malaya would prove just as successful as they had in Korea and Indochina. Native political leaders in Malaya, notably Tengku Abdul Rahman and Sir Cheng-lock Tan, suggested an amnesty and negotiations with the Communists. But British authorities were willing neither to grant a general amnesty nor to discuss negotiations in any form with the terrorists. The British felt, quite rightly, that their existing policy of offering attractive terms to individual defectors was already the most generous one possible.

The Tengku and Sir Cheng-lock Tan, influenced by the wave of Asian neutralist sentiment which reached its peak in 1955, favored granting lawful status to the Malayan Communist Party. They were left unmoved by British arguments that such concessions would not restore the country to normalcy but would merely guarantee the Communists a foothold in the soon-to-be-established parliamentary regime of an independent Federation. The coalition led by the Tengku and Tan won the country's first constitutional elections in the summer of 1955. After that, the British decided not to hold out any longer against negotiations, but they did quash a suggestion to have the insurrection arbitrated by a neutral power and they also managed to talk down the proposal to legalize the MCP. A formal amnesty was finally announced on September 9, 1955. Actually, it did not go much beyond the surrender policy already in effect. The Communists were told bluntly that they would be required to prove their loyalty to Malaya alone, to respect constitutional authority, and to abstain from any political activity proscribed by the government. Irreconcilables were to be deported, just as in the past. There was no chance that the leaders who had for years plotted and supervised the most grotesque acts of terrorism would be classified as mere "political criminals" and pardoned.

The MCP, probably fearing that it had been outmaneuvered on the amnesty issue—for the raising and the dashing of the guerrillas' hopes no doubt had a harmful effect on morale—stepped up its political offensive. The party made a new proposal for an immediate conference with the Tengku and Tan to discuss a total cease-fire, a satisfactory solution of the "emergency," and the creation of a peaceful, free Malaya once tensions had been relaxed. The Tengku, by then the Chief Minister of the Federation, agreed to meet Chin Peng, leader of the MCP, at Baling. Chin Peng asked for an international commission to implement the peace terms, as well as an alteration of the amnesty provisions. The Chief Minister bluntly refused to internationalize the peace arrangements. He was willing, however, to discuss the amnesty terms.

During the course of the Baling talks, the Communists tried to drive a wedge between the native leaders of the Federation and their British mentors by promising to halt the war just as soon as the native government should obtain complete control over internal security and local armed forces. But this tactic got the Communists nowhere. The Tengku made it perfectly clear that he had no intention whatsoever of sharing power in Mayala with Chin Peng, and after a few days the talks broke down. The Federation leaders, convinced that their amnesty offer had served little useful purpose except perhaps to placate neutralist opinion temporarily, began to speak of intensifying the anti-Communist drive. While the Federation mission was in London early in 1956 smoothing the way for Malaya's full independence within the Commonwealth, bombing attacks on terrorist hideouts were resumed. Once the country's independence seemed assured, national mobilization plans for the quick defeat of the MRLA appeared to disintegrate, and a "tacit truce" came to prevail. The guerrilla leaders, reckoning time to be on their side, settled back and waited for the day when they could return to the Malayan political scene and open the "constitutional phase" of their strategy.

The British moved to prevent a Communist victory by default. Upon becoming an independent Commonwealth dominion on August 31, 1957, Malaya concluded a defense agreement which provided that air, naval, and land forces of Great Britain, Australia, and New Zealand would remain in the country after it became free. Then the Federation made a final offer of amnesty to the some 2,000 terrorists still holding out in the jungle. Terrorists who surrendered before January 1, 1958, and renounced Communism were to be guaranteed freedom from prosecution for offenses committed under Communist orders prior to the date of independence. Those desiring "repatriation" to China—the term "deportation" was avoided— were promised free passage. The fortunes of the MCP guerrillas entered a period of eclipse, at least for the time being, when the new independent Federation of Malaya was recognized by both Moscow and Peking.

Several valuable lessons can be drawn from the British experience in Malaya. The policy adopted in the "emergency" showed what can be accomplished when Western and local native forces are meshed for close cooperation against Communist threats in the "Gray Areas." It also demonstrated the need for well-conceived measures to supplement military operations against guerrillas. Logistic ties between the guerrillas and the local community must be severed, and nowhere has this been achieved in the last decade as effectively and as humanely as in Malaya. Moreover, guerrilla armies in the underdeveloped areas of the world are doomed to ultimate defeat at the hands of technically superior Western powers unless they can succeed in gaining substantial political or military assistance from abroad. The British, controlling the sea approaches to Malaya, made it impossible for the MRLA to import arms aid. The chance of securing Chinese Communist help through Thailand faded when the latter country joined SEATO. The Communists' efforts to internationalize the guerrilla war were turned back. For the last eight of the ten years since the "emergency" began, the British have successfully thwarted the Communist guerrillas by conceiving the conflict in larger dimensions and by using a wider variety of weapons. The question for the future is: Which side possesses the greater reserves of strategic patience, or the will to wait for victory?

27

Major Anthony Crockett   **ACTION**
British Royal Marines

IN MALAYA

URING THE JAPANESE OCCUPATION of Malaya in WWII, the only serious, organized resistance to the enemy was provided by the "Malayan Peoples' Anti-Japanese Army." The hard core of this guerrilla force was provided by members of the Malayan Communist Party, the majority and most influential members of which were Chinese.

When peace came, the Communists possessed a battle-tested organization and an enhanced reputation amongst the civilian population. In the main, they refused to surrender the arms and ammunition supplied to them by the British and, under the threat of proscription, went underground. They proclaimed the birth of the Malayan Races' Liberation Army (the MRLA) and announced a program which included the overthrow of the government, with such of its instruments as the police, the expulsion of Europeans, and the redistribution of wealth. In much of this there was a popular appeal to the "have-nots" and to those infected by the rising tide of nationalism, which crept over Asia in the wake of the departing Japanese.

The Japanese had treated Malaya badly, had exploited and bullied its

From the *Marine Corps Gazette*, January, 1955. Copyright 1955 by the Marine Corps Association and reproduced by permission.

population, and had drained and pilfered its resources, and had allowed
the tin mines and rubber estates to go to ruin. While the British Military
Administration governed and maintained order, the country gradually began to recover. Europeans—officials, business men, planters and miners—
returned to their offices, estates, and mines and started to rebuild. The
police force, which had more or less disintegrated during the occupation,
was slowly reorganized, although many new officers and men had to be
recruited.

It was at this stage in the recovery of Malaya that the MRLA launched
the first phase of its intensive campaign. The brunt was on the police force.
It grappled manfully with the task, but it was only too evident that it was
not yet sufficiently large or well trained to cope with a state of affairs which
was rapidly deteriorating. With the declaration of a state of emergency and
the introduction of more troops, the struggle between the Communist organization on the one hand, and the security forces on the other, started
in earnest.

In the early stages the MRLA met with some success. Its tactics were
based on fear—intimidation, terrorization, murder, arson, abduction,
threats, and blackmail. It aimed to win over the Asian population, especially
the Chinese, who formed almost half the population of the Federation.

The Communist organization was split into three more or less independent bodies, which were yet closely interrelated; the armed and uniformed
bandits, who were formed in military units and were the MRLA proper;
the Min Yuen, who were its plain clothes workers living in the towns and
villages; and the Lie Ton Ten, or Killer Squads. These corresponded very
much to the strong-arm thugs of gangsterdom who were charged with the
"rubbing-out" of elements undesirable to the Communists and with minor
operations such as the slashing of rubber trees, cutting of telephone wires
and so on.

To keep their organization going and, in fact, to exist at all, the Communists needed money, food, arms, and ammunition. The last two they
had already had in fair amounts since the end of the war and they had
added to them since by raids on police posts and from what they had been
able to salvage from the dead bodies of armed men they had killed. For
money and food they relied largely on what they could extort from the
local population. This extortion they had worked out to a fine art. The
Chinese have a saying in which they liken themselves to the bamboo. When
the storm comes, they say, the straight, tall tree stands proudly in his resistance to it and when he can resist no longer, he breaks. But the humble
bamboo bends his head, bows before the storm—and survives.

The Communists made every small community responsible for supplying a quota of money from its weekly pay packets and each and every
family was found to provide food under arrangements laid down for them.
This system of supply was greatly facilitated by the presence of a vast

population of "squatters," nearly all of whom were Chinese. These Chinese, or their forebears, had entered Malaya, most of them illegally, and had settled down quite arbitrarily on a patch of ground where their isolated homes formed ideal staging posts for money and food destined for the bandits living in it. Others of them lived in squatter villages, which had grown in the course of time and which were far enough away from the main populated areas to make them only too accessible to the bandits.

In order to strangle this almost inexhaustible pipeline, a vast system of resettlement was undertaken by the civil authorities. All isolated squatters were concentrated into villages defended by barbed wire, protected by police posts and provided with such facilities as medical and welfare centers and schools. These measures not only protected the squatters from the easy depredations of the bandits, but afforded them such an extent of security that they began to lose some of their initial fear and passed information to the police.

It is necessary to know some of these facts about the origins of the present situation in Malaya to understand the differences between the struggle taking place there and the more conventional forms of warfare. In May of last year, shortly before he retired as High Commissioner, General Sir Gerald Templar stated that there were some 4,000 active terrorists operating in the Federation. To combat their activities and those of a far larger body of auxiliary supporters, it has been necessary to keep something in the nature of 35,000 troops active in Malaya for several years. This is surely an outstanding example of the efficacy of guerrilla warfare.

Another point to bear in mind when studying the Malayan situation is: it is not (in legal terms) war but a "state of emergency." The "military" are in support of the government and the police. While there are a number of emergency laws, and capital offenses now include such crimes as consorting with terrorists or possessing arms, civil and not martial law is administered in the courts by civil magistrates and judges.

In a country two thirds of which is jungle, the speedy deployment of large bodies of troops is impossible. In general, a battalion is responsible for an area, which is subdivided into smaller company areas. The 3 Commando Brigade, Royal Marines was deployed in the State of Perak, in northern Malaya. My unit, 42 Commando, had its Headquarters in the town of Ipoh. (There are five Rifle Troops and one Support Troop in each Commando. Each Rifle Troop in Malaya, with attached drivers, signalers, cooks, medical personnel, etc., numbered about seventy.) My troop camp was some five miles away. It was based on a four-roomed bungalow, around which were grouped tents, wash-houses, and latrines.

While remaining under the command of the CO, we were at the same time a self-contained outfit. My area comprised a long strip of flat country, two miles deep, containing tin mines, swamps, some small rubber estates, and a large number of Chinese small-holdings. Beyond this it embraced a

chain of high limestone outcrops and, on the far side of these, the jungle
—stretching away through the mountains to the borders of Pahang.

The terrorists' military organization was much akin to ours, with a chain
of responsibility for certain areas. Their bases were deep in the jungle. For
food, clothing, and medical supplies, they relied upon the Min Yuen, whom
they would meet inside or near the jungle edge. Occasionally, large
camps to accommodate as many as 60 men would be found. Generally they
lived in groups of from 10 to 30 shifting their camps frequently. They
were expert at living and operating in the jungle. Tough and hardy, they
could move swiftly and silently over long distances, even when wounded,
and were skillful in concealing their tracks. With a basic diet of rice and
dried fish, and a way of living which needed only the necessities of life, their
logistic problem was infinitesimal compared to that of British troops.

The uniformed MRLA carried out many forms of operation: ambushes
on roads, raids on isolated police posts, the destruction of mine-machinery
and smoke houses, the murder of Europeans and/or of Asians who had
failed to "cooperate" with, or were suspected of informing on, the bandits.
These are but a few examples. They were all governed by the same principles—surprise, swift action, good planning, excellent intelligence, and the
avoidance of a direct clash with military forces.

The fundamental requirement for us—pitted against an enemy with a
net, difficult to find and always on the move—was accurate and rapid information. With a civil population not actively hostile to the security forces
but cowed into silence by fear, this was not easy to obtain. In this respect,
we maintained the closest link with the police who, alone, were in a position to get this information. In Ipoh, a Joint Operations Room was set up
in the police station, manned by our Intelligence Officer and a Police Operations Officer. Here was built up a picture of bandit movements and strength.
Camps found and incidents reported often made it possible to gauge the
tenor of terrorist activity and to anticipate their actions.

As I have said, sometimes these joint Headquarters were on a com-
mando/battalion level. At other times, as for instance when my troop was
operating more or less independently in Selangor State, in central Malaya,
they were on troop level. This close cooperation between the military
forces and the police was the secret of all successful operations. Furthermore, it was cooperation at all stages, from the sifting and integration of
intelligence, through the planning, to the eventual execution. Like most
forms of cooperation, it depended also on the personal relationships between ourselves and the police.

To understand how the system worked, let us follow a hypothetical case
from its inception. The scene opens with the troop commander being called
to the telephone.

"Captain Walker, Sir? 10 here. The CO says you will come down to
police headquarters as quickly as you can."

Tim Walker grabs his carbine, calls for his driver, and in his armored scout-car makes tracks for the Joint Operations Room. There he finds his commanding officer, the Officer Superintending the Police Circle (OSPC), the 10, and the Police Operations Officer. They are poring over maps and a large air-photograph mosaic pinned on the wall.

"Tim," says the CO, "we've just had an interesting bit of news about your area. The pumping engine at the Liu Chin Mook mine was destroyed last night and the engine house burnt down. The watchman reports about 20 armed bandits. He thinks they were all Chinese—some of them wearing red-starred caps."

The OSPC chips in, "Luckily he recognized one of them, a lad who used to live in his village, called Ah Kee. Now we know Ah Kee is in 6 Platoon of the 3d Company and that that platoon has been working for some time from up the Sungei (River) Tembo. We also know that this is the third attack on tin mines in that district in the last fortnight. We've been hearing rumors of late that some of the owners are getting fed-up with paying their 'contributions.' It looks as if the bandits are putting on the pressure."

"The police think there may be more of these attacks planned," the CO continues. "An informer has got hold of some yarn that the Li Han Chow is next on the list—they say old Li is a pretty stubborn character—and that the raid is going to take place in a couple of nights' time. Our plan is roughly this. Soon after dark, two police squads will move into the rubber between the main road and the mine and will watch likely routes. I want you to deal with any of the possible ways down to the mine from the jungle."

"As you know, Sir," says Tim, "half my troop is out at the moment and they won't be back for 4 or 5 days. They're right up in the jungle on the other side of my area. Even if I recalled them, I doubt if they'd be back in time. However, I've got enough men in camp to deal with this. I know that part of the country well. If the bandits are lying up in the upper stretches of the Sungei Tembo, they'll probably use one of two tracks down from there towards the mine. I'll ambush both of them with small parties. They'll have to move out today."

Tim and the OSPC then coordinate the details of their plans, making quite sure that each knows where the other's men are going to be. This is vitally important in operations where it is often difficult to distinguish friend from foe and where the enemy, if encountered, is only visible for a few, fleeting seconds.

Back in his own camp, Tim briefs the ambush parties. A subaltern will command one and he will take the other. They will leave camp at 1500 hours by truck, one to the west and the other to the east of the area, taking 48 hours' rations with them. They will de-bus in the rubber (the rubber tappers will have left for the day by then) and strike through it to the jungle, where they will have to reach the ambush positions by a circuitous route, camping for the night on the way.

At 1430 hours the ambush parties fall in for inspection. Each is about 12 strong, including a sergeant, a signaler, with his set on his back, and an SBA (Sick Berth Attendant—a naval rating). They look a motley crew, in stained, shapeless shirts and slacks of olive green, their battered jungle hats worn with a rakish individuality. They carry the minimum of equipment— a small haversack contained their rations, washing and shaving gear, a change of clothing, sweater and an old pair of rubber sneakers—the last three for sleeping in. Below the haversack is strapped a green poncho. On the front of the belt are two pouches for ammunition. On one hip is a waterbottle, on the other a machete. They are armed with light machine guns, carbines, rifles, HE and smoke grenades. A bandolier of ammunition is slung round the waist, or a slatted satchel, filled with carbine or Sten magazines, is suspended from the belt.

The transport for the ambush parties is drawn up facing the camp gate. There is a 3-ton truck for each party, each escorted by an armored scout car. The men em-bus and the vehicles drive out, one pair turning to the right and the other to the left. We will follow the fortune of Tim Walker, who, with his party, is sitting in the 3-tonner which turned to the left.

The scout car and the truck speed along the main, tarmac road. The men sit facing outboard, their weapons at the ready and the tailboard down. There is always the possibility of an ambush to be borne in mind. Presently they reach a long stretch of road, lined on each side by rubber estates. It is away from all signs of habitation and there is no one in sight. Tim orders the driver to slow down, the men jump out, run quickly off the road and in amongst the trees. The truck and the scout car drive on.

They walk through the trees in extended line, their rubber-soled jungle boots making no noise. No one speaks—they have learned to move silently. Tim consults his compass from time to time. He has worked out beforehand the exact spot where the rubber ends—there he wants to enter the jungle. Presently the patrol senses they are reaching the limit of the rubber. Through the evenly spaced trees, they can see the tangled undergrowth which is the preliminary to the jungle proper. They have not met a soul since they left the road.

The bearing on which they have been advancing leads them to a narrow opening in the undergrowth. Shortly before they reach it, Tim halts the patrol and they form into single file, which is the only possible formation in which a body of men can move in the restricted space of the jungle. First goes the leading scout, armed with a machine carbine. A few yards behind is another scout, similarly armed. Then comes Tim, with the Bren group immediately in rear and the remainder of the patrol strung out behind them.

In the rubber, they had been able to see in all directions for two or three hundred yards, but now the visibility is reduced to a yard or two. The light filters gloomily through the trees, almost as if they were under water, and throws deep patches of shadow about them. It is much cooler, but there is an aura of damp and decay and a sense of airlessness. The ground at their feet is seeping with moisture, spongy with the leafmold of centuries, packed with twisted roots. The trees soar upwards, branchless for a hundred feet or more, reaching for the sun. It is deathly quiet.

The track they are following leads up a spur and along the spine of a ridge. These tracks, made by game and the aborigines who live in the jungle, have existed perhaps for hundreds of years and provide the only means of making reasonable progress. They nearly always follow similar formations of ground.

The aids for jungle map-reading are few. Available maps are of a small scale and can show little more than the configuration of the land, the rivers, and the larger streams. With these, a compass and the accumulated knowledge of the country obtained by his troop, a patrol leader has to be satisfied. It is seldom, if ever, possible to reach a point where he can fix his position in relation to another, owing to the confined visibility. In any case, landmarks hardly exist where dense jungle covers every feature.

The ground begins to rise sharply. It has rained during the afternoon, as it nearly always does, and the track, winding this way and that, is treacherous and slippery. Soon every man is soaked with sweat and is beginning to feel the weight of his equipment. They toil on until the track reaches the top of the spur and levels out along the ridge. There Tim Walker halts the patrol. They move off into the undergrowth and unfasten their equipment while two of their number act as sentries, watching the track in either direction.

Tim takes out his map and fixes his position as well as he can. From now on, he plans to move across the "grain" of the land in order to reach the ambush position unseen. This will entail moving where no tracks exist, up and down steep slopes and across rocky beds. It will undoubtedly entail cutting a way through thick undergrowth for a part of the trip. It will be grueling work and progress will be very slow.

He looks at his watch. In two hours it will be getting dark and he must find somewhere to camp for the night. preferably near a stream, and in sufficient time for the patrol to build shelters and have a meal. They press on again, slithering down the flank of the ridge supporting themselves as best they can by gripping saplings and creepers as they pass. A vast brake of bamboo bars their way. Cutting a way through it would make far too much noise and they have to work their way around it. Half an hour later Tim halts the patrol. They are almost in the bottom of the valley and, although he cannot see it, he knows water of some sort will be flowing nearby.

Camp is soon made. While the men construct 3-man bivouacs from branches and their ponchos, the signaler rigs an aerial ready for Tim to report back to base. Ration packs are opened. Tea is being brewed and tins of food are heated over Tommy cookers. Any minute now darkness will descend with tropical suddenness. The patrol stands-to until it is quite dark and then turns in. A pair of sentries are posted to squat, silently back-to-back. Should anyone approach their camp, which at night is unlikely, they want to be able to look upwards, if they are to have any chance of spotting a moving shape against the dark background of the jungle.

In spite of the fact that the sun has gone down, it is still very hot and, deep in amongst the trees, also very close. The outline of the sentries gradually merges into the pockets of blackness in the background as the night creeps down upon them. Soon the whole world is becalmed in silence.

Suddenly, about 20 yards away, there is a shrill whistle. An answering whistle sounds from the other side of the camp and is picked up by yet another from somewhere else. The sentries remain motionless.

This is a signal for the whole jungle to go crazy. As suddenly as the whistle starts, a thousand others burst in together. Every imaginable whistle, scream, rattle and wail is let loose on the night air, until the whole place sounds like a baseball game attended by a crowd of lunatics. For half an hour this tuneless din continues and then, as surprisingly as it started, it stops and the patrol is shrouded in deep, leaden silence.

As soon as it is light, they breakfast, dismantle the camp and hide all traces of occupation. The men have changed back into the sweat-sodden clothes of the day before, preserving their dry outfit for another possible night in the open. They cover the hundred yards to the stream at the foot of the valley. Here, looking up at the gap in the trees over the water, they get a clear view of the sky for the first time since they left their truck.

A body of men crossing a jungle stream is always very vulnerable. Should they by ill luck have been located by bandits, this is just the spot where they would be likely to run into an ambush. Many of these streams are fast-flowing with hidden pools, their beds littered with boulders. The Bren gunner takes up a position where he can cover the crossing point and the men, one by one, wade slowly to the other bank. The Bren gunner crosses last, covered by one of the patrol who has already reached the far side.

All day they push on, sometimes cutting their way, pace by pace, gaining only a few yards in an hour, slithering down the steep slopes of valleys and toiling up the other side of them. About three o'clock Tim halts the patrol. He reckons they are near the summit of the ridge, along which runs the track he is going to ambush. Taking one marine with him he goes forward, slowly and silently, lest he should be nearer to the track than he had estimated. When he finds it he stops and begins to search for a suitable ambush position. This takes some time, as he dare not move on to the track in case he should leave signs of his presence imprinted on the soft mud. He sends back the marine who is with him, with instructions that the patrol is to move another hundred yards down the hill and have a meal. He will join them as soon as his reconnaissance is finished.

They take up their positions some two hours before darkness. Tim has no idea how long they may have to maintain the ambush—perhaps 2 hours, 12 hours, 24 or 36 hours. Obviously, therefore, he cannot man it fully throughout this time. He divides the patrol into two watches, those off watch resting some 30 yards away, connected to the main position by a simple, string-operated signal.

The ambush lines one side of the track for about 12 yards. Here the path is straight but, just above it, in the direction from which the bandits might be expected, it vanishes round a corner. Half an hour ago the sergeant crossed it lower down, where it narrows, and laid a line of booby traps in the undergrowth a few yards in from the track and opposite the ambush position. Should the enemy walk into the trap and try to escape from the ambush party's fire, an unexpected reception will await them.

The men have concealed themselves in their individual positions and made certain that their fields of fire, restricted though they may be, are clear. There is nothing now for them to do save wait—and hope.

At this critical moment in the affairs of the ambush party, we will leave Captain Walker and his small group of marines. It might well have been that they were successful and that a silent-footed line of bandits, unaware of their danger, walked into the trap set for them. On the other hand— and far more akin to actual experience—they may well have waited, restless, uncomfortable and tensed, for another 24 or 36 hours and then, rations exhausted, have had to withdraw.

Such frustration, following on severe and prolonged physical effort, and at a sustained nervous tension, was typical of our work in Malaya. Constant patrolling of one's area, whether in the jungle or through the rubber estates and no-man's land between them, was essential. It kept the bandits guessing and on the move and, on isolated occasions, might lead to a surprise encounter or the discovery of a camp. Operations culminating in action, however, with enemy killed, wounded, or captured, were not everyday events. For the most part it was slog, slog, slog with very few concrete results to show for it.

The work was hard and the men got little rest. Any slackening of effort in an area, or part of an area, was immediately reflected in increased terrorist activity. It called for a high degree of physical fitness and stamina. In this respect it is interesting to note that the older men were inclined to stand up to the rigors of a prolonged patrol better than the younger lads.

High morale was essential. I have referred to the continual, nervous strain, which spared not even the most unimaginative and bore most heavily on the junior officers and NCO's. On operations, nerves were keyed to a constant intensity. In close country particularly, every yard of track, every overhanging bank or stream-crossing held a potential ambush. Round the next bend a leading scout might find himself face to face with a khaki-clad figure in a red-starred cap—the first to fire might well be the only one to survive. Patrols might return to camp after a week or several days away, looking forward to a day or two of rest and civilized comfort, only to be shot off again to cope with a sudden incident. Hours or days of waiting in mosquito-ridden ambush positions or on grueling patrols would end in nothing, with an expected enemy who never came or one who had fled a short time beforehand. These situations, aggravated by repetition, were met with patience, good humor and, generally, by a considerable amount of colorful invective. The response to a sudden emergency or to a test of endurance was a keenness which never flagged.

I think this state of morale can be attributed to four main factors. Good leadership on the part of the junior officers and NCO's; intense interest taken by all ranks in the day-to-day struggle against the terrorists; an existence which gave no one the time or excuse to be bored; and, pleasant camps, with decent living conditions for the troops when they had the opportunity to enjoy such facilities.

As a training and testing ground for leaders, particularly junior leaders, Malaya could not have been bettered. Subalterns, sergeants, and corporals had to take small bodies of men, sometimes for days on end, into country where they would be quite alone and cut off from all assistance. Contact with base was maintained by wireless, but with the thick jungle, the mountainous and hilly nature of the terrain, the severe weather conditions of heavy rain and tropical storms, wireless was often a doubtful aid.

A high standard of skill and personal leadership was required of a patrol leader; skill in not losing his way, in adapting the jungle to his own ends, in his instant reactions to a sudden emergency; personal leadership in his own example of stamina, cheerfulness, courage, and self-confidence. Some of this could be taught in the Jungle Training Center. The ability to live in the jungle, to master its difficulties and discomforts so that a man became confident in himself could be learned, to a certain extent, by careful training. There was, however, all too little opportunity for sparing sufficient officers and NCO's for such training and most had to learn the hard way—by experience.

It was the same with the troops. By the time they reached their unit, they had been a month at sea. While they gradually became acclimatized during this period, they had hardly advanced their physical fitness. Their first two weeks were spent on short patrols or simple operations, which did not involve the covering of long distances or lengthy periods away from camp. They were also given as much instruction as possible on the "jungle" range. Most troops were able to construct one of these. A small area of broken, over-grown country would be selected. In it, hidden here and there, would be figure targets which would appear for a few seconds as the firer approached them. This called for a quick eye and instant re-actions, both vital attributes in a warfare where contact with the enemy was, more often than not, unexpected and always fragmentary.

The care of his personal weapons, that basic lesson drummed into marines on both sides of the Atlantic, was never more important than in Malaya. Rain, streams, and sweat, any or all three, brought rust in their wake only too quickly. Mud, earth, broken twigs, and leaves fouled barrels and moving parts. Men learned to watch the state of their weapons con-stantly, to overhaul them thoroughly each night and to check them on patrol at every halt. A sudden meeting round a bend in the track—a bandit as surprised as you are—bringing his weapons forward to fire—and your carbine jams! It was a salutary thought, forgotten only by the foolish.

Jungle lore, the art of tracking, the ability to "read" the terrain and to "get the feel of it" are not learned in a day. We had splendid trackers in our Ibans (Dyaks from North Borneo) who were skilled and courageous and accompanied us everywhere. By the time we left Malaya there were some men who could almost match them in these skills, and there were few who actively disliked the jungle.

The jungle, however, was not the only scene of our operations. It was the type of country, however, in which we spent most of our time and from which we probably won the least obvious results, although the time and energy spent there were of paramount importance. Many Commando Troops met with their greatest successes in the outskirts of squatters' areas or in rubber estates. One of the more fortunate ventures of my own troop occurred among some overgrown vegetable gardens a quarter of a mile away from the Ipoh Golf Course!

A fact which distinguishes operations in Malaya from more conven-tional forms of warfare is their logistics. Once a patrol is committed to the jungle, it is, except for its wireless communications, cut off from the outside world. Each officer and man has to carry with him all that he and the patrol will need in the way of weapons, ammunition, food, clothing, wireless batteries, and so on. Depending on the country to be traversed (and it is seldom anything but difficult), this load is limited to three or, at the most, four days. Subsequent supplies, therefore, come by air.

At least 24 hours before the air drop takes place, the patrol leader signals his requirements back to base. His list is generally lengthy, a con-siderable portion of it being devoted to clothing. This takes a beating in jungle. Canvas, calf-length, rubber-soled, jungle boots wear quickly, sweat-soaked shirts and trousers tear easily on thorns and undergrowth; socks shrink to pygmy sizes. A drop zone has somehow to be found, enlarged, or constructed. Sometimes a natural clearing can be used, or a patch of abandoned, aboriginal cultivation on a hillside utilized. These DZ's are usu-ally very small, insignificant holes in miles and miles of tree-tops. Yet, somehow, the pilots never failed to make their drop, with little to help them save a map reference (which is probably at least a mile off), a thin column of smoke spiraling upwards through the trees and a call-sign on the radio.

Of the helicopter I can say but little. When 3 Commando Brigade was in Malaya, there were no troop-carrying machines as there are today and only three S51's, which were used for casualty evacuation—one of the worst problems of all in the jungle. The advent of the S55 must obviously have done much to redress the balance of jungle warfare and at last our troops can hope to achieve both speed and surprise in terrain where formerly they seldom had either.

In conclusion, it should be stated quite clearly—as it was to all of us who went out to join 3 Commando Brigade—that there is no black magic about operations in Malaya. Some of the problems of conventional warfare are minimized, i.e., the enemy possesses no aircraft, tanks, or artillery. Some of the problems are aggravated—the jungle has to be mastered and a guerrilla enemy found and brought to battle. Underlying everything, however, are the same principles, the same factors of morale and discipline, and, most important of all, the spirit, tenacity, courage, and sound training of the individual Marine.

Further References

BOOKS

Bartlett, V. *Report from Malaya*. New York: Criterion, 1955.

Campbell, A. *Jungle Green*. Boston: Little, Brown, 1954 (London: Allen & Unwin, 1953).

Communist Banditry in Malaya. Singapore: H.M. Stationery Office, 1951.

Crockett, A. *Green Beret, Red Star: Describing the Jungle Operations of 42 Royal Marine Commando*. London: Eyre & Spottiswoode, 1954.

Crawford, O. *The Door Marked Malaya*. London: Hart-Davis, 1958.

Hanrahan, G. Z. *The Communist Struggle in Malaya*. New York: International Secretariat, Institute of Pacific Relations, 1954.

Henniker, M. C. A. *Red Shadow over Malaya*. London: Blackwood, 1955.

Miers, R. *Shoot to Kill*. London: Faber, 1959.

Miller, H. *The Communist Menace in Malaya*. New York: Praeger, 1954.

Moran, J. W. *Spearhead in Malaya*. London: Davis & Heinman, 1955.

Oldfield, J. *The Green Hordes in Malaya, 1949–52*. Aldershot, England: Gall & Polden, 1953.

Percival, A. *The War in Malaya*. London: Eyre & Spottiswoode, 1949.

Pye, L. W. *Guerrilla Communism in Malaya: Its Social and Political Meaning*. Princeton, N.J.: Princeton University, 1956.

Slimming, J. *In Fear of Silence*. New York: Harper, 1961.

ARTICLES

Blare, T. "The Queen's 'Copters," *Marine Corps Gazette*, July, 1954.

Brazier-Ceargh, K. R. "Malaya," *Royal United Service Institute*, May, 1954.

Brooke, F. H. "Infantry and Air Power in Malaya," *Australian Army Journal*, December, 1954.

Clark, K. H. "Some Account of an Operation in the Malayan Jungle," *Journal of the Royal Army Medical Corps*, June, 1955.

Crook, P. E. "A Subaltern's War in Malaya," *British Army Journal*, January, 1953.

Duke, W. B. "Operation Metcalf," *Army Quarterly*, October, 1953.

"The Emergency in Malaya," *Army Quarterly*, April, 1954.

Forster, M. O. "A Long-Range Jungle Operation in Malaya—1951," *Journal of the Medical Corps*, November, 1951.

Fricker, V. "Flying against the Malayan Bandits," *Aeroplane*, 5 and 12, January, 1951.

Furby, S. W. "Malay Patrol," *Leatherneck*, January, 1953.

Garland, R. S. "A Tin of Sweet Potatoes," *Australian Army Journal*, January, 1959.

———. "Operations in Malaya," *Australian Army Journal*, April, 1959.

Harvey, M. "Malaya—Time for a Change," *Army Quarterly*, April, 1955.

Henniker, M. C. A. "Jungle War in Malaya," *Military Engineer,* January–February, 1953.

————. "Jungle Hunting Malaya Bandits," *ibid.*

————. "The Jungle War in Malaya," *ibid.,* November–December, 1953.

Hillard, J. L. "Tactics in Malaya," *Army Quarterly,* April, 1951.

Mackersey, I. "Jungle Crusade," *Royal Air Force Review,* February, 1950.

Maconochie, C. "A National Serviceman in Malaya," *Army Quarterly,* October, 1951.

Mellersh, F. "The Campaign against the Terrorists in Malaya," *Royal United Service Institute Journal,* August, 1951.

Meyers, B. F. "Malaya Jungle Patrol," *Marine Corps Gazette,* October, 1960.

Miers, R. C. "Ambush," *Army Magazine,* February, 1959.

Muros, R. L. "Communist Terrorism in Malaya," *U.S. Naval Institute Proceedings,* October, 1961.

Phipps, G. C. "Guerrillas in Malaya," *Infantry Magazine,* May–June, 1961.

Ranft, D. D. "Parachuting in Malaya," *Army Quarterly,* July, 1953.

Reynolds, J. A. C. "Terrorist Activity in Malaya," *Marine Corps Gazette,* November, 1961.

Roberts, C. "The Lighter Side of Bandit Hunting," *Army Quarterly,* January, 1956.

Robinson, R. E. R. "Reflections of a Company Commander in Malaya," *Army Quarterly,* October, 1950.

Saddier, G. T. "Malaya," *Australian Army Journal,* April, 1951.

Sendall, W. R. "The Royal Marines in Malaya," *Navy,* July, 1950.

Seymour, W. N. "Terrorism in Malaya," *Army Quarterly,* April, 1949.

"A Supply Dropping in Malaya," *Royal Air Force Quarterly,* October, 1950.

Tacchi, D. "Jungle Medicine," *Journal of the Royal Army Medical Corps,* October, 1951.

Whitehead, J. "What Price Malaya," *Royal Air Force Quarterly,* January, 1950.

Woodhouse, J. M. "Some Personal Observations on the Employment of Special Forces in Malaya," *Army Quarterly,* April, 1953.

DOCUMENTS

Technical Memorandum, Washington, D.C.:
Force-Tie-Down Capabilities of Guerrillas in Malaya, ORO-T, no. 72, 43p., 1957.
Guerrilla Warfare in the Federation of Malaya, no. 44, 11p., 1952.
Psychological Warfare and Other Factors Affecting Surrender and Disaffection among Communist Terrorists in Malaya, no. 296, 47p., 1955.

PART 8

THE CUBAN REVOLUTION AND
THE ALGERIAN REBELLION

Many nationalist revolutions of our time have been chiefly carried on by guerrilla forces. This is true in both Cuba and Algeria. Despite very different circumstances, both afford examples of guerrilla strategy and tactics that show how successful Communist techniques have been emulated. The leadership of these revolutions is obviously acquainted with the doctrines of Communist guerrilla and revolutionary warfare.

Despite the flood of pro-Castro literature still being produced, Fidel Castro is by his own admission an active Communist bent on spreading the socialist revolutionary spirit throughout the western hemisphere. The question of whether or not Castro's revolution was Communist-controlled from the start, or whether the Communists took over afterwards, is not germane to our purposes. Our concern here is with the over-all guerrilla principles, with the specific tactics used by Castro and his forces, and with the evident source of the Castro movement's theoretical bases in Communist revolutionary doctrine.

Here is one of the three English translations of "Che" Guevara's book, which is reportedly being distributed all over Latin America. Most guerrilla specialists recognize Guevara's work as an elementary imitation of Mao Tse-tung's writings, offering little new thought on the subject. A number of principles and prescriptions that Guevara promulgates seem to be applicable only to the situation in Cuba. Its significance lies in the fact that it may be used as a basic text for Castro-inspired revolutionary movements in other Spanish-speaking areas.

Preceding the Guevara piece is the Chapelle description of a segment of Castro's forces in operation, with her assessment of the superior morale of the revolutionists. Her study, more than any other, presents a description of Castro's use of basic psychological warfare. Most writers give Castro credit for defeating a regular army. This view is semantically correct, but the regular Cuban Army was far from being a disciplined war machine. Rather, it was run for the most part by politically appointed officers, caring little for the art of war but much for the conveniences a uniform provides in a dictatorship. Even if a Cuban Papagos had appeared, the morale of the Cuban Army was such that the Castro forces would probably have won eventually.

In comparing Chapelle's story to Guevara's work, it would appear that what Guevara implies was that his experience within the Cuban revolution was in reality only theory. Some of the principles Guevara advocates do not seem to have been put into practice in the hills. For example, he stresses conservation of ammunition, while Chapelle's account emphasizes the fact that the Cuban guerrillas were prodigal and indiscriminate in wasting it.

In Algeria an irregular type of war has been waged since the early 1950's. The principal participants are the French government's regular forces and the Front de Liberation Nationale (FLN) guerrilla forces—it might almost be called a guerrilla army. This war is complicated by a deep-seated political split between the French residents of Algeria and the government of France, which has profoundly affected the French army's role. This split on the French side has inevitably led to unusual developments in the FLN's strategy. A temporary truce arrangement has brought a cessation of most of the fighting to permit some diplomatic negotiations.

Our consideration here is limited to Braestrup's account of some of the guerrilla tactics employed by the FLN. Also included is Goraud's "Letter to the Editor" from *Army Magazine,* written in response to the Braestrup article. Though there is considerable literature in French, Braestrup's piece is the best brief description available in English of guerrilla activity in Algeria.

28

Dickey Chapelle   **HOW CASTRO WON**

JUST WEST OF GUANTANAMO CITY lies a bend in the Central
Highway which is a text-book ambush site—a horseshoe of asphalt almost
a mile from end to end lined every yard on both sides by steep ridges
thick with jungle growth. One hot morning early in December, 1958, the
curve was ready for its fate. At each end, several 200-pound mines lay
under the road surface and near them, a hidden *rebelde* rested with sweaty
hands close to the plunger. Seven light machine guns were emplaced in the
greenery of the rocky slope, the nearest 40 yards from the road and the
most distant almost on top of the ridge. More than 200 riflemen, many
with automatic weapons, were dug in, two and three to a hole, along the
rise.

But the bearded officer, Capitano Jose Valla, who before the war had
been a traffic clerk in an import firm, was not satisfied.

His people had been manning this ambush site now for thirteen days,
and in that time they had eaten thirteen meals. So he did not think they
were alert any more. As he walked his lines, he told them they could expect to be hit at any hour now by a column of Batista's troops many

From *Marine Corps Gazette*, February, 1960. Copyright 1960 by the Marine
Corps Association and reproduced by permission.

hundred strong. Other rebel forces were besieging one of the government's fortresses, that in the town of La Maya ten miles farther west, and he predicted a relief column would be dispatched to them from the army garrison at Guantanamo City.

But the captain was increasingly aware that he had given these same troops this same word every other morning on the site, too.

So today he decided to change the disposition of his forces.

He sent 40 riflemen and an LMG with its crew two miles up the road. There was an ambush spot there, too, a bush-covered slope lining the left of the road for a thousand yards. His orders to this advance guard he repeated twice. They were to hide in the jungle grass, fire on the relief column when it was at the point nearest them, then leapfrog in three's and four's back through the cane fields to the main ambush area, keeping the convoy under fire only as long as they could do it without exposing themselves.

"That will do no harm and make enough noise so everyone will be wide awake before we're really hit," he finished.

Just before noon, the enemy column did appear. There was a lead jeep, an armored car, a tank, three busses heavily loaded with troops, a rearguard jeep—and one element the captain had not thought about, air cover. Two Cuban Air Force B-26's were flying wide figure 8's along the road at an altitude of about 1,000 feet.

The rebels of the advance guard, well concealed behind chunky bushes and wide-bladed grass, opened fire. The machine gunner accounted for the driver and the officer in the lead jeep and a burst from a BAR killed three soldiers in the front seat of the first bus. The convoy halted dead in the road. A handful of soldiers in the crowded busses wrestled their weapons into firing position but they could not see a target. Neither could the tank crew, slowly traversing their 77mm.

Nor could the men in the B-26's. But they knew the fire had come from the green hillside and they began to strafe it from end to end. They so persistently stitched back and forth that the rebels one by one looked quickly up, hesitated and then fell back behind their concealment. A half dozen began to empty their weapons at the planes. One B-26 gunner opened fire with his 20mm. He hit downslope from the rebels, and most of them continued to empty clip after clip at the stalled convoy.

The men in the driverless bus panicked and fled back through the ditches to the cover of nearby cane fields; a score dropped their rifles as they ran and three fell wounded or dying. The drivers of the other two busses backed them for perhaps 50 yards, loaded the men who had been hit, then U-turned where they were to cover the busses. Then the whole column, leaving only the two wrecked vehicles, was grinding out, faster and faster, to the east.

It was all over in a matter of minutes—all over, that is, but for the verbal pyrotechnics of the rebel captain when the leader of his advance guard reported. The captain pulled him behind the deserted building of a cantina near the main ambush site.

"My orders were that you should fire and withdraw, fire and withdraw!" he shouted over and over at his red-faced junior.

"We would have, we would have, my captain, but that we had no cover from the B-26 and—" the lieutenant began.

"Your excuse shames our dead!" The captain interrupted. "If you had done what I told you to do, we would have captured the whole convoy," he went on, rocking on his toes. "This way, what do we have? Two wrecks and some blood on the Central Highway! And that is all there is to show—for 13 days of waiting!"

He opened his hands and put them over his bearded face. The lieutenant turned and walked slowly out of the yard of the deserted cantina.

Capt Valle probably stated the net tactical gain to the rebel campaign correctly. But to a looker-on and possibly to the historians, the action was more significant. It was almost a vignette of the Cuban revolution, an answer to the question: how did Castro's riflemen time and again turn back Batista's tanks and planes?

My own conclusion was that they earned all the real estate by making every mistake in the book—but one. They consistently delivered a high volume of fire. After they started shooting, they rarely let anything—the enemy's reaction or their own commander's orders—stop them from continuing to fire until there was nothing left to fire on.

They barely aimed and they did not conserve ammunition. But they unmistakably communicated their will to fight to an enemy whose superior equipment was unmatched by the will to use it.

Here is a report from the Cuban fighting:

Personnel

The forces of Castro at the time I knew them moved and fired as an army, not a band or mob. Fidel estimated there were 7300 in uniform (blue or green cotton drill fatigues) by the third week in December. They were directly supported by an equal number of personnel under military orders whose duties included work in towns still policed by Batista and who hence wore civilian clothing. One in ten of the fighters was a non-Cuban—Dominican, Mexican, Venezuelan, Nicaraguan, Argentinian. About one in twenty was a woman; except for one sniper platoon, the women in uniform were non-combatants who did housekeeping and supply assignments.

The basic unit of the rebel army was a 40-man platoon commanded by a second lieutenant. The rebels insisted there were no differences in rate among the non-officer personnel; in practice, I noticed many "natural NCO's" with their own following of from six to a dozen men. The officer ranks were the same as U.S. ranks up to major, or *commandante,* still the highest rank in Cuban military forces. (The single star on the Cuban Prime minister's epaulets today signifies this rank, as it did during the fighting.) In the field, I worked with the command groups of three majors beside the Castros. Each led about 500 men and 20-odd officers.

This simplified table of organization was reflected in the division of responsibilities. What we consider S-1 functions were almost entirely carried out by the senior officer or his top aides personally. The S-2 and S-4 work was done by men in mufti. This left the uniformed forces the single primary concern of operations.

The staffs had no problems of pay—no pay, hence no problem—or of recruitment, since there were more would-be *Fidelistas* than rifles with which to arm them. The sure method by which the volunteer became a *barbudo*[1] was to disarm one of Batista's soldiers (by force or purchase) and hike into a Castro command post with his rifle, ammo and canteen. One boy of 15 had to be accepted when he reported with a BAR which he insisted he had gotten the hard way.

More than half the *rebelde* fighters I knew had been field hands in the cane fields or coffee plantations of Oriente Province. But a high proportion of the others had city backgrounds and white collar experience, so the over-all literacy rate was very high for Cuba. Probably the most capable battalion officers (now G-3 of the Cuban Rebel Army) was *Commandante* Antonio Lusson, whose family owns a large cane plantation near to the Castro family's own fields.

Most of the enlisted men I knew had undergone a basic training stint of from two to four months in the most remote reaches of the Sierra Maestre mountains. They had learned scouting and patrolling there (one had a copy of FM 21-75 in his pack) but the primary purpose of the training obviously was to condition the men to extended periods of hunger and fatigue, to find out which would literally rather fight than eat. Not many had learned to use their weapons effectively nor to maintain them in the field; those who had became prized men. But the *barbudos* almost without exception had developed a genuine *esprit de corps.*

The wide dissimilarity of military capability among them was probably less significant than the one common motivation. All Castro's fighting men were terror victims to the extent that they believed they would be killed if they went back to their homes while Batista remained in power. I knew dozens who showed me what they said were marks of torture on

---

1. "Bearded one"—enrolled regular in Castro's army.

their bodies, or who told me how they had buried the bullet-riddled bodies of their fathers, sons or brothers.

"I always knew Latins could hate that much, but not that they could hate that long," is a comment I have heard about them. One explanation is the conviction most of them expressed that they as individuals could not expect to live if they did not destroy the *Batistianos* who were then still policing their home communities.

The other side of the coin—the personal motivation of government forces—was a particular target of psychological assault from the first.

Before I left the United States, the Castro underground in New York briefed me on the tactics this way: "We return prisoners without even intimidating them. We do not exchange them, you understand; not one of ours has ever been returned in the field. But we just disarm our enemies when we capture them and send them back through the Cuban Red Cross."

I was cynical about this claim and once in Cuba, I remarked to a rebel officer that I would be much surprised to see unintimidated, unwounded prisoners being returned, not exchanged, in the middle of a shooting war. This remark was a mistake.

That same evening, I watched the surrender of hundreds of *Batistianos* from a small town garrison. They were gathered within a hollow square of rebel Tommy gunners and harangued by Raul Castro.

"We hope that you will stay with us and fight against the master who so ill-used you. If you decide to refuse this invitation—and I am not going to repeat it—you will be delivered to the custody of the Cuban Red Cross tomorrow. Once you are under Batista's orders again, we hope that you will not take up arms agains us. But, if you do, remember this—

"We took you this time. We can take you again. And when we do, we will not frighten or torture or kill you, any more than we are doing to you at this moment. If you are captured a second time or even a third by us, we will again return you exactly as we are doing now."

This expression of utter contempt for the fighting potential of the defeated had an almost physical impact on them. Some actually flinched as they listened.

The following day, I could not question that these men were returned unharmed. I counted 242 across a border check-point marked by two burned-out car wrecks overlooking Santiago de Cuba.

On the matter of casualty figures over all for the two years of active fighting, I came to accept Castro's estimate of 1,000 rebel dead because I was able to verify personally that the rebel dead announced for the actions I saw were correct. (But an even more important and still controversial casualty figure is the rebel total loss from terrorism in the cities rather than military operations in the country. This is believed to be more than 10,000 over a five-year period.)

Intelligence

The *Fidelista* combat intelligence was superb. The Batista commanders could not go to the "head" without a perspiring runner arriving a few
minutes later to tell Castro about it. Most of the informants were volunteers—farmers or villagers.

While the bulk of such reports was hardly marked by accuracy, Fidel
himself placed the greatest reliance on them. The night we met for the
first time, he and his command group were standing within 600 yards of
where a huge enemy patrol was searching for him. I assumed he was there
to command an action to hit the patrol or cut it off.

"Oh, no," he explained. "It's too big. They are coming through the
woods in a body, with men in pairs on either side. When the nearest pair
is a few hundred meters away, people will tell me and we will leave."

Enemy scouts did in fact come in ten minutes after his departure. In
their asperity, they burned to the ground the farmer's house beside which
he had been conferring. The farmer became a fighting *Fidelista* before the
ashes of his house had cooled, bringing a Springfield rifle he had kept
buried apparently for just this eventuality.

One tradition of the Castro forces had a special usefulness to their
intelligence—the matter of the beards. The nucleus of the Castro forces
grew them because there were no razors on Pico Turquino where they hid.
But in time the beards served as an identification device. When you saw a
man with a six-month growth of hair and whiskers, you could be sure he had
not been in contact with the Batista soldiery for a long time, since to them
a beard was cause for summary arrest.

Operations

During the early months of the fighting, the only military tactic used
by the rebels was to ambush small government patrols for their weapons.
As the patrols grew larger, the *rebelde* underground furnished mines, and
the *Fidelistas* were able to turn back several punitive thrusts made at them
in the mountains by ringing their strongholds with the mines.

Their experience in stopping movement along roads and trails led to
the tactic by which they won much of Oriente Province. Its general objective was to isolate the government garrisons by halting all surface traffic.
The rebels blew up the railroad bridges first, then mined the side roads
and finally the main artery across Cuba, the Central Highway. They halted
and burned every bus, car and truck; even today, the wreckage of this
phase of the campaign still litters the ditches. Non-combatants were
walked at gunpoint back to wherever they came from—except for those

abducted, including the U.S. servicemen and technicians held for 27 days in July of 1958.

By early December, the roads and most of the countryside had come under rebel control after dark; by daylight, nothing moved but Batista's forces in not less than company strength and usually with tanks and air cover.

But most town and village *cuartels*[2] were still fully garrisoned, and the government controlled the built-up areas.

Against them, Castro's forces used three kinds of offensive action: combat patrols, assault and encirclement. But each of these terms is only correct in the most limited sense.

The patrols were night marches, off the roads, of one or two platoons with the objective of shaking up a garrison behind its concrete walls. Weapons included rifles, BARs, Tommy guns and one or two LMG. On one patrol, the men brought an 81mm mortar with five rounds for it. On another, they carried a 20mm cannon recovered from a wrecked Cuban Air Force plane. For it they had only notoriously undependable home-made ammo.

The patrols crept close to the *cuartel* walls (at Maffo, within 40 yards) and opened fire. They sustained it no matter what came back at them until their ammo ran low or, as happened twice, the garrison set fire to their trucks. At San Luis, the garrison resisted two such raids vigorously and the day after the second, withdrew in jeeps and a truck into the nearest larger *cuartel*. Their column tore by a rebel ambush which happened to be facing the wrong way and not a shot was fired.

The tactic which the rebels called an assault was not an assault at all as we use the word. It meant the rebel commanders would infiltrate their troops by dark to positions as close to an objective as they could find concealment. They would then keep it under uninterrupted small arms fire 24 hours a day. But they would not advance nor would they use demolitions.

In the fortress at La Maya, they so trapped 525 people, 125 of them the wives and children of government soldiers, for seventeen days. In Maffo, there were 150 *Batistianos* who held out for fourteen days and then surrendered. The artillery available on either side was negligible. The rebels used one 20mm cannon with comedy effect because of poor home-made ammo, and the garrison at Maffo one night expended nine mortar shells—presumably all it had—against a rebel sound truck that had been haranguing the troops to surrender. On this occasion, the accuracy was outstanding; four rebels were killed and 13 wounded.

In spite of the fact that small arms fire spattering concrete walls hardly sounds effective, these encirclements of the Batista *cuartels* were the decisive actions of the revolution. In the fight for Santa Clara, the final

---

2. Fortified barracks.

and largest action, it was a trainload of troops which the rebels encircled, not, a fortress. And in this one case those who could fire from buildings had better cover than the troops opposing them.

However, in the fighting which I saw, the rebels only sought out concealment and did almost without dug-in or sandbagged positions. Often they exposed themselves deliberately for no logical military purpose. Once, when a whole platoon was disconsolate because their rifle grenades were misfiring, their battalion commander himself led a dozen in a charge out of their concealment. An enemy blockhouse lay 150 yards away and perhaps some of his men assumed that he planned to flank it. But without grenades, demolitions or mortar fire, he charged out 50 yards, then disposed his men behind the foot-high cover of the foundation of a wrecked building, and from there emptied several BAR magazines into the concrete blockhouse walls. He then ran his people back through a crescendo of incoming fire from the blockhouse to their concealed positions. But for skinned knees and elbows, no casualties resulted. The effect on morale was excellent. But the blockhouse was no less lethal than before.

Why were the government garrisons unable to break out of their *cuartels* and blockhouses?

Surely they could have broken the ring of besiegers. But there would have been casualties, and the countryside was actively hostile.

Why were the *cuartels* not reinforced? Or better resupplied?

Until the last weeks of the fighting, the larger were, in effect, reinforced by the fleeing garrisons from the smaller.

But as to why these in turn did not hold out, purely tactical answers are not enough. When the 525 people from the La Maya fortress surrendered, they still had food, water and ammo. There were seven wounded, two of them dying, in the group. Nine people had been killed and buried inside the walls (and seven of the rebels had been killed, two from the air). The Cuban Air Force had not been successful in its resupply efforts. But it had never tried drops directly within the *cuartel* walls, presumably because of the risk of hitting some of the people with falling packages.

Which raises what was to me a great mystery of the actions I observed: the astonishingly poor performance of the B-26's. True, they bombed and strafed the town of La Maya twice a day at least and the roads around it at all hours. But they did this so badly that I was able to photograph them sometimes twice after they had begun their runs and then, usually leisurely, to move to shelter.

The Cuban Air Force B-26's—in pairs flying in echelon—usually committed in the adjoining county and then strafed from an altitude of 300 to 500 feet. They proved they knew how to do better when they were covering an unarmed DC-3 making a resupply drop; then they came in at right angles to each other and went up the streets with wingtips at housetop level.

I came to two conclusions about the curious B-26 performances:

First, the claims of the pilots at their subsequent trials that they did everything short of court-martial to avoid killing non-combatants are entirely valid. (You remember, Fidel set aside two trials acquitting flyers on this issue and ordered a third, after which came executions and prison sentences.)

Second, the psychological impact of the B-26 operations on the people of rural Cuba will be a major barrier to friendly U.S.–Cuban relations for a generation to come. It is no use to point out that we sent Batista these planes for another purpose and stopped sending them at all in March of 1958. The planes, no matter how poorly flown, utterly terrorized the province and, moral judgments entirely aside, the fact is that we are heartily hated because they caused such fear.

At the time, incidentally, the rebels, without aircraft or ack-ack, did not ignore the planes but emptied rifles and BARs up at them no matter what the range. I never saw a hit scored but the psychological effects were dramatic.

Supply

This was a controlling factor in the entire Castro offensive.

On the matter of food alone, the rebels' survival as a cohesive fighting unit was frequently in doubt. Being both guest and woman, I always had more to eat than anyone else, but at one point I lived on raw sugar cane for two days, and at another time I ate only one meal a day for five days in a row. The characteristic "hot chow" of the rebels in the field was a mush of rice with pieces of fresh-killed beef in it, served from a bucket hung on a pole which was carried by two runners from one foxhole to another.

Personal equipment was severely limited. Cotton drill shirts and pants were issued, but good footwear, canteens and blankets were not, and the *rebelde's* armbands, shoulder patches and insignia of rank were sewn and embroidered by his wife or one of the village women.

How Castro received his arms and ammunition was a subject of acrimonious international debate for a long time.

Before I went to Cuba, I was told that most weapons and ammo were smuggled in by air from the United States, Mexico and Venezuela. Dictator Batista's secretary of state once gave me a personal interview on a holiday to complain bitterly that American laxity in arresting the smugglers was the reason the government could not defeat the rebels.

But there is little evidence for this thesis. Recently I met a Cuban flier who had flown arms from the United States to Cuba for months during the revolution. He said he had been told in Miami that U.S. law enforcement agencies were alerted in early 1958 to look for a fleet of heavily-loaded station wagons and several DC-3's.

"So what we did was to fly the stuff in a pair of Cessna 182's. We got it out to landing strips near Key West in an outboard fishing boat loaded on a trailer. Once I was driving the trailer and I had a flat. The police helped me change the tire at the side of the highway without ever looking under the tarp which covered my boat. If they had folded it back, they would have found twelve Tommy guns and the ammo for them."

After I had been with the *Fidelistas* for a few weeks, I no longer questioned their on-the-spot insistence that only about 15 per cent of their weapons were so "imported." All the rest, they said, were captured.

The weapons which I saw were not new, and the great majority were of the type which we furnished to Batista—Springfields, M-1's, BARs and Tommy guns. And Colt .45 automatics, many of the latter demonstrably captured weapons with butt-plates still carrying the insignia of the Cuban Army.

In the case of .30 cal. ammo, I saw it being captured during the battle of La Maya. The action around the town involved more than 250 *rebeldes* actually firing on the line day and night for two and a half weeks. Yet when the battle was over, the rebel ammo inventory was fatter than when it began. Four times during the siege a government DC-3 had made an air drop (no parachute; they just pushed the packages out of the door) of ammo for the fortress, and four times the rebels had charged out under heavy fire and dragged the packages back behind their own lines. From these bundles the rebels also gained large quantities of medical supplies and some of the best cigarettes I ever smoked.

Two weapons widely used by the rebels were manufactured right in Cuba itself by the underground.

One was the 200-pound land mine, made at first from explosive salvaged out of unexploded aerial bombs that had been dropped by the Cuban Air Force. The mines usually were emplaced to be detonated electrically by a soldier on command.

The other homemade device was a rifle grenade which resembled no other grenade of which I've ever heard. It was a firecracker shape about eight inches long with a conical cap on one end. It was detonated by a fuse of cotton string. To fire it, you affixed it to the end of a rifle, lit the fuse and pulled the trigger. In theory, the grenade exploded four seconds later. I watched more than a score of these fired. Each time something inhibited the clean get-away of the grenade from the rifle and it detonated within 50 yards of take-off.

A special logistic problem to the rebels was motor transport. Their few dozen vehicles were jeeps, either captured from the government or expropriated at gunpoint from oil and mining companies. (I remember there was a "duty ambulance" at the battle Jiguani—a sky-blue enameled

DIES.) Impulsive driving and no main-
the availability of vehicles. But the
ıble tracks in rural Cuba probably re-
nsport to both sides in the fighting.

ı, the personnel in the field under Fidel
bout 15,000, half in uniform, including
lly and physically superior. There was
d discipline within small units was good.
king in marksmanship ability, conven-
perience in fighting as a cohesive force
of any size. Their attitude toward their enemies was one of contempt
leavened with compassion.

Their combat intelligence was unexcelled in quantity and of depend-
able accuracy. It was not organized on any military basis but originated
in the civilian population which felt itself a direct participant in every
action, and generally welcomed the rebels as liberators from terrorism.

The Castro defensive operations depended largely on this intelligence
and on foot mobility; the rebels simply did not remain where they were
sought.

Their offensive operations rested on tactics involving the highest degree
of surprise, the fewest men, the lowest risk and the greatest freedom to
disengage. These included road ambushes, raiding patrols, infiltration, and
sustained siege by small arms fire. No dependence on artillery or motor
transport was developed.

Their logistics were primitive and in other than the near-ideal weather
and terrain conditions of Cuba would have been disastrous. Their food
supply was not adequate by any ordinary standard. Their primary source
of arms and ammunition was the enemy, although perhaps 15 per cent
were smuggled into Cuba.

Their conspicuous military virtue was their ability to maintain a high
volume of fire under conditions which would have discouraged less motivated fighters. This virtue fully exploited the major weakness of the well-
equipped government forces, which was a near-paralysis of the will to
fire at all. If there is any military lesson from the Cuban revolution for
all Americans, in and out of uniform, I think this is it:

Machinery does not win wars. Men do.

29

Ernesto "Che" Guevara   ## LA GUERRA

DE GUERRILLAS

THE ARMED VICTORY OF THE CUBAN PEOPLE over the Batista dictatorship, an epic triumph recognized throughout the world, clearly demonstrates the ability of a people to free themselves, by means of guerrilla warfare, from a government that is oppressing them.

I. GENERAL PRINCIPLES

Essentials of Guerrilla Warfare

The Cuban Revolution made three fundamental contributions to the mechanics of revolutionary movements in America:
  1. The forces of the people can win a war against the army.
  2. It is not necessary to wait for the fulfillment of all conditions for a revolution because the focus of insurrection can create them.

Translated and condensed by *Army Magazine*. (Two long footnotes comparing official U.S. military doctrine have been deleted.)

From *Army Magazine,* March, April, and May, 1961. Copyright 1961 by Association of the U.S. Army and reproduced by permission.

3. The area for the armed struggle in underdeveloped America is the rural regions.

Independent of an analysis to be made later, we place the foregoing conclusions of the Cuban revolutionary experience at the head of this work as its basic contribution.

War is subject to a definite system of scientific laws. Anyone violating them will meet defeat. Guerrilla warfare is governed by the same laws but is also subject to special laws that derive from the particular geographic and social conditions in each country.[1]

Our present task is to analyze this type of struggle and the rules to be followed by a people seeking their freedom.

First, it is necessary to determine the combatants in a guerrilla war. On the one side is the center of oppression and its agent—the professional army. On the other side is the population of the nation in question. It is important to point out that guerrilla warfare is a struggle of the people.

The guerrilla force is merely the fighting vanguard of the people and derives its great strength from its roots in the mass of the population. The guerrilla force is not, therefore, to be regarded as numerically inferior to the army it is fighting although it is inferior in firepower. It is necessary to resort to guerrilla warfare when there is support from a majority group but only a limited quantity of arms to defend against oppression.

The guerrilla counts, therefore, on the support of the entire population of a locality. This is an indispensable condition. We can see this very clearly if we consider the example of bands of robbers operating in a region. The band has all the characteristics of a guerrilla army: homogeneity, respect for the chief, bravery, knowledge of the terrain and even, in many cases, complete understanding of the tactics to be used. The band lacks only the support of the people. Inevitably, therefore, the robber band is arrested and exterminated.

For the proper analysis of guerrilla warfare, it should be noted that there are two different types: first, the guerrillas supplement the effort of a large regular army as in the case of the Ukrainian guerrillas; second, an armed group is fighting against an established government. We are not interested in the first type. We are interested only in the type where an armed group is carrying on a fight against an established colonial (or other) power. This is a group that has its base in a rural region and is operating in and from that region.

It is important to remember that guerrilla fighting is only a beginning or preparation for conventional warfare. The possibilities for the growth of the guerrilla force and for changing the type of fighting to conventional warfare are as numerous as the possibilities for defeating the enemy in each of the separate battles or skirmishes that take place. For this reason,

---

1. See Mao Tse-tung, *Selected Works*, II, 124: "Guerrilla warfare is different from regular warfare only in degree and in the form of manifestation."

it is a fundamental principle that there must never be a lost battle or skirmish.

The fundamental tactic is to strike and flee continually so that the enemy gets no rest. Though this appears somewhat negative in character, it is, nevertheless, consistent with the general strategy of guerrilla warfare, which has the same final purpose as any other form of warfare: to annihilate the enemy and to secure victory.

War is a struggle in which both sides attempt to annihilate one another.[2] In order to achieve this purpose, they use force, subterfuge, trickery or any other device at their disposal. Military strategy and tactics reveal the aspirations of the military leaders and their methods of achieving objectives. The method always contemplates taking advantage of all the weak points of the enemy. If we compare a war of position with a guerrilla war, we can see that in a war of position the action of each platoon of a large unit corresponds to the action of a guerrilla force. The platoon may commit acts of treachery, will engage in night operations, and will attempt to achieve surprise. If it does not use these methods, it is only because it has not found the watching enemy off guard. However, the guerrilla force is a self-contained unit free to move anywhere, and there are always large areas unguarded by the enemy. Consequently, it is always possible to use the tactics described and to take advantage of surprise. Therefore, it is the duty of the guerrilla to use these tactics.

Guerrilla combat is a phase of warfare that cannot of itself attain complete victory.[3] It is one of the primary phases of a war of liberation and continues to grow in importance as the guerrilla army acquires the characteristics of a regular army. When the guerrilla army acquires a regular status, then it will be ready for decisive attacks on the enemy and thus secure victory. The triumph will always be the product of the regular army even though the regular army had its origins in a guerrilla force.

Guerrilla Strategy

. . . Strategy means the analysis of the objectives to be achieved in light of the total military situation and the courses of action available to achieve those objectives.

---

2. The interesting point here is that Guevara means there are no conventional type military objectives in a guerrilla war: a given hill or town is meaningless as an objective. The objective is always to annihilate whatever force the guerrillas attack. *Ibid.*, 121, uses this same type of thought when Mao says, "All guiding principles for military operations proceed without exception from one basic principle; that is, to strive as far as possible to preserve one's own strength and annihilate that of the enemy."

3. *Ibid.*, 151, says: "Since the war is protracted and ruthless, it becomes possible for guerrilla units to go through the necessary process of steeling and to change gradually into regular armies; consequently, with their mode of operations gradually transformed into that of regular armies, guerrilla warfare will develop into mobile warfare."

For a correct understanding of strategy to be followed by a guerrilla force, it is necessary to make a profound analysis of the courses of action available to the enemy. The guerrilla must analyze the resources available to the enemy, his strength in men, his mobility, his popular support, his armament, and his leadership. From this analysis, the guerrilla must adapt his own strategy so as to obtain his final objective which is to defeat the enemy army.

There are other fundamental matters to be studied: the enemy's tactics for using his equipment; exact estimates of the value of a tank in a struggle of this kind; the value of a plane; and the kind of arms and equipment possessed by the enemy. It is important to note here that if a guerrilla has a choice, he must always choose the weapons of his enemy because the guerrilla always lacks equipment and arms. Therefore, if he chooses the enemy's weapons the enemy will be the guerrilla's supplier. Once this study is made and the objectives evaluated and analyzed, it is necessary to begin planning for the achievement of the final objective. These plans will be made in advance but will be changed as needed to meet unforeseen circumstances that arise during the fighting.

In the beginning, the primary duty of the guerrilla is to keep himself from being destroyed. It will gradually become easier for guerrilla units to adapt themselves to the new manner of life involved in fleeing from and avoiding the enemy forces sent for their destruction. This objective attained, the guerrillas will find positions whose inaccessibility prevents the enemy from attacking them. Gradually, larger forces will be created and the process of weakening the enemy should begin. The weakening will take place initially in locations nearest the points of active fighting against the guerrilla army. Later, the weakening can be extended to deeper portions of the enemy territory where his communications and bases of operation can be struck and harassed to the maximum extent of the guerrilla capability.

The striking action should be constant. An enemy soldier in the zone of operations should not be allowed to sleep. The outposts should be systematically attacked and destroyed. At all times the impression should be created that the enemy is completely surrounded. This can be done by the use of patrols. To accomplish this, the complete cooperation of the people is necessary as well as a thorough knowledge of the terrain. These are two essential factors to which the guerrilla must constantly pay attention.

Certain well-organized groups that have shown ability in heretofore less dangerous work may now be used for sabotage duties. This is a terrible weapon which can paralyze entire armies or the industrial life of an entire area. It leaves the inhabitants without industry, light, water, communications, or even the ability to leave their homes except at certain hours. If this be accomplished, the enemy's morale, including that of combat units, will be weakened.

All of this presupposes an enlargement of the area involved in the guerrilla action although there should never be an exaggerated increase of this territory. A strong base of operations[4] must be maintained at all times, and it must continue to be strengthened during the course of the war. It is, of course, necessary to take measures to insure the indoctrination of the inhabitants of the base region as well as to take necessary precautions against the implacable foes of the revolution.

When the original guerrilla force has reached suitable strength in men and arms, it should form new guerrilla columns. Ultimately, the territory occupied by the various columns is too small to contain them. The columns advance toward the regions strongly defended by the enemy. Then, the columns unite to form a compact battle front able to engage in a war of position as in the case of a regular army. However, the old guerrilla army must not become separated from its base because the work of forming new guerrilla forces behind the enemy lines must continue. These forces then operate in the same manner as the first until the new territory is overcome.

Thus the moment comes for attacking, for besieging cities, for routing reinforcements, for increasingly daring action by the excited masses in all of the national territory, for the attainment of the final objective—victory.

Guerrilla Tactics

. . . In military terminology, tactics constitute the practical methods of achieving great strategic objectives.

Mobility is a fundamental characteristic of a guerrilla force. In a few minutes it can be far from the immediate scene of action, or in a few hours it can be far from the region of action, if this is necessary. This permits a constantly changing front and thus avoids any form of encirclement. Consistent with the phase of the war a guerrilla force can devote itself exclusively to avoiding encirclement and to prevent being trapped into a decisive, unfavorable battle, or it can conduct counter-encirclement operations. In these a small group of men is presumably surrounded by the enemy when suddenly the enemy finds himself surrounded by a larger contingent. The first men, situated in an impregnable position, were merely the decoy to lure the enemy into a trap to be surrounded or annihilated in some manner.

A characteristic of this war of mobility is what is called "minuet," by analogy with the dance of the same name. For example, the guerrillas surround an enemy column with small groups of five or six men in several locations (situated so that they will not in turn be surrounded). Then fight-

---

4. *Ibid.*, 134–144, says, ". . . Guerrilla warfare could not be maintained and developed for long without base areas, which are indeed its rear." He then gives a complete discussion of various types of base areas and the problems involved in establishing them.

ing is initiated at one of these points, and the enemy advances towards the attacking force. The guerrillas retreat, keeping contact with the enemy. Now, another group initiates an attack. The enemy will move to the new point and the guerrillas repeat their former action. With such successive operations an enemy column can be immobilized without great danger. The enemy is forced to use large quantities of equipment, and the morale of his troops is weakened.

This same procedure can be used at night, with greater aggressiveness because it is much more difficult to surround the guerrillas. We can say that night fighting is another characteristic of guerrilla forces. It permits them to advance and to maneuver in territory that is not well known and thus avoid betrayal by informers. The numerical inferiority of a guerrilla force requires that attacks take place by surprise. This is the great advantage that enables guerrillas to inflict casualties on the enemy, without loss to themselves.

A guerrilla soldier killed in action should never be left with his arms and equipment. It is the duty of every guerrilla soldier to recover at once the precious weapons and equipment of a fallen comrade. The manner of using weapons is another characteristic of guerrilla warfare. In any combat between a regular force and guerrillas, each side can be identified by the nature of its fire. The regular army fires heavy concentrations, but the guerrillas fire separate, accurate bursts.

Another fundamental characteristic of the guerrilla soldier is his ability to adapt himself to any conditions or to turn changing battlefield situations to his advantage. In contrast to the rigid methods of classical warfare, the guerrilla invents his own tactics for each moment of the fight and constantly surprises the enemy.

Primarily, there are three kinds of defensive positions: elastic positions, special positions which the enemy cannot pass, and positions suitable for diversionary actions. Instances are frequent where the enemy observes with surprise that a gradual, easy advance is suddenly and forcefully stopped, with no possibility of going farther. This is because the positions held by the guerrillas, when it has been possible to make a complete study of the terrain, are impregnable. It is not necessary to count how many soldiers may attack but how many can defend a position. Once this number is determined the position can be defended against a battalion almost always, if not always. The great task of the leader is to make the proper choice of the time and location for defending a position to the end.

The manner of attack of a guerrilla army is also different: it begins with surprise—furious, implacable—and suddenly the assault is completely stopped. The surviving enemy force believes the attackers have gone, becomes calm again and resumes normal activities within the position or besieged city. Suddenly the same kind of attack breaks out in another place. As another example, a post defending a sector is suddenly attacked, overcome, and falls to the guerrillas. The basic features are surprise and rapidity of attack.

Sabotage is always an effective weapon when well handled. Sabotage should never be used against unimportant means of production so that it needlessly paralyzes an unessential sector of the population and leaves people without work. Sabotage against a soft-drink factory is ridiculous, whereas sabotage against a central electric plant is absolutely correct and commendable. In the first instance a few workers are affected and there is no effect on general industrial activity. In the second, workers are also affected but this is entirely justified by the total paralysis of the life of the region.

Aviation is one of the favorite weapons of the regular army. However, this weapon cannot be used effectively in the first stages of guerrilla warfare, for there are only small, hidden groups of men scattered in rough terrain.[5] The effectiveness of the air weapon depends upon systematic destruction of organized and visible positions of defense. For these conditions to exist, there must be large concentrations of men in the defenses, but this is not true of guerrilla positions. Aviation can, nevertheless, be effective against marching columns in level or unprotected terrain. This danger, however, is easily avoided by night marches.

One of the enemy's weakest points is his highway and rail transport. It is practically impossible to guard every part of a road or railway. Therefore, traffic can be stopped by explosives placed at any unguarded point. Explosions can be caused when a vehicle is passing not only to make the vehicle unusable, but also to cause considerable loss of enemy lives and materiel.

There are various sources for explosives: they can be brought from other regions; they can be obtained from unexploded bombs or shells of the enemy; or they can be made in secret laboratories within the guerrilla area. There are many ways of using explosives; the manufacture of bombs and other devices depends upon the resources of the guerrilla forces.

The practice of concealing guerrilla groups along roads to explode mines and annihilate survivors is most remunerative against equipment and weapons. The surprised enemy does not use his ammunition and does not have time to escape. Thus, the guerrillas obtain considerable results at little cost.

As these blows are struck the enemy will change his tactics and instead of sending out vehicles separately will use motorized columns. Nevertheless, it is possible by proper choice of location to achieve the same results by breaking up the column and concentrating forces on one vehicle. In these

---

5. *Ibid.*, 127, says: "It is precisely because they are weak and small that they can appear and disappear mysteriously in the enemy's rear and completely baffle him—such great freedom of action is something that massive regular armies can never enjoy."

instances it is always necessary to observe the essential features of guerrilla tactics, which are:

1. Absolute knowledge of the terrain;
2. Safeguarding escape routes;
3. Knowledge and vigilance as to all secondary roads leading to the place of attack;
4. Knowledge of the populace of the area and its total capabilities as to supplies and transport;
5. Temporary concealment or permanent concealment when it is necessary to leave wounded comrades;
6. Numerical superiority at a particular point of the action;
7. Complete mobility; and possibility of counting on reserve forces.

If all these tactical requirements are fulfilled, surprise actions against the enemy's lines of communication can yield high dividends.

A fundamental part of guerrilla tactics is the manner of treating inhabitants of the region. The treatment of the enemy is also important. Toward the enemy the rule to follow should be one of absolute ruthlessness at the time of attack, absolute implacability toward all contemptible persons engaging in betrayals and assassinations; but the greatest possible clemency toward soldiers who in fighting are fulfilling, or believe they are fulfilling, their military duty. It is a good rule, so long as there are no important bases of operations or impregnable positions, not to take prisoners. Survivors should be left at liberty; wounded enemy should be given all care possible at the time of the action. Conduct toward the civilian populace should be governed by great respect for their traditions and customs, in order to demonstrate effectively the moral superiority of the guerrilla soldiers over their opponents. Except in special circumstances, there should be no executions without giving the accused person an opportunity to clear himself of the charges.

Favorable Terrain

. . . Guerrilla warfare will not always be waged in terrain favorable for the application of its tactics. However, when the guerrilla force is established in regions difficult of access, in wild and rough country, with steep mountains, or impassable deserts or marshes, the terrain is favorable. The general tactics will always tend to be the same and based on the fundamental postulates of guerrilla warfare.

The guerrilla force should fight from the first moment it has assured its survival. It must go out constantly from its place of refuge to fight. Its mobility does not have to be so great as when the terrain is unfavorable. It must adapt itself to the circumstances of the enemy but does not need to have the extensive mobility required in regions where the enemy can quickly concentrate large numbers of men. Nor are night operations so important in this kind of fighting, because operations and especially movement of forces often are possible by day, always subject to the enemy's vigilance on the ground and in the air. Also, the actions can last much longer in the mountains with smaller forces used, and very probably the enemy can be prevented from bringing reinforcements to the scene of the fighting. Vigilance over possible routes of access is, of course, an axiom that must never be forgotten by the guerrilla, but his aggressiveness (because of the difficulties of preventing the enemy from receiving reinforcements) can be even greater. It is possible to come closer to the enemy, to harass and fight him more directly and for a longer time, always subject to circumstances such as, for example, the quantity of equipment available.

Warfare in favorable terrain, and particularly in the mountains, in opposition to so many advantages, includes the disadvantages that it is difficult, because of the considerable precautions taken by the enemy in these regions, to seize in a single operation a considerable quantity of arms and equipment. The guerrilla soldier must never forget that the enemy should be the source of supply for arms and equipment. However, much more rapidly than in unfavorable terrain, the guerrilla force can become firmly established and form a center for carrying on a war of positions. It forms installations protected from aviation or long-range artillery, creates necessary small industries and activities such as hospitals, education and training centers and other essentials like warehouses and radio broadcasting stations.

The radius of operations of a guerrilla force of this type can be as wide as the conditions or operations of adjacent guerrilla forces permit. Everything depends upon the time required to proceed from a place of operations to a place of safety. This means assuming and calculating that marches will be made at night, that it is not possible to operate farther than five or six hours' march from the point of minimum safety. Of course, small guerrilla bands can radiate from the areas of safety weakening the territory.

Weapons preferred for this type of warfare are those of long range with little expenditure of ammunitions, with support from automatic and semi-automatic weapons. One of the weapons most recommended is the Garand M1 rifle, although it must be used by people with some experience, because it uses too much ammunition. Semi-heavy weapons such as machine guns mounted on tripods can be used in favorable terrain with a greater margin of safety for the weapons and their users, but they should always be used as defensive weapons and not for attack.

An ideal armament for a guerrilla force of 25 men would be 10 to 15 ordinary manually operated rifles, some 10 automatic weapons divided between Garand rifles and small portable machine guns, counting on the support of automatic weapons that are light and easily transported such as U.S. Browning machine guns and the more modern Belgian FAL and M14. Among the small portable machine guns, those of 9mm are preferable, as greater quantities of ammunition can be carried and their more simple construction the better facilitates changing replacement parts. All of this should be adapted to the armament of the enemy because we are going to use enemy equipment when it falls into our hands. The enemy will find that heavy armament is practically useless: the aviation can see nothing and serves no purpose, and tanks and artillery can accomplish little due to difficulty of advancing in these regions.

Supply is very important. In general, regions that are difficult of access have for that very reason a difficult supply problem because farmers, and therefore supplies of farm products, are lacking. It is necessary to have stable supply lines and a minimum of goods always on hand to provide against any unfavorable contingency.

In such areas of operations, possibilities for sabotage on a large scale are lacking because there are few constructions, few telephone lines, aqueducts or other facilities that can be damaged by direct action.

To assure supplies, it is important to have animals. For rough terrain mules are best. Adequate pastures must be available for feeding them. These animals can travel over extremely rough and difficult ground where other animals cannot. In the most difficult conditions, resort must be had to transport by men. A man can carry a load of 25 kilograms [say 55 pounds] for many hours a day and for many days.

Lines of communication with the exterior must have a number of intermediate points in the hands of persons who can be trusted. Here products can be stored and persons acting as intermediaries can be concealed at certain times. In addition, internal lines of communication must be established, depending on the degree of development reached by the guerrilla force. In some areas of operations during the last Cuban war, telephone lines many kilometers long were provided and roads were built. There was always an adequate messenger service to cover all areas in the shortest time possible.

Unfavorable Terrain

. . . Unfavorable regions are those without woods or other cover, that are not very rough, and have many roads or other means of communication. To wage war in this type of terrain all the fundamental features of guerrilla warfare are used. However, the manner of using them is changed. There is a change, we can say, in the quantity but not in the quality of these features. For example, mobility of guerrillas in such terrain should be exceptional; attacks should preferably take place at night and should be extremely rapid, almost explosive; withdrawals should be not only rapid but should be toward points different from the original location, as far as possible from the action. Always remember that it is not possible to find a protected place inaccessible to the repressive forces.

Men can march between 30 and 50 kilometers [say 18 to 30 miles] during the hours of night and into the early hours of daylight. However, the area of operation cannot be completely controlled, and there is danger that the inhabitants will see and hear the guerrillas pass and will report to the persecuting army. It is always preferable in such cases to act at night, although this rule will not always hold true, as there will be times when the hours of dawn will be better. The enemy should never be allowed to become accustomed to certain ways of fighting: the places, the time, and the manner of carrying out operations should be varied constantly.

Explosions of mines in roads and the destruction of bridges are very important methods to be taken into account. There can be less aggressiveness with regard to continuing attacks, but while they are occurring they can be very violent. Other weapons such as mines and shotguns can be used. The shotgun is a terrifying weapon for use against the usually uncovered vehicles carrying troops and also against unprotected vehicles (buses and similar vehicles).

The number of men in a guerrilla group of this kind should not be greater than 10 or 15. It is of great importance to consider always the limitations with respect to the number in a single combat group. Ten, 12 or 15 men can be concealed in some location and at the same time offer strong resistance to the enemy and support one another. On the other hand, four or five would be perhaps too few. However, if the number exceeds 10, the possibilities are much greater that the enemy may localize them in their original camp or on some march.

It should be remembered that the rate of marching of a guerrilla force is equal to the rate of its slowest man. It is more difficult to find uniformity of marching rate among 20, 30 or 40 men, than among 10. Also, the guerrilla of the plains should be a good runner. It is in the plains that the practice of striking and fleeing should be used to the maximum. Guerrillas of the plains have the great disadvantage that they can be rapidly surrounded and have no safe place where they can put up a firm resistance. For these reasons they must live for long periods under conditions of absolute secrecy, because they can trust only those whose loyalty has been completely proved. Repressions by the enemy are generally violent and brutal, reaching not only heads of families but also women and children. In many instances, pressure over persons that are not very strong-willed can cause them to give information as to the location of guerrilla forces and how they are operating, permitting immediate encirclement with consequences that are always disagreeable, if not mortal.

One of the weapons that can be used by a guerrilla force—a weapon of heavy type that is of great value because of easy handling and transport—is the bazooka (the antitank grenade for rifles can replace it). It will of course be taken from the enemy. It is ideal for firing on either armored or unarmored vehicles carrying troops, and for quickly overcoming small posts with reduced effort. However, only three shells can be carried by each man.

Naturally, none of the heavy weapons taken from the enemy must be wasted. However, there are weapons, such as the tripod-mounted machine guns and heavy machine guns of caliber .50, which, if taken, can be used temporarily with the thought of abandoning them eventually. There should be no combat, under the unfavorable conditions we are describing, to defend a heavy machine gun or some other weapon of this type. The weapon should be used only until the tactical moment arrives when it is advisable to abandon it. In our war of liberation, abandoning a weapon constituted a serious crime for which no excuse was permitted other than the one just pointed out; we specified this as the only situation that would not bring punishment. The ideal weapon for the guerrilla in unfavorable terrain is the rapid-fire personal weapon.

The very characteristics of easy access usually make the region populous, and the area usually includes a farming population. This greatly facilitates the problem of supply. By dealing with people who can be trusted, among those who make contact with establishments distributing provisions to the inhabitants, it is quite possible to maintain a guerrilla force without devoting time or much money to long and dangerous lines of supply. It should be emphasized, in this connection, that the smaller the number of men the easier it will be to supply them. Essential supplies such as hammocks, blankets, waterproof cloth, mosquito netting, shoes, medicines, and food are found directly in the region. They are objects of daily use by the inhabitants.

Communications will be greatly facilitated by being able to count on a greater number of men and many more ways of transmission. However, there will be much more difficulty as regards insuring that a message will reach a distant point, because trust must be placed in a number of persons. Thus, there will be a danger of the eventual capture of one of the messengers constantly crossing enemy territory. If the messages are not very important they may be transmitted orally; if they are important they should be transmitted in writing and in code, because experience shows that oral transmission from person to person can completely distort any message sent in this way.

For the reasons pointed out, in addition to being more difficult, industrial activities by guerrillas become less important. It will not be possible to make shoe soles or weapons. Activities of this kind will practically be limited to small well-concealed workshops for reloading cartridges, making some types of mines and detonating devices; in short, what is appropriate for the moment. On the other hand, it is possible to count on all the workshops of friendly inhabitants for the kinds of work that are necessary.

This brings us to two logical conclusions arising from what has been said. One is that conditions for guerrilla warfare are the reverse of those that favor the productive development of the region in question. All the favorable circumstances for production, all of the facilities to make human life easier, are unfavorable for the guerrilla forces; the more facilities there are for the life of the inhabitants, the more uncertain, the more difficult and nomadic will be the life of the guerrilla. The title of this section is indeed "Warfare in Unfavorable Terrain" because all that is favorable to human life, with accompanying means of communication, urban or semi-urban centers, large concentrations of people, and ground easily worked by machinery places the guerrilla at a disadvantage.

The second conclusion is that, if guerrilla activities must necessarily include important work among the masses, this work is much more important in unfavorable regions, in regions where a single enemy attack can result in catastrophe. In such regions there must be continual work in propaganda, continual effort to unite the workers, the peasants, and other social classes in the region, in order to arrive at a complete homogeneity of the internal front in favor of the guerrilla forces. This work among the people, this continual activity as regards relations between the guerrilla forces and the inhabitants of the region, must also take into account individual cases of recalcitrant enemies and eliminate such enemies without leniency when they constitute a danger. In such matters, guerrillas must be ruthless. There can be no enemies in dangerous places within the area of operations.

Suburban Areas

. . . When the guerrilla fight can be directed at harassing cities, and guerrilla forces are able to penetrate and establish themselves with a certain degree of security in the surrounding countryside, it will be necessary to give these forces special instruction or, we should say, organization.

It must be pointed out that a suburban guerrilla force cannot be formed by its own efforts. It can be formed only after the creation of certain conditions necessary for its existence. This indicates that a suburban guerrilla force will be directly under the orders of leaders located in other areas. Therefore, such a force does not carry out independent actions, except in accordance with previously established strategic plans. The action must support activities of larger groups located in another area. This is a smaller scale of operations than used by other types of guerrilla forces but it will definitely contribute to the success of some particular tactical objectives. A suburban guerrilla force will not be able to choose between sabotage of telephone services, or other forms of sabotage, or surprising a patrol of soldiers on a distant road—it will do exactly what it is told to do. If it is called upon to cut or damage telephone lines, electric power cables, sewers, railways, or aqueducts, it will confine itself to the performance of these duties to the best of its ability.

The numerical strength of such a force should not exceed four or five men. Limitation to this number is important because the surburban guerrilla force must be regarded as acting in an area that is exceptionally unfavorable; the vigilance of the enemy is much greater and the possibilities of reprisals and of betrayals increase enormously. A suburban guerrilla force is at a disadvantage because it is unable to withdraw very far from the scene of operations. Nevertheless some withdrawal, to remain completely concealed during the day, should be combined wtih rapidity of movement and action. Such a force is especially suited for night actions without changing its manner of operating until the insurrection has progressed to the point of besieging the city and the inhabitants can participate as active combatants.

Essential qualities of guerrillas of this type are discipline—perhaps to a greater degree than in the case of other guerrillas—and discretion. They cannot count on more than two or three friendly houses for shelter and food. It is almost certain that seizure under these conditions means death. Their weapons will not be the same as those of other guerrillas, and will consist of weapons for personal defense that do not prevent rapid flight and safe concealment. The best weapons are a carbine, one or two sawed-off shotguns, and pistols for the other members of the group.

Armed attacks should never be made except by surprise on one or two members of the enemy troops or of the enemy's secret service. The action must be concentrated on the sabotage ordered.

Ample supplies of equipment and tools should be provided for the work. There should be appropriate saws, large quantities of dynamite, picks and spades, and apparatus for tearing up railway lines. In short, adequate mechanical equipment is necessary for all that is to be done. The equipment should be concealed in safe places which can be easily reached by those who will use it.

If there is more than one guerrilla force, they will be under the command of a single leader who will give orders for the necessary work through trusted persons engaged in civil occupations. In certain instances, the guerrillas can continue their peaceful occupations. This is usually very difficult because the suburban guerrilla force is a group of men performing unlawful acts and operating under the extremely unfavorable conditions described.

There has been lack of appreciation of the value of guerrilla fighting in the suburbs, but it is, in fact, very important. Appropriate operations of this kind, extended over a wide area, can almost completely paralyze the commercial and industrial life of the area and cause disturbance and distress to the entire population. This makes the people anxious for violent developments to bring an end to their troubles. If thought is given at the beginning of the war to future possibilities, specialists can be organized for suburban fighting. Then action can be carried out much more rapidly and with a saving for the nation in lives and precious time.

II. BUSH WARFARE

The Guerrilla as a Fighter

... The first question which arises is, "what should the guerrilla fighter be like?" One must reply that preferably the guerrilla fighter should be an inhabitant of the area. There he has friends to whom he can turn for help. He will know the area because it is his. This personal knowledge of the terrain is an important factor in guerrilla warfare.

The guerrilla is a nocturnal fighter. This means he must have all the attributes required for night operations. He must be cunning; he must march to the battlefield over hills and dales so that no one becomes aware of his presence; and having the benefit of the factor of surprise he must fall upon the enemy. He must immediately exploit the panic which all surprises cause and throw himself violently into the struggle. He must allow no weakness on the part of his companions, and he must immediately correct any indication of weakness should it arise. He must fall upon the enemy like a typhoon, destroying everything, giving no quarter and expecting none if the tactical circumstances make this necessary. He must mete out justice to those who are to be tried and sow panic among the enemy. However, at the same time, he must treat benevolently the defenseless vanquished and also respect those that die.

A wounded soldier must be given medical treatment and must be given the best possible help unless his earlier life makes him subject to punishment by the death penalty. In this case, he will be treated in accordance with his past. One must never take a prisoner unless he can be brought to a solid base of operations impregnable to the enemy. Unless he is a well-known criminal, a prisoner is to be set free after he has been interrogated.

The guerrilla fighter must be ready to risk his life as often as necessary or to give it without the slightest hesitation at the required moment. But, at the same time, he must be cautious and never expose himself unnecessarily. All necessary precautions must be taken to prevent an adverse conclusion of any operation or battle. That is why it is so very important that, in any battle, total vigilance be exercised over areas from which enemy reinforcements can arrive, and also to prevent a siege. The consequences of a siege[6] are grave not only with respect to the physical disaster they can cause, but also with respect to the moral disaster which may bring a loss of faith in the outcome of the struggle.

Without reservation, there must be audacity. The dangers and the possibilities of an action must be correctly analyzed. There must always be readiness to take an optimistic attitude towards circumstances and to seek a favorable decision even when an analysis of the advantages and disadvantages may not warrant it.

If the guerrilla is to survive amid the conditions of the struggle and the actions of the enemy, he must have a quality of adaptability which will permit him to identify himself with the environment in which he lives. He must adapt himself to it as his ally and exploit it as much as possible. At the same time, he must have a quick imagination and instantaneous resourcefulness which will permit him to change the course of events by using a decisive course of action.

A guerrilla must never leave a wounded companion to the mercy of any enemy because it is virtually certain that his fate will be death. Regardless of the difficulty, he must evacuate the wounded from the combat zone to a safe place.

At the same time, he must be tight-lipped. Everything that is said or is heard in his presence must always be strictly reserved to his own knowledge, and he must never permit himself to utter one single word too many. This must even be the case among his own fellow fighters: obviously, the enemy will try to infiltrate agents into the guerrilla force in order to learn the plans, places, and means of existence available to and utilized by the guerrillas.

In addition to the moral qualities we have stressed, the guerrillas must possess some very important physical qualities. The guerrilla fighter must be untiring. There will be times when he will have to go to a still more distant place when his exhaustion appears intolerable. He must always have a radiant face and manifest the deepest of convictions. This will allow him to take still another step, still do his utmost, and follow it up with another, and another, and another until he arrives at the place designated by his leaders.

He must be long-suffering to the most extreme degree in order to over-

---

6. Throughout this work the fear of a "siege" is apparent. Actually, Guevara means encirclement. Mao also acknowledges that the encirclement is the thing to be most feared. German experience in Russia also indicated that the only really effective way of stamping out guerrilla activity was by encircling the effected area and completely exterminating the guerrilla band. For a description of German methods and the directive they issued to combat guerrilla groups see Dixon, *Communist Guerrilla Warfare* (Frederick A. Praeger, New York, 1954), 201–223. [A diagram provided by *Army Magazine* has been deleted.]

come the privations of hunger, thirst, and lack of clothing and shelter to which he is exposed at all times. He must also be able to withstand illnesses and wounds which many times will have to be cured without major medical care. His only doctor may be Nature's healing action. It *must* be this way, because the fighter who leaves the battle zone in order to seek medical help for some illness or wound is, in most cases, executed by the enemy.

Persons with such notable characteristics of devotion and firmness must have an ideal which permits them to be effective under the adverse conditions we have described. Such an ideal must be simple, not complex, without great pretension, and in general need not be profound. But it must be so firm and clear that without the slightest hesitation a man will give his life for the ideal. Among nearly all farmers such an ideal is the right to have a piece of land for himself in order that he may work it and enjoy the fruits of just social treatment. Among the workers such an ideal is to have work, to be paid an adequate wage, and also to receive just social treatment. Among students and professionals, more abstract ideals are found such as those of freedom, for which they fight.

All this leads us to ask how a guerrilla fighter lives. His normal pattern of life is the hike. Let us use as example a guerrilla fighter in the mountains situated in wooded regions, who lives under constant harassment by the enemy. Under such conditions, in order to change position, a guerrilla moves without stopping to eat during daylight. When darkness has fallen, an encampment is established in some clearing near some water course. Each group eats together and campfires are made from materials at hand.

The guerrilla fighter eats when he can, and all that he can. Sometimes fabulous amounts of rations disappear in the gullets of the fighters, while at others two or three days of fasting occur.

Under the conditions described, encampments must be easily movable, and no traces left which will give them away. Vigilance must be extreme: for every 10 men that sleep, one or two must be on watch. Sentinels must be continually relieved and all entrances to the encampment must always be under observation.

Within the pattern of the life of the fighter, combat is the most interesting event. It brings to all the greatest joy and makes them march with renewed spirit. Combat, the climax of the guerrilla's life, takes place at suitable moments when some enemy encampment has been found, investigated, and determined to be so weak that it can be annihilated. Alternatively, an enemy column may advance into the territory immediately occupied by the liberating forces. The two cases are different.

Against an encampment, action will be widespread and will fundamentally attempt to defeat the members of the column that come to break the siege, inasmuch as an entrenched enemy is never the favorite prey of the guerrilla. The ideal prey is the enemy in movement—nervous, lacking knowledge of the terrain, fearing everything, without natural protection for self-defense. An unfavorable condition exists when the enemy is entrenched and has powerful arms to repel attack. However, this is never the situation when a large column is suddenly attacked in two or three places and fragmented. Then the attackers can withdraw before any reaction can take place, because they cannot surround and completely destroy the enemy columns.

If it is not possible to rout the enemy through hunger or thirst or through a direct attack of those who are entrenched in the encampment, then the siege should be lifted after it has inflicted its destructive impact on the invading column. In cases where the guerrilla force is too weak and the invading column is too strong, action might be centered upon the advance guard. There are some who have a special predilection for this operation, whatever other result they may wish to achieve, and time after time they attack the same advance position. The enemy soldiers then come to the realization that those in the front places almost invariably are killed, and they refuse to occupy the advance positions. Thus, real mutinies are provoked. The advance guard must always be hit again, even though other points of the column might also be attacked.[7]

The degree of ease with which the guerrilla fighter can accomplish his mission and adapt himself to his environment depends upon his equipment. The guerrilla fighter has individual characteristics, even though he is attached to the small units that form his group of action. He must keep in his knapsack, in addition to his usual equipment, all the necessaries which will enable him to remain alone for some time.

In giving the list of equipment, we refer essentially to that which a fighter can carry in the sitautions existing at the beginning of the war, in difficult terrain, during frequent rains, in relative cold, and when being pursued by the enemy. In other words, we refer to the situation that existed at the beginning of the Cuban War of Liberation.

The equipment of a guerrilla fighter is divided into essentials and accessories. Among the first is the hammock which allows him to rest adequately. He will always be able to find two trees from which he can suspend it. In case he should have to sleep on the ground, the hammock can serve as a mattress. In case there is rain or when the soil is wet—a frequent event in the tropical mountain zone—the hammock is indispensable in order to be able to sleep if a piece of nylon waterproof cloth is used with it. Nylon can be stretched to form a roof to cover the hammock: a string is attached at each of the four corners, the middle resting on another length of string. The last string serves to divide the waters, and thus a small campaign tent is formed.

A blanket is indispensable because during the night it gets very cold

---

7. This is a favorite tactic evidently devised by Guevara himself. It is mentioned repeatedly and is an excellent example of psychological warfare of a rather unusual sort.

in the mountains. It is also necessary to carry some cover which permits one to face the great changes in temperature. Dress consists of work shirt and work trousers, be they uniform or not. The shoes must be of best possible construction, and one of the most important articles of which one should have a reserve are shoes: without them marching is very difficult.

Inasmuch as the guerrilla fighter carries his movable house in his knapsack his knapsack is also very important. Primitive ones can be made from any bag to which are attached rope handles; but better ones are made of leather and can be purchased or can be made by some leather worker.

The guerrilla fighter should always carry some personal food supply in reserve, in addition to that issued to the troops or eaten during rest stops.

The following are indispensable: butter or oil are the most important because they furnish the fats required by the body; canned goods that must not be consumed except in circumstances when it is not materially possible to obtain food for cooking, unless there are so many cans their weight hinders the march; canned fish, of great nutritive value; condensed milk, an excellent food because of the quantity of sugar it contains and for the taste, which gives it the character of a treat; powdered milk, which is always useful; sugar is another important part of the equipment; so is salt, which makes hardship more bearable. Also useful are seasonings for food. The most common are onions and garlic, though there are others which vary according to the characteristics of the country.

To care for his rifle, the guerrilla needs special greases which must be very carefully applied—sewing machine oil is quite good if special grease is not available. Scraps and bits of cloth will be useful in caring for weapons as well as a little pail in which he can clean them, for this must be done quite often. The cartridge belt should be of standard manufacture, or else home-made according to the circumstances; but it must be sufficiently good so that not a single round is lost. Bullets are the basis of the struggle. They must be guarded like gold for without them all else is in vain.

The guerrilla must carry a canteen or a water flask because he must drink in quantity and it is not always possible to find water when it is needed. He must carry general purpose medicines such as penicillin or other antibiotics, drugs such as aspirin to treat fever and those for the endemic illnesses of the locality. These might be tablets against malaria, sulfa drugs against diarrhea, antiparasite agents of various kinds—in other words, the medical supply must be adjusted to the characteristics of the area. All drugs should be well packed and of the oral type whenever possible. In places where there are poisonous animals it is well to carry the antidote serum. The rest of the medical equipment must be surgical. In addition, there might be small individual supplies of drugs for treating minor ailments.

Very important in the life of a fighter are cigars, cigarettes, or pipe tobacco, for the smoke that can be enjoyed during moments of rest is a great boon to the solitary soldier. A pipe is best, for it allows the fullest use, in times of shortages, of the tobacco of cigarettes and cigar butts. Matches are important not only in order to light cigarettes but also to light fires. Fires are one of the greatest needs of life in the mountains during rains. It is preferable to carry both matches and a lighter so that if one fails the other can be used.

It is convenient to carry soap, not only for personal cleanliness but also to clean eating utensils. Intestinal disorders are frequently caused by spoiled food which is mixed with new food in a dirty utensil. With all the described equipment, a guerrilla fighter can feel secure enough to survive in the mountains under any adverse condition for the time necessary to master the situation.

There are accessories which at times are useful and at other times constitute a hindrance but which, in general, are very useful. The compass is one. In any given zone, the compass is used mostly as a complement to orientation because increasing familiarity with the terrain makes that instrument unnecessary. Furthermore, the compass is very difficult to use in mountainous terrain because the route it indicates frequently is not the ideal one to move from one place to another. The straight route is likely to be interrupted by insurmountable obstacles. Also useful is an extra piece of nylon cloth in order to cover equipment during a rain. It must be stressed that in tropical countries rain is very constant during certain months and that water is the enemy of the warrior's equipment, his food, his weapons, his medicines, his papers, or his garments. A change of clothing may be carried, but usually this is something new recruits already have. Usually only a pair of slacks and underwear are carried and other articles such as towels omitted. The life of a guerrilla fighter teaches safeguarding energy to carry the knapsack from one place to another and rejects everything which is not essential.

The prerequisites of cleanliness are a piece of soap which will serve for washing of belongings as well as for personal cleanliness, and tooth brush and paste. It is also advisable to carry some books which can be exchanged among other members of the force. The books should be good biographies of heroes of the past, histories or economic geographies (preferably about the country), and some general works which will tend to raise the cultural level of the soldiers. These lessen the tendency to card games and other forms of distraction which sometimes loom too large in the life of the guerrilla fighter.

Whenever there is extra space in the knapsack, it should be filled with articles of food, except in areas which offer very advantageous conditions for food supply. Candy or foods of lesser importance might be carried to augment the basic diet. Hard biscuits might be among these, but they occupy much space and they easily crumble. In the mountains, it is useful to carry a machete. In more humid places, it is useful to have a small bottle of gasoline or to obtain some resinous material from pine trees which will permit quick starting of a fire even though the wood is wet.

Among the usual equipment of the guerrilla fighter must be a pencil and notebook to enable him to make notes, to write letters to the outside, or to communicate with other guerrillas. He should always carry a sewing kit.

A guerrilla who carries all these articles will have a solid house on his shoulders—a considerable weight, but adequate to make his life more comfortable amid the hard work of the campaign.

Organization for Bush Warfare

. . . The organization of a bush war cannot be described as following a rigid scheme.[8] There are innumerable differences resulting from adaptation to the environment to which the principles apply. For reasons of exposition, we shall assume that our experience has universal value. However, we must stress that as we explain it, there always exists the possibility that new ways of doing things can be found which are more suited to the characteristics of the particular armed group.

The number of units in a guerrilla force is one of the most difficult problems to define. There are different numbers of men, different organizations of troops, as we have experienced. We shall suppose a force located in favorable, mountainous territory under conditions that are not so bad as to force them to move continually, but not so good as to enable them to have a permanent base of operations. An armed nucleus located in such a setting should not have as its tactical unit more than 150 men. It may even be that this number is too many and the ideal might be 100 men. This constitutes a column, and it is commanded, following the Cuban military hierarchy, by a major (*comandante*). It may be well to repeat that in our war we abolished the ranks of corporal and sergeant because we considered these to be representatives of tyranny.[9]

Basing ourselves on these premises, a major commands a force of 100 to 150 men and has as many captains under him as there are groups of 30 to 40 men. The captain leads and organizes his platoon so that it fights almost always as a unit, and he is in charge of the distribution of supplies and the general organization of the units. In guerrilla warfare, the squad is the functional unit. Each squad has approximately eight to 12 men and

---

8. Mao, *op. cit.*, 154: "The principle of command in guerrilla war is opposed both to absolute centralization and to absolute decentralization; it demands a centralized command in strategy and a decentralized command in campaigns and battles."

9. Some readers may recall that Batista was a first sergeant in the Cuban Army before he seized power.

is commanded by a lieutenant who has duties analogous to those of a captain for his group, but who is always subordinated to his captain.

The operational reality of guerrilla warfare, which is waged in small groups, makes the squad the real unit. Eight to 10 men are the most that can act together in a fight under such conditions. Therefore the lesser groups must execute the orders of their immediate chief often while separated from the captain although active on the same front. One thing that must never be done is to fragment the unit and to maintain it as such at times when there is no fight. For every squad and platoon, the immediate successor must have been named in case the chief is killed; the successor must be sufficiently trained to be able to take immediate charge of his new responsibility.

One of the fundamental problems of this troop concerns food: lowest-ranking men must receive the same treatment as the chief. This is of prime importance not only with respect to chronic malnutrition, but also because the distribution of food is the only regular daily occurrence. The troop is very sensitive to justice and measures all rations in a critical spirit. Never, therefore, must the least degree of favoritism influence anything. If for any reason the food is distributed among the entire column, some order must be established and must be strictly respected. At the same time the quantity and quality of food allocated to every person must be specified.

In the distribution of clothing, the problem is different because here are articles of individual use. Two criteria must be considered. First, the claimant's need. Second, the system of seniority and merit. This is difficult to define and must be set down in special charts by someone entrusted with them and approved by the chief of the column. The same procedure must be followed with all other articles which may arrive and which are not for collective use.

Tobacco and cigarettes must be distributed according to the general rule of equal treatment for everyone.

The task of distribution must be handled by persons who are especially entrusted with it. It is advisable that these be part of headquarters. Indeed, headquarters has very important administrative tasks of coordination, and other tasks should normally be given to it. The most intelligent officers should be part of headquarters, and its soldiers should be diligent and imbued with the highest spirit of devotion, inasmuch as the demands made of them will, in most cases, be greater than those made of the rest of the troops. However, in matters of food they have no right to any special treatment.

Every guerrilla fighter carries his own complete equipment, but there are a number of articles of special social importance to the column which must be fairly distributed. For these two criteria may be established, depending on the numbers of unarmed persons in the troop. One solution is to distribute all the objects such as medical supplies, extra food, clothing, general surplus foods, and heavy weapons equally among all platoons. Each platoon would then be responsible for the custody of the material assigned to it. Every captain would distribute the goods among the squads and each squad leader would distribute them among his men. Another solution when there are unarmed men in the troops, is to form squads or platoons especially entrusted with the transportation of these supplies. Using these men will be very beneficial, since it unburdens the combat soldier while those who are unarmed do not have the weight or the responsibility of the rifle. In this manner, the danger of losing supplies is reduced; in addition, they are more concentrated. At the same time, this arrangement constitutes an incentive for the porters to carry more and to demonstrate more enthusiasm because one of the rewards may be the opportunity to carry a rifle in the future. Such platoons should march last in the column and should have the same duties and receive the same treatment as the rest of the troops.

The tasks to be executed by a column vary with its activities. If it remains permanently in the encampment, it must have special security teams. Seasoned, specialized troops should be detailed to this task which should entitle them to some premium. This, in general, might consist of some independence or in some surplus delicacies or tobacco to be distributed among members of units which have extraordinary tasks. Of course, these supplies must have been initially distributed to the entire column. For example, if there are 100 men and 115 packages of cigarettes, these 15 extra packages could be distributed among the members of the units to which I have referred. The vanguard and the rear guard, distinct from the rest, will have as their duty the primary responsibility for security. Nevertheless, each platoon must keep up its own. The more that areas distant from the encampment are kept under surveillance—if the camp is in open space—the greater the security of the group.

The places selected must be at some altitude; they must command a wide area by day and be difficult to approach at night. If several days are to be spent there, it is convenient to establish defensive works which allow and sustain adequate fire in case of attack. These defenses may be destroyed as the guerrillas withdraw from the site. If circumstances do not require the absolute obliteration of the column's tracks, they may simply be abandoned.

At sites where permanent encampments are set up, defenses must be clearly and perfectly established. It must be noted that in mountainous areas the mortar is the only effective heavy weapon. Using cover suited to the materials of the area (timber, stones), perfect shelters can be built which will impede the approach of enemy forces and protect your men from howitzer fire.

It is very important to maintain discipline within the encampment. Discipline must retain educational characteristics. The guerrillas must go to bed and arise at definite hours. They must not be permitted to engage in games which do not have a social function or which have a tendency to impair the morals of the troop. Alcoholic beverages and gambling must be forbidden. Supervision should be entrusted to a commission on internal order elected from among the fighters of greatest revolutionary merit. Among other duties they prevent the kindling of fires visible from a distance at night and betraying columns of smoke during daylight. They also make sure that the encampment is thoroughly policed when the column leaves it, if it is desired to keep secret the halt made at that site.

Much care must be taken with campfires because their traces remain a long time. It may be necessary to cover them with earth and to also bury papers, tin cans, and food waste.

During the march absolute silence must be enforced over the column. Orders are passed along by gestures or whispers from person to person until the last man is reached. If the guerrilla force marches through unfamiliar areas, clearing a path for itself or being guided by someone, the vanguard will precede it by some 100 or 200 meters as dictated by the terrain. In places where confusion may arise as to the route, one man is stationed at each fork in the road to wait for the next group, and so on until the last of the rear guard has been reached. The rear guard will also march separately from the rest of the column to watch the paths left behind and to attempt to conceal the column's tracks. If sidepaths offer danger, there must be a group to watch such paths until the last man has passed. It is most practical that these groups be provided from one special platoon. However, they can also come from each platoon, in which case each group would entrust its mission to the group of the next platoon and return to its place; and so on until the entire troop has passed.

Not only must the march be at a specified pace; it must always be maintained in an established order so that it shall be known that Platoon No. 1 is the vanguard; that Platoon No. 2 comes next; that in the middle is Platoon No. 3 with the headquarters; then follows Platoon No. 4; and finally, that the rear guard is Platoon No. 5. Regardless of the number of platoons in the column, their order must always be maintained. During night marches, silence must be complete and the ranks closed so that no one loses his way and thereby creates risks from voices being raised or lights being lit. At night light is the guerrilla's enemy.

Of course, if this march has as its object an attack, when the desired place has been reached to which all will return after the mission has been fulfilled, all superfluous equipment (knapsacks, pots, and so on) should be left behind so that each platoon will proceed only with its arms and other battle equipment. The target of the attack must have been studied by trustworthy men who will have made the contacts, observed the pattern of enemy guards, the layout of the position, the number of men defending it, and so on. Then the definitive plan of attack is made, and the fighters station themselves. It must be remembered, however, that a sizable part of the troops must be reserved to engage enemy reinforcements. The enemy's attack on the position may be only a ruse designed to lure reinforcements into an ambush. Therefore, one man must be able to quickly communicate with the command post because it may be necessary to retreat quickly in order to prevent being attacked from the rear. In any case, guards must always be posted along the approaches to the combat area when the siege is being initiated or a direct attack takes place.

When besieging, one need only to wait and to dig trenches which come ever closer to the enemy[10] thus always trying to come to grips with him by all means. Above all, one should try with fire to make him come out. When he is well encircled, the Molotov cocktail is extraordinarily effective. If one is not within range of a cocktail, he can use a shotgun with special attachment. This consists of a 16-gauge sawed-off shotgun to which a pair of supports has been attached in such a manner that with the end of the butt stock they formed a tripod. When so prepared, the weapon rests at an angle of about 45 degrees. This can be varied by moving the supports forward or backward. The weapon is loaded with an open cartridge which has been emptied of shot. The cartridge is then perfectly suited to receive a stick which becomes the projectile and protrudes from the mouth of the shotgun barrel. To the protruding end of the stick is attached a tin with a rubber buffer and a gasoline bottle. This apparatus will throw incendiary bottles 100 meters or more and can be aimed rather accurately. It is the ideal weapon for sieges in which the enemy has many fortifications made of wood or inflammable material. It is also good for shooting at tanks in rugged terrain.

Once the siege has ended with a triumph, or has been raised after the objective has been achieved, all the platoons retire in their normal order to pick up their knapsacks and return to normal life.

The organization, fighting ability, heroism and spirit of the guerrilla group will undergo their most crucial test during a siege—the most dangerous situation in a war. In the jargon of our guerrilla fighters during our war, the term "siege anxiety" was applied to the anxious expression some of the scared ones wore. The officials of the deposed regime pompously referred to their campaigns as "siege and annihilation." Nonetheless, for a guerrilla force familiar with the terrain, united ideologically and emotionally with the leader, this is not a serious problem. All that one need do is to take shelter, try to prevent the advance of the enemy, impede his use of heavy equipment, and await the night, the natural ally of the guerrilla fighter. When it becomes dark, then, with greatest silence possible, and after having explored

---

10. Oddly enough, for all his disdain for conventional warfare this is the classic seventeenth and eighteenth century method of conducting a siege.

and chosen the best path, the guerrilla force will utilize the best available means of escape while observing complete silence. Under such conditions it is very difficult to impede the escape of a group of men from a siege.

Combat

. . . During the first stage of guerrilla warfare, enemy columns will make deep incursions into rebel territory. According to the strengths of these columns, two types of attack can be made. One, systematically carried out over a period of months, will cause the enemy forces to lose their offensive capability. It habitually precedes the other type, and is carried out against the vanguards. Unfavorable terrain will prevent the column from advancing with adequate defense on their flanks. In this manner, there will always be a portion of the vanguard which penetrates and exposes its members as it seeks to assure the security of the rest of the column. The vanguard usually is a small force and cannot count upon reserves. Therefore, no matter how strong the remainder of the enemy's force, the destruction of this tip of the vanguard will always occur. The system is simple and requires only a little coordination. The moment the head of the vanguard appears at the pre-determined place, the attacking guerrilla force must, as suddenly as possible, break through to the designated men and deliver a devastating fire. Then a small group contains the rest of the column for a few moments so that weapons, ammunition, and equipment can be gathered. The guerrilla soldier must always be aware that the enemy is the source of his weapons. Except for special circumstances, he must not wage a battle which is not likely to gain him such equipment.

When the strength of the guerrilla force permits, the enemy column should be completely encircled. At least, this must be the impression created.[11] In such an instance, the guerrilla vanguard must be so strong and so well entrenched that it can resist a frontal assault. At the instant the enemy is held up in some special place, the guerrilla forces of the rear guard attack his flanks. Inasmuch as the selected place will have characteristics which will make flank maneuvers difficult for the enemy, it will be easy to station snipers who will be able to contain the entire column—perhaps eight or 10 time greater in number—within the circle of fire. When that happens (provided, of course, there are sufficient men), all routes must be blocked in order to deny him any reinforcements. Gradually, the circle must be tightened, especially at night. The guerrilla has faith in the night, but the enemy's fear will increase in the darkness.

---

11. Mao, *op. cit.,* 130: "Ingenious devices such as making a noise in the east while attacking in the west, appearing now in the south and now in the north, hit-and-run and night action should be constantly employed to mislead, entice and confuse the enemy." In addition, Mao gives a dissertation on the guerrilla view on encirclement.

In this manner, an enemy column can be totally destroyed with relative ease. Or such heavy losses can be inflicted upon it as to force a return to camp and require much time for regrouping.

When the guerrilla force is very small, and it is desired by all means to detain the enemy column or to slow its advance, groups of sharpshooters should be used. They should number from two to 10 men stationed at each of the four cardinal points around the column. In this manner, the enemy column will be fired upon from the right flank, for instance. When the enemy centers his attention on this flank and attacks it, he will, at that precise moment, be fired upon from the opposite flank. At still another moment, the rear guard will be attacked, or the vanguard, and so on. With a small expenditure of ammunition the enemy can be permanently held in check.

The technique for attacking a convoy or an enemy position must be adapted to suit the conditions or the site selected for combat. Generally, one must be certain that the first attack upon an encircled place will be a surprise during darkness against some advance post.[12] If one has the advantage of surprise, an attack carried out by fearless men can easily liquidate a position. For a regular siege, the escape routes can be controlled with a few men. Moreover, the access routes can be defended with men so dispersed and concealed that if one of them is passed, he can withdraw or simply yield while a second sniper remains, and so on. In situations where the factor of surprise does not exist, success or failure of the attempt to take the encampment will depend on the ability of the besieging force to contain the efforts of the relief columns. In such instances the enemy will usually have the support of artillery, mortars, and airplanes in addition to tanks.

In terrain suitable for guerrilla warfare, the tank is not very formidable. It must pass through narrow paths and is easy prey to mines. In general, the offensive capability which these vehicles have when in formation, loses its value because they must proceed in single file or, at the most, two by two. The best and safest weapon against tanks is the mine; but in hand-to-hand fighting, so easy to execute in rugged terrain, the Molotov cocktail is of extraordinary value. We have not yet mentioned the bazooka which can be a most decisive weapon for a guerrilla force. However, they are difficult to obtain at least during the early days of a guerrilla war.

A covered trench affords protection against mortar fire. The mortar is a formidable weapon against an encircled force. Conversely, its use against moving targets diminishes its power unless it is used in great numbers. Artillery is not very important in this kind of struggle since it must be sited in places of easy access, and it cannot reach targets which

---

12. *Ibid.*, 124: "The basic principle of guerrilla warfare must be one of offensive, and its offensive character is even more pronounced than that of regular warfare; furthermore, such offensive must take the form of surprise attacks. . . ."

move about. Aircraft are the principal arms of the oppressing forces, but their power of attack is much reduced by the fact that small, concealed trenches are their only targets. They can drop high-explosive bombs or bombs of jellied gasoline, but these are more a nuisance than a real danger. Moreover, whenever one has come as close as possible to the enemy's defensive lines, attacks by enemy aircraft endanger the positions of his vanguard.

A good means of defense against armored cars are steep ditches dug across their path in such a way that the vehicles easily fall into them, but have difficulty coming out. These ditches are easily concealed from the enemy, especially during night marches or when he cannot order infantry to precede the tanks because of the resistance of the guerrilla forces.

Another common form of enemy advance, in areas that are not very rugged, is in trucks that are more or less open. The columns are preceded by some armored vehicles followed by infantry in trucks. According to the strength of the guerrilla force, the entire column can be encircled, or it can be decimated by attacking some of the trucks and simultaneously exploding mines. Then one must act rapidly to gather up the weapons of fallen enemies and withdraw. If conditions allow it, a total siege can be executed.

The shotgun is an excellent weapon for attacking open trucks, and it should be utilized to the fullest extent of its power. The shot pattern of a 16-gauge shotgun loaded with buckshot can cover 10 meters, killing some of the truck's occupants, wounding others, and causing great confusion. Hand grenades are also excellent for such attacks.

Ammunition is the greatest problem of the guerrilla fighter. Weapons can almost always be obtained and kept by the guerrilla force. However, once ammunition is fired, it is gone. Usually, weapons are captured with their ammunition but only very rarely is ammunition alone seized. Not every weapon seized with its own ammunition can contribute to the total supply since there is no reserve stock. The tactical principle of conserving rounds is fundamental in this type of war.

No guerrilla leader who thinks of himself as such would neglect the retreat. A retreat must be well timed, nimble, and insure the recovery of all wounded men and equipment, be it knapsacks, ammunition, or other materiel. A rebel must never be surprised while in retreat, nor must he permit the course of the struggle to encircle him.

For all these reasons, the path selected must be watched at all points from which the enemy forces might possibly advance with troops in order to attempt to close a circle. A message system must be established which permits rapid warning to comrades that some force is attempting to encircle them.

During the battle, there should always be unarmed men. These men will recover the rifle of a wounded or fallen comrade, or seize the weapon

of a prisoner. They can be put in charge of prisoners, transport the
wounded, or carry messages. It is important to have a good group of
messengers of proved ability, and with feet of iron, who can forward the
necessary messages expeditiously.

There are many variations in the number of men that are required in
addition to armed fighters, but they may be reckoned at two or three for
every 10 fighters. Among them are some who aid the fight by acting as
rear guards, or defending the lines of retreat, or establishing the messenger
system.

When a defensive type of war is waged—that is, when the guerrilla
force is engaged in preventing an invading column from passing a specific
point—then the fight becomes a war of positions. The already mentioned
element of surprise must always be sought from the beginning. The entire
defensive apparatus must be established in such a manner that the enemy
vanguard always falls into an ambush.[13] A very important point to remember is the psychology connected with the fact that in a fight, invariably
the enemy in the vanguard are killed. This creates in the opposite army
a disinclination to be part of the vanguard. It is obvious that a column
which does not have a vanguard cannot move unless someone assumes
this responsibility.

It becomes clear that more men and more weapons are required in
defense than in offense. It is clear that many soldiers are required to block
off all the possible paths—and they can be many—leading to a zone. Here
additional use must be made of all traps and means of attack against
armored vehicles; and strict security must be established to protect trench
networks. In general, in this type of combat, the order must be given to
die in defense; but every defender must be given the greatest chance of
survival.

The more concealed a trench is from distant observation, the better.
Above all, it is well to cover it with a roof to neutralize the effect of
mortars. The shells of mortars used in the field—those of 60 or 81 milli-
meters—cannot go through a good roof well constructed out of the materials of the area. These may be a layer of wood, earth, or stones covered
with some material which hides the roof from the view of the enemy. The
shelter must always have an exit which will enable the defender to escape
in emergencies without greatly endangering his life.

In this type of war, the work of those not directly concerned with
fighting (those who do not carry a weapon) is extremely important. We
have already stated several characteristics of communications in places of
combat. These communications are a branch within the guerrilla organization. Communication with the farthest headquarters, or with the farthest

13. *Ibid.*, 125: "Gather a big force to strike at an enemy segment, remains one
of the principles for field operations in guerrilla warfare."

group of guerrillas, if there is one, must be so established that it is always possible to reach them by the most rapid method known in the region. This is as true in areas easily defended—that is, in terrain suited to guerrilla warfare—as it is in unsuitable terrain. It cannot be expected, for instance, that a guerrilla force fighting in unsuitable terrain would be able to use modern systems of communications. This is because such installations can be of use only to fixed garrisons that can defend such systems.

In all these situations, we have been talking of our own war of liberation. Communications are complemented by daily and correct intelligence concerning all the activities of the enemy. The espionage system must be very well studied, well worked out, and its agents chosen with maximum care. Enormous harm can be done by a counterspy. Even without referring to such an extreme example, great harm can result from incorrect information, regardless of whether it tends to exaggerate or underestimate dangers.

A most important characteristic of guerrilla war is the notable difference between the information the rebel force possesses and that known to the enemy. The enemy's agents must pass through zones that are totally hostile; they encounter the gloomy silence of the populace. In each case the defenders can count on a friend or a relative.

It is clear that preparation must be made to expel the enemy from the affected territory. Guerrillas must profoundly upset methods of supply and completely destroy lines of communication. The disruption of enemy efforts to supply himself forces him to invest large numbers of men in such attempts.

In all these combat situations, very important factors are reserves and, if at all possible, their proper utilization. The guerrilla army, by its very character, can count on reserves in only few instances. Therefore, when involved in an action, the efforts of even the last individual must be regulated and fully utilized. However, despite these characteristics a number of men must be kept ready to respond to an unforeseen situation, to contain a counter offensive, or to help decide a situation at a precise moment. Depending upon the organization of the guerrilla force and the situation at the time, a "general utility platoon" must be held ready for such necessities. Such a platoon must always reach those places in greatest danger. It might be called "the suicide platoon" or some other such name, but in reality it will have to accomplish the functions which the name indicates. This suicide platoon must get to all the places where the action will be decided: attacks designed to surprise the vanguard, defense of those sites that are most vulnerable and most dangerous, or any place from which the enemy may threaten to break the stability of the firing line. Such a platoon must be composed entirely of volunteers, and it should be considered almost a privilege for a guerrilla fighter to be admitted to membership. In time such a platoon will become the spoiled child of the guerrilla column, and any fighter in this unit can count on the respect and admiration of all his colleagues.

III. ORGANIZATION OF THE GUERRILLA FRONT

Supply

. . . Proper supply is fundamental for the guerrilla. The group of men, in touch with the soil, have to live off the products of that soil. At the same time they must allow the people who live in the area to continue to live.

In the beginning, one will live only on what the farmers may have. It will be possible to go to some store to buy something, but never to have supply lines, because there is no area in which to set them up.

Slowly, the area will be cleared, and then one can count on a greater ease in being able to act. The fundamental rule is to always pay for any goods taken from a friend. These goods may be the products of the soil or of commercial establishments. Many times these things are donated; but there are other times when the economic conditions of the same rural area make gifts impossible. There are times when the very needs of war make it impossible to pay simply because of lack of money. In such instances the businessman should always be given a requisition or an IOU—something that certifies the debt.

If conditions continue to improve, taxes can be imposed. These should be as light as possible, especially for the small producer. Above all, care must be taken to maintain good relations between the farmers and the guerrilla army which comes from that class of society.

Meat is of prime necessity. If a secure area cannot be had, farms should be set up by farmers not connected with the rebel army. These farms should be dedicated to the production of chickens, eggs, and livestock that can be killed and their meat preserved.

In this way, hides are also obtained. Then a tanning industry—more or less elementary—can be developed to provide the necessary material for shoes, a fundamental need for fighting.

Salt is vital. When near the sea, it is necessary to set up small salt-drying basins which will assure the required production to provide a surplus after supplying the troops.

There will come a time when problems of supplying food to the troops in the area will be solved. Yet many other products will be needed: hides for shoes, if a leather industry cannot be created that will supply the zone; material for clothing and other necessary things for the same troops; paper, newsprint, or a mimeograph machine, ink, and all the other accessories.

The need for articles from the outside world will increase as the guerrillas continue to organize and as their organization becomes more complex. In order to protect the organization adequately, it is vital that the organization for the line of supply functions perfectly.

In all supply lines that pass through the countryside, it is necessary to have a series of houses, terminals, or way stations where supplies can be hidden during the day, ready to continue the following night. These houses should be known only to those directly in charge of supplies. The inhabitants of the house should be told as little as possible, even though they are people in whom the organization has great confidence.

Civilian Organization

. . . The civilian organization of the insurrectionary movement is very important on both the internal and the external fronts. First, we will describe the work of the internal front.

We can say that the internal front is dominated, at least relatively, by the liberation forces. Also, it is supposed to be a region adequate for guerrilla warfare. When these conditions do not exist (that is, when guerrilla battles are developing in areas that are not suitable), the guerrilla organization extends but does not increase in depth. It makes channels into new areas, but it cannot have an internal organization because the whole region is permeated by the enemy. On the internal front, we can have a series of organizations which carry on their specific mission of better functioning of the administration.

It must always be kept in mind that the zone must never, for any reason, be impoverished by the direct action of the rebel army. Indirectly, however, such direct action may be the cause of impoverishment because it precipitates an enemy blockade. The enemy's propaganda will attempt to blame the guerrillas for the condition. For precisely this reason, direct causes of conflict should not be created. For example, there should be no regulations to prevent farmers in the liberated territory from selling their products outside this area, except under certain extreme or transitory circumstances which should be carefully explained to them.

Farmers should also have connections which will permit the organization of the guerrilla army, at any moment, to direct the disposal of harvests and sell them in enemy territory through a series of more or less benevolent middlemen benefactors (more or less) of the farmer class. In all such cases, along with the devotion to the cause which makes the merchant defy the dangers involved, cupidity naturally makes him take these risks for profit.

When the guerrilla group has achieved a certain measure of development, it should establish a series of routes varying from the tiny footpath, only wide enough for a mule, to the good truck road. As a general rule, these roads help overcome the supply problem in areas where there is no other solution. They should not be used except under circumstances where it is almost certain that the position can be maintained against an enemy attack. The roads should be established between points that make communications convenient but not vital. No danger should be involved in their construction.

Other means of communication can also be established. A very important one is the telephone, which can be spread across the mountains by using the trees as wire posts. The wires cannot be observed from above by the enemy. In the use of the telephone, we presuppose an area that the enemy cannot penetrate.

Storehouses are very important. In establishing a point where a beginning of permanent guerrilla organization may be undertaken, very well-kept storehouses should be set up to assure minimum care of merchandise and, above all, to control its equitable distribution.

On the external front, the functions are different as regards both quality and quantity. For example, propaganda should be of a national and educational type. It should explain the victories won by the guerrillas, call the attention of workers and farmers to successful battles and give news of victories achieved on the local front. Tax collecting must be totally clandestine, the utmost care being taken to protect the entire chain from the smallest collector to the treasurer of the organization.

This organization should be spread out in complementary zones to form a whole. The zones can be provinces, counties, states, cities, or villages, depending on the size of the movement. In all of these, there must be a finance committee which will take care of the organization of tax collections. Money can be collected by means of bonds or direct donations or even, if the war is far enough advanced, through taxes. The industrialist will have to pay taxes because of the great strength of the insurrectionary army.

Supply should be conditioned to the needs of the guerrillas. It must be so organized that merchandise moves in a chain. The more common articles are procured in nearby places. Scarce ones, or those impossible to get anywhere else, can be sought from the major centers. Thus, one tries to keep the chain a limited one: the mission must be known to as few people as possible in order to make the chain last longer.

This is the framework of a civilian organization inside and outside of guerrilla territory during a people's struggle. I repeat that I speak from my experience in Cuba. We are providing a framework, not a bible.

Role of Women

. . . The role that women can play, in the whole development of the revolutionary process, is extraordinarily important. It is well to emphasize this, because in all countries with a colonial mentality, a woman is underestimated to the extent that there is real discrimination against her.

Naturally, there are not many women combatants. When the internal front has been consolidated and the least indispensable combatants are being discharged, women can be set to work at a considerable number of specific occupations. One of the most important—perhaps the most important—would be communications between different combat forces; above all, those in enemy territory.

As a simple messenger, whether the message be oral or written, the woman is much freer than a man. She attracts less attention and, at the same time, inspires less of a feeling of fear in any enemy soldier, who often commits his brutal acts out of fear of an unknown force that may attack him, for that is the way the guerrillas operate.

Contacts between forces separated from each other, messages beyond the lines and even outside the country, including things of some size such as bullets, are carried by women in special underclothing. But all the time they also can carry on their usual peacetime pursuits. To be able to count on a well-prepared meal is very pleasing to a soldier subjected to the hard conditions of guerrilla life.

A very important job for women is the teaching of elementary reading and even revolutionary theory. Essentially, they teach not only the local farmers but may also teach the revolutionary soldiers. The school administration (part of the civilian organization) should rely fundamentally on women because they are able to inculcate greater enthusiasm in children and have the sympathy of the school population.

In health affairs, women play important roles as nurses or even doctors because they have a tenderness infinitely greater than that of a rude companion in arms, a tenderness which is so much appreciated when a man is defenseless, without any comforts, perhaps suffering great pain, and exposed to the many dangers of this kind of war.

Health

. . . The organization of hospitals depends greatly on the stage of development of the guerrillas. We can distinguish three fundamental types of hospital organizations which correspond to stages of development of the guerrilla's fight.

In this historic development, we have first the nomad phase. In this, the doctor, if this is what he is, travels constantly with his companions. He is simply one more man and very probably has to carry on all the other functions of a guerrilla, including fighting. Always he will have with him the tiring and at times hopeless task of treating casualties who could be saved with proper treatment. However, the means do not always exist for such treatment. In this state of the development of the guerrillas, the doctor fully realizes his character as a true altruist who brings to the men the necessary consolation from his poorly equipped knapsack.

In the course of normal events in guerrilla warfare, one becomes "semi-nomad." At this time, there are camps that are frequented by guerrilla troops. There are friendly houses that can be completely trusted, where things can be taken care of, where the injured may be left, and where each time the tendency of the troops to spend time is more marked. At this time the doctor's job is less fatiguing. He can have emergency surgical equipment in his knapsack, and at a friendly house a more complete set for less hasty operations. During this semi-nomad phase, if one can get to places completely inaccessible to the enemy, there can be hospitals or nursing homes where the sick and wounded can recuperate.

In the third phase, there are areas that the enemy cannot control and where a true hospital organization can be established.

When a man falls in the front line, some stretcher bearers, if the guerrilla organization has them, will carry him to the first-aid post. Then the soldier passes through the first hospital and on to a second center where there are surgeons and specialists, depending on the organization. At this center, all necessary operations are performed to save his life or to improve his condition. This is the second echelon.

Afterwards, in the third echelon, hospitals are set up with the greatest possible number of modern conveniences for the close examination of wounds or to diagnose any illness which may also affect the inhabitants of the area. These hospitals in the third group correspond to those in a settled community. They are not only centers of rehabilitation and of surgery that is not urgent, but in addition, are connected with the civilian population so that hygienists can carry on their teaching function. Dispensaries should also be set up which permit adequate personal attention. The hospitals of this third echelon will be able to have, depending on the supply capacity of the civilian organizations, facilities that will allow laboratory diagnosis and X-raying.

Necessary medicines should be obtained through contacts with health organizations in the enemy's rear area. Sometimes they can be had even from the International Red Cross. However, one should not count on this, especially in the early days of the struggle. It is necessary to organize an administration that will permit the rapid transportation of needed medicines in case of danger and to continue to supply everything necessary to all hospitals, military and civilian.

Sabotage

. . . Sabotage is an invaluable weapon of people who fight a guerrilla war. Its organization corresponds to the civilian or underground part, because sabotage should obviously be carried on only outside the areas controlled by the rebel army. But this organization should be commanded by and receive orders only directly from the guerrilla general staff which decides the industries, communications, or other types of objectives to be attacked.

Sabotage has nothing to do with terrorism. Terrorism and personal assassination are absolutely different phases. We sincerely believe that terrorism is a negative weapon which in no way produces the desired effects. It can turn people against a revolutionary movement, and it brings with it a loss of lives among those taking part which is much greater than the return. On the other hand, personal assassination is permissible under certain carefully chosen circumstances. It should be performed only when the head of the instruments of repression must be eliminated.

There are two types of sabotage: one on a national scale for certain major objectives, and a local one for the combat lines. On a national scale it is aimed directly at the destruction of all communications. Rapid communications are the enemy army's greatest weapon against the rebels in less rugged areas. We must, therefore, constantly attack this weapon by destroying railroad bridges, sewers, electric lights, telephones, and aqueducts. Lastly, everything necessary for a normal, modern life should be destroyed.

At certain times, the vital industries of each region will be destroyed with the proper equipment. When this is done, it is necessary to have an over-all concept of the problem and to be sure that one is not unnecessarily destroying the source of employment. Otherwise, hunger and a massive displacement of workers will result. Industries belong to supporters of the regime and should be destroyed unless the destruction brings about very serious social consequences. We must always try to convince the workers of the need for the destruction.

In the combat area also, sabotage should be carried out in the same way, but with much more daring, dedication, and frequency. In these cases, the tremendous help of the quick-moving patrols of the rebel army can be depended upon because they can go down into the zones and assist the members of the civil organization to do the job.

Sabotage includes appropriation of merchandise, cutting supply lines as much as possible, frightening farmers from selling their products, burning vehicles traveling on roads to create roadblocks. In each case of sabotage, it is desirable to have some contact with the enemy, whether at a distance or up close, and to follow the hit-and-run system. It is not necessary to make a big demonstration but only to point out to the adversary that, where there is sabotage, there also are guerrilla forces ready to fight. This causes him to keep his troop strength up and to move carefully or not at all.

In this way, all cities near the guerrilla zone of operations will slowly become paralyzed.

War Industry

. . . In the guerrilla army's view, war industry is the product of a fairly long development. Moreover, it should be well located geographically. As soon as zones are liberated and tight blockades set up around the enemy's supplies, the necessary different departments will be organized. We have already covered this.

So far as manufacturing is concerned, there are two fundamentals: shoe-making and leather-working. Troops cannot walk without shoes in rough and stony terrain. It is very difficult to march under these conditions, and only natives of the area, and not even all of them, can do it. The rest must have shoes.

The rebel shoe industry is divided into two parts: one applies half soles and repairs damaged shoes, the other makes crude shoes. The rebel force should be able to count on a small shoe machine, very easily come by in these areas, to set up a cottage type industry operated by many persons. Along with shoe-making should go the machine shop where all sorts of canvas or leather equipment used by the troops can be made and repaired. These include cartridge belts and knapsacks, which, while not vital, contribute to comfort and give the troops a feeling of self-sufficiency and well-being.

Another basic industry for small internal organizations of guerrillas is the gunsmith's. It also has a variety of functions: repair of small arms, the manufacture of some types of weapons invented locally, and the construction and handling of mines with varied mechanisms. When conditions are good, it is wise to join to this an outfit for manufacturing powder.

Someone should be in charge of communications, too. He would be not only in charge of communications relating to propaganda and with the outside world, such as the radio, but also the telephones and all types of roads, and he depends on the necessary civil organization to carry on his job. It must be remembered that we are at war, that we can be attacked by the enemy and that, at times, many lives depend on rapid communications.

To keep the troops content, it is well to have cigar or cigarette factories. Leaf tobacco can be purchased in selected places and then brought to the free area where it can be prepared for consumption.

Another important industry is tanning. These are simply undertakings which can be carried on anywhere and are adapted to the situation of the guerrillas. Tanning requires certain small concrete buildings and a great deal of salt. However, it is a tremendous advantage to the shoe-making industry to have its raw material right at hand.

Salt should be made in the territory of the revolution, concentrating it in large amounts. To make salt, it is necessary to go to areas of high saline concentration and to evaporate it. The sea is the best source. It is not necessary to purify the salt by removing all attached impurities because it can be eaten in its simple form. However, at first it doesn't taste very good.

Meat should be preserved as jerked beef. This is simple to do and is a means of saving many lives in a serious situation. For a long time it can be preserved with salt in large barrels. It can be prepared regardless of the external situation.

Information

. . . "Know yourself and your enemy and you will be able to fight a hundred battles without defeat." This Chinese maxim is as worthwhile for guerrilla war as a biblical psalm. Nothing helps a fighting force more than correct information. It should be spontaneously given by the inhabitants of the area where the army will be and it should deal with what is going on in a specific place. Moreover, it should be reliable. Women should infiltrate and make permanent contact with the enemy soldiers and slowly find out what we need to know. A coordinated system must be devised to permit the crossing of enemy lines into the guerrilla camp without a hitch.

If this is done well and by capable agents, it will be possible to sleep sounder in the insurgent camp.

In those areas where the guerrilla organization is dominant or which it frequently visits, all people are its information agents. Nevertheless, it is good to have people especially selected for this purpose because one cannot depend on the views of farmers, so accustomed to exaggerate and who know little of the precise language of war. One will be able to make the information machinery not only the very important auxiliary arm that it is, but also a counteroffensive agent. This can be done, for example, by means of the "sowers of fear" who may move about among enemy soldiers to sow fear and instability. Mobility, the primary tactic, can be developed to the maximum. By knowing exactly the places where the enemy troops are going to attack, it is very easy to run away or, in time, to attack them in the most unexpected places.

Training and Indoctrination

. . . The very life of the guerrilla leader is fundamentally the training of the liberating soldier, and no one can be a leader who has not learned his difficult job in the daily use of his arms. The soldier will be able to live with some companions who teach him something about the handling of arms, the basic notions of finding one's way, how to behave towards the civilian population, to fight, and other essentials. However, the precious time of the guerrilla leader should not be wasted in the details of instruction. That happens only when there is already a large liberated area, and large numbers of soldiers are needed to perform a combat function. Then basic training centers are established.

At such times these centers perform a very important function. They produce the new soldier who has not yet passed through that great sieve of formidable privations that convert him into a real fighting man. After he has passed through this difficult test, he reaches the stage of joining the circle of a beggar army that leaves no signs of its passing on any side. There must be physical exercises, basically of two types: agile gymnastics with instruction for the commando-type war which demands agility in attack and in retreat; and violent marching which stretches the recruit to the farthest point of endurance and hardens him for this life. He must, above all, get used to life in the open air. He must suffer all the changes of weather in close contact with Nature, as he will do when on guerrilla operations.

The training centers must have workers who take care of its supply functions. For that purpose, there must be stables, barns, orchards, dairy herd—everything to insure that it will not become a burden on the general budget of the guerrilla army. The students can be rotated in the work of supply, assigning it to the worst elements as punishment or simply on a voluntary basis.

All this depends on the characteristics peculiar to the zone where the training center is established. We think it is a good principle to put volunteers there and to fill up the details for necessary work with those who behave the worst or have the least aptitude for learning the art of war.

The center must have its small health organization, with a doctor or male nurse, as conditions allow, to provide recruits with the best possible attention.

Rifle practice is the fundamental element of instruction. The guerrilla must have much training in marksmanship and must be taught to expend the least possible quantity of ammunition.

The most important part of recruit training, and which must never be neglected, is indoctrination. It is important because men come in without a clear conception of why they came; they have vague concepts of personal liberty, freedom of the press, or other logical foundations. Therefore, indoctrination must be instilled for as long a time as possible and with the greatest dedication. During these courses, the elements of the history of the country are taught and economic facts are explained clearly as well as the facts which motivated each historic event. The reactions of national heroes to certain injustices are explained; and, afterwards, the domestic situation or the situation in the area is analyzed. This constitutes a single primer which can be well studied by all members of the rebel army as a guide for what will come later.

In addition, there must be a training school for teachers so they can agree on the textbooks to be used and on the experiences which each one may be able to provide in the educational aspect of the movement.

Of all measures of military training, one of the most important is disciplinary punishment. Discipline must be (it is necessary to repeat this again and again) one of the bases for the action of a guerrilla force. Discipline must be, as we also said previously, a force which springs from an internal conviction and which is perfectly reasoned out. In this way, a person develops an internal discipline. When this discipline is broken, it is always necessary to punish the guilty, regardless of his position. His punishment must be drastic, and must be applied in a way that hurts.

This is important, for in a guerrilla soldier loss of liberty does not manifest itself in the same way that duress affects a garrison soldier. Ten days in the guardhouse can be a wonderful rest for a guerrilla soldier: he eats, he does not have to march, he does not work, there is none of the usual guard duty. He can sleep as much as he wants, he can take it easy, he can read, and so on. From this it is deduced that the deprivation of freedom under guerrilla conditions is not advisable.

There are times when the combat morale of the individual is very high, and pride in himself is considerable. The deprivation of his right to bear arms can provoke positive reactions and constitute for him a true punishment. In these cases, it is correct to apply such punishment.

Long periods of guard duty at night and forced marches can also be punishments; but the marches have the grave drawback that they are not practicable because they have no other objective than that of punishment and of tiring out the guerrilla soldier. To insure such punishment requires other guards, who also get tired. Moreover, punitive guard duty has the inconvenient aspect that others must watch the offenders.

In the forces directly under my command, I established for minor infractions the punishment of arrest with deprivation of candy and cigarettes, and total deprivation of food in the worst. Although the punishment was terrible and is advisable only under very special circumstances, the results can be wonderful.

30

Peter Braestrup   *PARTISAN TACTICS—*

                                                     ALGERIAN STYLE

SINCE 1 NOVEMBER 1954, THE FRENCH ARMY has been embroiled in a war to suppress the Algerian rebel "National Liberation Front" (FLN), a cruel war of mutual terrorism, partisan tactics, and subversion in a mountainous, poverty-racked land nearly three times the size of Texas.

By early 1960, the French, largely withdrawing from other commitments, had slowly increased their Algeria forces from 50,000 to 500,000—draftees, reservists, paratroopers, the famed Foreign Legion. From *quadrillage* (local garrisons), the French had broadened their strategy through 1957–60 to include blocking off the rebels' vital supply "sanctuaries" in Tunisia and Morocco with heavily fortified lines; enlisting more than 100,000 Moslems as auxiliary troops; regrouping thousands of outlying villagers—potential rebel supporters—into "protected areas" using garrison troops on projects designed to attract Moslems to France; employing some 50,000 mobile reserves, mostly Legionnaires and *paras,* together with helicopters, close-support aircraft, and artillery, in repeated "comb-outs" of rebel-infested areas.

From *Army Magazine,* August, 1960. Copyright 1960 by Association of the U.S. Army and reproduced by permission.

Despite some considerable successes, notably the 1957 clean-up of Algiers and the reported semi-pacification of parts of western Algeria, the French failed to score decisively. And even as the French inflicted heavy losses, their own sacrifices were not trifling. By late 1959, the Army's announced dead totaled 13,000. Far greater civilian losses, both Moslem and European, continued to occur. France's failure to solve the Algerian "problem" led directly to the Fourth Republic's fall in May, 1958. For the Fifth Republic, the headache remains.

The military problem, in large measure, is to subdue an estimated 30,000 uniformed rebel regular troops, plus perhaps 100,000 irregulars (precise figures are impossible to find). These forces dominate most of rural Algeria outside the French-held towns, especially the Aures-Nemencha Mountains and Kabylia, east of Algiers. Financed heavily by the Arab League, but with its own "external" organization and a grass-roots internal network for sabotage, taxation, and propaganda among Algeria's nine million Moslems, the National Liberation Front has not only survived but, as guerrilla movements go, prospered in five years of war.

FLN tactics and organization, in an era of nationalist uprisings and limited war, seem worthy of study in the United States. The article that follows is based on my own continuing research and interviews with veterans of both sides, as well as observations as a reporter with the rebel forces in Algeria and Tunisia during September, 1958.

At a tin-roofed mud hut, just inside the Tunisian frontier, a half dozen officers and noncommissioned officers of the Algerian rebel 6th Battalion, *Base de l'Est,* were making ready to lead a typical night action against the French across the border in Algeria.

Shortly before 1800, a small, moustached, immensely professional *sergeant-chef* appeared. He carried a notebook, pencils, and binoculars. Nicknamed "The Mexican," he was chief of the Battalion's mortar section. Behind him came three chestnut mules and a dozen men in olive drab. Stashed away in the mud hut were the base plate, tripod, and tube of a World War II German 81mm mortar, plus battered metal cases of ammunition.

The Mexican, after much shouting, got his men to load up the three mules with the mortar components. They were taking 18 rounds for a mortar shoot of the 150-man French outpost at El Hamed, some 14 kilometers to the south and west. Also on hand would be a rifle company, split into sections, from the 6th Battalion, green replacements trained in Tunisia, with veteran sergeants, out for their first taste of war.

The mission: to harass El Hamed and, possibly, to provoke the French garrison into sending out a retaliatory force that could be ambushed. No direct assault over minefields and barbed wire against the bunkers and trenches of El Hamed was contemplated. The Algerians preferred, understandably, to catch the French in the open.

Convoying the mule-borne mortar was a 35-man rifle section and a small headquarters group. The rest of the company would precede us to the El Hamed area.

Just at twilight, the Mexican gave the word, and the little column moved out in single file across the pine-studded ridge to the southwest. Soon we were on a winding, French-built road that marks the Algerian side of the border valley.

Well spaced out, but, as usual, without flankers, and with the infantry section well forward, the column moved swiftly along the road under a slightly overcast night sky. The muleskinners cut occasionally at their charges with switches, growling *"Hrrh! Hrrh!"* ("Get a move on!"); the hoofs of the mules and the one officer's horse clopped loudly. Even the sneakers of the troopers crunched on the crushed rock of the road. It was hard to believe that the French did not patrol this obvious approach to El Hamed. Perhaps it was just too easy for the Algerians, as their officers said, to ambush the patrollers. The road, they added, was rarely used by the French even during daylight.

After three hours' march, we halted. Low whistles were heard. Shadowy forms appeared at the roadside. Linking up with the rest of the attack force, we were close to El Hamed.

Only a few kilometers to the east was the Tunisian sanctuary. Immediately to the south and west loomed the high dark outlines of the Algerian hills, silhouetted by the glow of El Hamed's searchlights. These, presumably, were alight to spot rebels and to guide friendly aircraft, and, in an emergency, relief columns.

An occasional, distant *crump* served notice that French artillerymen to the west were apparently relieving their nerves, if not the national budget, by spraying the countryside with 105mm harassment and interdictory fires.

During the halt, while the rebel troopers broke out canteens, a couple of political commissars began distributing crude red-and-green mimeographed broadsides along the road. INDEPENDENCE OR DEATH, they read in French and Arabic; THE WAR IS APPROACHING ITS CLIMAX. True to rebel doctrine, the mules had brought propaganda as well as mortar rounds.

Moving on, we halted once more, in the lee of a steep, rocky, lightly wooded slope that rose some 300 feet into the night above us. El Hamed was less than 2,000 meters away. Amid animated discussion—loud enough, it seemed, to rouse even the sleepiest Frenchman in El Hamed—the Mexican's mortar crew unstrapped their gear. The mules were led into a nearby gully, and we began the ascent of the hill.

That hill was a killer. A goat-legged young infantry lieutenant led the way up the zigzag, contour-jumping path. The mortar crew wrestled its heavy weapon and ammunition into a position just below the flat, pine-topped crest, and the protecting infantry section quietly spread out under the trees on each side. Other rifle sections were deployed on the hill's flanks.

Making Yourself a Target

The exuberant Mexican hastened to the forward slope for a look at the target. With him, we gazed down into a shallow valley, slightly hazed over, but illuminated by El Hamed's lights. Garrisoned, according to the Mexican, by the 8th Company, 153d Light Infantry Regiment, El Hamed was clearly demarcated by two brilliant searchlights sweeping lazily skyward as well as toward the surrounding hills. All the Mexican had to do, as he had already done, was to line up the mortar with the lights, and adjust for the range.

"There it is!" he exclaimed, adding optimistically, "Now we shall destroy them."

He shouted the range—900 meters—and the mortar crew, partly illuminated by a flashlight, noisily thunked out the first round. A familiar *whoosh* went up into the sky over our heads, and after what seemed a long wait, we heard a dim crash as the round landed. The Mexican peered down at the cluster of lights in El Hamed, and lengthened the range. Another round popped out and crashed.

After ushering us back to the reverse slope, the Mexican stayed on the crest, shouting orders. The morter crew worked smoothly—even when one round failed to fire and they had to up-end the tube.

Five or six minutes after the Mexican's first shell landed on El Hamed, the French reacted. A half-dozen rounds of 105mm, fired from a battery well to the west, landed on the next hill to our right, perhaps 2,000 yards away. The French counter-battery target was a mortar site which had been used by the rebels against El Hamed several months earlier. Apparently the French were relying on intuition rather than forward observers. At any rate, while the Mexican's helpers slowly popped out their 18 rounds, the French 105's continued to eviscerate the wrong hill.

All his ammo expended, the Mexican passed the word to the infantry leaders, who gave orders to move out, on the double. The mortar crew quickly dismantled their weapon; and everyone slid down the slope, scrambling, sliding, catching on the bushes to slow the mad descent. The noncoms hoarsely urged their young riflemen to move faster—"*Allez! Allez!*"

When the bulk of the rebels were more than halfway down the hill, the French in El Hamed finally caught on. The next rounds of 105mm smashed into the rocks and pine trees on the crest we had just vacated. The big shells continued to slam the ridgetop as the rebels streamed over the road, across a stubbled field, and into cover in a deep dry creek bed.

The young riflemen showed no panic. None was left behind. In the new moonlight, with the shells crashing and flaring on the hilltop behind them, most of the greenhorns looked quite elated, if anything, despite the obvious dangers of the exposed withdrawal.

No French Pursuit

The French did not seem inclined to pursue the matter. They did not box in the mortar site—although they must have known that the rebels did not risk their precious mortars without considerable infantry protection. Nor did they lift the range. Had the French done so, rebel losses might have been heavy. Instead, however, the French soon ceased fire.

The rebel column, rejoined by its mule train and by the covering units, quick-marched northward, following the creek bed under a full clear moon. Bren gunners covered the withdrawal; two- and three-man units met the column along the route, assuring that the way to Tunisia was open. There was no unfriendly interference.

Next morning, a postscript to the El Hamed affair further accentuated the impression of French garrison caution.

The Mexican had stayed behind on a hill near his mortar site to observe the reactions of the El Hamed Frenchmen. He was sure that he had scored some solid hits. At 0830 he saw coming slowly down the road from El Hamed two jeeps, a halftrack, and a truck. All were mounting machine guns, and were loaded with troops. The lead jeep bore several Moslems in the French Army. "Traitors," the Mexican called them. They got out of the jeep and swept the road with mine detectors. They carefully gathered up the propaganda throwaways left by the rebels the night before. Then, at extreme range, the Mexican opened up with his bolt-action Mauser.

He cranked off some 30 rounds. Without returning fire, the French hastily turned tail and scooted out of sight in the direction of El Hamed. Shortly thereafter, the Mexican's hill was subjected to a half hour of slow bombardment by 105mm howitzers. The Mexican, unscathed, turned up at a rebel post in Tunisia a few hours later, obviously delighted by the morning events: "That is a lot of money to waste shooting at one Algerian."

How has the rebel Army of National Liberation (ALN) managed to survive on the ground against western Europe's largest land army?

Rebel Organization and Tactics

French internal military and political problems and, importantly, outside Arab League financial and political support have helped sustain the rebel cause. Bases in the Tunisian and Moroccan sanctuaries obviously are crucial. Historically, Algeria's size and rugged terrain have encouraged rebellion. But, in large measure, the military answer lies in the doctrine, organization, and tactical effectiveness of the ALN.

With Marshal Tito's successful World War II partisan movement in Yugoslavia as one of their avowed models, the rebel leaders emphasize the dual military-political role of their army, with priority given to the political over the military, and to the "internal" organization over the external. The rebels' "collective leadership" in Tunisia—the Algerian Provisional Government—is officially headed by Ferhat Abbas, a veteran nationalist politician-lawyer; his cabinet, mostly French-educated, includes the powerful Belkacem Krim, hard-bitten combat veteran and Minister of War.

The tactical decisions are made by the ALN's seven regional commanders, each a colonel, who also have plenty to say on over-all strategy and logistics. They head six *willayas* (regions) within Algeria, and the crucial Base de l'Est (East Base) comprising western Tunisia and the eastern Algeria border area. Each *willaya*, in turn, is divided into districts, subdistricts, and sectors, with the corresponding TOE units of battalion (600 men), company (150 men), section (35 men).

Each unit commander is considered a political-military representative of the National Liberation Front's central authority. He has three officer or sergeant deputies responsible, respectively, for military activity, political action, and intelligence and liaison. The political commissars also raise taxes and food supplies from the Moslems and seek to rally Moslems to the FLN.

Most small-unit leaders in the ALN come up through the ranks, but in its transition from a loose, squabbling confederation of guerrilla bands into a Tito or Vietminh style partisan movement, the rebels had to revamp much of their early leadership. The original guerrilla chieftains won their spurs as tough, daring individual fighters; under the emerging political-military TOE many of these men proved unable to command others, and had to be replaced, often over their followers' protests. The interior organizations experienced wholesale purges, by French accounts. "Little by little," said Abdel Kader, a top rebel political commissar, "we are creating a nucleus."

His Rifle Is His Life

Most recruits are under twenty (like half Algeria's Moslem population), drawn from the tough, poverty-stricken Moslem peasantry. Volunteers are plentiful. They join for the excitement, to escape French police action at home, or to fight for "independence" and first-class citizenship. "We are fighting a twentieth century war with a sixteenth century people," observed one staff officer. "A young peasant lad who joins up has to learn to obey. A uniform is not enough. He says 'I joined my brothers to fight for independence. Why do I have to go here and there?' We give him a rifle, saying, this is your life. Keep it clean. It is hard to make him understand."

In the *willayas,* most recruit training is on-the-job. In the East Base sanctuary in Tunisia, sheltering some 15,000 rebel troops, the rebel army operates regular training camps (*Ecoles des Cadres*) for recruits and noncoms. Since early 1958, there have been reliable reports of schools elsewhere in Tunisia for armorers, radio operators, and demolitionists; of pilots training in Egypt; and of cadres training in the Eastern European satellites.

East Base recruit training, under the supervision of Algerian veterans of the French Army in World War II and Indochina, consists mostly of small-arms handling, partisan tactics, first aid, plenty of hiking, and enough French-fashion close-order drill to accustom the recruits to taking orders. Training may last up to three months.

Each training unit, inevitably, has its semi-educated commissar, charged with indoctrinating the troops with FLN propaganda. Here, as elsewhere, the rebels paid great attention to leaflet passing, political bull sessions among the troops, and distribution of the rebel newspaper *El Moujahid* ("Freedom Fighter").

It should be noted that the ideological spur to the ALN is "independence," not communism. While most of the political commissars I encountered expressed bitter dislike for "Western colonialism" and somewhat cloudy admiration for Karl Marx, they had no use for the Soviets or Communists as such. They admired the Vietminh—for Dienbienphu. Some rebel spokesmen claimed, indeed, that Communists were shot by the ALN where found. Not even the French Army has persisted in its early claims that the rebels were agents of the Kremlin.

Lean and Mean Fighters

Essentially, the Algerian troopers viewed themselves as Algerians first, "Arabs" second. Despite Radio Cairo, they were generally (and ungratefully) scornful of Nasser and the military pretensions of the Arab League. Some even regarded Irsael with some respect—for its Sinai victory. Amid the general resentment against the United States for supplying the French in the past with money and military equipment, there was also the image of the United States as a friend to such new Moslem nations as Tunisia and Pakistan.

Officers and men alike lived under stringent rules. They were forbidden women and alcohol. Some of the East Base troops had wives and children in Tunis; visits were forbidden. Only the badly wounded went to the rear. A private's pay was three dollars a month; dependents, theoretically, got a little more. There was no Universal Code of Military Justice. Disobedience, desertion, a hint of disloyalty, meant death.

This austerity made for a taut ship. Yet morale seemed high—a kind of hard, confident fatalism. Saluting in the field may have been ragged, but I never saw an order not obeyed with alacrity. Among line soldiers there was some disdain for the "politicians back in Tunis," but in the field the commissars played a discreet role. Marksmanship and fire discipline, as viewed at impromptu target practices, seemed up to U.S. recruit standards. The ALN was a soldierly looking army.

Just at sunset one day, I watched the veteran 3rd Battalion, East Base, getting ready to sally forth from Tunisia. It was like a scene from the Civil War.

The regulars stood at ease, two companies strong, on the reverse slope of a low, irregular scrubby ridge. They were gathered by 35-man sections, each behind its German MG42, LMG or Bren gun. They were in the bulgy, wrinkled, heavy olive drab of the regular ALN, with British water bottles, U.S. cartridge belts, and bandoleers. Slung from their shoulders were Lee-Enfields and Mausers (sent from Egypt) or, more rarely, a captured Garand or French MAS semiautomatic rifle. In their felt visored caps, their pantaloons, and sneakers, they reminded one of the Chinese Communist troopers in Korea. But the tough faces were as varied as the many races that mingle in Algeria. Variously, they looked Italian, Puerto Rican, Chinese, Turkish, or Cherokee. They talked quietly among themselves, calm and cheerful. Two or three troopers were off in the scrub to one side, bareheaded, on their knees in the bushes, facing Mecca in their sunset devotions.

On a small knoll, indifferent to the threat of French aviation, were grouped the bareheaded battalion staff and its commander, a tall grave Lincolnesque captain in his late thirties. He wore a Luger and carried French artillery binoculars.

Action, he said, had not been heavy in this area. The previous night, in a typical action, a half-dozen 3rd Battalion troopers had probed a French outpost to the northwest. Apparently, said the captain, the French CO was convinced that a major attack was in progress. The probers drew two hours of artillery fire, and, by the light of flares, the attentions of French aircraft. The two-hour embroglio left the rebels—and, presumably, the French —unscathed, but the French lost a night's sleep and a couple of thousand dollars' worth of ammunition and aviation fuel.

These 3rd Battalion troopers and others in the Army that we saw, operated on a shoestring.

Rebel Weapons and Rations

Cleaning materials for the standard weapons we have mentioned were scarce. Rebel doctrine on conserving ammunition was strict; it stressed recovery during combat of the weapons of the dead—both friendly and

French. Especially in the interior *willayas,* ammunition and weapons re-supply was a major problem.

As heavy weapons, the rebels relied on the above-mentioned German 81mm mortar, perhaps one or two per battalion. A few captured heavy machine guns were reported. During late 1958 there were propaganda photos of 20mm Bofors cannon, bazookas and recoilless rifles, but I saw none of these in action. The French reported some U.S. 57mm recoilless rifles in the East Base area after 1958.

Antitank mines (German) and bangalore torpedoes (from Egypt) seemed plentiful. Composition 3—*plastique*—was a favorite for sabotage. Stocks of hand grenades (French and English makes) were short. The mine, the automatic weapon, the rifle, and the mortar remained the basic ALN weapons, used sparingly.

On the whole, the rebel diet was austere: unleavened bread, peppers, coffee, *cous-cous* (a kind of rugged Wheatena), more rarely mutton, rice, and goat's milk.

Medical care was (and is) at best skimpy. The company aidman carried only the barest essentials. The badly wounded, when they could be brought out at all, were forced to travel on muleback without benefit of morphine, antibiotics, or proper bandages. In the *Base de l'Est* area, the survivors could expect hospital care at Le Kef in Tunisia; for the wounded in the interior, the prospects were less certain.

Communications Slow and Inadequate

Communications has constituted another headache for the rebels. At a 3rd Battalion farmhouse CP near Sakiet Sidi Youssef in Tunisia, we spotted a Canadian radio set comparable in size and appearance to those we remembered at battalion CPs in Korea. Since early 1959, both rebel Headquarters in Tunisia and interior *willayas* use new German Telefunken radios, but in units below *willaya* and battalion, communication is by runner.

Slow communications put scattered rebel units, once a planned operation has begun, strictly on their own. Thus each ALN operation tends to be a set-piece affair, of limited duration, with limited objectives. Prior to one scheduled 6th Battalion attack, a staff officer explained the plan:

"Tonight there will be night attacks. The French will be drinking to-night [Saturday night], and when they are full of wine, we attack. From long experience, the Army knows where the French artillery concentrations are. They know the routes by which the French will send relief columns to their outposts. Each [rebel] unit knows its role. To isolate the outpost, to ambush the reinforcing columns, to make diversions. Everything is ar-ranged."

But as it turned out, the situation changed. The French increased their activity in the 6th Battalion area during the next few hours (just prior to the September, 1958, referendum in Algeria); and the rebel plan was abandoned. It could not swiftly be modified. No major "offensive" occurred.

Hit-and-Run Tactics

As it affects the flexibility and duration of major rebel operations, so does the communications problem help to limit the strength which can be deployed against a single objective. For this and other reasons, seldom do rebel forces strike in more than company strength. On the other hand, to protect arms-carrying mule trains or to divert French units from the real objective, several companies have, on occasion, launched simultaneous attacks or probes at scattered points.

Most forbidding, of course, to larger concentrations and sustained "offensives" by the ALN is the French ability to counter rapidly in daylight with rocket-firing aircraft, artillery, and mobile reserves, once rebel positions are known.

Hence, the rebels, realistically, concentrate on hit-and-run tactics, the traditional small unit tactics of partisan warfare. When they have deliberately broken this rule—notably in major battalion-size thrusts through the newly built Morice Line in the winter of 1957–58—they have suffered severely; the lesson has been learned.

The "mosquito war" is favored by the rebels, especially against the shifting fringes of French strength. This is above all a night war, or a badweather war, when French tank and aircraft effectiveness is lowest. Each week, as many as 25 ambushes and 20 attacks on French units, convoys, and outposts are reported by the rebels across Algeria, in addition to countless unreported acts of sabotage and terror.

In every operation, the Algerians enjoy a basic advantage: their seemingly omnipresent civilian auxiliaries, who serve as "human radar," scouts, intelligence agents, and guides. These *moussebelline* infiltrate French-held villages, prowl the terrain ahead of regular ALN columns, and despite vigorous, if haphazard, French countermeasures, provide a constant stream of "hot" information to the ALN. As a result, French troops rarely achieve total surprise.

On one occasion, holed up on a mountainside near the Medjerda River, with a French armored column on the far side, I asked two *moussebelline* if they could get cigarettes. They not only brought back some passable French Gitanes—purchased in a French-occupied village—but also the unit designations of the French armor.

One of the principal keys to ALN survival is the impressive march endurance. ALN units are always on the move. Thirty to 40 miles in 24 hours over mountain paths is not considered arduous. The soldier carries a rifle, 100 rounds of ammunition, a full canteen, a blanket, and three pounds of bread. He doesn't bunch up, and when exposed in the open to aircraft he lowers his head and stands motionless until the aircraft drones away.

Whether on the march or in bivouac, rebel troopers prefer the high ground, just below the crest. If the ridges are bare (many of them have been burned off by French napalm) and daylight marching is required, the rebel leader will take his men into the heavily wooded draws and deep creek beds. While scouts and liaison units may precede a moving column by hours or days to the next bivouac for security, the column itself will depend on speed rather than flankers.

Ambush tactics vary with the type of target and the proximity of French supporting units. Most ambushes are squad-sized shoot-and-run actions, some are a kind of temporary roadblock, a few have involved whole companies of rebel troops and bloody retaliation by French aircraft, artillery, and mobile battalions.

One technique is to place a string of mines across an exposed French supply route, where the road passes through a defile or skirts a ridge nose. Scouts or *moussebelline* warn of the expected convoy's approach. When the lead vehicle hits the mine belt—or when the French point's mine detectors spot the mines and the convoy halts—the rebels open from both sides with automatic weapons and grenades as well as with enfilade fire down the road.

Then, if possible, one group of ambushers seeks to close with the survivors in the halted vehicles. Object: to grab weapons as well as to further confuse and destroy the enemy even at the risk of heavier friendly losses.

Speed and Shock

The accent is on speed and shock action. French armored escorts are attacked with Molotov cocktails or grenades, blinded with smoke, or deliberately blocked off by burning vehicles in the convoy. Vehicle-mounted machine guns are turned against the enemy. As soon as the French begin to rally, the rebels break off action, and, under cover of pre-arranged automatic weapons fire, the ambushers scatter with their casualties, prisoners, and booty, later to reunite. Seldom is a French convoy "annihilated"; but the rebels' success have forced the French Army to divert increasingly larger forces to protect its communications. Even so, losses continue.

Attacks on exposed garrisons—farmhouses, villages, iron mines, railheads, outposts—usually take the form of night or bad weather probes, mortar bombardment (such as the El Hamed affair), sniping, or, far more rarely, direct assaults and raids in company or section strength.

Using the lowest possible number of men, a stealthy close-in approach, and surprise and diversion are prime pre-assault elements of rebel attacks against outposts. Leading the way through the mine barrier, pathfinders with wire-cutters take care of the first aprons of barbed wire. Bangalores blow the final gaps. Simultaneously, the assault units rise, firing from the hip, and go in yelling, heedless of casualties. Unit leaders, including company commanders, join in the fire fight. They rely on the night assault's shock effect to hold down losses. Once a breach has been made, the rebels don't back off easily.

Sometimes mortars are used to reduce a die-hard bunker, once the bulk of the garrison has been subdued. In the rapid mop-up, weapons are recovered, ammunition collected, and prisoners, if any, are shepherded to the rear. "Sometimes," said a rebel officer, "the prisoners don't want to keep up with us during the withdrawal, and we have to shoot them. The French shoot our people, so why not?" Some prisoners, however, are kept alive. The FLN has exploited French prisoners, and particularly, for propaganda, German and Italian deserters from the Foreign Legion.

Unless trapped, seldom does the ALN try to make a stand or hold ground. Sometimes, a squad or section may be expended to delay a French sweep so that larger units can escape. However, the usual reaction to a major mountain comb-out (*ratissage*), which may involve several French regiments, is to avoid contact and seek safer ground. The accent is on living to fight another day, not on becoming fixed as a target for French aircraft, artillery, and the hard-worked Legion. As a result, most of the French Army's more massive punches land on air.

Realizing that its effectiveness lies as much in the mere fact of its existence as in any damage it inflicts on the French, the Army of National Liberation or its propagandists may talk of "offensives" and "Dienbienphus," but in practice seldom expends its slender material resources unless the rewards seem exceptionally promising. By choice and necessity, rebel tactics are opportunistic—pinpricks that harass rather than hammer blows that cripple.

Assaults on the Morice Line

Against the Morice Line, however, the rebels would like to have a hammer-blow capability.

Named after a former French Defense Minister, the Morice Line was completed in 1957 to block off the interior rebel *willayas* from the ALN supply dumps, training camps, and headquarters in "neutral" western Tunisia. Over the rugged terrain, the line runs roughly from Bône, on the Mediterranean, to Souk Ahras, guarding the Medjerda River corridor, to a point south of Tebessa at the Sahara's fringe. Total length is more than 100 miles. A similar line, facing the Moroccan frontier, was built earlier.

By rebel accounts, the Morice Line consists, through much of its length, of three parallel barbed-wire barriers. One barrier is electrified, all three are larded with minefields and backed up by patrols, artillery, and aircraft. Strongpoints are located at intervals of 2,000 to 3,000 yards. A road for armored car patrols and motorized units links the strongpoints. Radar is used to detect rebel approaches by night. It is reported that some 25,000 to 40,000 French troops garrison the line and its vicinity.

The mountainous approaches from Tunisia to the Morice Line constitute a No Man's Land, a dark and bloody ground, 15 to 35 miles across. Here, despite the abandonment of many small platoon-size positions, the French still maintained (in 1958) some two dozen isolated outposts in a style resembling that of Indochina days. Some were occupied by two companies of infantry with 105mm howitzers. These posts served as bases for French "Special Administrative Service" units in their social-political work among the remaining Moslem villagers. They serve as observation points, as centers for intelligence and counterintelligence activity. Prior to the 1958 referendum, the garrisons of these posts canvassed the local peasants and ordered them to vote.

One such post which had been recently abandoned when I saw it, was the fortified railway station at Sidi Bader on the Medjerda River, a few miles east of Souk Ahras. Sidi Bader consisted of an old-fashioned two-story station, a couple of sheds and outbuildings, sandbagged emplacements, a 15-foot-wide barbed-wire apron, and a belt of mines (unremoved). Once a shipping point for wheat, the outpost had been garrisoned, according to our ALN guides, by a half-company of infantry. Nearby was a small native village. Within mortar range of the ridges dominating the Medjerda Valley, and with the river bed and railroad embankment easy avenues of approach, Sidi Bader was less than ideal as an outpost.

However, the outposts, coupled with daily aerial reconnaissance, did put something of a crimp in rebel efforts to penetrate the Morice Line. They contested, however passively, complete rebel dominance of No Man's Land and its Moslem populace. By guarding the easiest approach routes, the outposts forced the rebel supply trains to take the more difficult, more circuitous paths. And, supplied by weekly armored convoys, the much-harassed outposts could provide supporting fires, blocking positions, and bases to assist mobile forces in their occasional counter-drives against the rebels.

Rebel tactics in breaching the barrier, usually after a zigzag approach march from Tunisia lasting several nights, followed the normal ALN pattern: diversionary night attacks, stealth, speed. Long-handled rakes are used to feel the way through the mines; rubber gloves are worn while handling the electrified wire. Having blown the wire with bangalores, it is imperative to rush the mule-borne supplies through the gap to the hills beyond before the French react in force. Delay is fatal.

Understandably, rebel (and French) losses have not been light in Morice Line operations. In the winter of 1957–58, the East Base command ran whole companies of Algerian riflemen through the line, each man carrying 600 rounds and an extra weapon to leave behind with the interior forces. Through 1958–60, the French gradually beefed up the line and made rebel breaches far more difficult. Indeed, in late 1958, several authoritative rebel sources stated that they knew of no major breakthroughs since the previous March. The rebels, however, later claimed additional successful, if costly, breaks, including several in late 1959 and early 1960.

The rebels' alternative supply routes are risky. The end run across the desert south of Tebessa is totally impractical save during the rainy winter months, when French aerial reconnaissance and water shortages become less pressing.

Attempts to land supplies by sea along Algeria's 650 miles of rocky coastline have been inhibited (but not eliminated) by French Navy patrols and the crust of French garrisons in the more heavily populated coastal zone. The Algerians prefer the costly breakthroughs from Tunisia, since the terrain immediately beyond the Morice Line is largely under rebel control.

Even as the rebel regular army kept up its mosquito war against the Morice Line and the French forces in the field, so did the rebel irregular commandos exert terrorist pressure in towns.

Commando Slimane, in the East Base area, was named after its leader, Slimane Genoun, a 26-year-old black marketeer and arc welder from Souk Ahras. Slimane had a price on his head, after walking into the central plaza of French-occupied Souk Ahras in broad daylight and emptying a concealed Sten gun at the midday crowd of French soldiers and civilians. He escaped unscathed in the bloody confusion that followed.

With their own comfortable hideout in Tunisia and their own blue denim garb, Slimane's "Commandos of Death" were loosely and reluctantly attached to the regular 3d Battalion. The commandoes were city boys: "We go right into the towns and blow up the French; the Army stays out in the countryside." Like their counterparts elsewhere in Algeria, the commandos specialized in minor ambushes, sabotage, assassination. Commando Slimane also specialized in probing the Morice Line. It avoided pitched battle.

Tactics of a Commando

A small, semi-autonomous band, Slimane's 40 men, aged 15 to 55, enjoyed better rations, lived more easily off the remaining peasantry, and felt little of the ascetic discipline imposed on the ALN. Instead of political tracts, the Commandos read comic books; they had no commissar and needed none. Their personal weapons were comparable to those of the regulars. For ease of control and concealment, Slimane usually split his force on the march. Like the regulars, he kept his automatic weapons well forward (a Bren, an MG42, submachine guns); his two-mule supply train stayed well to the rear. The pace was often a near-run. Once, when a young new recruit began to falter, Slimane bounded up, handed the laggard's rifle and pack to another man, and hissed: "Do not fall behind. The French will catch you and put a bullet in your neck." The recruit picked up speed.

My experience with Commando Slimane included an approach march toward the Morice Line through No Man's Land—four days of zigzag and dodge, moving mostly at night, holing up during the day in hillside peasant huts with scouts out and for security the Bren or the MG42 on the nearest high ground.

Peasants showed up with food, water, and information. Some showed the newly healed scars of French "interrogation." At hamlet after hamlet, some within sight of French outposts, the Moslem peasants provided *couscous*, lamb, milk, and coffee for the commando. They were friendly, hard-pressed, and scared to death of French retaliation.

Pressure of French Power

As he drew closer to the Morice Line, Slimane also felt the pressure of French power. One day two fighter-bombers, sided by a low-flying Piper spotter plane, gave the commando's hideout a thorough going over, then bore away to rocket another (empty) slope. Slimane's Bren gunner kept the Piper in his sights, but, following normal rebel policy, held his fire. (The rebels, it should be noted, have downed or damaged enough low-flying propeller-driven aircraft and scarce helicopters to bother French field commanders.)

Several times, Slimane's pickets and the *moussebelline* reported French ground patrols in the vicinity. Once the threat seemed serious enough to justify burying the commando's bangalores and rakes under a convenient haystack. Nevertheless, on another afternoon, Slimane did not hesitate to lead his column—crouching, to be sure—across a saddle in plain view of a French hill outpost a mile or so away. Following this dash, Slimane's troopers relaxed amid the bushes of a deeply cut gorge, listening to the comforting blare of Arab rock-and-roll on Slimane's portable radio, while the predictable French recon aircraft circled blindly in the sky overhead.

After quick-marching through one moonlit night along the Medjerda River and its chewed-up paralleling single railroad track, with great French-set forest fires blazing on the ridges to the north, past ruined railway stations and grain elevators, Commando Slimane reached its final jump-off point. This was a pair of stone huts perched on the reverse slope of a naked ridge high above the Medjerda. Sending out scouting parties and sentries, Slimane and his Headquarters group settled into one hut; his gold-toothed *sergeant-chef* and the others crowded together under their gray blankets in the other.

The Commando was within a dozen kilometers of Souk Ahras, hedge-hog of the Morice Line. The next move, said Slimane, would be to try to reach the line and go through, using the rakes and bangalores borne by his mules.

Armor in Open Country

The next morning, however, it was plain that the French had sallied forth to stage a major "demonstration."

On the dun-colored ridge crest just across the Medjerda Valley, a mile or so away, could be seen what at first glance looked like a procession of sluggish green beetles. Some were moving, some halted. They were headed eastward, toward Tunisia. A long line of French tanks, trucks, halftracks. The deep, throat-clearing grumble of tank engines was clearly audible.

As his troopers, a trifle tense and fidgety, strapped up their gear, Slimane was barking orders, sending out armed scouts disguised as civilians in loose white turbans and peasant smocks. The MG42 was sent to a wooded hillock above the huts.

Genuine peasants, some with children tagging along, drifted in to report another French column moving eastward to the south of Slimane's position, along the tank roads scraped out by French bulldozers early in the war. Commando Slimane was in the middle of what could become a regiment-size pincers movement.

The danger, as Slimane's *sergeant-chef* (an Indochina veteran) calmly pointed out, would come if the French turned the "demonsation" into a precautionary clean-up and closed the pincers with the full treatment—aircraft, artillery, helicopter-borne *paras.* "If they spot us," he said, "it could be very difficult."

Slimane himself stepped into the hut. "I have forty good men, well-fed, well-trained, well-treated. They are ready to die to the last man." He rubbed his forefingers together. "We are all brothers. All brothers."

The brothers went outside only when in civilian garb, and even then they kept to the available shadows. French motorized units across the Medjerda kept moving sluggishly along their long ridge. Despite its exposed, sunlit position, Commando Slimane was ignored. It would have seemed obvious that French patrols would investigate any habitations left standing on this virtually treeless high ground so close to Souk Ahras and closer still to their "demonstration" force. But they did not. Only two aircraft droned by, high overhead.

In late afternoon, Slimane said, "We are going to try another route tonight." The Commando was in for a long march and some fireworks.

Finally, the bright, hateful, revealing sunlight ebbed and the ridges shaded from sand color to rust to a cold grayish white. French tank engines still growled and grumbled across the valley as Slimane saddled up his troopers.

The Commando cleaned up the huts of all tell-tale evidence. Civilians brought up the mules. Scouts returned. The previously detached half of the Commando showed up for orders and moved out. The others, silent, a little dry in the mouth, snapped on their harness. The *sergeant-chef,* armed with a German MP40 submachine gun and British grenades in leather pouches, checked the troopers. Slimane was everywhere, pushing, ordering, his voice exploding in guttural Arabic. Two youngsters did something wrong; Slimane exploded in rage. He kicked and cuffed them. They both retreated to their hut to weep like children.

Knowing the Terrain

As night fell, the bangalores were loaded on the mules, and the column set off, zigzagging downslope to the broad, eroded, brush-dotted floor of the Medjerda Valley.

Split into small groups, Commando Slimane headed right up into the apex of the V created by the French columns. Our group doubled back and forth across the Medjerda in single file. The French are on the high ground? Slimane goes into the low ground.

Seven or eight miles of zigzag marching brought us to a rendezvous. Slimane and his *sergeant-chef* materialized out of the brush. After four years of war, these city boys had come to know their battleground without maps. Nevertheless, the Commando could not find a way through, despite several hours more of marching. Slimane's scouts discovered that there were just too many Frenchmen in the Medjerda area approaches for a slow moving mule train to penetrate. And, tomorrow, the demonstration might become a cleanup. Slimane decided to pull back.

"One group of mine will be making a little harassing attack [against the French column] tonight," he said. "Another group will cache the explosives. We'll take another way and try again in five or six days."

As this experience seemed to show, the French Army's massive effort was sufficiently strong to preclude any prolonged rebel thrusts, or any full-scale uprisings on the part of the Moslem populace. The French could protect Algeria's 1.2 million Europeans from any major rebel incursions in the towns and cities. The rebels could not seriously interfere with major troop movements.

Stalemate for Both Sides

Nevertheless, with the bulk of the 500,000-man army tied up in garrisons, the hard-worked mobile forces were insufficient to gain military decision over the elusive rebels. Only the Morice Line, and the periodic "cleanups," limited in time and area, gave rebel forces outside the cities a hard check. Not even the French claim to have "destroyed" any major rebel units.

For the lack of an over-all policy, the Army's "hard" measures (like forcible Moslem regroupment and haphazard repression) ran at cross-purposes with the work of its benevolent Special Administrative Service. Enough bitter Moslems remained, even in the Morice Line approaches, to supply recruits, information, and shelter to the rebels.

The French garrisons, from my observation, seemed relatively timid, despite the obvious rewards of aggressive patrolling and prompt reaction to rebel thrusts. Neither psychologically nor physically did the French Army, as a whole, seem prepared to cope with the rigors and subtleties of partisan warfare.

The rebels, adapting tactics to resources, coupled mosquito war with skillful, if crude, political action. Their cause gained strong emotional staying power among the Moslem masses, a power to which the French have devised no effective answer. The rebels relied on the long pull, militarily and politically. The French long sought, and have repeatedly claimed, imminent military victory.

In short, the Algerian war, thanks partly to France's slow initial reaction, has progressed after more than five years to the point where a purely military solution seems no longer possible. Both sides have arrived at a stalemate. Any breakthrough will have to be achieved at the negotiating tables.

* * *

Six months after Braestrup's article appeared the following letter was published in *Army Magazine* (January, 1961):

RECONSTRUCTED REBEL

It may be of interest to your readers, particularly those who studied the article "Partisan Tactics—Algerian Style," to know that Commando leader Slimane, mentioned in this article, surrendered on 31 October 1960. He is on record as having stated:

"The rebellion can no longer claim to work for the people, of which it is severed. France offered self-determination: why and for whom, therefore, to fight now.

"As for myself, I saw and I chose the way of truth. I pondered, I thought, I studied carefully and I came back.

"I surrender to generous France, and I ask her to forgive me in spite of my past errors and mistakes."

General PHILIPPE GOURAUD
Military Attaché
Embassy of France
Washington, D.C.

Further References

Cuba*

BOOKS

Du Bois, J. *Fidel Castro*. Indianapolis: Bobbs-Merrill, 1959.

Guevara, E. *Guerrilla Warfare*, Tr. by P. J. Murray. New York: Monthly Review, 1961.

Hubermann, L., and P. M. Sweezy. *Cuba—Anatomy of a Revolution*. 2nd ed. New York: Monthly Review, 1961.

Matthews, Herbert. *Cuban Story*. New York: Braziller, 1961.

Weyl, N. *Red Star over Cuba*. New York: Hillman Books, 1961.

Youngblood, J., and R. Moore. *The Devil to Pay*. New York: Coward-McCann, 1961.

ARTICLES

Castro, Fidel. "Why We Fight," *Coronet*, February, 1958.

Cline, H. F. "Mexico, Fidelismo and the United States," *Orbis*, Summer, 1961.

Fitzgibbon, R. H. "The Organization of American States—Time of Ordeal," *Orbis*, Spring, 1961.

Guevara, E. "La Guerra de Guerrilla," tr. and condensed by Major H. Peterson, *Marine Corps Gazette*, June, July, and August, 1961 (to be released by Praeger as *Che Guevara on Guerrilla Warfare*).

Macaulay, N. "Castro's Threat to the Hemisphere," *Marine Corps Gazette*, March, 1961.

McConaughy, J. B. "Latin America—Soviet Target," *Military Review*, October, 1961.

St. George, A. "A Visit with a Revolutionary," *Coronet*, February, 1958.

Vallet, R. "The Alternative of Castro," *Military Review*, March, 1961.

Algeria

BOOKS

Brace, Richard and Joan. *Ordeal in Algeria*. Princeton, N.J.: Van Nostrand, 1960.

---

* The editor has exercised some restraint concerning the Further References at the end of this section. While many books about Castro and the Cuban Revolution are available, most add nothing to an understanding of the problems in question and have, therefore, not been listed.

Clark, M. K. *Algeria in a Turmoil: A History of the Rebellion.* New York: Praeger, 1959.

Gillespie, J. *Algeria, Rebellion and Revolution.* New York: Praeger, 1961.

Kraft, J. *The Struggle for Algeria.* New York: Doubleday, 1961.

Mezerik, A. G., ed. *Algeria Development, 1959: De Gaulle, FLN, UN.* New York: International Review Service, 1960.

Roy, J. *The War in Algeria.* Tr. by R. Howard. New York: Grove, 1961.

Servan-Schreiber, J. *Lieutenant in Algeria.* New York: Knopf, 1957.

ARTICLES

Bethosuart, H. "Combat Helicopters in Algeria," *Marine Corps Gazette,* January, 1961.

Cottrell, A. J., and J. E. Dougherty. "Algeria: Case Study in the Evolution of a Colonial Problem," *U.S. Naval Institute Proceedings,* July, 1957.

Croizat, V. J. "The Algerian War," *Marine Corps Gazette,* December, 1957.

Halpern, M. "The Algerian Uprising of 1945," *Middle East Journal,* April, 1948.

O'Ballance, E. "The Algerian Struggle," *Army Quarterly,* October, 1960.

Paret, P. "The French Army and La Guerre Revolutionnaire," *Royal United Service Institute Journal,* February, 1959.

Riley, D. "French Helicopter Operations in Algeria," *Marine Corps Gazette,* February, 1958.

PART 9 COUNTERGUERRILLA PROCEDURES AND POLICIES

It was noted in the Preface that the Soviets are by no means the inventors of guerrilla warfare. We should recognize, however, that the Communist world has used this form of warfare with unprecedented success. They have gleaned many lessons from the history of guerrilla warfare and have set down a strategic doctrine of unconventional warfare that includes subversion, assassination, terrorism, and other weapons of a political, economic, and psychological nature. We have seen in previous sections of this book how these procedures have been utilized by Communist guerrilla movements.

A particular danger in the Free World is the fact that the Communists have learned to exploit wars of liberation regardless of the political leaning of the liberation movement in question. Cuba and Algeria are differing examples of this technique. The Communists recognize the fact that in wars of liberation the revolutionary leaders, when failing to achieve their goal, will often grasp at any outside assistance. The Communists are always willing to make this small down payment on a possible future satellite.

The purpose of this final section is to summarize the significance and dangers of Communist guerrilla activity, to analyze contemporary Communist techniques of unconventional warfare, and to present a discussion of possible countermeasures against revolutionary movements that are Communist inspired or directed. These complex problems are treated here in broader scope than in the preceding sections of the book.

In this section Jordan describes Communist techniques of guerrilla warfare and some counterguerrilla measures. Bjelajac discusses historic Communist strategy in underdeveloped areas and Soviet pronouncements on revolutionary warfare. Burnham advocates a more aggressive U.S. policy and utilization of unconventional warfare techniques with particular emphasis on psychological warfare. Kelly analyzes French experiments and experiences with psychological weapons in a revolutionary context. Bjelajac, in a second article, explains the growing importance of unconventional warfare in a nuclear age. Hilsman appraises the current Communist emphasis on internal war. Finally, Rostow sets forth the United States' purposes and its policy for countering Communist guerrillas.

31

Lt. Col. George B. Jordan
U.S. Army

OBJECTIVES AND

METHODS OF COMMUNIST

GUERRILLA WARFARE

*T*HE OVER-ALL COMMUNIST MENACE has focused attention on guerrilla warfare and its possible application by Communist elements in the Western Hemisphere. The Communists are experts in guerrilla warfare and use it as another means of fomenting revolution and debilitating those governments which are not economically or politically stable. Therefore, this article is written to provide background on the historical and military meaning of guerrilla warfare, on what guerrillas can achieve under favorable conditions to obtain their objectives, and on what can be done to counter guerrilla actions.

By definition, the word "guerrilla" means a "little war" and it has come to denote the irregular, nonprofessional civilian-soldier who takes up arms to fight against professional military forces. Guerrilla warfare also has been defined as that phase of Unconventional Warfare conducted by predominantly indigenous forces organized on a paramilitary or military basis to harass and eventually defeat the enemy. There are numerous recorded instances where guerrilla warfare has achieved its purposes when conventional type of warfare had failed.

From *Military Review*, January, 1960, and reprinted by permission.

Guerrilla warfare is as old as history, yet until recent times little heed has been paid to it by professional military men in studies of warfare in general. There has been a reluctance on the part of professional officers to participate in nonethical movements. History shows us that guerrilla action has chiefly been the weapon of partisans, revolutionaries, rebels, and more recently of Communist inspired movements. Well-known examples of guerrilla operations are to be found as far back as 360 B.C. in China and as recently as today in Cuba. The Communist nations of China and the USSR have produced professionals in the field of guerrilla warfare as evidenced by such leaders as Mao Tse-tung and Stalin. It was Stalin who utilized the teaching of Karl Marx that "The end justifies the means" and applied this concept to weaken his opponent while strengthening the Communist States. For example, the Soviet States are continually improving their own internal security while attempting to undermine the internal security of anti-Communist nations. Karl Marx' remarks on guerrilla warfare are especially noteworthy when considering Communist actions.

A nation fighting for its liberty ought not to adhere rigidly to the accepted rules of warfare. Mass uprisings, revolutionary methods, guerrilla bands everywhere; such are the only means by which a small nation can hope to maintain itself against an adversary superior in numbers and equipment. By their use a weaker force can overcome its stronger and better organized opponent.

Stalin, Mao Tse-tung, and Ho Chi Minh have been among Marx' most apt pupils.

Studies of historical examples have pointed out emphatically that to combat guerrillas is expensive in terms of manpower. For example, in World War II it was estimated that in two years of combating guerrilla warfare, the German Army employed in rear areas 300,000 soldiers or the equivalent of 15 German divisions in a period when every soldier was needed at the front. In the Korean conflict the United Nations forces had to assign four of its 10 divisions to combat partisans in rear areas. In Greece 200,000 Greek National troops were employed to defeat 30,000 guerrillas. In Cuba Prime Minister Fidel Castro with a small force which grew to a maximum estimated strength of 6,200 was able with some support of the Cuban people to overthrow the Batista forces.

Significant Problem

A few years ago General Alfred E. Gruenther, United States Army, estimated that it took 10 men from the regular forces to nullify one guerrilla. By simple arithmetic, one can see readily that the strength of military forces needed to combat guerrillas could reach phenomenal numbers; the significance of the problem cannot be underestimated. For example, if country

"X" were to have 3,000 personnel engaged in guerrilla activities, it is estimated by the above mathematical equation that it would take approximately 30,000 troops to neutralize them; and this figure in many countries far exceeds the strength of their entire military forces. Therefore, the importance of this problem cannot be overemphasized particularly as a tactic employed or exploited by international communism to achieve world domination.

Many military strategists believe that in the event of a nuclear holocaust the only type of ground action possible in the Western Hemisphere would be small unit actions for which guerrilla warfare is well-adapted. However, it seems unlikely that the Communists would risk a major nuclear attack as long as such action would bring massive retaliation. Such action would result in such general destruction on both sides that it would not serve their purpose. Therefore, it seems more probable that the agents of international communism will follow a course of action which will result in "brush type" wars or guerrilla actions.

Since guerrilla warfare is inexpensive and can be used to exploit an area where a foothold has been gained, it is necessary to be ready to combat this type of warfare and study its techniques and methods and their application. Communists are experts in the field of guerrilla warfare. It is imperative that the Free World study, understand, and prepare for such actions in any future conflicts, be they "brushfires," minor revolutions, or major conflagrations involving the use of nuclear weapons.

Objectives

In studying the historical precedents of guerrilla warfare and its form of employment, it can be concluded generally that guerrilla warfare is adopted for one or more of the following reasons:

1. To assist the regular armed forces in operations.
2. To defend the country as a last recourse when the regular armed forces have been routed.
3. To instigate a national action to regain the liberty of a country subjugated by the enemy.
4. To overthrow a dictatorial or tyrannical form of government.
5. To harass and weaken the existing government causing it to fall so as to permit the establishment of a new government.

There are many historical examples which can be used to support the statement that even though certain aspects of guerrilla warfare may be similar, there are many guerrilla operations conducted in which the motives and purposes differ. For example, Soviet guerrilla activities against the German Army in World War II were primarily to harass the German rear and function as an intelligence agency. This objective certainly varied from the motives of Ho Chi Minh in French Indochina and Mao Tse-tung in China; their purposes were to overthrow the recognized governments of that period.

An important point to remember about guerrilla warfare is that often Communists align themselves with what may be a justified revolutionary movement to implement Communist strategy of creating crises and weakening the political, economic, and military structure of a government. Once a government falls, the Communists move in and seize control.

Through the employment of guerrilla warfare, ultranationalistic and communistic movements now are able to achieve their purposes without resorting to an all-out conventional type warfare. The principles of war which are applicable to regular warfare are likewise applicable in varying degrees to guerrilla warfare and might well be termed the general rules of military strategy. In addition to the general principles of war, certain other conditions or characteristics have been found to be essential to wage successful guerrilla warfare.

Public Support Necessary

There are certain characteristics identified with successful guerrilla operations which include the exploitation of an unstable political situation, the gaining of general or local public support, or the emphasis on certain principles of war, such as the advantageous use of terrain and exploitation of surprise. Of these the political situation is of primary importance. There must be a cause or grievance against the constituted government behind which guerrilla units can rally support and sympathy of the civilian population. This sympathy can be built up through incessant propaganda so as to gain control of public opinion. Very often this is achieved through intense "hate" campaigns operating behind the popular theme of nationalism. This theme was used very effectively by Communist leader Ho Chi Minh against the French in the period of 1946–54 in Vietnam.

It is easy to visualize how a people with a strong national desire for independence, liberty, or other worthy causes might inadvertently fall under the control of the Communist Party and become a pawn in the international chess game of irregular warfare, cold or hot. Movements which start out as insignificant guerrilla activities with proper leadership sometimes can be expanded into large-scale partisan actions involving the masses of civilian populations, and can result in the overthrow of the duly constituted government. This is especially true when that government opposes Communist ideology. Communism associates itself with dissident elements, strives for popular support, and because its leaders are trained in organization, often gains control of the national movement in question.

To succeed, guerrilla forces strive to have the political sympathy of the local civilian population, because it is they who provide information, recruits, supplies, food, and funds. Since the guerrilla is a civilian who has taken up arms and springs from the people, he must have public support. This support, however, is not always given voluntarily, but at times is obtained through terrorizing the community.

The importance of maintaining a good public attitude and associating it with popular support to achieve political objectives is summarized quite well in the following quotation from Mao Tse-tung:

> If guerrilla warfare is without a political objective, it must fail; but if it maintains a political objective which is incompatible with the political objectives of the people, failing to receive their support, then, this too must fail. This is the basic reason why guerrilla warfare can only be a form of revolutionary war. This is because guerrilla warfare is basically organized and maintained by the masses, and once it is deprived of these masses, or fails to enlist their participation and cooperation, its survival and development is not possible.

The support of government, either its own, one in exile, or one sympathetic to the guerrilla's cause, is needed to provide special equipment, arms, ammunition, and direction. Policy guidance is provided at the highest level. This insures coordination and direction of the masses in the pursuit of national objectives. The need for centralized policy is summarized by Mao Tse-tung in his book, *The Strategy of Partisan Warfare,* in which he states:

> Without centralized strategic command the partisans can inflict little damage on their adversaries, as without this, they can break down into roaming, armed bands, and then find no more support by the population.

To insure unity of action, the organization and direction of guerrillas must emanate at the highest military and political level during hostilities. This direction should also continue after hostilities have ceased to prevent guerrillas from falling under control of dangerous political elements.

Control

Probably one of the most important principles is *control.* The general headquarters exercises absolute centralized control of policy, discipline, ethics, and political ideology. The actual conduct and basic responsibility for operations is decentralized to the guerrilla band leader. Centralized control insures coordinated action and forestalls the destruction of a facility or the assassination of a person who may be useful at a later date. Generally, the best results in guerrilla warfare have been obtained through using many small bands numbering about 50 men. Anything larger tends to become unwieldy and more difficult to conceal and to supply. Experience has proved that many small units, acting under independent leadership and centrally coordinated by a general headquarters, operate with maximum efficiency. Tactical missions can be carried out effectively only when the details of execution are decentralized to the small, self-contained guerrilla bands.

Simplicity, informality, and evasiveness provide the guerrilla with his strength. Since a guerrilla assumes the role of a "Dr. Jekyll–Mr. Hyde" character, he is difficult to fight because he cannot afford to be recognized. His effectiveness depends upon his ability to lead two lives. In Vietnam the French troops rarely came upon an enemy soldier in the daytime. By day, all appeared peaceful as the peasants worked their rice fields, and it remained that way until nightfall when these "peaceful peasants" became guerrillas and under the cover of darkness attacked the French forces. Thus the guerrilla can be the student, the farmer, the laborer, the next door neighbor, or the butcher who can strike and fade away like the mist. Since the guerrilla is a soldier of the shadows, he depends upon secrecy and nonrecognition for his survival. It is this informality which makes the guerrilla difficult to fight.

For the professional soldier to fight the enemy he must know who and where the enemy is. His training and experience have taught him to follow the maxim, "Find them, fix them, and fight them." If the guerrilla cannot be found to "fix and fight," then the professional soldier becomes frustrated. It is the fear of the unknown and not being able to strike back which wears the professional soldier down.

Offensive Spirit

In guerrilla operations the spirit of the offensive is essential to prevent stagnation. Units that are active and successful in the accomplishment of assigned missions build up a high *esprit de corps* and attract followers; success is contagious. Mao Tse-tung recognized the principle that guerrillas cannot afford to fight any losing battles. Therefore, his problem for many years was to maintain an offensive spirit without a major engagement so as to be able to fight another day. Mao Tse-tung laid down three basic principles for Communist warfare in Asia which were:

1. Yield any town or terrain you cannot hold safely.
2. Limit yourself to guerrilla warfare as long as the enemy has superiority in numbers and weapons.
3. Organize regular units and pass over to the counteroffensive when you are sure of victory.

He recognized that it was only through offensive that he could achieve final victory and implement his political objectives. To do this it is necessary to be both patient and flexible while awaiting the opportune time and place to launch a counteroffensive. Mao Tse-tung certainly exercised this principle in the fight against Japanese forces in World War II and later against the Chinese Nationalist Army. This guerrilla warfare was fought for many years in China before Mao obtained sufficient power to gain control in 1948. In the final phase, when the guerrillas are sure of victory, they organize regular units and operate openly. There is no doubt that irregular warfare can be used to great advantage when it is combined with regular operations or as a prelude to open warfare. To achieve victory and insure survival, guerrilla warfare must be offensive in nature because it is the only way that political objectives can be attained and opponents subjugated.

The element of surprise is another characteristic used most effectively in guerrilla operations. It is achieved through timing, direction, and method of attack, and is dependent upon receipt of good intelligence information often provided by trained observers, informants, and sympathetic civilians. Through the use of this information, appropriate objectives and plans are developed accordingly. Guerrillas generally attack at night using the cover of darkness or the concealment provided by forests or jungles to hide their movements to objectives. These targets could be an electric plant, radio station, telephone exchange, a key bridge, a person, or body of troops. If a band is operating in an area over a period of time, it frequently will change positions and routes of march to avoid detection. Surprise can be exploited further by hitting many widely separated objectives simultaneously so as to confuse the enemy about actual strength and to delay his commitment of counterforces.

In an ambush the guerrillas are very clever in selecting areas where the head of a column can be blocked along a defile and the main body saturated with automatic weapons fire. Often, guerrillas will combine a road or trail block with a swift vicious attack from the flanks to strike their objective, exploiting the element of surprise, then assemble promptly at a rallying point for return to their hiding places or "fadeaway" among the civilian population. These "hit-and-run" tactics often are accomplished behind the enemy's lines in areas where least expected—to reduce the effectiveness of the regular forces and exploit a psychological advantage—and are extremely effective.

If the assassination of an important political or military figure is the objective, then the methods and plans are varied accordingly. Guerrillas and partisans will use any methods or means to accomplish their mission and attack what they consider the weakest link in the chain of defense, whether by the use of murder, propaganda, or sabotage. The ends justify the means and their only law is that of survival.

Terrain

Another factor which is as important in guerrilla operations as it is in conventional warfare is terrain. To know the terrain and how to utilize it advantageously very often makes the difference between a highly successful or mediocre operation. One fact that stands out clearly is that guerrillas know how to use terrain efficiently and it makes very little difference to them whether it is the jungles of Vietnam, the mountains of Yugoslavia, or the tundras of Russia. This proficiency is obtained through reconnaissance and training at night. The guerrilla studies the terrain until he is thoroughly familiar with every trail, road, creek, hill, swamp, or jungle. The terrain must be known thoroughly in every locality for at least 50 miles in all directions.

Native guides or local sympathizers who are familiar with the area are used very often to good advantage to assist in raids. The vastness of territories such as China and the USSR with their long lines of communication passing through underdeveloped sections assists guerillas because it makes such communications vulnerable to attack and hinders the prompt reaction of counterforces. If the terrain is mountainous and rugged and covered with jungle forests or swamps, it provides concealment for logistical installations, bases or strong points, and tactical maneuvers. A lack of roads hampers counteractions by regular forces and reduces the effective use of heavy artillery and heavy equipment. In Greece during the period 1946–49 poor roads provided ideal conditions for Communist-led guerrilla operations against the existing government.

One aspect closely associated with terrain is the necessity for a base area. A base serves both a military function and a political purpose. Militarily it provides an area for training guerrillas, schools, communication facilities, supply points, hospitals, and headquarters. Also from the base, the political aims and high-level policy can be formulated into plans to accomplish military actions necessary to achieve the objective.

The skillful use of propaganda is another characteristic of guerrilla warfare frequently used by guerrilla leaders before and during a campaign. The purpose of propaganda is to maintain the loyalty of one's own forces; to enlist the sympathy of the local populace; and to weaken the enemy forces and the power of the government to control its people. Propaganda can be anything from a package of matches with a slogan to a sack of salt or a leaflet which will influence the opinion or attitude of any group to the guerrilla cause. Once guerrilla warfare has begun, it, in itself, is its best propaganda. If the propaganda is to be effective, it must be directed consistently and vigorously against the enemy, employing those themes which will arouse doubt, suspicion, mistrust, or discontent.

In exploitation of successful armed attacks by guerrillas, propaganda accompanied by deliberate rumor spreading will do much to spread terror and panic among the people and weaken their faith in the existing government and its leaders. Propaganda is an adjunct to guerrilla warfare which much be recognized for its true value and countered. Propaganda, in itself, is no substitute for actual guerrilla operations, but if properly used, can assist in the successful attainment of objectives.

Command and Leadership

Command and leadership among guerrilla bands is more of the authoritative than the democratic type. In many instances their leaders have been trained by the Communist Party or possess other attributes which qualify them for command; sometimes guerrilla leaders are named by the political party to command the group. In World War II fanatical party members with military training were brought through the frontlines or parachuted behind the German lines, to provide energetic leadership for Soviet guerrillas. In Malaya the Malayan Communist Party provided the leadership for guerrilla warfare in that area in 1948.

The motivating factor behind guerrillas is their strong belief in their cause for which they have the willingness and courage to face great hardship and even death. A guerrilla realizes when he takes a vow to support the cause that he is expected to adhere to the guerrilla oath and law, the violation of which can result in death. The guerrilla leader expects absolute obedience from his subordinates in operations, since to become guerrillas they have had to express willingness to be judged and punished by their comrades in the event of insubordination or cowardice.

The best type of guerrilla leader is the one who is ruthless and remains unperturbed in any grave emergency and is capable through his dominating personality to weld the individuals of his band into an efficient fighting unit. He must engender such a sense of loyalty among his men through his personal leadership in the accomplishment of difficult missions and endurance of hardships that each guerrilla feels proud to belong to the band. The accepted fact by a guerrilla that he faces judgment by his comrades provides the motivation for the accomplishment of difficult tasks.

Organization and Equipment

Most military leaders agree that with the advent of nuclear weapons, the large concentration of forces known in World War II is no longer practical, and that to survive, future land forces should be small, self-contained, highly mobile, hard striking, and capable of rapid concentration and dispersion. Guerrilla units normally operate as small independent bands, and their very organization provides them with the desirable characteristics advanced by many military leaders in the nuclear age. The organization of a guerrilla band provides it with a certain amount of built-in protection; its relatively small size facilitates concealment and prohibits its normal consideration as a profitable nuclear target.

The basic guerrilla band is a simple and flexible organization consisting of about 50 to 60 men headed by a chief. Often, the band is organized initially by a political commissar who later designates a chief to be the leader. The chief assumes the rank of lieutenant, captain, or other grade dependent upon the importance of his position and the number of men he controls. The strength, organization, and grades of leaders are variable. There is no standard table of organization to use as a guide, although there are different types such as combat units (light and heavy), and intelligence, supply, and sabotage units which are organized to perform certain missions. The smallest unit organized is a "cell" normally consisting of four men.

The Soviets have always contended that in guerrilla actions it is more effective to have a thousand bands of 50 men each, rather than 50 bands of one thousand each. Guerrillas seldom wear uniforms, but rather prefer to wear the native garb of the area in which they are operating. This practice helps to conceal their identity, and assists in evasion or detection if they are forced to mingle with civilian populations to cover a withdrawal. Their equipment usually is light and only sufficient to accomplish a particular mission. Individual weapons which are carried are knives, rifles, submachineguns, automatic rifles, or grenades.

In general, arms which are light and possess maximum firepower, and which can be brought into action quickly are preferred because they are not burdensome and assist the mobility of the units in tactical operations.

The mobility of the unit is sometimes further increased when guerrillas are mounted on vehicles or horses. With the development of improved communications and aircraft, it is now possible for guerrillas to increase the range of their operations. It has been estimated that it is possible for one unit to operate over an area 100 miles long and 80 miles wide. The development of light aircraft and helicopters will further increase their zone of operation and attack capabilities. Where possible, guerrillas do not like to be burdened with administrative sections and depend upon obtaining food from friendly civilian personnel. If the operation is an extended one or is one in which a unit is isolated or one being conducted in the rear of enemy lines, it is possible to be supplied by air. The airplane has enhanced the mobility and tactical capabilities of guerrilla raiders.

Tactics

The employment of guerrilla units is designed to accomplish certain tactical and strategical objectives. Therefore, the guerrilla leader must select his targets wisely to insure that each mission contributes to the accomplishment of the over-all objective. For example, Stalin felt that "the proper guerrilla field is the enemy's rear." By such employment, Soviet guerrillas in World War II were able to harass German communications, force deployment of troops for rear area security, and act as an intelligence agency. When the civilian population is friendly and supports a guerrilla movement, they are an invaluable source of information. Guerrilla agents can be planted in key spots to obtain information which will make it possible for the formulation and execution of plans that will weaken and wear down the opposition. The value of intelligence obtained by guerrillas is illustrated by a quote from a German corps report of 5 March 1942: "A guerrilla movement pays back a hundred times the costs which go into its making and maintenance of its intelligence work."

The conduct of raids, ambushes, and attacks must be based upon accurate information to insure success. The targets selected can be enemy troops, a bridge, telephone exchange, warehouse, a billet, or an ammunition dump. Whatever the target selected, it should be one within the guerrilla capability to assure, to a reasonable degree, successful accomplishment of the assigned mission.

Guerrilla raids normally are conducted at night and are characterized by their boldness, stealth, and the rapidity with which they are made. The cover of darkness provides concealment and is an effective ally to the guerrilla. He can strike in one area at sunset and by sunrise be miles away. His plans are based upon hitting quickly with minimum forces so that he can place as much distance as possible between his forces and the enemy.

The guerrilla uses his initiative and cunningness to the maximum advantage. The Communist guerrilla also uses terroristic methods and subterfuge as psychological weapons. One of his favorite tricks is to plant a time bomb in a locality such as an officer's billet, a club, or a theater where officers customarily gather at a certain time. Eleven officers were injured in such an operation in Vietnam in October, 1958. Often this type of ruse is timed to discredit a government when an important international conference is taking place so as to make the sponsoring government appear weak and unstable in the eyes of visiting dignitaries.

Other malicious acts which are committed to worry the opposition include putting sugar in gasoline of vehicles or mixing explosive charges with the coal of a locomotive. The guerrilla is secretive and ruthless in his actions and moves like a tiger in the night with the cunning of a fox to make his attacks. A guerrilla, with his hit-and-run tactics, terror, and assassination techniques does not pretend to have or follow the traditions of the military profession.

The guerrillas cannot afford to fight any losing battles or lose the initiative, but, sometimes, in the sequence of events, guerrillas are forced to defend a stronghold to prevent seizure or penetration of an important area. The defense generally is assumed to gain time or while moving to a new base of operations. It is most unusual for guerrilla units to defend because by so doing, the elements of mobility and surprise are lost. If the defense is assumed, it is done for a limited time only. The terrain is skillfully used in the area to be defended. Since guerrillas do not normally have tanks and artillery to engage in sustained operations against regular forces, one of their principles is to withdraw and avoid combat until such time as they can obtain sufficient power to mount an offensive and achieve success. By doing this they are able to live and fight another day while regular forces gradually are worn down and their manpower depleted.

Conclusion

Only a map study of the Western Hemisphere is necessary for one to realize that these countries possess ideal conditions and characteristics for the conduct of guerrilla warfare. The terrain, with its vastness of territories and long line of communications, the instability of some governments, and political conditions are but a few of the ideal characteristics which are found in the countries of the Western Hemisphere, and which make guerrilla warfare feasible in this area.

To be able to counter guerrilla warfare, one of the primary considerations is to recognize the danger of such warfare when used by Communists as a means to obtain their political objectives. The Communists are experts in applying the techniques and methods of guerrilla warfare as evidenced by their successes in the past.

Frequently, the Communists will align themselves with minority groups or ultranationalistic movements for the purpose of creating crises, and at the first opportunity, seize the powers of government. Guerrilla warfare is an inexpensive way to obtain objectives without resorting to a perhaps unacceptable conventional or nuclear war. For this reason it will continue to assume more importance in the future.

Therefore, to meet the problem of Communist guerrilla warfare, the first step is to acknowledge the serious threat that it poses to the security of the Western Hemisphere. Many of the guerrilla revolutions in this area have been prompted by groups of "outs" wanting "in" and have had neither popular support nor Communist direction. But, Communist inspired or exploited guerrilla operations can happen on the American Continent. The conditions which have permitted such action in other parts of the world exist also to a degree in the Americas. Stable government is characterized by high levels of education and economic stability. When public opinion is oriented to the strong support and belief in its government, then the chances for Communist guerrilla warfare are remote. A step in the right direction might be to give a higher priority to a Western Hemisphere program which would assist those countries that need economic or military help so that the reasons and causes for guerrillas do not exist.

Since the responsibility for the security of a nation generally rests with its military forces, renewed efforts should be made by them to plan and train for counterguerrilla actions, because there is no doubt that in the future the armed forces will continue to be a high-priority target of communism. Our combat arms generally are organized and equipped to fight any enemy on any type of terrain. However, to be more completely ready, units must be trained and appropriate plans developed based upon an understanding of how the guerrillas are organized, what their tactics and methods of operation are, how they can be defeated.

The answer lies in training which will teach our soldier to be better than the guerrillas in all phases, so that he is disciplined, is in superior physical condition, and is an expert in his weapons as well as in those of his enemy. He must be able to live and operate in the jungle, desert, and mountains. Combat training must include antiguerrilla operations because in the future many units of the armies in the Western Hemisphere may be fighting guerrillas. With this type of training program, soldiers with modern weapons and strong leadership can defeat the guerrilla at his own game and insure that Communists do not gain their ends of driving a wedge in the solidarity of Western Hemispheric nations.

32

Colonel Slavko N. Bjelajac   **SOVIET ACTIVITIES**
U.S. Army Reserve

IN UNDERDEVELOPED

AREAS

*The Soviets regard their friendly ties with national-bourgeois gov-
ernments pursuing a policy of neutrality as temporary. Their ultimate
goal is the assumption of power by the proletariat.*

THE SOVIETS ADMIT THE POSSIBILITY of temporary agreements and alliances with the bourgeois-liberation movement in colonial
countries. An indispensable condition for such a union is nonresistance of
the *bourgeoisie* (persons of middle rank having private property interests;
the midstrata of society opposed to the *proletariat* or working class, as
viewed by the radical Socialists) to communism.

Lenin has said:

> We as Communists must and will support bourgeois liberation movements
> in the colonial countries in those cases where these movements are
> genuinely revolutionary and their representatives do not prevent us from
> training and organizing the peasants and exploited masses in a revolution-
> ary spirit.

Stalin in a speech to the Central Committee and Central Control Commission stressed that in the colonial and dependent countries "the national
bourgeoisie may at a definite stage and for a definite period support its
country's revolutionary movement against imperialism." He regarded any
bourgeois-democratic revolution not as an end in itself, but exclusively as

From *Military Review*, February, 1961, and reprinted by permission.

a transitory stage which must inevitably be followed by the Soviet-type revolution.

The foregoing principles were prerequisite for the creation of a "united front" in the colonial and dependent countries with the goal of insuring that the Communists alone came to power. "A united front," Stalin insisted, "may be of revolutionary importance only in the event or on the condition that it does not hinder the Communist Party from carrying out its own independent political and organizational work . . . organizing the workers and peasants and thus preparing the conditions for the hegemony of the proletariat."

In the struggle for the liberation of the colonies and dependent countries from imperialism the task of the Communists is "to join the revolutionary elements of the *bourgeoisie* and peasantry against the bloc of imperialists and conciliatory elements in order to wage a genuine revolutionary struggle for liberation."

Applying this doctrine, in the Asian countries the Communists have endeavored to prevent the nationalists from coming to power and have waged a revolutionary struggle for the victory of communism. However, developments in the various Asian states outstripped the Kremlin's program. Turkey did not become Soviet. India and Burma became independent by peaceful means contrary to the Communist doctrine that rejects peaceful agreements with "colonizers."

Never abandoning the struggle to bring Communists in these countries to power, the Kremlin was anxious to draw these countries into the neutral camp in order to detach them from the West. This fact became clear after the Bandung Conference, which brought to light the role of new independent Asian states in world politics.

New Interpretation

The 20th Party Congress in 1956 gave a new interpretation of the role of national *bourgeoisie* in colonial countries. It was admitted that India, Burma, Indonesia, Egypt, and other countries had gained their sovereignty under leadership of the national *bourgeoisie,* but also established that there were differences in principle between the gaining of sovereignty under the national *bourgeoisie* and gaining of independence under the proletariat, particularly with regard to the final aims of the liberation movement.

The role of national *bourgeoisie* was admitted to be progressive, but not an end in itself. The proletariat was, as earlier, considered to be the only consistent fighter for national and social liberation. This reveals that the change in the Soviet attitude toward the national *bourgeoisie* who came to power in Asian countries was essentially tactical in nature.

Soviet political doctrine still maintains that "the leader of the national-liberation movement can only be the proletariat, the only consistently revolutionary class force of which is based on the broad masses of peasants."

The Party Central Committee magazine *Kommunist* states that:

> Bourgeois statesmen in the countries of East are . . . playing straight into the hands of the imperialists by their persecution of the Communists and by their anti-Communist outcries; and that whoever raises a hand against the Communists is in fact attacking the national-liberation movement in the East as a whole willy-nilly furthering the evil cause of colonialism and imperialism.

On further political development of countries in which the national *bourgeoisie* has come to power, the Soviet doctrine was expressed by Khrushchev at the 21st Party Congress:

> After the colonizers have been driven out, and when national tasks have been mainly solved, the peoples seek an answer to the social problems advanced.

This means that after the liberation from colonial dependence the people's struggle must continue and be directed against the national *bourgeoisie* in power which is holding up social reforms.

The statement of Khrushchev did not imply a change in Soviet policy as regards the problem of cooperation with the national *bourgeoisie;* it only demonstrated the temporary nature of such cooperation. These will play their role and go.

Soviet Cooperation

The policy of Soviet cooperation with national *bourgeoisie* of the Asian nations is the same, on a smaller scale, as the coexistence of the Communist world with the capitalist. Soviets consider them temporary phenomena. In the case of Egypt, for example, the Soviets have no intention of breaking off economic ties with the United Arab Republic because of Nasser's opposition to communism. Instead of tactics of sympathy for the national *bourgeoisie* in Egypt, the Soviets have switched to their basic and original doctrine of "the proletariat as the only class capable of achieving the final liberation of Egypt."

Expressing their political doctrine regarding African countries, the Soviet specialist in African affairs, I. I. Potekhin, writes:

> The colonial regime is replaced by the authority of the national bourgeoisie or even the local feudal lords, and then the economic dependence of a country on foreign capital is maintained for some time, even for a prolonged period.

He admits that in North African states the national *bourgeoisie* is playing the leading role in the national-liberation movement, since its interests conflict with the dominance of the foreign monopolies.

In those African countries with a predominantly Negro population, the Soviets have no intention of concluding an alliance with the national *bourgeoisie,* for these, the Soviets feel, are more likely to come to terms with colonizers and imperialists and are incapable of achieving social progress. Here, the Soviets are doing their utmost to bring to power the extreme leftwing and pro-Communist elements.

Use of Force

Potekhin says that in the African countries "the most consistent fighters for independence are the working class, for whom the gaining of complete independence opens up prospects for a further struggle for the reorganization of their native land."

Even more important for the Soviet policy is Potekhin's theoretical justification of the use of force. A resolution of the conference in Accra (December, 1958) stated that

> The conference of the peoples of Africa in Accra supports to the full all fighters for freedom, both those who use peaceful methods, resistance without the use of force and civil disobedience, and all those who are compelled to answer force with force.

The path for the transition to a Soviet-type revolution via the stages of a national and bourgeois-democratic revolution is regarded by the Kremlin as unsuitable for the colonial states of Africa. These states can jump into socialism of the Soviet type bypassing the Capitalist stage.

Based on these statements of Soviet policy and the context of their pronouncement, it may be concluded that the Kremlin's strategy and tactics are flexible and adjusted to fit their target area and situation; the Kremlin's final goal though remains the same.

The Kremlin is willing to sacrifice to a considerable degree the interests of the Arab and Asian Communists in the countries in which neutrality is important to the Soviets. On the other hand, it will support and encourage them covertly as much as it can.

While the Soviets are compelled to take into consideration the national *bourgeoisie* of India, Indonesia, Burma, the United Arab Republic, and Iraq, they do not have to pay any attention to the national *bourgeoisie* of the African countries. Here, the Communists are banking on the working class and peasantry.

Neutral States

In the states that are pursuing a policy of neutrality the Soviets will rely more on underground activities than on open acts or on critical statements which may be interpreted as hostile. Sapping the governments by

Communists within and a silent preparation of the masses for a revolution may be the main goals during the honeymoon of neutrality.

The Soviets regard their friendly ties with those national-bourgeois governments pursuing a policy of neutrality as a temporary alliance; the doctrine that the proletariat is the only consistent fighter for national and social freedom remains in force.

Soviet attitude toward national-bourgeois elements in colonial states of Africa will remain negative until these come to power or until they offer political and other support to the Soviets; a support leading toward the end of colonial rule over that country. In such states the Soviets will continue to support, with increased intensity, the extreme leftwing and pro-Communist groups opposed to national-*bourgeoisie* and colonial power. Preparation of resistance, uprisings, and revolts by the Soviets will continue in these states.

In newly emerging independent nations of Africa and Latin America, the Soviets will support the Communists and extreme leftwing elements and encourage them to use force. This is the Soviet plan supported by Communist China and the satellites. In a communique on a meeting of Communist leaders in Bucharest, it was asserted that "one must also base oneself on the possibility of the working class gaining the victory of the Socialist revolution by nonpeaceful means." Che Guevara in his book, *La Guerra de Guerrillas,* intended for the Latin American public, advocates the Soviet doctrine of use of force.

Soviet doctrine advocates that the African nations jump into Soviet-type socialism, bypassing the so-called capitalist stage. This is undoubtedly the most appealing doctrine to the uneducated and often still savage masses of Africa. Combined with the doctrine of use of force it may create a most dangerous proletarian force composed of semieducated, noneducated, and savage people capable of carrying blindly whatever may be the Kremlin's interest in the area. On the United Nations level this Soviet doctrine may result in an alliance of African nations with the Soviets and a force that may be more than embarrassing to the Western World. Khrushchev's visit to the UN may have had plenty to do with this.

Soviet political doctrine is in itself a strong and flexible weapon that requires an imaginative countering by the Free World. The implications are evident. There is little hope that the period of cold war may be over in the decade to come.

33

James Burnham

STICKS, STONES,

AND ATOMS

NOT LONG AGO, AFTER THE UNITED NATIONS patch-work expeditionary force was rushed or, perhaps better, sucked—into the Congolese maelstrom, a striking news photograph was widely printed in the American press. It showed a truckload of soldiers about to start off for the Léopoldville suburbs. The men were part of a crack, British-trained unit of the Ghana army.

As displayed in the picture, they were standing at attention in the truck, in two close smartly drawn ranks. Suspended from the left arm of each soldier was a round shield, looking as if it had been snatched from a museum's medieval armor collection or from the prop room of a grand-opera company.

A friend of mine, an able and hardworking officer now at the Pentagon, noticed this picture and smiled. "The Sir Galahad weapon system! How's that for defensive armament in the nuclear age?" he asked sarcastically.

Reprinted from *Ordnance* Magazine, January–February, 1961. Copyright 1961 by U.S. Army Ordnance Association and The Reader's Digest Association, Inc., and reproduced by permission. Another version of this article appeared in the July, 1961, issue of *The Reader's Digest* under the title "The War We're Not Prepared to Fight."

He was much surprised when I commented: "It's not too bad, as a matter of fact. Better than most."

In these Ghanaian shields, a light, strong aluminum alloy has replaced the wood, leather, brass, and iron of ancient bucklers. Their purpose is protection against the sticks, rocks, and stones thrown by rioting mobs. In the nuclear age, stones function as weapons a good deal oftener than nuclear bombs—and have won many more battles.

On both sides of the Iron Curtain many strategists believe that a curious law applies to the quantum jumps in firepower that have marked the weapons development of the past two decades. Beyond a certain limit— already passed by H-bombs—the more powerful the weapons become the less chance there is that they will be used. The reason for this is that fewer and fewer occasions would be taken to justify their use.

This is true even if one side had a monopoly. You are not going to start throwing H-bombs around to halt a border skirmish in the Cameroons or to block a change of government in Paraguay. When both sides possess the superpowerful weapons, the appropriate occasions are reduced to the brink of zero.

Indeed, many analysts are convinced that the only event that would be taken by either side as a sufficient motive for launching the most powerful weapons would be an attack with such weapons by the *other* side. If this puzzling conclusion is true, then an all-out unlimited war can take place *only* through faulty intelligence or an accidental launching.

Hurl an Invective, Not a Nike

In practice there seems to be a still more paradoxical corollary to this law of the inverse relation between the power and use of modern weapons. The more powerful the new weapons that *exist,* the more primitive the weapons that are actually *used.* Castro conquered Cuba with small arms, mimeograph machines, and portable radio transmitters.

The rioting mobs of Tokyo, Seoul, and Ankara that overturned governments and forced the cancellation of the visit of the head of the most powerful nation in the world were armed with nothing more than their fists, the staves used to raise their placards, and paving bricks, plus a few knives and revolvers. In the Congo, we have gone back to clubs, rocks, blow guns, and magical spells.

It is terribly hard for Americans to understand something so simple. In uniform and out, we have been dutifully trying to learn about grandiose "weapons systems" made up of infinitely complex aircraft, bases, carriers, nuclear devices, ballistic missiles, nuclear submarines, electronic computers, inertial navigators, and what not.

On a single system of this sort—for example, Polaris, Titan, Minuteman, or the B-52 complex—we are ready to spend five, eight, or ten billions of dollars as well as immense quantities of manpower, effort, technical ingenuity, and scientific intelligence.

It is well and good and necessary that this should be. But at the same time we seem to have difficulty in focusing our attention, not to speak of our brains and dollars, on the weapons systems by which the struggle for the world is in fact being fought.

We should more frequently remind ourselves that only two nuclear devices—crude, relatively low-power types at that—have ever been used for combat purposes. In the fifteen years since that parenthetic employment there have been many victories and defeats vast in scope and lasting in consequences. Power over many nations, whole regions of the earth, hundreds of millions of human beings, has changed hands—all without benefit of direct nuclear leverage.

Those rioting mobs of Tokyo, Seoul, and Ankara needed no A- or H-bombs, or planes or tanks or even guns to topple governments. Gandhi and Nehru had no strategic air force to help them drive the British Raj out of the Indian subcontinent.

Indonesia, Iraq, Cuba, Bolivia, Egypt, Guatemala, Vietnam, Cambodia, the Congo, the Rhodesias. . . . It is mostly sticks and stones, rifles and submachine guns—and the mobs of course: the mobs are a primary element of the weapons systems that have been deciding most battles and campaigns of the struggle for the world.

Words also, of course—the words of agitation and propaganda, zeroed in on minds—for in these battles of our age, unlike the old nursery rhyme, words as well as sticks and stones can break our bones.

From 1945 until some time after 1950 we possesed a monopoly in operative nuclear arms and thus overwhelming superiority in over-all firepower. But it is in those same years that our enemy made his greatest conquests since 1917, seizing eastern Europe, with 100 million inhabitants, and mainland China, with 600 million.

The weapons systems that he employed for these achievements were based, not on physical firepower, but on psychological and political warfare methods, both defensive and offensive.

Defensively, it was necessary for him to counteract, negate, and sterilize our nuclear capability. Communist reasoning never forgets that a weapon—any weapon—is only a powerless bundle of matter apart from human minds and wills.

Shoot at the Minds and Wills

The biggest bomb ever built or building is less than David's slingshot without a mind and will and arm able and ready to use it.

With atomic capability added to our force already in being in 1945, we were in a position, materially speaking, to enforce our views, to reduce the Soviet threat to manageable proportions, and thus to guarantee for a reasonable future both national security and world peace. This possibility conflicted with the Communist objective of world domination, so the Communists struck back, hard, brilliantly, and successfully. The main impetus of their strike was directed against the minds and wills of men.

Their agents, dupes, and ideas were already present in many strata of American life, including scientific circles, the institutions that affect public opinion, and certain of the agencies of government. They were thus in a position from the very beginning to counteract our nuclear projects and capability—from the inside as well as through external pressures and diplomacy.

The main thrust of the first Communist reply to our nuclear weapons monopoly was thus psychopolitical, against the minds of the men who were making the weapons (technicians and scientists) and the men who controlled it (the leaders of government and public opinion).

The Communist objective was to deprive the United States of the political benefit of its nuclear capability, to "denature" the bombs, not by the physical process described in the textbooks, but by political, psychological, and moral means. In this case, as more generally, the Communists acted to confuse and disorient their enemy, to entangle him in contradictory policies, and to destroy his will to resist.

Under this defensive psychic screen, which successfully counterweighed their enemy's material superiority, the Communists went ahead systematically with the phased subjugation of the east European nations. At the same time, in a theater still more vast, they carried through the conquest of mainland China and its absorption into an expanded Soviet Empire.

Although there was, of course, fighting, some of it rather large-scale, the China campaign was essentially a political-warfare operation. (I am using the term "political warfare" in its most general sense, as covering all types of agitation, propaganda, subversion, economic manipulation, rioting, terror, diversionary diplomacy, guerrilla and paramilitary actions, etc.: everything, in sum, short of the employment of the main formal armed forces.)

The Communists' polwar campaign for the conquest of China opened in 1920. It was completed in 1949 without the mass intervention of the main armed forces and with a total expenditure of probably less than half a billion dollars.

Although most professional military men, unlike their civilian counterparts, know that we are in a fight, I get the impression that very few of them can take a weapon system seriously unless it comprises a lot of firepower. They can analyze learnedly the merits of strategic manned bombers vs. submarine-carried Polaris vs. railroad-borne Minutemen.

They will thoughtfully debate the role of conventional limited-warfare forces. They can envisage, without qualms, spending ten or twenty billion dollars to develop weapons systems based on one or another or all of these concepts, together with the assignment of personnel and time and resources that go with money of that order.

But if you suggest—as I have often done in lectures at the various war colleges—spending any such sum, or a tenth such a sum, for systems based on Blanquist cadres, crowd manipulation, guerrillas, psychological warfare, paramilitary operations, subversion, bribery, infiltration, with specialized, mobile, ranger-type units in active supporting reserve—in short, if you suggest all-out political warfare (polwar)—the best response you can ordinarily hope for is a skeptical smile.

Yet it is the polwar weapons systems that have been winning all the battles. What good are Atlas and Polaris in Laos, Cuba, Algeria, the Congo, or in the swarming streets of Tokyo, Ankara, Jakarta, and Budapest?

It has been demonstrated over and again in the past fifteen years—indeed, since 1917—that modern polwar systems can smash governments and armies, and take over territory, peoples, and nations. Isn't a weapon system that can defeat the British, Dutch, and French armies, that can seize Czechoslovakia, China, and Cuba, worth spending a few billions on? The real worth of any weapon system, in the last analysis, should be measured by what it can accomplish, not by its size, complexity, cost, or physical firepower.

The Objective Is Power

Naturally I am not suggesting that a polwar system should operate in a military vacuum. B-52's, Atlas and Polaris missiles are not being used, but the fact that they might be is a solid foundation for every kind of conflict operation. And effective limited-warfare arms, present always as a threat and ready for appropriate use, naturally strengthen any sort of political-warfare campaign.

A conflict apparatus adapted to the mid-twentieth century struggle for the world consists of three primary forces, elements, or arms:

1. The massive retaliatory ("deterrent") force, which remains the ultimate reserve.

2. The mobile, limited-warfare ("brush-fire") force. This, too, remains normally in reserve but in more active posture than the retaliatory force, ready for quick intervention in any area where security or interest requires the direct presence or use of military power.

3. The political-warfare force. This force—which by its nature includes a multitude of activities and agencies, both governmental and

civilian—is the active vanguard. Under the shield of the retaliatory force, and backed up by the limited-warfare force, with which it collaborates, the polwar force continuously engages in the day-by-day operations of the protracted conflict.

True political warfare, as understood and practiced by our enemy, is not mere rivalry or competition or conflict of some vague kind. Political warfare is a form of *war*. It is strategic in nature. Its objective, like that of every other form of war, is to impose one's own will on the opponent, to destroy the opponent's will to resist. In simplest terms, it aims to *conquer* the opponent.

Within the frame of that general objective, the specific objective of each specific polwar campaign is always defined in terms of *power*. The purpose in conducting polwar operations is always to increase one's power in some definite way or to decrease the power of the opponent. In either case, positive or negative, the aim is to alter the power equilibrium in one's favor.

The power objective may be grandiose—conquest of a nation, disintegration of an empire; or the minor takeover of a trade union, scaring a parliament into defeating a bill, or the sabotage of a factory. But whether big or small, the objective is always power.

These are the principles in terms of which our enemy has planned and mounted his polwar operations since the summer of 1903 when, through the founding of the Bolshevik faction, he launched his enterprise for the conquest of the world. Moreover, although he realizes that polwar in some instances may not be able by itself to reach a decision and may have to be supplemented by full-scale military measures, he is convinced that in at least some cases political warfare alone *can* bring the decision.

By now he has ample evidence to support this belief. Czechoslovakia has been conquered twice in this century—once by Hitler and once by Stalin—by a purely polwar campaign, without the commitment of major armed forces. China also, as we have noted, was won essentially by polwar methods. By these same methods American nuclear testing has been stopped dead for more than two critical years.

Not a year passes but that these methods do not smash several governments. And right now they are swinging an island at our strategic doorstep into our enemy's power system.

Although we are in fact spending several billion dollars yearly on nonmilitary phases of the cold war, very few of these go for what can properly be called "political warfare" in the true sense—the sense accepted by our enemy. Our professional military leaders have traditionally regarded political warfare (or "psychological warfare," as it is more usually and inadequately termed), as being merely an auxiliary and relatively minor supplement to military operation.

The cold-war activities of nonmilitary agencies—"foreign aid," "truth (or information) campaigns," "student (or cultural) exchange," even much of the clandestine activity of CIA—are for the most part not true polwar operations. They are not political warfare because we do not really think of them as literally *war*.

We are trying to get the better of a competitor and opponent, certainly; to block certain of his moves, divert others, influence him to make certain changes in his behavior and policies. But we are not trying to impose our will on him in any general way, and certainly we are not trying to defeat him.

Foreign Aid Only a Key

In other words, we do not conceive our cold-war operations *strategically*. Often they have no clearly defined objective at all. When they do have an objective, this is seldom understood in terms of power.

In a genuine polwar system, foreign aid is only a key to open a national door for the conduct of field operations; information and propaganda are not a school to teach pale truths about how nice one is, but a psychological weapon to undermine, divert, and injure one's enemy; student scholarships are not a charity handout to the needy, but a cover for training activist cadres.

Because we decline to fight genuine, strategically conceived political warfare, a considerable part of our billions in foreign-aid dollars has been wasted, squandered on useless projects, filtered into the pockets of corrupt local residents, or used to build up industry for the enemy or his friends to inherit.

Let me point the contrast by returning in conclusion to the specific matter of riots and mob action, bearing in mind that this is only one of a hundred polwar fields. How many men and women (women are exceedingly important in crowd management) do we have in training today for the mission of exploiting crowds, mobs, and street riots to our political advantage? Do we have *any*?

How many persons in the agencies of our Government have ever made a thorough study of the historical, psychological, and technical problems of handling mobs and mass riots? Is there even a single one?

The Bolshevik approach to mobs, riots, and "command of the streets" is very serious indeed. In his design for the revolutionary party—the conflict apparatus—Lenin, like Bakunin and Nechaev before him, incorporated the ideas of Louis Blanqui, a French revolutionist who lived from 1805 to 1881. Blanqui first became prominent in the 1830 revolution and devoted the rest of his life, in and out of prison, to revolutionary conspiracy.

He believed that the key to successful revolt was the development of a small, secret "cadre" organization. Normally the cadres would remain underground, abstaining from political affairs. They were to be trained in the manipulation of crowds and the use of small arms and improvised weapons (sticks and stones) accessible to crowds.

In the 1848 and 1870 revolutions in France, the practical cogency of Blanqui's ideas was proved. In 1870 it was his cadres who were primarily responsible for the overthrow of the Third Empire and the establishment of the Paris Commune—the first revolutionary, proletarian-led dictatorship.

During the past two years there have been mass riots in the streets of many major cities of the non-Communist world: Caracas, Montevideo, Lima, Baghdad, Havana, Capetown, Léopoldville, Algiers, Seoul, Ankara, Tokyo, Vientiane, San Salvador, and Saigon, among others. Nearly all have been directed against political friends of the United States or against policies favorable to the United States.

Besides promoting fiercely anti-American attitudes, these riots played an essential part in the overthrow of no less than eight governments that were firm allies of the United States: in Venezuela, Iraq, Cuba, South Korea, Turkey, Tokyo, El Salvador, Laos. The governments were overthrown just as thoroughly as by outright military defeat. Unguided mobs may shake but they do not overthrow regimes. They do not spontaneously produce consistent slogans and select strategic targets.

Cinderella Politics Out

The coordinated operations of these recent riots, and their high measure of success, are the product of trained Bolshevik neo-Blanquists.

In the next year or so the Communized government of Cuba will either be overthrown, or the enemy will move on to the staged take-over of Central and South America. In the next year or so, non-Communist regimes must retain power in the Indochinese successor states, or the enemy will move on to the staged take-over of the entire Southeast Asian peninsula.

For both operations, H-bombs are useless. Is it not obvious that we are not likely to meet either of these challenges unless we decide to lift our Cinderella political-warfare system from the scullery floor where we have so far left her in rags and tatters?

34

George A. Kelly

REVOLUTIONARY

WARFARE AND

PSYCHOLOGICAL ACTION

WHILE ANGLO-SAXON OBSERVERS are unquestionably more familiar with the intricacies of the discussion that has taken place since 1954 (the year of the "massive retaliation" doctrine) regarding the prospects and conditions of nuclear war, there has been a no less spirited debate in France over the nature of a very different kind of conflict.

To qualify this type of war which has so seized the imagination of French military analysts, the comprehensive title of *la guerre révolutionnaire* has been given. It is construed as a function—perhaps the most serious one—of the "protracted conflict" described by Mao Tse-tung, and its alleged aim is nothing less than the undermining of the Capitalist camp through indirect, but, nevertheless, decisive military action. Continuing unabated for a long enough period of time, this subtle and steady revolutionary gestation could so weaken the West that any ultimate resort to nuclear war would become unnecessary.

La guerre révolutionnaire, consequently, whatever its manifestations, is

From *Military Review,* October, 1960, and reproduced by permission.

a manipulation of the policy centers of Moscow and Peking. It is itself *total* war on a *limited* scale, because it utilizes propagandistic appeal to whole populations and all economic, social, and political levers it can avail itself of. Wherever it erupts, it is one and indivisible, because the unitary aim of weakening the West is nowhere sacrificed. It is always conducted under a certain cloud of political ambiguity and generally is attached firmly to one or another nationalist or independence movement, thereby avoiding, in each instance, the provocation to general war in which the major powers might confront one another. There is little doubt in French military circles that this type of conflict exists—and exists permanently as a condition of global Marxist aggrandizement—and that it is doing irreparable damage to the position of the West and to the survival of "traditional Western values."

The only real point of dispute is the extent to which this phenomenon is actually controlled by the leaders of communism, whether they can indeed unleash *la guerre révolutionnaire* in widely scattered parts of the world at will or whether they have merely known how to attach their claims with great realism and sagacity to a broader "systemic" revolution which is basically not the prerogative of any ideology.[1] In either case, the effect is damaging and does not alter the fundamental perspective of the problem. If it is exaggerated to claim that all instances of *la guerre révolutionnaire* are directly inspired by the Soviet Union or Communist China, it is, nevertheless, clear—according to Claude Delmas, one of the best-balanced writers on the subject—that "the principles of the achievement of a national struggle of revolutionary character for the conquest of power were codified in the Marxist doctrine."

Commandant Jacques Hogard, another expert, maintains that if the long arm of the Kremlin is not evident in the first stage of a revolutionary crisis, it is bound to assert its presence in the second. The unlimited aspirations of Communist aggression are, therefore, the backdrop against which the nature of *la guerre révolutionnaire* must be understood.

Revolutionary Operations

Commentators emphasize that the Communist revolutionary conspiracy is like an iceberg, its great mass being hidden below the surface, from which isolated promontories appear to sprout. To win or lose a single battle or campaign does not in itself amount to an integral achievement; but success or failure in a series of conflicts can set in motion a trend either, respectively, toward containment of the menace or toward disordered retreat in the face of it. Seen in this light, Czechoslovakia, Indochina (Vietnam), Suez, Tunisia, Morocco, and Iraq were lost battles.

---

1. See the recent American work *Protracted Conflict,* by Robert Strausz-Hupé, *et al.,* New York, 1959, which analyzes this situation with exemplary insight.

Greece, Iran, the Philippines, Cambodia, and Malaya were, in their time, victories gained, albeit defensive ones. Algeria is seen as the critical turning point in this catalogue of revolutionary operations.

To the theorists of *la guerre révolutionnaire,* the *Front de Libération Nationale* (FLN) is equivalent to communism and the pacification of the territory is nothing less than the "defense of the Occident." Internal political problems aside, it is by this very simple standard that the characteristic attitudes of the French Army must be measured. Algeria is, above all, a war of the flank whose object is Western Europe itself, cradle of the "traditional values" on which French military writers unceasingly insist.

Jean Planchais, military correspondent for *Le Monde,* describes this attitude vividly:

> General Callies, inspector general of the armed forces in North Africa, scarcely ever moves about without a world map where he has drawn a large black arrow, which, issuing from the depths of Red Asia, pushes its point as far as the Maghreb. To him this is the best analysis of the Algerian situation.

Grand Strategy

It would be dangerous to reject the capital importance which the French have attached to the concept of *la guerre révolutionnaire,* however extreme some of the interpretations seem to be. But we must recognize some very precise psychological conditions that make this analysis highly compatible with national needs of morale and prestige. A decade and a half of nonpossession of nuclear armament in a world where its minatory power appeared omnipotent engendered in the French Army both a measure of chagrin and a requirement for formulating doctrines of grand strategy in which the emphasis would not be on the technical perfection of weapons or on statistical measurements of power.

The growing assumption of the "balance of terror" argued that as military potential approached the conceivable limits of destructiveness there was correspondingly less chance that the weapons of total cataclysm would ever be used, but rather that military activity would be carried on by less direct means. Whereas this likelihood led the nuclear powers to seek alternatives in the investigation of "limited wars" which would be essentially modifications of classical conflicts implying either the use or nonuse of nuclear arms, the French turned their attention to a much more restrictive, yet more total, phenomenon which their allies had sometimes mistakenly identified as "brush fire war" and to which furthermore they had given little concentrated study.

La guerre révolutionnaire claimed its essence from the celebrated maxim of Clausewitz and opposed itself not to total nuclear war but to total peace. For peace in the generally accepted sense and *la guerre révo-lutionnaire* could be, and demonstrably were, simultaneous and by no means exclusive. The tactics revealed by the enemy in the writings of his theoreticians (Lenin, Trotsky, Mao) and in the two colonial wars the French had fought in Indochina and Algeria enabled the planners to postulate theories for the novel kind of war they had perceived.

No Ultimate Weapon

The paradox of modern war so successfully posed by the theory of *la guerre révolutionnaire* was further abetted by French military sensi-tivities. If war was polyvalent (a favorite word of M. Bourgès-Maunoury while he held the portfolio of national defense in the Guy Mollet cabinet), then there was no ultimate weapon: both the knife and the tactical nuclear bomb might have their uses. If nuclear war was massively impersonal, the conditions of *la guerre révolutionnaire* imposed the primacy of the indi-vidual in the conduct of operations.

The resourcefulness of small units became paramount, and this fact had the tendency to restore to war some of the glamor so essential to the morale of many who engage in combat. It became a compliment to the French soldier and his military organization to proclaim this function of initiative as a specific national aptitude. Thus, as a result of the Indo-chinese and Algerian conflicts, it was alleged—again far from falsely— that the French among Western armies had the greatest experience and most adequate indoctrination for the new type of combat. As Colonel Némo wrote in the *Revue de Défense Nationale:*

> The French Army is practically the only one to have encountered com-munism in action in a vast land war of style and amplitude previously un-known. It can, therefore, open broadly the debate on the form of future war.

The doctrine of *la guerre révolutionnaire* was, it would appear, the result both of objective analysis of combat experience and of institutional self-appeasement. It would be incorrect, however, to suppose that the sub-jective arguments were of a nature to destroy the thesis as a whole. Again, it seems just to say that only the limits of the thesis are in question.

Military Conquest

La guerre révolutionnaire recognizes that military conquest of the enemy will be difficult and indeed prohibitive. If the adversary is bold enough to undertake a battle with regularly constituted fighting units and is beaten by the "forces of order," he still has the possibility of retiring to the *maquis* and reverting to continuous guerrilla activity, provided that his conviction in the war remains staunch. This was the precise case of General Giap of the Vietminh, beaten in Tonkin in 1951 in a regular engagement by the army of De Lattre. Customarily, a revolutionary army seeks a major military encounter only when it is sure of its numerical, technical, and strategic superiority in a given circumstance (for example, Dien Bien Phu). Until this time arrives the objective will be to drain the morale of the "pacification forces" through interminable raids, ambushes, skirmishes, reprisals, and a steady stream of carefully controlled propaganda.

Civilian Support

One particular condition is absolutely essential for the waging of revolutionary war: the support of the surrounding civilian masses. The revolutionary soldier must be able to disguise himself—sometimes in groups of regimental strength—among the population and reemerge when the time is ripe. He must be, as Mao Tse-tung puts it, like "the fish in water." Mao also writes that "revolutionary war is the war of the popular masses; it cannot be waged except . . . by enlisting their support." Therefore, it is to this "mass" that the counterrevolutionary army must likewise address itself: first, by the interdiction of the enemy's grasp over the indigenous population through both force and persuasion; second, by rallying the sentiments of the people to the cause of the "forces of order."

The mass, according to the most systematic theorists, is inert; it blows as the wind blows. Consequently, it becomes a question of employing a spectrum of means in the most advantageous manner if the allegiance of the mass is to be obtained. *"Cette masse est à prendre,"* declares Colonel Charles Lacheroy, former chief of the Psychological Action Service of the Ministry of Defense. *"Comment la prend-on?"* For it is elementary and undisputed in *la guerre révolutionnaire* that the first step is that of forming a base for revolutionary activity.

The axiom cuts both ways, because it is equally essential to the "forces of order" that their base of operations should be protected and a core of sympathy created among the surrounding inhabitants. With absolute military decision unavailable, the struggle becomes one for the allegiance and control of the population. This lesson has been analyzed frequently in the light of modern experience: where Ho Chi Minh succeeded brilliantly in extending his sway through the creation of popular support, Markos, the Greek Communist, failed in 1947 because of casual and ineffective methods of political indoctrination among the masses.

It becomes evident that if *la guerre révolutionnaire* is sometimes a war of terror and torture (as the experiences of Algeria have abundantly shown), it is also a conflict of persuasion, manipulation, and compulsion.

If there is nothing strikingly novel about this circumstance—for history is studded with the effects of illustrious persuasion—the scientification of the techniques employed is at least a significant innovation. This is, perhaps, the most confused and interesting aspect of *la guerre révolutionnaire,* and the one which we shall proceed to examine.

Psychological Weapons

The psychological weapon has been used in warfare since time immemorial, but never have its manipulators been so conscious of their activity as such as in this present "century of total war." The role of Communist "agitprop" and the function of the Hitlerian mass spectacles, hate campaigns, and "blood and soil" motifs are too well-known to require comment here. Today, propaganda technique and subsidiary uses of mass psychology may be at the total service of an aggressive ideology, one which either holds the formal levers of command in a nation-state or aspires to do so through subversion.

The French, more than any other Western nation, have experienced this pertinent factor in combat. The incessant psychological warfare of intense ideological character waged by the Vietminh against their own troops, the population of the country, the French Expeditionary Force, and the people of neighboring states easily convinced certain French officers that the Communist contagion could not be checked unless determined steps were taken to adopt some of these same methods in the West. The shattering experiences suffered in the prisoner of war camps of Ho Chi Minh furnished a final complement to the more indirect techniques of visual and audial propaganda.

An essential ingredient of *la guerre révolutionnaire* was the unprincipled use of psychological warfare. Increasingly, influential spokesmen in the French services, humiliated and smarting from the defeat of 1954, began to demand immediate action through improved methods of troop education and the establishment of psychological warfare services that could enable French forces to meet the revolutionary challenge on its own terms wherever it might break out in the future.

With regard to the psychological aspects of modern war, French military theorists divide the range of action into two components which they label respectively *la guerre psychologique* and *l'action psychologique.* Normally, the two terms would convey the dichotomy of "propaganda" as opposed to "information," but it is quite evident that these have become confused and that propaganda is paramount in both instances. *La guerre psychologique* comprises those elements of propaganda, psychological riposte, and demonstration which are specifically directed toward the forces of the enemy and designed to undermine his will to resist. In this sense it corresponds roughly with what the U.S. Army terms "tactical" or "strategic" operations in is Psywar doctrine.

L'action psychologique, on the other hand, embraces those efforts which either contribute to the morale and allegiance of the indigenous populations or to the fighting will of the "forces of order" themselves. This would recall a blend, in American military terms, of troop information and education and the aspect of Psywar known as "consolidation operations."[2]

It is not difficult to see that in a fluid campaign such as the Algerian, where small forces are individually engaged in combat and where the enemy fighter and the civilian, in conformity with the "fish in water" principle of *la guerre révolutionnaire,* are frequently indistinguishable, the two jurisdictions have a tendency and a temptation to overlap. Nevertheless, the distinction is clearly drawn in the significant instruction to the armed forces signed by the (then) Minister of the Armies, M. Pierre Guillaumat, on 28 July 1959, the ostensible purpose of which was to curb many of the independent and deep-rooted abuses of the psychological arm that the Algerian war and its surrounding political milieu had produced.[3]

Inasmuch as the province of *la guerre psychologique* is, at least in theory, fairly closely confined to those techniques familiar to the American military services (loudspeaker and leaflet operations, radio broadcasting operations, and special interrogation of prisoners), attention shall be devoted more exclusively to those elements comprehended in the term *l'action psychologique,* the direction of information and propaganda toward friendly or at least neutral targets.

Political Indoctrination

The origins of the pressure for a doctrine of psychological action in the French services were assuredly both theoretical and visceral. We have already spoken at some length of the theoretical in connection with *la guerre révolutionnaire.* Now we must briefly evoke the experience of Indochina on the human and emotional scale. In the compounds of the Vietminh the prisoners experienced constant political indoctrination, including compulsory study groups, lectures, and classes on Marxist texts. "Political progress" was encouraged through systems of rewards and punishments, creation of fear, doubt, and apprehension among the subjects, enforced autocriticism, and the whole battery of psychological manipulation which we collectively call "brain washing."

---

2. See Extension Course of the Psychological Warfare School, US Army, Subcourse 12, "Consolidated Propaganda Operations," June 2, 1954.

3. *Le Monde,* October 3, 1959.

This novel and debilitating process left deep scars on the returning officers. If it did not make many Communists, it did make a group of embittered professional soldiers who reserved whatever anger they could not muster for the Vietminh to the system, the politicians, and the insouciant civilian population of France in general—in short, the whole complex of democratic organization that had defended them and itself so badly against a little-understood menace. Liberal democracy stood, in a sense, condemned as ineffectual. "One will never insist enough on this point: propaganda directed from the base of a mild-mannered democracy loses nine-tenths of its chances, while on the contrary it achieves its maximum efficiency from the base of a clean, hard organization of parallel hierarchies,"[4] fumed Colonal Lacheroy, himself a former inmate of the Vietminh. Although this article does not touch upon the intense political ramifications of the *action psychologique* movement, it is appropriate to point out that variations of Lacheroy's attitude were instrumental in the unwillingness of the French services to defend the waning prerogatives of the Fourth Republic in May, 1958.

Generally speaking, the mode of thinking in 1954–56, when *l'action psychologique* was germinating, was the following: when the adversary is unscrupulous, what is fair is what works. And what works can be admired, even if the one who has delivered the hard lesson inspires nothing but hate. This was to lead a number of French officers to the detailed examination of the methods employed by the Vietminh in the Indochina War as well as to the study of a number of central Communist and psychological texts which provided both a justification and a methodology of the type of warfare they were proposing. The anguish of the Indochina defeat gave rise to serious questioning of democratic military doctrine. In a lecture given at Nice on 20 July 1957, Lacheroy exclaimed:

> In Indochina, as in China, as in Korea, as elsewhere, we observe that the strongest seems to be beaten by the weakest. Why? Because the norms we used for weighing our opposing forces, those traditional norms, are dead. We have to face up to a novel form of warfare, novel in its accomplishments and novel in its achievements.

Many of the officers who came back from Vietminh prison camps found themselves posted to the faculties of the war colleges and to the higher staffs in their quality as participants in the most recent war. Others "prepared certificates in psychology and sociology." They shared and compared experiences. A clarion article by the brilliant and dogmatic General Lionel Chassin, who had been De Lattre's air deputy in Indochina, served as a rallying point for the discontented. He wrote:

> It is time for the army to cease being the *grande muette*. The time has come for the Free World, unless it wishes to die a violent death, to apply certain

---

4. *Le Monde*, August 4, 1954. A "parallel hierarchy" denotes the omnipresent party organization in a totalitarian state, always seconding and "paralleling" the regular state administrative apparatus.

of its adversary's methods. And one of these methods—probably the most important resides in the ideological role which, behind the Iron Curtain, has been assigned to the military forces.[5]

In March and April, 1955, the review *Hommes et Mondes* furnished an operational sketch of proposals related to the Chassin criticism. Written under the collective nom de plume of "Milites," the article began with a section entitled *"L'Armée en Marge de la Nation."* Positive means for encouraging a common understanding of aims between the army and the French metropolitan population were urged. A later section called for the revitalization of the traditional values of the nation through educational reform, with a particular target being the younger citizens. The army, said the article, would be prepared to "give the citizens a 'moral armature' against an aggression which would be not only material but psychological . . . show him how to fight effectively on both the material and psychological planes."[6]

Army-Youth Committee

Partly as a result of the "Milites" study, an Army-Youth committee, established by the government in 1953, was revitalized under the presidency of General Jacques Faure. At a meeting of representatives of this group held at Chamonix in February 1956, Faure urged his young listeners to seek a "precise inventory" of national myths and to weigh "their emotional density." At the same time an ambitious troop information program was instituted at all echelons, making use of much psychological material in its presentation and particularly directed toward anti-Communist indoctrination. Thus the primary steps were taken in accordance with the doctrine of *la guerre révolutionnaire* to protect the base, *"protéger les arrières."*

In the meantime the military analysts addressed themselves to the matter of technique itself. Some of the extremists unquestionably would have preferred to see a more authoritarian line of political command proceeding from the highest government sources in Paris. This would have inhibited daily vacillations of policy and eased the task of imposing the new methods which had had such a startling fund of potency in the hands of Ho Chi Minh. Others, while endorsing the reorientation of psychological warfare to meet the needs of combating the enemy in Algeria, were more content to work within the traditional structures provided by modern democratic convention.

In any case, from 1956 on the fledgling Psychological Action Service (SAPI), which now had its own command channels and which furnished

---

5. *Revue Militaire d'Information,* October, 1954, p. 74.
6. "Enquête sur la Defense Nationale," *Hommes et Mondes,* May, 1955, p. 163.

an officer to all military staffs (*5ème bureau*), found itself—owing to the exigencies of the Algerian conflict—with considerable local license and autonomy, ample funds, and a constant ability to multiply its activities in what normally would be construed as the civilian sphere. A directive on the subject of the aims of the war by the Resident Minister for Algeria, M. Robert Lacoste, published in June, 1956, did much to regularize and legitimize the new concept of warfare which was increasingly thrown into the breach as the volume of the rebellion mounted.

Natural Laws

An intellectual substratum, sometimes misused or miscontrued, governed the French practice of psychological action, or at least was often used to justify it scientifically. It was believed—and indeed the belief is shared by many psychologists—that there were rules, almost amounting to natural laws, which could be discovered pertaining to the imposition of obedience on amorphous crowds, such as the Islamic peoples of North Africa. The works of Lenin and Trotsky were combed for all points relating to crowd behavior, and the unsystematic science behind the nefarious art of Hitler and Goebbels was studied. Other pioneer, and often native, crowd sociologists, such as Gustave Le Bon, hinted at laws and techniques that were introduced helter-skelter into the arsenal.

Probably the most influential *maître de pensée* was the Russian *émigré* psychologist Serge Tchakhotine, a disciple of Pavlov, who maintained in his book, *The Rape of Crowds by Political Propaganda,* that crowds could indeed be manipulated by clever oratory and skillful demonstrations through the induction of "conditioned reflexes." Tchakhotine, who, although himself a Marxist, had absorbed much of the Hitlerian method from residence in late-Weimar Germany, set great store in the mounting mass demonstrations, use of symbols (swastika, goose-step, and Roman salute); military music, crowd-leader dialogue, and other rhetorical and psychological tricks. More than a little of the Tchakhotinian style can be detected in some of the performances at the Algiers Forum in the days following the 13 May 1958 *coup d'état,* and directives of the psychological action services from this period clearly reveal the debt.

Although tentative efforts had been made in Indochina from 1952 on (under the auspices of a joint Franco-Vietnamese Psychological Warfare Branch headed by a Vietnamese official Nguyen Huu Long) to riposte against the Vietminh with their own methods, the first systematic use of the new techniques by a Western army was in the Algerian fighting. Three of four newly organized loudspeaker and leaflet companies (*Compagnies des Haut-Parleurs et Tracts*), formed on the American model, carried anti-FLN propaganda, entertainment, and educational material throughout the ravaged countryside in massive "consolidation operations." At the same time, the SAPI itself, through command directives and through the army's regular weekly publication *Le Bled* (which attained a circulation of 350,-000), concentrated its efforts on keeping morale and will to fight at a high pitch, counterattacking against "defeatist" propaganda from the *métropole,* and launching concerted campaigns aiming particularly at the conversion of the urban Moslem populations of the large centers.

A third, and most effective, type of *action psychologique* was performed by the SAS (*Section Administrative Spécialisée*) and SAU (*Section Administrative Urbaine*) officers, numbering more than 500, who had been given their missions in 1955 and 1957, respectively.[7] The former in the countryside, the latter in the cities, these men had no direct hierarchical connection with the *cinquièmes bureaux,* but it often happened in the smaller units that a single officer received both staff designations. The task was to work directly with the indigenous populations in the immediate zone of operations, helping to establish schools, giving sanitary and agricultural advice, distributing food, assisting resettlement, and, of course, winning native allegiances both actively and passively for *l'Algérie française.*

The terrorist campaigns of the FLN waged in 1955–56 had been extremely effective in depriving the "forces of order" of indigenous support, and it fell upon the shoulders of the SAS and SAU to deny this support to the enemy both through a variety of humane acts and the exercise of positive military control in the "spoiled" areas. A day-by-day account of these operations is furnished in the well-known *Nous Avons Pacifié Tazalt,* by Jean-Yves Alquier, a reserve lieutenant of the SAS.

Unquestionably, this experiment in civil-military relations bore much good fruit and some bad. It is, perhaps, the most extensive example of "consolidation operations" in the history of Western armies. It would, however, be mistaken to assign its entire origin to the new doctrine of *l'action psychologique,* for in many respects it resembles and conforms with the pattern of colonial relationship recommended by Marshal Lyautey, especially in his essay *"Du Rôle Colonial de l'Armée,"* written over 50 years ago.

New Techniques

Two aspects of the new doctrine which, however, owe little or nothing to French colonial tradition and have been of paramount importance in

---

7. Governor General Jacques Soustelle signed the decree creating these organisms on September 26, 1955, thereby reviving the old idea of "Arab bureaus," which dated as far back as a hundred years to the time of Marshal Bugeaud. See *Building the New Algeria—Role of the Specialized Administrative Sections,* Ambassade de France, Service de Presse et d'Information, September, 1957.

the conduct of the Algerian campaign are the techniques of relocation of populations and political reeducation. Usually, especially in the case of rural populations, the two operations are combined. It had been noticed that the relatively static role of village populations in Vietnam had worked to the advantage of the enemy. It had given him the opportunity to choose his targets like sitting ducks, unlimited means for subversion and infiltration (*pourrissement*), and a possibility of establishing his bases far to the rear of the outposts of the French Expeditionary Force.

In Cambodia, however, a mass resettlement of rural populations (about 600,000), made possible by the greater availability of arable land and the less emphatic association of the Khmers with their village community, had had the effect of snatching a malleable and easily terrorized population out of the enemy grasp, while the pacification could be pursued in earnest in the vacated territory. The enemy, no longer able to rely on levies and extortions from the intimidated villagers, was forced to fall back on his regular bases. In the meantime, the uprooted people were resettled in stockaded villages suited for autodefense, erected by military labor, and kept under close surveillance by the "forces of order." Often the facilities of the new habitations were much improved.

Because of the regular rectangular layout imposed in the reconstruction for reasons of internal security, the technique became known as *quadrillage* ("gridding"). *Quadrillage* also implied that spheres of authority in the area could be well-delineated. This produced, we may say guardedly, a measure of military control and guidance previously unexperienced in both city and country; at the same time it notably improved conditions of hygiene, diet, medication, and the general standard of living. The dislocated natives often became, in effect, wards of the army.[8]

Political Indoctrination

The program of resettling the population has been carried out at high speed in Algeria, a country topographically favorable for the operation. It is estimated that between a million and a half and two million Moslem Algerians have changed their residence under these conditions. As soon as they are regrouped in the new villages, it is current practice to grant them a liberal amount of political indoctrination according to the precepts of *l'action psychologique*. The themes of *intégration* and social evolution are steadily applied, confidence in General de Gaulle as a kind of totemistic figure is reinforced, and the lies and treachery of the FLN are exposed and condemned. What the effects of this massive undertaking will finally be is difficult to predict, but we may say that it has promoted the "pacification"

8. See Captain André Souyris, "Un Procédé Efficace de Contre-Guérilla," *Revue de Défense Nationale*, June, 1956, pp. 686–699.

of numerous sectors of the country despite the opposition of a stubborn and resourceful enemy, himself highly skilled in the practice of *la guerre révolutionnaire*.

Another undoubted success of *l'action psychologique* was the pacification of the Casbah of Algiers by Colonels Godard and Trinquier at the end of 1957 and beginning of 1958. Here, there was no question of relocating populations in an area honeycombed with FLN agents that were able to control the section through threats of terror and exemplary reprisals. Colonel Godard himself broke the enemy network by penetrating it in disguise and uncovering its operations. The *ratissage* that followed was neither lovely nor particularly humane, but the show of force had the effect of liberating the bulk of the people from the silent terror. Thereupon, the troops of the SAU proceeded to carry out the same kind of "consolidation operations" commented on elsewhere.

The events of the forum and the referendum of 1958, on the other hand, even if they do, in part, suggest the atmosphere of Tchakhotine, owe their success to much more "traditional" methods and to the personal prestige of General de Gaulle. It is appropriate also to remark that the General, himself a master of psychological action, has never taken a very kindly view of the new techniques, feeling them to be an abuse of the normal activities of the armed services. Consequently, it is not surprising that a more serious check has been placed on *l'action psychologique* in Algeria since 1958 than ever existed under the last four governments of the Fourth Republic. In the meantime, the controlled use of psychological methods for achieving military and political aims has become an approved part of French military doctrine, as has the concept of *la guerre révolutionnaire*.

Conclusions

It should be noted that these phenomena have attracted a great deal of attention in the French press, most of it unfavorable. I do not propose to judge this point. The excesses which the exponents of *l'action psychologique* on occasion permit themselves are quite obvious and need not be spelled out in an article which strives to avoid the polemical. The outstanding question apears to be this: How is it practical and morally defensible that "Western, Christian, and Mediterranean values" can be defended through recourse to the methods of the very enemy that is seeking to destroy these values? Is there a judicious balance? Where precisely can the line be drawn? Maurice Mégret, a distinguished writer on military topics, construes *l'action psychologique* as an "infantile malady of information." But perhaps the case is not quite so simple. Certain psychological warfare officers have unquestionably been carried away by the possibilities of the new role they have staked out for themselves. "Call me a Fascist if you like," said Colonel

Trinquier in an interview in 1958, "but we must make the people easy to manage; everyone's acts must be controlled."[9]

The association of certain *5éme bureau* officers with the leaders of the Algiers rebellion of January, 1960, has been widely noted, leading to the suppression of the SAPI in Algeria and to the indictment of its zonal chief. "Intoxication" is the word the political scientist Maurice Duverger uses to describe this attitude.

> What good does it do to fight in the name of a cause if one denies and destroys that which he justifies? . . . It is not a matter of replacing one "intoxication" (the Communist) with another but simply of putting an end to all intoxication.[10]

No other Western army has reached the point of crisis implicit in the French hesitation about psychological action. Perhaps this is due to the fact that our formal and political institutions are sounder and less subject to crisis. But it is also because we have not experienced the same bitter lessons, in length and intensity, of *la guerre révolutionnaire.* There may assuredly come a time when it will be necessary to fight such a war, not simply on our own territory or on that of a "modern" nation. Therefore, the French experience and its contingent problems are worth the most carefully detailed scrutiny by our qualified military experts.

9. *Le Monde,* July 10, 1958.
10. *Ibid.,* October 18–19, 1959.

35

Colonel Slavko N. Bjelajac
U.S. Army Reserve

UNCONVENTIONAL

WARFARE IN THE

NUCLEAR ERA

*M*ILITARY HISTORIANS OF THE FUTURE, looking back upon the convulsive developments of mid-century, may well characterize this as the age in which strategy was effectively dehumanized. The massive revolution wrought by nuclear weapons seems to have overwhelmed the thinking of strategists and statesmen alike, scattering in its wake all traditional concepts of international behavior. We stand as if transfixed before the awesomeness of the secrets which modern society has unlocked. We speak no longer of "victory" or "defeat," but of "survival"—and we compute "survival" in the time parameter of the countdown, and in the mathematical values of megatonnage launched and "acceptable damage" sustained.

No one can question seriously the fact that the nuclear weapon has become the prime mover of conflict techniques. Back of every event in international life today looms the terrifying specter of the mushroom cloud. Nuclear weapons may indeed become the final arbiters of conflict. Our military leaders have given us ample warning that the "balance of terror" is not a stable balance; that deterrence may fail; and that nuclear war may

From *Orbis,* Fall, 1960. Copyright 1960 by the Foreign Policy Research Institute, University of Pennsylvania, and reproduced by permission.

become quite "thinkable" to the leaders of the Kremlin—especially if Western weakness tempts them into taking this short-cut to global power.

The failure by the West to keep its strategic deterrent intact would be disastrous. It would be equally disastrous, however, if we permit ourselves to be blinded by the power of the new destructive forces and fall prey to the mechanistic assumption that "weapons mean everything." Our opponents do not subscribe to such a theory. Mao Tse-tung, who now must be ranked with the great classical strategists, has made the following observation: "We see not only weapons, but also the power of man. Weapons are an important factor in war but not the decisive one; it is man and not material that counts."[1]

The handwriting on the wall is clear. During the past year, there has been a profound shift in communist tactics vis-à-vis the West and its allies. The abortive summit meeting in Paris in June, 1960, seemed to herald the end of the Kremlin's emphasis upon the "soft sell" as a divisive wedge against the Free World's alliance system and the beginning of a violent campaign of missile threats from without, and riots, demonstrations and parliamentary obstructionism against elected governments from within. Under the umbrella of their newly acquired nuclear-missile power, the communists with renewed confidence and vigor are waging a form of combat in which they have excelled ever since the take-over of power in Moscow in 1917—unconventional warfare. Unless the West moves swiftly and purposefully to meet its opponents on this vast and shifting battleground, neither its massive nuclear stockpiles nor delivery systems may save it from final defeat in the protracted conflict.

I

Because it encompasses that broad and shadowy no man's land between formal peace and formal war, unconventional warfare defies satisfactory definition. Broadly considered, it is that diversity of actions and measures which a people can bring to bear against an enemy (either an invader or an oppressive government) short of confronting him formally on the battlefield. Unconventional warfare may consist of violent actions like guerrilla attacks, civil insurrections, mass riots, sabotage or terrorism —or of such "non-violent" techniques as propaganda, infiltration, strikes, boycotts and espionage. Indeed, its distinctive characteristic is that of blending violence and non-violence into a new synthesis of warfare. Paul M. A. Linebarger's description of one of its components, psychological warfare, applies to unconventional warfare as a whole:

---

1. Mao Tse-tung, *On the Protracted War* (Foreign Language Press, 1954), p. 54.

It is not controlled by the laws, usages, and customs of war; and it cannot be defined in terms of terrain, order of battle, or named engagements. It is a continuous process. Success or failure is often known only months or years after the execution of the operation. Yet success, though incalculable, can be overwhelming; and failure, though undetectable, can be mortal.[2]

There is nothing intrinsically novel about unconventional warfare as a method of conflict. The history of warfare teems with attempts by opposing armies to infiltrate each other's ranks, strike at the sources of the other's political and economic strength, and weaken each other's morale. As a consciously chosen vehicle of conflict, however, unconventional warfare did not come into its own until the advent of modern mass society. It did so for two principal reasons. First of all, the modern industrial and scientific revolution completely recast traditional concepts of warfare. In the past, victory or defeat hinged upon the outcome of isolated battles waged by small professional armies. The *levée en masse* instituted by the French revolutionary government in 1790 was the harbinger of an era in which warfare was no longer the purview of a handful of experts hunched over the chessboard of strategy, but drew instead upon the physical, moral and psychological resources of entire nations. The objective of war remained the same—namely, to shatter the opponent's will to resist. But whereas in the past the only target of this strategy was the soldier on the battlefield, in the new massive conflicts of the twentieth century this objective was broadened to encompass whole populations. Unconventional warfare provided the means whereby blows could be launched above the heads of contending armies at the sources of national power, to determine the outcome of battle long before it was registered by the tides of armed conflict in the field.

The second reason for the importance of unconventional warfare in modern conflict is its role as the ready-made instrument of insurrection and revolution. Basic to the communists' proficiency in this arena of conflict is the fact that, without specifically using the term, they have practiced unconventional warfare ever since the turn of the century—first against the Czarist regime in Russia, and then, after their accession to power, against the world at large. In the turbulent decades preceding World War I, bands of revolutionaries in Russia staged bank robberies, practiced terror on policemen, soldiers and officials, and conducted looting and pillaging forays in the countryside. Originally, the Russian Social Democrats had rejected terrorism, which was a major *modus operandi* of a rival group, the Social Revolutionaries. During 1905 and 1906, however, the incidence of terror increased greatly and the Bolshevik faction of the Social Democratic Party supported it wholeheartedly. Lenin early recognized the utility of this type of conflict, and defended its "Marxist" character in the following passage of his treatise on "Partisan Warfare":

2. Paul M. A. Linebarger, *Psychological Warfare* (Washington, 1948), p. 1.

What are the basic questions every Marxist must ask when he analyzes the problem of the types of struggle? First of all, unlike primitive forms of socialism, Marxism does not tie the movement to any particular combat method. It recognizes the possibility that struggle may assume the most variegated forms. For that matter, Marxism does not "invent" those forms of struggle. It merely organizes the tactics of strife and renders them suitable for general use. It also renders the revolutionary classes conscious of the forms of the clashes which emerge spontaneously from the activities of the movement. Marxism rejects all abstract thinking and doctrinaire prescriptions about types of struggle. It calls for a careful study of the *mass struggle* which actually is taking place. As the movement develops, as the consciousness of the masses grows, and as the economic and political crises are becoming more intense, ever new and different methods of defense and attack will be used in the conflict. Hence, Marxism never will reject any particular combat method, let alone reject it forever. Marxism does not limit itself to those types of struggle which, at a given moment, are both practical and traditional. It holds that, due to changes in social conditions, new forms of battle will rise *inevitably,* although no one can foresee what the character of these future encounters will be. . . . We know, as Kautsky stated when he was analyzing the different forms of social revolution, that the coming crisis will present us with new and unpredictable forms of action.[3]

It is through these "new forms of action"—terrorism, infiltration, subversion, propaganda and sabotage—that the Bolshevik minority swept to power in Russia. And it is through the same methods that the communist leaders tried to fan revolution throughout the rest of the globe. Until World War II, this campaign was launched from a position of relative weakness. Today it is being waged under the growing shadow of Soviet power.

Yet it is one of the ironies of history that the oppressed becomes the oppressor, and, in so doing, finds himself combatted by his own weapons. Nothing is more obvious than the fact that the Soviets, despite frenzied efforts, have not been able to resolve that painful dilemma posed by numerous insurrections within the Soviet Union since World War I and, more recently and dramatically, by the East German rising of 1953 and the bloody riots in Poznan and the Hungarian revolution of 1956. Nikita Khrushchev's description of West Berlin as a "cancer" in communist society attests to the abiding extent of resistance within the communist empire. The West has failed to exploit this dilemma partly because of the fear that, by so doing, it might trigger general war. Even more basic to this failure, however, is the West's lack of understanding of the full potential of unconventional warfare in the current struggle.

We have ignored this potential despite the objective lessons of World War II. True, most military historians are agreed that the unconventional warfare operations against Germany were poorly organized, haphazard and

---

3. V. I. Lenin, "Partisan Warfare" (translated from Volume X of the Third Edition of *Sochineniya* by Regina Eldor). [See also Chapter 6 of this volume.]

desultory. The emphasis was placed on guerrilla warfare to the neglect of other useful methods of internal resistance to the Germans. In almost all instances, Allied missions were hastily improvised and uncoordinated with the over-all operations. The concepts guiding such missions were narrow, unscientific and, in some instances, pernicious to the over-all effort. Unconventional forces deep in enemy territory were not mobilized by the Allied nations in any commonly understood sense of the term; sponsorship was generally of an agent-liaison type, which was generally distrusted by local resistance groups. There was little of that spirit of reciprocity which must guide any successful alliance effort against a common enemy.

It is significant to note, however, that despite these glaring shortcomings, unconventional warfare operations during World War II reaped a substantial strategic harvest. Former German Major General A. Ratcliffe, for one, believes that one factor which caused the collapse of the German fronts in Russia in 1944 was the inability of the German commands to cope with the Russian partisans. Elsewhere, Yugoslav guerrillas immobilized 35 German and Italian divisions. In a letter to the Allied Chiefs of Staff, Prime Minister Winston Churchill stated that "the guerrilla forces in Yugoslavia and Albania are containing as many (German) divisions as are the British and American armies put together."[4] General Eisenhower has acknowledged publicly the contribution made by resistance activities in Nazi-occupied territory to the Allied victory.

The lessons of the past and the opportunities of the future can be summarized in the following propositions: unconventional warfare is a vital segment of the total spectrum of conflict in the mid-twentieth century. We must take up this weapon if only to parry the thrusts of our opponent. Beyond that, however, unconventional warfare can play a decisive role in winning the Cold War, in deterring Soviet aggression, or, should deterrence fail, in bringing a hot war to a victory which would not be steeped in the ruins of nuclear devastation.

II

In order to understand more clearly the role of unconventional warfare in the total spectrum of conflict, it may be useful to review briefly the main trends in the current strategic efforts of the West.

Despite changes in official nomenclature, Western strategy continues to hew to the general guidelines of the doctrine of "massive retaliation" enunciated by John Foster Dulles in 1954. The shortcomings of this strategy have been described amply by a growing host of critics. Dean G. Acheson, for one, has observed:

---

4. Winston Churchill, *Closing the Ring* (Boston: Houghton Mifflin, 1951), p. 330.

It [the doctrine of "massive retaliation"] was a sensible theory, which contained but one flaw: it could not, and did not, last. As military men in our government had pointed out for a long time, nations of comparable power and techniques will, given equality of will, eventually achieve equality of power. . . . We waited until the Soviet Union possessed nuclear weapons and then announced the doctrine of complete reliance on them. This decision was the triumph not of intelligence, not of any military group . . . but of the Treasury Department, which does not always represent the highest form of human thought.[5]

Mr. Acheson's indictment may be a bit harsh. We can give the architects of "massive retaliation" the benefit of the doubt and assume that they did not expect their strategy to last. Massive retaliation was obviously designed as a short-term stratagem to redress quickly the imbalance between the conventional forces commanded by NATO and the Warsaw Pact countries in Europe, and as a purchase of time which would be used by the West to develop other weapons systems and strategies within the framework of a modernized and improved conventional military establishment.

If this was the intent, it has not been realized. True, there has been some modernization of NATO forces in Europe and of the Strategic Army Corps capable of rapid deployment to trouble spots throughout the globe. But the preponderance of communist conventional might has not been reduced to any significant extent.

The West, in short, continues to be committed to a strategy which places primary reliance upon strategic nuclear retaliation. Yet, the efficacy of such a strategy can be questioned on two decisive counts: (1) the *willingness* of the West to retaliate massively against every Soviet aggressive action, and (2) the *ability* of the West to carry out such a strategy in the rapidly changing nuclear equation.

The strategy of massive retaliation against any act of Sino-Soviet aggression is based upon the concept of the "first nuclear strike." It assumes that a communist thrust, with almost automatic certainty, would activate the West's strategic air and missile power. But is this assumption a plausible one? Is the idea of a "first strike" compatible with the very ethos of democratic pluralistic society? Conceivably, the West might take recourse to such drastic action if the provocation were sufficiently clear and severe. But, in the light of the communists' time-honored tactics of the indirect approach and the ambiguous maneuver, it is doubtful that the Soviet Union would ever present the West with such a clear-cut challenge.

The problem is compounded by the unhappy fact that the Soviet Union may soon have the means to rain massive distruction not only upon the allies and forward bases of the United States, but upon our own popula-

5. Dean G. Acheson, "The Premises of American Policy," *American Strategy for the Nuclear Age,* edited by Walter F. Hahn and John C. Neff (New York: Doubleday Anchor, 1960), p. 416.

tion centers. Under these circumstances, it may well be asked whether the United States would resort to its nuclear arsenal even in the case of an extreme provocation.

It is in the logic of the nuclear equation that a "first strike" strategy must be a "counter-force" strategy. The objective must be to cripple the enemy's offensive power to the extent that he will not be able to launch a large-scale riposte against American population centers. Two essential requirements of such a strategy are: (1) the quantitative availability of offensive weapons to destroy the enemy's installations, and (2) the intelligence through which enemy targets can be pin-pointed exactly and their destruction verified. It is doubtful that Western strategy, here and now, can meet these two conditions.

The Soviets, in short, appear to have the advantage of nuclear surprise attack. They clearly have recognized this advantage. Marshal Rostemisterov, in an article, "On the Role of Surprise in Contemporary War,"[6] made the following observation:

> It must be plainly said that in situations of employment of atomic and hydrogen weapons, surprise is one of the decisive conditions for the attainment of success not only in battles and operations but also in the war as a whole. The Soviet Union must be ready to strike a pre-emptive or forestalling blow in case the United States was about to attack.

Rostemisterov's position has since been restated by a growing number of Soviet military figures. Indeed, the concept of the "pre-emptive strike" seems to have become an integral part of Soviet military doctrine.

Under these circumstances, NATO strategy in Europe is impaled on the horns of a grim dilemma. As before, the armies of the United States and its allies in Central Europe confront superior communist forces. But now America's nuclear preponderance, which presumably placed a tight rein upon Soviet aggressive designs, has been compromised drastically. The next decade, therefore, is likely to witness a rapid acceleration of the Soviet's politico-military offensive in Europe. By mounting such challenges as the current threat to Western rights in Berlin, the Soviet leadership will seek increasingly to exacerbate the West's growing predicament—the choice between limited defeat and all-out nuclear conflict.

The West has sought to ease this predicament by arming its NATO contingents with tactical nuclear weapons. Yet, while these weapons have enhanced considerably the strength of the NATO forward shield, their utility is limited by three principal shortcomings. First, the deterrent value of tactical nuclear arms is compromised by the fact the the Soviet armies in Eastern and Central Europe, too, are armed with atomic weapons. Tactical nuclear arms may favor the defense to some extent. Their very existence in NATO hands could prevent the Soviets from massing their

---

6. *Vovinnaya Mysl'*, February, 1955.

troops for a concerted onslaught against Western Europe, thus precluding the lightning sweep to the English Channel which has haunted Western strategists since the end of World War II. But there is no reason to assume that in an extended engagement a big atomic army will not be superior to a small atomic force. Thus, it is questionable that tactical nuclear weapons alone would deter potential aggression in Europe.

Secondly, there is a distinct danger that a conflict waged with tactical nuclear weapons would quickly "spiral" into all-out nuclear conflict. The concept of a limited atomic war is based on the assumption that the contestants will adhere voluntarily to certain "ground rules" governing the nuclear firepower delivered and limiting the territorial extent of the battle. It is highly unlikely, to say the least, that such a "gentlemen's agreement" would be concluded by the combatants, or, even should it be adopted, that it will be observed in the mounting heat of battle.

Finally, there is the problem of the destructiveness of these weapons. A limited nuclear war in Europe would in all probability be waged, at least initially, on non-Soviet soil and in densely populated areas in which a separation of civilian and military targets would be well nigh impossible. For our NATO allies, contemplating their gutted territories, such a war would not be "limited" by any definition. And the destruction wrought beyond the Iron Curtain would take its toll in the lives not only of Soviet military personnel but of those millions of "invisible allies" who look to liberation, not nuclear cremation.

It is not inconceivable that the Soviets, recognizing the inhibitions which weigh heavily upon Western strategy, may be tempted to launch a conventional attack upon Western Europe with the declaration that they will not use nuclear weapons unless the West takes recourse to them. The West would then be confronted with the agonizing choice of engaging in an unequal contest with superior communist conventional forces or of accepting the onus of initiating nuclear war.

To summarize: a strategy of excessive reliance on nuclear weapons may maneuver the West into a dangerous quandary. We are approaching the time when deterrence may fail, when we may contemplate with increasing helplessness an accelerating series of new challenges. Requisite to our needs is a balanced strategy designed not only to deter war but, should aggression strike, to carry the struggle to victory. Unconventional warfare must form an integral part of such a strategy.

III

The West's excessive preoccupation with revolutionary weaponry is not a new phenomenon. It is perhaps one of the hallmarks of Western society that, basically antipathetic toward conflict and the sacrifices that it entails, it tends to put its trust in "gimmick" solutions which beckon as the easiest and cheapest road to security. Such solutions not only tend to be illusory, but they induce a climate of false optimism which suffocates purposeful national effort. Thus France, ensconced behind the Maginot Line during the gathering storm of the 1930's, experienced that attrition of will which marked her for defeat long before the German armored columns swept through the Ardennes Forest in May 1940.

Indeed, a strange paradox pervades Western concepts of peace and war. The individual, who occupies the highest place in the West's hierarchy of values, is singularly overlooked in the West's strategic computations. Even today, we tend to measure the power relationship between the West and the Soviet Union exclusively in terms of a cold balance sheet of physical assets—bomb against bomb, missile against missile, division against division, aircraft against aircraft and gun against gun. In the process, we tend to lose sight of the human factor in the strategic equation; we forget that the shiny facade of Soviet offensive power masks the discontent of millions of oppressed peoples.

Modern man under arms is and will remain nothing more than a part of the population of a country, and he will reflect the feelings of that population. He will fight for a cause with conviction, with reluctance, or not at all. He will fire a weapon or abandon it. If we have failed fully to grasp this fact, the Soviets have recognized it clearly. As one Soviet source has stated:

> The morale of the fighting front and the home front is of primordial importance to the Soviets, since an army in war gains full strength in mobilization. Among permanent operating factors which determine victory or defeat in a war, the most basic are the stability of the rear and the morale of the army. The nuclear era is not going to challenge the value of these operating factors; on the contrary, it should only be expected that these may grow in their importance.[7]

Since World War I, numerous revolts have challenged the rule of the Kremlin. Moscow needs no reminder of the fact that a total of two-and-a-half million Russian soldiers surrendered to the Germans within the first three months of World War II; nor that millions of Soviet subjects welcomed the German invaders as liberators. The East German youths who challenged Soviet tanks with stones in 1953, and the Hungarian Freedom Fighters who in 1956 pitted themselves against the might of the Red Army not only confirmed an obvious historical truth—that oppressed man, if sufficiently provoked, will challenge overwhelming odds to battle for freedom—but they also gave clear testimony of the explosiveness of the powder keg on which Soviet policy continues to be perched. Had the Hungarian rising, with outside assistance, flamed into other satellite countries—into

---

7. *Ibid.*

East Germany, Czechoslovakia, Bulgaria, Rumania, and Poland—the Soviets whould have been confronted with an insoluble problem.

One of the reasons the West has failed to exploit this latent force within the Soviet orbit has been the facile notion that the massive police apparatus which the Soviets keep in being throughout their empire can crush any rebellious movement before it gains dangerous momentum. This contention overlooks the fact that police forces, too, are composed of humans swayed by human emotions. We can assume that some of the men who patrol the communist empire are dedicated communists willing to stake all for the "revolutionary cause" and the survival of their regimes. We can assume with equal certainty, however, that the behavior of the great majority of them will be determined largely by the tides of events. Again, the lesson of Hungary is clear. During the turbulent October days before the Soviets rushed in reinforcements to crush the rebellion, Red Army soldiers defected to the rebels, satellite forces tore the Red Star from their uniforms and substituted the white band of the Freedom Fighters, and communist officials joined the insurgents.

There is no question that the memory of Hungary continues to haunt Soviet policy-makers. If the people of a country, armed only with make-shift weapons and grim determination, can effectively challenge communist power in peacetime, how much more powerful could a well-organized and well-armed rebellion be in time of war? Any Soviet plan of aggression, therefore, must take into account the prospect of debilitating rear-guard action, the breakdown of local authority—indeed, the potential crumbling of the entire communist empire.

IV

The above analysis yields the following conclusions:

1. Now that the Soviets are rapidly achieving the capability to inflict a high level of nuclear damage upon the continental United States, nuclear weapons alone may not be sufficient to deter all kinds of war. We must seek out additional deterrents in order to meet the full range of communist challenges. Unconventional warfare is one of these deterrents.

2. The use of nuclear weapons in a limited engagement runs the risk of triggering all-out nuclear war. The West, in order to create a deterrent which would be credible both to the Soviet Union and to its allies on both sides of the Iron Curtain, must have the capability, at least at the outset of a limited engagement, to fight with non-nuclear means. Unconventional warfare can play a significant role in such a defensive strategy. Indeed, unconventional warfare, in the sense of bringing the attitudes of the op-

pressed people behind the Iron Curtain to bear upon Soviet decision-making, may force the Soviets to forego the use of nuclear weapons.

3. A strategy of excessive reliance on nuclear weapons may increasingly and dangerously weaken the prestige of the West among the nations of Eastern Europe. Instead of promising them liberation, it extends to them only the nightmare of nuclear extinction. A Western strategy which embraces the contingency of conventional combat, supported by irregular warfare operations behind enemy lines, would be more compatible with the feelings and aspirations of the discontented masses behind the Iron Curtain.

4. Success or failure in any protracted military engagement depends upon the active support of populations in the entire theater of conflict. There is no doubt that powerful communist fifth columns in some Western countries could be activated by the Soviets in time of war. But these forces, both in terms of numbers and fighting morale, could not come close to matching the resistance potential which the Western powers could mobilize behind the Iron Curtain.

5. The military commitments of the United States, already vast, may burgeon significantly in the future. Massive sea and airlift operations will be required to meet conflict situations throughout the globe. In the light of logistic problems, as well as increased Soviet interception capabilities, considerable time may elapse before the United States can bring effective "staying power" into a given conflict area. Regardless of such factors as U.S. superiority in the quantity and quality of material, time will play the most crucial role in the strategy of the United States.

Unconventional forces would compensate for the lack of effective Western strength on the spot. Such forces, in conjunction with local troops supplied under the military assistance program of the United States, could brake a communist thrust pending the arrival of more firepower from the United States and allied bases. Unconventional forces could seriously disrupt, also, the enemy's supply lines and prevent the Soviets from moving up reinforcements to the battle zone from other areas in the Sino-Soviet empire.

6. The war-making power of the enemy is being dispersed and moved deeper into rear areas. Missiles with greater range are being developed, and launching sites located in the most remote corners of the Sino-Soviet empire. Unconventional forces not only can procure vital information on the sites from which destructive blows may be launched, but harass and sabotage these installations.

7. It is highly likely that insurrections will erupt in the communist orbit on D-Day, or possibly even before the outbreak of a conflict, if a period of prolonged tension or obvious Soviet preparations for a nuclear war will provoke the captive peoples into taking desperate steps to head off disaster. Given the fact that these rebellions may flare whether or not

the Western powers instigate or support them, it is up to the West to cast plans for exploiting the powerful forces of resistance in the satellite empire and harnessing them effectively to the Western war effort.

8. Whether a future war is fought with or without the use of nuclear weapons, the forces of the United States and its allies will be confronted with enemy ground forces greatly superior in number. Unconventional warfare forces can compensate for this inferiority by preventing enemy supplies from reaching the front and tying down enemy forces.

In the area between the Baltic and Black Seas alone live some 110 million people whose discontent with communist rule is a matter of record. If only one per cent of this population mass were willing actively to oppose the communists, an army of more than a million fighters could be organized to fight the Soviets within the confines of their own empire. By virtue of their location astride the logistic lines between the Soviet Union and the potential battle front in Central Europe, they could play a vital role in the defense strategy of NATO.

9. Unconventional warfare units could operate effectively behind enemy lines in the confusion following a nuclear exchange. They could provide, also, the cadres for military governments in occupied areas pending the conclusion of the war and in the chaotic aftermath of a nuclear conflict.

10. Unconventional warfare is a relatively inexpensive weapon. In fact, the weapon already exists; it needs only to be taken up and wielded with knowledge, imagination and purposiveness. At the cost of several hydrogen bombs, for example, the United States could increase her unconventional warfare capability to a significant degree. There already exist within the Departments of Defense and of the Army organizations dealing with the problems of unconventional and special warfare. The special forces groups and psychological warfare units organized by the Army should be greatly increased, both quantitatively and qualitatively, in order to prepare them for situations likely to arise in the countries of the Soviet orbit in the event of a future war. They should be coordinated intimately within the framework of our national defense strategy and that of our allies.[8]

11. The West, if it purposefully takes up the weapons of unconventional warfare and integrates them fully into the arsenal of the Free World, will find it less difficult to convince the Soviets that it can prevent them from starting a war or from obtaining even a limited objective. The leaders of the Soviet Union should be told openly that all means and forces, conventional as well as unconventional, will be put to use in order to prevent the further physical expansion of communism.

12. Peacetime planning for unconventional warfare in the West must

8. For further information on the U.S. Army's special warfare planning, see Colonel William H. Kinard, Jr., "This Is Special Warfare, U.S. Army Style," *Army Information Digest* (June, 1960), pp. 2–11.

include not only the alerting of the nations of the Free World to the potential of this weapon, but more importantly the preparation of the nations within the Sino-Soviet orbit. The first step would be to let the peoples of the Sino-Soviet empire know, by an extensive radio campaign, that the United States and its allies have no intention of provoking a war. This must be made crystal-clear and convincing to the target audience. Second, the West must convey to them that, if a war is started by their government, the United States and its allies will be forced to retaliate. The probable results of nuclear retaliation must be made vividly clear to them. Third, the captive peoples must be told that, in order to avoid a war and nuclear devastation, they must act so as to prevent their governments from initiating a conflict. This appeal should be directed to the civilian populations as well as to the military. Fourth, the captive peoples should be promised help in the event of a conflict. We should announce that material assistance will be given to resistance movements by the United States and her allies where necessary and practicable. The United States' special forces and psychological warfare units, trained for this purpose, will join resistance movements in the objective of bringing the war to a quick end and establishing a government acceptable to the indigenous population.

Unconventional warfare is not advanced as a panacea for the manifold problems besetting Western strategy in the nuclear age. In terms of the structure of Western defense, it can serve, at best, as a supplementary weapon: as a means of conducting offensive operations against the enemy deep in his territory, or, in the event of an enemy take-over of an area of the Free World, as a method of denying him the fruits of victory. Yet, as such, it can play an immensely vital role. Unconventional forces, if considered as an integral part of the Western defense scheme, could do much to redress the imbalance of military power in Europe and elsewhere. Indeed, if exploited to the fullest extent, they could serve as one of the most powerful deterrents to communist aggression.

36

Roger Hilsman

INTERNAL WAR:

THE NEW

COMMUNIST TACTIC

*T*HE COLD WAR WITH COMMUNIST RUSSIA has been with us for sixteen years. And each year the Communist tactics are more subtle and complex. In the 1940's, it was simple: the Soviet policy of expansion and the American policy of containment. The threat of direct Communist aggression remains, but new, more sophisticated tactics are added every year.

To most Americans, the basic danger over the past decade has been the threat of all-out thermonuclear war. The threat remains. It does and should demand our careful, constant attention.

Next there has been the threat of "limited war"—old-fashioned, foot-slogging fighting on the ground—with artillery, machine guns, and grenades. This is the dirty, bitter business of direct, personal killing, as we knew it in Korea.

Limited wars and total war are closely linked. A limited war can be the escalator carrying the world right up to the mushroom clouds.

But even as we have pondered this connection—and have tried to

Release by the U.S. Department of State, August 10, 1961. Reproduced by permission.

prepare for both eventualities—the Communists have found what they regard as a new chink in our armor. The new tactic is internal war—using military force not across national boundaries, but inside them.

This newest concept is guerrilla war—or, to use a more accurate term, *internal* war.

It was this that President Kennedy had in mind in his speech to the nation July 27 when he said:

> . . . We face a challenge in Berlin, but there is also a challenge in Southeast Asia, where the borders are less guarded, the enemy harder to find, and the dangers of Communism less apparent to those who have so little. We face a challenge in our own hemisphere.

Thus, even while reheating the Berlin crisis, Khrushchev has stressed this third approach of internal war over and over again this past year. He sees the possibilities for internal wars in Asia, Africa, and Latin America as the best way of using force to expand the Communist empire with the least risk. He argues that nuclear war is too disastrous even for Leninists. Apparently he has begun to have his doubts about even limited war on the Korean model.

We can take some credit for Khrushchev's change of heart. Our strategic force to deter nuclear war has paid its way. Our efforts to build ground forces, our alliances, and our sacrifices in Korea—the fact that we stood and fought—have all paid off.

In retrospect we can be proud of all this, though our pride should not lead to overconfidence. Moreover, we must beware of thinking that these different tactics were separate or unrelated.

Even in the early stages of the Cold War, the Soviets manipulated internal wars in Southeast Asia, Indonesia, the Philippines, India, and Guatemala and in vulnerable states in the Middle East. The Soviet leaders, bred as they were in an atmosphere of urban-based intrigue and revolutionary plotting, were pushed further in their thinking by the success of Mao Tse-tung's peasant-based Chinese Communist revolution.

New Developments

The result is that recently internal warfare has gained a new prominence in Soviet dogma. What Khrushchev calls "wars of liberation" or "just wars" are now considered the most promising paths to further expansion. The theory enables Moscow and Peiping to manipulate for their own purposes the political, economic, and social revolutionary fervor that is now sweeping much of the underdeveloped world. Since many governments are weak, since some are corrupt, since there is much injustice in the world, and since the Communist conspirators are well trained and supplied, it is usually fairly easy to start or take advantage of an internal war and to claim that years of blood and terror are in the people's interest.

Even when a government tries to undertake reform and keep the peace—as in Venezuela or Colombia—the Communists chant that the government is "repressive" and redouble their efforts.

A second development is the flexibility and sophistication in tactics of guerrilla terror and subversion. The Soviets continue to sponsor Communist rebellions overtly wherever possible. They also do their best to infiltrate nationalist movements against colonialism. They try especially hard to capture the extreme nationalists like Lumumba. They sponsor radical nationalism wherever they can find it, for the more violence there is in a country, the greater the Communists' opportunity.

If a democratic nationalist government is in power, Communists will advise that it separate itself from the West and permit the Communists to have "equal democratic rights"—that is, positions of power in the government, freedom to propagandize, and the right to officer regular forces or their own militia.

If a colonial or reactionary government is in power, the Communists direct efforts along the entire spectrum of subversion. They foster discontent in the cities, leading to demonstrations and strikes, perhaps to riots and mob action. Here their targets are student groups, labor unions, and left-wing intellectuals. In the countryside, they establish guerrilla forces in inaccessible regions, move to peasant areas, and, through a judicious mixture—on the Chinese Communist and Castro Cuban patterns—of social reform, administration, and sheer terror, establish a base of political rule. Whenever possible, in both urban and rural sectors, they endeavor to create "people's militias" as a device for organizing mass support to supplement their full-time combatants. Thus, they operate continuously to undermine an unfriendly government and differ in their handling of popular nationalist regimes only in the degree of their effort to influence the government directly and infiltrate its power centers.

Let me repeat that this new Soviet emphasis on internal war does not mean that we can forget about the other, greater levels of war. Moscow's willingness to raise the Berlin issue indicates that their so-called "peaceful coexistence" does not rule out manufactured crises that run the risk of conventional or even nuclear war. In fact, they could not get away with internal war, except for the inhibitions imposed by these other two possibilities.

The great advantage of internal war is that it is less risky and less conspicuous than the more violent wars. It also involves techniques that the Communists feel they have mastered and we have not. We must also remember that Khrushchev is using his recently increased capacity to wage the more violent kinds of war to expand his freedom of maneuver in guerrilla war and to threaten escalation if we try to stop him.

In short, the so-called nuclear stalemate has not served to inhibit violence. If anything, it has enabled the Communists to resort to a wider variety of force. Their new strength in nuclear weapons makes them all the more tempted to adventure with internal war.

How can we help stop the Communists from destroying independent states from within? At President Kennedy's direction—as outlined in his second "State of the Union" message—steps have been taken in several parts of the government to meet this threat. The people in the Pentagon and we in the State Department have devoted special attention to it.

Let me take up the question of how we stop the Communists from destroying independent states from within under three headings: military security, modernization and reform, and political factors, especially those unique political factors undercutting a regime's stability.

Here we must be very hard-headed, for there are several all-too-popular misconceptions.

Military Security

In my judgment, it is nonsense to think that regular forces trained for conventional war can handle jungle guerrillas adequately. Yet in spite of some very hard lessons—Magsaysay in the Philippines, the British in Malaya, and the French in Indochina and Algeria—we have been slow to learn.

Regular forces are vital to resist external aggression. But we must not be deluded by the desire of local generals for "prestige hardware" or by the traditionalist's belief that well-trained regulars can do anything.

Regular forces are essential for regular military tasks. But guerrilla warfare is something special. Conventional forces with heavy equipment in field formation tend to cluster together, centralizing their power on terrain that allows rapid movement. They rely on roads and consider strong points and cities as vital targets to defend; and so, when they do disperse, it is only to get tied down in static operations. In combat, rigid adherence to the principle of concentration keeps units at unwieldy battalion or even regimental levels, usually with erroneous stress on holding land rather than destroying enemy forces.

It is ironic that we Americans have to learn this military lesson again in the twentieth century. Have we forgotten that we were the ones who had to teach the British regulars "Indian fighting" back when we were still a colony? Have we forgotten that we taught the British regulars another kind of lesson in "Indian fighting" during our own revolution?

We Americans have also forgotten that it was we who fought one of the most successful counterguerrilla campaigns in history—in the Philippines back at the turn of the century. We learned some fundamental military lessons then, and it is time we remembered them.

After Aguinaldo's army was defeated and Aguinaldo himself captured, some of the extremists took to the hills to become guerrillas. And they were not alone. For 300 years the Spanish had been fighting a guerrilla war with bands of religious fanatics in the southern islands. And further south, in Mindanao, the Moro remained unconquered. All these roamed the jungles and mountains—raiding, ambushing, killing, and pillaging.

The army tried to fight the guerrillas, but with little success. The enemy faded into the jungle, and the unwieldy regular units were too burdened with equipment, too slow to follow. Regulars needed supply lines. They could not live off the country or do without ammunition trains or hospital corps.

The regulars tended to establish a fixed base from which they sallied out. Thus, the guerrilla always knew where they were and when their guard was lax. The stage was set for surprise attacks and massacre.

In fact, one of these massacres was famous in the old Army—second only to Custer's last stand. It occurred at Balangiga on the island of Samar, and involved Company C of the Ninth Infantry, one of the finest regiments in the Army. At 6:40 A.M., the men were lined up before the cook shack, the opposite side of the parade ground from where their rifles were stacked. Suddenly the jungle came alive as 450 guerrillas charged. The regulars of Company C never had a chance. They fought barehanded. One soldier killed several men with a baseball bat before he was overwhelmed. The cook accounted for several more with a meat cleaver. But soon it was all over. Twenty-four men escaped; the rest were killed and mutilated.

But, finally, the United States found the solution to the guerrilla problem in the Philippines. We recruited native Filipinos—men wise to jungle ways, men who knew the trails and mountains as their own back yard. These were divided into small groups of ten, fifteen, twenty, or fifty men, and over each group we put a trained American officer—a bold and determined leader.

This was the famed Philippine Constabulary and the history of their fabulous exploits is well worth reading. The story is told—and very well —in Vic Hurley's book, *Jungle Patrol*,[1] published about thirty years ago.

The trick was constant patrolling over every trail and careful attention to intelligence work. The jungle, night time, and surprise attack are the guerrilla's weapons. The solution is to adopt the same weapons to fight him.

During World War II our OSS guerrilla battalion operated behind the enemy lines in Burma. Nothing pleased us more in those days than to have a regular Japanese force take out after us. They operated in large unwieldy units that were easy to ambush. Their movements were simple to follow through the mountains and jungle. We felt that our own existence was well justified when the Japanese had to take regular forces from front

1. New York, Dutton, 1938.

line fighting to chase a guerrilla unit. At one stage my outfit—consisting of four Americans and about 200 Burmese—kept a whole Japanese regiment of 3,000 men marching and countermarching over the mountains far away from the front lines. What we would have feared far more were smaller groups patrolling steadily—especially cavalry.

In many parts of the world today counterguerrilla operations conducted by regular troops rely on the tactic of sweeps through the countryside like those of the Japanese regiments that chased our guerrilla battalion in Burma. The sweeps are too well publicized and too cumbersome to bring results. This tactic leads to antagonism between the regular troops and the population. Villagers fear reprisals and refuse their help. Soldiers sense they are in guerrilla territory and act accordingly toward the people. Military inadequacy leads to failure and so to defeat.

I also fear that in the past our military aid programs for countries fighting against guerrillas have often followed the mistaken assumption that all war is similar to the large-scale tank and artillery engagements so familiar in Western Europe. The tactics of guerrilla warfare and the customs and culture of the peoples, it seems to me, should determine the proper weapons for counterguerrilla forces. For instance, the mountain tribes of Burma prior to World War II conducted their wars with long knives—a kind of sword called a "dah"—and with one-shot muzzle-loading flintlocks. Burma's mountainous regions are sparsely settled and the seminomadic inhabitants constantly move from one mountain valley to another when the soil begins to wear out. Consequently, they see no point in holding ground or in taking ground, and their whole history in war is one of lightning raids, sneak attacks, and ambushes.

Those of us in OSS who tried to make our guerrilla troops attack a defended position or to stand by their own position reaped only disaster. We had to adapt our weapons and our tactics to the terrain and to the customs of the people. I found that my own troops, accustomed to fighting with knives, would wait until the enemy was within arm's reach before firing their guns. I also found that they saw no point in sticking around after exhausting the first clip-load of ammunition. They were brave in sneaking up on an enemy, they were brave in holding their fire in an ambush until an enemy was upon them, but their fundamental maxim was that the wise soldier lives to fight another day. The Americans who thought their purpose was to stand and hold found themselves all alone in standing and holding.

The lesson was obvious, it seems to me. I equipped my men with submachine guns of .45 caliber. The men wanted to wait until the enemy was close before opening fire, and the jungle itself rarely permitted a shot ranging more than a few yards. I needed weapons with a large volume of fire power but neither range nor accuracy. I equipped my eight-man squads with seven submachine guns and one light machine gun. One squad had

60mm mortars to lay down an umbrella of fire to cover our withdrawal. Our tactics were traditional for guerrillas—we ambushed, we hit, and we ran. This particular unit, operating behind the enemy line for six months, killed over 300 of the enemy, blew up many bridges and ammunition and supply dumps, and yet suffered less than a dozen casualties.

For effective counterguerrilla operations we need radical changes in organization, combat doctrine, and equipment. Our key units might be decentralized groups of fifty men, self-reliant and able to operate autonomously, fanned out into the countryside. The premium is on leadership, for only men of courage and great skill can make this system work. With such men, plus decent pay and training, a counterguerrilla force should not be difficult to maintain.

The operational concept is as follows: A guerrilla-infested part of the country is marked off and divided into sections. Each section is patrolled by one of these units, but all are in contact with a central headquarters, which in turn has a reserve force at its disposal. Upon contacting guerrillas, a patrol alerts headquarters and adjacent patrols. As the latter converge, headquarters dispatches paratroops or helicopter transports behind the enemy, who is surrounded and destroyed. Once an area is pacified, the government consolidates its control and moves its forces on to the next section of land to be cleared. The main ingredients then are constant patrols, good communication facilities, rapid mobility, and a capacity for rapid concentration.

One further point: the operations must cause minimum harm to the people, lest they become antagonistic to the government. The troops must be highly disciplined to respect civilian rights and property. They should offer help (ranging from field repairs to Magsaysay's offer of legal services in the Philippines). Cargo planes should carry in supplies, so that the forces do not have to live off the countryside. The onus for anticivilian behavior should be diverted squarely to the guerrillas themselves. They are the ones who are compelled to take to repressive measures, seizing rice or conscripting men in their desperation. As they lose popular support, they will have nothing to fall back on as they suffer military defeats.

Modernization and Reform

I hope that this last point indicates my awareness of how important it is to have popular support in conducting an internal war. Many observers argue that stability and physical security are basically political issues, depending on the popularity of governments. To this they add that economic development is the key to popular support and the criterion by which regimes will be judged.

In the long run, popular support is essential for stable governments and a stable world. And there is no question that economic development, modernization, and reform are key factors in creating popular support and stable governments. But in my judgment it would be mistaken to think that guerrillas cannot thrive where governments are popular and where modernization, economic development, and reform are going forward. And the usual corollary to this thought—the notion that the existence of guerrillas is proof positive that the government is unpopular and therefore not worth supporting—is even more mistaken. It is, in fact, defeatist. We need modernization, economic development, and reform to defeat guerrillas. But other things are also needed.

Let me draw on my personal experience once more. When we fought in Burma, about 10 per cent of the people were pro-West, another 10 per cent were pro-enemy, and the rest were indifferent or turned inward towards their own family and village. Yet our guerrilla group performed with great success. We recruited men not only from the 10 per cent who were pro-West, but also from the 80 per cent who were indifferent. We gave no quarter to the enemy and his supporters, but we did everything we could to avoid creating hardship for the rest and to help them when we could. We were careful to move around their growing crops. And when we had to ask them for food, we paid for it or arranged an airdrop of double the amount of rice we took. Before the war was over, it was the enemy and his supporters in the puppet government who appeared oppressive to the people—not we guerrillas.

The idea that guerrillas thrive only where the government is unpopular may apply to the more developed parts of the world. But in many parts of the world, states are underdeveloped in the political-administrative sense as well as economically. The number of people are few who have the training to perform the standard civil service jobs that we take for granted. Lacking that "steel frame" in which India takes such just pride, a government appears as a weak and distant entity to most villagers, except when it serves as a burdensome tax collector. In most lands, at least half the people are indifferent to a government. Even the active elements, ranged for or against the regime, are not too set in their political commitments.

In these circumstances, maintaining the bare minimum of national services is enough to determine a nation's fate in the short run. In the Congo, the collapse of two supports—the military *Force Publique* and Belgian technical service—revealed how far the state has to go before becoming an administrative entity.

By contrast, the Somali Republic, which gained its independence at the same time last year also faced a potentially difficult situation—of keeping newly joined regions and powerful tribal groups satisfied. As matters developed, no pseudopopular manifestation of discontent emerged, thanks in part to a small but efficient Western-trained civilian police force.

As for modernization, although essential for the long haul, it cannot help much in a counterguerrilla program. Modernization inevitably uproots established social systems, produces political and economic dislocation and tension, and cannot deliver results quickly enough to relieve these short-term pressures.

However, there is mounting unrest in rural areas all over the world. What peasants increasingly crave is social justice and reform—at a minimum, the old way of life with the cruelties removed.

This includes reform of land tenure arrangements, reasonable rent, credit, and market facilities, and simple modern tools. They may see ahead to the value of urban centers that buy their produce—instead of importing from abroad and forcing them to raise crops for export—and in turn manufacture for their simple needs. Finally, they crave peace and physical security.

Yet there is a growing link between urban and rural unrest. As modernization begins, the poorer farmers drift to the city, there to form the hard core of the unemployed slum-dwellers who overtax the rudimentary metropolitan facilities. These unfortunates form the recruits for the city mobs that Communists and demagogues have been turning out in the Middle East and Latin America for the past fifteen years. The political link between the two becomes clear when we see how the very poor are used as recruits for guerrilla forces in the rural areas and for "people's militia" in the urban regions. Communists have long made use of the former in sustaining a rebellion; Castro and "Che" Guevara have become adept at using both groups to support the present Cuban regime. In Latin America alone, Venezuela, Bolivia, Colombia, and Peru come immediately to mind as countries where the combined urban-rural problem exists.

What is required first is a program of social reform. Very often the conservative element in a community will struggle irrationally against all reform. As a consequence, we have encountered in several parts of the world the amazing and suicidal spectacle of conservatives giving secret aid to the Communists in order to undermine modest reformist efforts.

Equally important is the need to indicate some effort and progress on the long path to modernization. Small results, if they prove the intent of a regime, can inspire faith that will outlast the distress of early change. Finally, where these efforts are combined with democratic government and mass party organization, the government can broaden its base of physical power.

In Venezuela, for example, the ruling party has been fostering reform and change. It has also created a national organization, with loyal popular militia elements to support it. Though not professionals, militiamen can keep the peace in the face of provocative demonstrations and can perform useful services in supplementing the work of regular forces. A government that cannot get its image across to the peasantry or mobilize peasant support will find its functions in both these endeavors usurped by the Communists.

To summarize my feeling on popularity, reform, and modernization: (1) they are important ingredients but are not the determinants of events and (2) their role must be measured more in terms of their contribution to physical security than we generally realize.

Other Political Factors

Let me hurriedly refer to several other variations on the theme of internal security—the political factors that threaten the stability of new states. So far we have noted primarily the nature of the Communist threat and the issues of good government and economic development. Unfortunately, on top of these universal problems, most states have to grapple with specific difficulties that create further divisions, induce tensions, and propel even the best intentioned regimes to violence. Among these difficulties are the following:

1. *Antagonisms between Underdeveloped States.* The familiar pattern of rivalry between neighbors, as old as history itself, exists with even greater intensity today because so many new states have suddenly sprung into being. Territorial claims and other sources of friction are still fresh, as in the Persian Gulf or in India's nothern border regions. Such difficulties generate tensions, arms races, and nationalistic fevor that Communists try to exploit.

2. *Disagreements between Regions of a State or between a Region and the Center.* The issues of regionalism in India, separatist movements in Indonesia, and tribalism in the fragmented Congo are examples of serious challenges to governmental authority and stability.

3. *Social Class Antagonism.* It is characteristic of established economic elites that they feel themselves threatened from below and refuse to countenance the very reform that would ease the real dangers that they face. The great failures of old regimes in France before 1789 and Russia at the start of this century are but the outstanding instances of this historic problem that presents itself on almost every continent today.

4. *Intense Disagreement over Foreign Policy.* Iraq's adherence to the Baghdad Pact despite internal opposition and disapproval by all other Arab states is a case in point. Radical-nationalist African states accuse their neighbors of following a colonial, subservient line. In trying to get them on a comparable course, radical states engage in clandestine operations to subvert neighboring regimes or support opposition factions whose ideology resembles their own.

5. *Traditional Political Rivalries within a Social Class.* Colombia offers

the leading example of two parties that, without basic social or ideological differences, became embroiled in a long civil war, so bitter as to cause over 250,000 casualties. This war literally superimposed itself on all the other problems of security that normally confront a developing state. The ruling party in Burma split into hostile factions in 1958 and the army had to act to keep that situation from fragmenting the country.

6. *Lack of Popular Belief in the State as a Sovereign Entity*. In large areas of Africa and the Middle East, normal loyalties follow either tribal and provincial lines or grand dreams of regional African or Arab unity. The state does attract some loyalty because it is a going concern, one that can be used as a lever of power at both these other levels. With this overlapping of loyalties, it is only too easy for a government to meddle in the affairs of its neighbors and further weaken their internal cohesion—always, of course, in the belief that its cause is just.

7. *Ethnic or Racial Issues*. Rebellious tribesmen are constant drains on national military power in various states throughout Asia and Africa. The Communists found in Malaya's Chinese community ready hands for their bloody insurrection, partly because of interracial political rivalries. Indians in some Latin American countries are living at very low standards, are beginning to stir, and are potential bait for a Communist ethnic-economic appeal. Central African pagans have strained relations with Moslem Arab northerners in a crossroad land that is beset by outside pressures.

8. *Banditry*. Bandits (or armed rural gangs) that flout the authorities and exploit local neighbors have long existed in many parts of the world —colored perhaps with varying degrees of political or ideological overtones, but essentially dedicated to violence. One thinks of recent illustrations in the Philippines, of traditional sporadic outbreaks in Java, of troubles experienced by the new state of Burma. These actions impoverish the peasant, ruin the government's authority, paralyze public morale, and open the path to similar Communist tactics or, conversely, to establishment of Communist authority in that region.

9. *Constitutional Crises*. Unconstitutional extension of presidential power, so often exemplified in the history of Latin America, is one example of a constitutional crisis that may lead to political turmoil when such excesses are traditionally resented and countered by violence. The seizure of power by a military junta is another.

There are other obvious factors, such as the outburst of nationalism that may follow independence, proximity to Sino-Soviet territory, the existence and strength of a Communist party and its orientation toward Moscow or Peiping, and, of course, revolts against colonial rule and white-minority rule in certain areas. The addition of just a few of these special hazards to the basic difficulties I described earlier places a tremendous strain upon a government's staying power. You can clearly see why I am saying that internal security is a problem in its own right and not simply a function of good government or economic growth.

CONCLUSION

There are many things we can do to help responsible and friendly governments attack this problem all along the line. I have already illustrated how the training of armed forces can be better geared to the specific war against guerrillas. Equally important is the training of police and other forces to cope with the lesser manifestations of violence, not only in detection and surveillance but also in handling actual outbursts. We may find ourselves encouraging reformers to organize mass parties, and in certain tense circumstances we may need to help create citizens' militia forces. We are seriously interested in broadening the will and capacity of friendly governments to augment social and political reform programs as a basis for modernization.

We must also look for ways to ease the access of beleaguered states to ouside assistance. The Communists use the concept of state sovereignty as a device to seal off a land from "intervention" once they have made sufficient inroads. They use international law, appeals to neutralist neighbors, the unpleasant reactions to what is called "Western imperialism," and the threat of force in this effort. We must foster the growth and use of international organizations as sources of help on all the problems I have mentioned—help that can be on the scene and in action before the crisis reaches its peak. In this way we may ward off a showdown or at the very least have elements there to indicate outside support in being and on the way.

In any event the United States must be prepared to become deeply involved. This effort may be costly, but careful and early involvement is far less expensive or dangerous than a crash program. The Communists are already committed everywhere, and unless we approach the problem in a systematic way, with considerable thought, we will simply be paving the way for Mr. Khrushchev in his new and potent tactic—internal war.

37

Walt W. Rostow   **COUNTERING**

                                    GUERRILLA

                                    ATTACK

WHEN THE KENNEDY ADMINISTRATION accepted the responsibility of government it faced four major crises: Cuba, the Congo, Laos, and Viet Nam. Each represented a successful Communist breaching —over the previous years—of the Cold War truce lines which had emerged from the Second World War and its aftermath. In different ways each had arisen from the efforts of the international Communist movement to exploit the inherent instabilities of the underdeveloped areas of the non-Communist world; and each had a guerrilla warfare component.

Cuba, of course, differed from the other cases. The Cuban revolution against Batista was a broad-based national insurrection. But that revolution was tragically captured from within by the Communist apparatus; and now Latin America faces the danger of Cuba's being used as the base for training, supply, and direction of guerrilla warfare in the Hemisphere.

From *Army Magazine,* September, 1961. Copyright 1961 by Association of the U.S. Army and reproduced by permission. This article is drawn from an address by Dr. Rostow before the graduating class of the Counter Guerrilla course of the Army's Special Warfare Center at Fort Bragg. Of the eighty students in the class, sixty-three of them were from twenty different nations and only seventeen from the United States.

More than that, Mr. Khrushchev, in his report to the Moscow conference of Communist parties (published January 6, 1961), had explained at great length that the Communists fully support what he called wars of national liberation and would march in the front rank with the peoples waging such struggles. The military arm of Mr. Khrushchev's January, 1961, doctrine is, clearly, guerrilla warfare.

Faced with these four crises, pressing in on the President from day to day, and faced with the candidly stated position of Mr. Khrushchev, we have, indeed, begun to take the problem of guerrilla warfare seriously.

To understand this problem, however, one must begin with the great revolutionary process that is going forward in the southern half of the world, for the guerrilla warfare problem in these regions is a product of that revolutionary process and the Communist effort and intent to exploit it.

The Old Order Changes

What is happening throughout Latin America, Africa, the Middle East and Asia is this: old societies are changing their ways in order to create and maintain a national personality on the world scene and to bring to their peoples the benefits modern technology can offer. This process is truly revolutionary. It touches every aspect of the traditional life: economic, social and political. The introduction of modern technology brings about not merely new methods of production but a new style of family life, new links between the villages and the cities, the beginnings of national politics, and a new relationship to the world outside.

Like all revolutions, the revolution of modernization is disturbing. Individual men are torn between the commitment to the old and familiar way of life and the attractions of a modern way of life. The power of old social groups—notably the landlord who usually dominates the traditional society —is reduced. Power moves towards those who can command the tools of modern technology, including modern weapons. Men and women in the villages and the cities, feeling that the old ways of life are shaken and that new possibilities are open to them, express old resentments and new hopes.

This is the grand arena of revolutionary change which the Communists are exploiting with great energy. They believe that their techniques of organization—based on small disciplined cadres of conspirators—are ideally suited to grasp and to hold power in these turbulent settings. They believe that the weak transitional governments, that one is likely to find during this modernization process, are highly vulnerable to subversion and to guerrilla warfare. And whatever Communist doctrines of historical inevitability may be, Communists know that their time to seize power in the underdeveloped areas is limited. They know that, as momentum takes hold in an underdeveloped area—and the fundamental social problems inherited from the traditional society are solved—their chances to seize power decline. It is on the weakest nations—facing their most difficult transitional moments— that the Communists concentrate their attention. They are the scavengers of the modernization process.

Scavengers of Modernization

They believe that the techniques of political centralization under dictatorial control—and the projected image of Soviet and Chinese Communist economic progress—will persuade hesitant men, faced by great transitional problems, that the Communist model should be adopted for modernization, even at the cost of surrendering human liberty. They believe that they can exploit effectively the resentments built up in many of these areas against colonial rule and that they can associate themselves effectively with the desire of the emerging nations for independence, for status on the world scene, and for material progress.

This is a formidable program, for the history of this century teaches us that communism is not the long run wave of the future towards which societies are naturally drawn. On the contrary. But it is one particular form of modern society to which a nation may fall prey during the transitional process. Communism is best understood as a disease of the transition to modernization.

What is our reply to this historical conception and strategy? What is the American purpose and the American strategy? We, too, recognize that a revolutionary process is under way. We are dedicated to the proposition that this revolutionary process of modernization shall be permitted to go forward in independence, with increasing degrees of human freedom. We seek two results: first, that truly independent nations shall emerge on the world scene; and, second, that each nation will be permitted to fashion, out of its own culture and its own ambitions, the kind of modern society it wants. The same religious and philosophical beliefs which decree that we respect the uniqueness of each individual, make it natural that we respect the uniqueness of each national society. Moreover, we Americans are confident that, if the independence of this process can be maintained over the coming years and decades, these societies will choose their own version of what we would recognize as a democratic, open society.

Commitments to Freedom and Independence

These are our commitments of policy and of faith. The United States has no interest in political satellites. Where we have military pacts we have them because governments feel directly endangered by outside military action, and we are prepared to help protect their independence against such military action. But, to use Mao Tse-tung's famous phrase, we do not seek nations which "lean to one side." We seek nations which shall stand up straight. And we do so for a reason: because we are deeply confident that nations which stand up straight will protect their independence and move in their own ways and in their own time towards human freedom and political democracy.

Thus, our central task in the underdeveloped areas, as we see it, is to protect the independence of the revolutionary process now going forward. This is our mission and it is our ultimate strength. For this is not—and cannot be—the mission of communism. And in time, through the fog of propaganda and the honest confusions of men caught up in the business of making new nations, this fundamental difference will become increasingly clear in the southern half of the world. The American interest will be served if our children live in an environment of strong, assertive, independent nations, capable, because they are strong, of assuming collective responsibility for the peace. The diffusion of power is the basis for freedom within our own society; and we have no reason to fear it on the world scene. But this outcome would be a defeat for communism—not for Russia as a national state, but for communism. Despite all the Communist talk of aiding the movements of national independence, they are driven in the end, by the nature of their system, to violate the independence of nations. Despite all the Communist talk of American imperialism, we are committed, by the nature of our system, to support the cause of national independence. And the truth will out.

The Vitals of the Victory

The victory we seek will see no ticker tape parades down Broadway— no climactic battles nor great American celebrations of victory. It is a victory which will take many years and decades of hard work and dedication—by many peoples—to bring about. This will not be a victory of the United States over the Soviet Union. It will not be a victory of capitalism over socialism. It will be a victory of men and nations which aim to stand up straight, over the forces which wish to entrap and to exploit their revolutionary aspirations of modernization. What this victory involves—in the end—is the assertion by nations of their right to independence and by men and women of their right to freedom as they understand it. And we deeply believe this victory will come—on both sides of the Iron Curtain.

If Americans do not seek victory in the usual sense, what do they seek? What is the national interest of the United States? Why do we Americans expend our treasure and assume the risks of modern war in this global struggle? For Americans the reward of victory will be, simply, this: it will permit American society to continue to develop along the old humane lines which go back to our birth as a nation—and which reach deeper into history than that—back to the Mediterranean roots of Western life. We are struggling to maintain an environment on the world scene which will permit our open society to survive and to flourish.

The Dimensions of Independence

To make this vision come true places a great burden on the United States at this phase of history. The preservation of independence has many dimensions. The United States has the primary responsibility for deterring the use of nuclear weapons in the pursuit of Communist ambitions. The United States has a major responsibility to deter the kind of overt aggression with conventional forces which was launched in June, 1950, in Korea. The United States has the primary responsibility for assisting the economies of those hard pressed states on the periphery of the Communist bloc, which are under acute military or quasi-military pressure which they cannot bear from their own resources; for example, South Korea, Viet Nam, Taiwan, Pakistan, Iran. The United States has a special responsibility of leadership in bringing not merely its own resources, but the resources of all the Free World to bear in aiding the long-run development of those nations which are serious about modernizing their economy and their social life. And, as President Kennedy has made clear, he regards no program of his administration as more important than his program for long-term economic development, dramatized, for example, by the Alliance for Progress in Latin America. Independence cannot be maintained by military measures alone. Modern societies must be built, and we are prepared to help build them.

Finally, the United States has a role to play . . . in learning to deter guerrilla warfare, if possible, and to deal with it, if necessary.

A Battle for the Mind and Spirit of Man

I do not need to tell you that the primary responsibility for dealing with guerrilla warfare in the underdeveloped areas cannot be American. There are many ways in which we can help—and we are searching our minds and our imaginations to learn better how to help; but a guerrilla war must be fought primarily by those on the spot. This is so for a quite particular reason. A guerrilla war is an intimate affair, fought not merely with weapons but fought in the minds of the men who live in the villages and in the hills; fought by the spirit and policy of those who run the local government. An outsider cannot, by himself, win a guerrilla war; he can help create conditions in which it can be won; and he can directly assist those prepared to fight for their independence. We are determined to help destroy this international disease; that is, guerrilla war designed, initiated, and supplied, and led from outside an independent nation.

Although as leader of the Free World, the United States has special responsibilities which it accepts in this common venture of deterrence, it is important that the whole international community begin to accept its responsibility for dealing with this form of aggression. It is important that the world become clear in mind, for example, that the operation run from Hanoi against Viet Nam is as clear a form of aggression as the violation of the 38th parallel by the North Korean armies in June, 1950.

In my conversations with representatives of foreign governments, I am sometimes lectured that this or that government within the Free World is not popular; they tell me that guerrilla warfare cannot be won unless the peoples are dissatisfied. These are, at best, half truths. The truth is that guerrilla warfare, mounted from external bases—with rights of sanctuary —is a terrible burden to carry for any government in a society making its way towards modernization. As you know, it takes somewhere between 10 and 20 soldiers to control one guerrilla in an organized operation. More-over, the guerrilla force has this advantage: its task is merely to destroy; while the government must build and protect what it is building. A guerrilla war mounted from outside a transitional nation, is a crude act of interna-tional vandalism. There will be no peace in the world if the international community accepts the outcome of a guerrilla war, mounted from outside a nation, as tantamount to a free election.

The sending of men and arms across international boundaries and the direction of guerrilla war from outside a sovereign nation is aggression; and this is a fact which the whole international community must con-front and whose consequent responsibilities it must accept. Without such international action those against whom aggression is mounted will be driven inevitably to seek out and engage the ultimate source of the aggres-sion they confront.

Alternatives to Guerrilla Aggression

I suspect that, in the end, the real meaning of the conference on Laos at Geneva will hinge on this question: it will depend on whether or not the international community is prepared to mount an International Con-trol Commission which has the will and the capacity to control the borders it was designed to control.

In facing the problem of guerrilla war, I have one observation to make as an historian. It is now fashionable—and I daresay for you it was com-pulsory—to read the learned works of Mao Tse-tung and Che Guevara on guerrilla warfare. This is, indeed, proper. One should read with care and without passion into the minds of one's enemies. But it is historically inaccurate and psychologically dangerous to think that these men created the strategy and tactics of guerrilla war to which we are now responding. Guerrilla warfare is not a form of military and psychological magic created by the Communists. There is no rule or parable in the Communist texts which was not known at an earlier time in history. The operation of Marion's men in relation to the Battle of Cowpens in the American Revolution was, for example, by rules which Mao merely echoes; Che Guevara knows nothing of this business that T. E. Lawrence did not know or was not practiced, for example, in the Peninsular Campaign during the Napoleonic wars, a century earlier. The orchestration of professional troops, militia, and guerrilla fighters is an old game whose rules can be studied and learned.

My point is that we are up against a form of warfare which is powerful and effective only when we do not put our minds clearly to work on how to deal with it. I, for one, believe that, with purposeful efforts, most nations which might now be susceptible to guerrilla warfare could handle their border areas in ways which would make them very unattractive to the initiation of this ugly game. We can learn to prevent the emergence of the famous sea in which Mao Tse-tung taught his men to swim. This requires, of course, not merely a proper military program of deterrence, but programs of village development, communications, and indoctrination. The best way to fight a guerrilla war is to prevent it from happening. And this can be done.

Similarly, I am confident that we can deal with the kind of operation now under way in Viet Nam. It is an extremely dangerous operation; and it could overwhelm Viet Nam if the Vietnamese—aided by the Free World—do not deal with it. But it is an unsubtle operation, by the book, based more on murder than on political or psychological appeal. When Communists speak of wars of national liberation and of their support for "progressive forces," I think of the systematic program of assassination now going forward in which the principal victims are the health, agriculture, and education officers in the Viet Nam villages. The Viet Cong are not trying to persuade the peasants of Viet Nam that communism is good: they are trying to persuade them that their lives are insecure unless they cooperate with them. With resolution and confidence on all sides and with the assumption of international responsibility for the frontier problem, I believe we are going to bring this threat to the independence of Viet Nam under control.

Assassination of a Rising Culture

My view is, then, that we confront in guerrilla warfare in the underdeveloped areas a systematic attempt by the Communists to impose a serious disease on those societies attempting the transition to modernization. This attempt is a present danger in Southeast Asia. It could quickly become a major danger in Africa and Latin America. I salute in particular those among you whose duty it is—along with others—to prevent that disease, if possible, and to eliminate it where it is imposed. As I understand the course you are now completing, it is designed to impress on you this truth: you are not merely soldiers in the old sense. Your job is not merely to accept the risks of war and to master its skills. Your job is to work with understanding, with your fellow citizens, in the whole creative process of modernization.

From our perspective in Washington you take your place side by side with those others who are committed to help fashion independent, modern societies out of the revolutionary process now going forward. I salute you as I would a group of doctors, teachers, economic planners, agricultural experts, civil servants, or those others who are now leading the way in the whole southern half of the globe in fashioning new nations and societies that will stand up straight and assume in time their rightful place of dignity and responsibility in the world community; for this is our common mission.

Each of us must carry into his day-to-day work an equal understanding of the military and the creative dimensions of the job.

I can tell you that those with whom I have the privilege to work are dedicated to that mission with every resource of mind and spirit at our command.

Further References*

BOOKS

Atkinson, J. D. *The Edge of War.* Chicago: Regnery, 1960.

Burnham, J. *Containment or Liberation?* New York: John Day, 1953.

————. *The Coming Defeat of Communism.* New York: John Day, 1950.

Dougherty, J. E. *American-Asian Tensions.* New York: Praeger, 1956.

Fuller, J. F. C. *Russia Is Not Invincible.* London: Eyre & Spottiswoode, 1951.

Hann, W. F., and J. C. Neff, eds., *American Strategy for the Nuclear Age.* New York: Doubleday, 1960.

Hilsman, Roger. *Strategic Intelligence and National Decisions.* New York: The Free Press, 1956.

Possony, S. T. *Century of Conflict.* 2d ed. Chicago: Regnery, 1960.

Strausz-Hupé, R., W. R. Kinter, J. E. Dougherty, and A. J. Cottrell. *Protracted Conflict.* New York: Harper, 1959.

ARTICLES

Asprey, R. B., comp. "Nato and Guerrillas," Special Guerrilla Warfare Issue, *Marine Corps Gazette,* January, 1962.

Atkinson, J. D. "American Military Policy and Communist Unorthodox Warfare," *Marine Corps Gazette,* January, 1958.

Barnett, F. R. "A Proposal for Political Warfare," *Military Review,* March, 1961.

Bjelajac, S. N. "Strategy of Protracted Defense," *Military Review,* June, 1960.

Brazier-Creagh, K. R. "Waging a Cold War," *Royal United Service Institute Journal,* May, 1954.

Daley, S. A. "Twentieth Century Irregulars," *Infantry Journal,* June, 1941.

Delaney, R. E. "A Case for a Doctrine of Unconventional Warfare," *U.S. Naval Institute Proceedings,* September, 1961.

Downey, E. F. "Theory of Guerrilla Warfare," *Military Review,* May, 1959.

Engels, F. "Frederick Engels on Guerrilla Warfare," *Labour Monthly,* August, 1943.

Fisher, T. L. "Limited War—What Is It?," *Air University Quarterly Review,* Winter, 1957–1958.

Gellner, J. "Partisans as a Weapon of War," *The Roundel,* March, 1956.

Hargreaves, R. "Communism and the Resistance Movement," *Royal United Service Institute Journal,* August, 1949 (condensed, *Military Review,* April, 1950).

---

* See "Research Bibliography on Guerrilla Warfare" for counterguerrilla procedure references.

Harris, A. E. "Partisan Operations," *Military Review,* August, 1950.

Hart, H. G. V. "United States Employment of Underground Forces," *Military Review,* April, 1946.

Heelis, J. E. "Guerrilla Warfare and Its Lessons," *United Service Institute of India,* July, 1947.

Hellner, M. H. "The Communist Strategy of Time," *Marine Corps Gazette,* August, 1961.

Jacobs, W. D., and N. de Rochefort. "Ideological Operations in Unconventional Warfare," n.p., 1961. (W. D. Jacobs, 4948 33d Rd., North, Arlington 7, Va.)

Kinter, W. R. "Para-Military Warfare: The Nation's Security Planning," *Marine Corps Gazette,* March, 1951.

Kvedar, Dusan. "Territorial Warfare—a Yugoslav View of Partisan Warfare," *United Service Institute of India,* April, 1959.

————. "Territorial Warfare," *Foreign Affairs,* October, 1950.

Leaske, T. "The Problems of Cold War Operations," *Army Quarterly,* July, 1957.

Lindsay, F. A. "Unconventional Warfare," *Foreign Affairs,* January, 1962.

Linebarger, P. M. A. "Propaganda—Mobilized Nonviolence," *Orbis,* Winter, 1959.

Livengood, F. W. "We March with Braddock," *Infantry Journal,* January, 1949.

Metcalf, G. T. "Offensive Partisan Warfare," *Military Review,* April, 1952.

Methvin, E. H. "Mob Violence and Communist Strategy," *Orbis,* Summer, 1961.

Miksche, F. O. "The Organization of Future Armies," tr. and condensed by *Military Review,* January, 1957.

Nickerson, H. "Irregular Warfare—the Role of Irregular Troops in Modern Conflict," *Army Ordnance,* November–December, 1941.

Paret, P. "The French Army and La Guerre Revolutionnaire," *Royal United Service Institute Journal,* February, 1959.

————, and J. W. Shy. "Guerrilla Warfare and U.S. Military Policy: A Study," *Marine Corps Gazette,* Special Guerrilla Warfare Issue, January, 1962.

Raeder, J. C. G. "Guerrilla Warfare," *Army Quarterly,* January, 1956.

Rice, E. E. "Generals, Guerrillas, Diplomats," *Foreign Service Journal,* September, 1961.

Rigg, R. B. "Twilight War," *Military Review,* November, 1960.

Rostow, W. W. "Guerrilla Warfare in Underdeveloped Areas" (another version of the address reprinted as "Countering Guerrilla Attack," page 464 of this book), *Marine Corps Gazette,* Special Guerrilla Warfare Issue, January, 1962.

————. "Countering Guerrilla Warfare" (still another version of the article on page 464), *The New Leader,* July 31–August 7, 1961.

Sheard, K. S. "Irregular Warfare," *Australian Army Journal,* June, 1953.

Strausz-Hupé, R. "Soviet Psychological Strategy," *U.S. Naval Institute Proceedings,* June, 1961.

Velde, R. W. "The Neglected Deterrent," *Military Review,* August, 1958.

Woodhouse, C. M. "Prolegomena to a Study of Resistance," *Nineteenth Century*, November, 1948, February, 1949.

DOCUMENTS

Air Force. Human Resources Research Institute. Maxwell AFB, Ala.:
  Organization and Control of Partisan Movements, no. 6, 67pp., 1954.
Air University. Maxwell AFB, Ala.:
  Shinkle, E. G. *United States Support of Guerrillas,* 33pp., thesis, 1953.
U.S. Government Printing Office. Washington, D.C.:
  Analysis of the Khrushchev Speech of January 6, 1961, Testimony of Dr. Stefan T. Possony, June 16, 1961.

RESEARCH BIBLIOGRAPHY

ON GUERRILLA

AND UNCONVENTIONAL WARFARE*

---

* Items listed in this Bibliography do not duplicate the Further References at the end of each section of this book.

24. Ireland, 1916–1923
25. Israel (Palestine), 1946–1949
26. Italy
    A. 1848–1860
    B. World War II
27. Kashmir, 1957–1958
28. Korea, 1950–1953
29. Malaya, World War II
30. The Netherlands, World War II
31. Nicaragua, 1927–1931
32. Norway, World War II
33. Philippines, World War II
34. Poland
    A. World War II
    B. Polish Revolution, 1956
35. Russia
    A. War of 1812
    B. Civil War, 1917–1918

36. Siam, World War II
37. Spain
    A. Peninsular War, 1811–1813
    B. Civil War, 1936–1938
    C. Post-Civil War
38. Yugoslavia, World War II
39. North America (U.S.A.)
    A. French and Indian War, 1755–1763
    B. American Revolution, 1776–1781
    C. Civil War
    D. Indian Warfare
    E. American Ability to Wage Guerrilla Warfare in the United States

General Miscellaneous

Strategy, Tactics, Theory

BOOKS

Brett-James, A. *Wellington at War 1794–1815: A Selection of His Wartime Letters.* New York: St. Martin's, 1961.

Casserly, G. *Manual of Training for Jungle and River Warfare.* London: Laurie, 1918.

Chorley, K. *Armies and the Art of Revolution.* London: Faber, 1943.

Heneker, W. C. G. *Bush Warfare.* London: Rees, 1907.

Hobsbawm, E. J. *Social Bandits and Primitive Rebels: Studies in the Archaic Forms of Social Movements in the 19th and 20th Centuries.* New York: Free Press, 1960.

Hunter, R. *Revolution: Why, How, Where?* New York: Harper, 1940.

Idriess, I. L. *Guerrilla Tactics.* Sydney: Angus & Robertson, 1942.

———. *Shoot to Kill.* Sydney: Angus & Robertson, 1942.

———. *Trapping the Japs.* Sydney: Angus & Robertson, 1942.

International Conference on the History of Resistance Movements (papers presented in English, French, and German). London: Pergamon, 1960.

Kerr, A. *The Art of Guerrilla Fighting and Patrol.* London: Jarrolds, 1940.

———. *Guerrilla.* London: Jarrolds, 1943.

Kornhauser, William. *The Politics of Mass Society.* New York: The Free Press of Glencoe, 1959.

Levy, B. *Guerrilla Warfare.* Washington, D.C.: Infantry Journal–Penguin Special, 1942.

Lockwood, R. *Guerrilla Path to Freedom.* London: Angus & Robertson, 1942.

Matthews, B. F. *The Specter of Sabotage.* Los Angeles: Lymanhouse, 1941.

Miksche, F. O. *Secret Forces.* London: Faber, 1950.

Ney, V. *Notes on Guerrilla War.* Washington, D.C.: Command Publications, 1961.

Paret, P., and J. W. Shy. *Guerrillas in the 1960's.* New York: Praeger, 1962.

Shore, C. *With British Snipers to the Reich.* Georgetown, S.C.: Small-Arms Technical Publishing Co., 1949.

Wintringham, T. *The Story of Weapons and Tactics.* Boston: Houghton, 1943.

ARTICLES

"Ambush," *Australian Army Journal,* May, 1958.

Amery, J. "Of Resistance," *The Nineteenth Century,* March, 1949.

"Atomic War and Partisans," tr. and condensed by *Military Review,* June, 1957.

Austin, M. "Some Thoughts on Ambushes in Tropical Warfare," *Australian Army Journal,* June, 1958.

Banks, C. L. "Austerity and Victory," *Marine Corps Gazette,* August, 1951.

Bjerke, A. "The Social Group, Infiltration, and War," tr. and condensed by *Military Review,* March, 1952.

————. "Concerning Strategic Depth," tr. by L. Dale, *Military Review,* September, 1959.

Blindheim, S. "The Strategy of Underground Warfare," tr. and condensed by *Military Review,* June, 1951.

Crawford, T. J. "Korean Ambush," *Australian Army Journal,* March, 1953.

Crisol, J. M. "Guerrilla Warfare," *Philippine Armed Forces Journal,* December, 1948.

Donovan, J. A. "Guerrilla," *Leatherneck,* July and August, 1961.

Dupuy, R. E. "Nature of Guerrilla Warfare," *Pacific Affairs,* June, 1939.

Dodson, C. A. "Put Your Mind to Mayhem," *Army Magazine,* November, 1961.

Frankel, E. "One Thousand Murderers," *Journal of Criminal Law and Criminology* (vol. 29), 1939.

Gottschalk, L. "Causes of Revolution," *American Journal of Sociology* (vol. 50), 1944.

Graca, J. R. da. "Guerrilla Action Leads to Victory," tr. and condensed by *Military Review,* April, 1947.

Gruenther, R. S. "Guerrilla Warfare," *Infantry,* April, 1957.

Gubbins, C. "Resistance Movements in World War II," *Royal United Service Institute Journal,* May, 1948 (condensed by *Military Review,* January, 1949).

Haig, G. "Organization of Guerrilla or Raider Units," *Field Artillery Journal,* February, 1941.

Hargreaves, R. "Thorn in the Flesh," *Military Review,* June, 1961.

Harrigan, A. "A New Dimension in Special Operations," *Military Review,* September, 1961.

Harrington, S. M. "The Strategy and Tactics of Small Wars," *Marine Corps Gazette,* December, 1921.

"Home Guard—Guerrilla Warfare," *Fighting Forces,* February, 1942.

Hopper, R. D. "The Revolutionary Process: A Frame of Reference for the Study of Revolutionary Movements," *Social Forces* (vol. 28), 1950.

Htaik, T. "What It Takes: Essentials of Special Operations," *Military Review,* August, 1961.

Hughes-Hallett, R. J. "The Mounting of Raids," *Royal United Service Institute Journal,* November, 1950.

Igot, Y. "The Underground Army Must Become the Army of the Future," tr. and condensed by *Military Review,* August, 1951.

Levy, B. "Guerrilla Warfare," *Infantry Journal,* March and April, 1942.

Macaulay, N. "The Strategy of Guerrilla Conquest," *National Guardsman,* September, 1961.

Mason, L. M. "A Practical Jungle Formation," *Marine Corps Gazette,* April, 1945.

Malinowski, W. R. "The Pattern of Underground Resistance," *Annals,* March, 1944.

Miers, R. C. H. "Both Sides of the Guerrilla Hill," *Army Magazine,* 1962.

Miksche, F. O. "The Third Front," *Military Review,* September, 1944.

Nemo, Colonel (pseud.). "The Place of Guerrilla Action in War," tr. and condensed by *Military Review,* November, 1957.

Ney, V. "Bibliography on Guerrilla Warfare," *Military Affairs,* Fall, 1960 (reprinted, *Marine Corps Gazette,* September, 1961).

————. "Guerrilla Warfare—Annotated Bibliography," *Military Review,* November, 1961.

Osanka, F. M. "Guerrilla War: A Paperback Bibliography," *Marine Corps Gazette,* February, 1962.

Postel, C. "Occupation and Resistance," tr. and condensed by *Military Review,* December, 1948.

"Revolutionary War," tr. and condensed by *Military Review,* August, 1959.

Rezin, P. "Tactics of Ambush," *Field Artillery Journal,* December, 1942.

Rigg, R. B. "The Guerrilla—a Factor in War," *Army Cavalry Journal,* November–December, 1949.

Riezler, K. "On the Psychology of Modern Revolution," *Social Research* (vol. 10), 1943.

Rocquigny, Col. de. "Urban Terrorism," tr. and condensed by *Military Review,* February, 1959.

Roucek, J. S. "Sociology of Secret Societies," *American Journal of Economics,* July, 1960.

"Secret Forces and Sabotage in Maneuver," *Military Review,* January, 1951.

Simonds-Gooding, H. "Guerrilla Warfare," *United Service Institute of India,* April, 1946.

Speier, H. "Treachery in War," *Social Research,* September, 1940.

Suhosky, R. A. "Ambush," *Leatherneck,* March, 1954.

"Swiss Partisans," tr. and condensed by *Military Review,* October, 1952.

Tomasic, D. "Ideologies and the Structure of Eastern European Society," *American Journal of Sociology,* March, 1948.

Waldenstrom, S. "Resistance Movements," *Military Review,* May, 1952.

Walker, F. L. "Your Next War," *Infantry Journal,* June, July, August, 1947.

Widder, D. J. W. "Ambush—The Commander's Attrition Punch," *Army Magazine,* November, 1961.

Wilkins, F. "Guerrilla," *Cavalry Journal,* September–October, 1941.

Ximenes, D. "Revolutionary War," tr. and condensed by *Military Review,* August, 1957.

Zawodny, J. K. "Unconventional Warfare," *Annals of the American Academy of Political and Social Science,* May, 1962.

————. "Unexplored Realms of Underground Strife," *American Behavioral Scientist,* September, 1960.

————. "Guerrilla Warfare and Subversion as a Means of Political Change" (Center for Advanced Study in the Behavioral Sciences, 202 Junipero Serra Blvd., Stanford University, Stanford, Calif.), 1961.

DOCUMENTS

Air University. Maxwell AFB, Ala.:

Carleton, L. A. *Are You Prepared?* Air Command and Staff College, Student Monograph, 12pp., 1955.

Greene, C. C. *Logistics and Guerrilla Warfare.* Air Command and Staff College, Study, 38pp., 1951.

Army. Assistant Chief of Staff. Intelligence. Washington, D.C.:

Guerrilla Warfare, "Surface" Warfare, Revolutionary Warfare. Intelligence Translation, no. H-2064, 15pp., 1957.

The Seven Principles of Guerrilla Tactics, n.p., Translation registry no. G-4084, 57pp., 1954.

Army. Deputy Chief of Staff for Logistics. Washington, D.C.:

Logistics Support of Guerrilla Warfare. Logistics Directive, no. 163–700, 6pp., 1959.

Army. Headquarters, Washington, D.C.:

Guerrilla Warfare, FM–31–21, 93pp., 1955.

Guerrilla Warfare and Special Forces Operations. FM–31–21, 144pp., 1958.

Guerrilla Warfare and Special Forces Operations. FM–31–21A (Classified), 1960.

Army. Intelligence Division. Washington, D.C.:

Lesson from the War. Translation registry no. F–6252, 28pp.

Army. Special Warfare Center, Fort Bragg, N.C.:

Readings in Guerrilla Warfare, December, 1960.

Johns Hopkins University. Operations Research Office. Washington, D.C.:

Condit, D. M. *A System for Handling Data on Unconventional Warfare: Including a Bibliography of Open Sources,* ORO–T–339, 185pp., 1956.

Hanrahan, G. Z., and W. M. Rossiter, *Military Potential of Combat Units Isolated in Enemy Rear Areas.* Technical Memorandum ORO–T, no. 297, 23pp., 1954.

Townsend, E. C. *Espionage, Underground Forces and Guerrillas.* Fort Leavenworth, Kan., 13pp., 1946.

Marine Corps. Historical Branch. Washington, D.C.:

Johnstone, J. H. *An Annotated Bibliography of the United States Marines in Guerrilla-Type Actions.* Headquarters, G-3 Division, Historical Bibliographies, no. 5, 16pp., 1961.

Ney, V. *Guerrilla Warfare and Propaganda,* Washington, D.C.: Georgetown University. Unpublished M.A. thesis, 106pp., 1958.

Special Operations Research Office. The American University. Washington, D.C.:

Miller, H., W. A. Lybrand, *et al. A Selected Bibliography on Unconventional Warfare.* 123pp., October, 1961.

Counterguerrilla Operations

BOOKS

Callwell, C. E. *Small Wars: Their Principles and Practice.* London: H.M. Stationery Office, 1906.

U.S. Marine Corps. *Small Wars Manual.* Washington, D.C.: Government Printing Office, 1940.

ARTICLES

"Anti-Guerrilla Operations," *Officer's Call,* March, 1951.

Bealer, A. W. "Command Post Minute Men," *Marine Corps Gazette,* September, 1952.

Bellinger, J. B. "Civilian Role in Antiguerrilla Warfare," *Military Review,* September, 1961.

Booth, W. "Operation Swamprat," *Combat Forces Journal,* October, 1950.

Bruehl, P. E. "Are We Prepared to Defend Our Highway Lines of Communications?," *National Defense Transportation Journal,* March–April, 1952.

Collier, T. W. "Partisans—the Forgotten Force," *Infantry,* August–September, 1960.

Clutterbuck, R. L. "Bertrant Stewart Prize Essay, 1960," *Army Quarterly,* January, 1961.

Decker, J. R. "Anti-Guerrilla Warfare," *Marine Corps Gazette,* August, 1951.

Dilke, C. W. "Guerrillas and Counter-Guerrillas," *Fortnightly Review,* December, 1901.

Dragojlov, F. "War against Partisans," tr. and condensed by *Military Review,* June, 1958.

Donovan, W. T. "Strategic Services in 'Cold War,'" *Naval War College Review,* September, 1953.

Firth, J. B. "The Guerrilla in History," *Fortnightly Review,* November, 1901.

Gray, D. W. "When We Fight a Small War," *Army Magazine,* July, 1960.

Grinland, N. G. "The Formidable Guerrilla," *Army Magazine,* February, 1962.

Htaik, T. "Encirclement Methods in Antiguerrilla Warfare," *Military Review,* June, 1961 (extract of the same, *Marine Corps Gazette,* August, 1961).

Jenkins, M. H. "Hannigan Learned the Hard Way," *Infantry,* January–March, 1959.

Johnson, J. R. "Antiguerrilla Exercise," *Marine Corps Gazette,* December, 1955.

Langtry, J. O. "Total Implications of the Human Factors in War," *Australian Army Journal,* April, 1958 (condensed in *Military Review,* February, 1959).

Lyke, J. P. "Protection for Rear Areas," *Military Review,* March, 1960.

Mangold, H. B. "Defense of the Rear Areas," *Infantry School Quarterly,* July, 1952.

Moore, P. N. M. "The Other Side of the Kampong," *Army Quarterly,* July, 1946.

Murphy, A. P. "Principles of Anti-Guerrilla Warfare," *Infantry School Quarterly,* July, 1951.

Oatts, L. B. "Guerrilla Warfare," *Royal United Service Institute Journal,* May, 1949.

Pickert, W. "Antiairborne and Antiguerrilla Defense," tr. and condensed by *Military Review,* August, 1957.

Puckett, R., and J. G. "Lancero," *Infantry,* July–September, 1959.

Rigg, R. B. "Get Guerrilla-Wise," *Combat Forces Journal,* September, 1950.

Rodgers, R. F. "Guerrilla Warfare," *Australian Army Journal,* November, 1957.

Saundby, R. "Irregular Warfare," *Air Power,* Winter, 1956–57 (condensed in *Military Review,* December, 1957).

Spark, M. "Guerrillas, Small Wars, and Marines," *Marine Corps Gazette,* Special Guerrilla Warfare Issue, January, 1962.

Warnbrod, K. "Defense of Rear Areas," *Infantry School Quarterly,* April, 1952.

Wilkinson, J. B. "The Company Fights Guerrillas," *Marine Corps Gazette,* Special Guerrilla Warfare Issue, January, 1962.

DOCUMENTS

Army. Headquarters. Washington, D.C.:
  Operations against Airborne Attack, Guerrilla Action and Infiltration. FM–31–15, 95pp., 1953.
  Operations against Guerrilla Forces. FM–31–20, 146pp., 1959.
Army. Special Warfare Center. Fort Bragg, N.C.:
  Readings in Counter-Guerrilla Operation. April, 1961.
Johns Hopkins University. Operations Research Office. Washington, D.C.:
  Japanese Operations against Guerrilla Forces, no. 263, 38pp., 1954.
Marine Corps. Marine Corps Schools. Quantico, Va.:
  Guerrillas and Anti-Guerrilla Operations. MCECO, p. 3430, IA TIP (T), 1960.
United States. The Engineer Schoool. Fort Belvoir, Va.:
  Combatting Guerrilla Operations. A. 020–57, 14pp., 1951.

Psychological Warfare

BOOKS

Auckland, R. G. *Aerial Propaganda Leaflets Dropped by the R.A.F. in the Far East between 1942–1945.* 60 High Street, Sandridge, Herts, England, 11pp., 1957.
Carroll, W. *Persuade or Perish.* Boston: Houghton, 1948.
Daugherty, W. E., and M. Janowitz. *A Psychological Warfare Case Book.* Baltimore, Md.: Johns Hopkins, 1958.
Dyer, M. *The Weapon on the Wall: Rethinking Psychological Warfare.* Baltimore, Md.: Johns Hopkins University, 1958.
Farago, L., ed. *German Psychological Warfare.* New York: Putnam, 1941.
Field, J. C. W., comp. *Aerial Propaganda Leaflets: A Collector's Handbook,* Sulton Coldfield, England: Field, 1954.
Lerner, D. *Sykewar.* New York: Stewart, 1949.
Linebarger, P. M. A. *Psychological Warfare,* 2nd ed. New York: Duell, Sloane, and Pearce, 1960.
White, J. B. *The Big Lie.* New York: Crowell, 1956.

ARTICLES

Araldsen, O. P. "Norway and Soviet Psychological Warfare," *Royal United Service Institute Journal,* November, 1961.
Barnett, F. R. "4th Dimensional Warfare and Our Foreign Policy," *Reserve Officer,* February, 1956.
Connolly, R. D. "The Principles of War and Psywar," *Military Review,* March, 1957.
Crossman, R. H. S. "Psychological Warfare," *Australian Army Journal,* June, 1953.

DeHuszar, G. B. "The Communist War of Ideas," *Officer,* February, 1959.

Diesen, E. "Psychological Preparedness," tr. and condensed by *Military Review,* October, 1954.

Ferrus (pseud.). "The Menace of Communist Psychological Warfare," *Orbis,* April, 1957.

Fleming, C. H. "Psychwar—A Neglected Weapon," *Marine Corps Gazette,* November, 1960.

Kahn, L. A., and T. G. Andrews. "A Further Analysis of the Effectiveness of Psychological Warfare," *Journal of Applied Psychology,* October, 1955.

King-Hall, S. "The Alternative to the Nuclear Deterrent: Non-Violent Resistance," *Royal United Service Institute Journal,* February, 1958.

Lockhart, R. H. B. "Political Warfare," *Royal United Service Institute Journal,* May, 1950.

McConaughy, J. B. "A Review of Soviet Psychological Warfare," *Military Review,* December, 1960.

May, R. E. "Fighting with Words," *Marine Corps Gazette,* March, 1961.

Possony, S. T. "Communist Psychological Warfare," *Officer's Magazine,* January, 1959.

Riley, J. W., Jr., and L. S. Cottrell, Jr. "Research for Psychological Warfare," *Public Opinion Quarterly,* Spring, 1958.

Taylor, E. "Political Warfare: A Sword We Must Unsheathe," *The Reporter,* September 14, 1961.

Warren, J. W. "War of Words," *Infantry Magazine,* January, 1958.

DOCUMENT

George Washington University. Human Resources Research Office. Washington, D.C.:
   Factors Affecting Credibility in Psychological Warfare Communications, no. 5, 58pp., 1956.

Role of Air Power

BOOK

Tickell, J. *Moon Squadron.* New York: Doubleday, 1956 (London: Wingate, 1956).

ARTICLES

Claunch, J. E. "Jungle Resupply with L-19," *Army Aviation Digest,* September, 1955.

Mertel, K. D. "Air Resupply," *Combat Forces Journal,* November, 1950.

Muir, J. I. "Air Supply," *Military Review,* November, 1945.

Norris, G. "Pimpernels of the Air," *Royal Air Force Flying Review,* August, September, and October, 1957.

Pointer, P. "They Blasted Amiens Jail," *The Roundel,* December, 1954.

DOCUMENTS

Air Force. Maxwell AFB, Ala.:

> *The Role of Air Power in Partisan Warfare.* Research Study no. 6, Vol. 3, 48pp., 1954.

Fisher, J. L. *Local Ground Defense of Air Bases.* Vol. 1, 1957.

Horne, C. G. *A Concept for the Employment of Tactical Air Forces in Combatting Guerrilla Warfare in the Middle East.* Air Command and Staff College, Study, 73pp., 1958.

Melchar, C. E. *A Concept for Employing Air Forces in Combatting Guerrilla Warfare.* Air Command and Staff College, Study, 68pp., 1958.

Guerrillas and International Law

BOOK

Lieber, F. *Guerrilla Parties Considered with Reference to the Laws and Usages of War.* New York: Van Nostrand, 1862 (22pp.).

ARTICLES

Baxter, R. R. "So-Called Underprivileged Belligerency: Spies, Guerrillas, and Saboteurs," *British Yearbook of International Law,* 1951.

Hazard, J. N., and J. P. Trainin. "Question of Guerrilla Warfare and the Laws of War," *American Journal of International Law,* July, 1946.

Nurick, L., and R. W. Barrett. "Legality of Guerrilla Forces under the Laws of War," *American Journal of International Law,* July, 1946.

Wilson, G. G. "Guerrillas and the Lawful Combatant," *American Journal of International Law,* June, 1943.

DOCUMENT

Special Operations Research Office. The American University. Washington, D.C.:

> Thienel, P. M. *The Legal Status of Participants in Unconventional Warfare.* 90pp., October, 1961.

Special Forces

1. COMMANDO OPERATIONS

BOOKS

Arnold, R. *The True Book about the Commandos.* London: Muller, 1954.

Austin, A. B. *We Landed at Dawn.* London: Gollancz, 1943.

Buckley, C. *Norway—the Commandos—Dieppe.* London: H.M. Stationery Office, 1951.

Durnford-Slater, J. F. *Commando.* London: Kimber, 1953.

Fergusson, B. *The Watery Maze.* New York: Holt, 1961 (London: Collins, 1961).

Holman, G. *Commando Attack.* New York: Putnam, 1942 (London: Hodder & Stoughton, 1942).

Lepotier, A. *Raiders from the Sea.* Tr. by M. Savil. London: Kimber, 1954.

McDougall, M. C. *Swiftly They Struck: The Story of No. 4 Commandos.* London: Odhams, 1954.

Mills-Robert, D. *Clash by Night: A Commando Chronicle.* London: Kimber, 1956.

Phillips, C. E. L. *Cockleshell Heroes.* London: Heinemann, 1956.

————. *The Greatest Raid of All.* Boston: Little, Brown, 1960 (London: Heinemann, 1958).

Reyburn, W. *Rehearsal for Invasion.* London: Harrap, 1943 (Toronto: *Glorious Chapter.* Oxford University Press, 1943).

Ryder, R. E. D. *The Attack on St. Nazaire, 28th March.* London, 1947.

Samain, B. *Commando Men: The Story of the Royal Marine Commando in Northwest Europe.* London: Stevens, 1948.

Saunders, H. St. George. *Combined Operations.* New York: Macmillan, 1943.

————. *The Green Beret: The Story of the Commandos, 1940–1945.* London: Joseph, 1949.

————. *The Red Beret: The Story of the Parachute Regiment at War, 1940–45.* London: Joseph, 1950.

Young, P. *Storm from the Sea.* London: Kimber, 1958.

ARTICLES

Andrews, R. D. A. "Special Boat Section—Royal Marines," *Marine Corps Gazette,* December, 1955.

Churchill, T. B. "The Value of Commandos," *Royal United Service Institute Journal,* February, 1950.

Close, C. C. S., "An Early Attempt at Combined Operations," *Royal United Service Institute Journal,* May, 1954.

"Commando Classroom," *Canadian Army Journal,* August, 1951.

Croft, A. J. "Commando Course, R.M.," *Marine Corps Gazette,* October, 1961.

Drysdale, D. B. "41 Commando," *Marine Corps Gazette,* August, 1953.

Gravrand, C. J. F. "French Marines," *Marine Corps Gazette,* September, 1957.

Hargreaves, R. "The Value of Commandos," *Royal United Service Institute Journal,* August, 1949.

Horan, R. H. E. "Combined Operations, 1939–45," *Royal United Service Institute Journal,* February, 1953.

————. "Operation 'Chariot': The Raid on St. Nazaire, 27th & 28th March, 1942," *ibid.,* May, 1954.

Laycock, R. E. "Raids in the Last War and Their Lessons," *Royal United Service Institute Journal,* November, 1947.

Lovat, L. "Training Commandos," *Cavalry Journal,* March–April, 1944.

"Operation Commando," *Australian Army Journal,* March, 1952.

Owens, P. J. "A History of 41 Commando—Korea 1950–52," *The Globe and Laurel,* August–September, 1960.

Stacey, C. P. "The Raid on Dieppe," *Military Review,* May, 1949.

Tompkins, R. M. "British Combined Operations," *Marine Corps Gazette,* December, 1948.

Twohig, J. P. "Are Commandos Really Necessary?," *Army Quarterly,* October, 1948.

2. SPECIAL WARFARE GROUPS

BOOKS

Connell, B. *Return of the Tiger.* New York: Doubleday, 1961.

Cowles, V. *Who Dares, Wins.* New York: Ballantine, 1959 (London: *The Phantom Major: The Story of Daniel Stirling and the S.A.S. Regiment.* Cassell, 1957).

Crichton-Stuart, M. *G. Patrol.* 2nd ed. London: Kimber, 1958.

Farran, R. *Winged Daggers.* London: Collins, 1954.

Foley, C. *Commando Extraordinary.* New York: Ballantine, 1956 (London: Longmans, 1954).

Harrison, D. I. *These Men Are Dangerous: The Special Air Service at War.* London: Cassell, 1957.

Howarth, P., ed. *Special Operations.* London: Routledge, 1955.

Lowick, J. *The Filibusters: The Story of the Special Boat Service.* London: Methuen, 1947.

McKie, R. *The Heroes.* New York: Harcourt, 1961 (London: Angus & Robertson, 1961).

Owens, D. L. *The Desert, My Dwelling Place.* London: Cassell, 1957.

Peniakoff, V. *Popski's Private Army.* New York: Crowell, 1950 (London: Cape, 1950).

Shaw, W. B. K. *Long Range Desert Group: Its Work in Libya, 1940–43.* London: Collins, 1945.

Skorzeny, O. *Skorzeny's Secret Missions.* New York: Dutton, 1950 (London: Hale, 1957).

Smith, D. M., and C. Carnes. *American Guerrilla Fighting behind Enemy Lines.* Indianapolis: Bobbs-Merrill, 1943.

Yunner, P. *Warriors on Wheels.* London: Hutchinson, 1959.

ARTICLES

Bellah, J. "Long Range Penetration Groups," *Infantry Journal,* October, 1944.

Burke, D. "Carlson of the Raiders," *Life,* September 20, 1943.

Crichton-Stuart, M. "The Story of a Long Range Desert Patrol," *Army Quarterly,* October, 1943.

Drysdale, D. B. "Special Forces," *Marine Corps Gazette,* June, 1954.

Fleming, P. "Unorthodox Warriors," *Royal United Service Institute Journal,* November, 1959.

Hackett, J. W. "The Employment of Special Forces," *Royal United Service Institute Journal,* February, 1952.

Heinl, R. D. "Small Wars—Vanishing Art," *Marine Corps Gazette,* April, 1950.

Hood, B. F. "The Gran Sasso Raid," *Military Review,* February, 1959.

"Operation Grief," *Military Review,* January, 1960.

McWhine, C. "The Case for a Strategic Assault Force," *Infantry*, June–July, 1960.

Oman, C. "A Commando Raid of 1460," *Army Quarterly*, October, 1944.

Wyatt, T. C. "Butcher and Bolt," *Army Magazine*, May, 1960.

3. FROGMAN UNDERWATER OPERATIONS

BOOKS

Bekker, C. D. *K-Men: The Story of German Frogman and Midget Submarines.* Tr. by G. Malcolm. London: Kimber, 1955.

Brow, W. C. *Combat beneath the Sea.* Tr. by Edward Fitzgerald. New York: Crowell, 1957 (London: Muller, 1958).

Fane, F. D. *The Naked Warriors.* London: Wingate, 1957.

Fraser, I. *Frogman V C.* London: Angus & Robertson, 1957.

Strutton, B., and M. Pearson. *The Beachhead Spies.* New York: Ace Books, 1958 (London: *The Secret Invaders.* Hodder & Stoughton, 1958).

Waldon, T. J., and J. Gleason, *The Frogman,* New York: Berkley, 1959 (London: Evans, 1950).

Warren, C. E. T., and J. Benson. *The Midget Raiders.* New York: Sloane, 1954 (London: *Above Us the Waves.* Harrap, 1953).

4. U.S. OFFICE OF STRATEGIC SERVICES

BOOKS

Alsop, S., and T. Braden. *Sub Rosa: The O.S.S. and American Espionage.* New York: Reynal & Hitchcock, 1946.

Donovan, W. J., and J. S. Roucek. *Secret Movements.* New York: Crowell, 1958.

Ford, C., and A. MacBain. *Cloak and Dagger.* New York: Random House, 1946.

Hall, R. *You're Stepping on My Cloak and Dagger.* New York: Norton, 1957 (London: Kimber, 1958).

Morgan, W. J. *The O.S.S. and I.* New York: Pocket Books, 1957.

O.S.S. Assessment Staff. *Assessment of Men.* New York: Holt, 1948.

ARTICLES

"A Good Man Is Hard to Find," *Fortune*, March, 1946.

Sakoda, J. M. "Factor Analysis of OSS Situation Tests," *Journal of Abnormal and Social Psychology*, October, 1952.

5. U.S. ARMY RANGERS

BOOKS

Altieri, J. *The Spearheaders.* New York: Popular Library, 1961.

Gilchrist, D. *Castle Commando.* London: Oliver & Boyd, 1960.

ARTICLES

Shipley, A. P. "Infantry Intern," *Infantry*, July–September, 1958.

Stroupe, R. M. "Rescue by the Rangers," *Military Review*, March, 1947.

Young, L. M. "Rangers in a Night Operation," *Military Review*, July, 1944.

6. U.S. ARMY SPECIAL FORCES

ARTICLES

Asprey, R. B. "Special Forces: Europe," *Army Magazine,* January, 1962.

Chapelle, D. "Our Secret Weapon in the Far East," *Reader's Digest,* June, 1960.

Dodson, C. A. "Special Forces," *Army Magazine,* June, 1961.

Gleason, F. A. "Unconventional Forces—The Commander's Untapped Resources," *Military Review,* October, 1959.

Goodman, G. J. W. "The Unconventional Warriors," *Esquire,* November, 1961.

Hamlett, B. "Special Forces: Training for Peace and War," *Army Information Digest,* June, 1961.

Hanrahan, G. Z. "Guerrilla Warfare," *Marine Corps Gazette,* March, 1956.

Kinard, W. H. "This Is Special Warfare U.S. Army Style," *Army Information Digest,* June, 1960.

McGlasson, W. D. "Have Guts, Will Travel," *National Guardsman,* April, 1960.

Mainard, A. G. "Special Warfare," *Leatherneck,* February, 1958.

Ortner, E. H. "U.S. Special Forces—The Faceless Army," *Popular Science,* August, 1961.

Pezzelle, R. M. "Special Forces," *Infantry,* April–June, 1959.

Raff, E. D. "Fighting behind Enemy Lines," *Army Information Digest,* April, 1956.

Troxel, O. C. "Special Warfare—a New Appraisal," *Army Information Digest,* December, 1957.

7. OTHER U.S. SPECIAL FORCES GROUPS

ARTICLES

Collins, J. M. "Deep Penetration Parachute Patrol," *Army Magazine,* December, 1959.

Devins, J. H. "Long Range Patrolling," *Infantry,* October–November, 1960.

Lyon, H. C. "Recondo," *Infantry,* January, 1960.

Meyers, B. F. "Force Recon," *Marine Corps Gazette,* May, 1961.

Nickerson, H. "Force Recon—by Land, Sea, and Air," *Marine Corps Gazette,* February, 1959.

Williams, R. C. "Amphibious Scouts and Raiders," *Military Affairs,* Fall, 1949.

Geographic Areas

1. AFRICA

A. The Boer War, 1899–1902

BOOKS

Cloete, S. *Against These Three: A Biography of Paul Kruger, Cecil Rhodes, and Lobengula, Last King of Matabele.* Boston: Houghton, 1945.

Doyle, C. *The Great Boer War.* New York: McClure & Phillips, 1902.

Kruger, R. C. *Good-Bye Dolly Gray: The Story of the Boer War.* Philadelphia: Lippincott, 1960.

Millin, S. G. *General Smuts*. Boston: Little, Brown, 1936.

Reitz, D. *Commando: A Boer Journal of the Boer War*. New York: Charles Boni Paper Books, 1930.

Smuts, J. C. *Jan Christian Smuts*. London: Morrow, 1952.

Wilson, H. W. *After Pretoria: The Guerrilla War*. 2 vol. London: Amalgamated, 1902.

ARTICLES

"Guerrilla Warfare: A Historical Parallel," *Blackwood's Edinburgh Magazine*, 171:102–108, 1902.

"With the Boers Round Mafeking, 1899–1900," *ibid.*, 16–27, 1902.

B. Mau Mau Uprising, 1952–1956

BOOKS

Corfield, F. D. *Historical Survey of the Origin and Growth of Mau Mau*. New York: British Information Service, 1960 (London: H.M. Stationery Office, 1960).

Henderson, J., and P. Goodhart, *Manhunt in Kenya*. New York: Doubleday, 1958.

Wills, C. *Who Killed Kenya?* London: Roy, 1953.

ARTICLES

Blackburn, R. J. "Aircraft versus Mau Mau," *Flight*, November 12, 1954.

Croker, G. W. "Mau Mau," *Royal United Service Institute Journal*, February, 1955.

Erskine, G. "Kenya—Mau Mau," *Royal United Service Institute Journal*, February, 1956.

Esmond-White, D. C. "Violence in Kenya," *Army Quarterly*, July, 1953.

Horne, N. S. "On Patrol against Mau Mau Terrorists," *Forces Magazine*, March, 1955.

Moyse-Bartlett, H. "Kenya: A Political-Military Problem," *Forces Magazine*, June, 1954.

Slane, P. M. "Tactical Problems in Kenya," *Army Quarterly*, October, 1954.

Whittlesey, D. "Kenya, the Land and Mau Mau," *Foreign Affairs*, October, 1953.

2. ALBANIA, WORLD WAR II

BOOKS

Amery, J. *Sons of the Eagle*. London: Macmillan, 1948.

Davies, T. *Illyrian Venture: The Story of the British Military Mission to Enemy-Occupied Albania, 1943–44*. London: Lane, 1952.

Filman, H. W. *Where Men and Mountains Meet*. Cambridge: Cambridge University, 1946.

Kemp, P. *No Colours or Crest*. London: Cassell, 1958.

ARTICLE

"Albanian Mission," *Fighting Forces*, February, 1945 (condensed in *Military Review*, July, 1945).

DOCUMENT

U.S. Army. Intelligence Division. Washington, D.C.:
   Resistance Factors and Special Forces Areas: Albania. Project no. A–229, 248pp., 1957.

3. ARABIA, WORLD WAR I

BOOKS

Armitage, F. *The Desert and the Stars: A Biography of Lawrence of Arabia.* New York: Holt, 1955.
Edmunds, C. *T. E. Lawrence.* New York: Appleton-Century, 1936.
Hart, L. *Colonel Lawrence: The Man behind the Legend.* New York: Dodd, Mead, 1934.
————. *Lawrence in Arabia and After.* London: Cape, 1936.
Lawrence, A. W., ed. *Oriental Assembly.* London: Williams & Norgate, 1937.
Lawrence, T. E. *Revolt in the Desert.* New York: Doran, 1927.
————. *Secret Dispatches from Arabia.* London: Golden Cockerel, 1939.
————. *Seven Pillars of Wisdom.* New York: Doubleday, 1935.
Lonnroth, E. *Lawrence of Arabia: An Historical Appreciation.* Tr. by R. Lewis. London: Vallentine, Mitchell, 1956.
Storrs, R. *Lawrence of Arabia, Zionism, and Palestine.* Harmondsworth, Middlesex, England: Penguin, 1940.
Wevell, A. P. *The Palestine Campaigns.* London: Constable, 1928.
Young, H. *The Independent Arab.* London: Murray, 1933.

ARTICLES

"Extracts from Lawrence's Twenty-Seven Articles," *Military Review*, October, 1954.
Lawrence, T. E. "The Evolution of a Revolt," *Army Quarterly*, October, 1920.
————. "Guerrilla Warfare," *Encyclopaedia Britannica*, Vol. 10, 1948.
Patton, O. B. "Colonel T. E. Lawrence of Arabia," *Military Review*, October, 1954.
Pavey, R. A. "The Arab Revolt," *Marine Corps Gazette*, July, 1956.

4. ASIAN AREAS

BOOK

Payne, R. *Red Storm over Asia.* New York: Macmillan, 1951.

ARTICLE

Hanna, W. A. "Three Men and Three Revolutions," *The Reporter*, February 16, 1961.

DOCUMENTS

Air University. Maxwell AFB, Ala.:
> Steele, R. J. *Employment of Tactical Air Forces against Guerrillas i Southeast Asia.* Air Command and Staff College, Study, 1958.

Johns Hopkins University. Operations Research Office, Washington, D.C.:
> Hanrahan, G. Z. *Asian Guerrilla Movements: Annotated Bibliography of Source Materials on Guerrilla Movements in East and Southeast Asia.* 117pp. (Technical Memorandum ORO–T, no. 224), 1953.
>
> ———. *Salient Operational Aspects of Para-Military Warfare in Three Asian Areas.* 241pp. (Technical Memorandum ORO–T, no. 288), 1953.

5. BALKANS, WORLD WAR II

BOOK

Dunsany, E. *Guerrilla.* Indianapolis: Bobbs-Merrill, 1944.

DOCUMENTS

Army. Washington, D.C.:
> *German Anti-Guerrilla Operations in the Balkans, 1941–1944,* no. 20–243. 82pp., 1954.

Army. Headquarters. European Command.
> *Partisan Warfare in the Balkans.* Tr. by the U.S. Army from General Lanz's article, "Warfare against Partisans in a Mountainous Wooded Terrain," 1952, APO 403.

6. BELGIUM

BOOKS

Goffin, R. *The White Brigade.* Tr. by C. L. Markman. New York: Doubleday, 1944.
Goris, J. *Belgium.* Berkeley, Calif.: University of California, 1945.

ARTICLES

Dreze, R. "The Liberal Party," *The Annals,* September, 1946.
Terfve, J. "The Communist Party," *The Annals,* September, 1946.

DOCUMENTS

Tanham, G. K. *The Belgium Underground Movement, 1940–1944.* Stanford, Calif.: Stanford University, 1951. (Unpublished Ph.D. Dissertation.)
U.S. Office of Strategic Services. Washington, D.C.:
> *The Belgium Underground,* 24pp., 1944.

7. BORNEO

BOOK

Harrison, T. *World Within.* London: Cresset, 1959.

8. BRAZIL, 1896–1897

BOOK

Cunha, E. da. *Rebellion in the Backland*. Tr. by S. Putnam. Chicago: University of Chicago, 1960 (first English edition published in 1944).

9. BULGARIA

DOCUMENT

Army. Intelligence Division, Washington, D.C.:
   Resistance Factors and Special Forces Areas: Bulgaria. Project no. A–394, 266pp., 1957.

10. BURMA, WORLD WAR II

BOOKS

Beamish, J. *Burma Drop*. London: Elek, 1960.
Branard, J. *The Hump*. London: Souvenir, 1961.
Brelis, D. *The Mission*. New York: Pocket Books, 1959.
Burchett, W. G. *Wingate's Phantom Army*. Bombay, Thacker, 1944.
Calvert, M. *Prisoners of Hope*. London: Cape, 1952.
Chamales, T. *Never So Few*. New York: Scribner, 1957.
Fellowes-Gordon, I. *Amiable Assassins: The Story of the Kachin Guerrillas of North Burma*. London: Hale, 1957.
Fergusson, B. E. *Beyond the Chindwin: Being an Account of the Adventures of Number Five Column of the Wingate Expedition into Burma, 1943*. London: Collins, 1945.
———. *The Wild Green Earth*. London: Collins, 1946.
Friend, J. *The Long Trek*. London: Muller, 1957.
Guthrie, D. *Jungle Diary*. New York: Longmans, Green, 1946.
Halley, D. *With Wingate in Burma*. London: Hodge, 1945.
Irwin, A. *Burmese Outpost*. London: Collins, 1945.
Jeffrey, W. F. *Sunbeams Like Swords*. London: Hodder, 1951.
MacHorton, I., and H. Maule. *Safer than a Known Way: One Man's Epic Struggle against Japanese and Jungle*. London: Odhams, 1958.
McKelvie, R. *The War in Burma*. London: Methuen, 1948.
Morrison, I. *Grandfather Longlegs*. London: Faber, 1947.
Moseley, L. *Gideon Goes to War*. London: Barker, 1955 (New York: Scribner, 1956).
Ogburn, C. *The Marauders*. New York: Fawcett Crest Books, 1960.
Rolo, C. J. *Wingate's Raiders: An Account of the Fabulous Adventure That Raised the Curtain on the Battle of Burma*. New York: Viking, 1944.
Sykes, C. *Orde Wingate: A Biography*. Cleveland: World Publishing, 1959.
Wilcox, W. A. *Chindit Column 76*. London: Longmans, Green, 1945.

ARTICLES

Bellah, J. "Encirclement by Air," *Infantry Journal*, June, 1944.

"The Burma Campaigns," *Military Review*, February, 1946.

Crocker, H. E. "Dacoits in Burma," *Fighting Forces*, August, 1947.

Fergusson, B. E. "Behind the Enemy Lines in Burma," *Royal United Service Institute Journal*, August, 1946.

————. "The Burma Rifles," *United Service Institute of India*, January, 1945.

————. "Two Years under Wingate," *Cavalry Journal*, May–June, 1946.

Hilsman, R. "Burma Ambush" (digest of paper that appears as Chapter 9 of this book), *Marine Corps Gazette*, Special Guerrilla Warfare Issue, January, 1962.

Mead, P. W. "The Chindit Operations of 1944," *Royal United Service Institute Journal*, May, 1955.

"Mobility in the Jungle," *Air University Quarterly Review*, Winter, 1954–55.

Ogburn, C. "Merrill's Marauders—The Truth about an Incredible Adventure," *Harper's*, January, 1957.

Osburne, W. L. "Shaduzup," *Infantry Journal*, April, 1950.

Peers, W. R. "Guerrilla Operations in Northern Burma," *Military Review*, June and July, 1948.

Rumsey, J. R. L. "Air Supply in Burma," *Army Quarterly*, October, 1947.

Sewell, H. S. "Fighters behind Jap Lines in Burma," *Military Review*, June, 1945.

Stone, J. B. "The Marauders and the Microbes," *Infantry Journal*, March, 1949.

Wilkinson, W. C. "Problems of a Guerrilla Leader," *Military Review*, November, 1952.

Wilson, W. K. "Logistical Support of British Operations in Burma in the Winter of 1944–45," *Military Review*, March, 1946.

11. CUBA, 1895–1897

BOOK

Reporaz, D. G. *The War in Cuba: A Military Study*. London: (publisher unknown) 1898.

ARTICLE

"The Spanish Crises," *Blackwood's Edinburgh Magazine*, 163:238–253, 1898.

12. CYPRUS, 1955–1959

BOOKS

Alastos, D. *Cyprus Guerrillas: Grivas, Makarios, and the British Doros Alastos*. London: Heinemann, 1960.

Barker, D. *Grivas: Portrait of a Terrorist*. New York: Harcourt, 1960.

Foot, S. *Emergency Exit*. London: Chatto & Windus, 1960.
Tremayne, P. *Below the Tide*. London: Hutchinson, 1958.

ARTICLES

Gourlay, B. I. S. "Terror in Cyprus," *Marine Corps Gazette*, August and September, 1959.
Leopold, L. "The Cyprus Bastion," *U.S. Naval Institute Proceedings*, March, 1952.

13. CZECHOSLOVAKIA, WORLD WAR II

BOOKS

Burgess, A. *Seven Men at Daybreak*. New York: Dutton, 1960.
Hronek, J. *Volcano under Hitler: The Underground War in Czechoslovakia*. London: Czechoslovak Independent Weekly, 1941.
Mackworth, C. *Czechoslovakia Fights Back*. London: Drummond, 1942.

14. DENMARK, WORLD WAR II

BOOKS

Bertelsen, A. *October '43*. Tr. by M. Lindholm and W. Agtby. New York: Putnam, 1954 (London: Museum, 1955).
Lampe, D. *The Danish Resistance*. New York: Ballantine, 1961 (London: *The Savage Canary*. Cassell, 1957).
Muus, F. B. *The Spark and the Flame*. Tr. by V. Muus and J. F. Burke. London: Museum, 1957.

ARTICLE

Leistikow, G. "Denmark under the Nazi Heel," *Foreign Affairs*, January, 1943.

15. ETHIOPIA, WORLD WAR II

BOOKS

Allen, W. E. D. *Guerrilla War in Abyssinia*. Baltimore: Penguin, 1943.
MacDonald, J. F. *Abyssinian Adventure*. London: Cassell, 1957.
Schaefer, L. F., ed. *The Ethiopian Crisis, Touchstone of Appeasement?* Boston: Heath, 1961.

16. FINLAND, WORLD WAR II

BOOKS

Jakobson, M. *The Diplomacy of the Winter War: An Account of the Russo-Finnish War, 1939–1940*. Cambridge, Mass.: Harvard University, 1961.

Langdon-Davies, J. *Invasion in the Snow: A Study of Mechanized War.* Boston: Houghton, 1941 (London: *Finland—The First Total War.* Routledge, 1941).

ARTICLES

Mikola, K. J. "The Finnish Wars, 1939–1945," *Revue Internationale d'Histoire Militaire,* no. 23, 1961.
"Motti Tactics," *Infantry Journal,* January, 1950.
Schuler, E. "Fighting in the Forest of Finland," tr. and condensed by *Military Review,* December, 1960.

DOCUMENT

Army. Intelligence Division. Washington, D.C.:
   Guerrilla Activities in the Winter War and Development from 1941–1944. n.p., n.d. (translation registry no. F–6685A).

17. FRANCE, WORLD WAR II

BOOKS

Astier, D. E. D. *Seven Times Seven Days.* Tr. by H. Hare. London: MacGibbon & Kee, 1958.
Benouville, G. de. *The Unknown Warriors: A Personal Account of the French Resistance.* Tr. by H. G. Blockman. New York: Simon & Schuster, 1949.
Bergier, J. *Secret Weapons—Secret Agents.* Tr. by Edward Fitzgerald. London: Hurst & Blackett, 1956.
Buckmaster, M. J. *Specially Employed: The Story of British Aid to the French Patriots of the Resistance.* London: Batchworth, 1952.
———. *They Fought Alone: The Story of British Agents in France.* New York: Norton, 1958 (London: Odhams, 1958).
Churchill, P. *Duel of Wits.* New York: Putnam, 1955 (London: Hodder & Stoughton, 1953).
Fuller, J. O. *No. 13 Bob.* New York: Little, Brown, 1955 (London: *Madeleine.* Gollancz, 1952).
Grenier, F. *Franc-Tireurs and Guerrillas of France.* London: Cobbett, 1944.
Kessel, J. *Army of Shadows.* Tr. by H. Chevalier. New York: Knopf, 1944.
Liebling, A. J., ed. *The Republic of Silence.* New York: Harcourt, 1947.
Marsden, A. *Resistance Nurse.* London: Odhams, 1961.
Marshall, B. *The White Rabbit.* Boston: Houghton, 1952 (London: Evans, 1952).
Millar, C. R. *Waiting in the Night.* New York: Doubleday, 1946 (London: *Maquis.* Heinemann, 1945).
Nicholos, E. *Death Be Not Proud.* London: Cresset, 1958.
Rémy, G. *Courage and Fear.* Tr. by L. C. Sheppard. London: Barker, 1950.
Scott, L. *I Dropped In.* London: Barrie & Rockliff, 1959.
Shiber, E. *Paris Underground.* New York: Scribner, 1943.

Teare, T. D. G. *Evader*. London: Hodder & Stoughton, 1954.

Vaculik, S. *Air Commando*. Tr. by E. Fitzgerald. New York: Dutton, 1955 (London: Jarrold, 1954).

Vomecourt, P. de. *An Army of Amateurs*. New York: Doubleday, 1961.

Waldheim-Emmerick, R. *In the Footsteps of Joan of Arc: True Stories of Heroines of the French Resistance in World War II*. Tr. by F. Gaynor. New York: Exposition, 1959.

Walters, A. *Moondrop to Gascony*. London: Macmillan, 1946.

Wighton, C. *Pin-Stripe Saboteur: The Story of "Robin," British Agent and French Resistance Leader*. London: Odhams, 1959.

ARTICLES

Cass, L. M. "The Maquis Republic of Vercors," *Infantry Journal*, April, 1957.

Combaux, C. "Military Activities of the French Resistance Movement," *Military Review*, July, 1945.

Grell, W. F. "A Marine with the O.S.S." *Marine Corps Gazette*, December, 1945.

Parker, G. "A Surgeon in Guerrilla Warfare," *Military Review*, April, 1947.

Sawyer, J. A. "The Reestablishment of the Republic in France: The DeGaulle Era, 1944–1945," *Political Science Quarterly*, September, 1947.

Siegfried, A. "The Rebirth of the French Spirit," *Foreign Affairs*, July, 1945.

Vinde, V. "The Spirit of Resistance," *Foreign Affairs*, October, 1942.

18. GERMANY, WORLD WAR II

BOOKS

Andreas-Friedrich, R. *Berlin Underground, 1938–45*. Tr. by B. Mussey. New York: Holt, 1947 (London: Latimer, 1948).

Dulles, A. W. *Germany's Underground*. New York: Macmillan, 1947.

Fraenkel, H. *The Other Germany*. London: Drummond, 1942.

Jansen, J. B., and W. Stefan. *The Silent War: The Underground Movement in Germany*. Philadelphia: Lippincott, 1943.

Rothfels, H. *The German Opposition to Hitler: An Appraisal*. Chicago: Regnery, 1948.

Trevor-Roper, H. R. *Last Days of Hitler*. New York: Macmillan, 1947.

ARTICLE

Almond, G. A. "The German Resistance Movement," *Current History* (vol. 10), 1946.

19. GREECE, WORLD WAR II

BOOKS

Byford-Jones, W. *The Greek Trilogy*. London: Hutchinson, 1945.

Fielding, I. *Hide and Seek: The Story of a War-Time Agent*. London: Secker & Warburg, 1954.

Jerchinis, C. *Beyond Olympus: The Thrilling Story of the "Train-Busters" in Nazi-Occupied Greece.* London, Harrap, 1960.

Lincoln, J. *Achilles and the Tortoise: An Eastern Aegean Exploit.* London: Heinemann, 1958.

McNeil, W. H. *Greek Dilemma: War and Aftermath.* Philadelphia: Lippincott, 1947.

Moss, S. *Ill Met by Moonlight.* New York: Macmillan, 1950 (London: Harrap, 1950).

———. *A War of Shadows.* New York: Macmillan, 1952 (London: Boardman, 1952).

Myers, E. C. W. *Greek Entanglement.* London: Hart-Davis, 1955.

Psychoundakis, G. *The Cretan Runner: His Story of German Occupation.* Tr. by P. L. Fermor. London: Murray, 1955.

Rendel, A. M. *Appointment in Crete: The Story of a British Agent.* London: Wingate, 1953.

Smothers, F. *Report on the Greeks.* New York: The Twentieth Century Fund, 1948.

Turton, E. B. *I Lived with Greek Guerrillas.* Melbourne: The Book Depot Co., 1945.

Woodhouse, C. M. *Apple of Discord.* London: Hutchinson, 1947.

ARTICLES

Black, C. E. "Greece and the United Nations," *Political Science Quarterly,* December, 1948.

Stavrianos, L. S. "The Greek National Liberation Front (EAM): A Study in Resistance Organization and Administration," *Journal of Modern History,* March, 1952.

20. HAITI, 1915–1934

BOOK

McCrocklin, J. H. *Garde d'Haiti.* Annapolis, Md.: United States Naval Institute, 1956.

ARTICLE

Greathouse, R. H. "King of the Banana Wars," *Marine Corps Gazette,* June, 1960.

21. HUNGARY, OCTOBER–NOVEMBER, 1956

BOOKS

Bain, L. B. *The Reluctant Satellites: An Eyewitness Report on East Europe and the Hungarian Revolution.* New York: Macmillan, 1959.

Fejto, F. *Behind the Rape of Hungary.* New York: McKay, 1957.

Kecskemeti, P. *The Unexpected Revolution: Social Forces in the Hungarian Uprising.* Stanford, Calif.: Stanford University, 1961.

Laskey, M. J., ed. *The Hungarian Revolution.* New York: Praeger, 1957.
Lettis, R., and W. E. Morris, eds. *The Hungarian Revolt.* New York: Scribner, 1961.
Vali, F. A. *Rift and Revolt in Hungary: Nationalism versus Communism.* Cambridge, Mass.: Harvard University, 1961.

ARTICLES

Gellner, J. "The Hungarian Revolution: A Military Post-Mortem," *Marine Corps Gazette,* April, 1958.
————. "What Went Wrong in Hungary?," *United States Naval Institute Proceedings,* June, 1957.

DOCUMENT

Army. Intelligence Division. Washington, D.C.:
  Resistance Factors and Special Forces Areas: Hungary, 1957. 278pp. (Project no. A–914).

22. INDOCHINA, WORLD WAR II

ARTICLES

"The Indochina Resistance," *Military Review,* February, 1947.
"Military Operations in Indochina, 1940–45," *Military Review,* March, 1948.
Villiers, A. "French Indochina," *Marine Corps Gazette,* June, 1949.

23. INDONESIA, POST-WORLD WAR II

BOOK

Kamin, G. *Nationalism and Revolution in Indonesia.* Ithaca, N.Y.: Cornell University, 1952.

ARTICLES

Chaplin, H. D. "Indonesian Incident," *Army Quarterly,* April, 1950.
————. "The U.N. Military Observers in Indonesia," *Army Quarterly,* April, 1952.
Menefee, S. "Guerrillas in the Indies," *Cavalry Journal,* March–April, 1945.
Van Vook, H. J. "Indonesia and the Problems of Southeast Asia," *Foreign Affairs,* July, 1949.

24. IRELAND, 1916–1923

BOOKS

Barry, T. B. *Guerrilla Days in Ireland: A First Hand Account of the Black and Tan War, 1919–1921.* New York: Devin-Adair, 1956.
Briscoe, R. *For the Life of Me.* Boston: Little, Brown, 1958.

Colum, P. *Ourselves Alone: The Story of Arthur Griffith and the Origin of the Irish Free State.* New York: Crown, 1959.

Figgis, D. *Recollections of the Irish War.* New York: Doubleday, 1927.

Holt, E. *Protest in Arms: The Irish Troubles 1916–1923.* New York: Coward-McCann, 1961 (London: Putnam, 1960).

Jones, F. P. *History of the Sinn Fein Movement and the Irish Rebellion of 1916.* New York: Kenedy, 1917.

Joy, M., ed. *The Irish Rebellion of 1916 and Its Martyrs.* New York: Devin-Adair, 1916.

Kerryman, Ltd. *With the IRA in the Fight for Freedom.* Tralee: Kerryman, n.d.

O'Callagnan, S. *The Easter Lily: The Story of the I.R.A.* New York: Roy, 1958.

O'Donnell, P. *There Will Be Fighting.* New York: Putnam, 1931.

O'Grady, R. *O'Houlihan's Jest.* New York: Macmillan, 1961.

O'Malley, E. *Army without Banners: Adventures of an Irish Volunteer.* Boston: Houghton, 1937.

25. ISRAEL (PALESTINE), 1946–1949

BOOKS

Begin, M. *The Revolt: The Story of the Irgun.* Tr. by S. Katz. New York: Schuman, 1952.

Dekel, E. *Shai: The Exploits of Hagana Intelligence.* New York: Yoseloff, 1959.

Kimche, J. and D. *A History of the Foundation of Israel and the Arab-Jewish War.* New York: Praeger, 1959.

Meridor, Y. *Long Is the Road to Freedom.* Tujunga, Calif.: (P. O. Box 18) Barak Publishers, 1961.

Pearlman, M. *The Army of Israel.* New York: Philosophical Library, 1950.

Sacker, H. *Israel.* London: Weidenfeld, 1952.

Syrkin, M. *Blessed Is the Match: The Story of Jewish Resistance.* Philadelphia: The Jewish Publication Society, 1947.

Wilson, R. D. *Gordon and Search.* Aldershot, England: Gale & Polden, 1949.

ARTICLES

Anderson, R. N. "Search Operations in Palestine," *Marine Corps Gazette,* April, 1948.

Ne'eman, Y. "The Unorthodox Israeli Army," *Marine Corps Gazette,* November, 1961.

26. ITALY

A. 1848–1860

ARTICLE

Wood, M. M. "From Gauchos to Guerrillas: The American Education of Giuseppe Garibaldi," *Americas,* January, 1961.

B. World War II

BOOKS

Battazilia, R. *The Story of the Italian Resistance.* Tr. by P. D. Cummins. London: Odhams, 1958.
Bonciani, C. *"F" Squadron.* Tr. by J. Shillidy. London: Dent, 1947.
Carter, B. B. *Italy Speaks.* London: Gollancz, 1947.
Delzell, C. F. *Mussolini's Enemies: The Italian Anti-Fascist Resistance.* Princeton, N.J.: Princeton University, 1961.
Dunning, G. *Where Bleed the Many.* London: Elek, 1955.
Farron, R. *Operation Tombola.* London: Collins, 1960.
Lelt, G. *Rossano: An Adventure of Italian Resistance.* London: Hodder & Stoughton, 1955.
Luzzatto, R. *Unknown War in Italy.* London: New European Publishers, 1946.
Maugeri, F. *From the Ashes of Disgrace.* New York: Reynal & Hitchcock, 1948.

ARTICLES

Roselli, A. "Guerrilla Warfare as It Really Is," *Harper's,* August, 1952.
Salvadori-Paleotti, M. "The Patriot Movement in Italy," *Foreign Affairs,* April, 1946.

DOCUMENT

Johns Hopkins University. Operations Research Office. Washington, D.C.: *Allied Supplies for Italian Partisans during World War II.* no. 269, 72pp., 1954.

27. KASHMIR, 1957–1958

ARTICLE

Haight, R. K. "The Bridge at Kotli," *Army Magazine,* November, 1958.

28. KOREA, 1950–1953

BOOKS

Clark, M. *From the Danube to the Yalu.* New York: Harper, 1954.
Gugeler, R. A. *Combat Action in Korea.* Washington: Combat Forces, 1954.
Karig, W. *Battle Report.* New York: Rinehart, 1952.

ARTICLES

Beebe, J. E. "Beating the Guerrillas," *Military Review,* December, 1955.
Kleinman, F. K. "Designed for Your Destruction," *Infantry,* February–March, 1960.
Larrabee, E. "Korea: The Military Lesson," *Harper's,* November, 1950.
Montross, L. "The Pohang Guerrilla Hunt: 1600 Square Miles of Trouble," *Marine Corps Gazette,* January, 1952.

DOCUMENTS

Johns Hopkins University. Operations Research Office, Washington, D.C.:
U.N. Partisan Warfare in Korea, 1951–1954, no. 64, 209pp., 1956.
RAND Corporation. Santa Monica, California:
North Korea Guerrilla Units. RM–550, 7pp., 1951.

29. MALAYA, WORLD WAR II

BOOKS

Chapman, F. S. *The Jungle Is Neutral*. New York: Norton, 1949 (London: Chatto & Windus, 1949).
————. *Living Dangerously*. London: Chatto & Windus, 1953.
Chin, Kee Onn. *Silent Army*. New York: Ballantine, 1953.
Cross, J. *Red Jungle*. London: Hale, 1958.
Thatcher, D., and R. Cross. *Pai Noa: The Story of Nona Baker*. London: Constable, 1959.

30. THE NETHERLANDS, WORLD WAR II

BOOKS

Boas, J. H. *Religious Resistance in Holland*. London: Allen & Unwin, 1945.
De Jong, L. *Holland Fights the Nazis*. London: Drummond, 1941.
Dourlein, P. *Inside North Pole: A Secret Agent's Story*. London: Kimber, 1953.
Duren, T. *Orange Above*. London: Staples, 1956.
Giskes, H. J. *London Calling North Pole*. London: Kimber, 1953.
Kessel, A. W. L., and J. St. John. *Surgeon at Arms*. New York: Norton, 1959.

ARTICLE

Meerloo, A. M. "Psychological War Experiences in a Small Army," *Psychiatric Quarterly Supplement* (vol. 21), 1947.

31. NICARAGUA, 1927–1931

ARTICLE

Peard, R. W. "The Tactics of Bush Warfare," *Infantry Journal*, September–October, 1931.

32. NORWAY, WORLD WAR II

BOOKS

Astrup, H., and B. L. Jacot. *Oslo Intrigue: A Woman's Memoir of the Norwegian Resistance*. New York: McGraw-Hill, 1954.
Hauge, E. O. *Salt-Water Thief*. Tr. by Malcolm Munthe. London: Duckworth, 1958.
Haukelid, K. *Skis against the Atom*. Tr. by F. H. Lyon. London: Kimber, 1954.

Howard, D. *Across to Norway.* New York: Sloane, 1952 (London: *The Shetland Bus.* Nelson, 1951).

Manus, M. *9 Lives before Thirty.* New York: Doubleday, 1947.

Oluf, R. O. *Two Eggs on My Plate.* Chicago: Rand McNally, 1953 (London: Allen & Unwin, 1952).

Saeler, F. *None But the Best: The Story of "Shetlands."* Tr. by K. A. Lund. London: Souvenir, 1955.

33. PHILIPPINES, WORLD WAR II

BOOKS

Abaya, H. *Betrayal in the Philippines.* New York: Wyn, 1946.

Doromal, J. D. *The War in Panay: A Documentary History of the Resistance Movement in Panay during World War II.* Manila: Diamond Historical, 1952.

Galang, R. C. *Secret Missions to the Philippines.* Manila: University Publishing Co., 1948.

Haggert, J. E. *Guerrilla Padre in Mindanao.* New York: Longmans, 1946.

Harkins, P. *Blackburn's Headhunters.* New York: Norton, 1955 (London: Cassell, 1956).

Hawkins, J. *Never Say Die.* Philadelphia: Dorrance, 1961.

Ingham, T. *Rendevous by Submarine: The Story of Charles Parsons and the Guerrilla Soldiers in the Philippines.* New York: Doubleday, 1945.

Monaghan, F. J. *Under the Red Sun: A Letter from Manila.* Garden City, N.Y.: McMullen, 1946.

Panlilio, Y. *The Crucible.* New York: Macmillan, 1950.

Phillip, G. *Manila Espionage.* Portland, Ore.: Binford & Mort, 1947.

St. John, J. F. *Leyte Calling.* New York: Vanguard, 1945.

Spencer, L. R. *Guerrilla Wife.* New York: Crowell, 1945.

Utinsky, M. *Miss U.* San Antonio, Tex.: Naylor, 1948.

Volckmann, R. W. *We Remained: Three Years behind Enemy Lines in the Philippines.* New York: Norton, 1954.

Wolfert, I. *American Guerrilla in the Philippines.* New York: Simon & Schuster, 1945 (London: *Guerrilla.* Transworld, 1958).

ARTICLES

Bautista, A. N. "East Central Luzon Guerrilla," *Military Review,* March, 1946.

Espiritu, N. "The First Filipino Guerrilla Regiment in World War II," *Philippine Armed Forces Journal,* August, 1956.

Fertig, C. E. "American Engineers with Philippine Guerrillas," *Military Engineers,* September–October, 1949.

Fink, S. "A Marine Guerrilla's Diary," *Leatherneck,* August, 1945.

Sanchez, J. A. "Guerrilla Warfare in Luzon," *Armoured Cavalry Journal,* July–August, 1947.

Taylor, J. G. "Air Support of Guerrillas on Cebu," *Military Affairs,* Fall, 1959.

Volckmann, R. W. "The Raid on Los Banos," *Infantry Journal,* October, 1945.

DOCUMENTS

General Headquarters. U.S. Army Forces. Pacific:
  The Guerrilla Resistance Movement in the Philippines, Vol. 1, 1948.
Military History. Department of the Army. Washington, D.C.:
  Ney, V. *Guerrilla Warfare in the Philippines, 1942–1945.*

34. POLAND

A. World War II

BOOKS

Bor-Kamorowski, T. *The Secret Army.* New York: Macmillan, 1951 (London: Gollancz, 1950).
Jordan, P. *In the Field and Underground.* London: Polish Ministry of Information, 1944.
Karski, J. *The Story of a Secret State.* Boston: Houghton, 1944 (London: Hodder & Stoughton, 1945).
Korbonski, S. *Fighting Warsaw: The Story of the Polish Underground State, 1939–1945.* Tr. by F. B. Czarnomski. London: Allen & Unwin, 1956.
Sosabowski, S. *Freely I Served.* London: Kimber, 1960.
Tennenbaum, J. *Underground: The Story of a People.* New York: Philosophical Library, 1952.
The Unseen and Silent: Adventures from the Underground Movement. Narrated by Paratroopers of the PHA. Tr. by G. Iranek-Osmecki. London: Sheed & Ward, 1954.
Zajaczkowska, A. *The Underground Struggle: An Untold Story.* Bombay: Associated Advertisers, 1945.

ARTICLES

Bor-Komorowski, T. "Sewer Warfare in the Warsaw Rising," *The Nineteenth Century,* July, 1950.
"The Polish Home Army," *Military Review,* November, 1944.
Stableford, P. E. "Supplies to Warsaw," *South African Air Force Journal,* January, 1950.

B. Polish Revolution, 1956

BOOKS

Gibney, F. *The Frozen Revolution: Poland, A Study in Communist Decay.* New York: Farrar, Straus & Cudahy, 1960.
Shneiderman, S. L. *The Warsaw Heresy.* New York: Horizon Press, 1959.
Syrop, K. *Spring in October: The Story of the Polish Revolution in 1956.* New York: Praeger, 1958.

35. RUSSIA

A. War of 1812

BOOK

Caulaincourt, A. de. *With Napoleon in Russia: Memoirs.* New York: Grosset, 1935.

B. Civil War, 1917–1918

BOOK

Kowimakoff, S. *Russia's Fighting Forces.* New York: Duell, Sloane, and Pearce, 1942.

36. SIAM, WORLD WAR II

BOOK

Smith, N., and B. Clark. *Into Siam, Underground Kingdom.* Indianapolis: Bobbs-Merrill, 1945.

ARTICLES

Chakrabandhu, C. K. "Force 136 and the Siamese Resistance Movement," *Asiatic Review,* April, 1947.

Chandruang, K., and C. Prabha. "Our Siamese Underground," *Asia,* November, 1945.

37. SPAIN

A. Peninsular War, 1811–1813

BOOKS

Ford, G. *The Unchanging Character of the War in Spain: A Treatise.* (publisher unknown) 1889.

Forester, C. S. *Rifleman Dodd and the Gun.* New York: Readers Club, 1942.

Forestier, M. *The Fort of San Lorenzo.* London: Hodder & Stoughton, 1960.

Napier, W. F. P. *History of the War in the Peninsula.* 4 Volumes. Philadelphia: Carey & Hart, 1842.

Rocca, M. de. *Memoirs of the War of the French in Spain.* London: Murry, 1816.

Thomason, J. W., ed. *Adventures of General Marbor.* New York: Scribner, 1935.

ARTICLES

de Beer, G. R. "The Peninsular War," *Army Quarterly,* August, 1943.

"Guerrilla Warfare—A Historical Parallel," *Blackwood's Edinburgh Magazine,* 171:102–108, 1902.

"The Guerrillero," *ibid.,* 163:540–551, 1898.

B. Civil War, 1936–1938

BOOKS

Borkeraw, F. *The Spanish Cockpit: An Eyewitness Account of the Political and Social Conflicts of the Spanish Civil War.* London: Faber, 1937.

Brenan, G. *The Spanish Labyrinth: Social and Political Background of the Civil War.* New York: Cambridge University, 1960.

Cardozo, H. *The March of a Nation: My Year of Spain's Civil War.* New York: McBride, 1937.

Cattell, D. T. *Communism and the Spanish Civil War.* Berkeley: University of California, 1955.

Hemingway, E. *For Whom the Bell Tolls.* New York: Scribner, 1940.

Koestler, A. *Dialogue with Death.* Tr. by T. and P. Blewitt. New York: Macmillan, 1960.

Lunn, A. *Spanish Rehearsal.* New York: Sheed & Ward, 1937.

Palencia, I. de. *Smouldering Freedom: The Story of the Spanish Republicans in Exile.* New York: Longmans, 1945.

Temperley, A. C. "Military Lessons of the Spanish War," *Foreign Affairs,* October, 1937.

Thomas, H. *The Spanish Civil War: The First Comprehensive History.* New York: Harper, 1961 (London: Eyre & Spottiswoode, 1961).

Wintringham, T. *English Captain.* London: Faber, 1939.

C. Post-Civil War

BOOK

Castillo, G. R. *Communist World Offensive against Spain.* Madrid: Diplomatic Information Office, 1949.

38. YUGOSLAVIA, WORLD WAR II

BOOKS

Armstrong, H. F. *Tito and Goliath.* New York: Macmillan, 1951 (London: Gollancz, 1951).

Brown, A. *Mihailovic and Yugoslav Resistance.* London: Lane, 1943.

Caffin, J. *Partisan.* London: Collins, 1945.

Davidson, B. *Partisan Picture.* Bedford, England: Bedford Books, 1948.

Dedijer, V. *With Tito through the War.* London: Alexander Hamilton, 1951.

————. *On Military Conventions.* Lund (Sweden): Gleerup, 1961.

Inks, J. M. *Eight Bailed Out.* New York: Norton, 1954 (London: Methuen, 1955).

Jones, W. *Twelve Months with Tito's Partisans.* Bedford, England: Bedford Books, 1946.

Lawrence, C. *Irregular Adventure.* London: Faber, 1947.

Maclean, F. *Escape to Adventure.* Boston: Little, Brown, 1950 (London: *Eastern Approaches.* Pan Books, 1949).

Maclean, F. *The Heretic: The Life and Times of Josip Broz Tito.* New York: Harper, 1957. (London: *Disputed Barricade,* Clarke, Irwin, 1957).
Martin, D. *Ally Betrayed: The Uncensored Story of Tito and Mihailovich.* New York: Prentice-Hall, 1946.
Neill, R. S. *Once Only.* London: Cape, 1947.
Piyade, M. *About the Legend That Yugoslav Uprising Owed Its Existence to Soviet Assistance.* London: Yugoslav Embassy, 1950.
Rogers, L. *Guerrilla Surgeon.* New York: Doubleday, 1957 (London: Collins, 1957).
Rootham, J. *Miss Fire: The Chronicle of a British Mission to Mihailovic, 1943–1944.* London: Chatto & Windus, 1946.
Sava, G. *The Chetniks.* London: Faber, 1942.
Shaw, W. B. K. *Milhailovic, Hoax or Hero?* Columbus, Ohio: Leigh, 1953.
Thayer, C. *Hands across the Caviar.* London: Joseph, 1953.
Tosevic, D. J. *Third Year of Guerrilla.* Toronto: Periscope, 1943.

ARTICLES

Mansfield, W. R. "Marine with the Chetniks," *Marine Corps Gazette,* January, 1946.
Petrovich, M. B. "The Central Government of Yugoslavia," *Political Science Quarterly,* December 1947.
Pickett, G. B. "The Pilsen Story," *Combat Forces Journal,* April, 1951.
Tito, I. B. "The Yugoslavian Army," *Military Review,* September, 1945.

39. NORTH AMERICA (U.S.A.)

A. French and Indian War, 1755–1763

BOOKS

Roberts, K. L. *Northwest Passage.* New York: Doubleday, 1937.
Rogers, R. *Journals: Reprinted from the Original Edition of 1765.* New York: Citadel's Corinth Books, 1961.

ARTICLE

Cuneo, J. R., and J. C. Scharfer. "Rogers' Rangers—Recon Company 1775," *Marine Corps Gazette,* March, 1961.

B. American Revolution, 1776–1781

BOOKS

Bakeless, J. *Turncoats, Traitors and Heroes.* Philadelphia: Lippincott, 1960.
Peckham, H. H. *The War for Independence: A Military History.* Chicago: University of Chicago, 1958.
Pratt, F. *Eleven Generals: Studies in American Command.* New York: Sloane, 1949.

ARTICLES

Cuneo, J. R. "The Early Days of the Queen's Rangers," *Military Affairs*, Summer, 1958.

Weller, J. "Irregular but Effective: Partizan Weapons Tactics in the American Revolution," *Military Affairs*, Fall, 1957.

———. "The Irregular War in the South," *Military Affairs*, Fall, 1960.

C. Civil War

BOOKS

Breihan, C. W. *Younger Brothers*. San Antonio, Tex.: Naylor, 1961.

Brownlee, R. S. *Gray Ghost of the Confederacy: Guerrilla Warfare in the West, 1861–1865*. Baton Rouge: Louisiana State University, 1958.

Burch, J. P. *Charles W. Quantrill: True History as Told by Captain Harrison Trow*. Vega, Tex.: Burch, 1923.

Butler, L. L. *John Morgan and His Men*. Philadelphia: Dorrance, 1960.

Connelley, W. E. *Quantrill and the Border Wars*. New York: Pageant, 1956. (Originally published by the Torch Press, Cedar Rapids, Iowa, 1910.)

Edwards, J. N. *Noted Guerrillas: or The Warfare of the Border*. St. Louis: (publisher unknown) 1877.

Jones, V. C. *Gray Ghost and Rebel Raiders*. New York: Holt, 1956.

Keller, A. *Morgan's Raid*. Indianapolis: Bobbs-Merrill, 1961.

McCorkle, J. *Three Years with Quantrill*. Armstrong, Mo.: Armstrong Herald Print, 1914.

Mosby, J. S. *Mosby's War Reminiscences and Stuart's Cavalry Campaigns*. New York: Pageant, 1960.

Munson, J. W. *Reminiscences of a Mosby Guerrilla*. New York: Moffat, 1906.

Roske, R. J., and C. Van Doren. *Lincoln's Commando*. New York: Pyramid, 1960.

Russel, C. W., ed. *The Memoirs of Colonel John Singleton Mosby*. Bloomington: Indiana University, 1961.

ARTICLES

Bissell, S. L., and A. Castel. "Bloodiest Man in American History: With Eye-Witness Account of Raid on Lawrence, Kansas," *American Heritage*, October, 1960.

Grant, C. E. "Partisan Warfare, Model 1861–65," *Military Review*, November, 1958.

Johnson, J. R. "Morgan's Men," *Marine Corps Gazette*, June, 1953.

Jones, V. C. "The Problems of Writing about the Guerrillas," *Military Affairs*, Spring, 1957.

D. Indian Warfare

BOOK

Wellman, P. J. *Death in the Desert: The Fifty Years' War for the Great Southwest*. New York: Macmillan, 1935.

ARTICLES

Mahon, J. K. "Anglo-American Methods of Indian Warfare, 1676–1794," *Mississippi Valley Historical Review*, 45:254–275, 1958.

Rattan, D. V. "Antiguerrilla Operations: A Case Study from History," *Military Review*, May, 1960.

Trussell, J. B. B. "Seminoles in the Everglades," *Army Magazine*, December, 1961.

E. American Ability to Wage Guerrilla Warfare in the United States

ARTICLES

Alsop, S., and S. B. Griffith, "We Can Be Guerrillas Too," *Saturday Evening Post*, December 2, 1950.

Lowry, E. E. "Could It Happen?," *Military Review*, March, 1957.

Rhoades, E. M. "Guerrilla Warfare," *Armoured Cavalry Journal*, November–December, 1947.

GENERAL MISCELLANEOUS

BOOKS

Chapelle, D. *What's a Woman Doing Here?* New York: Morrow, 1962.

Fleming, P. *Invasion 1940: An Account of German Preparation and the British Counter-Measures*. New York: Simon and Schuster, 1957 (London: Hart-Davis, 1957).

Fuller, J. F. C. *The First of the League Wars*. London: Eyre & Spottiswoode, 1936.

Huntington, S. P., ed. *Changing Patterns of Military Politics*. New York: Free Press, 1962.

Richardson, H. *One-Man War: The Jock McLaren Story*. London: Angus & Robertson, 1957.

Seth, R. *The Undaunted: The Story of Resistance in Western Europe*. London: Muller, 1956.

Seton-Watson, H. *The East European Revolution*. London: Methuen, 1950.

INDEX